"In *Adoptive Youth Ministry* some of the finest thinkers and writers in youth and family ministries explore a timely and penetrating metaphor for ministry in today's world. That metaphor is adoption, and it begs consideration of a strong commitment to faltering families, churches, and communities in our society. *Adoptive Youth Ministry* summarizes much of recent research, articles, and books. It can hardly be neglected by anyone wanting to be informed about the current state of, and challenges facing, youth ministry."

—**Dean Borgman**, founder and director,
Center for Youth Studies;
author of *Foundations
for Youth Ministry*

"Youth ministry is at a critical turning point. It's time for pastors, youth leaders, and youth ministry professors to engage in authentic dialogue regarding how to help teenagers embrace Jesus's message and mission at the deepest core of their beings. Chap Clark's *Adoptive Youth Ministry* will stimulate the kinds of discussions that will form and forge the nature of youth ministry for decades to come."

—**Greg Stier**, author of *Gospelize
Your Youth Ministry*; speaker;
founder and CEO, Dare 2 Share

"Popular youth ministry models of even a few years ago have quickly become outdated. Chap Clark's adoption youth ministry paradigm offers a reenvisioned lens through which to see youth ministry—a radically welcoming and inclusive spiritual kinship with teens linked together through a solidarity of love, grace, and mercy. The breadth of *Adoptive Youth Ministry* thoughtfully and honestly engages this paradigm in dialogue with the social sciences, theology, and youth ministry, addressing trends that show what we in the academy and in the field already know—that teens are not attending church and are not believing and embracing 'traditional' faith. With the acceleration of technology, globalization, and instantaneous connections, the field of youth ministry must ever adapt to remain effective, relevant, and authentic. *Adoptive Youth Ministry* attempts to address these issues and move the conversation forward by answering the question, now what?"

—**Fernando Arzola Jr.**, dean, College
of Arts and Sciences, Nyack College;
author of *Toward a Prophetic
Youth Ministry*

"This is not just a book. It's a youth worker's toolkit essential for building a deeper and more effective youth ministry."

—**Megan Hutchinson**, adult ministries
pastor, St. Andrew's Presbyterian Church,
Newport Beach, California

"*Adoptive Youth Ministry* is essential reading for anyone working in Christian education. In a single volume it provides a compilation of engaging research that spans the psychosocial nuances necessary to understand both human development and spiritual formation. The standard processes for integrating adolescents in many faith communities have unfortunately proven dysfunctional. Now, more than ever, is the time for a change, and *Adoptive Youth Ministry* provides the necessary metaphor for conceptualizing this change."

—**Chris King**, president,
Dallas Christian School

ADOPTIVE
YOUTH
MINISTRY

Youth, Family,
and Culture Series

Chap Clark, series editor

The Youth, Family, and Culture series examines
the broad categories involved in studying and
caring for the needs of the young and is dedicated
to the preparation and vocational strengthening of those who are committed to the spiritual
development of adolescents.

ADOPTIVE YOUTH MINISTRY

Integrating Emerging Generations
into the Family of Faith

edited by chap clark

Baker Academic
a division of Baker Publishing Group
Grand Rapids, Michigan

© 2016 by Chap Clark

Published by Baker Academic
a division of Baker Publishing Group
P.O. Box 6287, Grand Rapids, MI 49516-6287
www.bakeracademic.com

Printed in the United States of America

Library of Congress Cataloging-in-Publication Data
Adoptive youth ministry : integrating emerging generations into the family of faith / edited by Chap Clark.
        pages cm.— (Youth, family, and culture)
    Includes bibliographical references and index.
    ISBN 978-0-8010-4970-5 (cloth)
    1. Church work with youth. 2. Adoption (Theology) I. Clark, Chap, 1954– editor.
  BV4447.A335 2015
  259'.3—dc23   2015034302

In keeping with biblical principles of creation stewardship, Baker Publishing Group advocates the responsible use of our natural resources. As a member of the Green Press Initiative, our company uses recycled paper when possible. The text paper of this book is composed in part of post-consumer waste.

16 17 18 19 20 21 22   7 6 5 4 3 2 1

Contents

Acknowledgments   ix

Contributors   xi

Introduction: Adoption—
Reenvisioning Youth Ministry and
the Family of God *Chap Clark*   1

Part 1: The Context of Adoptive Youth Ministry

1. The Strategy of Adoptive Youth
   Ministry *Chap Clark*   11

2. Understanding the Changing
   Adolescent *Steven Bonner*   22

3. Welcoming Wounded and Broken
   Adolescents into the Family of
   God *Marv Penner*   39

4. Technology and Adoptive Youth
   Ministry *Bradley Howell*   52

5. Screen Time: A Window into Teens'
   Dreams *Craig Detweiler*   67

Part 2: The Call of Adoptive Youth Ministry

6. Reflective Youth Ministry: Youth
   Ministry as Critical, Ongoing,
   Communal Reflection *Almeda M.
   Wright*   85

7. Thinking (Practical)
   Theology *Michael McEntyre*   97

8. Youth Ministry, Adoption, and
   Culture *Walt Mueller*   115

9. Thinking Ecclesiologically:
   Teenagers Becoming Part of the
   Church *Mark Cannister*   136

10. Thinking Critically about Families
    and Youth Ministry *Allen
    Jackson*   150

11. Thinking Globally: An
    Asian American Case Study
    Approach *David Jia Hwa Doong
    and Jinna Sil Lo Jin*   165

12. Thinking Long Term *Cheryl A.
    Crawford*   180

Part 3: The Practice of Adoptive Youth Ministry

13. Adoption Extended: Creating a Welcoming Space *Pamela Erwin* 197

14. Spiritual Formation: It's a Matter of Time *Tony Jones* 212

15. Can I Ask That? Imagining a Church Big Enough for Teenagers' Hard Questions *Kara Powell and Brad Griffin* 221

16. A Call to Adoptive Ministry: Middle School Distinctives *Heather Flies* 233

17. No Church in the Wild: Urban and Multiethnic Contexts as the New Frontier of Youth Ministry *Daniel White Hodge* 246

18. Adoptive Youth Ministry: A Latin American Perspective *Howard Andruejol* 256

Part 4: The Skills for Adoptive Youth Ministry

19. Adoptive Leadership *Bill MacPhee* 273

20. The Communication of Adoption: Hearing and Making Known *Duffy Robbins* 288

21. Teaching for Adoptive Ministry *Jay Sedwick* 302

22. Rethinking Church Strategies and Structures *Steven Argue* 316

23. A Call to Adoption: Integration of Youth Ministry to the Church *April L. Diaz* 335

Notes 347

Scripture Index 369

Subject Index 373

Acknowledgments

This book has been years—if not a lifetime—in the making. For me, as first a parachurch staff member singularly devoted to inviting teenagers into an authentic, vibrant faith in Jesus Christ, and then as a trainer and teacher for others who shared that same calling, *Adoptive Youth Ministry* represents a theological evolution for the church and also for me. I therefore have lots of people to thank.

First, to the visionary and impassioned staff and volunteers of Young Life. You taught me the root structure of what we now know as contemporary youth ministry, starting with the early years of Jim Rayburn and passing on what you learned as pioneers of ministry to adolescents: Bill Starr and Bob "Mitch" Mitchell, Jim Shelton, Cliff Anderson, Don and Patty Taylor, Randy Giusta, Shelley Sadler, and countless others. These lessons are alive and well in thousands of men and women who serve Christ on the front lines of ministry around the world.

Thanks to the faculties of Denver Seminary and Fuller Theological Seminary. Thank you for helping me to see that teaching is the tip of the iceberg and that who we are is what matters most as seminary professors. Thank you also for teaching me how to think, how to reason, how to wrestle, and most of all how to hold that tension between, as Alan Jones puts it, "the dreaming and the coming true."

Thanks to those youth ministry friends who have encouraged and taught me how to communicate and lead with graceful conviction: Mike and Karla Yaconelli, Tic Long, Wayne Rice, Marv Penner, Duffy Robbins, Walt Mueller, Rich Van Pelt, Doug Fields, Kara Powell, Cheryl Crawford, and Mindy Coates Smith.

To all those people who believe that it is worth time and effort to "waste time" with kids, in the name of and for the sake of Jesus Christ and his kingdom (we call you "youth workers"), you are the gatekeepers for future generations. You are the ushers who invite them to participate in God's family feast. You are the relational models and interpreters of the gospel of the kingdom in a world of performance expectations, hollow messages, and stagnant faith. You are the ones who help the young to see the church as their family and who make it possible for them to live into that reality in Christ.

Last, to the family that God has graced me with. Each of you has pursued your own unique journey, fought complacency, and struggled to hold on to authentic belief in the God of mercy, justice, and grace. In a world where self-interest and self-promotion are all that seems to matter, you compel me to continue to try to live on the margins, pushing the borders of conventional belief into the unknown mystery of risky abandonment to Jesus and his kingdom. You have helped me to see with new eyes the pain of injustice, the subtle savagery of status quo faith, and the radical call of the kingdom. "Your sons and daughters will prophesy" (Joel 2:28).

Chap Clark

Fuller Theological Seminary, in partnership with Baker Academic, has created a website dedicated to this book at youthministry.fuller.edu. This site will provide supplementary content for *Adoptive Youth Ministry* as well as video and print resources that assist the faithful in thinking carefully and creatively about youth ministry. Our desire is to create a community where we can learn from one another in applying the ideas and principles from *Adoptive Youth Ministry*. We look forward to learning from one another.

Contributors

Howard Andruejol is the senior pastor at El Mensaje de Vida Church in Guatemala City. He is also the director of the Instituto Especialidades Juveniles (Youth Specialties Institute), faculty member at Universidad San Pablo de Guatemala, and the executive editor of *Revista Líder Juvenil*, the first specialized journal in youth ministry in Latin America. He has close to twenty-five years of youth ministry experience, has authored books on youth ministry in Spanish, and has edited the *Biblia para el Líder Juvenil*.

Steven Argue (PhD) is an assistant professor of youth, family, and culture at Fuller Theological Seminary and applied research strategist for the Fuller Youth Institute in Pasadena, California. Steve researches, writes, and speaks on topics surrounding adolescent and emerging adult spirituality. He has worked in academic, church, and parachurch contexts and uses his experience and research to teach, train, and coach on formational approaches, teaching and learning, and internship strategies. You will likely find him running long distances, eating vegetarian, and searching for local coffee shops.

Steven Bonner (DMin) is an associate professor of youth, family, and culture at Lubbock Christian University, where he trains, prepares, and equips future ministers to effectively step into the lives of youth and their families. With nearly two decades of ministry experience, Steve's research includes the study of youth culture, adolescent psychosocial development, precocious puberty, student athletics, and ministry to rural churches.

Mark Cannister (EdD) serves as professor of Christian ministries at Gordon College and as executive administrator of the Association of Youth Ministry Educators. He is the author of *Teenagers Matter: Making Student Ministry a Priority in the Church* (Baker Academic). He has served as president of the Society of Professors of Christian Education and the Association of Youth Ministry Educators, and as senior editor of the *Journal of Youth Ministry*. Mark has also served in a variety of leadership capacities at Grace Chapel in Lexington, Massachusetts.

Chap Clark (PhD) is professor of youth, family, and culture, and coordinator of Fuller Studio at Fuller Theological Seminary. Prior to teaching, Chap served on the Young Life staff for fifteen years, was associate staff for youth specialties for over three decades, and served in a variety of ministries along the way, including senior editor of *YouthWorker Journal*, executive and senior pastor, consultant, and speaker. Chap is the author or coauthor of twenty-four books, including *Hurt 2.0: Inside the World of Today's Teenagers*, *Starting Right: Thinking Theologically About Youth Ministry*, *Sticky Faith*, *The Performance Illusion*, and *Youth Ministry in the 21st Century: Five Views*.

Cheryl Crawford (PhD) is professor of practical theology and director of the youth ministry program at Azusa Pacific University. She is also the senior editor of *The Journal of Youth Ministry*, which is dedicated to promoting research that will help faculty prepare future youth workers. Cheryl has been involved in the research design, implementation, writing, and presentation of *Sticky Faith* and continues to follow fifteen emerging adults as they transition into adulthood. Cheryl has served in pastoral roles over the past thirty-plus years in church, parachurch, and camp settings. Most importantly, Cheryl enjoys teaching, mentoring, and being with students.

Craig Detweiler (PhD) is professor of communication and director of the Institute for Entertainment, Media, and Culture at Pepperdine University in Malibu, California. He has written comedies for the Disney Channel, directed award-winning documentaries, and is the author of several books, including *iGods: How Technology Shapes Our Spiritual and Social Lives*, *Foreword*'s Silver winner for best books about Popular Culture. Other books include *Into the Dark*, which explores the top-ranked films on the Internet Movie Database, and *Halos and Avatars: Playing Video Games with God*. Craig is grateful for Young Life, InterVarsity, and the youth ministers who dared to care about him.

April Diaz has pastored in the local church for over seventeen years. Secretly, she's a total girlie girl, reads more than she can put into practice, and is still crazy about her high school sweetheart, Brian. Together, they co-parent their beautiful Ethiopian children, Judah and Addise, and their biological son, Asher. April's first book, *Redefining the Role of the Youth Worker: A Manifesto of Integration*, is a compelling vision for the church's role in the lives of teenagers.

David Jia Hwa Doong (PhD) is pastor to young Chinese immigrants in southern California at Evangelical Formosan Church of Los Angeles, where he served for nine years. He is currently studying the state of Chinese emerging adults in America through the lens of perceived loneliness among them, exploring ways for the church to faithfully respond to this people group. David leads workshops and teaches seminary courses on ministry to Chinese emerging adults in North America and East Asia. He is married to Joy Chung and has two sons.

Pamela J. Erwin (DMin) is professor of youth ministry and practical theology and dean of professional programs at Bethel University.

Pamela is fascinated by the influence of culture for shaping how young people see the world and their place in it. As a parent, pastor, and teacher, she delights in encouraging young people to think and act creatively in engaging their world as kingdom-minded folk.

Heather Flies (MA) is the junior high pastor at Wooddale Church in Eden Prairie, Minnesota. Outside the walls of Wooddale Church, Heather spends a great deal of time as a communicator. She is invited into local junior and senior high schools to present on a variety of topics, such as self-esteem and abstinence. Heather also brings truth, hope, and fun to students at various camps, seminars, and retreats locally and across the nation.

Brad Griffin (MDiv) is associate director of the Fuller Youth Institute, where he develops research-based training for youth workers and parents. He is a speaker, blogger, and volunteer youth pastor, and is coauthor of *Deep Justice Journeys* and several books in the Sticky Faith series, including *Can I Ask That?* He has also authored a number of youth ministry book chapters and journal articles. A native Kentucky youth pastor, Brad now lives in southern California with his wife, Missy, and their three children and leads the youth ministry at Mountainside Communion in Monrovia.

Daniel White Hodge (PhD) is the director of the Center for Youth Ministry Studies and assistant professor of youth ministry at North Park University in Chicago. His research interests include the intersections of faith, hip-hop culture, and young adult emerging generations. His two books are *Heaven Has a Ghetto: The Missiological Gospel and Theology of Tupac Amaru Shakur* and *The*

Soul of Hip Hop: Rims, Timbs, and a Cultural Theology. He is currently working on books titled *The Hostile Gospel: Finding Religion in the Post Soul Theology of Hip Hop* and *Between God and Kanye: Youth Ministry in a Post-Civil Rights Era.* You can find him at www.whitehodge.com.

Bradley Howell (DMin) is a researcher, speaker, and writer on the adolescent use of social media and bridging the adult-adolescent digital divide. He also designed and teaches the course Youth and Family Ministry in a Culture of Digital Relationships at Fuller Theological Seminary. He earned his master of arts in youth ministry and counseling ministries from Denver Seminary and his doctor of ministry in youth, family, and culture from Fuller. Brad authored "Social Media Myth Busting" and "Finding Love One Byte at a Time" for *YouthWorker Journal* and the article "Using Social Media to Strengthen Family Bonds" as well as participating in the Sex and Social Media Roundtable for the Fuller Youth Institute. As a regional campus director for Fuller's San Francisco Bay Area and Sacramento campuses, he and his wife reside in Sacramento, California.

Allen Jackson (PhD) is professor of youth ministry at the New Orleans Baptist Theological Seminary as well as founder and director of the Youth Ministry Institute. He joined the faculty in 1994 after ministering to students in several local churches. Allen has served in interim positions in local churches throughout his academic career and is active as a speaker for Discipleship Now weekends, youth and family camps, and training conferences. Allen has written extensively for youth publications and has authored or coauthored seven books, including his latest, *Disciple: The Ordinary Person's Guide to Discipling Teenagers.*

Jinna Sil Lo Jin (PhD candidate) was born and raised in Korea and is director of international relations at Fuller Theological Seminary and a PhD candidate in practical theology with an emphasis in youth, family, and culture. She has been serving Korean immigrant youth in the greater Los Angeles area in various ways for eight years. Her passion for diversity and cultural sensitivity based on personal, ministerial, and professional experience helps and encourages people to broaden their perspectives of cross-cultural relationships and ministry.

Tony Jones (PhD) is the author of *Did God Kill Jesus?* and the theologian-in-residence at Solomon's Porch in Minneapolis. He teaches theology at Fuller Theological Seminary and United Theological Seminary of the Twin Cities. He has written a dozen books on the topics of youth ministry, prayer, spirituality, and the emerging church movement. He lives in Minnesota with his wife and children.

Bill MacPhee (DMin) serves as a teaching pastor at The River Church of the South Bay on the Palos Verdes Peninsula and has recently served as the associate head of School for Spiritual Life at Village Christian Schools in Sun Valley, California. He has thirty years of experience as a pastor in large churches serving in youth and family ministries and is an affiliate professor at Fuller Theological Seminary in youth, family, and culture. Bill also speaks for ParentTeen in an effort to help communities take seriously their role in understanding and nurturing the next generation of young people so they might more easily find their place in the adult world.

Michael McEntyre (DMin) is the associate pastor to youth and young adults at First Baptist Church in Columbia, Montana. A native of east Tennessee, Michael and his family moved to Missouri in July 2012 when his wife, Carol, was called as the senior pastor of First Baptist. He and his wife have one son, Nate, and are in the process of adopting a little girl from China. He has served in student ministry at churches in Texas, Georgia, Tennessee, and Missouri since 1999.

Walt Mueller (DMin) is the founder and president of the Center for Parent Youth Understanding, a nonprofit ministry organization that has served churches, schools, and community organizations worldwide for nearly twenty years. He is a sought-after authority on youth culture and family issues and has appeared on CNN, Fox News, and the BBC.

Marv Penner (DPhil) is a lifetime youth worker with more than four decades of frontline work with teenagers and their families. As a veteran member of the Youth Specialties speaking team, an associate staff member at the Center for Parent/Youth Understanding, a seasoned college professor, and a respected coach and counselor, he has equipped thousands of students, parents, and young leaders with practical tools to make their lives more effective. Marv's books cover a range of topics but recently have focused on work with kids whose stories and choices put them at high risk. He has been married to Lois for as long as he's been in ministry and can't imagine retiring from the joy of working with young people.

Kara Powell (PhD) is the executive director of the Fuller Youth Institute and assistant professor of youth ministry at Fuller Theological

Seminary. Named by *Christianity Today* as one of "50 Women to Watch," Kara serves as an adviser to Youth Specialties and also speaks regularly at parenting and leadership conferences. Kara is the author or coauthor of a number of books, including *The Sticky Faith Guide for Your Family*, *Sticky Faith Curriculum*, *Can I Ask That?*, *Deep Justice Journeys*, *Essential Leadership*, *Deep Justice in a Broken World*, *Deep Ministry in a Shallow World*, and the *Good Sex Youth Ministry Curriculum*.

Duffy Robbins (DMin) is professor of youth ministry at Eastern University in St. Davids, Pennsylvania, and a thirty-five-year veteran of youth ministry. Duffy is one of the most prolific speakers and writers in youth ministry, both in the United States and around the world. His books include *This Way to Youth Ministry* and *Ministry of Nurture*. He is widely respected as one of the leading voices in both youth and family ministry.

Jay Sedwick (PhD) is professor of educational ministries and leadership and has served on the faculty at Dallas Theological Seminary for eighteen years. Jay has more than thirty years of youth ministry experience as a volunteer, part-time, and full-time youth minister. An ordained minister who teaches youth at a large Dallas-area church, Dr. Sedwick is also a popular conference and seminar speaker. His research and teaching interests include youth development, biblical education for youth, curriculum design, and legal and financial issues in ministry. He and his wife, Laurie, have been married for twenty-eight years, during which time God blessed them with four children and one son-in-law.

Almeda M. Wright (PhD) is an assistant professor of religious education at Yale Divinity School. Her research focuses on African American religion, adolescent spiritual development, and the intersections of religion and public life. Almeda is currently completing a book on the spiritual lives and questions of African American youth. She is also the editor, with Mary Elizabeth Moore, of *Children, Youth, and Spirituality in a Troubling World* and contributed to an exciting new student Bible, the *Common English (CEB) Student Bible*. Almeda is an ordained minister of the American Baptist Churches and has worked with young people for almost twenty years, including as a fifth- and sixth-grade teacher, a youth minister, and the assistant director of the Youth Theological Initiative at Emory University.

Introduction

Adoption—Reenvisioning Youth Ministry and the Family of God

CHAP CLARK

> We are the family of God,
> Yes, we are the family of God,
> And He's brought us together
> To be one in Him,
> That we might bring light to the world.
>
> —"We Are the Family of God,"
> John Byron, 1976

Of all the metaphors used to describe who we are as God's people in both the Old and New Testaments, in most contexts *family* is the least considered. We talk about being a "community," a "body," and a "gathering." We envision our relationships in the church to be a collection of networked people, which is usually practiced through the default program of "small groups." When we do sing songs that recognize we have come together to give praise to God (what many call the "worship" time), we sing as if our words are true. Yet when we run across lyrics that force us to consider what these words actually mean, some of us might chafe at the idea. Perhaps you have heard or sung, for example, Hezekiah Walker's "I Need You to Survive":

> I need you
> You need me
> We're all a part of God's body . . .
> You are important to me
> I need you to survive[1]

Pastors learn in seminary that the word we translate "church," *ekklēsia*, actually means "gathering" or "assembly."[2] Thus the local gathering of Christ's followers, then and now, is what Jesus called into being as his people. The church (local, historical, global) and the Church (those across time and culture and geography who are "called according to his purposes," Rom. 8:28) are those who gather "in [his] name" (John 14:13). This gathered group, who are the "sent" ones (John 20:21), are the collection of people that God has called together to be his "witnesses" (Acts 1:8) to the world of the Creator's goodness, mercy, and love. God's declaration of who we are, then, is embedded within this notion of "we-ness": "*We* are his people, the sheep of his pasture" (Ps. 100:3, italics added). Not only are we his gathered people but we also become siblings, even as we have "become children of God" (John 1:12). We, as God's people, are all God's children: welcomed, accepted, embraced, empowered, and united, with God as our Father (Matt. 6:9, "Our Father in heaven . . .").

Adoption as Ministry

A child who is accepted and taken in by non-biological parents as a permanent, actual, and "full" son or daughter is referred to as *adopted*. Merriam-Webster defines this as the "act of transferring parental rights and duties to someone other than the adopted person's biological parents. The practice is ancient and occurs in all cultures."[3] To be adopted is to be fully accepted as a member of the family, with all the rights and privileges of a natural-born child. Previously, God was not our Father, but in Christ we are now included in the family of God. This is a theological and ontological fact that is made plain throughout Scripture. As Paul writes in Ephesians 2:19, "Consequently, you are no longer foreigners and strangers, but fellow citizens with God's people and also members of his household." In Christ, we are not only called God's children, but we also are God's *adopted* children. While this is a powerful image for who we are in Christ, what little attention theologians give to this fact is limited to either human adoption in a family or a debate over our standing as God's children. I have been able to uncover very few voices who explore in depth

what this means for how we live together as "members of God's household."[4] Nonetheless, the fact remains that we, as God's adopted, are invited—indeed, called—to live out of this reality in community as we gather together as the family of God.

The metaphor of family provides the theological framework for how we are to live together as God's people. The ministry of adoption, then, invokes the following four foundational premises:

> #1: Adoption recognizes that in every church or organization there are insiders and outsiders.

The primary critique people have with the concept of adoption as a basis for all ministry is that it sounds paternalistic; they consider the idea as starting from the church as parent. The power of adoptive ministry is not that we are adopted by a group of "surrogate parents" (the older people in the church) but rather that *the inner circle of the gathering does whatever it needs to do to make sure that the adopted person experiences the family of God as a fully embraced and included participant.* Adoptive ministry recognizes that in every group or gathering, church or organization, some people are dominant and many are not—and the many who are not often feel like they are on the outside of the community or group. Adoptive ministry mandates that it is the responsibility of those in power to draw in, to include, and to equip all those who feel like outsiders so that they feel included in the very center of the family of God.

> #2: I am adopted into God's family as a child with other children.

Because some are in power and many are on the systemic outside of power, adoption as the primary metaphor for God's family requires that those in power see themselves as siblings to all others who trust in Christ (John 1:12). God is our Father, and we together are his children (Eph. 3:14–15). When Jesus told his disciples that they must "receive the kingdom of God like a little child" to "enter it" (Mark 10:15), he was reminding them of this central message: *you have one Father, and you are all siblings.* While this requirement is often reduced to the exhortation that adults should come to God with a "childlike faith," the text itself does not allow for that interpretation. "Like" is a simile, not a metaphor, and every sixth grader knows that a simile means what is compared is functionally equivalent. We not only are to have a faith that is "like a child," but we must also "receive the kingdom" like a child, which demands the whole person. Adoptive ministry begins with the creation of an environment in which there is an ethos of familial mutuality. The child, then, has something to bring to the adult; the teenager has something to bring to the senior; and vice versa. This is the essence of family.

#3: Jesus has his eye especially on the vulnerable.

Adoptive ministry means that while all are siblings—all are children of the same Father, whether they are eighty or fifteen years old—those who are mature must take the lead on ensuring that those who are vulnerable *for any reason* are protected. Thus adoptive ministry is not simply a grounding theological framework for youth ministry, though it obviously applies to both youth and children's ministry. *Adopting the vulnerable means that those who are mature must see it as their responsibility to ensure that those who are not are cared for, included, and empowered, and can grow into well-established life and faith.*

Therefore, adoptive ministry includes all those who may be or feel vulnerable, such as the elderly, the single parent, the divorced, the outcast, the hurting, the lonely, the lost, and the broken. God has already received and identified outsiders as his children and adopted them into the kingdom. What they need, and therefore what those in leadership must initiate and sustain, is the experiential reality of what God has declared to be true.

#4: Adoption is not limited to the gathered but includes the outsider as well.

With its roots in the historical body of Christ, adoptive ministry begins with the local community of faith and extends to the global people of God. Adoption means all those who are called God's children are taken seriously, welcomed as part of the family as siblings. As God's people gather, worship, and are equipped for ministry both to God's people and to the world God loves, the theological calling of partnering in God's work of adopting children into his family becomes the primary external expression of life together. Evangelism is not about shouting a message to the world, whether on a T-shirt or through a flashy musical production hosted by a church. Biblical evangelism is about living together as witnesses to Jesus Christ by the power of the Spirit in the world God created—"You will be my witnesses" (Acts 1:8)—and living as salt and light (Matt. 5:13–16) amid those God has come "to seek and save" (Luke 19:10). Justice and acts of mercy cannot be separated from verbal proclamation of witness to Christ; these are all part of our calling as witness, salt, and light. *Adoptive ministry is vital because we are witnessing to the fact that in Christ God has invited those who "believed in his name" to "become children of God" (John 1:12). This is the message of the good news. Therefore our message—in our lifestyle, service, and word—is adoption.*

These four principles form the basis of *Adoptive Youth Ministry*. The conviction driving every chapter in this book is that all youth ministry practice is an expression of this theological mandate. Those in power—that is, the mature and the leadership—have the responsibility to ensure that every child, every adolescent, every young adult, and every other vulnerable outsider is brought into the center of the family as a participant in the community. This does not mean that there is not the place and even need for leadership (both lay and paid staff) to take on the role of initiator and ultimate decision maker of a given organization or community. What it does mean is that those who are vulnerable must be included and invited to participate even while they are being nurtured, trained, and empowered to grow into a peer level of engagement with the mature. This is the role of youth ministry in the twenty-first century. *Adoptive Youth Ministry* is designed to equip you to be the voice of adoption and to be the catalyst for this dual task of nurturing and empowering participation.

Why "Adoption"?

Several years ago, in a doctor of ministry cohort class in youth, family, and culture, a student beginning the second year shared how her congregation had received the teaching she had absorbed during year one. A senior pastor, she came home from class excited and motivated to lead her congregation into a greater awareness of what it means to live together as God's family. In response to the training she had received, Rev. (now) Dr. Andrea King delivered an impassioned sermon proclaiming the need to "assimilate" children and youth into the church family. Her congregation's immediate and visceral negative reaction stunned her, until she realized what she had tapped into (prompted by her professor, yours truly).[5] In using the term *assimilation* to describe the church's call to welcome and integrate the young into the life and participation of the faith community, she had used a word that, in her primarily African American community, had been forced on them by a dominant ethnic culture that would gladly welcome someone, so long as he or she adapted to the lifestyle, culture, and rhetoric of the dominant community. In other words, as Andrea shared with the class, *assimilation* to her congregation means that I "*get* to join you, so long as I *become* you!" Andrea discovered that this meaning of *assimilation* misses what God intends for his family.

In response, we spent the next two days wrestling with an appropriate way of thinking about dealing with the twofold call of youth ministry, especially in a world where kids have been isolated by adult-controlled systems. The discussion led us to examine how the apostle Paul describes the coming together of two very different and oppositional communities: those who grew up in the Jewish tradition and received Jesus as the Messiah as the culmination of their faith, and those who were outsiders—gentiles (non-Jewish) who came to faith in Jesus Christ without the history and experience of Jewish practices. Paul settles this throughout his writings by appealing to the unity that is in Christ (e.g., Gal. 3:26–29, "There is neither Jew nor Gentile, neither slave nor free, nor is there male and female, for you are all one in Christ Jesus"). He uses the term *adoption* four times to describe the familial privilege both Jewish and gentile Christians have with God and one another in Christ.[6]

As we examined Paul's use of this term, we came to see that what youth ministry leaders and influencers had been leaning into for years (if not decades) but had yet to put together into a straightforward framework with clear language came together in the term *adoption*. Certainly youth ministry is interested in younger generations owning their faith; the goal of youth ministry is often described as faithful lifelong discipleship. Likewise, there is general agreement that the church is the place where God calls his people to experience, embody, and express their faith—and somehow parents fit into the mix. What remained unclear was how to put together these three convictions. Reclaiming the biblical metaphor of family for the community of faith through adoption seemed to be a clear and unifying concept that was biblically based and theologically grounding. Although some may wrestle with the way people think about adoption across cultures and in various contexts (especially the possibility of it being hierarchical and paternalistic, since it is more about what God has done than about what we do, and therefore all ministry—including evangelism and justice—is envisioned as participating in God's work), I believe that adoption is an appropriate way to conceptualize youth ministry practice.

In the recent book *Youth Ministry in the 21st Century: Five Views*, I detail the rationale for youth ministry—and *all* ministry—as the ministry of adoption.

> In terms of youth ministry, where for years the young were not only seen as a separate population but have been programmatically structured to maintain and even reinforce that separation, the only way the church can begin to realize its calling to live as a family is by literally adopting the young. *This is the theological and sociological rationale for Youth Ministry as Adoption.* Youth ministry is, by definition, ministry to and for teenagers, typically middle and high school students aged eleven to eighteen, and sometimes includes college ministries. As a group, this population rarely experiences their relationship with the dominant population of church, or society at large, as being something to which they belong. If the church is indeed intended to be a network of familial relationships, a "family of families," then the need for a comprehensive ministry strategy to make this happen trumps all other programmatic goals. If people do not know one another, if they do not feel cared for or necessary, and if they do not sense that the rest of the community values them, the church is simply not the church. The church must adjust vision and structure to ensure that everyone in God's family experiences their faith as a vital member of God's household as expressed in the local faith community.[7]

The Purpose of *Adoptive Youth Ministry*

Since what has been called "modern youth ministry" emerged on the ecclesial landscape in the mid-twentieth century,[8] every decade or so a book has been published that gathers together the current (and assumed future) array of philosophies, perspectives, and practices that make up what most agree is "youth ministry" in order to ground and shape the practices and scope of the movement. Around the turn of the twenty-first century, a trend to more specialized youth ministry books and texts became the standard way of thinking about and doing youth ministry. Many dozens of important, compelling, and ministry-altering youth ministry books have been published over the past few decades, with many making a significant if not widespread impact on youth ministry. Yet even as publishing in youth ministry increases, conferences abound, and more authors and speakers experience wider circulation and audiences (to say nothing of Twitter and blog followers and Facebook "friends"), few foundational youth ministry books containing multiple authors and perspectives or multiple, across-the-board ministry topics (like Mark Senter and Warren S. Benson's *Complete Book of Youth Ministry*) have emerged that can help youth ministry students and practitioners sort through the plethora of viewpoints and frameworks.[9] The most recent of the multitopic foundational books is *Starting Right: Thinking Theologically about Youth Ministry* (edited by Kenda Creasy Dean, Dave Rahn, and myself). One of the more direct outcomes of *Starting Right*—a collaborative project of Zondervan Academic and Youth Specialties, authored by well-known and respected youth ministry leaders from a wide swath of the youth ministry landscape—was the way it set the groundwork for what would soon become the theological framework for many in the field, both in the United States and internationally. Since its publication, practical theologians from a variety of theological traditions have produced a diverse, rich, and helpful way of thinking about and doing youth ministry. Today it is common to attend a youth ministry conference and participate in a seminar, if not several, on the "theology" of youth ministry, which is almost always framed within the rubric of practical theology.

Because so much has changed over the past two decades in both the culture at large and the diversity of youth ministry perspectives, there is once again the need for a single volume that will help to ground and shape the way we think about and do youth ministry. *Adoptive Youth Ministry* brings together diverse and well-respected scholars and teachers, practitioners and researchers, and speakers and writers who come at the field of youth ministry from many angles and yet are drawn together by the idea that the church is the vital center of all youth ministry practice.

Three Issues Facing Contemporary Youth Ministry

Even as the greater focus on practical theology in recent years has provided the theological framework for ministry and most youth workers have been more theologically deliberate in their ministry thinking and efforts, three related but distinct issues have emerged. While they have come from different people and directions and for different reasons, none of the three seems to have been the catalyst for the other two, yet all three now make up the bulk of our collective discourse. Each of these issues impacts the other two, but up to this point little has been done to pull them together. In no particular order, the three issues are:

- The struggle related to youth ministry's long-term effectiveness, in that we are "losing" kids once they leave our ministry programs
- The concern that people in contemporary culture, including an increasing number of young people, report to have written off "traditional" faith (a movement labeled the rise of the "Nones"). Current literature seems to confirm that many young people do not even want to give youth ministry a chance, and there

is ample evidence that great numbers of adolescents and emerging adults have a negative view of the church and confirm wanting nothing to do with "us," meaning the institutional church.

- The widespread recognition that as the world has changed dramatically over the past few years and decades, these changes not only affect how we do ministry but also who we do ministry with—primarily adolescents and their families. The world the young now inhabit is the precarious, often painful, clearly confusing, and "abandoned" reality that middle adolescents (fourteen- to twenty-year-olds) and emerging adults (twenty- to early-thirty-year-olds) live within.

Each of these issues and the corresponding focus that results has created a new day for youth ministry. Over the past decade we have come to recognize and admit that we are losing ground in terms of our ability to theologically engage students in a way that engenders both current and lifelong faith even while we try to go theologically deeper ourselves. While each issue has received a great deal of attention, there is a growing consensus that these three are born of the same parent. Today's and tomorrow's youth worker cannot simply be aware of the dynamics that affect ministry to the young; they must thoughtfully and theologically engage them head-on, recognizing that the day of gathering kids in a dedicated youth wing or living room and getting them to sing and play and listen to a clever talk (regardless of how well delivered it is) no longer guarantees lifelong spiritual interest, much less life transformation. Without question there remain pockets where the "add water and stir" youth ministry model of an adult "leading" a group of five to fifteen teenagers within the framework of a carefully crafted and strategically produced program works. Many of the kids in these churches do come through with an owned faith that they are able to take with them into the future. But that result is a rarity and almost certainly due to a great many other factors, such as deeply invested parents and a system that highly values the young (or momentum and budget). Even if we dig deeply into highly touted or stable ministries, it is hard not to see the same issues nipping at the heels of these highly "successful" model programs.

In surveying the literature on each of these questions in youth ministry circles and in society at large—the shallow, temporary faith of adolescents, the lack of trust in faith institutions, and the systemic isolation of hurting kids—there is a common denominator that bubbles to the surface and is consistently affirmed: our young desperately need and long for authentic community. For example, one of the central tenets of the Sticky Faith work of Kara Powell, Brad Griffin, Cheryl Crawford, and the faculty of the Fuller Youth Institute is that in order to contribute to the long-term faith of an adolescent, that adolescent must believe that he or she is known, valued, actively engaged, and proactively loved within a community (usually described as being composed of at least five nonparental Christian adults).[10] In David Kinnaman's work (especially as it is informed by practical theologian Andrew Root's reminder that the gospel calls us to participate "in Christ's risen presence" regardless of a young person's response),[11] ministry to the "Nones" must provide "authentic community" and "build bridges."[12] According to my research and continuing study of behaviors and attitudes of mid-adolescents in my book *Hurt 2.0*, the reason we have a generation that feels so alone is that they lack the social capital—that is, genuine, non-self-serving relationships—of knowing they have people in their corner to help them navigate their entry into an adulthood that is amorphous and a psychosocial moving target. In sum, each of these issues points us to not only the human condition throughout history but also our increasing collective individualism and atomization, which has created a generation of young people who need us more proactively than ever.[13] These three issues culminate in the recognition of the dearth of adult presence in the lives of children and teenagers in contemporary society around the world and comprise the context for youth ministry in the twenty-first century.

Adoptive Youth Ministry seeks to address each of these issues by appealing to and building from the core reason they exist: an erosion of what is sometimes called "social capital," which is necessary for any child to become an adult, and the lack of an adult community committed to the support and nurture of the young.[14] This is a book on youth ministry practice. Our premise is that any activity targeting the church's mission to the young must recognize and address the central reality that every young person faces, not only in the church but also in every aspect of their young lives. For teenagers and emerging adults to be included, welcomed, embraced, and invited as participants into a community of faith presupposes that the adults in that community want them around. This notion is the foundational prerequisite for youth ministry in today's society around the globe.

The Goal of Adoptive Youth Ministry

Adoptive Youth Ministry seeks to equip youth ministries, churches, and organizations that have been charged with the spiritual development of the young to facilitate a ministry of adoption into the local and global family of God. No chapter specifically details this new way of grounding our work, but each offers a specific strategy and theology for connecting the young into the larger faith community. While some chapters speak more directly to adoption, others do not. Each chapter and every author invited to speak in this volume (as well as on the website dedicated to the adoptive youth ministry conversation at youthministry.fuller.edu) is committed to this overall goal, which culminates in youth being received and embraced as full participants in the community of faith as siblings with other members of the body, even as they still need the social capital and nurture of the adults. The driving theological foundation of this book is the idea that all kids have gifts, talents, vision, and energy to bring to the family table. In bringing together a wide array of youth ministry leaders, thinkers, professors, practitioners, authors, and speakers who are committed to this single trajectory of ministry to help shape youth ministry practice for the next several decades, this book is unique. As you read you will be invited to reflect on many of the issues and responsibilities of youth ministry practice while being grounded in the theological foundation of familial adoption. As you read, discuss, and even connect with an author through the website, you will be able to do your work—to create ministry strategies, programs, events, and structure—in a way that is fully embedded within the community of faith and, more important, faithful to God's intent for passing the faith on from generation to generation as we serve our Lord in the work of the kingdom.

Part 1

The Context of Adoptive Youth Ministry

The Strategy of Adoptive Youth Ministry

CHAP CLARK

Consider this unsolicited email from an eighth-grade boy to his youth pastor about the multigenerational mission event that people from his church were going to attend.

> "One of my biggest reasons of why I want to go is to worship God in that *huge* mass amount of people! If I think church camp is amazing then this has to crazy awesome, and I think it's great! Not only we get to have fun and worship but we get to have a work experience too! I can't wait to meet people and *find new siblings*!"
>
> There's no easy way to say this: The American evangelical church has lost, is losing and will almost certainly continue to lose our youth. For all the talk of "our greatest resource," "our treasure," and the multi-million dollar Dave and Buster's/Starbucks knockoffs we build and fill with black walls and wailing rock bands . . . the church has failed them. Miserably.
>
> —Marc Yoder, "10 Surprising Reasons Our Kids Leave Church"[1]

Adoptive ministry is the biblical calling describing our role in recognizing and par-ticipating in God's declaration that in Christ we have been called "children of God" (John 1:12). As churches attempt to build community among those who gather together as God's people, *adoption* is the term used as the biblical foundation for drawing disparate people into the family-like intimacy we have been invited to in Christ. Adoptive youth ministry, then, provides the biblical foundation for the inclusion of young people into the core of the Christian community.

When I first began using the term *adoption* to describe how we are called see ourselves as connected siblings of one another in the church—and therefore how we envision ministry to the body and beyond—not everyone immediately jumped on board. Essentially, those who struggled landed in two basic camps.

First, some people believe the term is confusing because it is most commonly used for families adopting children into their home. Clearly the word is embedded within a very specific context. Wouldn't it confuse people to use the term in a different, albeit broader, way? This is actually a strength of its use. For this very reason, Paul chose this term to break down the walls dividing the early church. Using *adoption* to describe what it means to live together in God's family concisely raises the bar of the relational connectedness and intimacy we are called to in Christ. People already know that to adopt a child changes everything—not only for the child but also for the receiving family. By using this familial language, this same intentionality is applied to who we are and how we function in the community of faith, thereby capitalizing on the term's familiarity. In using *adoption* we are more readily able to embrace the complexity, the messiness, and the emotional energy that comes with taking in a child who, by nature of the choice the family makes, is endowed with all the rights and privileges of a biological child. Those I have talked with who have adopted children or are adopted themselves have overwhelmingly resonated with the concept of adoption as a grounding theological base for youth ministry, and every ministry.

The second objection involves the implicit implication such a label will have on the term *intergenerational*, which is currently in vogue. As many churches have come to recognize fragmentation in the church and how it creates multiple communities within a single congregation, they have instituted programs and strategies to connect people of various groups and ages. Some who have embraced the concept of "intergenerational ministry" wonder whether *adoption* is too top-down a word. However, this assumes that intergenerationalism levels the playing field of communal engagement and that as young people and older people are given the opportunity to know one another they will be drawn to one another as equals, or at least co-participants. Last year at a summit of youth ministry writers and leaders, I was given a few minutes to pitch the idea of adoptive ministry. One participant remarked, "I don't think 'adoption' is an especially helpful metaphor for youth ministry. It is hierarchical and devalues kids." This comment and the resultant conversation forced me to think more deeply about what I mean by *adoptive ministry*. Any ministry concept that devalues young people is clearly not what is appropriate in the desire to integrate young people into the life of the church community. As mentioned in the introduction, adoptive ministry is not about adults "adopting" the children or adolescents of a church as their own. Rather, because God is the one who adopts all of us, adoptive ministry is more directly communal and inclusive, more straightforward and therefore easily explainable, and far more radical than any previous foundational theology of youth ministry practice.

Participating in what God declares as truth is the reality of who we are *together* as his children. In the course of teaching, writing, and speaking about this subject in various contexts, this discussion has not only caused me to describe more carefully the implications of adoptive ministry but has also given me greater confidence that adoption is the most helpful and direct biblical metaphor for the church in today's atomized society. Since it has been declared by God that we are *siblings* of one another, we are members of the same household and family, and we hold the same standing before the God who has called us. Nothing could be *less* hierarchical.

Adoptive ministry, however, is less about fostering diverse relationships and more about changing our fundamental mind-set of how we relate to one another in the church. It is first and foremost about attitudinal change; structural change will follow. The shift from where we are to where we need to be is significant, but in today's culture of disinterest and disdain we are losing both kids and relevancy; we simply have no choice. We must move from the historical complacency of institutional and programmatic defensiveness into the uncharted, mysterious, and uncontrollable waters of abandoned life together in Christ. This is what adoptive ministry means.

Adoptive Ministry

The Move from Institution to Organism

Several years ago, while trying to integrate various perspectives on organizational dynamics and group leadership, it occurred to me that anything of merit begins with an idea (e.g., "we need more efficient transportation"). With any idea that matters, we must create a structure that promotes the idea in a specific context (a contextual application of the idea, as in "we need a car with four wheels and rubber tires"). As we refine the application, we almost always begin to see the structure as being essentially one with the idea, and we end up protecting and controlling the structure that promotes the idea (e.g., "Consider a car; how many wheels does it have? Of course. Four.").[2] Yet to keep an idea alive in a changing environment, the temptation to control or contain how it is applied and constantly seek to restructure the essence of the idea must be resisted. ("Why not five wheels, on plastic tires?") To maintain the integrity of an idea in any fluid climate means we must be willing to change how we envision the idea in different settings and contexts. What matters, then, is the idea, not how it is structured or applied.

I have come to see all change in these terms. Ronald A. Heifetz and Marty Linsky remind that "people do not resist change, per se. People resist loss."[3] There is such great power in maintaining what we know and what we have become comfortable with that anytime a "fixed" idea is challenged—even by simply asking a question or proposing a new way of thinking—our default response is to become nervous. We wonder what will happen if what we have believed in and relied on is lost. Yet this must happen in order to change how youth ministry has been practiced for decades. We must move from running a program to being a family—from functioning as an institution to living as an organism.

The Evolution of the Idea

For an idea to go anywhere, it must have some sort of structure to give it legs. Once a rudimentary structure is in place, especially in its early iterations, the structure may go through fits and starts; yet if the idea has merit, eventually the structure enables the idea to gain momentum. At this stage, whoever owns the idea is forced to choose. Most typically, the choice is made to commit to and therefore formalize the structure by creating an organization with

The Evolution of the Idea

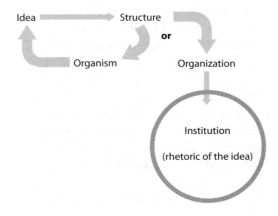

layers, hierarchy, tenets, and procedures in the attempt to ensure that the idea continues in its current iteration. Once this happens, however, the idea becomes subject to the power of the organization itself and has only one trajectory—to become so codified and rigid that it becomes an institution. In this use of the term, an institution is an organization that is in the business of perpetuating itself by using the power of the organization to keep it going and the rhetoric of the idea to give it perpetual legitimacy. Once this occurs, the idea is no longer what drives practices and structure because the institution is now in control. Depending on the power of the institution and how deeply the leaders cling to it, changing or even questioning the assumptions, tenets, and reasoning of the institution is extremely difficult. It becomes, in essence, a closed system in which outside forces and voices are perceived as threats to the integrity of the institution's reason for being. The idea is considered to be alive, but the idea has been strangled by the power of the institution. If not dead, the idea is buried so deeply it is only a matter of time before the institution becomes an empty shell devoid of meaning.

In my experience, this process is inevitable without dedicated and deliberate leadership. As an example, take the idea of socializing the young in a society. The child needs to be taught not only concepts but also history and values and must be given the opportunity to observe these in action. So a society may choose to gather the children together in order to pass on the story so that the children will be ready to enter the greater community as peers when the time is right (this signifies the structure, the contextual application of an idea). Over time, as curriculum is developed and teachers are trained, the structure gains traction and

soon becomes an organization. But unless the caretakers of the idea fight to keep the idea at the center, the organization will become so formalized, with layers of hierarchy and tenets that maintain the status quo, that it will morph into an institution that retains the idealized rhetoric to "socialize the young" but is now so powerful and solidified that it has become an idea unto itself.

What, then, is the antidote to institutionalism? How can an idea be maintained with integrity, even in changing environments? At the point where the idea begins to take shape as a structure, the crucial decision needs to be made by those who control the idea: either we commit to our structure—what we have learned, how we think about what the idea means in a given context—and evolve into an organization that eventually slips into an institutional morass, or we continually campaign on behalf of the idea and become an organism, an open system that seeks out any and all input in order to keep the idea alive. The choice is always the same: commit to the messy, unknowing life of a living entity by being willing to experiment with new structures and pursue any questions that would cause the idea to thrive, or settle for a fixed (and proven?) structure that may appear healthy but in the end will ultimately self-destruct the idea. Interestingly, the two most common uses of the term *institution* (besides marriage) are education and the church, both of which are hugely powerful institutions with long histories, time-honed practices, and sacred assumptions that only the most "out there" are willing to attempt to improve.

Let's return to the education example mentioned above. With all of the data available on how growing up is changing—how boys and girls develop differently and the way in which the brain matures—should the way contemporary education is delivered be reconsidered? Are we willing to go back to the original idea, that is, to develop mature, healthy adults who will take what has been given them and move the story forward? Can we ask questions like why middle school? What if schools were made smaller? What if boys and girls were educated separately? Why five days a week? Don't ask. The goals of education have become so limited for most kids that the surface of socialization is barely scratched as educational institutions seek to develop "competencies" in order to stay "competitive" with other societies. Education is now about *data* (raw content) and *information* (integrating data into categories). Socialization and the making of healthy, interdependent adults *begins* with data and information. Young people need help to move beyond mere content into *knowledge* (connecting the dots created by data and information into a cohesive landscape where true interdependent interaction and deliberation can take place), with the ultimate goal of producing men and women who embody *wisdom*—who can use knowledge to contribute to the greater good.

Now, what about the church? How do we "do" church? How is staff hired? How is the church going to be structured? Most important, what is the strategic goal for ministry?

For the church to become a family—which, in terms of health, means our life together needs to be experienced as an open system, or essentially as an organism—we must be open to thinking differently about how to operate as a community. We must be strategic and holistic, but we also must be willing to ask any and every question that would keep us from living into who we are called to be. After all, the first church (Acts 2) did not have a preordained plan or organizational structure in place. All that is known is that those in the early church quickly bonded to one another, and the family grew: "All the believers were one in heart and mind. No one claimed that any of their possessions was their own, but they shared everything they had. . . . More and more men and women believed in the Lord and were added to their number" (Acts 4:32; 5:14).

Even within the time frame that the New Testament was written, over time the structure of the local church morphed into a more visible and boundaried entity. Local "overseers" were identified, vetted by carefully crafted qualifications (Titus 1:7–9), and apparently appointed by centralized leadership from the outside (Titus 1:5). These leaders were organizationally, at least somewhat, trained by and under the authority of the apostles or their designates, and "God's flock" was instructed to follow their leaders.

> To the elders among you, I appeal as a fellow elder and a witness of Christ's sufferings who also will share in the glory to be revealed: Be shepherds of God's flock that is under your care, watching over them—not because you must, but because you are willing, as God wants you to be; not pursuing dishonest gain, but eager to serve; not lording it over those

Four Levels of Education

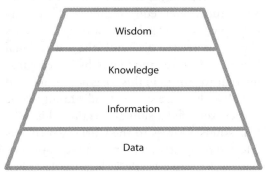

entrusted to you, but being examples to the flock. And when the Chief Shepherd appears, you will receive the crown of glory that will never fade away.

In the same way, you who are younger, submit yourselves to your elders. All of you, clothe yourselves with humility toward one another, because,

> "God opposes the proud
> but shows favor to the humble."
> (1 Pet. 5:1–5)

This structure apparently held for several generations: "overseers" or "bishops" led, and people followed. The New Testament documents, however, consistently stress that there is one Head, that is, Christ, and we are all his children, each endowed with gifts and called to unity.[4] Similar to Aristotle's vision of leaders functioning as peers—"first among equals" (*primus inter pares*), which is based on what one scholar has described as "friendship"[5]— the appeal is to "make every effort" to maintain the unity of the Spirit regardless of role or status within the body.

> As a prisoner for the Lord, then, I urge you to live a life worthy of the calling you have received. Be completely humble and gentle; be patient, bearing with one another in love. Make every effort to keep the unity of the Spirit through the bond of peace. There is one body and one Spirit, just as you were called to one hope when you were called; one Lord, one faith, one baptism; one God and Father of all, who is over all and through all and in all. (Eph. 4:1–6)

During the writing of the New Testament, this hierarchical structure seemed to be less about power and authority and more about maintaining the integrity of the idea of the gospel, but over time it slipped into organizationalism and ultimately morphed into an institution. As early as the second century the body of Christ became functionally stratified, separating the body into those who were in control and those who were not. Depending on the integrity of the leadership (along with other factors such as geographical location, local history, and applied theology), the local community has struggled ever since to be faithful to the biblical mandate of living as an organism while generally finding itself operating under the weight of an institution. For centuries, this institutionalism has encouraged some to be heard and expected, even forced, others to be silent. In most places and across most theological expressions throughout church history, this struggle has led to the almost complete dismantling of the biblical metaphor of the family-church.

With so many people feeling so deeply isolated and disconnected, now is the time for the body of Christ to reimagine biblical community and to reinvigorate family life together. That is what adoptive ministry is about. *Primus inter pares* ("first among equals") is not simply a philosophical ideal to be co-opted as mere rhetoric by the power of institutionalism; it is how we are called to live. In terms of youth ministry, this means that young people are co-siblings with all others in the community—functional "equals" even while needing to be nurtured and led into maturity. In today's church we need to dismantle the institutional baggage of power and hierarchy by recognizing that we are all in this together, young and old alike, because we are God's family. Pope Francis sounded a similar refrain in his 2014 Christmas address to the Curia, which was referred to by news outlets as a "scathing critique of Vatican officials." The pope described the Vatican's leadership as having "spiritual Alzheimer's. . . . We see it in the people who have forgotten their encounter with the Lord . . . in those who depend completely on their here and now, on their passions, whims and manias, in those who build walls around themselves and become enslaved to the idols that they have built with their own hands."[6]

Anything less is not New Testament Christianity. As the world has changed and as the church has seen not only its status but also its impact significantly decrease, we have no choice but to reexamine who we are and how we are called to live together. Jesus calls us salt and light (Matt. 5:13–14); Paul calls us Christ's body (Rom. 12:5); God the Father calls us his children (John 1:12). In Christ, we are not an institution—we are a living, breathing, messy, and powerful organism. We are family.

Adoption and the Current State of Youth Ministry

In 1988, Stuart Cummings-Bond wrote an article that was to become an important marker on youth ministry's developmental journey. His concept of the "One Eared Mickey Mouse"[7] got very little play initially, as most wondered why this could possibly be a negative thing. Youth ministry was focused on kids and Jesus Christ, not the church, so to be an appendage to the larger "head" seemed almost natural. When Mark DeVries wrote *Family Based Youth Ministry*[8] a few years later, leaders in the field (especially those who had been doing youth ministry for a while) knew that youth ministry was missing something by going it alone apart from the church. Within a few years several books and dozens of articles had been written in an attempt to get youth ministry to take parents seriously, as

youth ministers began to realize that adolescents need more than a few dedicated adults and a viable peer support system to become mature, interdependent adults. At the turn of the twenty-first century, most youth workers understood that youth ministry meant some level of parent ministry.

As Mike Yaconelli decried that "youth ministry as an experiment has failed,"[9] the most prominent discussion in youth ministry circles was why so many active youth ministry graduates were walking away from faith after high school, and several emphases emerged in the practice of youth ministry. Some advocate a much deeper partnership with parents, even to the point of questioning whether youth ministry is doing more harm than good.[10] Others push for strengthening the practices of youth ministry so as to "expect more" from youth group students. Leaders of this view seek to raise the bar on what is demanded of ("challenging") early and late adolescents. The proponents of this perspective encourage adolescents to become more active in their faith—from "acquiring fire" to "daring to share" their faith and doing "hard things" to change the world.[11] However, what has picked up considerable steam across the entire youth ministry world and is being accepted in widely divergent circles is the conviction that youth ministry work must be deeply embedded within the ministry of the church, regardless of the specific emphasis. This perspective, perhaps most notably expressed in the Sticky Faith project of the Fuller Youth Institute,[12] recommends structuring youth ministry practice as a holistic partnership between youth ministry, congregational leaders, parents, and the congregation at large. Even youth ministry parachurch organizations, which for the most part have been insulated from youth ministry practice trends, have recognized the necessity for a more holistic and ecclesial approach to their ministry.[13]

The pieces, then, are in place for reimagining youth ministry as integrated into the life of the church. For years many youth ministry leaders have recognized the importance of multiple people in a child's life for developmental health and have also promoted both parental and church-wide participation in the discipleship life of adolescents. The trend toward intergenerational relationships is obviously a theologically and psychosocially positive trajectory. What has emerged to date, however, is more akin to a programmatic adhesive patch to a flawed historical problem. Youth ministry, in fact *any* ministry, that fundamentally segregates a congregation into parts as its primary thinking and mode of ministry will inevitably hinder the work of the Spirit in creating a new community within the church. While done with the best of intentions, creating an environment of intergenerational relationships without actually enabling deep and lasting, intimate, intentional connectedness among various members of a congregation will have little sustainable impact on the life of either the young or the old. Though heightened interest in getting diverse populations within the church together is a positive trend, the conceptual or theological framework has not been available to take youth ministry as far as it needs to go. So long as parents are equipped and encouraged and young people and adult congregants develop relationships, the prevailing hope is that a strategically and programmatically fragmented congregation will develop long-term faithful followers of Jesus. Simply tweaking what has always been done—a parent class here, an intergenerational mission

day there—isn't enough. The goal and practices of youth ministry and *all* ministry need to be thoroughly reenvisioned so as to become God's visible family on earth. We are the family of God, and all ministry must be strategically and programmatically oriented to reflect this reality.

The Strategy of Adoptive Ministry

In *Starting Right: Thinking Theologically about Youth Ministry* (2001), I proposed a new structure of ministry programming. Unlike other models that use a similar "funnel" format, this model—"The Funnel of Programming"[14]—urges programming targeted to the level of interest expressed by those we serve. In the chapter titled "The Myth of the Perfect Model," I use the following categories of expressed interest and appropriate "levels" of programming:

- Outreach—people who would choose not to attend a "Christianized" event or program
- Entry level—people who are willing to attend a Christian-branded program or event but are not interested in being a part of a significantly spiritual activity or event
- Community building/discipleship level— those who are willing to be a part of a significant spiritually focused event or program
- Intimate relationship level—this level is for those who are not only willing to attend significant spiritual events and programs but are also willing to personally connect themselves to others in the pursuit of spiritual growth. This level

serves as the training ground for developing spiritual community in Christ.

- Mentoring level—as the final stage of this strategic process of integrating (in this case) adolescents into the body of faith, this is the level at which an adult personally mentors a young person, "assimilating" them (as I called it at the time) into the community of faith.

The Funnel of Programming provides a strategy for attempting to connect young people to the church as the goal of youth ministry. Guiding this strategy is the philosophy that a person needs to be "in" Christian family-like community in order to be "in" Christ." The flaw of this model, as I now see it, is that assimilation should not be the goal of ministry to outsiders, including the young. As mentioned in the introduction, assimilation requires the person being assimilated to adapt to the dominant group. This is not only offensive but it is also a stumbling block to authentic communal engagement. In using the model represented in *Starting Right*, we may do all the right programmatic things to mentor young people into the body, but what this inevitably means is that they "get" to sit in church, enjoy our music, appreciate the talking points, and make themselves "feel" a sense of attachment to the programmatic gathering of adults. This is not the idea behind *Adoptive Youth Ministry*.

The categories, however, do provide a helpful starting point for thinking critically about a strategy for participating in God's adoptive process. I propose, therefore, a revised version of the Funnel, which I would like to title "Strategy for Adoptive Ministry." Note that this strategy is not limited to youth ministry but is an intentional approach to helping

Strategy for Adoptive Ministry

The Faith Community

anyone who feels disconnected from the center of the community to come into the family-like intimacy that God's household promises.

Outreach. It is important to remember that many people not only feel disconnected from the community of faith but are also intentionally left out of the Christian community. The strategic concern, then, is to offer adoptive ministry as the motive and message of evangelism. We seek not to make adoptive children of those who are not interested in being part of the community; rather, we are witnesses to God's invitation to them to join the family the Spirit creates in Christ (John 1:12). Thus evangelism is less about "making converts" than about serving others (Matt. 25:31–46) and witnessing to God's desire to gather his children for the wedding feast of the Son (Matt. 22).

Welcoming level. For a person who is willing to participate on at least the periphery of the community of faith, even if they are resistant to full participation in faith practices or spiritual engagement with others, strategic adoptive ministry seeks to create space and an environment where he or she feels welcomed. This is one of the places where targeted ministry can be valuable (e.g., youth ministry, women's ministry, senior ministry); most people need to feel safe with their peers prior to investing in relationships outside their relational comfort zones. However, this assumes that while delivering "targeted ministry" programs and structure, leadership is so committed to adoptive ministry that anything they do within the mini-community is to be strategically located as a segue to adoption.

Engaging level. When a person has expressed an interest in personal faith, the role of adoptive ministry is to encourage this individual journey while framing the full experience of faith within the context of Christian community. This is where most ministries fail because when we promote private faith we sometimes communicate that personal faith is the end goal. This level is the place where leadership affirms a person's individual journey while engaging him or her toward a deeper, more intimate familial expression and corporate experience of faith.

Diverse relationships level. This level is the strategic place of connecting people to the broader family of faith, which leads to a recognition that all believers—whether in a local church, a given denomination, across town, or around the world—are part of the same family. By investing in a microcosm of intimate family-like relationships with a diverse community of faith siblings, men and women—both young and old—are encouraged and equipped to live differently as members of God's historical and global family.

Adoption level. As the community gathers—whether in small groups, for missions and service, or to serve the family internally or intentionally as they seek to engage with those outside the family of faith—the rhetoric, style, and experience of the gatherings must be an intentional recognition of the reality of our station as family. For example, this means that "worship" is never limited to singing certain songs with a particular flavor; gathering together is a comprehensive communal opportunity to collectively thank the Father who calls us his own.

Conclusion

Adoptive youth ministry means we participate in what God has declared and is in the process of realizing throughout his human family, the church. To create an environment where all community members believe that they belong, are welcome, and are part of the visible family of God, we must first recognize how institutional the church has become and proactively work to move toward becoming an open-system organism. This requires leadership, rhetoric (verbally and in print) that is more than mere words, and a change in attitude across the entire community. Once we have done the hard work of being willing, as a Spirit-led family, to align with God's work among us, the next step is to assess and appropriately respond to the different needs of those who are furthest out. In terms of youth ministry, we must rethink our practices—programs, events, structure, and everything we "do" in the name of youth ministry—so that those who need to feel welcomed are embraced, those who are called to move beyond "personal" faith are proactively engaged with Jesus's "one command" to love one another, and those who have few or no authentic relationships are provided the encouragement, training, and opportunity to participate in the community as a family member in the full body of faith.

This is the reason for *Adoptive Youth Ministry*, and every chapter will address various aspects of youth ministry as a whole. Rarely does an author use the language of this particular chapter, but each writes so as to help the reader strategically move forward with a commitment to adoptive ministry. We encourage you to visit the website dedicated to this book and concept at youthministry.fuller.edu. By engaging in a community that is going after adoption as the core concept for youth ministry, our desire is that we will all learn from one another.

Understanding the Changing Adolescent

STEVEN BONNER

Dr. Steve Bonner is not primarily a college professor, although he is a sought-after and excellent teacher. He has not spent his life and career sitting in libraries, offices, and classrooms, yet he is a solid scholar. He is a pastor and a youth pastor who has spent years in the trenches of ministry with kids and families. He is also a deliberate and thoughtful researcher, someone who has taken that experience and history and immersed himself in what people are saying about the changing adolescent landscape in order to better serve young people and their families. His "day job" is being a college professor, but Bonner has stayed deeply involved in and connected to the church and to adolescents, their families, their communities, and their world.

Bonner was asked to draw together the latest and best research on adolescent development so that at the outset of this book the reader can understand what growing up is like for today's youth. Employing the metaphor of flying in a helicopter across the rolling countryside (Bonner was a flight engineer and senior crew member in the Army), he helps us

to see the bigger picture. Bonner knows and understands childhood and adolescence both from the ground and from several thousand feet up. His insights and perspective provide valuable insight for those entering into adoptive youth ministry. As described in the introduction, our goal is not to get a church to "adopt" kids as their "own" children but rather to train and encourage adults to think of themselves as a family and to see children, teenagers, and emerging adults as their siblings who need them as they grow in their lives and faith. The task in youth ministry, then, is to help connect the young to their older brothers and sisters in the body of Christ through adoptive ministry. This takes a working knowledge of the basics of adolescent development, and Bonner gives a good start in that journey.

A historic tenet of youth ministry has been that in order to serve kids well we cannot only be concerned with the spiritual development of the young people we walk with, but we must also be aware of who they are and where they are in their journey as adolescents. Human development cannot be separated from spiritual development. What is appropriate teaching, counseling, guidance, and ministry to and for a twelve-year-old must be different from how we walk alongside a nineteen-year-old. In any ministry—but especially in one so volatile and precarious as adolescent ministry—we must understand who adolescents are, what they need, and what they are going through. Our call is to try to understand this from both a general and a specific perspective, which is the purpose of this chapter. Generally, it is important that youth workers—volunteers and staff alike—have a basic understanding of what all adolescents go through as they grow up, what we call a macro *awareness of adolescent development. As we work among them, we must also develop a* micro *understanding of each one's unique story within that general context.*

As you read this chapter, consider these questions:

1. *Bonner writes about an incident where he had not taken the time to know the young people he worked with and it cost him in his ministry. He laments, "I wish I could have that one back!" Think of a time or event when you reacted to something or said something, only to realize later that had you slowed down your reaction, done a little more digging, and looked a little harder, you would have been more helpful in your response. Ask yourself why you reacted out of ignorance instead of seeking to understand.*

2. *In light of the issues that adolescents experience today, as highlighted in this chapter, what does this mean for youth ministry and how can we help adults to participate in adoptive, welcoming youth ministry?*

3. *What is "systemic abandonment"? How does the active presence of adults in the lives of adolescents help to diffuse the power and impact of "systemic abandonment"?*

4. *Many people believe that in order to become adults, young people need to become more "responsible"—to get married, commit to a "stable" career, or save to buy a house as soon as possible. But these are external markers that may or may not (and usually do not) point to someone becoming an adult. How does this chapter describe becoming an adult? What are the factors, and what is the process?*

Introduction

A Bird's-Eye View

Several years ago I served in the US Army as a Chinook helicopter flight engineer, logging nearly five hundred hours of flight time throughout my enlistment. Early on in my training I took a trip that has ever since been etched in my mind.

The mission was to deliver supplies to a base on the East Coast. The route took us directly over the Smoky Mountains just as the leaves were changing.

Growing up in southern California I had never experienced the changing of the seasons. The landscape that spread out before me that afternoon takes my breath away to this day. A quilt of fantastic and brilliant colors seemed to hover in midair, intricately woven together by green fields, blue streams, and brown dirt roads. It spread out underneath me for miles in all directions. Millions of trees were changing, literally before my eyes. It was a tremendous sight, and on this flight I realized what a "bird's-eye view" really meant. I could see the country roads crisscrossing through the trees, bridges suspended over rivers, trucks meandering on their journeys, the occasional hawk, and the farmhouses that occupied space in open fields.

As I contemplate adolescent development and its importance for ministry to adolescents within the theological conception of adoptive ministry, I cannot help but recall that early fall afternoon and my encounter with the Smoky Mountains. My perspective enabled me to see so much more than if I were on the ground. I was able to see the journey ahead and where we had come from. I was able to see the contours in the terrain and the changes in elevation. In a sense, I was able to anticipate where we would be and what the journey to that point would require. In this chapter we will take a similar bird's-eye view. What might the youth worker see from this perspective regarding the adolescent landscape? What insight into the adolescent journey could we gain if we were able to see the lay of the land, and how does this insight enable adoption in our churches?

The Ying-Yang CD

I had been the youth pastor in a growing rural church for a few years. In the short time that I was there I was able to make significant inroads into the local school systems. One-third of the members in our congregation were schoolteachers in these systems, and our pastor of nearly thirty years at the time (he is still there!) had, in a real sense, become the community pastor. I rode these coattails right into the school systems and started building relationships.

One Wednesday afternoon I received a call from a distraught PE teacher asking for help. He and his colleague had confiscated a CD player from a student with an illegal (what we used to call "burned") copy of the Ying-Yang Twins. To make matters worse this teen was from my youth group. They hoped I could shed some light on the situation. With eagerness beyond my maturity, I agreed to help.

To be honest, I had never heard of this bombastic duo. With the CD in hand, I went home and did some research. If you are acquainted with the Ying-Yang Twins' music, then you might have an idea of what I was walking into as a youth minister in a relatively conservative part of the country and denomination. It didn't take long for my self-righteous indignation to boil over. I resolved to address the matter that night at youth group. I tossed out what I had been working on and quickly pieced together the most articulate, doctrinally prepared argument for cultural criticism and engagement I had ever written. It was a masterpiece. They would be persuaded by sound theology, Scripture quotations, and sheer logic.

I failed miserably. First, in my exuberance I had failed to spend any time in prayer, and God certainly was not about to bless what I was determined to do. Second, in my zeal I had not even considered that the person who had prompted my lecture might actually be present. For that young man and his friends, it was not one of my finer moments. Third (this one came out of thin air), as I was hitting the finer points of my theological argument a most terrifying thought occurred to me: *this is not limited to a single incident with a single person in the youth group; they are all listening to this music!* I stopped midstream and asked them outright. Yes, the majority of them had their own burned copies (another issue, I know), but then came their retaliation. They had listened to me, and now it was my turn to listen to them. They were indignant. I had insulted them and their music. I didn't realize it at the time, but when I left the church building that night, not only had my arrogance taken a hit but also my lack of awareness of who I was called to lead. I had begun a new journey of discovery that brought with it new challenges and new questions.

A New Perspective

As I reflect back on that turning point in my youth ministry journey I can definitely say that I wish I knew then what I know now. Certainly those kinds of situations can initiate rich periods of growth and development. In particular, that experience helped me to ask questions of adolescent development that I had not been prepared to ask. Had I been able to look at the situation from above rather than from below (where I was firmly rooted), I would have been able to see more of the landscape. I would have seen the obstacles in the journey—both directly ahead and down the road. Taking in the adolescent journey from above could have enabled me to be much more sensitive. Looking back, I could have seen the origins of pain and suffering so prevalent in the teens I worked with. Specifically, I might have been reminded of the broken families and grandparents struggling to raise their grandkids. I might have remembered that my teens were being raised in broken and fractured systems that often did not have their best interests at heart. With a view from above, I could have anticipated and avoided the relational setbacks that occurred as a result of my blunder. All these years later, I wish I could have that one back.

Why a Different Path?

The study of adolescent development is a field exploding with innovation, research, and growing and varied perspectives. What was certain a few years ago in the landscape of adolescence is now questioned. Adolescents in today's culture are changing quickly, and research struggles to keep up. Just a few short decades ago it was common to think of adolescence in terms of early and late, with young adulthood beginning as one graduated from high school and transitioned to college. As the 1980s gave way to the '90s, practitioners working with this age cohort began to recognize significant changes in the way adolescents negotiated their environments. It was not long before the term *middle adolescence*, or mid-adolescence, began to show up in academic and even popular literature. Generally speaking, early adolescence corresponded to junior high. Middle adolescence was understood to be the new high school phenomena, while late adolescence was pushed to the college years and beyond. The explanations for this apparent shift have been wholly unsatisfactory, and the continued divergence in the literature points to this uneasiness. Research has produced very little in the way of progress toward a universal agreement or even understanding of these developments. Perhaps this is because those in the field of adolescent research have persisted in studying adolescence through the lens of *age and stage* rather than through *markers* of development.

Much of the focus and history of adolescent development has zeroed in on identifying the *age* at which one transitions from one *stage* to another. Complicating the landscape further are the many prominent and classical theories of adolescent development. John Santrock identifies four theoretical orientations:

psychoanalytic (Freud and Erikson), cognitive (Piaget and Vygotsky), behavioral and social cognitive (Skinner and Bandura), and ecological (Bronfenbrenner).[1] I do not disagree with those who would argue that these various theoretical orientations provide different pieces to the "adolescent developmental puzzle."[2] Each should be considered in turn. However, many of these classical developmental theories contradict one another and were written before the development of mid-adolescence in the 1990s. Developmental psychologist Susan Harter even goes so far as to suggest that the traditional developmental icons "have fallen from theoretical grace" as they "held little explanatory or predictive power in furthering our understanding of specific behaviors."[3]

In this chapter I aim to chart a different course rather than argue for a particular age-and-stage perspective of adolescence. While perhaps appropriate for children and adults, the age-and-stage means of identifying growth in developmental maturity during the adolescent process is becoming more tenuous. The lack of consensus in the literature with regard to the age that adolescence begins or ends, whether two or three stages exist, or how age corresponds to these stages is evidence enough that, at best, the landscape is constantly changing and, at worst, something is amiss. Harter acknowledges that in her long history of research, writing, and teaching development she has come to realize that the breakdown of age and stage all blend together.[4] Therefore, I intend to take the reader to an altitude at which we can see and identify the significant markers of development that dot the adolescent landscape. I believe these markers have widespread agreement and are supported by the literature. Further, I contend that both the youth pastor in training and the youth pastor

in the trenches benefit from having identified the hazards (markers) that are interspersed along the adolescent landscape so they can be more effective companions on the journey. As a result, youth pastors, parents, and the church at large are in a better position to facilitate and encourage adoption within the local church.

Markers along the Adolescent Landscape

If you will, imagine climbing into my CH-47D helicopter (you may have to google it to get the image). The blades quickly beat the air into submission as it climbs to an altitude suitable for giving us a perspective on the adolescent journey. Below we see the fourteen-year-old whose CD was confiscated. Looking behind him we can see the terrain he has already traversed. Sharp unanticipated curves in the road, such as the divorce of his parents, mark a significant transition in this young life. We can see where his dad abandoned him and left his mom to handle the strain of raising him on her own. Immature and unable to support him, she arranged for the boy to be raised by his grandfather. Looking ahead, we can see several markers in the journey that he will have to navigate to make it successfully to adulthood.

These markers are interrelated. They crisscross and fold into one another, much like a patchwork quilt. While none of these markers are wholly dependent on one another, each informs and helps to shape the others, thus providing a more holistic picture of the adolescent landscape. Separately, each is significant and needs to be thoroughly understood in order to better assist the developing adolescent in successfully navigating the approaching terrain. Taking these markers together enables us to successfully assemble an adult ground team to assist the adolescent in traversing the oncoming landscape.

As I consider the adolescent developmental landscape, three significant markers need to be pointed out: the timing and duration of adolescence, the reality of multiple selves, and the growing reality of objectification. It is my opinion that if one has a working knowledge of these current markers, how they intertwine, and how they serve as the impetus to many other developmental issues, then the youth pastor, with the help of the adopting church, will be able to assist the developing adolescent traverse the terrain of adolescence.

Timing and Duration of Adolescence

After the Ying-Yang devotional (that's what I began to call that unfortunate Wednesday night youth group gathering) I began to ask the adolescents I served questions about their perception of life and faith and also the role the church played in their lives. Their collective response awakened something that had been dormant inside me: young people, when given the chance, hold storehouses full of experience and perception to share that I, and most adults I knew, rarely access. In the wake of that evening I began to realize that, without a greater understanding of what they were going through, I could not help them to learn how to discern between competing values and longings, grow through a rugged and difficult adult terrain of expectation and agenda (including in the church), and take on faith at a deep, lifelong level. What also became clear is that these kids needed adults in their lives other than me; there was no way a single leader who planned and orchestrated events, gave talks, and ran programs could make a dent in what

they needed. I knew their journey through adolescence was longer and more difficult than mine had been, but I really did not know how so. I soon realized that if I was going to actively involve more adults in the lives of my youth, I needed to better understand the experience of adolescence, which begins with getting a handle on the timing and duration of adolescence. What are the markers of adolescent development? It begins with timing.

Is Adolescence Extending?

Our country has transitioned through some massive cultural shifts in the past century. Two shifts in particular deserve mention: the loss of a shared corporate story (what some call a metanarrative) and the steady rise of systemic abandonment and resultant isolation of children and youth from adults. These major transitions gave way to a new stage of development in the human lifespan—adolescence. As I intimated above, this stage of development has been thoroughly studied and exhaustively documented. As our country transitioned from the twentieth to the twenty-first century, developmentalists acknowledged that this stage of the journey was taking longer to navigate. The contributing factors are varied and complex, but one common thread runs through them all: kids are increasingly separated from adults. While the diminishment of adult relationships will be seen throughout this chapter, this reality deserves brief mention here because it hints at larger systemic issues that have contributed to this malaise. For as long as adolescence has been a field of study it has been accepted that adolescence begins in puberty and ends when the individual becomes an adult. This presupposition presents two significant issues for those interested in helping adolescents on their journey. First, current research suggests that puberty is progressively starting earlier, especially for females. If it is starting earlier, this complicates and necessitates a rapid and careful response. Second, while no one can precisely label (especially chronologically) when adolescence ends, it is clear that its beginning is rooted in the process of the body and mind changing in preparation for adulthood and that the transition into adulthood is rooted in the social environment and how the particular person responds to that environment, both externally and internally. If researchers are in disagreement (even those late adolescent/emerging adults/young adults who were interviewed don't know, though the culture at large agrees with the latest brain studies that it is somewhere between the mid- to late twenties), then we must adjust our ministry strategies toward both ends of the spectrum as we seek to adopt young people into full and active participation in the family of God. In what has become a rather colloquial saying, author John Santrock suggests that "adolescence begins in biology and ends in culture."[5] This statement seems to capture, rather succinctly, the elusive and rapidly shifting nature of adolescence.

Decrease in the Age of the Onset of Puberty

In the United States and in Europe,[6] data on the age of the onset of menarche has been collected and recorded. "Declines in the age of menarche have been reported from the late 1800s to the mid-1900s."[7] This trend continued downward until the middle of the twentieth century, when it seemed to level off.[8] At this point, two independent works—the Pediatric Research in Office Settings study and the population-based National Health and Nutrition

Examination survey, which were published in 1997 and 2002—reported earlier sexual maturation in American girls. The study published in 1997 of 17,000 girls indicated that the initial signs of puberty were occurring much earlier than had been recorded previously.[9] The most recently published research continues to support this downward trend. S. Cesario and L. Hughes report that girls in the "United States appear to be maturing at an earlier age and documented incidence of precocious puberty is on the rise."[10] The obvious question is, why?

While many theories have been reported, the most popular in the media is the obesity or BMI (body mass index) theory. The BMI theory holds that there is a correlation between the onset of the age of puberty and weight. Early weight gain is often cited as the culprit since the chemical leptin, which is produced by fat cells, is a component necessary for the progression of puberty.[11] With the percentage of overweight kids nearly doubling between the decades of the 1970s and 1990s, this correlation was easily made.[12] While on the surface there seems to be a correlation, what has not been reported widely in the media are the studies that point out the inconsistencies with the BMI theory. Though there are too many inconsistencies to discuss here, three important studies deserve mention. These studies report that an early relationship to BMI was not apparent in African American girls and was negative in boys;[13] furthermore, BMI remained constant where researchers found that the onset of puberty dropped from a mean age of 10.9 in 1991 to 9.9 in 2006.[14] While the BMI hypothesis is predominant in the mainstream consciousness of American culture, its standing in published research is undecided.

Given the growing body of research, it is interesting that the ecological predictors of the earlier onset of puberty have not received the same attention in the media as the BMI predictor has. Numerous studies have linked the earlier onset of puberty to ecological and psychological stress.[15]

Collectively, this research demonstrates that the early onset of puberty cannot be attributed exclusively to BMI. Any childhood practitioner has long known that a healthy and stable home life is important to healthy outcomes. For the better part of two-plus decades of research, ecological and familial stressors have predicted the onset of puberty. Certain of this relationship, Julianna Deardorff and her team state, "Environmental conditions, particularly those in the family domain, influence the timing of puberty in girls. Specifically, the absence of a biologically related father has been shown to accelerate reproductive development."[16] While this assertion may seem shocking, it does not surprise those of us who work with children in the church. A growing body of current research demonstrates that chronically stressful ecological environments influence the onset of puberty. If adolescence begins in biology, as Santrock has suggested, then ministry to youth in the church must adapt to this changing reality. Programming for children's and youth ministry programs needs to be revisited in light of this significant marker of development, which presents crucial implications and opportunities to the church that seeks to adopt its youth. Given this new reality, is it too far a stretch to ask, what constitutes ministry to adolescents?

Difficulty Determining When Adolescence Ends

I have taught for some time that if we are going to be effective in reaching adolescents, then we need to know where they are and the obstacles that prevent or slow down their psychosocial and spiritual development. The continuing challenge, however, is that adolescence is a moving target; it is constantly changing. I have marshaled evidence that demonstrates, biologically, that adolescence is beginning earlier. Interestingly, youth ministry's collective eye has focused on the other end of the journey. If Santrock is correct in that adolescence ends in culture, this strongly suggests that youth ministry is taking place in an environment never before realized.

Determining when adolescence ends and adulthood begins is extremely difficult. Prior to our current cultural context (a couple of decades ago) a person was considered to be an adult when he or she graduated from high school. At that point a person was said to have individuated and developed a core self. Whether one went on to college or directly into the workplace, he or she was understood to be an adult. Generally speaking, this is no longer the case. Citing years of his own research, J. J. Arnett suggests that those on the upper end of the adolescent journey should be known as emerging adults rather than late adolescents or young adults.[17] While his argument as to why this age group (eighteen to twenty-one) is not known as late adolescents or young adults has only muddied the already murky waters of adolescent developmental research, his suggestion that the top three criteria for adulthood are accepting responsibility for oneself, making independent decisions, and becoming financially independent is helpful.[18] These criteria are true of anyone in that age range, though they are accomplished gradually and occur incrementally. That it is taking longer for young people to transition into adulthood is well accepted; perhaps it is best to leave it there. Crossing the threshold of adulthood is generally taking more time, and recognizing the rather fluid nature of the landscape is important in helping young people navigate the journey. In my estimation, emphasis and debate on this age and stage effectively turned the researchers' focus from the important developmental changes taking place in junior high and high school that, as will be demonstrated below, have contributed to the lengthened duration of adolescence.

Multiple Selves

My research into the timing and duration of adolescence supported what I knew instinctively—adolescence was changing. But the Ying-Yang devotional revealed something I was not expecting: my teens seemed to be leading double lives! I was not expecting the backlash I received, especially from my most spiritually active teens. How could they profess obedience and allegiance to Christ on the one hand, and then listen to this music on the other? It didn't make sense. Were they hypocrites? Were they intentionally duplicitous? Did they just not care? Did they even know? These questions led me to our second marker of adolescence: the reality of multiple selves.

Cognitive Propagation

It is widely understood that the transition from childhood to adolescence brings with it dramatic physical, emotional, and cognitive advances. While much has been written about these developmental changes and their implications for youth ministry, the development of the cognitive is most important for our current discussion. As adolescents move deeper into this transition it becomes evident that their sense of self becomes increasingly differentiated. With the development of abstract thought, they become aware that their self-representations begin to shift; that is, their sense of self is not internally consistent and leads to a "proliferation of selves."[19] Harter says that for junior high students "a critical developmental task, therefore, is the construction of multiple selves that will undoubtedly vary across different roles and relationships."[20]

Cognitive advances facilitate this propagation and, in concert with social pressures, perpetuate the development of multiple selves. When young adolescents develop the ability of abstract thought they actually lack the developmental-cognitive ability to integrate the abstractions that develop within each socially constructed self. Thus, while an adult is able to fully and intelligently engage adolescents in each self-representation, adolescents do not have the ability to apply abstractions across the many socially constructed selves. Each self (or persona) is, in effect, compartmentalized. The adult who seeks to engage the adolescent will encounter inconsistencies in the adolescent's self-presentation. Ironically, this inability to integrate abstract thought across their multiple selves actually serves to protect young adolescents from opposing and contradictory characteristics. In other words, the contradictory characteristics do not generalize to the other selves, are generally undetected, and thus reduce potential conflict. As the adolescent ages, however, their cognitive-developmental abilities continue to develop, and they soon are able to make comparisons.

The young adolescent progressing in age and maturation (typically understood to be middle adolescence) not only develops the ability to compare self with friend, self with mother, self with father, and so on, but will also pick up on the inconsistencies. Now the adolescent can overlay realizations, attributes, and characteristics developed in one role-related self and compare and contrast those realizations in other selves. While these contradictions are realized, the adolescent does not yet possess the cognitive-developmental ability to integrate these multiple selves. The "awareness of these opposites causes considerable intrapsychic conflict, confusion, and distress given the inability to coordinate these seemingly contradictory self-attributes."[21]

The Ying-Yang devotional unfolded among a group of junior high and high school adolescents. What I could not have foreseen that night was their immediate negative reaction to my harsh critique of their music. Their response shocked me. At the time I could not reconcile the contradictory behavior I was suddenly faced with. I had experienced phenomenological whiplash! The experience opened my eyes (and my ears), and I quickly tuned in to this emerging reality by turning my attention to facilitating integration rather than perpetuating proliferation.

Proliferation of Selves

I learned that I was facilitating the proliferation of multiple selves among the adolescents in my youth group. While I certainly did not do this intentionally, I soon realized that as children cognitively develop the ability of abstract thought in adolescence they begin to pull away. That is, they develop self-protective mechanisms. The most drastic of these mechanisms is the development of multiple selves.

As youth transition from elementary to middle school, and later to high school, they are introduced to increasingly public social comparisons and adult conditional support.

The transitions that come with education (and parallel transitions in church, inasmuch as the local church models their education program after the local school system) heighten the young adolescent's self-consciousness. The priority in most elementary schools is on effort. A child is encouraged to work hard and do better. When one transitions into adolescence, however, schools "heighten the salience of social comparison."[22] In junior high and above, poor performance is equated to a lack of academic ability—an association that is often processed publicly. "The emphasis on social comparison is a pernicious new influence that leads to the conclusion that everyone but those at the top of the academic ladder [is] intellectually incapable. This, in turn, ushers in a need to protect the self."[23] This performance pressure facilitates the development and proliferation of multiple selves, which is a function of self-protection and preservation.

When we couple the social comparison perpetuated by adults with the conditionality of adult support, adolescents struggle to keep up. Adults force adolescents to adopt a new self when they communicate that their approval is conditional. Of course, this is not really support; the conditions placed on the adolescents are actually socially constructed hoops they must negotiate in order to please the adults in their lives.[24] This performance-based acceptance is particularly damaging when it comes from trusted adults: parents, grandparents, coaches, and ministers. When the adolescent experiences high levels of conditionality, hopelessness is the result, and high levels of hopelessness translate into low levels of self-esteem. Consequently, the adolescent experiences the developmental need to protect the emerging self, causing the proliferation of multiple selves.

Integration

If low conditional support facilitates the perpetuation of multiple selves, then high levels of unconditional adult support facilitate integration of the selves. Adult-driven systems contribute, enable, and perpetuate multiple selves, but significant psychosocial research has shown that adults can also help to facilitate the integration of adolescent multiple selves. Research demonstrates that higher levels of cognitive development require higher sustained levels of adult support and scaffolding.[25] When this support is not present, adolescent cognitive development may even be delayed.[26] Research reveals the benefits of adult support or scaffolding at progressively higher levels of cognitive development.[27] My own research, which will be discussed below as an emerging concern, demonstrates that adolescent cognitive attainment is taking longer. Collectively, research persuasively shows that when adolescents (and by extension, children) are effectively left on their own to develop, cognitive attainment slows down. When adult support and scaffolding is consistent from childhood through adolescence, higher levels of cognitive development are facilitated at younger ages. Could the lengthening of adolescence and the proliferation of multiple selves be tied directly to increasingly lower levels of adult support? I believe so.

The call to adoption is particularly poignant given the realities described above. What adolescents need are more faithfully committed adults who are willing to be fully present in their lives. The church is strategically and theologically positioned to offset the proliferation of multiple selves in adolescents. By providing high levels of unconditional support through a network of loving adults, the adolescent reality of multiple selves can be arrested and higher levels of cognitive attainment achieved. What this research demonstrates beyond a shadow of a doubt is that kids desperately need adults to become healthy adults. Furthermore, they need faithful, committed adults to become faithful, committed believers.

Objectification

I stated above that these markers are interrelated. While they can stand alone they tend to fold into one another. Taken together they present a formidable landscape for the adolescent to negotiate. The marker of objectification is particularly iniquitous because it cuts theologically to the heart of personhood. What's more, this marker tends to run just below the surface of the other markers, enabling the rupture that continues to grow between youth and adults. The objectification of our young is also the most difficult to pinpoint as it is most often clothed in the language of love and sacrifice and is, therefore, laden with emotional weight.

Adolescents need a core group of adults to journey with them in order to reverse the effects of these markers and successfully traverse the adolescent landscape. I examine this marker last because it so often goes undetected, even though it is present in every arena of an adolescent's life, especially where adults are present. It was Chap Clark's term *systemic abandonment* in *Hurt* that slowly opened my eyes to this reality and my own objectification of youth in my sphere of influence. I could not agree more with Clark; *more* adults are needed to undo and reverse the trends of systemic abandonment. Ironically, either through outright neglect, abuse, or objectification—which are all forms of systemic abandonment—the very adults who can reverse the tide are the ones enabling these very markers of the adolescent landscape to persist. As we turn our attention to the objectification of our young, we will first consider the theological issue of personhood and then take up three primary ways in which objectification occurs in the lives of adolescents.

Denial of Personhood

Christianity has long affirmed the fundamental theological assertion that to be human is to be a person. Created from the triune community, relationship is essential to personhood. To be a person is to be in relationships.[28] As John Zizioulas says, "There is no true being without communion. Nothing exists as an 'individual' conceivable in itself. Communion is an ontological category."[29] Our culture tends to perpetuate the unhealthy notion that people are their interests or their functions. Christianity, with its commitment to personhood, claims that people are their relationships and as imagers of Christ are "communal structure[s] because Christ is in communion with the Father and the Spirit."[30] As preconditions for the ontology of personhood, being and relationship are rooted in the reality that humans are image bearers of God.[31] Humanity created in the image of God has dignity. Therefore, a person "cannot be used merely as a means by any[one] . . . but must always be used at the same time as an end."[32] The dignity of every person must be protected and never exploited or manipulated and certainly never used as a means to an end. Consider the words of Louis Pojman:

> We cannot think of our personhood as a mere thing, for then we would have to judge it to be without any value except that given to it by the estimation of someone else. But then

that person would be the source of value, and there is no reason to suppose that one person should have unconditional worth and not another who is relevantly similar. Therefore, we are not mere objects. We have unconditional worth, and so must treat all such value-givers as valuable in themselves—as ends, not merely means.[33]

Objectification is the act of turning a human being into a thing or commodity. When this happens the person is depersonalized. When a person's humanity is ignored, used, or not properly acknowledged, that person is harmed; his or her personhood is denied. Being reduced to a *thing* diminishes the humanity of the one being objectified. Using a "person as an object, in the sense of a mere instrument for someone else's purposes" consequently reduces "this individual to the status of a mere instrument."[34] It is my contention that adolescents are being used by the adults in their lives as means to adult ends. This objectification occurs in the many adult-controlled and adult-driven systems, organizations, and institutions that adolescents find themselves in.

Extracurricular Life

Student athletes, student dancers, band members, and drama students (to name a few) are all commodified and objectified by the adults in their lives when they are used for any adult-driven end. When parents use students vicariously to recover something from their own childhood, they are objectified. When commercial interests commodify students, they are objectified. When coaches, instructors, and directors use students to win competitions and thus secure their own status, adolescents are objectified. And, as alluded to above, objectification is made worse when the adolescent trusts the one doing the objectifying. Thus when the cognitive-developmental ability of abstract thought progresses, the adolescent is able to reflect on how adult-driven agendas have used them for adult gain. Ontologically, they may not fully understand the depersonalization that has occurred, but they can feel it. They learn early on what it feels like to be used. When this occurs at the hands of trusted adults, the betrayal and damage are magnified. It is objectification that helps to facilitate and speed up the protective mechanism of multiple selves mentioned above.

Adults are present in every arena across the adolescent spectrum of extracurricular life. When adults engage adolescents solely through adult-driven performance agendas, kids are harmed. These very systems, originally for the benefit of children and adolescents, perpetuate the self-driven agendas of adults. While they are often clothed in the rhetoric of play and physical/emotional benefit, they actually serve the needs and desires of the adults who perpetuate these extracurricular activities.

Education

As a youth pastor I actively sought creative ways to engage my students outside their involvement in church. Doing so permitted me access to the other selves my students had developed. Since adolescents spend the majority of their time in school, I became a substitute teacher. Access to the hallways and lunchrooms of my teens enabled me to learn a great deal about adolescents and youth culture; however, I was not prepared for what I would learn from the adults. As the months passed, I got to know many of the teachers at the middle and high school levels and eventually gained

their trust. The frustrations they aired around the lunch table were telling.

Frustration, fatigue, and burdensome federal and state regulatory requirements had, over time, created calloused hearts. Many of these teachers were simply going through the motions. Whatever zeal or passion they had when they answered their calling had long dissipated. As they discussed issues in their classrooms it became clear to me that they were not engaging their students as persons; instead, students were treated as objects to be sorted out and negotiated. Of course, there were exceptions. The freshly minted teacher would offer idealized words of hope, but they were quickly reprimanded and put in their place.

Around the table teachers would share names of the exceptional students and lament those who were poor performers, troublemakers, or both. The less than desirable students were more often than not described in negative and dehumanizing terms. I knew many of these students; I knew about their home lives and the daily struggles they had to overcome simply to make it to school. These teachers were trusted by the community to educate and mold young minds, but their students had become mere objects to be negotiated. These students were viewed and treated as some*thing* to be sifted and sorted, not persons to be engaged and loved.

The descriptions and treatment of their students bothered me greatly. As I dug deeper and asked more questions, I discovered what I have come to understand as an innate institutional malaise. What I experienced then is now considered common knowledge—if anything, it has gotten worse. Our educational model is still perpetuating the factory model of education: input raw product (the student), then shape, mold, and manipulate the product to produce a society-worthy end product. While there are noteworthy exceptions, thoughts concerning the student's humanity, development, and family are hardly considered or are seen as obstacles to overcome. Furthermore, many school systems place an inordinate amount of weight on their student's standardized test scores. When a teacher's performance review or the job security of school administration is tied to these scores, we should not be surprised. Teachers now commonly train their students to test well on these exams.

Adolescents who have grown up in these systems have been conditioned to believe that their self-worth is tied to their performance on these (and other) tests. Here we see conditional approval and support at its worst. Those who score high receive praise and adoration, and those who do not are often derided. Approval and support from teachers and administration depend on successful performance, and the adults running the education system determine what successful performance looks like. Ultimately, adolescents are being used as a means to the adult end of promotion, recognition, and job security. Students raised in these systems are taught conditional support and approval. They are conditioned to believe that their self-worth and their sense of self is tied to these performance-driven adult agendas. These adult-led systems (along with the extracurricular activities) actually force adolescents to pull away from adults and cognitively drive them to develop multiple selves. In the end, they are only trying to protect themselves. The lack of genuine and authentic adult support coupled with adult objectification of adolescents facilitates and perpetuates this troubling reality. Do they trust adults? Generally, no, and why should they? As abstract thought kicks in they are able to differentiate and reflect on how

adults have used them as means to an end; as a result, they pull away. This objectification sets up the dilemma we now see prevalent across the spectrum of adolescence, even in youth ministry.

Youth Ministry

I hinted briefly above that I inadvertently contributed to the development of multiple selves in those adolescents to whom I was called to pastor. I now believe that objectification occurs in youth groups across the country, and it is particularly hazardous to the spiritual and cognitive development of the emerging adolescent. First, when objectification occurs in youth ministry it compounds the objectification that is taking place in the other arenas of the adolescent's life. Our churches must be places of refuge and safety, not another system of adult-centered performance-driven agendas that must be carefully negotiated by the growing adolescent. Second, the objectification of adolescents (and children) in our churches undermines the very theology we profess. When we objectify our students we fracture the *imago Dei* in their developing self-concept. Consequently, their spiritual and developmental journey is lengthened, and their transition to healthy, God-fearing adults is jeopardized. When they begin to sense this abuse, the gospel we proclaim becomes hollow and meaningless because they are being forced into the all-too-familiar performance-driven agendas they negotiate everywhere else.

If we are honest with ourselves, as church leaders we have a lot in common with the teachers mentioned above. While we quietly convince ourselves that we are not like them, our leadership and peers deem us successful if we are able to bring in the numbers, even if our current rhetoric says size and number are not important. We fall back on techniques and fads geared to generate numbers, and our teens are objectified in the process. Often, youth pastors tend to gravitate to those teens who seem to be more likable, though perhaps I am the only one who has done this. We massage our guilt with hollow and empty arguments. Ultimately, when we sift through, label, and categorize our students, are we not also objectifying them? Sometimes we even publicly trumpet the more spiritual. And when the athletes, dancers, and musicians in our groups perform well do we not celebrate them openly while often ignoring the "lesser" achievements of others? Isn't our support and approval often tied to their performance? While there are certainly exceptions, my intention here is to illuminate what has perhaps become the default practice rather than the exception.

Our churches can be places of safety and security for adolescents, but the silent denial of teenage personhood must be addressed. The church is uniquely positioned to address and reverse this trend and live up to the high calling of ministering to adolescents. When the adults in an adolescent's life artificially impose the marker of objectification, adults within the church can offer their presence, suffer alongside, and model hopeful lives. The youth pastor cannot help adolescents to navigate this terrain alone. Full adoption by the church is necessary for successful navigation of the adolescent landscape.

Emerging Concern

Early in this chapter I presented a brief argument for taking a different path when considering the development of adolescents. I agree with Susan Harter. The old standby theories need to be reconsidered when it comes to adolescence, especially when we realize that the most prominent of those developmental theorists were doing their work before the onset of mid-adolescence. Culture has changed. Families have changed and so too have adolescents. My position on considering a different path involves my own experience and research. Though I have alluded to the central concern above, I will treat it here in full: cognitive attainment of adolescents is taking longer. While this could certainly be one of the markers discussed above, I feel it deserves to be set apart because, when woven together, the other three markers and sub-aspects of those markers are contributing to and perhaps even creating this reality.

Delayed Cognitive Attainment

I transitioned into full-time teaching of youth ministry at the university level in the fall of 2008. In my first semester of teaching I discovered that the majority of my freshman and sophomore students were manifesting many of the same psychosocial characteristics as the high school students I had just left; they had not yet integrated their multiple selves. Moreover, I found myself in conversations with colleagues who reported that their students seemed to be less mature. I verified these anecdotal findings with colleagues at other universities and, after a series of events and a couple of years' time, a colleague and I presented research at the annual national conference of the Southern Association of Colleges and Schools Commission on Colleges (SACSCOC).[35]

In that SACSCOC session we presented qualitative and phenomenological evidence that contemporary college students are not as cognitively prepared for the overall college experience as students several decades ago. We attributed this diminishment to the psychosocial phenomenon of extended adolescence and then suggested ways that student services, faculty, and assessment leaders might respond. That session generated substantial discussion and was well received. While the evaluations expressed the need for quantitative data—a lacuna we admitted at the time—the overwhelming response of our colleagues in that session encouraged a redoubling of efforts to understand just what and why this was occurring. Blaming cognitive diminishment on extended adolescence seemed rather vague. I soon realized that the key to understanding the diminishment could be found in understanding the psychosocial reality that turned me on to this issue in the first place: mid-adolescent multiple selves.

Was I experiencing a lengthening of mid-adolescence among my students? Though this question runs counter to some of the prominent theories surrounding this age group, it was plain to us that our incoming students lacked the cognitive developmental acumen to integrate their selves. My colleagues and I were (and are) experiencing diminished cognitive abilities in our undergraduate students. In the spring of 2013, we launched a longitudinal study to gather new quantitative evidence. After one year of data collection, our research suggests the rate at which eighteen- to twenty-year-olds are attaining the level of cognitive development expected of them in previous decades has slowed.[36]

What Extended Mid-adolescence Means

This new psychosocial reality has significant implications on the expected academic, moral, and social performance of incoming students. With this evidence (both qualitative and quantitative) in hand, the current developmental paradigms need to be revisited. Our research demonstrates that it is taking longer for young people to transition through adolescence. Holding to a particular age or stage at this point is irrelevant. The issue is not that young people (whether one refers to them as teens, adolescents, mid-adolescents, or late adolescents) are less capable cognitively but that they are not reaching cognitive attainment as soon as they once did. The speed of attainment has slowed, thus their ability to get out of or emerge from adolescence has slowed. It is simply taking longer for adolescents to attain the requisite cognitive abilities to transition into emerging adulthood/young adulthood. When we witness diminished ability in the classroom and across campus we tend to hold the opinion that students are coming to us dumber, but this is not the case. Students are arriving on our campuses less cognitively mature, but why?

The larger purpose of *Adoptive Youth Ministry* seeks to address this reality. I suggest that what we are experiencing in our classrooms and what our data demonstrates is the result of the cumulative effects of adolescents who have, essentially, been left alone to journey through adolescence. Chap Clark recognized the damaging effects of systemic abandonment in his *Hurt* research.[37] When kids are systematically left to their own devices to individuate into adulthood, their progression is slowed. The evidence for increased adult support is convincing. Susan Harter cites recent and credible research that indicates that "cognitive solutions will not necessarily emerge automatically with development. Nor will the potential benefits of movement to late adolescence necessarily accrue. Development may be delayed or even arrested if there is not sufficient support for the transition to higher levels of conceptualization . . . [there is] compelling evidence for the role of support or scaffolding at higher levels of cognitive development."[38] Additionally, R. E. Dahl argues that it is absolutely crucial for adolescents and young adults to have access to adult social scaffolding.[39] As adolescents progress through adolescence there is greater need for social scaffolding from adults if adolescents are going to achieve optimal cognitive development. If this is true of adolescents, how much more so is it true of children? Is it possible that what we are witnessing on college campuses is the cumulative effects of years of diminished adult support? The implications and opportunities for the church are substantial.

Moving toward Adoption

From the vantage point of that CH-47D helicopter, we can much more effectively survey the adolescent landscape. We can see the main hazards/markers of the adolescent journey and how they intersect and enable the others. Now that we have taken the bird's-eye view of adolescent development, we are in a better position to identify the central reality that ties all of these markers together: the lack of loving adult relationships. Simply stated, adolescents need adults—a great many more than we realized! Through loving and sacrificial adult relationships, adolescents will transition through adolescence much faster. Through the abundance of adult relationships, adolescents will integrate their selves much earlier than is currently the norm. Through theologically grounded and prophetically positioned adults, adolescents will be able to realize their full potential as persons created in the image of God. The church is uniquely positioned to turn the tide. By being fully connected to, embraced by, and included in the historic body of Christ, adolescents can safely and securely transition into and become healthy adult believers.

Welcoming Wounded and Broken Adolescents into the Family of God

MARV PENNER

Dr. Marv Penner is widely considered one of the most significant and influential youth ministry leaders anywhere. Penner, a Canadian, spends most of his time teaching, leading, consulting, training, and equipping youth ministry scholars, practitioners, and students in Canada and the United States but also travels extensively throughout the world, helping people to think deeply about today's adolescents and helping them to respond faithfully in the name of Christ. Whether he is teaching in Korea, speaking in Latin America, or consulting in Europe, Penner brings a wealth of ministry experience, comprehensive knowledge, and global sensitivity to those who serve the young. Among Penner's primary ministry foci, he is particularly well known for helping kids and families in crisis, which is what we have asked him to share in this chapter.

As Penner writes about "wounded and broken adolescents," it is important to know and remember two things. First, although Penner is describing young people who have experienced a relatively serious brokenness that presents itself in a variety of ways, his perspective

is that most kids will encounter some level of similarly traumatic experience along the way. Penner is not addressing an isolated occurrence—just in case we encounter a child, teenager, or emerging adult who is broken or wounded. He is expecting us to realize that we will regularly and consistently encounter woundedness in ministry. Emphasizing the necessity for community involvement (what we have already described as the essence of participating in God's work of adoption), Penner points out that we must be prepared to recognize and respond to kids and families in a way that promotes not only short-term relief but also long-term communal engagement.

The second issue at the heart of Penner's chapter, which consistently surfaces in his speaking and teaching ministry, is that he has come to believe that all kids are bruised and wounded as a result of today's performance- and image-oriented society. Penner's work contributed significantly to my books on this subject, Hurt *and* Hurt 2.0: Inside the World of Today's Teenagers. *He has been an advocate for helping the church and youth* workers in particular to be very careful as they lead and serve young people in the name of Christ. What I call "systemic abandonment"[1] (when adults abandon their responsibility to consistently protect, nurture, and guide the young as their primary legacy) Penner and others sometimes refer to as "systemic isolation," which describes the effect of the loss of social capital and adult nurture. While the upfront message of this chapter regards the extraordinary brokenness that young people sometimes experience, the subtext is vital: every single teenager or emerging adult we serve has their own share of wounds they are dragging along behind them.

As you read this chapter, you may notice that Adoptive Youth Ministry is not a cookie-cutter, one-formula-fits-all type of book. As we drew together a wide variety of thinkers, scholars, and leaders who have influenced and continue to influence youth ministry thinking and practice—and whom we believe should continue to influence youth ministry for years to come—we decided to invite them to write out of their own history, experience, and style. Thus Penner's chapter has a unique flavor and style that is particular to him. Instead of trying to edit the authors into stylistic conformity, we have chosen to go this route because we feel they have earned the right for their individual voices to be heard, especially those who have a long and distinguished track record as key influencers and leaders. We believe this adds to the richness and diversity of expression in this book.

As you read, consider these questions:

1. This chapter underscores the basic longings and developmental needs all of us have, which obviously includes the young people we serve in ministry. Where in your own story do you resonate with what Penner shares in this chapter? (If this chapter brings up for you unresolved or deeply personal experiences and/or events, we encourage you to maintain boundaries if need be but to take steps to work through anything in your own history and background that keeps you from being free.)

2. Penner notes that while people tend to deal with crisis in two simplistic categories—those who have been victims and those who have made "bad choices"—the reality is that life is never that clean or simple. What is your understanding of how the chapter deals with this dilemma?

3. How can adoptive youth ministry, by which we are proactively participating in God's work of calling us his children, foster hope and healing for teenagers or emerging adults dealing with crisis?

The email came in just before midnight. The despair in its words was almost palpable. "I'm so lost. I'm so alone. There is nothing in my life that feels good. Just don't let me cut. I got no one and nothing. Please don't let me cut."

Sadly, the writer's situation was so highly dysfunctional that self-injury seemed almost like a rational response to the brokenness of her circumstances. Her family was destructive in the worst sense of the word. Abandonment, neglect, abuse, and betrayal were all she had experienced in her short fifteen and one-half years of life. Granted, it had turned her into a survivor—a fighter, a gutsy street kid who was determined to make it on her own—but in order to ensure her safety she had cocooned herself in a shroud of attitude that none but the most persistent would ever get inside.

Our paths had crossed by the will of the Child Protection Agency in our community. After a few standoffs she must have realized that I wasn't going away, so she reluctantly opened up. Once she had trusted me with her story and recognized that I wasn't put off by it, she began to invite me into the day-to-day realities of her complicated world. The late-night email that day was her way of checking in and letting me know that things weren't okay.

I replied with a quick (and likely too clichéd) response that told her I believed in her, Jesus loved her, and that I was looking forward to seeing her in the morning at a coffee shop near where she was staying. But only a few minutes later she responded in the form of a one-line email and attached photo. "I cut agin. Pleez don't be mad. Pleez don't give up on me." It was the photograph that really told the story. A cell phone picture of her left hand with the word *Daddy* roughly carved into her palm. I found out later it had been a sharp shard of glass. I responded with a much less clichéd message to this much more urgent cry for help, communicating my profound sadness for her, making sure she didn't need a trip to the emergency room, and reconfirming our breakfast arrangements.

When I met with her in a coffee shop the following morning, I knew I was in for a tough conversation. Not sure where to start, I gently asked her, "If your hand could speak, what would it tell me?" Without even raising her head she used her wounded, still-oozing left hand to pull up the sleeve on her right arm, revealing the words *ugly*, *stupid*, *worthless*, and *unlovable* carved in her skin in the same macabre font. Gently rubbing her forearm with her *Daddy* hand she quietly said, "Maybe if I had a daddy I wouldn't feel this way about myself." And then, with what felt like a rhetorical question she asked, "Is it wrong for me to wish I had a daddy?"

The deep longing to belong, to be loved, and to be valued that was expressed in her question is at the heart of much of the brokenness experienced by teenagers in the world today. Desperate for meaningful relational connection but often finding only disappointment, they manage their loneliness in whatever ways work best. For some, it's the bizarre cycle of self-harm; for others, drugs or alcohol numb the pain; for still others, parties and promiscuity distract them from the deep loss they are feeling inside. Some find a form of community in street gangs or clusters of friends that become surrogate family; some become citizens of the global community of gamers and spend every waking moment participating in what feels like very significant work. For too many the predictable plot lines of pornography provide them with a fantasy role to play in which, for brief moments, they can pretend they belong. Sadly for some the pain of rejection and loneliness has become so intense that they detach themselves from any meaningful relationship and live their lives resigned to a lonely and isolated existence, often creating a relational buffer by communicating an angry, sullen, or indifferent attitude that defies anyone to enter.

What all of these young people have in common is that their exterior behaviors, attitudes, relational patterns, and emotional symptomology mask their complex and often unrecognized interior cries for response. On the basis of visible evidence they are labeled as cutters, anorexics, gang bangers, shoplifters, addicts, fighters, problems, sluts, runaways, troublemakers, and losers, and most adults in their world sincerely believe that if "the outside" could simply be rearranged everything would be fine.

Like my young friend who bared her soul when she bared her arm that morning, there is so much more going on that must be understood if we are going to provide a place of safety and belonging for wounded and broken adolescents among us. We cannot simply assume that calling them to behavioral or attitudinal conformity represents a victory in their lives (or in our ministries).

A "Look under the Hood"

Although in many ways adolescence represents a unique chapter in the human development story, individuals who are navigating the transition from childhood to adulthood appear to have at least one significant thing in common with all people. At their (our) core are some powerfully motivating needs that have potential to fuel choices and behaviors. Many keen observers of human nature—both academic and nonacademic—have attempted to identify these innate longings of the human soul. Some examples include the longing to be loved unconditionally (apart from performance or achievement); to know that one's life has a purpose (making some sort of significant impact in the world); to be desired (being pursued is tangible evidence); and, of course, the longing to belong (to live in relationship or community.) These represent a sampling of the most commonly identified internal forces that have been observed and experienced.

While some might be intrigued by the exercise of determining which of these longings should be included in or excluded from the "official list," there is perhaps a more productive exercise to be undertaken. We need to ask ourselves why the longings are there in the first place—both in the souls of the young people we serve and in each of our own hearts.

If, in fact, these longings are common to all (whether consciously experienced or not), it stands to reason that they are part of God's sovereign design. In his infinite wisdom, why would the Creator have wired his human progeny with profound needs that demand satisfaction? It may be the simplest theological question to answer, given that God is a God of relationship.

Clearly, he placed these longings in each of us for the divinely ordained purpose of drawing us to himself. He knew that no human would ever be fully satisfied until his or her deepest longings were met in him.

The Scripture actually uses a commonplace metaphor to help us understand the intense urgency of satisfying these longings. Thirst is something all humans are familiar with. Psalm 42:1–2 declares,

> As the deer pants for streams of water,
>   so my soul pants for you, my God.
> My soul thirsts for God, for the living
>   God.

Isaiah 55:1 is an enthusiastic invitation to

> Come, all you who are thirsty,
>   come to the waters;
> and you who have no money,
>   come, buy and eat!
> Come, buy wine and milk
>   without money and without cost.

And certainly the conversation between Jesus and the Samaritan woman in John 4 puts all of this into a New Testament perspective when a woman—clearly longing to be loved, significant, pursued, and welcomed—is offered living water. Jesus promises that those who drink the water he gives them will never thirst again (John 4:14).

But there's a problem. In spite of the open invitation from the ultimate Source of thirst-quenching satisfaction, our natural predisposition as post-fall human beings is not to run to our heavenly Father to quench our thirst. Instead, we look for ways to satisfy our longings that will not require us to remain in a relationship of dependence on the true Thirst-Quencher. Jeremiah 2:13 describes the two-sided coin of our inherent self-reliance and independence.

> My people have committed two sins:
> They have forsaken me,
>   the spring of living water,
> and have dug their own cisterns,
>   broken cisterns that cannot hold
>   water.

The prophet is saying that we look for ways to quench our thirst that allow us to manage and control our sources rather than to rely deeply on the One who finds his greatest delight in seeing us satisfied. Of course, the satisfaction we experience is short-lived and in the end disappointing. The cisterns simply do not hold water.

So, you may ask, what does this little theological side trip have to do with understanding and responding to wounded and broken teenagers? What I am suggesting is that adolescents often find themselves involved in personally and relationally destructive behaviors in a desperate need to have their thirst quenched. Any veteran youth worker or high school teacher has plenty of stories of young women who have compromised their moral convictions for the sake of experiencing the feeling of being loved. They will tell stories of young men who, in a desperate need to feel like they belong, will surround themselves with people of violence and evil to be part of the gang. Stories of students who cut, or drink, or shop to distance themselves from the pain in their lives are common. The cycle of brokenness is not easily interrupted.

When a faith community provides a young person with a welcoming place to belong, a meaningful way to make a difference in their world, and a family that loves and pursues them unconditionally, God's people are responding, in the name of Jesus, to the deepest core needs that a youth can experience. When we understand that, as God's family, we have been entrusted with this "ministry of reconciliation" that Christ began (2 Cor. 5:18), we can serve as his ambassadors, speaking on his behalf into the lives of the young people who cross our paths.

The thirst that I have been talking about is not unique to adolescents. The longings I identified are common to humans of all ages, young and old. What makes them a significant factor for adolescents is that the thirst becomes palpable during these crucial years. It is the first time in an individual's young life that they have the capacity for a conscious awareness of their desire to be loved, to be significant, and to belong. What this means in practical terms is that early adolescence is also the stage of life where, for the first time, they have the emotive capacity to process the deep pain and disappointment of not feeling loved, believing they don't have any significance, and experiencing the loneliness of being on the outside looking in. This can make adolescence a trying time for young people and creates an opportunity for ministry that cannot be ignored by those who want to make an eternal difference.

But . . . It Gets Even More Complicated!

As a specialist in cognitive development, Jean Piaget spent much of his life helping us to understand the transition from childlike to adultlike thinking. In its most basic terms he pointed out that children tend to think in simplistic, literal, black-and-white ways while adults are able to process complex concepts, conflicting ideas, and more sophisticated problems. During adolescence the transition to more mature cognitive approaches takes place. This shift has enormous implications for understanding what is going on in the minds of the adolescents we work with.

Because of their more limited cognitive aptitude, children tend to experience life in simple, literal terms. They generally live in the moment, experiencing life as a series of isolated, consecutive events or "snapshots" that may or may not eventually find their way into long-term memory. This is not to imply that the experiences of childhood have no impact on future development. When preadolescent children experience the absence of love, significance, and belonging, there is an unmistakably erosive effect on their souls. They simply don't have the cognitive capacity to contextualize and sort out the events that are occurring until later in life.

Mid-adolescence, ages fourteen to twenty, changes all of that. The brain undergoes some significant changes in terms of neurological complexity (a miraculous process that we are learning more about as a result of new technologies that allow us to "look inside"), and as a result, early evidence of "formal operations" (Piaget's name for adultlike thinking) begins to emerge. This newly discovered cognitive sophistication allows mid-adolescents to begin thinking about their world at a much deeper level. They are able to process conflicting ideas, combine concepts in their head without any concrete evidence, think creatively at a whole new level, and begin to imagine the outcomes

of certain choices, even though they have never experienced them before.

A practical outcome of this new level of thinking is that for the first time in their young lives they become aware of their personal narrative. At this point, the adolescent is able to look back over the "snapshots" of childhood memories and begin to weave them together into his or her own story. When those snapshots are marked primarily by pain and disappointment, the story that emerges tends to read like a tragedy. A series of memories where love was absent, relational attachment (belonging) was negative or unavailable, and feelings of worthlessness or insignificance were common result in a story line that often expresses itself in low self-esteem or even self-loathing.

When the notion of thirst/longing is combined with this new capacity to process one's own personal story line we begin to understand how complex life can be for a mid-adolescent who has experienced the pain of rejection, loneliness, and self-doubt. The opportunity to provide for these young people a place of relational safety, community, and significant involvement represents one of the highest callings of any faith community. But it gets even more complicated than that!

The Perfect Storm of Mid-adolescence

One more crucial element must be factored in if we truly want to understand what is going on at the deeper levels of a young teenager's life. Developmental psychologists have examined the journey through adolescence from a variety of perspectives, and many of them agree that a primary challenge/task of this stage of life is identity formation. The "Who am I?" question looms large for teenagers—whether they are consciously aware of it or not.

It's not that a person has no identity until they reach adolescence. For most children, their identity is well-defined from quite a young age. But what their identity is based on needs to change in order for a healthy transition to adulthood to take place. In early childhood, their identity is linked directly to their family of origin. They are "Bob and Susan's son," "Jeff and Lisa's daughter," or "Josh's little sister." As they enter early adolescence they begin to intuitively sense the need to establish themselves as individuals apart from the ties to their family of origin, but since the brain is still developing they cannot yet reflectively consider their life in relationship to others. To further complicate matters, puberty has brought about significant changes, endowing the adolescent with the body of an adult and the brain of a child. It is in mid-adolescence, when the brain begins the process of moving from concrete, "first person" thinking and awareness to the abstract abilities of the mature brain, or "third person" thinking and awareness, that they are able to consider in a more objective way who they are compared to others.

The first stage of this process commences when they begin to chafe at being known only in relation to their parents or siblings. As early adolescents they often begin to assert their individuality by pushing back on their relationship with parents and siblings as a means of creating some distance. This stage is often disconcerting for parents, who may experience it as personal rejection and react by holding on tighter, linking their own identity to that of their child, and creating tension that simply makes the transition more difficult. This process of discovering one's self is essential to establishing a coherent adult identity and can be as terrifying for the adolescent as it is for the parent.

At this point, all of the dimensions of early to mid-adolescent development come together. The emerging personal story line is shaped by a growing sense of disappointment in relationships that are not providing unconditional love, significance, and belonging commensurate with the longing for those things that are bubbling into the adolescent's consciousness. This becomes the backdrop against which important identity formation decisions are made. The word *decisions* is used intentionally. Adolescents begin to make some identity assumptions based on their interpretation of what they have experienced in life so far. Understanding these assumptions is crucial to responding appropriately to adolescents in transition.

The vocabulary of personal identity in adolescents generally consists of adjectives or metaphorical images. When my young friend (whom I introduced at the beginning of this chapter) carved those self-deprecating words into her forearm that night, she was simply reminding herself of who she believed herself to be. The assumptions that led to the conviction that she was ugly, unlovable, stupid, and worthless were simply her best attempt at making sense out of her personal story. Although the adjectives she chose are painfully negative and patently inaccurate, she embraced them as her own because they made complete sense of her story. Her desire to be loved, valued, taken seriously, and seen as attractive had been ignored by the people closest to her. Instead, she had experienced the opposite—hence the words by which she chose to define herself.

For some, a picture or metaphor more accurately portrays how they see themselves. They identify as a bag of trash, a piece of crap, a little lost puppy, or a bird who can't fly as a way of illustrating the subjective experience of what their lives feel like and how they see themselves. One young woman I was working with (who gave me permission to quote from her journal) expresses it so articulately:

> Life works for me as long as I view myself as a worthless piece of crap. If I see myself as a whore, a nothing, then everything makes sense. All the pain, betrayal, and powerlessness of my past becomes clear. I am a whore so that's why I was sexually abused when I was ten years old. I am worthless, so that is why my mom drank. I am a slut, so that is why I was assaulted when I was eighteen. I am a hard, cold, calloused, tough woman hiding a frightened little girl inside. A little girl who is convinced that being female is what got her into trouble in the first place, so she cut off her beautiful long hair and gained weight. All this little girl wants is to be held in the big strong arms of her Daddy. The whore image protects the little girl from ever being hurt again but it also keeps her from running into Abba's open arms of love. You see he is male, so therefore he will hurt me.

As she reviews the events of her life—the memories of an alcoholic mother, the abuse she experienced at the hands of one of her mom's many boyfriends, the date rape in her senior year of high school—she clearly comes to some conclusions about how those events define her identity. The images combine to give us a sense of how she sees herself. The worthless piece of crap, the whore, the slut, the nothing, the terrified little girl hiding behind the tough exterior of the calloused young woman she has become give us a sense of just how deeply entrenched these assumptions can be.

Perhaps the saddest part of seeing young people who have defined themselves with such painfully negative assumptions is that they often go through life without ever having those assumptions challenged in a loving, caring relationship or healthy, supportive community. Instead, they build a precarious existence on the foundation of the words and pictures that define them.

Obviously, young people who have lived in a traumatic or dysfunctional relational environment as children tend to have more deeply entrenched identity issues to work through.

The Source of Adolescent Pain

Some young people are broken or wounded because painful things have happened to them. The range of hurtful circumstances that teenagers find themselves in seems endless. Perhaps they are caught in the middle of a painful family breakup; it could be the tragic loss of a parent, sibling, or friend in an accident or suicide; the diagnosis of a terminal disease is devastating news for some. Sexual abuse, public humiliation, bullying, being dumped by a boyfriend or girlfriend, being cut from the team, struggling with weight or complexion, living with a learning disability, an emotionally absent dad, a demanding or verbally abusive mom—the list can go on and on, and as I compile this list, each entry represents a young person I know. We identify them as victims because the pain they live with came about as a result of someone else's choices or circumstances, which were completely beyond their control. The pain they live with is not of their own doing.

But not all of the pain young people live with comes about as a result of victimization. Some are hurting because of choices they made themselves. Perhaps they chose the wrong friends and now find themselves in destructive relationships. They may have chosen to make their studies a low priority and have eliminated a whole range of options for the future as a result. They have chosen drugs, alcohol, self-injury, or pornography as a means to self-medicate and now find themselves trapped in an addiction that seems impossible to break. They chose to quit school, to have unprotected sex, to run away from home, to play video games instead of doing their homework. Again, the list of ill-advised choices that teenagers make could go on forever, but in this case the painful outcomes are a result of their own doing.

Wouldn't it be convenient if we could simply classify hurting teenagers as victims or agents? On the one hand, we would immediately know how to respond. If we were dealing with a victim, our role would be to come alongside and provide support, encouragement, and empathy. We would remind them that what happened was not their fault and assure them that it was not fair. We would do all that was possible to protect them from further victimization and surround them with a community that was committed to helping them find healing.

On the other hand, if we were dealing with an individual who was the agent of his/her own pain, we would firmly hold them responsible, help them to understand the connection between their choices and the unanticipated outcomes, and exhort them to make wiser choices in the future.

Of course, it is not that simple. I am reminded of a conversation I had with the person sitting next to me on a flight one day. I was on my way to train a group of social workers on how to care for teenagers who self-injure, and I was editing a few presentation slides on my computer screen. My seatmate glanced over, saw what I was working on, and asked incredulously, "What is up with those kids?" I replied, "It's complicated." He continued, "Do you work with those kids?" After I told him that I do work with those kids, his next question made me smile just a little. "Why doesn't someone just tell them to stop?" It was a reminder that many people make the assumption that behavioral choices are made in isolation. But those of us who work with hurting teenagers know that it is complicated; very often people make bad choices *because* bad things have happened to them. The pain of victimization expresses itself in behaviors that are destructive in ways the individual might never have anticipated. The complex interplay of victimization and agency requires us to take a much more thoughtful approach than simply offering a hug for the person who appears to be a victim or a kick in the pants for the person who seems to have chosen his or her lot in life. Compassion always looks through both lenses and forces us to see the connection. When the apostle John introduces us to Jesus he says, "The Word became flesh and made his dwelling among us. We have seen his glory, the glory of the one and only Son, who came from the Father, *full of grace and truth*" (John 1:14, italics added). In this beautiful description of the Savior we see the balanced approach we are called to make in response to the brokenness of teenagers around us. Jesus was "full of grace and truth." Grace takes into account the woundedness that is often a precursor to unhealthy choices young people make, and truth calls them to a higher level of volitional intentionality as they sort out how they will respond to the pain that is inherent in their story.

The Call to Adoption

The promise of Psalm 68:6 (NLT) is that "God places the lonely in families." As faith communities committed to the spiritual well-being of next generations, we must embrace the opportunity to be family for the young people around us. Whether their need for connection is rooted in the painful reality of a family of origin that was abusive and neglectful or they simply find themselves in the normal adolescent transitions of disengaging from their biological family, we are called to invite young people in and welcome them as Jesus would. It should be noted, however, that the cost of adoption is greater than many faith communities are willing to pay, and the integration of young people, particularly those who come with "baggage," may feel like an intrusion. But when we reflect on the price that was paid for our adoption into God's family and the baggage we brought, we can more generously and gratefully open our doors and our hearts.

The truth is that most of the young people we work with today are hurting much more deeply than they or we are willing to acknowledge. They camouflage and cover up their pain for a variety of reasons. Most often, when I have asked them why they hid their stories of brokenness from the people around them, their reasons were rooted in mistrust. They have tried to reach out for help in the past and have been ignored, belittled, exposed, rebuked, or given clichéd advice that seemed to have no relevance to the depth of their pain. The implications are obvious: we must create communities in which trust is nonnegotiable. Until a youth is able to trust an adult there will be no opportunity to talk about the issues that really matter. This means calling leaders to lives of absolute integrity. It means vetting

and training our volunteers carefully to ensure that they understand what a precious and fragile gift the trust of a young person is and that they must guard that trust carefully. It means living our lives transparently and honestly so that students can see what it looks like when imperfect people are committed to growing spiritually through painful or difficult circumstances.

But it's not only the young people themselves who live in denial. As youth leaders and parents we also have a tendency to diminish the seriousness of what young people are dealing with. Again, when I have asked youth workers and parents why they prefer to pretend that everything's okay, the issue is either pride or inadequacy. Pride declares that "our kids" don't struggle with those sorts of things because if they did it would be a reflection on us. Inadequacy tells us that if the struggles young people describe are true, we don't have a clue where to start them on their journey toward healing.

Step 1: Know That Adolescent Pain Is Real

The first step in responding to the brokenness of hurting young people around us is to admit that the pain is real. The world is a cruel place for kids today. Our churches are called to stand as islands of safety in the midst of the cultural chaos that young people must navigate today. Pious platitudes, clichéd "steps to victory," Bible verse Band-Aids, and guilt trips for those who fail to conform are simply not helpful within the family of God. The prophet Jeremiah speaks out against the spiritual leaders of his day. Sadly, the indictment he declares could be addressed to many church leaders today.

From the least to the greatest,
　all are greedy for gain;
prophets and priests alike,
　all practice deceit.
They dress the wound of my people
　as though it were not serious.
"Peace, peace," they say,
　when there is no peace. (Jer. 6:13–14)

Ignoring and belittling the pain of young people is not an option.

Step 2: Adults Need Young People, and Young People Need Adults

Families are intergenerational. When young people are invited into a family of faith it is important that they are invited into a relationship that crosses generational lines. While a strong case can be made for peer-based ministry structures, it is important for a young person exploring faith to be exposed to individuals at all stages of spiritual maturity. In healthy families, grandparents provide wisdom, stability, and a sense of longevity. Parents offer guidance, relationship, and intentional involvement. Siblings create opportunity for shared experiences, camaraderie, friendship, and mutual accountability. These generational benefits can be experienced in a faith community that understands the value of breaking down age-based silos[2] and creating opportunities for all the generations to connect with one another. The benefits that come about as a result of pursuing intentional intergenerational interactions are numerous and broad, reaching across generational lines.

The faith experience of senior saints in the community is enhanced when young people are invited to challenge the status quo and call congregations to remain relevant in the face of cultural changes. The passion and energy of youthful presence can give older folks confidence that the mission of their church will continue into the foreseeable future. On the other side of the equation, young people benefit from the wisdom and experience of older believers who choose to make themselves relationally available and share the lessons they have learned in a long life of faith. They must be caretakers of the young, who, while they have a great deal to offer the faith community in their energy and perspective, still need adults to nurture and guide them without judgment or condemnation. Older believers offer a picture of what mature and seasoned faith looks like to young believers who are just beginning their walk with Jesus. Their prayers and encouragement can give a struggling young person the courage to press on, even in the face of difficult or painful circumstances.

Because young people are caught in the awkward stage of detaching from their family of origin they often need the involvement of other adults to be the voice of "parental wisdom" and provide nonjudgmental presence in the face of life's challenges. In this way, the church can be a great example of a "village" raising children. Youth workers, mentors, teachers, coaches, and small group leaders fall into this category of men and women, one generation ahead of the young people they serve. Teenagers who have the benefit of at least one committed nonparental adult in their life reap enormous benefits. Imagine the benefit of a fully committed community of believers who each see themselves as significant to the spiritual well-being of the young people in their midst—a whole congregation of "youth workers." By the same token, those adults who are intentionally invested in the spiritual lives of younger individuals are motivated to make their faith their own. They find themselves helping young people wrestle with biblical truth and in the process of doing so are forced to solidify their own convictions. Everyone wins.

Being the Family of God Changes Everything!

My family adopted a newborn baby girl when I was thirteen. As we eagerly anticipated her arrival we made some significant changes to our home. We paid careful attention to potential safety hazards around the house, and we prepared a room in which our new little sister would be comfortable. Our shelves were stocked with food that would be suitable for her infant palate. Lifestyle and scheduling adjustments had to be made when she came to live with us. In short, everything changed when the dynamics of our family were impacted by the arrival of the new and needy little member. When a church decides to get serious about opening their family to young people with unique needs and challenges, it will require them to make enormous adjustments. It can no longer be "business as usual."

In the face of this realization too many congregations simply decide the cost is too great. Inviting the "wrong kind of kids" into the family will destroy the peaceful predictability of what currently exists. There's a chance that some of their "badness" will rub off on the good kids who currently occupy the pews. Staffing adjustments might need to be made to address the greater demands that come with young people who have issues. Liturgy might need to be adapted to create a more user-friendly environment for young people who are unfamiliar with traditional

worship. Sermons will need to be rethought to ensure that they are relevant and helpful for honest young people who won't put up with clichés and pat answers. Just like any family that adopts a new member, life is never the same. *But it is what we are called to, and the benefits are immense.*

I began this chapter thinking about the deepest longings of the human soul. The thirst to be loved, to know that one's life has purpose and meaning, and to find a place to belong is something that every one of us identifies with deeply. I discussed the fact that the natural predisposition of sinful humans is to find ways to quench their thirst on their own terms—often with disastrous outcomes. Is there an alternative?

When young people who consider themselves to be unworthy and unlovable encounter the gospel they are invited into a relationship that is marked by absolutely unconditional love. Romans 5:8 reminds us that God demonstrated "his own love for us in this: While we were still sinners, Christ died for us." Thirst quenched!

When young people who identify as weak, stupid, and worthless discover that God has a completely different view of them—and has laid out a specific plan and purpose for them—it radically changes their view of themselves and their future. "For we are God's handiwork," Paul tells us in Ephesians 2:10, "created in Christ Jesus to do good works, which God prepared in advance for us to do." Thirst quenched!

When young people who see themselves as outcasts, losers, or undesirable are invited into a community where they are welcomed and invited to participate—in some cases even before they believe—it provides them with the assurance that they belong. First Corinthians

12 uses the metaphor of the body to describe the interdependent nature of the family we are all invited into. In verse 27 Paul summarizes by saying, "Now you are the body of Christ, and each one of you is a part of it." Thirst quenched!

The self-deprecating assumptions that are made by young people in response to their pain and disappointment are meant to be challenged in healthy community. This is the context in which the lies of the enemy (you are unlovable, ugly, stupid, worthless) can be exchanged for the truth of the gospel that declares, "Those who are led by the Spirit of God are the children of God. . . . Now if we are children, then we are heirs—heirs of God and co-heirs with Christ" (Rom. 8:14, 17). There is no higher calling than this.

Technology and Adoptive Youth Ministry

BRADLEY HOWELL

Everywhere I go parents, pastors, and youth workers want to talk about technology. "Technology" is a broad topic with many facets and aspects, to say nothing of the myriad debates concerning the impact of various technological media. In one recent seminar, I received the following five questions back to back:

- *What does social media do to kids' relationships?*
- *How much time should my kid spend playing video games and watching Netflix?*
- *How does texting affect my son's ability to have a conversation?*
- *At what age should my child get a smartphone?*
- *Is "cyber counseling" a helpful trend?*

This is a book about youth ministry, primarily a textbook but also a handbook for anyone who desires a comprehensive resource about the practice of adoptive, or communally driven, youth ministry in today's complex society. Because this is a book, we run the risk of talking about the issue of "technology" in a way that makes the content obsolete before this book even goes to print. This chapter, then, does not attempt to specifically answer any of these questions, especially the more contextual, cultural, or even timely queries that youth ministers will be asked about in a parent's meeting or seminar. Instead, Dr. Bradley Howell helps us to think about technology, especially as various issues relate to the concept of adoptive youth ministry. After providing a general overview of how technological advances are received in the three stages of adolescence—early (ages roughly ten to fourteen), middle (fifteen to twenty) and emerging adult (twenty to mid- to late twenties)—Howell then provides a primer on "Perspectives on Digital Connectivity" and closes with a resource list for further study and discussion. While a good and important starting point for the conversation, this chapter is simply intended to get you thinking about this vast area as you develop a healthy and contextually appropriate adoptive youth ministry.

This highlights why we have added to this book the component of digital connectivity with our authors. On the website youth ministry.fuller.edu, Howell, like every author, has a page for this chapter's topic (as well as his contact information). As a scholar and professor who is constantly looking at issues related to youth ministry and technology (like all of the authors in Adoptive Youth Ministry*), Howell has made himself available for a conversation or a web interview for an individual or a class. For this topic in particular, he will continually add to the website new resources, articles, and information. Howell is committed to the continuing study of the impact and power of technology, especially as it relates to youth ministry, and he is a helpful resource as we head into a future of more technological uncertainty.*

As you read this chapter, consider these questions:

1. *What were the most significant technological issues for you in middle school? In high school? As an emerging adult? What made them significant?*

2. *List and prioritize the top five most significant technological issues that youth ministry leaders will have to deal with in the next few years. How does this chapter help you to understand them and give you the ability to critically reflect on them?*

3. *What from this chapter is important to share and discuss with parents to help them get a better handle on dealing with technological issues?*

4. *Howell closes the chapter with the assertion that the issue is really not about technology but about how people use technology (i.e., digital connections) in*

a changing society. His caution is to remember that our role as youth workers is to be about people, which is especially true for those committed to participating in God's adoptive work. What are some ways we can use technology to enhance adoptive youth ministry?

Gun in one hand and a camera in the other, the frustrated father targets a small black laptop lying unceremoniously on a patchy, dying lawn. As had already been explained earlier in his video,[1] his teenage daughter's efforts to hide her social media rants about her parents had failed. Apparently, being grounded for months on end did nothing to change the heart of this adolescent digital lamenter. As a repeat offender, she was about to enter a whole new level of paternal discipline (likely without her knowledge): the digital twilight zone of viral video parenting.

Fully loaded with hollow-point rounds and fueled with self-justified enragement, her father effortlessly squeezes the gun's trigger. As the first shots ring out, the viewer's imagination intuitively fills in the stunned cheers of exasperated parents everywhere. Shot after devastating shot discharge from the gun until the ammunition is spent and the object of the father's wrath resembles something more akin to a black mangled mass of plastic Swiss cheese than a gateway to the digital realm. If this father's daughter is to have any future rants, they will not be hurled at the digital world stage from this computer.

Perhaps we should be thankful that the vast majority of families would never seriously consider posting their pain, disappointments, and dramatic acts of retribution online as casual enjoyment for tens of millions of people. However, not unlike the undernourished grass backdrop to the digital spectacle, too many households struggle to maintain a well-nourished, healthy family in a culture of digital relationships. Whether adoptive youth ministers love or hate technology, they know all too well that many of the families entrusted to their spiritual care are being torn apart by digital behaviors. We see it on our teens' online posts, we hear about it in small groups and parent meetings, and every once in a while we are conscripted to the unenviable task of digital referee.

Yet the technological world juxtaposes the digital pressures families navigate with another pressure an adoptive youth minister must tackle: the artful task of actually using technology to augment an adoptive ministry. This frustration is amplified when videos like the one described above go viral while the (of course) deeply life-changing and spiritually important youth group digital messages often appear to go unnoticed. On one hand, technology seems to promise that, with just a few well-placed keystrokes or a creative viral video, any one individual could have most of the earth's population as their audience. On the other hand, many youth workers find they struggle to grab their own students' attention, much less discover some utopian technological promised land. Complicating this dichotomy is the sea of competing digital applications, voices, and digital tools. Employing the right one in the best way to reach the most youth feels like a never-ending uphill battle.

How did we get here?

"You've Got Mail!"

That phrase, with its corresponding squeaks, squawks, and bleeps summarizes well the transitional marker of the internet's incursion into the general public's mental awareness. During much of the 1990s through the dawn of the new millennium, homes and businesses were relentlessly infiltrated by heaps of AOL CD-ROM disks. These discs would arrive daily through technology magazines, office supply stores, and what was increasingly being labeled as snail mail—the traditional post office. This colossal marketing campaign invited the user to become a cyberspace pioneer, with AOL as the virtual gateway. This all took place barely two decades ago—a nanosecond in world history but an eon in the digital age.

The internet adopted in the 1990s was itself an innovative tool for passing information and enabling multicomputer collaboration. At some level it even had the capacity to augment human relationships through online chat rooms and Instant Messaging (IM). But chat rooms required coordination if two people who actually knew each other were to use them at the same time. Plus, only half of the US population at that time ventured onto the internet, and only about a quarter of those folks were even willing to try chat rooms; consequently, people primarily relied on email to digitally connect.[2] So, at its core, the first public rendition of the internet was a platform for sending and receiving information.

Of course, emails were not the only data that the internet was useful for. The entertainment industry, the business world, national sport teams, governments, and even religious communities voluntarily (in response to social pressure) began to explore website design and development. This quickly developed into an impressively massive worldwide web of interconnected bits of data that, to some extent, put the individual user at the center of it. The mental image of the internet as an information superhighway was born.

For the youth worker who finds him- or herself caught between parents who adopted this mental model of the internet as an information superhighway and a generation of young people who did not, this is a subtle but important distinction. The information age shaped the perspective of modern parents and their spiritual communities toward an internet that existed to give and receive information, but it was considered to be a virtual world—a shadow of the real thing—and socially isolating. That understanding of the internet is a far cry from the mental model that a new generation of internet adopters would soon take.

At the dawn of the new millennium (or "Y2K," as it had been labeled), three-quarters of adolescents were active internet users.[3] Unlike adults of that time, teens were multitasking; they kept IM applications open while they were doing homework, gaming, or listening to music, and consequently, they found they had many friends available to exchange emails or IM with.[4] But the mental model that adults were using to understand the internet had no framework for interpreting this type of activity. In an information superhighway model, the internet is "virtual," not real; it is about information, not people. Despite how teens were actually using the internet, the popular "socially isolating" label stuck.[5] The fragmentation had begun, and the digital divide, an antithetical mind-set to an adoptive ministry, was taking root and about to explode.

In 2002, an innovative social platform arrived in the virtual universe that would radically alter the trajectory of a document-based interconnected digital network. Utilized first by Friendster and then MySpace, this development cultivated a remaking of the internet into a beta version of itself: Web 2.0.[6] The fundamental change that Web 2.0 brought over the next half-decade was to make the internet synonymous with the humans who would adopt it. Increasingly, people did not merely send and retrieve bits of information between each other—they digitally re-created themselves, their likes, their activities, and their friendship structure online. The internet was morphing from an interconnected web of documents into an inter-webbed connection of humans.

The implications of this relational shift were huge, but during the shift it was difficult to make sense of what was actually happening. The revolution would be commonly likened to the invention of the Gutenberg press. Not surprisingly, with the dominant paradigm of the internet being an information superhighway the rhetoric of thought leaders centered on a shift concerning information control. Likened to the days of the Reformation, the old guardians of information would be replaced. Yet no one was quite sure what the fallout was actually going to be.

During this period it became increasingly evident that there was an oversimplification of adolescent internet use and a general acceptance of treating teens as a "monolithic social entity."[7] Fast forward to our current time. Teens today are not all using the internet in exactly the same way, but they continue to be treated as if they are. Where this cultural oversimplification mind-set enters the spiritual community, it is more like a cancer to the human body, threatening to distort, destroy, and devour the spiritual body. Terms like "digital native" and "internet addiction" marginalize an entire generation while simultaneously relieving adults of the responsibility to bridge the digital divide. Furthermore, marginalization allows adults to expect teens to act at adult standards of digital behavior yet abandons adolescents to discover on their own what that even means.

Marginalization remains a significant concern not only among the general population but among researchers and ministry experts as well. Consequently, contemporary researchers typically need to wade deep into the data to extrapolate the differences of how early, mid-, and late adolescence each approach their digital decisions. For adoptive youth ministry leaders, though, understanding how the different adolescent stages of development play out in the digital universe is of foundational importance if they want to be caring adults who can truly come alongside adolescents.

The Digital World for Adolescents

Concrete Minds in the Bounce House of Conceptual Space

Observe a group of early adolescents (roughly middle-school aged)[8] for fifteen minutes and they may appear to be consumed by technology. It may also seem like they are making their own decisions about which digital activities they choose to engage. However, because they are closer to childhood than adulthood (in terms of their brain development), their sense of self and the freedom of leisure options are more shaped by their family then something as abstractly reflective as digital choices. Even their friendships are not exempt from this family influence.

Across the developmental spectrum, adolescent offline friendship networks are almost exclusively with other young people of the same age, and these networks extend themselves into the digital world.[9] For these young adolescents, their peer groups consist of the natural relational pools that, for most eleven- to fourteen-year-olds, are a reflection of their family's lifestyle and relational commitments and connections. These pools include extended family, school, and extracurricular activity. An early adolescent's digital activities are constrained both by these peer groups and the technology that is available to them.[10] If given the choice, early adolescents report to adults that they would prefer to interact face-to-face with their friends then play online with them.[11] But for the most part, that option is beyond their control. Early adolescents generally go where they are taken, so digital interactions are the only available substitute for face-to-face ones.

Mentally speaking, even though early adolescents are only beginning to be capable of reflecting on their own perspective as well as the perspective of others, most adults believe they should be able to frame their actions in line with what the broader society would consider as being socially appropriate.[12] While they have been compelled to deal with thorny issues of adolescence at this age—how I see myself and how I think others see me—consistent and rational "third person" thought applied to the concrete problems that they encounter remains an elusive goal. This means that the concrete dynamic of early adolescence requires that they approach digital tools from their own limited sense of reality. What matters to an early adolescent is what is happening in the here and now, which has fairly dynamic effects for the conceptual world of digital tools.

When concrete thinking is the mode of operation for early adolescents, interesting scenarios begin to ensue. I had the opportunity to observe one such development unfold while exploring how digital relationships affect offline ones. During my research I was spending many afternoons observing adolescents in public settings. One particular gender-mixed group kept passing through a local fast food restaurant on their way home from school, and over a period of days a drama unfolded that was rooted in their concrete thinking. They had all joined the same digital community that required raising and selling animals while building an online farm. They had shared login information with everyone in the group in order to demonstrate to the novices how the site worked, reveal various insider shortcuts, and help one another keep their farms growing. To the concrete-minded young people involved, this made perfect sense.

After a few days though, an adult dropped what may as well have been a virtual grenade on this group of aspiring digital farmers. One mom made her daughter change her login credentials. According to the daughter who had to report this to her friends, Mom had threatened to ground her from the computer if she were to share her login with her friends again.

Now, without having a chance to hear from the mother, the most likely conclusion a reasonable adult would come to is that Mom could envision the complications of someone else pretending to be her daughter online, while these middle school students clearly had not. But what mom did not envision was the relational fallout that was about to occur among this specific group of friends.

Without any conceptual framework to navigate this new development (appeals to a mother's discipline were not enough), tempers quickly soared, friendships were questioned, and name-calling ensued. The girls in the group demanded access to their friend's site; the boys more or less just sat there, nodding their heads back and forth to the verbal volley. Then, as quickly as it started, the fight ended unresolved with the girls darting out of the

restaurant in tears. The poor guys were left sitting at the table, ice cream dripping down their fingers, completely dumbfounded. They had just witnessed the inadvertent fallout of a parent's best intentions but had no conceptual understanding of what they were experiencing.

While I have no way to know for certain what (if anything) happened in the next stage of the fight, it does not take much imagination to understand that name-calling in person oozes into digital space. Without anyone being able to articulate it (at least for this particular group), sharing login credentials had subconsciously become a measuring stick of friendship validation. When one of the friends could no longer measure up, the response was to turn on that girl.

How to deal with middle school girls being extremely mean to each other, both online and off, continues to be among the most common concerns that youth ministries, teachers, school administrators, and families face. Early adolescent girls appear to be constantly on relational high alert and are quick to determine relational status. Research appears to confirm this.

In a report conducted by the Pew Research Center's Internet & American Life Project on teens and cruelty online, almost every single twelve- or thirteen-year-old female had an opinion as to whether others were mean or kind to each other in digital space—about two-thirds chose kind, one-third chose mean, and about 3 percent chose "it depends."[13] No other grouping of teens comes even close to this level of certainty about their peers, and the report makes special note that this is statistically significant.[14] Early adolescent females are the most relationally intuitive people on the digital landscape. Their male counterparts, however, were the most likely of any adolescent group to report that their peers were kind; they were also the most likely to give a nebulous answer on the quality of digital relationships. So, unlike their female peers, it seems that most early adolescent boys think everything is just kind of, sort of, well . . . fine.

For an adoptive youth ministry, this implication is noteworthy. These girls are actively listening to digital conversations and deciding whether people like them or not in their online interactions. Actions of adults both online and off will be constantly and relentlessly weighed. The implications do not end in the youth worker's relationship with girls in this age group; they carry over into other relationships that early adolescent females are trying to balance. Thus an adoptive ministry-minded adult must always keep in mind a young person's context with each digital engagement.

There are other land mines as well. Concrete-minded early adolescents do not have the intrinsic ability to anticipate the emotional disruption their own actions can cause others online. Students regularly do multiple activities on their computers or leave themselves logged in after they have left the screen. On occasion they can even leave in the middle of an online activity if their attention is snagged or if their parents demand it. With all of these demands for attention, it is little surprise that their likeminded peers find themselves in half-finished conversations and activities, but middle school students are unaware of this.

Adults, however, are deeply concerned about how young people treat one another online, and rightly so. It turns out that "being ignored" is the most common reported form of adolescents being mean to each other online.[15] Yet concrete-minded early adolescents who physically leave their computers while being logged in, engage in multiple activities simultaneously, or even send comments of retaliation to others who ignore them online have little intuitive awareness of how their actions affect others online. Even something as simple as understanding that their friend at the other end might not actually be there may be difficult to understand without being prompted to do so.

Youth leaders, parents, coaches, and teachers can all step into this gap. Middle school students need adults who are a part of their offline world to experience the online world along with them—to get in there and play games online together, to share, care, and be a pastoral presence in a digital landscape. They need adults who will take the time to understand the digital world from the context of the early adolescent. This means we cannot merely take the internet in terms of how we want it to be or how we wish to use it. We need to take it as it actually is. Early adolescents need adults who do not accidently ignore them because of their own adult tendencies to multitask. They need adults to be living, walking, and intentionally modeling grace in day-to-day digital life together.

Mid-adolescents and the Internet

Friendship Clusters Offering 24/7 Emotional Support

It will be another generation before mid-adolescents (ages fourteen or fifteen to nineteen to twenty-one, on average)[16] will have parents who grew up with digital relational tools as a significant aspect of everyday life. By then it is quite possible that some new technological innovation will have been introduced that will change the nature of human interaction as it is commonly understood today. This is not a prediction that something never heard of before is about to be launched but rather a reflection on the fact that parents often ask why teens today can't talk on the phone like they did when they were teens. In interactions with parents, my normative strategy is to remind them of what life was like for them as teenagers: if their parents were at all like mine, they were not as concerned about teenage telephone habits as today's parents are about internet habits. Yes, my parents were frustrated with how much I tied up the telephone, but no one accused me of losing an ability to hold a conversation, not being able to look adults in the face, or that my brain was being rewired (arguments that accentuate fragmentation). The concerns of parents when I was a teenager were basically about convenience—there was often only one phone line, and the teens were typically clogging it up.

The problem with the fragmenting statements is not whether they are true; the concern is expecting a different outcome without actually being involved in day-to-day life. Research consistently affirms that most adults simply are not all that present in the digital lives of adolescents.[17] Many adults likely do not even know where to start. In addition to the difficulty of personally monitoring the online and digital world of their children is the proliferation of new digital tools, apps, and technologies that allow and even encourage mid-adolescents to diversify their online practices. The development of new apps and updates to existing ones are relentless, and with every new technology and option teens are drawn deeper into the digital environment. Web 2.0 is the perfect digital environment for egocentric, newly abstract mid-adolescents.

Mid-adolescents, by definition, are shifting from the childlike concreteness of awareness and integration into the ability for abstract thought. In their everyday interactions, however, they have not fully developed an internal, autonomous self or a central, formalized identity that integrates how they behave and operate in their various relational contexts.[18] Parents, teachers, coaches, and others who interact with mid-adolescents online see the result of this phenomenon when they happen along a post that they were never meant to see. Mid-adolescents understand that their actions affect others, but they do not have the life experiences that provide a realistic perspective on the intricacies and nuances of human communication and relationships.[19] Even if a person of authority never deliberately meant to come across a digital post that they were never intended to see, the mid-adolescent perceives this as a breach of trust. From the adolescent's perspective, he or she is completely justified in being appalled by such an act, regardless of the propriety or appropriateness of the original post.

As Web 2.0 reached its first decade of existence, many of the social media sites still collected all of a participant's contacts into a single, mass group. This caused the various relational boundaries to bleed into one another in digital space; in geophysical space they would have been more isolated.[20] While connecting with adults has never been the primary intent of mid-adolescents when they initially engage with digital tools, adults are coming in and out of their digital interactions, at least at some level. As they do, adults expect mid-adolescents to behave online as if they are adults—that is, as if they are fully individuated and therefore aware of the possible consequences of how they interact online, especially toward those who are not in their inner circle of peers. Of course, this is not typically at the forefront of a mid-adolescent's thinking when he or she is flying in and out of various digital environments. Consequently, in digital networks mid-adolescents are rarely even aware of what adults would consider a mature ability to present a cohesive and integrative mature "self" across all platforms and websites. When their inconsistency and perceived lack of integrity in their online identities have been exposed to adults, the most common response is to blame the adults who "caught" them at being somehow "less than" they presented themselves in direct interactions and to dive deeper into the relative safety and anonymity of their peer group—what Chap Clark calls the "Worth Beneath" in *Hurt 2.0*.[21]

As mentioned earlier, teens connect online with those they know offline. It is not the technology itself that is the most captivating for teens; it's the access that tech gives them to their friends.[22] Among mid-adolescents, there is a general belief that digital tools increase a sense of connectedness among their peer group.[23] This social network consists of their friendship cluster—a very loyal and typically gender-exclusive small group of friends who watch out for one another. These clusters are described in friendship terms by mid-adolescents, yet recent research of this age group tends to support the notion that the cluster is more a "network of mutual self-protection" rather than support system of adultlike, self-sacrificing friendships. Because the point of the mid-adolescent friendship cluster is mutual self-protection and the ability to navigate the mid-adolescent years in perceived community and relative enjoyment, the basic structure demands a loyalty to the values of the cluster.[24] While previous generations were safely bound by direct interpersonal modes of communication, mid-adolescents, through offline relationships, are increasingly being exposed in the

online world for all to see. As the adults in their lives adopt each new technological tool, they increasingly need to find new ways to keep the world beneath hidden from adult view. However, digital space is increasingly becoming the only location where adults are bumping into teens.

Lack of Geophysical Space in an Ever-Changing World

One increasing change in our culture is the amount of space available to adolescents. Typically, physical space has been an important ingredient for developing friendship networks that promote individual identification and group distinctiveness.[25] However, actual space set aside for adolescent use has been shrinking.[26] Furthermore, any space that is created for adolescents often leaves them out of the design process; they are frequently presented with environments that they find foreign, unusable, and even hostile to their desire to connect with one another.[27] Given that adolescents are actually losing space for relational development, they are understandably turning to the internet to facilitate peer socialization.[28] The result is that digital space is now a place where adolescents interact with the various social groups in their lives, each of which develops its own unspoken norms to guide behavior and from which teens are learning to differentiate their identity from others.[29] This systematic removal of teens from public spaces reduces opportunities for intergenerational interaction and a broader sense of social solidarity, more so than in any other time in history.[30] The result is a series of generational silos that are becoming increasingly foreign to one another.

Early in social media, adolescents were limited to creating alternative user profiles within a specific social media site to balance their demonstration of loyalty to their friendship group and navigate the expectations of adults. Some social media sites have been developing ways that a person can more easily distinguish between their natural circles, but young people tend to find those tools somewhat cumbersome and awkward. It is becoming increasingly easier for friendship clusters to migrate to different digital tools that allow for both a wide audience of peers to invite themselves into the intended interactions and relationships of the more dedicated cluster group and for adults to digitally wander among their most sacred of friendship groups. They may feel betrayed and violated by those who observe their digital life uninvited, yet at the same time mid-adolescents continue to expose themselves in places and ways that summons the masses to enter. While teens are more comfortable than the general public about displaying themselves on the internet, this does not mean they have the life experience or skills to deal with the ripple effects of the increased visibility.[31] This confusing dichotomy is the trademark of mid-adolescent online interaction. Adolescents need to be included in the design, development, and use of physical space where they can interact with adults who will fully embrace mid-adolescents for who they are. Then, in the same way that teens use tech themselves, life lived in the physical world will have the opportunity to reflect itself in the digital.

Emerging Adults and the Internet

Emerging adults (between twenty and the late twenties) have learned to use online interactions with a greater sensitivity to how they present themselves to the world at large. While they do not have the geophysical restraint

issues that they exhibited when they were younger, they continue to use digital tools primarily to remain connected with those whom they have an existing, or promising, personal connection.[32] Similar to mid-adolescents, emerging adults find that digital tools add a positive dimension to their already existing relationships.[33] In a way that is comparable to mid-adolescent behavior, the quality and nature of offline relationships are mirrored in the digital ones.

However, there is something different about how emerging adults understand and utilize the web in their social interactions and behavior. Increasingly, young adults are turning to the internet to meet new people, and it appears (although the research is preliminary at best) that many emerging and young adults believe using social media to expand their relational network is not only appropriate but also a sound strategy for finding romantic partners. According to research, meeting new people was rated as the most positive reason to engage in online dating sites; conversely, wading through piles of false profiles was rated as the most negative aspect of these same sites.[34] While this has proved to be a necessary part of the online dating experience, the process is like using a machete to forage through a dense jungle: even when the false or misleading profiles are cleared away, the path is not necessarily all that clear to users, especially those who are new to the process.

Even among legitimate profiles, it appears to be a common practice to manipulate content or pictures to emphasize or enhance one's appearance and to a lesser degree social standing in order to be successful on digital dating sites.[35] This was especially true for women, with men being more critically aware of a potential date's attractiveness than females were.

Complicating this further, emerging adults are only beginning to learn to balance self-promotion with desirability, so these online dating sites become a kind of hyperrelational tool in developing one's own sense of identity and then filtering that identity through a vast sea of others' hyperrelational attempts at public identities.[36] For emerging and young adults, negotiating the social media landscape in order to find meaningful relationships requires the delicate and often significantly difficult task of balancing three competing factors: garnering attention to one's self by enhancing (or at least highlighting) one's characteristics and attractability and attempting to grow into an integrated, mature person who is recognized and received as an interdependent and individuated adult while trying to determine the maturity and authenticity of others on the social network.

Given this struggle, it is astonishing that emerging adults are also more likely than their younger counterparts to post sexually explicit material online (astonishing because this behavior is an appeal to attract potential suitors by exposing one's external attributes while actually wanting desperately to be attractive for much more intrinsic and enduring qualities).[37] Among a majority of males and a minority of females, a social acceptance of pornography is developing, and this attitude spills over into online behaviors.[38] Increased levels of sexual activity are in line with Erik Erikson's theory that in the oldest stage of adolescence there is an increased concern with sexual attractiveness and identity.[39] The issue, of course, with the casual excesses of sexuality and promiscuity represented in contemporary digital networks, is that it sets up both men and women for almost certain disappointment in the quality and longevity of ensuing

relationships. However, relational land mines are not limited to digital promiscuity.

Perhaps surprisingly, some emerging adults are turning to online gaming sites to discover and develop relationships. While online gaming remains a relatively limited research field, one online gaming study suggests that emerging adults are also using these sites for relational and even romantic connections. Yet, in an ironic twist, those who turn to online gaming communities for the specific intent of meeting new people report a greater sense of loneliness and family fragmentation than those who play with friends or family.[40] Playing massive multiplayer online games with friends and family strengthens those relational bonds, while searching out new people weakens existing relationships.

Technology is not merely an exception to physical presence; it can be a partner. But turning to technology to meet one's needs for human relationships seems to lead to a cycle of turning back to digital connections and away from face-to-face human connectivity. This fragmenting cycle will potentially estrange their existing relationships, putting at risk their very desire to find someone to love and be loved by.

The implication for adoptive ministry then is found in how we view technological tools. Similar to other stages, we must always begin with the people we desire to serve, and those people need to be people with whom we interact in and around our geophysical spiritual community. While online gaming accountability groups may have some value, attempts to build relationships and evangelize strangers online may well result in our facilitation of the estrangement of other relationships. Instead, spiritual communities need guidance in building bridges with emerging adults in their geophysical relationships—bridges that will develop into relationships that can be augmented with digital tools.

Other Current Perspectives on Digital Connectivity

Adolescent development was chosen as a primary way to consider adolescent tech use because it easily provides a framework for understanding adolescent context, giving the astute youth worker a simple structure from which to evaluate the conflicting voices of tech guidance. Therefore, this information serves only as a conversation starter for the reality and impact of tech on an adoptive youth ministry. The effects of social media on brain development as well as formational concerns, the cultural acceptance of multitasking, and privacy issues are just a few of the myriad digital realities with ministry implications that could be addressed. Formational ideology and multitasking are highlighted here.

Formational Concerns

Psychologist and MIT professor Sherry Turkle is a researcher and specialist on how technology interacts with human sociability. While Turkle initially believed that the internet held promising opportunities for human identity and relational exploration, she now has the conviction that Web 2.0 reduces opportunities for identity experimentation, primarily because most digital self-representations are archived.[41] By this, Turkle is talking about digital footprints: posts, texts, uploaded videos all can remain present online and follow students into their future. From Turkle's perspective, these activity logs keep adolescents somewhat stuck in past expressions of identity, thus hindering their ability to experiment with new expressions and forms of identity, as is required in order to grow into healthy adulthood.

Another concern is reflected in the title of Turkle's book, *Alone Together*, where she proposes, "At the extreme, we are so enmeshed in our connections that we neglect each other."[42] In Turkle's research, the effect of digital technology is a growing dependence on the digital tools to build and enhance relational intimacy instead of the actual people these represent. Turkle, for example, demonstrates how cell phones have so come to embody a person's social safety net that "having a feeling without being able to share it is considered so difficult that it constitutes an emergency."[43] Perhaps we see this in how teens (and adults) keep their phones beside their beds in order to be fully available to others in their life, when what they might really need to be a good friend tomorrow is a good sleep tonight.

Danah Boyd, however, believes that concerns about how our digital connections affect the human condition are really a concern of the adult population. For Boyd, adults, on the one hand, tend to focus on the tech over the deeper formational issues because the technology is the easiest to see.[44] Teens, on the other hand, are more concerned about what it means to participate in the public sphere and treat technology tools as a given.[45] Similarly, though from the perspective of a marketer, Paul Adams suggests that successfully using digital tools requires being less focused on the tech and more focused on people.[46] The formation of individuals, as well as their inclusion into community, begins with people, not the technology.

Exposing the Myth of Multitasking

To many, multitasking is a style of handling daily life that is not only acceptable but also preferable. The research, however, tells us that if someone is in the habit of engaging in multiple media activities at the same time, he or she is likely not doing any of them very well, or at least as well as if he or she were focused on a single event or experience. As it turns out, it might even be destroying a person's ability to think clearly about even the most mundane tasks. In a Stanford University study, compared to their more focused peers, those who engage in heavy media multitasking had a more difficult time focusing on important information, ignoring irrelevant data, or even being able to switch between tasks without constantly thinking about many other things.[47] Heavy media multitasking means it is likely taking longer to do everything and none of it is probably getting done as well as it could. Likely this includes relationships. What is more troubling than the consequences associated with adults who embrace this way of living is that there is an even more significant effect on children and adolescents.

Similar research, led by Stanford University professors Roy Pea and Clifford Nass, indicates that multitasking appears to be having a negative social and emotional developmental effect on "tween"-aged girls (ages eight to twelve).[48] Preteen girls who were heavy media users, whether social media or entertainment-based, trended toward feeling more isolated and different from others (in a negative way), got less sleep, and had more friends that their parents thought were bad influences on their daughters. While this sounds depressing, the solution that researchers discovered was a relatively simple one.

Preteens need face-to-face interaction if they are going to develop a positive sense of social and emotional well-being. Children need adults who will not only walk alongside them but who will also look at them face-to-face and engage together in conversations. But this solid research has simply not been able to make a dent in the overwhelming cultural commitment to advertising directed at the very young that encourages and manipulates them to engage deeply in all forms of the individualistic and impersonal activities of social and entertainment media. The marketing of the Amazon Fire phone from AT&T is a prime example. In this ad, seemingly independent, multitasking hipster kids, coffee press and all, school adults on how to maximize the technological capabilities of their new phones. The boy proclaims, "I've been on this earth nine years, and I've never seen anything like it." At the time of this writing, this commercial last aired on the Cartoon Network, implying a strategy to have kids convince their parents that this is the best phone to buy.[49]

Looking beyond the Flux Capacitor: It's Not Really about the Technology

When young people are not around older people outside structured and controlled settings—such as a classroom, a practice, or even riding in a car to a competitive sporting event—they do not learn the rules and norms of the society. As the culture has become more fragmented[50] and children have less access to downtime, or *any* nonspecifically regulated time with adults living out their metanarrative, they have a hard time learning how to think, how to behave, and how to move forward as productive and assimilated members of society. At the heart of this generational and time segmentation, technology further isolates the young from the adult in society, which becomes problematic for the culture as a whole. Historically, children and newcomers learned the landscape of the culture by simply being together, by rubbing shoulders with one another. When someone—a child, an immigrant, or a young adult who, for whatever reason, had not received the proper experience or environment—did not seem to live up to the societal norms and values of that society, he or she was considered as someone who needed to be trained. Whether this was reflected in acts of communication (i.e., interrupting), an invasion of social space (i.e., crowding into each other), or any other behavior, attitude, or expression that represented a violation of the rules and norms of society, the perpetrator was generally considered to be merely naive, or sometimes intentionally rebellious. Historically, no culture has deemed the child or outsider to have "lost" some seemingly innate ability. It was understood that this person had just not properly learned what was socially appropriate (or was somehow deliberately pushing against the rules). For those who needed training, the typical response was to help the child or outsider become a greater part of the community through time, interaction, and deeper exposure to the culture.

This is not to suggest that mediated interactions between generations do not have their place. Christianity has relied heavily on media technology throughout its history: Scripture can be viewed as a form of mediated communication between God and humanity; Paul's letters are deeply personal writings with greetings to very specific individuals; and the Reformation was fueled by mediated tech developments. Therefore, mediated tech is not foreign to the human reality.

Fairy tales, for example, served the purpose of teaching adult lessons and community values to children. The difference is that adults told these stories to their children while they lived life alongside and together with them. Children observed and experienced how to live in community as adults modeled it. While almost every parent of an adolescent today deals with their children and teenagers regarding their perception of the dangers of the internet, only about a third of parents actively engage with their adolescents or their adolescent's friends online.[51] The result is that children and adolescents are defining and learning interpersonal social interaction without the opportunity to shape these within the context of adult interactions. For adolescents, this diminishing of mutual participation in everyday life means that they are often left to their own peer groups, somewhat mediated by the limitations of social interactions, to determine socially acceptable values, expectations, and practices. For parents, it likely means that their role has been reduced to more of a police officer or a protective detail. Teenagers then discover—either unintentionally or in hindsight—that they have a different set of values, rules, and norms from the dominant, adult-controlled society.[52] Parents are thereby left by default as the last line of training and equipping for adult life that young people have. Many parents do not feel equipped or, frankly, do not have the capacity to fully respond to the social deficits that separation and fragmentation has created in their children. They need a community to join them.

While it might be possible for adults relatively to stay up on what adolescents are doing online, many wish that their children would be more responsible and "web savvy" and avoid those parts of the web that hinder their socialization and development. In both cases—monitoring web access and activity and trying to influence web behavior creates an adversarial relationship between the child and parent, and thus places the relationship focus on the behavior of the child. What is almost always missed in this parental dance is that all the while something incredibly significant is happening. Young people are developing and consistently reinforcing patterns of behavior and values that are unique social interactions separate from the larger community. They are in the process of developing a multitude of microcultures of which adults themselves have become naive outsiders. Each of these developing online cultures requires adult missionaries who will step into, understand, and engage with that unique relational world.

Conclusion

Digital tools are embedded in everyday life. The rapid pace of innovation, the ongoing proliferation, and the societal willingness to adopt new digital technologies suggest that digital connectivity is going to be the ongoing and daily reality for all young people for the foreseeable future. Those who appreciate that technology is not the enemy per se of physical presence will recognize it as a tool to be understood and utilized as an invitation to deepen existing human relationships. As adolescents are pushed to society's margins and their social interactions are increasingly developed apart from adults, technology will likewise continue to augment this reality and further isolate adolescents from adults. This is what parents, teachers, coaches, and youth workers must avoid.

The idea that someday technology will unite the world under a common message is a utopian myth. Instead, geophysical presence will need to combat fragmentation by being more intentional, more gracious, and more seeking of interpersonal understanding. To accomplish this, adoptive youth workers will need to see themselves as missionaries, seeking first to understand the students they serve and their relational context in order to facilitate deeper personal connections, foster a sense of being embraced by the community, and promote greater inclusion of the youth within the ongoing body of Christ. Only by focusing on people will digital tech become a tool that augments an adoptive reality.

Screen Time

A Window into Teens' Dreams

CRAIG DETWEILER

There is no one like Craig Detweiler. He is a first-rate thinker, filmmaker, scholar, teacher, and passionate advocate for justice and integrity. We consider Detweiler one of the most important voices in the national discussion on the intersection of pop culture and theology. Detweiler, a PhD theologian who lives in Malibu, California, is widely respected in Hollywood and in film schools around the world. His voice is an important one, and we are grateful to have him as an author in Adoptive Youth Ministry.

I first got to know Detweiler when we were on the team facilitating a youth leadership program cosponsored by Young Life and Fuller Theological Seminary and funded by the Lilly Endowment. His role was to help our young prodigies wrestle with and integrate their understanding of the Christian faith with the rich texture of popular culture, mostly experienced through film. When he showed the film Dogma (starring George Carlin as Cardinal Glick) to our first-year class of Young Life high school juniors who had been nominated as "student leaders," I remember the somewhat

heated and profoundly impressive conversation with a few of us in the hallway. Detweiler was convincing, but only because he knew what we had yet to discover—film reflects us and often reflects God in ways that most people fail to recognize. Using film to expose the underbelly of cultural faith and helping teenagers discuss movies and thereby see and experience God in new and deeper ways is Detweiler's greatest gift; he is a faithful, honest, insightful, and highly gifted facilitator. This chapter, which weaves together a convincing tapestry of cultural observation and examples of God shining through a variety of creative expression, is quintessential Detweiler; you are in for a treat.

As with many of the chapters in Adoptive Youth Ministry, *this chapter does not overtly point to participating in adoption as the ultimate goal of all ministry, especially ministry to the young. He seeks a deeper engagement with society and with our God, inviting us to bring that into our ministries. As we do and as we explore what Detweiler shares with us, it is our job to find ways to bring adults and *the young together so that we can, as siblings and regardless of our ages or backgrounds, explore our society together in the interests of the mission of God in the world ("thy kingdom come, thy will be done").*

As you read this chapter, consider these questions:

1. *How can "pop culture" be a "conduit for God's general revelation"? What is Detweiler's point when he describes popular culture as a way God communicates with the world he loves?*

2. *When you were in high school, did your parents watch what you watched? Were they interested in being students of your culture and world? What was your interaction like with your parents regarding television, video games, movies, the phone, and the internet?*

3. *Detweiler spends a great deal of time in Acts 8. Look carefully at this text, and consider what is he saying about our interaction with popular culture and society in the name of Christ. What are some tangible ways to engage in today's society?*

4. *Why do you watch what you watch? Think of a recent movie you saw that some in your church might be critical of. What drew you to that film? How did it make you feel? What did it say to you and say about you? Do the same with a favorite television show or band/song.*

Years before Facebook started asking us to list our favorite movies, music, and shows as a way to define ourselves, I would ask my college students about what stories spoke to them. What was their all-time favorite film? For many years, two consistent answers emerged. The guys' favorite film tended to be *Se7en* (1995). The women in my film classes loved *Pretty Woman* (1990). I found these answers frightening and fascinating, particularly given the demographic I was teaching. These were students from Christian colleges and universities who chose to pursue a semester in Hollywood at the Los Angeles Film Studies Center.[1] These were the most media-savvy students from Christian college campuses, and their all-time favorite films were about a serial killer enacting the seven deadly sins on his victims and a romance/fantasy about a hooker who wins over a corporate raider.

Were the students suffering from a slippery rather than a sticky faith?[2] These sounded like half-baked, "almost Christian" responses devoid of a thoughtful ethic regarding entertainment.[3] While the inclination may have been to shout "What?!" I decided to adopt a posture asking "Why?" Why did these R-rated stories speak into these students' lives? Could seemingly disposable pop culture become a conduit for God's general revelation? And if so, how could I learn to listen carefully to pop culture?

Perhaps my students had been so sheltered in their upbringing that they found the horrors of *Se7en* sobering, a disturbing wake-up call about the depths of evil. Maybe director David Fincher's vision was so visually arresting that they couldn't resist its dark, nihilistic allure. What if they were drawn to *Se7en* because it illustrated the wages of sin that they heard so much about but hadn't dared to test? In this case, *Se7en* became a remarkable cautionary tale, a visceral warning. These messy, repellant images may have approximated the impact of Jonathan Edwards's famous sermon, "Sinners in the Hands of an Angry God."

What about *Pretty Woman*? Julia Roberts's iconic role was rooted in her considerable charm and easy laugh. It was fun watching her undercut the snooty attitudes of those Rodeo Drive salespeople who judged her. Had Cinderella stories been so normalized for young Christian women that they found *Pretty Woman*'s journey from prostitute to trophy wife enlivening? Or did the women in my class find the love of Richard Gere for a woman of ill repute remarkably affirming and biblical? Hadn't Hosea married a prostitute as a prophetic act? Didn't Jesus undercut the Pharisees' judgment by inviting them to cast the first stone of aspersion at a woman in similar circumstances? Maybe *Pretty Woman* actually reflected Jesus's enduring love for us, despite our self-denigrating actions.

Whatever the reasons for the students' pop cultural attachments, the roots of their fandom may be far more spiritual than we or they realize. In studying what they watch, we may uncover students' hopes and dreams and nightmares. By engaging in deep, empathetic listening, we may find points of connection for Bible studies, sermons, and counseling situations. Pop culture burrows into teens' hearts and minds in ways that sermons or Sunday school may never touch. So I'd rather start from that soft, soulful space than try to work from my agenda to their passions.

I study adolescents' cinematic inspirations because a profane, violent R-rated film transformed my teenage years and accelerated my spiritual search. As a high school senior, I was scared straight by *Raging Bull*, an uncompromising portrait of self-destructive World Middleweight Champion Jake LaMotta. I felt many connections with how this boxer cut himself off from friends and family, shunning the brother and wife who loved and supported him. Even as an angry young man, I didn't want to end up like Jake, alone and in a jail cell,

banging my head against a wall and shouting, "Why? Why? Why?" When the movie ended and the credits rolled, *Raging Bull* hooked me with the seemingly obscure conclusion, "All I know is this: once I was blind and now I can see." I didn't know at the time that it was drawn from John 9:25, but I inherently sensed it was true. I had watched a brutal two-hour portrait of blindness that opened my eyes. The talks I'd heard at Young Life about a personal relationship with Jesus Christ suddenly took on a new urgency and appeal. Six months later at Young Life's camp Windy Gap, I committed all I knew of myself to all I understood about Jesus. It was a revelatory, life-giving turning point.

How can God use profane pop culture to spark sacred searches? This question has dominated my work as a youth minister, a filmmaker, an author, and an educator.[4] I have invested years of study into general revelation, natural theology, and the power of God to use talking donkeys and mere stones to speak.[5] From *Braveheart* to *Bruce Almighty*, I compiled stories of how movies moved people from despair toward hope. Real-life role models in *The Blind Side* and fantastical heroes in *The Book of Eli* model the power of faith to transform lives. Television series like *Lost* invited us to consider the divergent values of faith versus science (the whole of Psalm 23 was recited on *Lost* during prime time). Religious questions that were rare in the era of *Touched by an Angel* have become commonplace on shows that range from *Bones* to *Glee*.

As a parent of two teenagers, I watch what they watch. But I want to do more than monitor the content they consume to check for inappropriate words or scenes. I want to potentially help them find God amid all the electronic inputs. The Kaiser Family Foundation reported that American kids ingest almost eleven hours of media content every single day (with the amount rising annually via multitasking).[6] Is that time away from God, removed from divine influence? If so, then heaven help us all. Given our kids' limited time in Sunday school or youth group, I hope and pray that God might speak through their extensive screen time. Their playlists are a window into their worries. Their favorites may form a picture of their passions or aspirations. I want to watch and listen carefully.

My fourteen-year-old daughter's favorite television show was *Glee*. It was an unabashed celebration of outsiders, the Gleeks who occupy school bands and choruses and clubs. The Fox show's creators turned even the most painful high schoolers' questions of identity into an opportunity to burst into song. My daughter's favorite character was Blaine, a gay teenager engaged in a fairly intense romance with Kurt, the talented soloist and central protagonist of the series. Why did she have such a rooting interest in Blaine and Kurt? Why did she resonate with their songs? Listening to pop culture is far more than an academic exercise. It is central to my calling as an educator, a screenwriter, and a parent.

Biblical Models for Pop Cultural Plunges

Who can teach us how to come alongside our students' or our children's spiritual search? Who models cultural engagement in the Scriptures? The incarnation is the paramount example of entering into others' shoes. In *The Message*, Eugene Peterson translates John 1:14 as "The Word became flesh and blood, and moved into the neighborhood." Jesus literally stepped into our situation. His public ministry

occurred in the marketplace. It was rooted in compassion. When I see students walking past one another, staring at their smartphones, scrolling for updates, I recall that when Jesus "saw the crowds, he had compassion on them, because they were harassed and helpless, like sheep without a shepherd" (Matt. 9:36).

In Acts 17, we find Paul engaging in public debates in the marketplace of Mars Hill. He studies the Athenians' cultural artifacts as an entry into gospel proclamation, connecting what they have made for an Unknown God to the God revealed in Jesus Christ. He quotes from popular Greek poetry as both a bridge from their thinking to his thinking and as a point of contrast. Jesus engaged in the same shift when he declared in the Beatitudes, "You have heard that it was said . . . but I tell you" (Matt. 5:21–22). He raises the stakes of discipleship by building upon the things people already know, discuss, and embrace. Careful listening and familiarity with the lingua franca, the language of the day, precedes effective proclamation.

In studying the Scriptures, I found the first cross-cultural Christian was actually Philip in Acts 8. He was on the run, fleeing persecution in Jerusalem, when he headed toward Samaria. As an outsider and exile, he was able to communicate with a marginalized community. An angel told Philip to head south toward Gaza. Perhaps his experience in a foreign land enabled Philip to receive the angel's instructions more clearly. We often think we need to be in a place of safety, security, or peace to find God's call. But the unfamiliar surroundings in Acts show us that a place where we are challenged or off-kilter may sharpen our spiritual antennae.

Philip encounters an Ethiopian eunuch who had gone to Jerusalem to worship. While the eunuch may have longed to serve the God of Abraham, Isaac, and Jacob, his ethnicity and especially his physical alteration would have prevented him from entering the holy temple. The removal of his sexual organs ensured that he was not a threat to the queen he served. Yet it also separated him from the purity codes observed by God's people according to the Torah. The eunuch's spiritual hunger had not been satisfied.

The Spirit instructed Philip to go to the chariot, where he heard the man reading from the book of Isaiah. Their exchange is a model for how we may dream our evangelistic endeavors will unfold. As Philip approaches, a spiritual search is already under way. Philip asks a simple question, "Do you understand what you're reading?" In Greek, you hear the wordplay, "*ginoskeis ha anaginoskeis?*" The difference between reading and understanding (just an *ana-*) is small but significant. We may challenge students in youth group to read the Bible. But all too often they lack sufficient background or context to unpack the powerful implications. The same could be said for their favorite pop cultural plunges. They know when they love a movie or a show, but they may not fully grasp why it pierces their heart or expresses their deepest longings. Seeing, they may not see. Reading, they may not understand.

The Ethiopian eunuch answers Philip's question with a question, "How can I (understand) unless someone guides me?" Eugene Peterson notes the subtle but significant difference between an invitation to explain and an invitation to guide. Both words are rooted in the Greek verb "to lead." Peterson distinguishes how "the explainer, the *exegete*, leads the meaning out of the text; the guide, the *hodegete*, leads *you* in the way (*hodos*) of the text." Drawing on his years in ministry, Peterson suggests, "Pastoral-biblical hermeneutics presupposes exegesis but involves more. The African invites Philip into the chariot to accompany him as his guide. This is going to take some time. . . . Philip decides on *hodegesis*. He climbs into the chariot and shares the journey."[7] This is youth ministry at its best. It starts by getting in step with God, following the Spirit's lead. It expands by paying attention to what the Ethiopian eunuch is already reading (or watching or texting). It gets deeper when we're invited into their world, to accompany them on the journey. Philip's story provides us with a sound ministry method: listen to the Spirit, listen to what people are listening to, and get invited to guide their understanding of God's ways. Surely we can all practice the art of listening and ask the simple question, "Do you understand what you're reading, watching, or listening to?"

Why We Watch What We Watch

Our pop cultural habits reflect our passions, interests, and needs. Our favorite shows offer something we need—from surrogate friends and family to a laugh or a cry. When my children were young, Winnie the Pooh served as a calm, comforting friend. In elementary school, *The Suite Life of Zach and Cody* offered a silly alternative to their constricting classrooms. In adolescence, *Supernatural* enabled my daughter to deal with dark forces that she couldn't always name or explain. It exposed her to the scary and wondrous reality of the ineffable. The summer she watched eight seasons of *How I Met Your Mother* on Netflix coincided with confounding mating rituals. While not every relationship needs an intervention and their Bro Code doesn't always work, she was able to gain perspective on her own romantic entanglements via the comedic spouse seeking portrayed on the show. *Glee* offered a space to wrestle with myriad adolescent issues, from teen pregnancy to sexual identity. The characters learn to embrace their otherness, to find a place in the world as an artist or creative force (both in high school and beyond).

We turn to pop culture when we can't quite name our dilemmas. We may go to the movies as a way to buy time. It holds our demons at bay for a couple of hours. It offers some distance or perspective, a chance to worry about somebody else's quandaries. The best films and television series offer a vicarious experience where we can enter into the suffering of another and perhaps gain control or mastery over our own struggles. Surely, Jesus offers the most vicarious example of taking on our suffering, entering into our world and our pain.

Pop culture invites us to identify with a character. It is an opportunity to see ourselves in someone else's story—both our siblings in God's household and those whom we are called to love—and step into their struggles. The film or show might be aspirational (like the teens overcoming the odds in *The Hunger Games*, *Harry Potter*, or even *Pretty in Pink* and *Ferris Bueller's Day Off*). These Hollywood stories offer happy endings and reassurance. Independent films offer darker, more cautionary tales, such as *The Perks of Being a Wallflower*, *Garden State*, *Fruitvale Station*, and *Short Term 12*. These are hard-won hopes that may leave viewers more disturbed than when they arrived.

The arc of pop cultural icons can also serve as instructive stories. Tweens who grew up watching *Hannah Montana* are confronted by the outrageous habits of an older, saucier Miley Cyrus. Those who once idolized Britney Spears or Justin Bieber may find their faith in their teen idols tested. What used to be pure and simple may look much grainier in later adolescence. Twenty-somethings are only starting to put their faith to the test. They can potentially avoid making the same mistakes as their fallen idols, or they can slide into the same prolonged adolescence. Conforming one's convictions and behavior takes a long time and continues into later adolescence (aka the twenties).

Youth ministry must be thought of as something that extends far beyond high school or college.[8] Following the arc of both fictional characters and tabloid celebrities is a way to talk about hard choices and bad decisions. The travails of former teen stars illustrate how tough the transition to adulthood can be. More freedom also means more temptation. Discussions of the arrested development of a Lindsay Lohan or Justin Bieber may prove a far more effective springboard than a Bible study leader imagines. When Cory Monteith of *Glee* died from a drug overdose, his fans were forced to wrestle with addiction, mortality, and the consequences of actions. A special episode of *Glee* offered the characters (and the audience) an opportunity to grieve. Hopefully, adolescents will also learn from the comebacks of Demi Lovato, who struggled with eating disorders, or Robert Downey Jr.'s recovery from substance abuse.

Pop culture often takes us places we haven't been. Film noir like *Memento* or *The Dark Knight* may take us to scary places we don't want to dwell in. Horror films like *The Exorcism of Emily Rose* and *Sinister* offer a safe way to wrestle with literal demons. From fantasies like *Lord of the Rings* and *Harry Potter* to science fiction like *Star Wars* and *Star Trek*, movies can open up vistas and possibilities we have never imagined. It can expand our vision. Documentaries may raise our awareness of communities in crisis and deepen our hunger for justice. The intensity of the movement that arose from *Invisible Children* and the subsequent YouTube campaign, "Kony 2012," caught even its creators by surprise. My daughter has been challenged toward a healthier diet by documentaries like *Super Size Me*. Fifth graders in our community protested a class field trip to Sea World after seeing the plight of orcas in *Blackfish*. Independent films made outside the Hollywood system will often afflict the comfortable with a prophetic edge.

Television traditionally offers comfort. Sitcoms like *Cheers* center on a bar where everybody knows your name. The formulaic nature of television formats offers up familiar feelings (and repetitive patterns), from the warmth of *Modern Family* to the procedures on *Law & Order* and *CSI*. As more channels compete for our fragmented attention, reality television often depends on outrageous personalities and behavior. It is a form of shock TV rooted in titillation. Television is increasingly taking us to disturbing places we haven't been, inviting us inside the mind of a serial killer like *Dexter* or meth dealers like Walt and Jessie on *Breaking Bad*. As youth ministers compete for teens' limited attention, we may be tempted to take teens to places they have never been rather than creating a comfortable space. It is tough to compete with $200 million entertainments laden with special effects. I do not suggest that youth ministers attempt to compete with pop culture via various stunts. Perhaps we need to recover the comforts and familiarity of beloved television shows; a safe space where everybody knows your name can be a great gift to harried teens.

YouTube is a boundless resource for both oddities and familiarities. Viral videos arrive via strange and unexpected found footage. The outrageous and outlandish often pop out from the crowd. We can subscribe to YouTube stars who look/think/act like us. Popular channels are often built upon direct address—adolescents talking to one another, building an audience of peers; followers become a surrogate family. From writing a song to just putting our feelings out there, YouTube promotes the feeling that we are not alone. Pop culture allows us to process our pain via solidarity. Whether through traditional media outlets or the burgeoning world of social media, YouTube, Vimeo, or Vine, teens find comfort and refuge in screen time.

"Grilled Cheesus": A Case Study

Glee tackled faith and doubt in an episode that series creator Ryan Murphy predicted "would be our most controversial yet."[9] "Grilled Cheesus" premiered October 5, 2010, and attracted an audience of over 11 million viewers in the United States alone, the highest rated scripted program for the week among viewers aged eighteen to forty-five.[10] The copresident of the New Directions glee club, Finn Hudson, is shocked to discover the face of Jesus on his grilled cheese sandwich. Although he's not the most religious person ("he sort of worships Eric Clapton and Chad Ochocinco"), Finn takes this appearance as a sign and decides to pray. He kneels before the sandwich and asks "Grilled Cheesus" to please let the McKinley High football team win its first game. In return, he offers to "make sure we honor you this week in glee club." The episode is about why we pray, what kind of bargaining we do with God, and how we respond when our prayers are or aren't answered. It begins with an incidence of general revelation and unfurls in all kinds of unexpected ways.

"Grilled Cheesus" also deals with questions of religious liberty, particularly what is allowable in a public school setting. Does singing religious songs in Mr. Schuester's classroom violate the separation of church and state? When Finn suggests the glee club "pay tribute to Jesus" in music, students like Kurt Hummel resist: "Sorry, but if I wanted to sing about Jesus, I'd go to church, and the reason I don't go to church is because most churches don't think very much about gay people or women or science." Mercedes, an African American student with Christian convictions, retorts, "I don't see anything wrong with getting a little church up in here." Throughout the episode, the producers of *Glee* go to great lengths to ensure that every attack on religion is followed by an affirmation of faith; each salute to the Divine is met by a skeptic's objection. The show mirrors the cultural tension between Christians and atheists who continue to argue about how much religious expression is allowable in the public square. Are we promised freedom of religion or freedom from religion?

Having rallied the New Directions glee club to sing songs for Jesus, Finn returns to the sandwich with an additional request. He admits, "I didn't go to Sunday school, so I don't know if God works the same as a genie and I only get three wishes, but here's the thing . . .": Finn wants to get to second base with his girlfriend, Rachel. He makes a deal with God: "Considering that I've devoted a week of my musical life to you, I hope that you can see it in your heart to answer my prayers. Amen." While such reasoning may seem absurd, it is not too far from the type of magical thinking used by many adolescents. In what has

been famously termed "Moralistic Therapeutic Deism," many students perceive faith as being a pretty good person in order to please a fairly remote deity.[11] Religion is seen as a merit system in which God rewards good behavior. They may see success in life as an appropriate gift commensurate to their faithfulness.

Beyond Finn's deal making with Grilled Cheesus, the efficacy of prayers is tested in a sensitive, life-threatening situation. When Kurt's father has a heart attack, Kurt's friends and teachers rally around him in the hospital room. With Burt Hummel hooked up to tubes and monitors in the hospital, Kurt seeks a sign of life, but his father fails to squeeze his hand. Back at school, Mr. Schuester says, "Our thoughts are all with Kurt." Mercedes sings a gospel song about "being in a very dark place and turning to God," Whitney Houston's hit "I Look to You." While Kurt appreciates her musical gift, he admits he is an atheist who doesn't believe in God. He thinks, "God is kinda like Santa Claus for adults." (Certainly that's how Finn has approached "the Cheesy Lord.") Kurt also sees God as kind of a jerk, especially for making him gay and then having Christians tell him it's something he chose, "as if someone would choose to be mocked every day of their life." The scene reflects the ongoing cultural tensions swirling around gay rights, gay marriage, and some Christians' responses. Kurt tells his friends, "I appreciate your thoughts, but I don't want your prayers." He walks out of the class.

The nemesis of the glee club, cheerleading adviser Sue Sylvester, goads Kurt into filing a formal complaint with the school board. Haven't his rights been violated by religious intrusions in Mr. Schuester's classroom? The guidance counselor, Emma (who is also Mr. Schuester's girlfriend), is furious. Emma bursts into Sue's office and asks, "What happened to you, Sue, that made you such a miserable tyrant?" In perhaps the most vulnerable scene in Sue's bombastic history on *Glee*, she talks about her childhood hero, her big sister, Jean. Sue recalls the cruel things that others said about Jean, mocking her Down syndrome. Sue tells Emma, "I prayed every night for her to get better and nothing changed. So I prayed harder and after a while I realized it wasn't that I wasn't praying hard enough. It was that no one was listening." Earnest, unanswered prayers can turn into doubt and even bitterness. Sue comes to see that "asking someone to believe in a fantasy, however comforting, isn't a moral thing to do. It's cruel." She cannot reconcile a loving God with her sister's unchanging condition.

Here is the crux of the entire episode. While it may be tempting to see the show as mocking religion (via Jesus's face on grilled cheese) or advocating for gay rights (through Kurt's speeches), a deeper, core question slowly emerges. Those engaged in empathetic listening will recognize that objections to faith are usually rooted in far more painful, personal issues. We may respond too quickly to surface objections and never get to deeper issues of doubt. As Philip paused beside the Ethiopian eunuch's chariot, so we have an opportunity to listen in to ancient questions reposed for twenty-first-century teens. Several core questions lie beneath all of *Glee*'s jokes, songs, and political posturing: "Why doesn't God answer my prayers?" "How can I believe in God amid all the suffering (in my life, in my family, in the world)?" "Grilled Cheesus" is about far more than how gay people have been treated by Christians. It raises timeless questions of theodicy, how to reconcile a good God with a cruel world. *Glee* reveals how a young, hopeful,

and faith-filled Sue Sylvester slowly became the angry, volatile, and scheming Coach Sue. Show creator Ryan Murphy summarizes the situation: "Sue's an atheist, but I love that she doesn't want to be. . . . She and [Kurt] are both saying to the world, 'Prove us wrong: If God is kindness and love, make me believe in God.'"[12] This is the challenge of theodicy: explaining how a loving God can preside over a fallen and broken universe. It is a blatant cry for meaning, for hope, and for answers. Murphy calls it "the scene I'm most proud to have been involved with in my entire career."[13]

We will often find these enduring problems of theodicy expressed in Psalms and in contemporary pop songs. As with the best musicals, *Glee*'s songs express characters' feelings and advance the story line. In the center of the episode, Rachel lights a candle and sings Barbara Streisand's hit "Papa, Can You Hear Me?" from *Yentl*. It is a highly particular and appropriate expression of Jewish faith and devotion. In the hospital, Rachel, Quinn, and Mercedes take turns praying for Kurt's father. Yet, when Kurt discovers them, he is offended by their actions. He has brought a Sikh to apply acupuncture to improve circulation in Burt's brain. Kurt mocks their prayers: "Amazingly, needles pierce the skin better than Psalms." What makes Kurt so curt with his friends, so bitter toward God and resistant to prayer?

Before Mr. Schuester's class Kurt admits, "I need to express myself." He reflects on his mother's funeral, when they were lowering her body into the ground, and he was crying. He goes to his life moment of the greatest pain, confusion, and crisis. Kurt remembers the assurance that came from his father squeezing his hand: "Knowing that those hands were there to take care of me, that was enough."

He sings the Beatles' "I Want to Hold Your Hand" for his father, turning a song rooted in romance into a prayer for healing. This is the kind of deep listening that pop culture (at its best) invites. An adolescent in crisis may interpret a show or a film in ways that the creators never intended. Our job is to figure out why that pop cultural form speaks so profoundly to their hearts. While Kurt sings, the class falls silent. Flashbacks to a young Kurt, learning to ride a bicycle with his father's help, provide a poignant glimpse into his backstory. Father and son engage in a tea party, with a young Kurt teaching his dad the proper protocol. It is clearly suggested that Kurt's gay identity was forming from an early age. The flashbacks conclude at the funeral, where Kurt's father reaches back and grabs Kurt's hand, offering comfort and reassurance in his hour of deepest need. The song concludes with Kurt (and the class) in tears. In Kurt's deepest existential crisis, he found comfort not in God but in his father's hand. With his father potentially dying, Kurt cannot take comfort in his friends' prayers (or God). By listening to Kurt's song, we see where his faith resides (in his father's hands) and why even that hope is now being threatened and undermined.

After class, Mercedes reaches out and challenges him not to cut himself off from "a world of experiences that might surprise you." She says to him, "Do me a favor. One thing: come to church with me this Sunday." They have dedicated their upcoming Sunday worship service to Kurt's dad. Kurt agrees to attend even if worship is just genuflecting to "the Great Spaghetti Monster in the Sky." Mercedes asks the church to direct their prayers toward Burt Hummel and to her friend Kurt. She acknowledges his unbelief but challenges him to believe in something more "because life is too hard to go through it alone, without something to hold on to, and without something that's sacred." Mercedes dedicates a rousing gospel version of "Bridge over Troubled Water" to Kurt. Here we see a common and lovely Christian response to a friend in crisis. Perhaps he cannot pray, but the body of Christ, as a caring community, still seeks to surround him with love and support, adopting him as one of their own.

Finn's quick conversion is followed by an equally fast renunciation of faith. He bows down in the locker room for a third prayer and asks for another favor. Finn prays that he will become the starting quarterback again. He reasons, "I can deliver your message to the world more powerfully if I'm the most popular guy in the school again." Having lived and worked in Hollywood for years, I have heard many versions of this prayer—from athletes, politicians, and entertainers. We vow to praise God if and when we are lifted up: "Make me rich, famous, and powerful and I will shout your name across media formats." It echoes the deal that Salieri tries to strike with God in the Oscar-winning drama *Amadeus* (1984). As a dedicated Christian, Salieri promises to praise God through his songs. And yet he wonders what kind of capricious God would lavish far more profound musical gifts on a lewd, faithless fop like Mozart. Instead of praising God's gifts revealed through Mozart, Salieri turns bitter and vows to destroy his musical rival. When we make deals with God that fail to unfold according to the terms we have outlined, our faith can quickly devolve into doubt, anger, or even revenge.

Finn's prayers are seemingly answered when the starting quarterback, Sam, gets injured in the game. This outcome seems rather twisted to Finn. Feelings of guilt and confusion prompt him to confess to the guidance counselor. He feels terrible about Sam being injured because of his prayers. But Emma explains that Finn's prayers toward a grilled cheese sandwich didn't result in divine intervention, saying, "You didn't hurt Sam," and "God didn't let you touch Rachel's boobs, Rachel did." Emma reframes Finn's nascent theology, telling him, "God works in all kinds of mysterious ways, but I'm pretty sure he doesn't spend a lot of time trying to speak to us through sandwiches." There is general revelation, but there is also foolish attribution or misguided deal making with the divine. Finn is disappointed; he thought he had a direct line to God. He doesn't want to feel like everybody else, like he's just floating around through space. He responds to his shattered view of God as genie with an angry version of REM's hit song, "Losing My Religion." He identifies with Kurt's doubt. In a defiant, direct address to God, he sings/shouts, "I thought that I heard you laughing / I thought that I heard you sing," but it turns out, "That was just a dream / Just a dream." He tells the class, "I used to think God was up there looking over me. Now I'm not so sure."

Are we meant to see Finn's entire experience as foolish and comic? Two concluding scenes suggest where the producers' intentions reside. Sue plays chess with her big sister, Jean. Sue asks Jean whether she believes in God. While Sue holds fast to her atheism, which is rooted in the world's cruel behavior toward her sister, Jean says, "God never makes mistakes. That's what I believe." Jean asks, "Want me to pray for you, Sue?" Sue replies, "That would be nice."

After his church experience, Kurt talks to his still-comatose father. He admits his mistakes: "I should have let those guys pray for

you." Through tears he says, "I don't believe in God, Dad. But I believe in you. And I believe in us. You and me, that's what's sacred to me. And I'm . . . I'm so sorry that I never got to tell you that." As Burt's finger begins to move, Kurt springs to his feet. Tears of sorrow shift into tears of joy and relief. He may not have been uttering a prayer, but his hopes are answered with this sign of life.

As always, the episode concludes with a song. The New Directions sing Joan Osborne's 1996 hit, "One of Us." It asks a series of timeless theological questions like "If God had a name, what would it be?" and "What would you ask if you had just one question?" before the chorus ponders, "What if God was one of us?" In the audience, Mr. Schuester and Sue listen to the choir. He wonders whether she will press the issue of a religious song being performed by the students at a public school: "Will you get me fired? Will you report me?" Listening to the song with a furrowed brow, Sue answers with a simple "No." The church/state question has been put aside for now. Finn finishes eating his grilled cheesus sandwich. He no longer preserves it as a magic totem. The unexpected appearance of Jesus that sparked his short-lived faith has been devoured.

Did the producers try to make our search for God look ridiculous? Were they mocking those moments when we try to find the face of God in a cloud (or a sandwich)? Ryan Murphy admits they played the Cheesy Lord for laughs but that "you read stories about it every week. People see the face of God in, like, bird droppings or corn flakes. To me, what that says is that in our society right now, people are just so desperate to believe in something."[14] Cocreator Ian Brennan described the episode as "a very honest take on how we think about religion today."[15] When thinking about *Glee*'s youthful audience, Brennan said, "Some of the kids don't know yet what they believe."[16] Murphy reflected on his own religious upbringing (quite similar to Kurt's) as a gay teenager in Ohio. He told *TV Guide*, "I do believe in God," adding, "I think religion gave me great structure and discipline and order. . . . The older I get the more I feel like God is a collective good. I think that's what the episode is saying. That's what all these kids are desperately trying to find in their lives."[17] Surely youth workers can find points of connection with such an earnest search. Murphy acknowledged his overriding goal with *Glee*: "I wish there had been something to launch conversations about feelings and emotions in my household when I was younger."[18] Murphy concludes, "When the show is at its best, that is what I think we're doing."[19]

Considering Contexts

Would I recommend that youth ministers show the "Grilled Cheesus" episode to their teens? Not necessarily. Every city, school, church, country, and culture has particular sensitivities and interests. What sparks a conversation in one setting may shut down discussion in a different context. By following Philip's lead in listening carefully to what students (and their parents) are watching and discussing, youth leaders can discern what shows and what theological questions are bubbling to the surface. Denominational concerns may make a show like *Glee* too incendiary in particular settings. Yet in churches that are already asking teenage members to vote regarding denominational ties, this episode of *Glee* may offer a way to wade into contentious issues. I would recommend that youth ministers watch the episode regardless of their particular feelings about

gay marriage and denominational divides. Watching what our adoptive siblings watch does not mean we necessarily agree with or even endorse the beliefs and practices of Hollywood. We engage pop cultural activities in order to have a deeper understanding of and humble discernment toward teens' proclivities. "Grilled Cheesus" raises issues that extend far beyond political flashpoints. Questions of theodicy follow in the wake of deaths from cancer, car wrecks, and natural disasters. Teens seeking to make sense of the world will invariably find their childhood faith challenged by real-world situations. The producers of *Glee* may be asking questions parents and youth workers might not be prepared to deal with, but if pop culture has raised the question, then our teens are already wrestling with the theological implications of pain, suffering, and death. Teens need caring adults and role models to come alongside their questions, to see what they're watching, thinking, and feeling. Like the eunuch, adolescents may desperately need someone to explain it to them.

Engagement with pop culture has traditionally diverged along denominational lines. With more churches opting for nondenominational status, how might a youth minister discern what is timely, appropriate, and wise to watch? H. Richard Niebuhr provided an insightful survey of historic theological responses in his classic, *Christ and Culture*.[20] Protestants tend to vacillate between avoiding pop culture whenever possible to justifying movie watching for the sake of ministry. In his seminal book, *Reel Spirituality*, Robert K. Johnston describes these positions as Avoidance, Caution, and Dialogue.[21] Sacramental traditions (Catholic, Orthodox, Episcopalian) tend to view Christ as "of" or "above" culture. They may focus less on how much sex, violence, or profanity occurs in a pop cultural form than the overriding theme or values expressed in the picture or show. While some may avoid watching *Glee* because of the homosexual characters who express their disgust with the church, other Christians may find it offers moments of "divine encounter" in which God speaks through unlikely means. What some denominations might consider blind embrace and compromise, others may consider a source of natural theology and spiritual breakthrough. Wherever a church tradition may fall on the theological spectrum, all members of the body of Christ are encouraged not to judge one another.

Christians have always debated what cultural standards and practices should be embraced or avoided. In Paul's letters to the Romans and Corinthians, he challenges Christians with different understandings of how to live not to judge one another. While our pop cultural diets are not equivalent to the ancient debate about meat sacrificed to idols, the concern that we are to carry toward others' relative strengths or weaknesses carries on. We are not to cause our brothers and sisters to stumble in their faith (1 Cor. 8), yet we often get confused about our responsibilities and roles in regard to Paul's references to being weak or strong in faith. We may judge those who will not watch R-rated movies as weak while they consider themselves to be strong or mature. We may feel judged (as weak or worldly) for something we watch when it genuinely doesn't cause us to stumble (thanks to the strength of our faith). When we lord our convictions and conscience over others and condemn their practices, we are falling into the divisive practices that Paul warns against.

In *Grey Matters*, Brett McCracken discusses how we (mis)use the Bible to justify our choices in relation to what we watch, what we eat, and what we drink.[22] He sees far too much ethical compromise in the name of ministry or cultural dialogue and calls his generation of believers to rise above the hipster Christian pose and rationale. Sometimes we turn Paul's promotion of unity into categories we use to judge one another or divide ourselves. Yet the conclusion in Romans seems abundantly clear: "The one who eats everything must not treat with contempt the one who does not, and the one who does not eat everything must not judge the one who does, for God has accepted them" (Rom. 14:3). Whatever our choices and practices regarding pop culture, Paul asks us not to judge one another.

Responses to pop culture may also diverge widely according to race, gender, and age of the audience. Others may ignore programs we consider "must-see TV." Shows we have never watched may be essential viewing for communities beyond our purview. The Nielson ratings for television programs vary widely between Caucasian, African American, and Hispanic viewers. While Caucasian viewers may have made *NCIS* a top-ten show, African American viewers prefer *NCIS: Los Angeles* (perhaps because it stars LL Cool J). *Scandal* is the top-rated show among African Americans, but enough "other people" watch it to place it in the top-ten programs overall.[23] *Scandal* creator and executive producer Shonda Rhimes remains one of the few African Americans to run multiple networks programs (like *Grey's Anatomy* and its spinoff, *Private Practice*). She brings a distinctive voice to her programs and leans into the racial diversity reflected in her cast and characters. Millions of Hispanic viewers tune to Univision and their hit programs like *Que Vida Me Robo* and *Que Pobres Tan Ricos*. Univision caters to a demographic that is expanding (and perhaps youth ministry should follow suit with more Spanish-speaking staff and volunteers). Advertisers are increasingly interested in reaching targeted markets. The Nielson ratings subdivide audiences into particular age groups (ages 2–11, 12–34, 18–49, over 50). Nickelodeon programs like *SpongeBob SquarePants* or *iCarly* attracted the most kids ages two through eleven, while teens gravitated toward Fox programs like *Family Guy*, *The Simpsons*, and *Glee*.[24]

The Internet Movie Database separates their lists of the top-ranked films by genre and gender. Women's all-time favorite films may diverge from men's lists. A savvy youth ministry leader will tailor his or her events and talks to reflect the interests of the local group. Attention to subtle and sometimes significant differences in favorite songs, shows, or films should be factored in before choosing illustrations for talks or Bible studies. Pop culture offers an easy way for teens to express their passions as well as their likes and dislikes and provides a way for youth professionals to enter into dialogue around those significant stories. Pop culture that moves us (like *Raging Bull*!) might be offensive or even reprehensible to others. God may speak to us through a program that causes others to stumble. Such is the mystery of God and the elusive nature of general revelation.

The days of a singular youth culture united around a particular text or show are waning. The proliferation of television networks and channels has splintered adolescent interests across a wide variety of programming. Time-shifting devices like the DVR or an online streaming service like Netflix allow teens to binge watch or catch up on a program when it is convenient. Only live events like the Super Bowl or MTV's Video Music Awards may capture a large swath of teen attention in a singular moment. Massive series like *Harry Potter*, *Twilight*, and *The Hunger Games* may capture large segments of teens' imagination, but adolescents may reserve a greater passion for a story they feel as if they have discovered. My daughter's interest in Blaine's relationship with Kurt on *Glee* was rooted mostly in her love for actor Darren Criss's music career. She followed his theater troupe, StarKid Productions, and their satire, *A Very Potter Musical*. Thanks to social media, teens can rally around particular stars, bands, or shows in remarkably personalized ways. Adolescent culture is best understood as a series of smaller cultures. The fragmentation of our taste and resulting fan clubs and followings has become a form of culture making itself. The smartphone and social media have turned every adolescent into a potential broadcaster and marketer.[25]

While pop culture morphs into new media forms, a global perspective can make us aware of the biases inherent in American entertainment. The ideologies embedded in Hollywood's productions (young is better than old, rich is better than poor, sex is the ultimate expression of love) may appear strange to international audiences. Americans raised on a steady diet of gun-toting action films may not realize how abrasive and violent our "entertainment" may appear to foreign audiences. The villains we choose for our movies may castigate those who do not deserve to be stereotyped on the big screen. I can recall feeling embarrassed by our cultural exports playing on television screens in Mongolia. To see Jay Z singing "Big Pimpin'" on a massive yacht outside an American culture of affluence was downright disgusting. Muslim nations may be right to reject TV series that sexualize and objectify women (and men). Yet Americans may be scandalized by the sexuality and violence that permeates Japanese manga. Our values are reflected in what we create. We may not realize how much influence pop culture has exerted on our desire to be famous, to be noticed, or to be loved for something beyond our looks, our power, or our riches. Youth ministers need to develop discernment to see through the messages being sent across our screens. A countercultural youth ministry may need to elevate films or programs that question the status quo and promote kingdom values.

If the tendency in pop culture is to break down audiences according to race, culture, or age, perhaps youth ministry should focus on opportunities to bring people together across ages and interests. It is the rare film franchise like *The Fast and the Furious* that offers substantive roles to actors across the racial spectrum. It celebrates a diverse family onscreen, where people's unique gifts (for car theft!) create a stronger whole. A band of outsiders is adopted into a loving gang that covers one another's back. The healthy box office receipts for the *Fast* franchise suggest how much interest follows those who can aggregate audiences across race and culture. Perhaps youth ministries could be known by their ability to bring teens together from a variety of backgrounds and heritages. Consider how prophetic and powerful it would be if churches could bring together teens who separate themselves at school. Imagine drawing all of those separate tables in the cafeteria around one common table, united around the body and blood of Jesus celebrated in communion.

Perhaps one of the (not so) secrets of *Glee*'s success is the remarkable diversity in the cast and characters. Mr. Schuester makes room for every kind of adolescent in the New Directions.

Kids who have lost parents like Kurt join forces with teens raised by two dads like Rachel Berry or those born into mixed marriages like Tina Cohen-Chang. There is room on the football team for Artie Abrams in his wheelchair and a place on the cheerleading squad for Becky Jackson, despite her Down syndrome. Such radical inclusiveness can be considered as either a television fantasy or an aspirational challenge. *The Glee Project* was a reality TV contest that offered fans a chance to win a part on the show. Winners ranged from the cross-dressing Divine Adams to "a teenage Jesus," Samuel Larsen. Both were added to the choir, pushing the boundaries of what adolescence includes. We live and minister within such confounding and challenging times.

How does the Bible deal with such cultural collisions? In Acts 8, the Ethiopian eunuch wanted to join a Jewish tribe, but his background separated him from their worship practices. Philip crossed cultural lines in coming alongside this African. Even after Philip explained the good news about Jesus, the eunuch may still have wondered whether this wondrous love applied to him. When the eunuch spots some water he asks, "What can stand in the way of my being baptized?" This can be read as an exclamation and affirmation (nothing!) or as a hesitation and question. Did one have to become a Jew to be baptized? Was there a racial, cultural, gender, or sexual barrier to following Jesus? Having faced rejection in Jerusalem, the eunuch might have wondered, "What are the rules of your tribe, Philip? Is there room for someone like me?" Philip baptized the Ethiopian eunuch, extending the early Christian community beyond its Jewish roots. The first non-Jewish Christ follower was a sexually ambiguous black man. Philip fulfilled the kinds of promises that the prophet Isaiah had imagined. In Isaiah, the Lord promises to the eunuch who keeps his Sabbaths, "I will give them an everlasting name which shall not be cut off" (56:5 RSV). Talk about a divine sense of humor. Imagine the glee that occurred when the eunuch discovered the Lord offers assurance that "my house shall be called a house of prayer for all peoples" (56:7 RSV).

Part 2

The Call
of Adoptive
Youth Ministry

Reflective Youth Ministry

Youth Ministry as Critical, Ongoing, Communal Reflection

ALMEDA M. WRIGHT

Adoptive Youth Ministry *is committed to creating a theological base from which to engage and nurture the young into the life and practice of faith. Dr. Almeda Wright, from Yale Divinity School, provides an insightful, personal, and applicable description of what it means to help young people become critical theologians. Her understanding of youth ministry takes us far beyond traditional programming and practices and what has become for many an individualistic personal piety that promotes an "add quiet time, a small group, and a mission trip and stir" type of faith. Her approach provides us with a theological foundation for the practice of participating in adopting young people into the community of faith by helping them to become reflective participants in God's kingdom work, even as they are nurtured and welcomed by adults who model critical reflection.*

Wright's ultimate goal is to help youth workers ensure that our young people learn how to become critical thinkers and theologians. She breaks down critical reflection into three parts, each of which is an essential element to

growing mature faith: reflection on our tradition and practices of faith, reflection on our lives and calling, and reflection on the needs of the world. Thus youth ministry is centrally about calling forth and helping to develop a young person's perspective and voice in terms of how faith interacts not only with our "spiritual lives" but also with our daily practices and our understanding of and interaction with the world at large. She reminds us that when young people are encouraged and led to actively engage in critical reflection, it will inevitably spill over into the greater church community, possibly upsetting those committed to the status quo. When this happens, leaders must be ready to create a safe space and proactively receive these young people as they grow, reflect, and invest in God's mission in the church and the world. Wright makes clear what seasoned youth ministry people know and frequently talk to one another about: many if not most churches may say they want mature, growing disciples of Jesus Christ, but to give them voice and conscience is another matter altogether. As Wright states, "Critically reflective youth ministry is transformative youth ministry, or ministry that changes how we see and live in the world." This is vital as church communities are led to embrace and empower young people to participate in God's household, which is the essence of Adoptive Youth Ministry.

As you read this chapter, consider these questions:

1. *What does "critical reflection" look like in youth ministry? How could it result in people becoming upset? When is this good, even important? When is disruption a destructive force?*

2. *Wright talks about encouraging kids to question. What are a few ways that questioning can be done poorly or even destructively? How can it be done in a way that encourages and fosters relationship and community and even enhances the movement toward adoptive youth ministry?*

3. *Wright talks about youth ministry needing to encompass three aspects of our faith: tradition and practices, personal response, and what it means to engage the world in God's name. Which of these do you see as the most common or prominent way of thinking about youth ministry? Which is the weakest? What could be done in your context to integrate all three aspects of faith development in order to help kids become theologians?*

4. *Respond to this statement: "Missions and service projects are almost always* not *a critical engagement with what God intends for the world. Participating as an agent of the kingdom of God is what it means to live the Lord's Prayer ("thy kingdom come, thy will be done, on earth as it is in heaven").*

A Tale of Two Abnormal Communities

The Sacred Canopy of Church Communities

Every Sunday since before I can remember, my family has gone to church. Our first church was a small, rural congregation. It consisted primarily of my extended family and generations of people who had lived in that part of Virginia *forever*. I am and have always been the "overly churched" kid. My parents dragged me to church before I knew to kick or scream. I never thought to challenge this practice until it was too late, until church had become such an essential part of my social and spiritual life that I would not have had any friends without it. So I happily came to church to see my friends and get "loved on" by all the "aunties" and "uncles" gathered there each Sunday.

My earliest memories of my family are connected with church—with a community of people who came together weekly to reaffirm their faith and its power to shape their daily lives. In this community, the foundations of my faith were established and nurtured. I learned about a God who loves us, cares for us, and would go to some pretty strange lengths for us. I have innumerable memories of learning Scripture and hymns, reciting Easter poems, and attending classes and conferences. In this small church, we did not always have a large number of youth, so I spent a great deal of time in adult Sunday school, Bible study, and church meetings. I observed adults in the serious work of church and as they often struggled to articulate what Scripture and faith meant to them.

Though it surprises me a little now, this community also taught me that faith and questions are more than compatible; they actually enhance each other. Even as this community formed me to take as a matter of fact that God is great, that we were religious, and that we would consistently fellowship, it also granted me the space to question. One of the unique gifts of this community and my family is that we talked a lot. We asked questions. We studied. We reflected critically and remained committed to the community and the life of faith through many transitions in leadership and conflicts among members. My parents modeled for me the art of asking tough questions in Bible study, sometimes playing devil's advocate and sometimes vulnerably sharing the deep inner musings of their hearts. As I watched them teach and participate in this community, I learned the nuanced and complex nature of community. I learned that community is essential for faith development; it is the ecosystem within which people, young and old, can try on, question, and live into religious practices and ideas.

However, I have to pause often and remember that my experiences in a small, family-based church in the rural South are *not* normal. Today, most young people do not grow up in a community that is so small that church is *the* event of the week.[1] This type of connection and community—while it is no longer (or maybe never was) normal—has tremendous value. In some ways it reflects the legacy of Horace Bushnell, who advocated "*christian nurture*" as the primary model of religious education and formation in the mid-1800s. It also reflects many of the world-constructing and world-maintaining characteristics of the "sacred canopy," described by sociologist Peter Berger. Berger argues that religion plays a crucial role in creating a *nomos*, or normative worldview, which offers humanity a way to make sense of the world around us. According to Berger, humans create and maintain this sacred canopy under which we live in such a way that we are unaware of its constructed nature. In many ways, my family and church community not only created a sacred canopy that helped shield me against terror and not knowing but also created an environment in which I was shaped in faith (from birth through college) as I learned the norms of the community.[2]

In other ways, this community offers youth a paradigm for faith that expands far beyond orthodoxy (believing the right thing) or orthopraxy (doing the right thing) to include critical, communal reflection on faith. It offers a paradigm of youth ministry and faith development that esteems community and connection as a goal of faith development and holds communal formation in tension with critical reflection on the faith. In other words, from my experience what sustained my faith was not simply good people (because all church folks were not), harmony (as an overly churched child, I endured way too many raucous church meetings and conversations), or even common beliefs. Instead, I was sustained by the enduring power of that community, which demonstrated that regardless of who showed up or what arguments we got into we would come, pray together, and trust God to make a way out of no way.

To be very clear, I cannot foresee a time or a place when we will be able to force young people back into the model of my religious upbringing. I do not romanticize this community or attempt to map it onto our present realities. However, I am left to ponder what we can learn about young people and their growth in faith from this small, rural community and the ideals it instilled in me.

A Community of Questioning

As I fast forward a few decades, my faith and ministry journey encountered a different but equally transformative community. During my doctoral studies, I was privileged to work with the Youth Theological Initiative (YTI) at Emory University.[3] YTI stands in direct contrast to my rural church in that it exists for only a few weeks each summer, after which the youth and leaders return to other communities, but during these few weeks a type of metamorphosis occurs in the lives of most participants.[4]

YTI is a place where the religious lives and questions of young people are taken seriously and nurtured. The motto of YTI is "exploring questions that shape us." Youth participate in classes, covenant groups, and service projects, and the goal is always the same: to create the space for them to explore their faith and ask tough questions. Many questions emerge as youth engage the course readings and their classmates. Some youth raise the expected questions about the existence of God, how God could allow pain and suffering in the world, or whether they were *really* Christian, as they come to see that they are not exactly like the other Christians in this ecumenical group. Others push deeper and challenge the hypocrisy, sexism, racism, and imperialism that many of them are recognizing within parts of the history of Christianity, while even more youth engage in (sometimes heated) debates about interpretations of Scripture and meanings of particular doctrines of faith. To be honest, even after attending seminary I was not always prepared for the questions raised by young people in this community.

However, the questions and social justice issues are not the only dimensions of the YTI community. At the center of the YTI curriculum is worship. Worship is the unifying and centering ritual that helps the young people and staff remain focused on the larger goals and reasoning behind the daily struggles and challenges. The entire community attends nightly worship services, which means that the community always ends the day together, united around a common purpose and ritual. During my time there I noticed that the nightly worship experience empowered the youth to keep moving, to stay connected to the larger community when they were being challenged by new ideas (contrary to their personal experience or family's teaching about God and/ or the world), and to move beyond feelings of anxiety or animosity to a place of shared practice, shared prayer, shared faith, and shared commitment to God. Worship helped the youth to cope with the immediate community; what's more, the youth experienced models of Christian theological reflection and practices of social justice. They experienced the power of worship to transform individuals into a community and to give them the support to do the work that they were each called to do.

In the same way that I paused to reflect on the "abnormality" of my rural church family, I must also note that YTI is not normal. It happens over the course of two to four weeks. It is an experience, not a sustained community in a traditional sense. And while I was amazed at the power of worship in this community and its ability to help youth explore questions that shape us, one of the potential pitfalls of programs like YTI is that it could leave an entire group of young people without the ongoing supports needed to remain faithful as they continue to ask big questions. In some cases youth leave with their religious foundations completely shaken only to go home as if nothing has changed about them.[5] To be fair, there are myriad experiences like this for adolescents—including mission trips, a journey away from home, an encounter with a friend of a different culture, or a world history project about different religious traditions. The disruptive nature of these experiences points to the fact that as adolescents grow and expand their worlds they have to learn to incorporate new experiences and knowledge into their current experiences. Questions and reflection are the hallmarks of adolescent maturation. And as such they should become part and parcel of congregation-based youth ministries.

But what would it look like for questions and reflection to be the norm of youth ministry? What would happen if congregations modeled critical reflection rather than resisted it? Can communities shape youth in a shared praxis of faith and support youth in their questions of faith?[6]

Critically Reflective Youth Ministry

Within recent decades, writings about youth ministry have more fully situated its identity as a theological enterprise. Varied examples across the theological spectrum invite youth and youth workers to embrace their roles as theologians and to offer practical theological reflection on their ministries with youth.[7] This turn initially excited me and has more recently disheartened me. For example, I celebrated the reminder that youth and youth workers are theologians. I encouraged youth to define for themselves and embrace the title of theologian. I argued along with many, including authors Howard Stone and James Duke (*How to Think Theologically*) that to "be a Christian is to be a theologian."[8] And while that adage makes for a great T-shirt or bumper sticker, I didn't

slow down to invite people into a fuller process of what that really means.

Beyond the limited practical instructions of living into this idea of theological youth ministry, I began to notice that in some ways we have now "routinized" theological reflection. As a side of effect of this routinization, theological reflection on youth ministry and with youth is no longer the thing that enlivens young people or calls our ministries to a higher level. This is not simply a critique that theological reflection has become blasé; it is that we have failed to fully realize the implications of making ongoing theological reflection and reflection in general part of the habitus of our congregational life together with youth.

In other words, we have attempted to domesticate theological reflection. We have attempted to ignore the prophetic and often disruptive nature of theological reflections and proclamations. For example, I recently encountered a youth ministry curriculum that purported to lead youth in theological reflection on a host of youth issues. As I gazed at the shiny cover and glossy pages, I was amazed (in a bad way). The editors offer *their* theological reflection on certain issues, but only a very limited number of ways are offered for youth to engage in the process. And there is a predetermined outcome (or foregone conclusion) that youth are supposed to reach. To be certain, the best any one person can do is to offer his or her individual theological assessment of a situation. But is that all that we can hope for as a community of faith? Can we live into what it means to critically reflect within communities, even if this leads to different answers? For a season I wholeheartedly embraced the naive idea that if we all just go through the same process of theological reflection and rational thought, we will all reach the same conclusions. Like so many, I presumed that right process led to right beliefs (or at least same beliefs), only to encounter time and again that this was not the case and that I was often not prepared for the conclusions that were reached.

Instead of a process of leading youth to the *right answers*, theological reflection primarily means having an ongoing dialogue. It is wrestling with tough questions: Where is God? What is God doing? What is God calling us to do? How is God calling us to act in response to this particular situation? Asking these questions is not a one-time exercise. Youth (and adults) must continuously ask these questions and struggle with the answers that emerge. In some cases, we struggle because we feel that no answers emerge. At other times, too many answers emerge. We have to learn the art of communal discernment, seeking wise counsel, and other practices, which have evolved through the life of faith across the history of Christianity.

In sum, my disenchantment with the "theological turn" in youth ministry is that in some ways we have attempted to short circuit the process and reinscribe fixed answers. Knowing fully who God is and what God is calling us to do in every situation would be lovely, but this is not the case and has never been the case in the history of Christianity. Even biblical, transcendent truths have to be interpreted and applied to our lives and various communities. Being able to offer youth fixed answers to all of life's questions would also be wonderful, but that isn't possible either. Therefore, we have to empower young people to wrestle and respond to the questions of their lives and communities. We have to remain open to the onslaught of questions and conclusions that will emerge as we invite them into critically reflective youth ministry, into a community and ministry that values ongoing critical reflection.

Some Definitions

Critically reflective youth ministry points to the essential role of questions and reflection for the life of faith in community. Critically reflective youth ministry, as I am defining it, has two foci interrelated with three tasks. The foci convey the dual meaning of *reflective*. *Reflective* describes the ability or capacity to provide a reflection (as in a reflective glass), and it describes someone or a thing that is characterized by deep thought (as in a reflective young person). Therefore *reflective* youth ministry focuses on nurturing young people to reflect the image and life of Jesus Christ and to think deeply, or reflect on, what it means to be a follower of Christ today. This model of ministry reminds us of the importance of helping youth to develop lives that reflect the *imago Dei* within them and the ministry of Jesus. It pushes youth toward a thoughtful, intentional way of being in the world. For the most part, we want to emphasize only one of these foci, but truly reflective youth ministry reminds us that young people must grow both in terms of how they follow Christ and in how they love God with their hearts, souls, bodies, and minds (and fully incorporate their God-given skills of thought and reflection into their life of faith).

The threefold task helps us to flesh out our critical reflection on the life of Christ. For many of us theological reflection (and religious practice) ends at the personal level. We often see young people who pray about tests, college, boyfriends, and family. But critical theological reflection is not and cannot be limited to our personal and individual lives. Instead, critically reflective youth ministry includes three areas:

1. Critical reflection on our religious traditions (including practices and beliefs)
2. Critical reflection on our individual lives in Christ
3. Critical reflection on the world around us

Ministry with youth, like all Christian ministries, involves walking with young people as they live and grow in the life of faith. It involves pushing youth to think fully about what God is calling them to do and be as part of the body of Christ in the world.

Ongoing Tasks of Critically Reflective Youth Ministry

Task 1: Critical Reflection on the Tradition, Content, and Practices of Faith

The first task of ongoing critical reflection is often the hardest to sell, which is not surprising. By nature a tradition or core belief has been around for a long time, or it holds a special place in the life of a community of believers. Our religious traditions are deeply connected to our understanding of the truth of Christianity and not merely with the ways of humanity. However, the traditions, practices, and content of faith cannot be above questioning or critical reflection. Even as we rest on God's revelation as essential for our being, what we say about God and how we worship God still must be the subject of critical reflection with young people. In every generation, young people emerge who have not been part of the Christian community, and just as we must invite them into the stories of faith, we must also invite them to make the faith their own by fully engaging it. In particular, as

reflections of Christ youth must question the traditions that have been handed down and seek to fulfill them like Christ.

If we reflect on the kinds of faith formation that are offered in the Bible and through the life of Jesus, we see Jesus crossing boundaries, questioning the establishment, and hanging out with more sinners than saints. In some ways we see Jesus as *the one who questions everything*. If we truly want youth to follow in his footsteps, we must create the space for them to question and critically reflect—on the religious tradition as well.

As a tween, Jesus inaugurates his ministry of questions at the age of twelve. He sits in the temple among the teachers inquiring. He not only questions but also begins to amaze those who encounter his preteen zeal for knowledge: "Everyone who heard him was amazed at his understanding and his answers" (Luke 2:47). In true adolescent fashion, Jesus gets caught up in what he is doing, loses track of time, and fails to tell his parents where he is going to be. When he is chastised for getting left behind, he sasses his mother, saying, "Didn't you know I had to be in my Father's house?" (Luke 2:49). From this starting point, we see numerous examples of Jesus's direct challenges to the religious practices of his day.

Jesus questions the traditions of not healing on the Sabbath (Mark 3:1–6). Jesus questions social structures by lifting up little children as models for the kingdom of God (Mark 10:14–15) and teaching that "many who are first will be last" (Mark 10:31). He challenges the corruption in the Jerusalem temple when he reminds the people that God's house is supposed to be a house of prayer but that they have made it into a den of thieves (Matt. 21:12–13). He questions the generational relationships between Samaritans and Jews, and he esteems the Samaritan as a model of care for one's neighbor (Luke 10:25–37). He also questions some of the traditions concerning how men and women interact by engaging with the Samaritan woman at the well (John 4). In general, he questions the sociopolitical and religious norms by embodying a compassionate vision of the kingdom of God, which has very little in common with contemporary political structures.

This idea of Jesus having a ministry of "questioning everything" is not simply an intriguing interpretive lens for reading about the life of Jesus. For me it is also a reminder of an essential element of effective youth and young adult spirituality: each generation is involved in a journey of making faith its own.

Young people look at the traditions that have been passed down to them. They strive to see whether or how the tradition works and how it can shape their lives. In my observation, the traditions that hold are not primarily the ones young people take on without question. Instead, the enduring traditions are those that youth are allowed to wrestle with, to try on, and to eventually become shaped by. I often remind students preparing for youth ministry that the last thing they want is a group of young people who take everything they say about God and life without challenge. When youth fail to question, they most often fail to engage and make the tradition their own.[9]

While we are not asking or hoping that youth will come into the church on Sunday morning and turn over the offering table, what would it look like for us to listen with youth as they imagine how the church can become more faithful to its ministry? I am always amazed at the ways that youth, in an often innocent and carefree manner, push us to think differently and be more faithful to the traditions we have "taught" them.

For example, from time to time I get impassioned calls from my nephew. It is typically after Bible study or Sunday worship. He jumps straight in with an obscure question about a biblical text because he is certain that what they have been discussing is open to multiple interpretations (that is his nice way of saying that he thinks the teacher is wrong). So we walk through the particular biblical passage or topic of the day; I send him links to commentaries and websites where he can study more on his own, and eventually I give him my interpretation of the passage. At first my nephew resisted and wanted me just to affirm or deny that the teacher was right or wrong. But in the process, he learned that "aunty wasn't going to do that" and that he needed to learn to study and reflect on the content of his faith so that when his heart said something was not right he could check it with his mind.

I share my nephew's zeal and cell phone Bible sidebars as one example of the ways that young people can and do wrestle with the core of our Christian tradition and critically reflect on the content of their faith. But his story is not unique. I have myriad stories, typically from the youth who have been in church for a long time, who have been shaped in the life and narratives of the community but who perceive that there is more than the superficial answers they are getting in Sunday school. I remember vividly the challenge of a youth who read the book of Job for the first time in senior high Bible study and told me adamantly, "This can't be right—God doesn't tempt people. How could we have the devil chatting with God and God letting the devil mess with Job?" In those moments, we can either offer young people platitudes—signaling that youth group or church is not the place to ask these questions—or we can encourage them in their questions. We can encourage their zeal to know more and to wrestle with texts that many adults and scholars have wrestled with and to see how it does or does not fit into what we understand about the larger story of faith and life in Christ.

Task 2: Critical Reflection on Our Lives and Our Callings

Critical reflection as a model of youth ministry also reminds us of the inward work that we must invite young people into. Often we discuss growing in faith and discerning a future path with youth as one of vocation, or calling. Vocation centers on the existential questions of the lives of youth as they struggle to confidently answer the questions concerning who they are and what they are called to do. In particular, these questions entail answering what God is calling youth to do within the purpose and kingdom of God. James Fowler writes that our vocation is to be in reflective partnership with God.[10] As communities of faith, how do we invite youth into this partnership, and what specifically is the task of critically reflecting on their lives and calling?

Quaker educator Parker Palmer invites us to journey with youth as they listen to their lives. In *Let Your Life Speak*, he recounts numerous stories from his own life in which he struggled to figure out what to do with his life and what his purpose in life was supposed to be. At first he attempted to emulate the lives of great leaders like Gandhi, Martin Luther King Jr., or Mother Teresa, but he then discovered that his calling was not to *live their lives*. His calling did not emerge from the lives of others

but from listening and reflecting on what God placed inside him.[11]

Often I encounter students who are trying to figure out who they want to be or what they want to do with their lives. Pressure comes from every side. Youth experience pressures to be successful, to make good grades and go to a good college, to be a leader, to be a good friend, to be popular, athletic, obedient, professional, rich, famous, cool, and so much more. But the one thing Palmer tries to help us understand is that we need to practice "letting our lives speak" in order for us to be able to make sense of all the pressures and competing messages around us. We have to practice listening *with* youth to their inner passions and to see the things that God has placed inside them. Instead of trying to change youth or their natural abilities so that they can be like someone else, we should ask God to show them how to use what God has given them for God's glory.

Often, when we invite youth into processes of critical self-reflection, we are inviting them to better themselves or "clean up their act." While we all need moments of introspection so that we can correct the course of individual behaviors and sins, far more often we need to model for youth the process of seeing their genuine worth and abilities as they reflect the image of God in and around them. Too often youth display a caricature or mask of who they really are. This is because, in part, they are still struggling on their vocational journeys to see themselves as wonderful creations of God.

They are struggling to demonstrate their maturity in faith and to demonstrate their full humanity. Paulo Freire argues that the one vocation of all persons is *humanization*—that is, the process of becoming fully human.[12] In the revolutionary contexts in which Freire worked, the idea that all could be seen as full humans, as men and women—not as mere pawns or workers who have no control over their lives or the direction of their futures—was a truly radical idea. But a calling to become fully human may strike Christian ears as somewhat problematic, especially if we have been shaped in a community that holds a strict dichotomy between humanity, flesh, or carnal natures and the spiritual or sacred sides of our nature. For some Christians, becoming fully human is the last thing we want to do; we'd rather become fully divine. However, the paradox of the Christian faith is that we are offered a savior who is fully human and fully divine—who is God and the Son of God at the same time. This paradox reminds us that we are not inviting youth to a place where they can forget their humanity but rather where they can embrace the unique ways that their bodies are created—even the varied pigments or imperfections that they will invariably obsess over. We are inviting them to a place of living into the fullness that God has created them to be.

Task 3: Critical Reflection on the Needs of the World

Effective youth ministry also compels us to look beyond our individual lives and to reflect critically on the world around us. The world-as-it-is is not the world-as-it-should-be. As people of faith, this simple truth serves as a constant reminder of the work that we are called to do with youth and with ourselves. For many generations we have focused youth ministry inwardly on the development of personal relationships with Jesus and on commitments to congregational or denominational life. While these are important, I cannot help but think through the life and ministry of Jesus

and wonder at the power of his life in changing the communities around him. To be certain, he did not run for political office or become an earthly messiah, but his ministry included and addressed the world around him. What does it mean to live a life of faith as the communities around us remain unchanged?

The possibility of transforming the world is designed to be daunting. It is in the best interest of oppressive powers and structures for young people to buy into the idea that "there is nothing that they can do" or that all they can hope for is survival in a world over which they have no control. However, many critical theorists and radical educators have worked for centuries to remind students that the world and humans are interconnected. Looking again at the work of Freire: "Education as the practice of freedom—as opposed to education as the practice of domination—denies that man [woman] is abstract, isolated, independent, and unattached to the world; it also denies that the world exists as a reality apart from people."[13] The significance of this interconnection is that it reminds us that the world can be changed and influenced by the collective work of individuals. Freire (who is best known for his criticism of the banking model of education in which students are simply the depositories of expert knowledge and narratives) underscores the ways that critical reflection transforms the world. Freire pushes for "problem-posing education" that builds on the questions and critical reflections of persons in community as the basis for education. This method of education and ministry resists any notion that the world, systems, and society are unchangeable realities.[14]

Allen Moore, in his work *Religious Education as Social Transformation*, expounds on the interconnections between religious education and transformation within society and societal structures. Moore's vision is that religious education is an ethical way of life that serves to transform religious platitudes into concrete social structures that are just and serve the welfare of all people.[15] In other words, the transformative elements of ministry with youth require inviting youth into the practices of critical reflection—imagining or dreaming of an alternative reality and acting to achieve these alternative visions. Freire outlines the practice of critical consciousness in conjunction with his idea of dialogical education. The process of coming to critical consciousness about the world and being in the position to truly transform the world requires both reflection and action, or what Freire defines as *praxis*.[16]

Directly connected with the work of transforming the ways that young people see themselves and their vocations is the need to engage youth in the process of conscientization, that is, coming to critical consciousness. Coming to critical consciousness is not simply raising awareness about issues in the lives of young people. Critical consciousness includes transforming how youth perceive the world around them and awakening within youth the ability to critically reflect on and take action in their worlds.[17]

Religious educator Katherine Turpin expands on Freire's understanding of conscientization and proposes the idea of ongoing conversion, which emphasizes the idea that within each youth there remains a paradox between what one is aware of and how one chooses to act in the world. Ongoing conversion emphasizes that critical reflection, transformation of the world, and how youth act in the world are not a "one time thing"; neither does conversion emerge from simply seeing things

differently. Turpin argues that conversion requires a "deeper change" and explains that "conversion, then refers not just to a change in awareness and understanding, but to a change in both our intuitive sense of the way the world is (imagination) and our capacity to act in light of that intuitive sense (agency)."[18]

Building on Freire's understanding of conscientization and Turpin's understanding of ongoing conversion, I argue that critically reflective youth ministry must include an ongoing process of critical reflection and action in the world.[19] In other words, critically reflective youth ministry entails both thinking critically about the conditions of the world and taking action to reflect the light of Christ in the world.

Conclusion: Making Space for Disruption

Critically reflective youth ministry is transformative youth ministry—ministry that changes how we see and live in the world. If we are serious about creating the space for youth to critically reflect as well as reflect on the life of Christ and if we are not simply interested in forming youth in our preconceived understandings of the life of faith, then we must always remain open to the ways that youth will stretch us and in many ways speak disruptive, prophetic words into the world around them (particularly into our communities of faith). As we journey with youth and encourage them to constantly listen for and expect God's new and ongoing revelation, we will recognize that revelation is often revealed in the cries and deep passions of the people—often the passions of young people. Evelyn Parker discusses the ways that African American youth experience rage and anger. These emotions do not fit well within the religious or cultural norms; however, in many cases this rage is an indication of the passions and outrage of black youth and their responses to perceived and real injustices. Parker argues that youth should not be forced to simply tone down their anger; rather, we should foster listening and encourage youth as they experience these moments of truth within systems of injustice and oppression.[20] Parker outlines a framework of *holy indignation*, which she defines as a "form of constructive rage. It is the freedom to express anger against injustice in the sacred space of the Christian church."[21] Parker's framework opens the sacred space of religious institutions to include the prophetic and sometimes enraged reflections of youth.

As I continue to ponder the lessons from the abnormal communities presented at the beginning of this chapter, I come to understand that the journey of faith and maturity is hard work. It is work that can easily overwhelm us and make us uncomfortable. It is work that disrupts us because we cannot script it or plan it out completely. Yet these communities also remind us that we are joint heirs with Jesus and part of the family of God. They remind us that our response to the ongoing work of God in the world is also to listen and discern how God is speaking and where God is pushing us to work. When what we see overwhelms us we can come together to pray, worship, and hold the disruptions under the sacred canopy of God's love.

I invite you to begin an inventory to gauge what type of community of faith your congregation and family represents:[22]

- Are you modeling ongoing growth and maturation/journeying in faith?
- Do your actions, images, prayers, and liturgies reflect a place that values critical reflection and aligns people's lives with the image of Christ?
- Are the questions of youth valued, and can youth learn to critically reflect on their tradition, vocations, and world?
- Can we hold the disruptions that emerge as they share their emotions, passions, or God's revelations?

Thinking (Practical) Theology

MICHAEL McENTYRE

We as editors are committed to continuing the conversation concerning the best thinking and practices that youth ministry brings us. Beginning with the book When Kumbaya Is Not Enough: A Practical Theology for Youth Ministry, *by Dean Borgman in 1995, the field of practical theology has been the primary theological launching pad for theologically oriented youth ministry.*

For those who are steeped in practical theology literature, there are many different ways to describe the process, and the field is far from clear in terms of what and how practical theology actually operates. While this conversation is obviously beyond the scope of this book, we do need to make this point: what sets practical theology apart from other theological perspectives is its emphasis on the starting point of theological inquiry. Practical theology starts with the context, or the current practices, of what it is we are seeking to understand. In general terms, practical theology's four basic questions and tasks (as summarized by Princeton's Richard Osmer) are:

- *What is going on?*
- *Why is this going on?*
- *What ought to be going on?*
- *How might we respond?*

Our intent in Adoptive Youth Ministry *is not to wholesale replace that grounding perspective but to learn and grow from the way practical theology has defined the practice of youth ministry. This chapter, by Michael McEntyre, is the way we have chosen to make that connection between practical theology and participation in God's adoptive work in the church. As we work to consider youth ministry as the church's participation in drawing those who are not included in the dominant community of faith into the family of God—which obviously includes adolescents and emerging adults—we can and should continue to rely on the insights of practical theologians who specialize in youth ministry. This chapter and the webpage dedicated to practical theology as an aspect of adoptive youth ministry are intended to help you understand how the work of youth ministry has been theologically conceived over the past several years.*

As you read this chapter, consider these questions:

1. *This chapter uses Urie Bronfenbrenner's* Ecology of Human Development *to describe growing up (a model some find difficult to understand on first glance). In this chapter, how does McEntyre explain and make use of this "ecological model" to explain practical theology in youth ministry?*

2. *What is the definition of practical theology? In reading this chapter, why is practical theology important? How does it help us to be theologically grounded, and how is it reflected in how we "do" or "practice" youth ministry?*

3. *Practical theology is basically a process by which we reflect as a community on what we need to do in order to think critically about how God would like us to better align ourselves with our Lord's purposes in creation. List five or more areas of ministry that might need to be examined critically and reflectively in order for a community of faith to move in the direction of adoptive youth ministry.*

When I was in seminary, I went to see a professor with a question about a grade he had given me. As I sat down across the desk from him, he leaned back and asked, "What's your story?" Not quite sure what he meant, I began to ask my questions about the assignment he had given. He interrupted me and said, "That's not your story; that's your problem. Before we get to your problem, I want to know about your story. Tell me about you." The conversation

that followed was simple, yet its impact on our relationship and my approach to ministry would prove to be profound.[1]

Much of my time in seminary was spent learning about God's story. My Old Testament classes focused on how God's story has been revealed to us throughout history. My New Testament classes examined how the fullness of God's story was reflected in the work of Christ. My Greek and Hebrew classes helped me to appreciate the original languages first used to share God's story found in Scripture. My theology classes explored how humanity has sought to understand and interpret God's story over the ages. My preaching classes honed my skills on how to best communicate God's story to a congregation. All of these classes came together to proclaim the beautiful and complex symphony of God's story.

As I entered my first ministry position, I was excited to share what I was learning with the students in my youth ministry. As each new revelation about God's story was introduced to me, I would eagerly form it into my next Sunday school lesson to "enlighten" my middle school and high school students. I would love to say that my messages were received with as much enthusiasm as they were taught, but I think you can imagine what happened. My well-crafted monologue with three points and a clever illustration didn't make it past the second paragraph before the interruptions began. Amazingly, the students did not seem to care what it meant that a particular passage was written in the middle voice in Greek. And my quotes from Barth and Augustine might as well have been pulled from a fortune cookie. You see, in my eagerness to share God's story, I didn't take the time to listen to the stories of the students who were right in front of me. That's when I remembered my professor's comment to me: "Before we get to your problem, I want to know your story." Looking back, this was the moment when I began to realize the power and value of practical theology.

This chapter will explore why it is important for youth workers and leaders to develop an accessible framework of practical theology for ministry. The content will explain how practical theology has come to be defined and how it has emerged as a discipline. The goal will be to identify and explain the characteristics that are generally seen as unique to the discipline of practical theology in order to create a framework to engage the use of

practical theology for guiding our ministry. In conclusion, I will share why I believe incorporating practical theology into ministry is not just good practice but also essential to the work of adoptive youth ministry.

The world is, to paraphrase a famous novel by Charles Dickens, a tale of two stories. We have God's story of the world and humanity's story of the world. In response to God's story, prominent Canadian theologian Douglas John Hall writes, "Humanity is telling its own story, improvising scenarios, creating roles for itself—for all the other creatures, too, and of course for God!"[2] Taking the time to

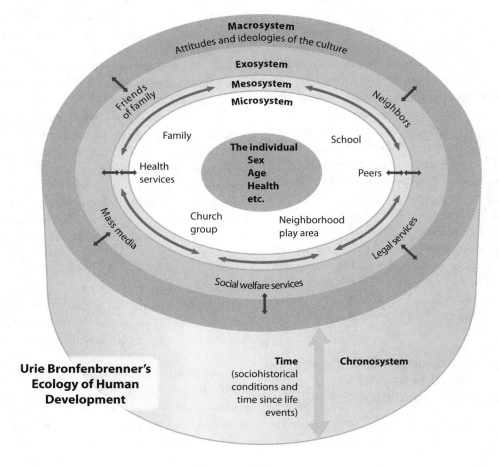

understand these stories is important. A person's story is about more than information. Our story is our life, the narrative of who we are. Stories hold power, enable perspective, foster respect, build relationship, and create space for community. Our personal stories shape and are shaped by the stories around us and combine to create the stories of our neighborhoods, our schools, our churches, our culture, and so on. All of these stories play a part in what Hall refers to as humanity's story.

Psychologist Urie Bronfenbrenner describes in depth how these stories influence one another in his book *The Ecology of Human Development*. Bronfenbrenner suggests that our development, our stories if you will, have a ripple effect through the various systems of context in which we live. This ripple does not simply travel outward but flows back and forth, allowing layers to mutually affect one another. Observing and interpreting how these layers affect one another is crucial to understanding our context. Our context is the setting of our story. It includes the "unique place, people, history, and story" that surround us.[3] Everything we do is done in context. We are caught up in its current, and without careful and deliberate investigation we are blissfully unaware of the ebb and flow it creates in our lives. As those who minister to students, our task needs to be to seek to understand how both God's story and humanity's story are at work in our ministry. This is where a framework of practical theology is essential.

Why Is It Important to Have a Good Framework for Practical Theology?

When I first was introduced to practical theology as a concept, my immediate thought was, "I am already doing that." Student ministry is known for its ability to connect with students where they are and seeks to understand the world of adolescence. Being up to date with student culture, or the context and stories of students, is something on which most student ministers pride themselves. In the same way, I believed that I was pretty good at thinking theologically when it came to preparing my lessons and trying to help students grow in their faith. I worked hard to make God's story applicable to the lives of my students in a way they could connect to. Yet as I began to learn about how to use practical theology in my ministry, I realized that being familiar with parts of the process is not the same as knowing how the process works. As I began to use practical theology to shape my ministry, I also realized that my end goals were being shaped more by unspoken expectations and traditions than by the kingdom of God.

After my first ten or so years of working in student ministry in three different church settings, I came to a realization: being a church youth minister was fairly easy. Before you write me off, hear me out. Helping students to understand the love of our Creator and the need for the community of faith (that is the church) to join with God in the ongoing work of the kingdom in this world is not easy. Sharing your life and faith in an incarnational presence with others is not easy. Working to see the bride of Christ fall deeper in love with God and care for those God cares for is not easy. But keeping my job, as it turns out, was a relatively simple affair.

Through numerous life/ministry lessons, I learned that there were really only a few unwritten expectations I needed to follow if I wanted to keep my youth parents, my church members, and my senior leadership happy (so that I could keep my job). For my senior leadership, the students needed to be seen (not necessarily heard) in the worship services, preferably sitting together in a nice big group. For our church members, it was important to know that there were lots of activities and discipleship opportunities going on for our students constantly. And for my youth parents, they needed to know I was working hard to keep their kids from making bad choices that could "ruin" the rest of their lives. While this is all very cynical and simplistic, at times it felt like as long as I followed these secret guidelines, everything else was good to go.[4]

It is easy to let cynicism creep into our ministry efforts. As ministers, when we become cynical about the church we tend to take on a hero complex, acting as if we have to do it all ourselves. Since student ministers often feel like they have little voice in the direction of the larger church, our efforts turn to making our ministries the bastions of all that is good and holy in the church. In essence, we stop focusing on the kingdom of God as our end goal and focus on what we are doing instead. This may sound like a harsh generalization, but if I'm honest it is more of a confession. Without good mentors, the care and wisdom of countless "senior adults," youth and youth parents who were not afraid to examine our ministry practices and partner with me to make a difference, the encouragement of family, and an awakening to the destructive changes occurring in adolescence, my approach to ministry would be very different today.

I say all of that to show why having a good framework of practical theology is important to us as student ministers. Ministry of any sort is messy. People will offend you; your schedule will push you. Interruptions will come at the worst possible time. It can be overwhelming,

and even our best intentions can fall by the wayside. Over time, the comfort of routine can replace the work of ministry. Engaging the process of practical theology pushes us to move past our cynicism and routine. By forcing ourselves to "begin with the end in mind,"[5] as Stephen Covey says, we must hold everything we do up to the inbreaking work of the kingdom. With this as our goal, we come to see humanity's story and God's story in a different light. Understanding the stories in this way helps us to see people, not problems. Our focus moves from assimilation into our student ministry or our congregation to acceptance into the family of God. For this reason, I think having a good framework of practical theology is essential to our goal of adoptive ministry for us and for our leaders.

What Is Practical Theology?

Prior to the 1960s practical theology was simply seen as "the fourth move in the four-fold encyclopedia behind biblical studies, church history, and dogmatics; the first three did the science, practical theology applied it."[6] In the past five decades, practical theologians have successfully argued that practical theology is more than simple application. Richard Osmer summarizes the reasoning for this change well.

> Practical theology as an academic field has its own distinctive research program. It makes its own constructive contribution to the theological enterprise as a whole and to the ongoing conversation of humankind in its quest for intelligibility. It carries out four mutually related intellectual operations: the descriptive-empirical, interpretive, normative, and pragmatic. This distinguishes practical

theology from the social sciences, even as it overlaps these fields in certain ways.[7]

Don Browning is often credited with making the shift from pastoral (applied) theology to practical theology. "Browning proposed a new conception of practical theology based on an interdisciplinary correlation occurring between theology and the human sciences. He corrected the concept of practical theology as applied theology (theory-to-practice), and proposed a *praxis-theory-praxis* model using a comprehensive model of practical moral reasoning."[8] James Fowler also picked up on this shift, describing practical theology as "theological reflection and construction arising out of and giving guidance to a community of faith in the praxis of its mission. Practical theology is a critical and constructive reflection on the praxis of the Christian community's life and work in its various dimensions."[9] Ray Anderson later defined practical theology as "critical and constructive reflection on ecclesial praxis . . . the process of ongoing critical reflection on the acts of the church in the light of the gospel and in critical dialogue with secular sources of knowledge with a view to the faithful transformation of the praxis of the church in the world."[10] Osmer would use his four intellectual operations (the descriptive-empirical, interpretive, normative, and pragmatic) to craft a definition and process of practical theology that would set the standard for discussion in this discipline.

> Practical theology is that branch of Christian theology that seeks to construct action-guiding theories of Christian praxis in particular social contexts. In part, it focuses on "how to"—how to teach, preach, raise children, influence society, and so forth. But this "how to" is informed by a strongly developed theory of "why to"—why we ought to practice the Christian way of life in certain ways in light of an interpretation of a particular social context and the normative claims of the Christian community.[11]

While all of these definitions shape the way we intellectually approach the work of practical theology, it is important to remember God's role in the process. Mark Lau Branson recognizes that practical theology is "an ongoing transformational initiative of the Holy Spirit with a church."[12] As such, the Holy Spirit should be the guiding impetus throughout this process. When the Holy Spirit illumines God's work in our midst, it raises questions about our current practices, revealing the opportunity for the work of the kingdom to break through. The work of practical theology gives Christians the tools to faithfully respond to the prompting of the Spirit in order to best join in what God is doing.

What Has Shaped the Process of Practical Theology?

Since the rebirth of practical theology in the 1960s, there have been many ideas, theories, methods, and approaches as to how practical theology should be done. While there are still a wide variety of opinions on how to arrive at faithful action, there does seem to be some consensus on what elements must be included in the process. Andy Root writes that "even in the midst of this diversity, practical theologians seem to be unified regarding a set of common tasks. Richard Osmer has done the most work in providing an account of these larger shared tasks."[13]

Osmer uses four questions to guide his interpretation:

- What is going on?
- Why is this going on?
- What ought to be going on?
- How might we respond?

Answering each of these questions is the focus of one of the four core tasks of practical theological interpretation:

- *The descriptive-empirical task*. Gathering information that helps us to discern patterns and dynamics in particular episodes, situations, or contexts.
- *The interpretive task*. Drawing on theories of the arts and sciences to better understand and explain why these patterns and dynamics are occurring.
- *The normative task*. Using theological concepts to interpret particular episodes, situations, or contexts, constructing ethical norms to guide our responses, and learning from "good practice."
- *The pragmatic task*. Determining strategies of action that will influence situations in ways that are desirable and entering into a reflective conversation with the "talk back" emerging when they are enacted.[14]

Osmer's tasks form the building blocks for the practical theology process. While various nuances and reworkings continue to add to the discussion of this discipline, these tasks continue to drive the process of practical theology forward. Along with these core tasks, practical theology is shaped by at least two other important characteristics.

First, practical theology does not begin with theory, as other branches of theology do; "it is *at least* a praxis-theory-praxis process of constant dialogue and interpretation, communal reflection and challenge, and a never-ending quest to hear God's voice and follow his call."[15] Thomas Groome states that "instead of theory leading to practice, theory becomes or is seen as the reflective moment in praxis, and articulated theory arises from that praxis to yield further praxis."[16] It is important to recognize that the Aristotelian term *praxis* is not the same as practice. The term *practice* is sometimes mistakenly used synonymously with *praxis* in practical theology literature. Hyun-Sook Kim explains:

> The Greek term *praxis*, frequently translated into English as "practice," implies more than the typical English definition for "practice." According to *A Dictionary of Philosophy*, practice was described as something pertaining to action, whereas *praxis*, itself, meant action or activity. Practical (Greek *praktikos*) referred to anything related to action, whereas the Greek *theoretikos* is classified as the theoretical or related to thought.[17]

Consider the game of golf, for example. You could seek to be a competent golfer and thereby practice your swing, putting, judging the distance to the green, and understanding what club to use when you hit the ball. All of these elements are clearly important to becoming a good golfer, but none of these elements is, in and of itself, the actual game of golf. Practicing golf is not playing golf; rather, playing golf would be our praxis.[18]

As noted in Kim's definitions earlier, practical relates to action while theory focuses on thought. Thus practical theology begins by examining our current actions and practices and then bringing the weight of theological reflection to bear in order to create action that is faithful to a kingdom-oriented trajectory yet lived out effectively within our current context. That is why one will often hear practical theology described as "doing theology from below."[19]

In his essay "Youth Ministry as Practical Theology," Chap Clark argues that our praxis should be understood in light of our *telos*. He defines *telos* as "the culmination of God's intended purpose for creation and redemption."[20] Clark notes that the conclusions of practical theology should always be mindful of God's current action and God's future intent for all of creation. This can also apply to understanding God's story of the world. Clark believes that our praxis—the action/activity that drives us—should be the inbreaking of the kingdom of God. It is the "already and not yet" that seeks to permeate our existence and lead us toward the *telos*. Scott Cormode calls this "faithful action," which must be "faithful, effective, contextual, and communal."[21] Our faith practices should help us to move toward faithful action, and therefore we must continually evaluate our practices in light of the trajectory, or inbreaking reality, of God's kingdom in the world.

Second, practical theology draws on an interdisciplinary conversation between the secular disciplines[22] and theological reflection in order to faithfully evaluate and reorient our praxis. Root explains: "Using theories from fields as diverse as sociology, evolutionary biology, literary studies, existentialism, object relations psychology, and education, to name but a few, the practical theologian seeks to provide an interpretation, a particular theoretical lens that helps explain why such an occurrence is happening."[23] Ballard and Pritchard describe it this way:

At a theoretical level [a hermeneutical dialogue] will be a critical correlation between theology and the social sciences, together

illuminating the human condition. This method of "critical correlation" has become central to much recent practical theology, not least in North America, developing a theme found in Paul Tillich and elaborated in more recent hermeneutical theology such as that of David Tracy.[24]

The essay "Youth Ministry as Practical Theology" argues that

practical theology is in its essence a correlative relationship between theology and any other data set that can inform and illuminate God's call to his people. Whatever the source of these data sets, anything that speaks into the human condition such that believers can receive a deeper and more thorough understanding of the context in which the Gospel is to be lived out is an important part of a practical theology method.[25]

As you can see, this concept has the general support of the practical theology community.

Osmer's four tasks, the progression of praxis-theory-praxis, and the use of the interdisciplinary tools of both secular disciplines and theological reflection all contribute to the uniqueness of the work of practical theology. Understanding how these elements work together to lead our actions toward the inbreaking of God's kingdom is our next step. While I find it helpful to describe this process in a more technical-rational nature, I recognize that the process of practical theology can and perhaps should, at least at times, be more organic than systematic. I appreciate David White's reminder that "life in the Holy Spirit is more appropriately akin to dancing than engineering, more aesthetic than technical."[26] While the following guide is linear in nature, I affirm that any time the Holy Spirit introduces new revelations that call into question our previous assumptions, we must be willing go back and work the process again.

Before We Continue

An important question to answer before we tackle the "how" of practical theology is the "when" and "what." When do we use practical theology and on what? Practical theology applies anytime we want to bring something more in line with what God is doing. That may seem vague, but it is true. The secret to success is working to refine your question or issue down to the core of the matter. What is the Holy Spirit prompting you to respond to? The process of practical theology will help you do this if you are faithful to the work. As with most things in life, the more effort you put into the process (making use of a wider array of secular disciplines, working to understand your faith traditions, looking for the connections between the stories, seeking the wisdom of others, praying through your implementation, etc.), the more you will get out of it. However, that does not mean that without volumes of research the process holds no value. The process of practical theology is ongoing. God is always creating, always redeeming. As such, God is always inviting us to join in the work of bringing the kingdom near. In some instances our work may result in a gigantic leap forward. At other times it may feel like a baby step. Remember, the distance isn't as important as the direction; our goal is faithful action.

Putting It All Together: The Process of Practical Theology

Practical theology starts by recognizing that the Holy Spirit is constantly inviting us to join in God's ongoing work of redemption and creation. In this discipline, when we realize a specific way in which God is inviting us to be involved, our proper response should be to first step back and try to observe what is going on. Try to determine what stories are involved. Think back to Bronfenbrenner's *Ecology of Human Development*. By examining the interactions of the various layers, we hope to better understand our context and bring clarity to the praxis that the Holy Spirit is revealing.

As the process begins, the urge to immediately jump in and respond must be resisted. We must develop the discipline to hover above any situation or setting and observe the context from a bird's-eye view: What can we see? What do we notice? What is God drawing our attention to?

When I took a CPR/first aid class the instructor taught us that when arriving on the scene of an accident, our first action should be to look around and survey the scene. Your instinct is to immediately address the problem, but doing so may jeopardize yourself and the person(s) you are trying to help. First, you need to assess and try to understand the factors involved and how they have affected the situation. The same is true with the process of practical theology.

Root explains it this way: "Because the objective of practical theology is to attend to God's action in the locations and practices of human individuals and communities, practical theologians must describe what is going on in concrete locales. In the descriptive task, therefore, the practical theologians will seek to answer the question 'What is happening?' in a rigorous manner that sets forth a thick description of location."[27] Osmer gives an important warning regarding this process: "It is worthwhile for students and leaders to learn the skill of attending to the words and actions of others without filtering them through interpretive and normative judgments. This is very important in the descriptive-empirical task of practical theological interpretation, which focuses on *what* is going on before reflecting on why it is going on or what ought to take place."[28] At this early stage of the process it is important to avoid assigning meaning and creating assumptive categories too quickly. To best assign meaning, we need to first take the time to hear the stories that are involved.

Let's return to the story of my meeting with my professor. While I do not believe my professor was intentionally working through the process of practical theology during our meeting, what transpired that day lends itself to parallels that can help us to understand the process better. When I went to my professor to ask about my grade, he did not immediately address my concerns. Instead, he seized the opportunity to learn more about the situation. He asked what I was studying. He asked about my undergrad work. He wanted to know about where I grew up. He asked about my family. When he found out that I had recently been married before coming to seminary, he asked how the transition was going. He wanted to know about the church I was serving in and how the student ministry was going. He asked all kinds of questions that had nothing to do with the B on my assignment. As we talked, I believe he made observations about what was important to understanding my story and what wasn't. In the important areas, he would dig a little deeper. He would ask follow-up questions and allow more time for the story to unfold. When he was satisfied with the conversation, he redirected us back to the reason I had come to see him.

Once we have thoroughly observed and described the context in which the Holy Spirit has prompted us to act, we can begin the next step of practical theology. Osmer refers to this as the interpretive task, in which we answer the question "Why is this going on?" I would recast the question of the interpretive task as "How does humanity's story of the world contribute to what is happening?" Either way, the second step of the framework of practical theology is trying to better understand the context and stories that are involved in shaping God's ongoing creation.

To bring clarity to how our specific area of context is affecting our observations, we turn to practical theology's interdisciplinary strength.[29] As we have noted, practical theology draws from both the secular disciplines and theological reflection to help interpret our context and uncover the stories involved. Beginning with secular disciplines, we often use tools such as sociology, psychology, psychiatry, ecology, family systems, and the study of culture, race, ethnicity, and class to create a thick interpretation of our context.[30] To again borrow from Hall's imagery, these are all ways in which humanity tells its own stories. Learning to listen to these stories helps us to identify the root issue that God is inviting us to realign with the ongoing work of redemption and creation. The secular disciplines act as a lens to bring into focus how the context affects our story and influences our practices.

Examining our context can be an exhaustive task. To help guide this process, I find Clark's focus on internal and external factors to be helpful. Clark states, "There are two significant areas of influence that shape a context: relational (or *internal*) factors and environmental (or *external*) factors."[31] Internal factors are by and large "those that are primarily relational and are generally located within the familial systems, structures, and experiences that shape how a person or people group view themselves."[32] These would be the stories uncovered in the microsystems and mesosystems in Bronfenbrenner's bioecological model. Clark goes on to say that external factors

> include anything outside of the individual and their familial history that influences how a community and even a collection of individuals will think about a given issue. These include the various messages that mold opinion and perspective (including media, advertising, etc.), the ecological dynamics and resultant push of the context (how the whole shapes the specific), the various expressions (both overt, such as film, music, and other forms of directed message, and just as potent but less institutional, like language, humor, and the like) that comprise the elements of a collective narrative and continually swirl in and throughout a community while providing meaning and a sense of belonging to those living within the context, and any other cultural force that has been forged over time that influences and guides a collective perspective.[33]

These would include the larger stories generated by the exosystem and macrosystem found in Bronfenbrenner's model. By arranging our context into internal and external factors, we allow the "lens" of secular disciplines to better guide our process.

Getting back to my original story, when my professor asked me why I had come to see him I asked him why I had received a B on my assignment. He asked me what grade I had wanted. I responded, "An A." Without a word he picked up my paper, took a pen out of his desk, marked through the grade, wrote an A beside it, and slid it back across the desk to me.

Then he asked me a question that was simple, yet profound: "Why is it important for you to get an A?" I responded without really thinking, "Because it's the best." Without hesitation he replied, "Why is it important for you to be the best?" In a moment our conversation shifted from a discussion about a few points on an assignment to a deep-seated truth about myself that I had never realized. This is what the tools of secular disciplines bring to the work of practical theology. They take our observations and peel back the layers of façades and defenses that cover the core of the issue that the Holy Spirit is revealing about our current praxis. With this newfound clarity we are able to move forward in the work of practical theology.

Once our issue within its context has been uncovered, the issue and process is then brought into the work of theological reflection. Theological reflection brings to bear the fullness of the Christian faith understanding (the richness of God's story revealed throughout history) to the issue at hand in an attempt to discern God's call to faithful action. In practical theology, I would espouse that true theological reflection cannot occur without first doing the work of the descriptive-empirical and interpretative tasks. The reason? One relies on the other. As Hall observes, "Theology lives *between* the stories—God's story of the world, and humanity's ever-changing account of itself and all things. *Theology is what happens when the two stories meet*."[34] While these two movements are both necessary for the work of practical theology to happen, it does not mean that their contributions are equal influencers in determining our faithful action. Hall goes on to say, "It is of course the particular vocation of the disciple community to keep listening especially for God's story."[35] Root lays out this idea more clearly:

The heart of practical theology, the organ that pumps the blood through the organism, is theology itself. Therefore, the practical theologian's work should not only possess deep reservoirs of reflection on experience, but also it must seek to reflect on God's continued action in the world. Theology should never be used functionally as a kind of add-on. Rather it should provide direction for how the empirical task is done. Theology must remain the heart of the field, because its core objective is to discuss the association between divine and human action. While empirical work provides invaluable perspectives on human action, the divine can only be articulated theologically.[36]

When working with students, we must not neglect the work of theological reflection. It can be tempting at times to simply celebrate the breakthrough that uncovers the core issue and not press on. For example, say you have an active student who suddenly stops coming to church. Through observation and inquiry you discover that her parents are struggling with their marriage. In your conversations with her you discover that she blames herself and has even thought about taking her own life. Let's say that somehow, by engaging the power of secular disciplines, you help this young lady realize that her parents' struggles are not her fault, and as a result she no longer wishes to harm herself. Let's go one step further and imagine that in the process of working with the family you all stumble across the core issue that has caused the marital turmoil and it is easily resolved. This is cause for celebration; the family has been restored. Given the situation, most people would be content not to press the issue. But what has the family learned about God's plans for their life through this struggle? Has the young lady who was ready to take her life realized the value she holds in God's eyes, or is she just content that Mom and Dad aren't fighting anymore? How is God wanting to bring the work of the kingdom into this situation? As youth ministers, we must train ourselves to reflect theologically about the situations in which God invites us to take part. We cannot rely on observation and action alone.

If my conversation with my professor had ended with the revelation that my need to be the best was not based on a healthy work ethic but on insecurity and a need for acceptance, it may have helped me be a better person, but it would not have changed my approach to ministry. The biggest God moment of that conversation was not the unpacking of my family issues or how I defined myself by my achievements. The psychosocial analysis was helpful in uncovering the deeper issue, but it was my professor's theological inquiry that most shaped the work of the kingdom for me that day. In a profound moment of clarity my professor asked me, "How does your need to be the best affect how you see God?" That was when my story and God's story collided and the work of theological reflection began.

Theological reflection helps us to understand God's story in the world, both presently and historically. The goal of theological reflection is to bring our issue into alignment with the work of the kingdom; or to put it another way, we work to align humanity's story with God's story in order for humanity to more clearly see the work of the kingdom of God. As the process unfolds, the desired outcome is a more deliberate alignment with God's work and purpose than we had at the outset. This is referred to as the kingdom trajectory: "movement towards God's ultimate trajectory for us as he brings his kingdom to fruition."[37]

This is what Kenda Creasy Dean calls "the radical congruency between God's action and our action."[38] Richard Osmer refers to theological reflection as the normative task necessary to answer the question "What ought to be going on?" It is appropriate to note that the revelation of new information may call into question our previous assumptions. Anytime this occurs, we must revisit each step of the process to make sure that our perceived kingdom trajectory is an appropriate expression of God's revelation.

Practical theologians use different descriptors and approaches to describe the actual process of theological reflection, but despite the various labels, I believe one can find common elements essential to the process. Synthesizing the current work regarding practical theology, I see four main standards by which, through the guidance of the Holy Spirit, we bring the weight of theological reflection to bear: theology, tradition, experience, and Scripture. To help establish my practical theological framework for theological reflection, I envision the first three standards as interlocking circles within a larger circle. The larger circle represents all that is bounded by the process of theological reflection while the smaller circles within represent theology, tradition, and experience.

These three elements of theological reflection each bring a unique series of questions to bear on the contextual issue. Theology encompasses all of the ways in which we think about God. It draws from such rich disciplines as systematic, philosophical, historical, contextual, and ethical theology to reveal kingdom truth about our current issue. Tradition includes both historical and local church history. Through tradition we bring to bear the timeless wisdom and practices of the church as well

as unique denominational views, doctrines, and congregational beliefs that influence our issue in light of specific context. Experience acknowledges the revelation of God in both our corporate and individual stories. It provides space for the beauty of "worship, discernment, and prayer" to permeate the issue at hand.[39] All three elements are essential to the task of theological reflection. Each circle balances and tests the other in order to eventually lead to kingdom trajectory.

Continuing with this imagery, in the center of the circle where theology, tradition, and experience overlap, is the revelation of Christ as revealed through Scripture. In the work of theological reflection all of these elements must be seen and interpreted in the light of Christ as revealed through Scripture by the Holy Spirit. Anderson uses the term *biblical antecedent* to address this idea: "As nearly as I can see, for every case in which eschatological preference (kingdom trajectory) was exercised by the Spirit in the New Testament church, there was a biblical antecedent for what appeared to be revolutionary and new."[40] While the biblical antecedent guides our course, it is the light of Christ that illuminates our path toward kingdom trajectory and ultimately faithful action. Once the process of theological reflection is satisfied, any action we choose to move forward with needs to be supported by a biblical antecedent and true to our kingdom trajectory. (This model of practical theology can be found on the website dedicated to this book: youthministry.fuller.edu.)[41]

As stated earlier, practical theology is a discipline of praxis-theory-praxis. When we recognize the Holy Spirit's invitation to join the ongoing work of creation, we respond by observing the elements of our current praxis. We use secular disciplines to help us interpret what humanity's story is telling us about the context in which the Spirit is moving. Having gained new insights, we turn to theological reflection (theory) to understand how God's story is calling us to transform our actions to align more with the work (trajectory) of the kingdom. A new praxis emerges out of our theological reflection, but here we must be careful to continue on and complete the work of practical theology in order to ensure that our action is faithful action.

Osmer's fourth task of practical theology is the pragmatic task, and he uses the question "How might we respond?" to describe it.[42] While Osmer's intent is on target, I believe that we must dig deeper than Osmer's question prompts. There is more to the end of the model than just our response. To simply respond to our theological reflection runs the risk of action that is less than faithful.

As followers of Christ, we need to remember that our new praxis should promote the inbreaking of the kingdom of God, not just the ministry of the church. These goals are by no means mutually exclusive, but often our temptation can be to focus our outcome on what is best for our ministry or our members. For our actions to be as faithful as possible, we want to keep the focus of our praxis on our kingdom trajectory, not just on our congregation. Gerben Heitink, a leading international figure who was one of the first to attempt to formulate a complete theory of practical theology, states that "the exercise of practical theology does not have the church, but rather society, as its horizon."[43] Practical theology is constantly working toward the inbreaking of God's kingdom "on earth as it is in heaven" (Matt. 6:10). By returning to humanity's story of the world and reengaging the tools of secular disciplines, we can determine the best way to introduce

our new praxis so that humanity's story will move toward aligning with God's story, allowing the work of God's kingdom to be further established on earth as it is in heaven.

When my professor asked me how my need to be the best affected how I saw God, the answer was clear, although I didn't say a word. I had built my identity on achievement, and when I honestly examined my spiritual life the lines of works and grace had become very blurred. I was constantly *doing* ministry for God, but rarely did I seek to just *be* with God. Logically, I understood Paul's rebuke in Philippians 3 about the confidence of the flesh and counting all of our own attempts at righteousness as garbage when compared to knowing Christ. But practically, I wanted others to see me as a "Hebrew of Hebrews" (Phil. 3:5). Being seen as zealous and faultless sounded pretty good. I guess my professor sensed my discomfort and brought our meeting to a close by saying, "Michael, there are more important things in this life than grades. What good is it if you get an A in this class but a D at being a husband? Who does it serve if you have a great GPA but are too busy for the students in your ministry? God will still love you if you make a B. If you want to be the best you can be, learn to be present with your family, your friends, and your ministry. If you want to be successful in this calling, you need to learn balance."

Not many professors would be advised to tell their students that grades are not *that* important. But I believe my professor understood what it meant to align our praxis with the work of the kingdom. He wanted my actions to be as faithful as possible and in that moment that was exactly the lesson I needed to learn. In our brief conversation, my professor (knowingly or not) used the tools of secular disciplines to uncover a deeper issue in my life, brought the power of theological reflection to bear on that issue, and reoriented my praxis to align more faithfully with what God was doing by helping me to understand what that meant in my context. It was pretty impressive. As my seminary career continued, I often had to remind myself that God would still love me if I made a B. It was an easy mantra that encapsulated the incredible experience I had with my professor and helped me to continually evaluate where my story was headed.

Once our theological reflection leads to a kingdom trajectory that is informed by the tools of secular disciplines to best understand how to live out faithful action in light of our current context, we come to the end of Osmer's four core tasks and our cycle of praxis-theory-praxis is complete. Yet one step still remains. In this process we have worked to make our praxis faithful to the work of the kingdom, but we must remember that this is a tale of two stories. As we come to the close of this process, I think it is important to pick up on the work of Ray Anderson. Whereas Osmer asks, "How might *we* respond?" Anderson asks, "What is *Christ* doing in this situation?" (emphasis added to both questions). He calls this *Christopraxis*.[44] For Anderson, Christopraxis is a continuation of Christ's own ministry of revelation and reconciliation. The process of practical theology invites us to journey with the Holy Spirit, offering our faithful action to Christ's ministry of reconciliation (Christopraxis) to usher in the inbreaking of the kingdom of God (on earth as it is in heaven) in our particular context (or story). The inbreaking of the kingdom ultimately leads to further revelations of new praxis that need to be examined. Thus the work of practical theology is actually an ongoing process of revelation, reflection, reaction

to the work of the Holy Spirit, and partnership in the reconciliation of Christ.

How Practical Theology Can Lead to Adoptive Youth Ministry

Understanding practical theology has changed the way I approach ministry. It has given me the focus to keep first things first (to borrow again from Stephen Covey). By keeping my attention on the inbreaking of the kingdom, I find it easier to resist cynicism and build the church, not just my ministry. Beyond equipping me with a good framework and tools by which to engage in ministry, understanding practical theology has shaped my philosophy of ministry and my understanding of my Creator. Because of these insights, I have come to embrace the ministry of adoption as the best narrative for my ministry practices with adolescents.

Below is the revelation of what I believe the Holy Spirit has shaped in me over the past several years. You do not have to agree or disagree with me in order to appreciate the work of practical theology or the ministry of adoption. I offer it because it has proved to be important to my ongoing praxis of aligning with God's kingdom work.

One of the greatest strengths of practical theology is that it begins by respecting humanity's story, our story. Hopefully God's story can clearly be seen weaving in and out of the fabric of our own narrative; nevertheless, it is still our story—and one of God's greatest gifts. By inviting us to join in the ongoing work of creation, to become co-laborers with Christ, God makes room for the beauty and tragedy of the stories we share. James Fowler writes, "God can and does call us to a *partnership* in the divine praxis."[45] By examining our story and God's story, practical theology allows us to faithfully join in this work to move us toward the work of God's kingdom.

In this chapter I have referred often to the kingdom, God's kingdom, the kingdom trajectory, the work of the kingdom, the inbreaking of the kingdom, and so forth. I realize that many of us will have preconceived notions of what those terms refer to, but nowhere in the chapter have I explicitly defined what I believe these terms incorporate. I want to argue that the work of the kingdom, and ultimately the work of practical theology, has two main overarching thrusts.

The first thrust is the one we are probably more familiar with. Anderson focuses on this with his discussion of Christopraxis. We are called to join with Christ in the ministry of reconciliation, which is clearly seen in 2 Corinthians 5:17–21.

> Therefore, if anyone is in Christ, the new creation has come: The old has gone, the new is here! All this is from God, who reconciled us to himself through Christ and gave us the ministry of reconciliation: that God was reconciling the world to himself in Christ, not counting people's sins against them. And he has committed to us the message of reconciliation. We are therefore Christ's ambassadors, as though God were making his appeal through us. We implore you on Christ's behalf: Be reconciled to God. God made him who had no sin to be sin for us, so that in him we might become the righteousness of God.

When I talk about the work of the kingdom or the inbreaking of the kingdom, part of what I am referring to is the gospel news that because of Christ our relationship with God can be reconciled, redeemed, and restored. This is

the joy that was set before Christ as described in Hebrews 12:2. Humanity can once again be in right relationship and community with its Creator.

In the magnitude of this revelation it is easy to focus our ministry efforts on us (humanity) being in relationship with God. Songs like "Give Me Jesus" and "Turn Your Eyes upon Jesus" lift our focus toward God's kingdom and the perfection of our community with our Creator that awaits us in heaven. We long for that day and echo that chorus, "You can have all this world / But give me Jesus." However, relationships work two ways. Yes, we want to be reconciled in our relationship to God, but I believe God also wants to be reconciled in God's relationship to us—and not just us (those who are in the church) but also the world. We may know John 3:16, "For God so loved the world . . ." When we place those words in the context of Jesus's prayer in Matthew 6:10, "Your kingdom come, your will be done, on earth as it is in heaven," we don't need to be so quick to leave this world behind. God is not done creating yet. This is the second thrust of the kingdom work that I think we do not give enough attention to. Yes, the church should be drawing humanity closer to God, but in the process the church needs to be drawing closer to humanity because God so loved the world. If it is important to God it needs to be important to us.

Practical theology begins with the Holy Spirit's invitation to join in what God is creating. This profound statement does not need to be glossed over. Gilbert Bilezikian's book *Community 101* has been one of the most influential works in helping me understand the depth of this revelation.[46] The Bible begins with God's invitation for humanity to join in the creation process. Have you ever stopped to wonder why God created a garden that needed tending (Gen. 2:15)? Why not put everything on autopilot and give Adam and Eve a continual all-you-can-eat buffet? If you have ever eaten a tomato that you watched mature from a vine you planted, you know the answer. If you buy a tomato at the grocery store and it falls out of your shopping bag in the parking lot and busts, you are probably not going to worry that much about it. If you pick the first tomato of the season off a plant you have nurtured for months and accidently drop it on the way into the house, there is a twinge of pain and loss. (I know not everyone likes tomatoes, but you get the point.) Why is this? Because God invites us to connect with creation and to share in the beauty of cocreating. God does not simply place us in the midst of God's creation as pawns; God also invites us to participate in the creation process.

God didn't stop with the garden either. In Genesis 1:28 God tells Adam and Eve to "Be fruitful and increase in number"; humanity is given the gift of giving birth. God allows us to participate in the creation of life. It is important to God that we are a part of the process. And it's not just a little important; God chose for us to be involved even though humanity would reject God and inflict pain and suffering on its Creator and itself. In the Genesis story it is clear to me that God wanted us to be involved in what God was creating. So when we say that the work of the kingdom that God invites us into includes the ongoing work of creation, we need to ask: What is God creating?

To understand that question we need to start at the beginning. Look back at the creation story in Genesis 1. In this story, our God is set apart as the creator of everything. As God's creation progressively unfolds, God makes a judgment about each movement of creation. God says, "It is good." What we often miss in this reading is that God created something that was deemed not good.

Genesis 2:18 tells us that it was "not good for the man to be alone." It is astounding to think that Adam was in God's presence when this decree was made. At this point in the story, God had already filled Adam's lungs with the breath of life, created a place for Adam to live, and provided food to eat, water to drink, and careful instructions by which to live. God had established a relationship with Adam, but it was not good for Adam to be alone? What could possibly be better than one-on-one time with our Creator?

According to the story, God gets creative and forms all kinds of animals and birds from the dirt and brings them to Adam, but nothing cures Adam's loneliness. Then God chooses a new medium. He takes from Adam and creates Eve. From the one God creates two. Human becomes humanity, and at the pinnacle of creation stands God's crowning achievement: community. In God's infinite wisdom, God chose to purposefully design humanity to be in relationship with God *and* one another. God calls this "very good."

To be clear, while I propose two main thrusts within the work of the kingdom, our relationship with God has to be primary. Yet if we pursue that relationship while ignoring our community, we are falling short of God's invitation. Christ's response to the expert in the law who asked, "Which is the greatest commandment in the Law?" (Matt. 22:36) demonstrates this idea. "Jesus replied: 'Love the Lord your God with all your heart and with all your soul and with all your mind.' This is the first and greatest commandment. And the second is like it: 'Love your neighbor as yourself.' All the Law and the Prophets hang on these two commandments" (Matt. 22:37–40).

As Christians we have to recapture the beauty of community. We need to renew our efforts to love God and one another. As a church we need to draw people closer to Christ, and we (as a church) need to be drawn closer to the people. We need to move away from the "us" and "them" mentality of assimilating people into our membership and instead open ourselves to the transformative work of the ministry of adoption. As Galatians 4:4–5 (NRSV) says, "But when the fullness of time had come, God sent his Son, born of a woman, born under the law, in order to redeem those who were under the law, so that we might receive adoption as children." Through Christ we become children of God and coheirs with Christ. This is the miraculous work of God's kingdom, the revelation of Christ's reconciliation for creation. In that revelation it is important for us to remember that this reconciliation is for our relationship with both God and one another. This is why practical theology is the best approach for student ministry today. A model of ministry that is built on a process that values humanity's story as well as God's story is the only way the church can grow in true community.

Youth Ministry, Adoption, and Culture

WALT MUELLER

If there is any single voice who has helped youth ministry practitioners around the world to think critically and theologically about culture, it is Walt Mueller. Mueller has served the church as an author, consultant, encourager, thinker, speaker, and teacher for nearly three decades. While some decry people with influence and degrees, assuming that they do not understand the field or the trenches, Mueller has always been deeply engaged in both. He understands the demands of youth ministry;

The scope of this chapter, as it relates to culture, is limited. While there are a multitude of youth ministry issues, skills, and sensitivities that must be pursued and developed in response to culture, the task before us in this chapter is to develop a cursory and basic understanding of how those of us in the older generations (in this case, anyone post–high school age) can begin to understand, address, and cross the cultural-generational gap that exists between generations as a result of rapid cultural change. While the definitions, explanations, and basic understandings presented here do apply at some level to all manner of cross-cultural ministry, the focus of this discussion is specific to the engagement of teenagers and their unique youth culture. This chapter is deliberately introductory in nature and therefore limited in scope and depth.

he spends most of his time walking alongside those who are working in churches and parachurch organizations with teenagers, and he is one of the most respected leaders in helping parents, educators, and youth workers to understand the cultural pond they find themselves immersed in.

This chapter, like a few other chapters in Adoptive Youth Ministry, *is an example of a significant leader's particular and unique perspective. As representative of his other writings, this chapter both describes the world in which we all live and helps us to navigate what today's culture brings and does to all of us, especially young people. The way that Mueller leads us is by looking at the specificity of what he calls "youth culture." His intent from the outset is threefold: first, to help us realize that our ministry to young people is cross-cultural; second, our understanding of how young people see and experience their cultural setting will help us to be more deliberate and careful in our ministry to them; and third, by having a greater awareness of the changing culture in our kids' lives we will be better able to "contextualize" our ministry to speak into the world in which they live.*

On this chapter's webpage, not only will you be able to look more deeply at Mueller's perspective and the work of the organization he leads, the Center for Parent and Youth Understanding, but you will also be able to stay on top of the trends and issues that he mentions. His organization is also available for seminars and consultations for churches, communities, and denominations.

As you read this chapter, consider these questions:

1. *What is Mueller's definition of culture? Put it in your own words.*
2. *The chapter provides six "characteristics of culture." Which of these do you most resonate with, and why? Which of these do you most struggle with or not understand, and why?*
3. *This chapter's purpose is not only to describe culture but also to give us the ability to engage with culture and to interpret culture so as to be more effective in our ministry to emerging generations. What is the danger of not paying attention to our cultural setting, especially as we are engaged in youth ministry?*
4. *In light of this chapter, what are two to three takeaways that will impact how you think about youth ministry in the future?*

My good friends Ben and Cindy starred in a reality show. The show tracked the stories of couples who chose to adopt. In every instance, the individual stories were embedded in good lighting, strategic camera angles, and carefully edited video clips, all of which were held together with perky narration and a musical soundtrack designed to elicit heart tugs, tears, and warm feelings from viewers. That was certainly the case for me as I watched Ben and Cindy's very touching televised story of adopting three elementary-aged siblings out of an orphanage in South America.

We *should* cry tears of joy at adoption stories. Adoption is about making rights out of horrible wrongs and wholeness out of brokenness. It's about working to bring shalom into young and vulnerable lives struggling to live in the wake of the effects of sin, brokenness, and systemic abandonment. It's about offering a place to call home to those who have no real home, providing familial love and relationship to those who have had no family due to choice or circumstance, and bestowing a standing and inheritance that didn't exist before the adoption. In so many ways, adoption is about belonging. How can we not be moved by adoption?

But any family that has gone through the process of adoption will also tell you that adoption, like everything else in life, includes a good dose of messiness. Shouldn't that be expected when broken people adopt broken people?

For my friends Ben and Cindy, their TV show only told the feel-good part of the story. Their decision to adopt was also a decision to enter into a clash of cultures as they were integrating three young children from another country who spoke another language and lived by another set of customs and rules into an American family. While family life (adoptive or biological) is never easy, smooth, and squeaky-clean, Ben and Cindy faced even greater difficulties due to cultural differences. They had to learn not only how to be parents but also how to be cross-cultural missionaries.

The story of the growth and expansion of God's family—the church—in today's rapidly changing world is similarly complex. God's family is made up of broken people who await the day when they and everything else will be made new. God is not only bringing together a family made up of people, tribes, and nations separated by geographical and cultural differences ("all the world"), but he is also calling and adopting children and teens who live in our homes and communities into his family. And while these adopted children of God (John 1:12–13) may live with us, their world is very different from ours. We cannot assume that they think, talk, believe, or act the way that we do. Consequently, the family of God—both globally *and* locally—will always be multicultural in some way, shape, or form. This reality necessitates our willingness as older and more mature sisters and brothers in Christ (including parents, pastors, youth workers, Christian educators, and mentors—the entire local church body!) to see ourselves as cross-cultural missionaries who must assume a cross-cultural posture if we are to effectively communicate the message of the gospel (*invite* them into the family), nurture them in the gospel (*integrate* them as growing members of the family who both contribute to and benefit from their place as siblings), and send them forth with the gospel (*equip* them to be kingdom bearers in the world who interact with and function in culture to the glory of God).

I have found it helpful to visualize cultural change through what has become known in the world of technology as "Moore's Law." In the mid-1960s, Gordon Moore, the cofounder of Intel, postulated that the number of transistors a circuit board could hold would double every two years. All of us who are computer users have benefited from the reality of what Moore predicted, as this kind of exponential growth has resulted in rapid changes in computer technology and speed. (Have you ever considered that the smartphone in your hand has more power and potential than the NASA computer that landed the first astronauts on the moon?) In the same way, the rate of cultural change is reaching speeds that those of us who were doing youth ministry in the 1970s and 1980s could never have imagined! The size and scope of the world is expanding far beyond our familiar surroundings and experience. The world of the emerging generations is not our world. Their distinct youth culture is not our culture.

A few years ago, I spent a day speaking to a group of youth workers about the changes taking place in youth culture and the cultural trends they needed to address in their ministries. A young youth worker came to me afterward and said, "Thanks for today. Everything you talked about I'm seeing in my ministry. This has been very helpful." "Where are you doing ministry?" I asked. He replied, "I'm working in the high school I graduated from. It's an after-school mentoring program for at-risk kids. I go back on that campus and the culture of these kids is so different from when I was a student." Curious about his age and how long it had been since he had graduated, I asked, "When did you graduate?" His answer: "Last year." Indeed, culture is changing at breakneck speed.

If we are to answer God's call to reach out to the mission field of the emerging generations and incorporate those among them who are called and adopted by God into the life of our churches as our siblings in the faith, we will experience three inevitable and inescapable realities related to youth culture. First, we will have to embrace the reality that we are engaging with a culture that is different from our own. Our living together as brothers and sisters adopted into the family of God will be cross-cultural in nature. Second, when we go from our culture into theirs, we will experience some amount of culture shock. But the level and intensity of that shock can be buffered if we take the time to understand culture and how it functions in people's lives, particularly in the lives of those from the emerging generations God brings in to our midst. And third, our ministries of evangelism and nurture to the young in our midst will require us to know their culture, contextualize our efforts, and speak to the unique issues and challenges they face that come with following Jesus in the midst of this rapidly changing culture.

These realities are not at all unique to our times. The model for this type of cross-cultural adaptation is the incarnation of the God-man, Jesus Christ. God sent his son Jesus, a particular man, into a particular world at a particular time and to a particular place. "The Word became flesh and blood, and moved into the neighborhood" (John 1:14 Message). Jesus lived among those to whom he ministered. He participated in their lives by sharing in their day-to-day activities and tasks. He became intimately familiar with their language, values, beliefs, customs, and thoughts.

The Scriptures also give us numerous models of unique people (messengers and missionaries) sent to unique cultural groups to communicate the unchanging message of the gospel. The apostle Paul stands out as one who adapted not the message but his presentation of the message, depending on the audience and their culture. When we read the book of Acts we see how his presentation changed and adapted from audience to audience. Of course, he wasn't just thinking on his feet. This man who became "all things to all men" had, as

Jerram Barrs says, "done his homework. He respected his hearers sufficiently and had a deep enough care for them that he had worked at understanding their ideas and their religion."[1] He learned their "language" so that they were able to understand the message he was called to communicate.

The New Testament is filled with letters written to communicate clearly with individuals and churches who had unique spiritual needs that had to be addressed in the contexts of their distinctive cultures. Church history and missions are filled with these same types of examples, but so are the fields of missiology, translation, and contextualization, which have burgeoned as Christians throughout history have realized the necessity of knowing both message *and* audience if effective communication and ministry is to take place.

This task is especially important for anyone hoping to evangelize and nurture young people in a rapidly changing world. In an interview with *Time* magazine, twentieth-century theologian Karl Barth said that he advised young theologians to pursue knowledge of both Scripture and culture when he said, "Take your Bible and take your newspaper, and read both. But interpret newspapers from your Bible."[2] Barth knew how essential it was to know both the message and the cultural issues to which that message had to respond.

Theologian John Stott believed that the foundation for effective cross-cultural communication and ministry is what he called "double listening." This is the ability and resolve to listen to two voices at one time. He says that all Christians are called to "stand between the Word and the world, with consequent obligation to listen to both. We listen to the Word in order to discover evermore of the riches of Christ. And we listen to the world in order to discern which of Christ's riches are needed most and how to present them in their best light."[3] With our understanding of the Word (Bible) *and* the world (newspaper/culture) we can then contextualize the gospel and our ministry efforts in meaningful ways that speak to the emerging generations *and* to the unique cultural challenges and pressures that they are facing in today's world.[4]

In *A Many Colored Kingdom: Multicultural Dynamics for Spiritual Formation*, Gary Parrett offers guidance on how to become a "culturally sensitive minister." He relates a helpful real-life example of the importance of an exhaustive and multilayered approach to getting to know a young person and his or her culture.

To illustrate, let us consider the case of a young woman who was part of a church project that I and several others worked on years ago. I will call her Sandy. Suppose I was a new pastor in Sandy's church and desired to minister to her in a culturally sensitive way. How could I equip myself for the task? As a shepherd, I would be committed to knowing my sheep, each one, individually, seeking the same spirit in which our Lord Jesus, the Good Shepherd, ministers to his own (see John 10:10–30). I might ask the question, "Who is Sandy anyway?" How might I answer this query? Sandy is a Korean-American teen-aged girl. These few descriptive words, by themselves, evince the complexity of the challenge. I must understand something about the meaning of "American" and of "Korean" and of the hybrid form, "Korean-American." But there is also the matter of being a teenager in America. Thus, I must also know something about so-called youth culture and the various potential influences it can have on Sandy. She is a young woman, not a young man, and this too is a critical piece of who Sandy is. But the case is more complex still. Sandy lives in a particular geographical region of the United States. She is part of an evangelical church youth group. It is a Korean-American youth group. She reports to me that it is very different from the other Korean-American youth groups in her area. She thinks the "climate" is more spiritual in her church than it is in others she has visited. She attends a particular high school and, at that school, "hangs" with a particular group of friends. We could, of course, continue the exercise, but the point should be clear. A person's culture is multilayered and exceedingly complex.[5]

This task of contextualization is an essential ingredient in effective youth ministry. *Contextualization* is defined both as "taking the gospel to a new context and finding appropriate ways to communicate it so that it is understandable to the people in that context"[6] and "the practice of declaring or depicting and living out the gospel message in cultural forms and terms drawn predominantly from the frame of reference of those you are communicating with."[7] Again, the book of Acts and Paul's New Testament letters show the apostle's consistent commitment to contextualize his message to his hearers, shaping his presentation to each unique audience in order that they might have the opportunity to hear the good news. He was "faithful and relevant, not merely trendy."[8]

We are all responsible to be on our toes, knowing not only our rapidly changing culture and its effect on the emerging generations but also how culture is subtly changing as it develops and how it is uniquely affecting the individual young people God places in our lives. In other words, it is necessary to search for, recognize, and understand the unique aspects that mark the culture of *your* particular mission field of young people. Missions theorist Sherwood Lingenfelter says that "we must be learners and let them teach us before we can hope to teach them and introduce them to the master Teacher."[9] In effect, we must become like the men "from Issachar, men who understood the times and knew what Israel should do" (1 Chron. 12:32). Dean Borgman challenges us to realize that one of our main tasks "is to make divine revelation (the Bible and especially Jesus Christ) relevant and coherent to any particular age and society. To fulfill that task with regard to young people, we must learn a great deal about culture."[10] For example, what does their culture say about issues like identity, materialism, vocation, play, relationships, marriage, sexuality, racism, entitlement, narcissism, and so on?

Consequently, our youth ministries must not only grapple with some foundational questions about culture but must seek, develop, and communicate well-framed answers to these questions among our individual church family, along with the pursuit of the practical implementation of each:

- What is *culture*?
- What are the elements of culture?
- What are the characteristics of culture?
- How does culture function in the lives of kids?

What Is Culture?

Culture is what we believe, what we do, and how we live our lives from day to day. It is the identity that defines us individually and binds us to others who think, do, and live in a similar manner. Stott describes culture as "a tapestry, intricate and often beautiful, which is woven by a given society to express its corporate identity."[11]

While most spiritual siblings from across the generations in our churches generally speak the same language and share a common faith in God, there are markedly different cultures present. These differences are occasioned by a multiplicity of factors including our ages, where we grew up, and the kinds of families that we come from. Our life experiences and contexts are different. We all engage with different cultural influences and artifacts. The "tapestries" of our lives do share some common threads, but each is unique. Our individual cultural tapestries contain "values and assumptions which are expressed in a life style"[12] that are unique to ourselves and those like us. Our cultures transmit the meaning that life has for each of us. Our cultures are where, how, and what we have lived, are living, and will live in the future.

Social scientists define and describe culture in a variety of ways. Missiologist Harold Netland has studied the need to understand and know culture as a necessary step in engaging those who have been shaped by the pluralism of our twenty-first-century times. He says:

It is helpful to think of culture as a historically transmitted pattern of meanings embodied in symbols that are reflected in behavior, values, ideas and institutions through which people understand the cosmos and their place in it, communicate with each other and structure communal life patterns. As such, culture includes the products of a wide variety of human activities—reflection upon life experiences and the world around us; communication with others; the establishment of normative patterns of individual and communal behavior; relationships with others; social and political institutions, artistic expressions and so on. Culture includes the many dimensions of social life through which people make sense of their experiences and pass on to succeeding generations the wisdom and expectations thus acquired.[13]

William Romanowski offers a simpler and more direct definition of culture as the way that "humans define and live in God's world."[14] It is "a collection of ideals and beliefs, values, and assumptions that makes up a kind of master plan for living and interpreting life."[15]

When I speak to those who desire to understand and minister to the emerging generations, I offer them a simplistic working definition of culture that captures the essence of how we can most easily begin to understand how our children and teens define and live in God's world. Simply stated, culture is "the soup" that the emerging generations swim in every day. Consequently, if we want to engage the young for the sake of the gospel, we'd better take the time to know what's in the soup.

The soup bar at one of our local megabuffets serves as a great example of how to understand and examine the cultures of our young. In this particular restaurant, the soup bar typically features three soup selections every day. I have watched how people choose their soup. As they arrive at the soup bar, they grab a bowl before making their selection. Then they step back and scan the small cards on the counter that name the type of soup in each of the large steel soup tureens. Before placing soup in their bowl, they will lift the steel lid off the tureen, grab the ladle, and stir the soup so that the ingredients are evenly distributed. Then, after the soup has been stirred, they will lift a ladleful and examine it visually. They want to know the soup's ingredients. If they like what they see, they'll fill their bowl. If not, they may

move on to examine the next selection in the same manner.

If we and our church families are to effectively engage our children and teens with the truths of the gospel in ways they can hear and understand, we must step up to their world, lift the lid, stir it up, and look carefully at the unique and ever-changing mix of cultural elements and forces they live and swim in every day. We cannot escape the reality that those elements—which may seem strange, unusual, and even frightening to us—make up their environment, shape the way they look at the world, and define and govern how they live their lives. We might even be tempted to close the lid because we don't like what we see. But if we hope to effectively communicate God's unchanging good news and nurture the faith of the young in our midst, it's not an option to avoid facing and understanding the culture that reveals so much about who they are, why they're that way, what it is that gives them meaning in life, and how they choose to live that life in God's world.

For the cross-cultural missionary called to go into the world of the young (i.e., *every* member of our adopted faith family), it's important to approach our observations and perceptions of each unique culture by understanding three foundational aspects of culture that are shared by all cultures in all times and all places. These foundational aspects include the *characteristics* of culture, the *elements* of culture, and the *functions* of culture.

What Are the Characteristics of Culture?

What are the characteristics of culture that we must understand if we are to prepare ourselves and our churches to effectively take our place and fulfill our role as cross-cultural missionaries to children and teens growing up and living in the twenty-first-century world?

First, we must understand that culture is a *good* thing that has been created by God and given to humanity as a gift to use and perpetuate. In the book of Genesis, we read about the wonder of God's creation as he spends six days forming and filling the heavens and the earth. On the sixth day, the Creator of the universe creates the crowning point of his creation:

> Then God said, "Let us make mankind in our image, in our likeness, so that they may rule over the fish in the sea and the birds in the sky, over the livestock and all the wild animals, and over all the creatures that move along the ground."
>
> So God created mankind in his own
>   image,
>   in the image of God he created
>   them;
>   male and female he created them.
>   (Gen. 1:26–27)

On the seventh day, God rested. But even though God was done creating, the work of creation carried on. His image bearers now inhabited what he had made, and he gave them the responsibility to enjoy, care for, and develop all he had made. He gave them the responsibility to "work it and take care of it" (Gen. 2:15). Before resting, he blessed the image bearers he had made and commanded them to "be fruitful and increase in number; fill the earth and subdue it. Rule over the fish in the sea and the birds in the sky and over every living creature that moves on the ground" (Gen. 1:28). As theologian Albert Wolters says of God's instructions to the people he made in his image and of their responsibility to his created order, "People must now carry on the work of development: by being fruitful they must fill it even more; by subduing it they must form it even more. Mankind, as God's representatives on earth, carry on where God left off. But this is now to be a *human* development of the earth. The human race will fill the earth with its own kind, and it will form the earth for its own kind."[16]

In effect, "We are called to participate in the ongoing creational work of God, to be God's helper in executing to the end the blueprint for his masterpiece."[17] As God-imaging and God-commanded cultivators of the creation, our creativity results and is expressed in human culture. We become, as Andy Crouch so effectively explains, "culture makers."[18] Culture is a good gift given to us by God, entrusted to us by him to develop as responsible stewards. This implies not only that it is wrong for us to label culture as "evil" or a place for Christians to avoid (as so many have!) but also that we need to nurture the emerging generations into embracing culture as "a playground" on which to celebrate and indulge the *imago Dei*.

Second, culture is universal among all humans. While our cultures will differ from generation to generation, place to place, and time to time, everyone lives in and does culture no matter who they are. Wherever there are people, there is culture. The songwriter who prayerfully constructs her music to the glory of the one who has redeemed her *and* the unredeemed songwriter whose only desire is to bring glory to himself are both made in the image of God. As a result, both have been made and called to cultivate the creation. Whether they do so consciously or not, to the glory of God or not, both are making culture. Culture is a common human endeavor.

Third, culture is shared as a system for living by those in a particular society.[19] The same is true for subcultures within a society. A visit to a local high school reveals that while there is a general culture of students with shared values, attitudes, and behaviors, the larger student population can be divided into several unique subcultures. There are the band members, the athletes, the scholars, the goths, and the cowboys, among others. Each particular group is marked by a unique mix of beliefs, behaviors, interests, language, dress, and so on that binds them together while distinguishing them from the other groups. They are little "societies" sometimes populated by no more than a handful or "cluster"[20] of students. But each individual finds his or her identity and some sense of security in the group because of a shared culture.

Fourth, culture is not something we're born with. Rather, we are born into it, and it is learned. Missiologist David Hesselgrave points out that culture "is not biologically determined or restricted by race."[21] We learn and live our culture as we grow up in our families, schools, churches, and communities. For the most part, we unconsciously assimilate the culture that is lived around us, including all of its rites, habits, rituals, and behaviors. It is what becomes normal to us because "it's always been that way." But in a rapidly changing world full of options that are easily accessed through our globalized media, more and more young people are consciously choosing to adopt and live out cultures that are markedly different from those within which they have been raised.

Fifth, culture is an integrated whole.[22] Like a living organism, every culture is made up of many different parts that are all interrelated; it is an ecological system. Add a new ingredient, eliminate a component, or change something ever so slightly, and the entire composition is altered. Each part affects the others. If a culture places high value on human life, that value will be reflected in human relations, in conflict resolution, in medical practices, in how business is conducted, and so on. If humanity is devalued, that will be reflected in attitudes and behaviors related to issues like abortion, euthanasia, treatment of workers, friendships, and so on. The responsibility of the cultural observer is to discover and understand each part of the cultural soup and how those parts combine and relate as a whole.

Sixth, culture isn't static. In a rapidly changing world, cultures will not only grow, change, evolve, and develop, but they also will do so at a faster and faster pace as the years go by and the rate of change continues to accelerate. Cultures will develop new elements on their own, assimilate elements of other cultures, and discard those elements that are either outdated or no longer necessary. Consequently, those who desire to understand the culture of the emerging generations can never assume that their job is a once-and-done endeavor. It is an ongoing process that requires continued and diligent observation on a day-to-day basis. While we may stand in the same spot in our yards day after day, the air that we breathe at that spot changes from minute to minute. It's never the same air twice. So it is with culture in our fast-paced world. Every minute brings change.

What Are the Elements of Culture?

As the cross-cultural missionary stirs the soup, there are certain ingredients to look for, examine more closely, and seek to understand. While they might at times seem small and insignificant, these individual ingredients are nevertheless important because they are part of the whole system and can offer us valuable insight into who young people are, how they think, what they value, why they do what they do, and—most important—how we can best reach them with the gospel and then nurture them into integrating Christian faith into all of life.

No doubt the growing list of social media miscommunications occasioned by the cultural ignorance of the older generations who didn't grow up in a social-media-saturated world reveals the need to examine two levels that exist in every culture. Consider this now-famous text exchange (thanks to the viral nature of social media!) between a mother (digital immigrant) and her teenaged son (digital native). Mom: "Your great aunt just passed away. LOL." Son: "Why is that funny???" Mom: "It's not funny David! What do you mean?" Son: "Mom lol means laughing out loud." Mom: "Oh my goodness! I sent that to everyone. I thought it meant lots of love. I have to call everyone back. Oh God."

This simple illustration offers an example of the two levels of cultural ingredients that always exist and the importance of looking for, examining, and understanding both. There is the level of culture that we empirically see, feel, hear, taste, and touch every day of our lives. In this case, it was the texting slang "LOL." But the fact that the same texting slang was used by two different people from two different generations with two different meanings reveals a deeper level of culture. That second level is the unseen foundational level that lies beneath the outward expressions that we encounter every minute of every day. It is the level of underlying meaning. Foundationally, the mom used "LOL" as she understood the abbreviation in the vocabulary of her culture—to indicate to her son and other relatives that she was concerned for them in the midst of hearing this grievous announcement. To her son, "LOL" not only meant something entirely different, but it was also entirely inappropriate in light of Aunt Martha's death!

Our examination of *both* levels of cultural elements helps us both to understand the meaning of the outward expressions of another culture that are unfamiliar to us and also to understand and address the tension that exists when the same expression—whether a word, behavior, or texting slang—is used and understood by different people from different cultures in different ways.

Cultural analyst Patty Lane likens these two levels to an iceberg. The "objective culture" or visibly expressed parts of the culture are the part of the iceberg that can be seen above the surface of the water. The hidden aspect that lies beneath the surface of the water is what Lane calls the "subjective culture."[23] As I have looked, examined, and analyzed youth culture over the years, I have found it helpful to understand these two levels of cultural elements this way: the underlying level of a culture is best described as a "worldview,"[24] and the visible upper level of a culture that expresses that underlying worldview is best described as what the "world views" when they observe people from that culture living out their lives every day. What then are the distinctives of each level?

What lies beneath, at the level of worldview, is the "subjective culture," which is made up of the values, attitudes, assumptions, beliefs, knowledge, and ideologies held by the people in that culture. As one who studies youth culture I want to stir up the soup young people swim in every day and seek to understand what they believe—either consciously or unconsciously—about God, humanity, life's purpose, relationships, and so on. I want to seek to discover how they are answering the basic worldview questions.[25] What lies beneath at the level of worldview supports, guides, and defines everything that lies above. "This is the internal part of culture that drives or motivates the visible, objective culture."[26]

Above the worldview level is the level of what the "world views." This is the culture that is expressed in daily life. It includes everything we do, everything we make, and how we do and make it all. Because it is more visible, it's easier to recognize and describe, but it can be puzzling, strange, and difficult to understand. Sometimes our assumptions about the meaning beneath what we see can be totally off base, thereby jeopardizing our ability to connect. Lane refers to this dangerous practice as "misattribution." It's that tendency to assume or assign our own sense of meanings and motives to someone's behavior or objective culture based on what we think those meanings or motives are.[27] If we fall into that easy-to-fall-into trap, our ignorance will cause us to miss the mark on what those meanings and motives really are. To fully understand the meaning of the objective aspect of culture that the world sees, we have to know the underlying worldview, or subjective culture. With time and practice spent observing culture and asking the right questions, we can begin to learn how to use the objective cultural expressions that are seen to help us discern and understand the underlying unseen worldview. The seen and unseen are interrelated, and both must be understood. When approached and examined together, they can help us to understand the emerging generations with a depth and accuracy that will open doors for communicating God's good news in ways that can be heard and understood by our young audience.

One example that illustrates how this reality works out in life is tattoos. For the most part, the members of the older generations in our churches grew up in world where tattoos were relatively rare in the mainstream culture. Tattoos were limited mostly to the subcultures of bikers and combat vets. Not so in today's world. Tattoos have gone mainstream. However, many in the older generations look at the objective culture inked onto the bodies of those who are young and have no idea what they mean or why they have them. Based on my own observations of adults, we sometimes view tattooed young people negatively or with scorn. At first glance, some might think that the markings are repulsive, meaningless, faddish, or something that will cause regret later in life. In some cases this might be true. But usually we have fallen into the trap of misattribution, and we haven't even come close to understanding tattooed young people, their lives, and their culture. If the older generations would take the time to probe deeper by asking about the underlying meaning of someone's tattoos, they would be able to establish rapport with those who are tattooed and learn so much more about them and their lives.

Ask some young people about their tattoos. Their eyes will light up with excitement. Our question and their response indicate two realities. First, it says "I have an interest in you." They know that I care enough about them to take the time to let them speak, to listen, and to understand. Second, it tells me that their tattoos mean something important to them. When it comes to tattoos, every picture *does* tell a story; we need to ask questions and then listen. More and more young people are telling their stories—their subjective culture—through the visible and objective culture on their bodies. Once we know the story, we are better able to speak the gospel to the real issues, questions, needs, and brokenness that exist. Consequently, our audience will be able to hear and understand. If we try to talk to our young people before listening to their reality we will, as Francis Schaeffer has said, "only beat the air."[28] Schaeffer writes, "We must realize that we are facing a rapidly changing historical situation, and if we are going to talk to people about the gospel we need to know what is the present ebb and flow of thought-forms. Unless we do this, the unchangeable principles of Christianity will fall on deaf ears."[29]

The subjective worldview of the emerging generations is being expressed in their objective culture in a variety of ways and through a variety of channels. As we seek to understand and reach the emerging generations, we must look for and analyze those channels of behavior and expressions that will give us further insight into who young people are, how they think, and how they live in the world. The following list, while not exhaustive, highlights a few of the main visible and objective ingredients in the youth culture soup that warrant attention as we seek to understand and reach young people. Like tattoos, each can give us great insight into young people, their worldview, and their culture.

- Language and slang
- Race
- Ethnicity
- Socioeconomic status
- Geographic location
- Gender
- Physical condition (disabilities, etc.)
- Religious heritage, preferences, and practices
- Mannerisms and gestures

- Dress and clothing style
- Facial expressions
- Habits
- Social organization and hierarchy
- Apps
- Social media sites
- Music
- Movies
- Books
- Television shows
- Musical preferences
- Automobiles or other modes of transportation they use
- Hobbies and interests
- Extracurricular activities
- Heroes and role models
- Art
- Jobs
- Peer group
- Favorite websites
- Magazines
- Piercings, tattoos, body markings
- Food
- Favorite place(s)
- Observable patterns of behavior
- How money is spent
- How time is spent
- Social activism

How Does Culture Function in the Lives of Kids?

I spent a good portion of my childhood summers swimming in the neighbor's pool. By the time my mom would call me out of the pool and home for dinner, you could see the effects of being in the water for hours all over my body. My eyes were red, my skin was shriveled, and my head was clogged from the time I had spent underwater.

Swimming in the soup of today's youth culture isn't any different, except that our kids are in the "water" twenty-four hours a day. It affects every square inch of their lives in powerful ways. To assume that culture has no influence or function in their lives would be to make a mistake that would lead us to misunderstand who they are and ultimately forfeit our ministry effectiveness. What are the influences, effects, and functions of culture that we need to understand as we shape our cross-cultural ministry approach to the emerging generations?

Culture Is a Map

I remember one of my college professors—a man who had served for many years as an overseas missionary—telling us a story about one of the clashes he experienced as an American living as a foreigner in another culture. One day as he was walking down the street, he saw a man blowing his nose in a curious and strange way, which he had seen many others doing as well. My professor watched as the man stopped walking, leaned forward, covered one nostril with his thumb, and proceeded to exhale hard through his other nostril, emptying the contents of his sinuses right there on the busy sidewalk. This time, his curiosity—and disgust—finally got the best of him. When the man was done, my professor walked up to him and boldly asked in the native language, "Excuse me, sir. Why is it that you blow the contents of your nose onto the sidewalk? I find that to be unhealthy and rather repulsive." The man looked at my professor and responded, "That's not repulsive at all. What's

repulsive is what you Americans do. Why do you blow it into a rag and carry it around in your pocket all day?" Both saw the other as odd, while each was doing what they had been taught was normal.

The story serves as a simple illustration of how each man had been taught the "proper" and appropriate way to tend to a runny nose by his respective culture and the powerful role the culture played in teaching him how to live his life. Their cultures had functioned (as all cultures do) as maps, pointing them down the "roads" and to the "destinations" of what was accepted and normal in each particular culture. That didactic role and function of culture exists everywhere in all cultures, and it is especially strong in the lives of children and teens.

The power of culture to teach and shape the young is always strong and significant because of where young people are in the process of physical, emotional, intellectual, social, and spiritual development. On a journey from point A, the dependence of childhood, to point B, the independence of adulthood, the emerging generations are on a quest to discover the meaning of life and find answers to the questions they have about life. Living in the midst of a developmental period marked by more earthshaking change and uncertainty than they'll ever experience again in their lives, they wonder what is happening to them, where all the change is leading, and where they will wind up. Consequently, they are constantly looking consciously and unconsciously for a map to guide them along the way. The map that unfolds before their eyes in today's world is the map of their 24-7 youth culture. The map functions as an effective teacher, telling them how to think, what to think, and how to live in the world. The culture defines and shapes their reason for getting up in the morning and guides their decisions on how to spend their day once they're out of bed.[30]

In effect, culture is *directive* in that it serves to transmit "the meaning life should have for people."[31] It is an inescapable fact that we are all products of our culture, and the young are no exception to this rule. It would be a great mistake to miss the simple fact that they are passing through the change-filled period of life that leaves them most open and vulnerable to the influence of culture. Culture's influence on them during their teenage and young adult years will shape the way they view the world, relate to the world, and live the rest of their lives.

While culture's mapping influence is always strong, our current globalized and technology-driven culture has created an environment in which the volume has been turned up on culture's power to shape and teach the emerging generations. In today's world, elements of popular culture such as music, media, marketing, and digital technology increasingly fulfill this directive role, which has been abandoned by parents who are either physically absent by choice or circumstance from their children's lives or emotionally and/or spiritually detached because they take little or no interest in the emotional and spiritual nurture of their kids.

Because of their nature and developmental stage, children and teens are like sponges. This fact can be seen in Deuteronomy, where God charges parents and the community to live out his commandments and to "impress them on your children" by talking about them everywhere and at all times (Deut. 6:4–9). But when parents and the community fail to fulfill these "mapping" responsibilities in a deliberate and unified manner, the lessons concerning a biblical worldview can't and won't be heard.

Of course, even though the lessons are absent, young people continue to probe, question, and learn. They seek out maps and teachers who speak to their needs. In his ongoing analysis of media, George Gerbner has found that its power to teach young people has increased vigorously in recent years. He says, "For the first time in human history, the stories are told not by parents, not by the school, not by the church, not by the community or tribe and in some cases not even by the native country but by a relatively small and shrinking group of global conglomerates with something to sell."[32] Those conglomerates reach out through the expansive media network for the purpose of generating profit. They do so through advertising products to a generation they have targeted because that generation is loaded with disposable income. Not only are the conglomerates selling product, but they are also selling a worldview and a way of life that will live on in the hearts and minds of young people long after the product has been used and forgotten.

In centuries past, this "mapping" function of guiding the young into what to believe and how to live was an essential part of Christian education, which took place in both the home and the church community. Adopted children of God who were older and more mature in their faith took seriously their responsibility to deliberately and carefully teach, nurture, and equip the young among their number. Though not always consistent, the history of the church recounts how those who were converted to the faith and adopted into the family of God were nurtured in the faith "carefully, prayerfully, and intentionally, with thorough understanding at each stage" of life.[33] This educational "mapping" process is known as *catechesis*, a word derived from the New Testament word for teaching, *katēcheō*. "The primary definitions of this term are 'to share a communication that one receives' and 'to teach, instruct.' Its overtones point to the weight and solemnity of the instruction being given."[34] J. I. Packer and Gary Parrett define the task of catechesis as "the church's ministry of grounding and growing God's people in the gospel and its implications for doctrine, devotion, duty, and delight."[35]

When the church and home do not intentionally engage in answering the questions of curious young people in ways that will shape them as Christians while grounding them in the gospel for life, young people will still long for and look for answers. In other words, they will seek out and find surrogate teachers and instructors. Because the culture is omnipresent, pervasive, attractive, enticing, and powerfully convincing, it is the culture that will shape their lives. In other words, catechesis will always take place for the simple reason that kids are like sponges. When the church and home aren't doing the catechizing, the culture will assume that role, offering a 24-7 education that maps out belief and behavior for kids.

Consequently, this is why we need to embrace Barth's idea of Bible and newspaper and Stott's practice of "double listening." We need to know both Word *and* world. On a practical level, we must read what our kids read, watch what they watch, and listen to what they listen to. This practice of examining their cultural soup allows us to see how the culture is mapping life. Next, it is our responsibility to respond by either affirming the cultural map's directions because it conforms to God's will and way or challenging and correcting the cultural map because it is sending them in the wrong direction.

Theologian Darrell Guder gives some guidance when he says that the role of Christians as we interact with other cultures is not primarily to identify the visible characteristics (the objective aspects that the worldviews) of a culture and then apply Christianity to it. The "primary issue, instead, is to identify, name, and critique the ways in which various social realities form or make—cultivate—a people."[36] In other words, we are not only to come to an understanding of the visible, objective scenery of what lies along the way as the map of culture serves to direct the path of young people, but we also must discover *where* it's sending them and *how* it's telling them to get there. We must ask, "How is culture shaping them, and what is it teaching (catechizing) them to think and live? How is it shaping their worldview?"

What the map of culture teaches is a way of life. It is our responsibility as cross-cultural missionaries to deconstruct the map and understand how it guides the young each step of their way. To know their map is to know them. Then, and only then, can we enter their lives with a truly Christian response that answers their questions, affirms what's right with the culture, challenges what's wrong, and thereby correctively guide their steps in line with the map of a biblical world and life view.

Culture Is a Mirror

My friend Denis Haack understands the reflective power of culture. He writes that one of the reasons Christians should be monitoring, observing, and understanding culture is that it can be "a window of insight into a worldview we do not share."[37] I like to envision myself standing behind young people as they look into the mirror—or window—of their culture. As I look over their shoulders at the reflection of their lives I want to look at *their* art, music, advertising, social media, and film, as well as all the other elements of culture mentioned earlier in this chapter. It is especially helpful to look at their habits and observable patterns of behavior, as these offer us great insight into who they are and what they believe. What is reflected back helps me to understand them at a deepened level.

Haack encourages us to actively seek out these "windows of insight" and mirrors into cultures with different worldviews for two reasons.

> First, it will give us information about that worldview, about the ideas and values which it contains, and second, it will help us to see life from the perspective of that worldview. If we are to understand those who don't share our deepest convictions, we must gain some comprehension of what they believe, why they believe it, and how those beliefs work out in daily life. In other words, a window of insight allows us a tiny glimpse inside a worldview we do not share.[38]

Understanding the reflective power of culture and its ability to function as a mirror can serve us in powerful ways as we seek to understand values, attitudes, trends, behaviors, and ideas that have taken hold of the emerging generations and their culture. In addition, by viewing and using young people's culture as a mirror, those called to minister cross-culturally to the emerging generations will raise their level of understanding of how their own culture has functioned specifically in their lives as a map. It's another way that we are able to increase our ability to listen and understand. Once we have listened to both Word *and* world, we can bring the light of God's Word (through our teaching and modeling) to either correct or affirm the cultural messages.

Culture Is Always Moving and Never Neutral

While culture is never neutral regarding where it comes from (it always references a worldview), it is also never neutral in terms of where it's going. Just like his human image bearers, God created culture as something good. And just like humanity, culture is marred and polluted as a result of the fall of humanity into sin. Paul tells us that creation joins humanity in "groaning" for redemption and liberation from its "bondage to decay" (Rom. 8:18–23). Until that time of ultimate and final redemption comes, culture and all its elements will be involved in a process of pushing and pulling as its elements, values, attitudes, and behaviors either reflect and bring glory to the kingdom of God or reflect and bring glory to the world, the flesh, and the Devil. As C. S. Lewis describes this reality, there is "no neutral ground in the universe: every square inch, every split second, is claimed by God and counterclaimed by Satan."[39]

Theologian Albert Wolters offers helpful clarification as he differentiates between "structure" and "direction." Wolters says that "structure refers to the order of creation, to the constant creational constitution of any thing, what makes it the thing or entity what it is."[40] When the "thing" we're talking about is "culture," we understand its structure to be something positive and good. In its substance, essence, and nature culture was brought into existence by God at creation as part of his perfect created order. "Direction, by contrast, designates the order of sin and redemption, the distortion or perversion of creation through the fall on the one hand and the redemption and restoration of creation in Christ on the other."[41] In other words, all the ingredients in the cultural soup (language, art, social media, apps, books, etc.), all societal institutions (schools, corporations, marriages, churches, families, etc.), and all human functions (emotions, sexuality, rationality, etc.) are marked by the fingerprint of the Creator *and* the fingerprint of the fall. As a result, they are moving in the direction of either obedience or disobedience to his law. They are never neutral. "To the degree that these realities fail to live up to God's creational design for them, they are misdirected, abnormal, distorted. To the degree that they still conform to God's design, they are in the grip of a countervailing force that curbs or counteracts the distortion."[42]

As we look at the culture of the emerging generations, every element must be viewed as a map and a mirror. In addition, we must go a step further and discern, under the authority of God's Word, between those ingredients in the soup that are moving in a direction away from God's order and design, which must be renounced, and those that are worth retaining, transforming, and enriching because they are moving in the direction of God's order and design for the world.[43]

I have encountered the complexity of this task repeatedly in my years of speaking to people about contemporary youth culture. I usually encounter the greatest amount of resistance, protest, and disagreement when I show an audience of Christian adults a music video or film clip from the culture of the emerging generations. As you can imagine, the experience forces many adults out of their cultural comfort zone.

In the early 1990s I began showing a powerful music video, "Jeremy," from the band Pearl Jam. To this day, the video is not only relevant but also listed consistently as one of the top-five music videos of all time. The song and video tell the horrible story of a struggling

thirteen-year-old boy who is cut off relationally from his parents and peers. His parents constantly fight, and they fail to give him the attention and love he needs. In school, his peers make fun of him and pick on him every chance they get. As the song comes to its ugly climax, the lyrics tell us that "Jeremy spoke in class today." The video shows him "speaking" as the powerless and pained young man takes his destiny into his own hands. He walks into the classroom, throws an apple on the teacher's desk, pulls a pistol from his pants, and proceeds to shoot himself in the head in front of his classmates (the act itself is implied rather than shown).

People wondered what kind of sick and sinful man I was to show such a dark and violent video to a group of adults in a church. Despite the protests, I continued to show the video for years. Why? First, it offered adult viewers a powerful "mirror" experience. The video's popularity and staying power were testimony to the fact that it was putting into words and pictures the reality of many young kids—kids whose cries for love, time, acceptance, and direction were not being heard by adults. In effect, it was a powerful wake-up call.

Second, I always processed the video with adult viewers by explaining that I thought what they had just seen was one of the most powerful and biblical music videos they'll ever encounter. No, Pearl Jam's lead singer and songwriter Eddie Vedder makes no claims to be a follower of Christ. But the song and the video combine in a creative package that truly reflects creative excellence. In that way, Vedder is imaging God. In addition, the song's message clearly shows the downside of what happens when God's order and design for the family is not followed. As a piece of art, "Jeremy" was not neutral. In its direction, it was sending a strong message of truth about God and his design and order for his creation, calling all those who viewed it to see how our sinful, culturally accepted distortions of family and relationships have deep and abiding negative consequences. The message is clear: something is wrong, and it must be made right. The video opens tremendous doorways for discussion regarding the answers to the questions posited by a truly biblical worldview.

What Now? Faith, Culture, and the Family of God

Over my years of ministering to youth and studying culture, I have learned that certain core commitments are essential if we hope to speak the truth and nurture the young among us to live the truth in the midst of our rapidly changing world. I'm convinced that we must embrace and pursue these core commitments—in cooperation with the Holy Spirit—to build the church. They should be part of our individual and corporate makeup, marking every nook and cranny of our lives every minute of every day. Two of these commitments are especially relevant to our current discussion of culture.

A Commitment to Be a Student of the Word

As the emerging generation cries out for redemption, they are not ultimately crying out for a relationship with another human being. They are crying out for a restored relationship with their Creator. It is a cry for adoption. If the crux of my ministry is to point them to that relationship, not only must I be in that relationship myself, but I must also studiously seek to grow in both my knowledge of the One

who has adopted me and my knowledge of myself as an adopted child of God.

After twenty-five years of what most would say was a successful and fruitful ministry, Henri Nouwen came face-to-face with a simple question that caused him to rethink and evaluate every aspect of his ministry: "Did becoming older bring me closer to Jesus?"[44] He says that he found himself praying poorly, living isolated from others, and preoccupied with the tyranny of the urgent. In his words, he felt he was experiencing "spiritual death."[45]

No doubt, each of us has experienced the same struggle at some time and at some level. When we submit ourselves to the painful yet helpful process of self-examination, we begin to see the source of our struggle with greater clarity. We soon realize that not only do we experience spiritual death, but we also begin to lose our missional effectiveness as our passion for Christ and our knowledge of the Savior diminish and disappear. We are left powerless and passionless, with nothing to give.

The antidote is to maintain single-minded commitment as a student of the Word—a commitment that involves three crucial and complementary elements that are characteristics of spiritual vitality.

First, we must prayerfully seek to grow closer to the resurrected and incarnate Word, Jesus Christ. Nouwen says that "Christian leaders cannot simply be persons who have well-informed opinions about the burning issues of our time. Their leadership must be rooted in the permanent, intimate relationship with the incarnate Word, Jesus, and they need to find there the source for their words, advice, and guidance."[46] Nouwen believes the avenue to this intimacy is through the disciplines of contemplative prayer and theological reflection, where time spent with Christ yields the benefit of "thinking with the mind of Christ."[47] Perhaps part of the blame for the ineffectiveness of the church in reaching the emerging generations is rooted in our lack of consistently exercising these disciplines. While we may be taking the time to know the culture and developing well-planned strategies (based on that cultural knowledge) to be relevant, our lifeline will be cut, and our strategies will cause us to connect to young people without life if we are not first and foremost committed to nurturing our own relationship with Christ.

Second, we must prayerfully seek disciplined study of God's written revelation of himself. Not only does God have much to say to us, but his Word addresses our contemporary situation and the unique issues facing the emerging generations. Our theological reflection should focus on systematic and disciplined study of the written Word. The failure to know and study the Scriptures as the truth that serves as the foundation for *all* of life is both a horrible mistake and a recipe for certain ministry disaster and ineffectiveness. Perhaps without knowing it, we have allowed our faith journey to begin and end through a faulty and unconscious literal misunderstanding of Jesus's words to Nicodemus, "You must be born again" (John 3:7), as if birth—or getting "saved"—is all that is required of us. We come to faith but fail to foster and *live* the faith in a consistent, integrated fashion. Marva Dawn speaks to the importance of knowing the written Word in today's postmodern culture if we hope to reach the young: "Raising genuinely Christian children in a culture that rejects as oppressive any comprehensive meta-narrative is NOT a lost cause IF the church stands as an alternative community formed by the meta-narrative of God's revelation to humankind."[48]

Third, I must consciously guard against the temptation to reinvent, redefine, or reimagine the Word in my own image—a mistake encouraged and easily (often) made in our twenty-first-century world. It will become easier and easier to sacrifice true biblical faith and understanding on the altar of relevance as our culture shifts deeper and deeper into a post-Christian worldview. Consequently, we must focus on rediscovering and treasuring the truths of orthodox biblical faith, which continue to be relevant from era to era. Thomas Oden's own spiritual journey from liberalism led him to conclude that classical orthodox Christianity—"the consensual core of beliefs that has been held by a majority of the church throughout the span of its historical existence"—will prove to be a vital source of postmodern orthodoxy.[49]

With the culture catechizing and shaping the thinking, believing, and living of the emerging generations, how can we steer them in the right direction? It starts with our commitment to live in that direction ourselves by being students of the incarnate, resurrected, living, reigning, and written Word. We cannot live, share, or communicate what we do not possess. To lead, we must seek to be led.

A Commitment to Be a Student of Culture

When the apostle Paul finds himself in the unfamiliar pagan culture of Athens (Acts 17), he first walks around the city with his mouth shut and ears and eyes open. He absorbs as much as he can about the culture not only so that he can find evidence of their spiritual hunger but also so that when he opens his mouth to communicate the good news about Jesus Christ he can speak in a language and manner that will invite the Athenians to truly engage with and hear what he has to say. Paul has it right. He realizes that he must not only engage in disciplined study of and reflection on God's written and incarnate Word, but he must also work to intimately know the culture of those to whom he has been called to minister.[50]

Dean Borgman affirms that "theology begins with an awareness of God and with the exegesis of Scripture."[51] It is not enough to simply know the Word, even though it might sound like it's the "holy" and "spiritual thing" to do. We must also know the world. Borgman says, "We often overlook the necessity of an exegesis of culture or world in which we were raised and to which we minister. . . . Theology is a systematic expression of God's Word in a particular time and space."[52] Listening and understanding the unique cultural situation of the audience is a necessary prerequisite to effective ministry, that is, ministry that our audience is willing to listen to and able to understand because they have first been listened to and understood. As Gene Veith says, "To ignore the culture is to risk irrelevance."[53]

Because the culture is changing quickly day by day and is never identical from person to person, group to group, or place to place, cultural literacy is an ongoing process rather than a once-and-done exercise. Even if we find it to be frightening or threatening, we must "stir the soup" and "lift the ladle" regularly. This requires us not only to be aware and wise to the values, attitudes, allegiances, and behaviors of the members of the emerging generations we know and love but also to be aware of what they are reading, watching, and listening to. Then we must engage these elements by reading, watching, and listening to them ourselves. Failing to know the music, films,

television, social media, advertising, magazines, and other expressions of young people will lead to failure in ministry. The current shift in worldviews and the rapidity of cultural change require our diligence in cultural exegesis and cultural awareness more than ever before. Dawn writes that there is ample evidence of our failure to do so: "It seems to me that much of the poor child-raising I observe arises because pastors and parents, churches and communities don't understand what they are up against in their endeavor to form Christian character in young people."[54] Cross-cultural missions theorist Duane Elmer knows that the remedy lies in understanding what they are up against: "The better we are at interpreting culture, the fewer conflicts we will experience, the more we will be able to build authentic relationships, and the greater will be our ability to communicate God's truth."[55]

Our ability to connect with the emerging generations and to establish credibility in their eyes is facilitated through our commitment to diligently work to understand their cultural context. As Myron Augsburger has said, "Unless we so immerse ourselves in the Muslim way of viewing things that we are tempted to become Muslims, we will never reach the Muslim."[56] The same holds true for our approach to the emerging generations. We must be committed to know and understand their culture better than they understand and know it themselves.

Conclusion

Kids are like the rest of us: broken, groaning for redemption, and longing for a place to belong and to call home. For many, their yearning is amplified by the fact that broken family situations and the lack of healthy peer relationships have left them with a huge relational void.

Regardless of whether or not their lives are marked by excessive relational brokenness, all members of the emerging generation are looking for a place to call home and a people to call "family." They want connections, relationships, and community. The larger body of Christ should integrate the emerging generations as it assembles for worship, missions, fellowship, education, and service. In other words, we must stop our destructive practice of implementing programs that separate the body of Christ along generational lines because we believe that the only way to effectively minister to and reach the young is to keep them separate. For example, we must ask ourselves why we are so quick to remove teenagers from the opportunity to worship with the older, wiser, and spiritually gifted brothers and sisters in our congregation. Why do we want to start a separate culturally relevant "youth worship" experience just for students? Doing so robs the body of Christ of its ability to function properly. Do we really believe that the young have nothing to offer the old, and vice versa?

One of my heroes of the faith, Francis Schaeffer, knew all too well the importance of understanding and knowing culture. At times, he was criticized for his engagement with people and their cultures. People would ask him, "Why don't you just preach the simple gospel?" He answered, "You have to preach the simple gospel so that it is simple to the person to whom you are talking, or it is no longer simple."[57]

We are a family, a multicultural family. Let's start listening to each other and living like it.

Thinking Ecclesiologically

Teenagers Becoming Part of the Church

MARK CANNISTER

The topic of this chapter is where our calling in youth ministry firmly resides: the nature and activity of the church (what is called ecclesiology). Dr. Mark Cannister, longtime professor at Gordon College, opens his chapter this way: "Transformation happens most deeply in the lives of teenagers when they are engaged in the broader life of the church and connected to a network of caring adults." As Cannister describes what this means in terms of the church's calling, he helps us to see how the idea of adoption embraces both the nurture of the young by adults as well as the responsibility of the congregation to help young people engage as participants in the community of faith. Making use of Don Coryell's notion of young people as "reservoirs" provides an additional theological foundation for youth ministry as a place of nurture and training as well as contribution and participation.

Unique to this chapter is Cannister's emphasis on the role of the youth ministry's participation with the leadership of the local church through the strategic promotion of practices that enable and enhance adoption (although

he rarely uses the term). The role of membership, for example, is a case in point. If you are part of a church or denomination (or even a parachurch organization) where membership is not emphasized, not important, or simply operates differently than Cannister describes, that does not mean this section doesn't apply to you or your ministry. He makes it clear that the meaning behind membership, and therefore any other activities that may signify or encourage inclusion and connection to the body, is an important element of connecting young people to the whole. However a given church formalizes or invites children and teenagers into the relational and participatory community of faith is the responsibility of both the church leadership and the youth ministry leadership.

As you read this chapter, consider these questions:

1. How does my church formalize children, teenagers, and emerging adults' entry into the community? How well is this strategy and structure working to actually accomplish that goal?

2. *How have you seen or experienced a local church or parachurch youth ministry as being a "launching pad of adolescent faith transformation," as Cannister puts it? How intentional is this "launching pad"? Does this particular youth ministry simply hope adoptive ministry will happen or that someone else will do it? What are the critical pieces in play here?*

3. *What does Cannister say is the way to encourage young people to make connections in the church? Do you agree or disagree, and why?*

The movie *Failure to Launch* is a romantic comedy about three men in their thirties who, having failed to take the leap into adulthood, are still living at home with their parents. They are not ready to engage fully in adult society, and in many respects the adult world is not ready to embrace the three of them. They simply refuse to grow up and embrace the transition from adolescence to adulthood.

This transition is less mysterious than once imagined. The reality is that *we are who we were*, and our faith commitments tend to follow a rather predictable pattern. The research of the National Study of Youth and Religion, led by Christian Smith, found a significant amount of religious stability and continuity among those moving from adolescence to emerging adulthood. Even those who are likely to decline in their religiosity as young adults can be identified in the adolescent years by observing key factors related to religious decline. Smith notes that

> the lives of many teenagers who are transitioning into the emerging adult years reflect

a lot more religious stability and continuity than is commonly realized. Everything simply does not change. The past continues to shape the future. This is important to know, because it means that religious commitments, practices, and investments made during childhood and the teenage years, by parents and others in family and religious communities, matter—they make a difference.[1]

While Smith identifies several factors that contribute to high levels of faith among emerging adults, personal relationships with adults (parents and other caring adults) who connect teenagers to the faith community in the middle and high school years are necessary in almost all cases.[2] Further, Lisa Pearce and Melinda Lundquist Denton found that teenagers who were the most committed to their faith reported that, in addition to having parents and close friends who shared their beliefs, they were also connected to a faith community that provided "a welcoming, challenging atmosphere that *values and integrates youth*."[3]

Transformation happens most deeply in the lives of teenagers when they are engaged in the broader life of the church and connected to a network of caring adults. This is not meant to minimize the role of student ministries, which are the launching pads of adolescent faith transformation. Nothing is more reflective of healthy student ministries than students who launch into the full and robust life of the church. For this to happen, however, the broader church must be prepared for and committed to receiving teenagers into its midst by valuing them for who they are and allowing them to contribute to the whole life of the church. This perspective is very countercultural, as few institutions embrace the notion of allowing students to contribute to the adult world.

Dave Coryell suggests that most churches view students from one of three perspectives: as rocks, receivers, or reservoirs.[4] Churches that view teenagers as *rocks* do not see much, if any, value in their young people. Adolescents are understood to be adults-in-waiting who must patiently wait their turn to take on significant roles in the church. Their opinions on leadership decisions in the church are not valued, and they typically have few meaningful relationships with adults. Worship services in these churches are rarely designed to engage or involve teenagers.

Churches that view teenagers as *receivers* foster a culture of "passing it on," which places adolescents as recipients of the church programs, values, norms, ethics, traditions, and beliefs. Students become static receptacles of the church's teachings and are offered few, if any, avenues of contribution outside the student ministries programs. While there is much for teenagers to learn, faith formation requires contribution and involvement that is more significant than a faith passed down from the previous generation.

Churches that view teenagers as *reservoirs* understand that students have much to contribute to the life and ministry of the church. Adults in these churches are willing to build relationships with teenagers and invest the time necessary to develop their gifts and talents, encouraging them to contribute in nearly every aspect of church life. In this sense, students are contributing and connected to the life of the whole church.

Making Connections

In our technological society, life is predicated on connections. We are constantly connecting with people via text messages, cell phones, email, video chats, and Facebook. As long as these connections remain viable, all is well, but as soon as a network drops a call or a server goes down we feel helpless and disconnected. All of this technology certainly makes connecting easier, when it works, but it also has the potential to proliferate superficial connections.

Our technology certainly keeps us connected with more people faster than ever before, but what level of connection is being maintained? Is the church increasing or decreasing in its ability to live out the "one another" passages in Scripture? More than fifty times following the ascension of Christ, the Scriptures remind God's people how to live in community with one another as the early church is being established. For example, we are called to accept (Rom. 15:7), admonish (Col. 3:16), build up (Eph. 4:29), care for (1 Cor. 12:25 KJV), comfort (1 Thess. 4:18 KJV), confess to (James 5:16), be devoted to (Rom. 12:10), encourage (1 Thess. 5:11), fellowship with (1 John 1:7), forgive (Eph. 4:32), greet (Rom. 16:16), honor (Rom. 12:10), love (Rom. 13:8), pray for (James 5:16), serve (Gal. 5:13), and submit to (Eph. 5:21) one another.

Living in community is different today than it was in the early churches of the New Testament era. Life is demanding and fast paced, but in some ways our technology helps us to stay connected and live out these "one another" passages. In other ways, our technology interferes with our ability to live out these commands. No matter where we land in a conversation concerning things that compromise community, it is important to realize that we are not the first generation to struggle with the issue. As the author of Hebrews encourages the Hebrews to persevere in their faith, he emphasizes the importance of community. "Let us hold unswervingly to the hope we profess, for he who promised is faithful. And let us consider how we may spur one another on toward love and good deeds, not giving up meeting together, as some are in the habit of doing, but encouraging one another—and all the more as you see the Day approaching" (Heb. 10:23–25). Staying connected is essential to caring for one another, and churches that care for one another are churches in which people are connected to one another in authentic and meaningful ways.

For students to become connected to the whole church, the whole church must highly value community. Many churches, large and small, work tirelessly to ensure that everyone feels connected and welcome in the faith community. For churches of only a few hundred people this is easier, as everyone knows everyone and gathering the whole fellowship together in one place is not too difficult. Churches that number more than a thousand people tend to develop small groups, regional groups, or some kind of community-group system that helps people to connect with others who live in close proximity, are in a similar stage of life, or are interested in similar issues. There are myriad strategies for fostering fellowship in large churches, and most make community development a priority because of how easily people can fall through the cracks in the setting of a large church.

Churches that are most at risk for failing in the area of fellowship are those in the five- to eight-hundred-persons range. These churches, which are often growing fast, have outgrown the small, family-church size in which connection and community happen almost naturally. But they may not have realized that people are falling through the cracks. Once they begin pushing the one-thousand-persons size, it will become obvious that a community strategy is essential. In the meantime, they are in danger of believing that everyone is connecting as if they are still a small, family church.

To place a high priority on connecting students to the larger congregation, the church must be committed to the value of community and "one anothering" among its adults. Such modeling is essential to the success of inviting adolescents into the fellowship of the whole church. Once a church has established a deep commitment to community, the assimilation of adolescents becomes the responsibility of the entire community, the whole pastoral staff, and all parents of teenagers. This is not an endeavor that can be executed by the youth minister alone.

Making connections usually begins in the student ministry itself, as faithful adult leaders connect with students. It is essential that these connections happen not only at the regularly scheduled programs but also between programs. Adults make connections with teenagers by demonstrating a curiosity about the interests of teenagers. This type of relational ministry is often the lifeblood of student ministries, yet it doesn't always translate to assimilating students into the life of the broader church. Assimilating teenagers into the whole life of the church requires making connections with multiple adults who will speak into their lives in a variety of aspects of the church.

Many teenagers already have multiple adults in their lives. They have teachers, coaches, youth leaders, scout leaders, and music teachers. When my daughter was in high school she regularly connected with her small group leader at church, her flute instructor, her track coach, her yearbook adviser, and her Young Life leaders, all of whom are wonderful role models and most of whom are Christians. They are not all part of our church community, and there is nothing wrong with that. But what if there were another two or three or four adults from our church with whom she was connected as well? There were, and I will talk about them a little later. Each of these connections, large and small, helps teenagers to feel engaged and connected to the local congregation that is their church home.

Consider for a moment the places in which teenagers make connections with adults on a Sunday morning at church in addition to the student ministries venue. Perhaps each week at the front door they shake the hand of the same greeter, who knows them by name. Perhaps they sit in the same seat of the sanctuary each week with family or friends, surrounded by the same adults who know them and who offer a friendly inquiry into the happenings of their week.

A few times every year most churches baptize or dedicate children, depending on the tradition of the church. The occasions are marked by the joy of parents and grandparents, the endearing innocence of babies, and often the baby's surprised reaction to the experience. One aspect common to all such rituals involves asking the congregation a question, and the question is always something like: "Will you promise to love, support, and care for these children as they live and grow in Christ?" To which the congregation gives a rousing: "We will!" But do they? And how? Unfortunately, if you asked most church members to name the children they had promised to love and support, they would be at a loss for words.

But what if, in that moment, rather than everyone in the congregation (especially a large congregation) pledging to love and support every child, a small handful of adults pledged to love and support one child, or one adult small group pledged to care for one child

and his or her family? Children's baptism and dedication pledges were designed in the context of small, family-style congregations and still function well in that context. Larger churches, however, need to consider adapting these pledges for their context in such a way that it is truly meaningful. Imagine a family coming forward with their child *and* ten or fifteen other adults and children who compose their life community or small group, who commit to walking alongside this child in faith for the next two decades.

Connecting children and teenagers to a broad range of adults in the church must be done with great intentionality. But connections alone are not enough. While it feels very supportive for students to be known by other adults in the congregation, formation of individuals and communities requires contribution. When teenagers matter and student ministry is a priority of the church, students are afforded opportunities to contribute to the whole life of the church.

Making Contributions

After every big win, the stars of a sports team always say the same thing: it was a team effort, and everyone contributed to this win. Sure, some players may contribute more than others, but in order to win in team sports, everyone must contribute. This is not just a phenomenon in sports. The same is true in the arts. There may be lead actors in a play or musical, but the whole cast contributes to the performance. Leonard Bernstein, the great conductor, was once asked which instrument in the orchestra is the most difficult to play. His quick-witted response was "second fiddle." Bernstein went on to explain that he had no problem recruiting people to play first violin, but finding someone to play second violin or second trumpet or second flute with as much enthusiasm was always a challenge. Yet if nobody played second, there would be no harmony in the music.[5]

Every instrument contributes to the majesty of a concert. Every player contributes to the beauty of a game. Every believer contributes to the splendor of the church. Without the contribution of every person of every age group, gender, ethnicity, and stage of life, the church does not radiate her full splendor as the bride of Christ. It is as though players have been left on the bench or musicians have been left backstage, and while the spectators may not notice their absence, the coach and conductor are keenly aware of the deficiency. Coaches and conductors quickly recognize when something is missing from their group because they understand what a complete team or orchestra looks and sounds like. I fear that we have forgotten what the splendor of church looks and feels like because we have segregated age groups for so long. We have accepted a new definition of normal in which children and teenagers are spectators in most settings and contributors only in their age-appropriate contexts. Sometimes children and teenagers remain spectators in their age-appropriate contexts as well.

Allowing teenagers to contribute is not only important for the faith formation of adolescents; it also benefits the entire community and the faith formation of everyone who is a part of it. We hear this truth whispered on a regular basis from volunteers in children's and student ministry when they say, "I get more out of teaching Sunday school than I give"; "I learn more from the teenagers in my small group than they learn from me"; "Those young people keep me young at heart." These are testimonies to the mutual contribution that is apparent in our lives. A few moments of reflection brings a sea of examples of the ways in which people younger, older, and peers contribute to our lives. Theologian Marcia Bunge reflects on the important contributions children make to adult faith formation:

> Many Gospel passages turn upside down the common assumption held in Jesus's time and our own: children are to be seen but not heard; and the primary role of children is to learn from and obey adults. In contrast, the New Testament depicts children in striking and even radical ways as moral witnesses, models of faith for adults, sources or vehicles of revelation, representatives of Jesus, and even paradigms for entering the reign of God. . . . Viewing children as models for adults or vehicles of revelation does not mean that they are creatures who are "near angels," "closer to God," or "more spiritual" than adults. However, these passages [Matt. 18:2–5; 19:14] and others do challenge parents and other caring adults to be receptive to the lessons and wisdom that children offer them, to honor children's questions and insights, and to recognize that children can positively influence the community and the moral and spiritual lives of adults.[6]

Bunge further suggests,

> The idea that children can be teachers, bearers of revelation, or models of faith has often been neglected in Christian thought and practice. However, throughout the tradition and today, we do find theologians who have grappled seriously with these New Testament passages, forcing them to rethink their assumptions about children and exploring what adults learn from them. For example, Friedrich Schleiermacher emphasized that adults who want to enter the kingdom of

God need to recover a childlike spirit. For him, this childlike spirit has many components that we can learn from children, such as "living fully in the present moment," being able to forgive others, or being flexible.[7]

The church is a wonderfully multifaceted community in which there is great opportunity for individuals of all ages to contribute. When I was a teenager, my family belonged to a church that had blended services long before blended or contemporary worship was popular. One of the more traditional aspects of the service was the processional in which the choir and clergy marched down the center aisle during the opening song and took their seats on the platform. Teenagers walked in the procession carrying flags and serving as acolytes. One acolyte led the procession with a cross just ahead of the choir while two others served as flag bearers just behind the choir; the fourth acolyte proceeded just behind the flags and in front of the clergy. I remember as a teenager thinking that I was playing an important role in the worship service. No doubt the choir members could find their way down the center aisle and into the choir stalls without me leading them with a cross in hand, but in my teenage mind I felt that the worship service could not begin without me leading the procession. I felt like I was contributing to something important and something larger than myself.

When I was serving as a youth minister, I regularly received calls from people in the church asking whether some teenagers could help with the women's luncheon, the men's breakfast, child care for an event, or the annual fall festival that raised money for missionaries. My response was always the same: "I can think of several students who would do a great job for you. I'll send you a list of their names and phone numbers so that you can contact them directly."

This simple yet strategic response accomplishes several things. First, when youth ministers are constantly asking students to do things, they communicate the subtle message: "He or she only calls me when they want something." That's not healthy for an authentic relationship, and this strategy cuts down on the amount of asking that the youth leader needs to do. Second, this gives other adults in the congregation an opportunity to connect with teenagers. By naming a specific person to contact (not the whole student ministry mailing list), a youth minister is placing a high level of confidence in the student, and the adult's connection to the student will likely be a positive experience..Third, students are empowered when other adults see value in them and reach out to them. Time and time again, I would walk into a youth meeting, and a student would come up to me saying, "You'll never guess who called me last night!" The notion that another adult in the church—worship pastor, children's minister, chair of the women's guild—would ask them to contribute to a church program outside student ministry blew their minds. Students feel valued, empowered, and honored when other adults ask them to contribute to meaningful ventures.

When my kids were teenagers, I worked hard to find ways both large and small for my son and daughter to connect with other caring adults and contribute to the ministries of the church. When they were younger and my wife and I were part of the communion-serving team, we would involve our kids. When we left our seats in worship to acquire the communion trays, they came with us. My wife and daughter would take one aisle as my son and

I took another aisle, moving the communion trays from one row to the next. After the service we all helped to wash the dishes in the church kitchen, along with other adults. This monthly act of service offered a brief, simple, and stress-free moment of connection with caring adults and the opportunity to contribute to the ministry of the church.

Both of my kids know and are known by our pastor of adult discipleship, Doug Whallon, who has nothing to do with the student ministries of the church. Because I regularly taught or hosted an adult Sunday morning class, our family would arrive at church early, and I would ask Kasey and Ryan to help set up the room by distributing handouts around the tables while I fussed with the technology and my wife organized the food. Each Sunday, without fail, Doug (and often his wife, Mary) came by the room, thanking all of us for our service and taking an interest in the happenings of Kasey's and Ryan's lives that week. Each fall Doug and Mary would have a picnic for the adult discipleship committee members *and* their families—yet another opportunity for children and teenagers to connect with adults of the church.

My daughter served with the student worship team in the high school ministry. Every few months, that worship team leads music for the church worship service. This is not designated as a youth Sunday; the high school pastor will not let the teenagers be introduced as if they were guests leading worship. He wants teenagers leading worship to become the norm, not the exception. Students have the opportunity to contribute to worship among their peers in the student ministry as well as to the all-church worship service. This brings a unique life and vitality that would otherwise be absent from the congregation.

My son has been obsessed with acting since he was in elementary school. From time to time the worship arts ministry of our church performs short dramas to frame the sermon, so I asked the drama leader whether she would consider casting teenagers in some sketches. She agreed to give Ryan an audition, and he was cast as an iPhone-wielding teenager in the Christmas Eve drama about a family struggling with the real meaning of Christmas. The role required weeks of rehearsals on Wednesday evenings and performing in five Christmas Eve services over the course of three days. This is a significant commitment, but for several years he was a regular in the Christmas Eve dramas. I am thankful to the worship arts ministry for helping him to connect with other adults in the church and allowing him to make a significant contribution to the most well-attended services of the year.

Other students in our church serve in the nursery, children's ministry, Vacation Bible School (VBS), and the café. From time to time students play in the orchestra in worship. My hope is that as time goes on, other avenues for students to contribute will emerge. There's nothing to wake you up on Sunday morning like a high five from a teenage greeter at the door. And what teenager wouldn't want to tell adults where to park their cars?

Some churches have been even more strategic in assimilating teenagers into the life of the church. From the very start of North Point Community Church in Atlanta, Andy Stanley and his team decided not to offer any programs for high school students on Sunday morning. They have a great high school ministry on Sunday afternoon, but Sunday morning is designed for high school students to contribute to the ministries of the church. Most students contribute to the nursery, children's ministry, or middle school ministry during one hour of the morning and attend the worship service during the other hour of the morning. Their vision for high school students on Sunday morning is for them to serve for an hour and worship with the whole church for an hour.

People often suggest that there simply are not enough roles for all the teenagers to have an opportunity to contribute to the faith community. At Second Presbyterian Church in Memphis, Todd Erickson is so committed to having every teenager contribute to the church that he pulled the staff together and they took the time to identify all the possible areas where teenagers could contribute. Eventually they came up with enough areas that every one of the hundreds of students in their church has the opportunity to make a significant contribution each year. Todd believes that discipleship is an active, not a passive, process and that real success in student ministry is plugging students into the church in such a way that they are contributing to the church family. As in many churches that value the contributions of teenagers, Todd has dozens of high school juniors and seniors serving on the middle school ministry team, with the mentoring of adult volunteers. Freshman and sophomore high school students take responsibility for leading the VBS program under the mentoring guidance of caring adults. These students don't simply show up for a week to serve as counselors. They are involved in the entire ministry development process, beginning with planning meetings in the winter and contributions to creating and implementing the VBS program in the summer. Another group of students leads the sixth-grade transition program, which includes several events throughout the year designed to help kids make a smooth transition from children's ministry to middle

school ministry. They have created a tradition of Tuesday morning prayer groups, which are organized and run by teenagers. The church is committed to a local community program for tutoring the refugee population in Memphis, and teenagers are fully integrated into the leadership of that program as well.

Likewise, Jim Byrne at The Falls Church in Virginia seeks every opportunity for teenagers to contribute to the ministries of the greater church body. In the summer, numerous high school students serve as leaders for the middle school day camp operated by the church. In worship services, some students play in the worship band while others serve as acolytes. In this Anglican church, Jim has created an acolyte program that is respected by teenagers and parents alike, raising its level of importance and allure. While in many churches mission trips are segregated by generation, Jim took the forward-looking approach to short-term mission trips by emphasizing family mission trips and mainstreaming students into adult mission experiences. While he occasionally still offers a mission trip just for teenagers, the emphasis is on encouraging people to contribute to church missions as a family, with parents and teenagers experiencing outreach together.

Perhaps the boldest strategic decision Jim made, with the full support of the church leadership, was to eliminate the high school Sunday school class in favor of offering students opportunities to contribute to the Sunday morning experience. Students serve in the children's ministries, set up various rooms for Sunday morning programs, and direct traffic in the numerous parking areas surrounding the church.

When students contribute to the church, they become an authentic part of the family, and once you are part of a family, you go where the family goes. One of my mentors taught me long ago that people do something for one of two reasons: either it's fun or it's important—and fun never lasts! While there's nothing wrong with using fun and entertainment to engage students in ministry, at some point ministry, church, and faith have to become important as students genuinely become integrated into the family of God. When I call my kids for dinner, they show up because it's dinnertime, not because of the entertaining meal that is being served. (Sorry, but we don't serve a lot of entertaining meals.) As Erickson says, "When kids are coming to contribute, the church becomes family, and they show up for family dinner no matter what we are serving."[8]

When students are invited to contribute to the life of the church, they are afforded opportunities to put their faith in action and experience meaningful engagement with the broader community of faith. Inviting students into this kind of contribution must be done intentionally, and it is the responsibility of the entire leadership of the church.

Membership Matters

Once upon a time, membership in a local church had its privileges. Members were afforded certain accommodations that were not available to visitors. Old North Church, one of the oldest remaining church buildings in Boston, is famous for its two lanterns, which signaled Paul Revere that the British were heading toward Lexington by sea as he rode his horse through the county warning the patriots. Revere was never a member of Old North Church; his family was Congregationalist, not Anglican. But those who were members in 1775 were able to purchase a pew

for their families. Not unlike purchasing seats for a concert or ball game today, the practice of purchasing church pews assumed that the better the location of the pew, the higher the price. Touring historic churches on the East Coast reveals that church members often owned family pews. Ownership was indicated by a brass medallion, engraved with the family name and affixed to the pew.

Another historic example of privileged membership in the church was the common policy of church members receiving discounted fees for church events. I remember churches offering member prices and nonmember prices for attending VBS as late as the 1970s. One would be hard-pressed to find churches with such a fee structure today. On the contrary, as evangelicalism became more popular, churches began to eliminate as many barriers to attendance as possible. Programs such as VBS became outreach oriented, and everyone was charged the same price or none at all.

Likewise, participation in nearly every aspect of the church has been opened to regular attenders rather than limited to members only. No longer does a person need to be an official member of the congregation to sing in the choir, contribute to the worship team, join a pastoral care ministry, or do almost anything else. In many churches nonmembers can participate and serve in nearly every aspect of the church except on the church board. Even the way churches determine their size has changed from the number of members to the weekend worship service attendance number. Denominational churches often have a greater number of members on the rolls than people in worship, while independent churches often have far more people in worship than they have members. All of this raises the question: Does membership matter?

Anyone who has led a confirmation class or a baptism preparation class for teenagers (depending on your tradition) has faced the question of the relative importance or unimportance of membership for teenagers. Rarely do teenagers see any value in becoming official members of the church, even when they have grown up in the church. Their posture is typically that there is no payoff for them to become members. Why bother to become a member if the only reward is being allowed to vote at the annual congregational meeting? This is a self-centered response, to be sure, but few churches have offered teenagers any other significant reasons to engage in the membership process. When churches ignore the issue of membership, they communicate to young people a poor understanding of theology and a poor understanding of community.

Theologically, membership is about belonging and contributing to a community of faith. Our misunderstanding of the very nature of membership is exposed regularly when we ask one another, "Where do you go to church?" Fundamentally, we must understand that the church is not a place to which we go. The local church is not a building or a location; it is a community of believers committed to the work of God's kingdom. In one of their final gatherings with Jesus, the disciples asked whether he was about to restore the kingdom of Israel. His response was that they were to be his witnesses in Jerusalem, Judea, Samaria, and to the ends of the earth (Acts 1:6–8). They were looking for a Jesus to establish a kingdom, and he said, essentially, "*You* are the kingdom. *You* are the church. *You* are the community of God." The kingdom of God is nothing less than the community of God's people, committed to one another and empowered by the Holy Spirit. Mark Dever describes the importance of church membership:

> A temple has bricks. A flock has sheep. A vine has branches. And a body has members. In one sense, church membership begins when Christ saves us and makes us a member of his body. Yet his work must then be given expression in an actual local church. In that sense, church membership begins when we commit to a particular body. Being a Christian means being joined to a church.
>
> Scripture therefore instructs us to assemble regularly so that we can regularly rejoice in our common hope and regularly spur one another on to love and good deeds (Heb. 10:23–25). Church membership is not simply a record of a box we once checked. It's not a sentimental feeling. It's not an expression of affection toward a familiar place. It's not an expression of loyalty or disloyalty toward parents. It should be the reflection of a living commitment, or it is worthless.[9]

The New Testament never establishes a dichotomy between membership in the church universal—that is, a believer's commitment to Christ along with all believers past, present, and future—and membership in the local church. Once people professed their faith in Christ they were baptized, symbolizing their new life in Christ *and* their commitment to the community of faith. Membership in the early church was never a second step after baptism. When people accepted Christ they also accepted his bride, the church, and they immediately entered into fellowship with other believers in the local church. Today membership has often become an entirely separate process from confirmation or baptism, suggesting that a personal commitment to Christ is more important than a commitment to the community of faith. New life in Christ is viewed as essential, while commitment to the church is seen as optional. This dichotomy further undermines the value of community in the church by creating a system of elitism. When we do not enthusiastically view teenagers as potential members of the church, we communicate that they are not worthy of such a status. This is expressed in the teenager response to the question of why they do not become members of their church: "Because nobody really cares whether I'm a member." Once again, the church becomes another institution in teenagers' lives that is perceived as not caring about them.

Becoming members of the local church upon their profession of faith in Christ is an important aspect of assimilating teenagers into the community of faith. Membership matters for teenagers for a variety of reasons, which require us to rethink membership as an important aspect of the assimilation process.

Taking a Stand

Membership declares before God and others that we are part of a particular local faith community that has been entrusted with the gospel, and it is through the visible church that God expects us to live out our faith. The majority of Paul's letters are written to local congregations or to their pastors. Nowhere in the New Testament are there individuals floating around in "just me and J. C." land. Yet that is exactly what many faithful teenagers are doing because the church has not embraced them as committed, contributing members of their fellowship. Christians have always belonged to a local church, because the visible church is a witness to the invisible body of believers.

Membership provides a visible commitment to Christ and his people in the same way that a marriage covenant provides a greater level of commitment than simply living together. As a wedding ring is a clear and public statement concerning one's identity as a committed spouse, so church membership makes a clear and public statement about one's identity as a committed Christian. This commitment is directly tied to the "one another" passages mentioned earlier. We are called to love, comfort, serve, forgive, admonish, and exhort one another, among other things, but this occurs only among those who are committed to one another in a healthy faith community. Such a community provides a place where we can live out these characteristics of a life in Christ, with real people who have real needs and real problems and real faith. While this often happens within a student ministry group, it must also happen throughout the church. Teenagers must become members of the larger church community, "one anothering" the whole family of God and demonstrating their commitment to the bride of Christ, not just to the youth group.

Living in Obedience

Paul uses the image of the body as a metaphor for the church (1 Cor. 12; Rom. 12; Eph. 4). Being a part of the body requires connection. An arm that is not connected to the body is not part of the body. The family of God is connected to and belongs to one another: "For just as each of us has one body with many members, and these members do not all have the same function, so in Christ we, though many, form one body, and *each member belongs to all the others*" (Rom. 12:4–5, italics added). Membership is a visible sign of being connected to the body and a commitment to obey all that Christ has commanded. Joshua

Harris suggests that the best thing the church does is to bear witness to new life in Christ, and that is best done in community:

> One thing a local congregation does best is to show your non-Christian neighbors that the *new life* made available through Jesus's death and resurrection is also the foundation for a *new society*. By living the Gospel as a distinct community, the church down the street accomplishes the important mission of displaying the transforming effects of the gospel for the world to see. Others won't be able to see this larger picture if we remain detached from each other and go our separate ways.[10]

Scripture contends that believers are to submit to and obey the leadership of the community of faith (Heb. 13:17), and the only people who are charged with being accountable for leading God's people are pastors, elders, and overseers of the local church. Chuck Colson writes, "Of course every believer is part of the universal church. But for any Christian who has a choice in the matter, failure to commit to a particular church is failure to obey Christ."[11] Without being a faithful member of a local church, it is impossible to follow this model of Christian community.

Further, the leaders of the church are instructed to care only for those who have committed themselves to their care and become faithful members of the local church (Acts 20:28). Without making a commitment to a local faith community, it is impossible to function as part of the body and enter into a caring community that provides the accountability essential to fostering faith formation. As Mark Dever suggests,

> The practice of church membership among Christians occurs when Christians grasp hold of each other in responsibility and love. By identifying ourselves with a particular local church, we are telling the church's pastors and other members not just that we are committed to them, but that we are committed to them in gathering, giving, prayer, and service. We are telling them to expect certain things from us and to hold us accountable if we don't follow through. Joining a church is an act of saying, "I am now your responsibility, and you are my responsibility."[12]

This is a countercultural statement that says we are committed to one another and we are more interested in giving than receiving. When this attitude is reversed and membership is more about receiving than contributing, we become a reflection of our consumer-driven culture, focused on engaging others only for what they can do to benefit us. There are few areas of our contemporary culture that challenge students to sacrifice for the good of the community, and the church should take its rightful place at the head of that line. Holding students accountable in a manner that offers grace and truth contributes to their humanity and to the common good of the church and society at large.

Building Up the Body

It is hard to imagine effectively contributing to the growth of a local church as a detached and autonomous attender. The church comprises many people with a variety of gifts and talents for the clear purpose of equipping one another and building up the body of Christ (Eph. 4:11–16). We understand the growth of the church to be the continual transformation of lives as more people come to faith and faithful people are continually sanctified. The strength of the body determines the power of our witness to the gospel. A church that is a strong and faithful body of believers is a powerful witness, while a church that is weak, divisive, and self-centered produces a poor witness. The unity of a faith community is a strong witness of Christian living in a secular culture. Together we proclaim to the world the character of God by loving one another, persevering through tough times, and serving the community at large as the bride of Christ.

Together we grow in maturity by building one another up, challenging one another, and learning from one another, "attaining to the whole measure of the fullness of Christ" (Eph. 4:13). Only then are we no longer susceptible to false teachings and evil temptations. Instead, we become a community marked by Christ and held together by every supporting member as each person contributes to the body of believers.

Intergenerational ministry extends well beyond student ministries and incorporates every generation and all ministry areas of the church. The term *intergenerational student ministry* is an oxymoron; intergenerational ministry must always be owned by the entire leadership of the church and infiltrate the entire faith community.

Thinking Critically about Families and Youth Ministry

ALLEN JACKSON

When it comes to parents and youth ministry, opinions tend to span a single continuum. On one end are the parents, who serve as the primary disciplers of their children; in this context, youth ministry is best when it supports the parental role or even gets out of the way ("youth ministry's job is to support families"). On the other end of the spectrum is youth ministry, whose task it is to represent the gospel to children and adolescents; in this scenario, parents are encouraged to support the work of the church or even get out of the way ("the parent's role is to support the youth ministry"). Allen Jackson, professor at New Orleans Baptist Theological Seminary and longtime youth ministry author and trainer, takes on this conversation by removing the polarity of the positions. With personal (and painful) honesty and thoughtful reflection, Jackson demonstrates that there does not need to be an inherent battle between parents on the one hand and the church (or other Christian youth ministries) on the other. We need each other.

Jackson writes from the perspective of a mountain sage. He is gently casual but well read; he is humble, yet he offers deep insight; he is willing to ask questions as a learner, yet his conclusions land with conviction. In this chapter, we are given the opportunity to hear what various voices are saying as well as a deeper glimpse into what the fuss is about. Yet Jackson allows us to see that we are all in this thing called youth ministry together, that adoption must happen both within families and within larger groups of people, and that the church is called to be unified.

In the course of your ministry, you will likely be handed a job description (at some point) that ignores parents altogether. When you are in the midst of the work of youth ministry—giving talks and lessons, leading trips and small group, recruiting and training leaders, handling budgets and meetings and expectations—it is vital that you keep in mind the reason for this book and the essence of this chapter. The goal of youth ministry is that every young person—every child, every adolescent, every emerging adult—is to be embraced, known, encouraged, and equipped to participate in the body of Christ as a full *participating member by the entire community. Parents matter, as do the elderly, the nursery workers, and the staff. This is our calling.*

As you read this chapter, consider these questions:

1. *How does your experience as a follower of Christ compare with how Jackson describes his son, Steven? What was your parents' relationship to your faith journey, and how did the church encourage/discourage that journey?*

2. *If you had to choose a side, which would you land on: "parents are the primary disciplers of their children" or "the church is the primary discipler of the young"? What are some of the downsides of taking the position you chose over the other?*

3. *What has been your experience of nonparental adults being close to you in your faith formation? What are the hallmarks of your relationship with them? How can we foster the best of those characteristics in ministry to adolescents?*

Steven's Story

Steven was a junior in high school and riding the wave of athletic success and popularity. His adolescent growth spurt had produced dramatic results—he grew almost a foot taller and close to a hundred pounds heavier in less than two years. On an August weekend in 2005, he had a spectacular game in the preseason football "jamboree" and was looking forward to a great year on the gridiron.

His family was intact and traditional. His parents were involved in leadership positions at church. Mom and Dad had been faithful to attend ball games, Bible drill competition, awards ceremonies, and anything else in which Steven was involved. Family time was important, and devotions were common (not so regular as to say they never missed, but regular enough that he would remember that they took place). His dad was a former youth minister and still working in ministry. His mom had been a youth ministry intern and Young Life volunteer in her younger days and remained very active in church.

Steven was very social. He gravitated toward groups of boys and girls who shared his interest in athletics and who went to school with him at the small Christian school he attended in New Orleans. He seemed to take turns between being influenced by his friends and being an influencer among his friends. He had a streak that resisted authority, not unlike his dad, but he rarely got into trouble at school. His coaches were his heroes, and their rules and approval were sufficient to keep him focused on the positive.

He also found a groove in a small group at church. Even though his family was very active at church and Steven went regularly—including the trips, the concerts, the Disciple Now weekends, camps, and retreats—he never bonded with the youth pastor. In his junior year, however, he bonded with his small group leader. He talked about spending time with the group and looked forward to time at church with them and the adult leader who guided the group. It seemed that "Mr. Clint" said all the same things that his family said at home, but when he said them, it was cool.

On that particular August weekend, the Friday football game was followed by the game film on Saturday, but by that time the news and weather folks were talking about a weather event that would affect the New Orleans area.

Her name was Katrina, and she hit New Orleans as a category 3 hurricane on August 29, 2005. The levees that were supposed to protect the city breached, and the entire city was flooded. Like most other students in New Orleans, Steven evacuated with his family. He would not return to his home for a year.

Steven gravitated to a different group of friends in the city to which his family relocated. He attended a new school, lived in a new neighborhood, and worked a part-time job in a different place. He was not as connected with sports, and he met some people who helped him along a path that would result in behavior that his family and church didn't embrace. He would return to his original school for the spring semester, but sports injuries and the instability of most structures in New Orleans meant that his life was not the same. He had changed.

The small group at church would not meet again. Mr. Clint moved permanently to Texas, and the youth pastor moved to Tennessee; the guys in Steven's small group scattered with their families. Whatever impact the group made on Steven's life was minimized by the short time that they were together, yet the impact of being a part of the group was not lost on Steven's family, especially as they reflected back years later.

I will summarize the rest of the story (though it is still being written) by confessing that Steven is my son. His journey into young adulthood included destructive alcohol and drug use, four different colleges, and almost two years in a faith-based rehabilitation program to help deal with his demons. I often wonder whether his life would have been different if the small group had continued to nurture both faith and friendship during that critical junior year. I am grateful to God that as a young adult he seems to have the substance abuse issues under control. However, like so many in his generation, he has only a marginal interest in church and/or spiritual conversations.

As many parents do, I began to beat myself up. Did something go wrong? Did I mess up as a parent? What could I have done/not done? Should the church/youth ministry have done more? How could I have partnered with the youth minister to reach out to Steven? Should I have spent more time with him? Was his attention deficit disorder a factor? I know I cannot answer most of these questions, nor can you if you are a parent who is going through a similar journey. I know that as a youth minister I have dealt with desperate parents who have blamed everything and everyone for the poor choices made by their son or daughter; some spent years in desperate guilt over what they perceived they could have done differently.

How can the church or youth ministry partner with parents who are in pain? What is the role of the church or youth ministry? Is youth ministry, as some have suggested, an outdated and obsolete aspect of church life? I believe that God brings groups of families together in this thing we call church in order to allow us—in community—to worship him and to journey through life in this fallen world.

Help from the Community of Faith

Another story about an adolescent and faith can be found in Luke 2. While most of us consider the nativity to be the main feature in this particular chapter, the events at the very end of the narrative are interesting to me.

Every year Jesus' parents went to Jerusalem for the Festival of the Passover. When he was twelve years old, they went up to the festival, according to the custom. After the festival was over, while his parents were returning home, the boy Jesus stayed behind in Jerusalem, but they were unaware of it. Thinking he was in their company, they traveled on for a day. Then they began looking for him among their relatives and friends. When they did not find him, they went back to Jerusalem to look for him. After three days they found him in the temple courts, sitting among the teachers, listening to them and asking them questions. Everyone who heard him was amazed at his understanding and his answers. When his parents saw him, they were astonished. His mother said to him, "Son, why have you treated us like this? Your father and I have been anxiously searching for you."

"Why were you searching for me?" he asked. "Didn't you know I had to be in my Father's house?" But they did not understand what he was saying to them.

Then he went down to Nazareth with them and was obedient to them. But his mother treasured all these things in her heart. And Jesus grew in wisdom and stature, and in favor with God and man. (Luke 2:41–52)

The reader might not notice that twelve years passed between verses 40 and 41. The Christ child has become the Christ adolescent, and Joseph and Mary have taken him to Jerusalem. At the time, faithful Jewish families living in the kingdom of Judah made three trips to Jerusalem each year (see Deut. 16:16) for the observance of major religious holidays. One of them was Passover, which celebrated the deliverance of the Israelites, under the leadership of Moses, from the Egyptians.

Usually it is noted that Jesus was mature beyond his years; it was only natural that he would be in the temple teaching, even though his parents were frantic over his absence. It intrigues me that he was missing for twenty-four hours before they even thought to look for him. As a parent of middle schoolers, I would have been concerned if I could not locate my children for an hour, much less a day. The key is in verse 44: *Thinking he was in their company, they traveled on for a day.* The phrase "in their company" means that Joseph and Mary thought Jesus was walking home with another relative or friend of the family. They figured he was walking with Uncle Mordecai and talking about the Torah, which was good because it reinforced the lessons they were teaching at home.

What a great reference point for youth ministry. While I admit I may have embellished the narrative, the essence of the verse (which I believe I have put in context) highlights that, according to the traditional Jewish mind-set, the community of faith came alongside parents to help raise children. Samuel was sent to Eli at a young age when his calling was recognized. The wilderness wandering of the Israelites depicts the community of faith traveling together. At the risk of exposing my thesis early, I believe the best possible faith formation environment is a partnership between family and the community of faith. Richard Ross, a passionate voice for students and their families, says, "When church and home link arms in mutual support, teenagers are the most likely to prosper as adults with a lifetime faith."[1]

My first experience in Sunday school came as the result of a man in the church who drove an aging school bus through the neighborhoods to pick up children; my sister and I got on the bus. My parents loved me and provided for me, but church was not a part of our weekly rhythm. I owe my first glimpse of what it means to follow Jesus to a gentleman who got up early on Sunday, put gas in the bus, kicked the tires, and greeted every adult or child who boarded the bus with a smile and a word of encouragement.

My first experience with a youth group was in a small church in Georgia. While I had other ways to get to church besides the bus, I still attended with my sister. Though tiny by mega-standards, my church had adults who stepped forward as youth ministry volunteers. I was "raised" spiritually by adults in the church who treated me like family. I believe I was better for the examples of men and women who volunteered to work with teenagers. My own father was drawn to faith in his later years because he saw the growth of spiritual seeds that had been planted in his children by other adults in the church.

I also know of instances in my church where empty nesters helped young moms—especially single ones—who had to work to make ends meet. In an age of cocooning, it is important for parents to realize that other parental voices are speaking into the lives of their children. Parents instinctively reach out to other adults to help in areas where they feel inadequate—coaches, music teachers, and tutors in higher math—but having a Mr. Clint as a faith mentor or a couple as parenting mentors or a Sunday school teacher who simply validates the spiritual conversation inspires confidence that wisdom is being shared.

Where This Chapter Fits

In a book that is a compilation of the work of a number of contributors, there will likely be some ideas, concepts, strategies, or even research that seem redundant. I apologize ahead of time for any repetition here. The main question that drives me—both from my own story and as a professor in a seminary—is, "What is the best model of interaction between youth

ministry and family with the goal of authentic discipleship?" This chapter is about the context of the church partnering with families in youth ministry. I happen to teach youth ministry at both undergraduate and graduate levels in a seminary. I hear youth pastors describe their ministry settings with regard to families. I desperately wish I had a magic pill or an automatic formula to help them help their churches to see genuine discipleship—incubated in the home, modeled by godly parents, and supplemented by quality spiritual formation at church.

Our task in youth ministry is to join parents in helping students set and reach spiritual (discipleship) goals that complement the academic, social, and career goals that help them to launch. I joke with parents that our job as parents and as youth ministers is to get rid of these teenagers. What if we helped parents articulate goals that finish a sentence that goes something like this: By the time they graduate from high school, they will be able to . . .

- describe their own faith story.
- recognize the value of commitment as a disciple.
- understand how to study and interpret the Bible.
- practice spiritual disciplines.
- develop and demonstrate Christ's character.
- make wise decisions.
- develop godly relationships.
- make an intentional impact on others.

If you are a parent or a youth minister perhaps such a list can be a point of discussion for you and other adults who speak into the lives of your teenagers.

Youth Ministry Takes a Beating

A few years ago, research began to emerge that youth ministry was broken. Most studies indicate that students who had been active in youth ministry, active in church, and active in spiritual practices were still "leaving" the church. The common phrase "what we have been doing hasn't worked" supported the evidence: the church was not retaining students as young adults. Youth ministry was criticized as having become one more source of entertainment with rock-climbing walls, video arcades, and youth rooms that environmentally and technologically rival a nightclub. A major accusation was that youth ministry was being done "in silo," away from the watchful eyes of parents and other church members.

As a professor and youth culture observer, I see that parents bear some responsibility for the detachment and outsourcing mentality of youth ministry. Sure, youth ministers sometimes (in error) feel that they know better than parents how to spiritually nurture youth, but I have been amused to discover the different ways that parents outsource. There are etiquette counselors to coach manners, specialty coaches to train athletes, tutors for academics, and therapists for discipline and anger management.

Also, the vocabulary of "church" and "spirituality" indicate that at least some of these students are disillusioned with organized religion but may have an affinity for God. While the definition of "leaving" is a bit fuzzy (some students left the church but did not necessarily leave their faith), the numbers point to a kind of exodus.

Some studies claim that as little as 4 percent will remain Christian (an oft-repeated but seldom-verified number), while others suggest there's virtually no exodus. The following is a summary of the most-cited studies that point toward the departure from church by the millennials:

- The Southern Baptist Convention's Family Life Council study in 2002 indicates that 88 percent of students leave after high school and do not return to the church.[2]
- A LifeWay Research study in 2007 found that 70 percent leave, although 35 percent eventually return.[3]
- An Assembly of God study indicates that 66 percent of students check out.[4]
- A 2006 Barna study, titled "Most Twenty-somethings Put Christianity on the Shelf . . . ," indicates that 61 percent leave the church.[5]

A fair estimation, according to Timothy Paul Jones, a professor at Southern Seminary, is the LifeWay research assertion that about 70 percent of students who had attended church twice a month or more for at least a year during high school dropped out after high school.[6] Jones also points out that the trend of declining attendance in church among young adults is not new. At least since the 1930s, involvement in religious worship services has followed a similar pattern.

The National Youth Study of Religion was (and is, as of this writing) a massive longitudinal study of American teenagers designed to "enhance our understanding of the religious lives of American youth from adolescence into young adulthood, using telephone survey and in-depth interview methods."[7] Christian Smith, the lead researcher of NYSR, told us that evangelicals "behaved badly with statistics" and quickly dispenses with the 4 percent statistic. Smith and his team conducted extensive research on the spiritual attitudes of American students and published their results in a number of books and articles, including three books and a movie that summarize the attitudes of a generation toward religion and spirituality.[8]

It is beyond the scope of this chapter to go into depth about the study, but the results served as a wake-up call for youth ministry in three major ways. First, the exodus has been confirmed, though not to the extent that some alarmists have pronounced. Too many students detach from the church following their youth group days, though some return as middle-aged adults. Second, too few students possess the devoted mind-set of a disciple. Third, too few families are involved in actively discipling their students, but when they are, devoted discipleship is more likely to occur.

Several books followed the NYSR research: *Almost Christian*, by Kenda Creasy Dean; *Youth Ministry in the 21st Century*, compiled by Rick Lawrence and *Group* magazine; *The Family Friendly Church*, by Ben Fruedenburg and Rick Lawrence; *Rethink*, by Steve Wright; and *Transforming Student Ministry*, by Richard Ross. All of these books are important interpretations of the NYSR, and all agree that in many cases moms and dads have dropped the ball with discipleship; they also agree that outsourcing to the church is not a healthy model for discipleship. Peter Benson, president of Search Institute, in the foreword to *Passing on the Faith* by Merton Strommen and Richard Hardel, parallels the trend in outsourcing at church to that of the modern school system.

Families have extraordinary power to shape the lives of their children. This is so obvious that one would think it unnecessary to say. Unfortunately, a conspiracy of social forces has diminished the influence of family. Take, for example, the importance of a child's educational achievement. Educators know that the highest level of learning occurs when family and school interact as partners, moving in the same direction during a child's educational development. Families create positive learning environments at home—modeling, encouraging, and rewarding learning, while schools respect and encourage this family engagement. The family-school partnership is reinforced by frequent parent-teacher dialogues and parent engagement in school policies and programs. This partnership is essential. Unfortunately, it is also uncommon. National studies tell us that all too often families give away their power and depend on schools alone to promote their children's achievement. And then the finger pointing begins. Teachers blame parents for being too busy with work and personal agendas to be attentive to the family role in learning. Parents blame schools for being out of touch with family pressures. Certainly, the reasons for parents' lack of involvement are complicated. But the reality is that family influence on learning has gone underground; it has become a latent, dormant power. Families' influence on faith development parallels this reality. We know from documented studies and from our own intuition that parents are essential actors in their children's faith journey. Theoretically, congregations should support families in activating and using this power. Just as quality learning results from a strong family-school partnership, family strength results from a solid congregation-family partnership.[9]

Some have suggested that the title of Dan Kimball's book *They Like Jesus but Not the Church* is the rationale for the attitude of some in the emerging adult generation who disdain the politics and the perceived message of "being against" in many churches but who have an affinity for God (or at least a "higher power"). Yet for whatever reason and using whatever metaphor, young adults are leaving the church at least for some period of time. Much of the blame for this trend has been laid at the feet of churches who do youth ministry "in silo" or apart from the dynamics of discipleship within the family.

A Weed in the Church

A movement has arisen in the past few years that sees youth ministry as a harmful element in the discipleship of teenagers, even going so far as to label it as a "weed in the church."[10] According to some who propose a model called the Family Integrated Church, youth ministry *is* the problem. The premise is that age-segregated ministry in general and youth ministry in particular has become a place where the discipleship of students is outsourced. I strongly affirm the criticism of a youth ministry that has a drop-off lane. The last thing that youth ministry needs is to become a place where the discipleship of students is turned over to the experts.

The solution, according to the voices in the Family Integrated Church, is to eliminate age-segregated ministry and return the responsibility of spiritual nurture solely to parents, and especially fathers. I agree wholeheartedly with half of their objective. Parents are the primary disciple makers for their children. Are some youth ministries alienating parents and becoming their own kingdom? Perhaps. Do fathers need to take their duties seriously? Certainly. Should youth ministry and families partner for shared goals? Absolutely.

While this book is a helpful corrective to the abuse of age segregation, I think the greater problem harming youth and families is what both Jon Neilson (a pastor to collegiate students at a church near Chicago) and my children identify: both families and youth ministries have allowed a widespread ignorance of the gospel, Scripture, and the place of a disciple in the world.

What of Those Who Stuck Around?

On a blog post titled "3 Common Traits of Youth Who Don't Leave the Church,"[11] Jon Neilson suggests three characteristics of students who do not leave the church:

1. They are converted.
2. They were equipped and not entertained.
3. Their parents preached the gospel to them.

The post is not necessarily based on research, and an appropriate critique is that Nielson's list is too simplistic. He proposes that if a student is genuinely converted, participates in a youth ministry that equips him or her for service, and has parents who preach (and live out) the message of Jesus, he or she will not leave the church as an emerging adult. However, some of the comments in response to the blog post are as revealing as the post itself. One example:

> Here's why the youth are leaving the churches, they've wised up. They realize the dogma of 2000 years does not apply to them. They are learning that a good, loving God does not need continuous praise or strict adherence to a Book that still can't be translated correctly. Most of all though, kids are leaving the church because they see the hatred that is

spewed from the pulpit against anyone who isn't conforming or might be different. I'm glad the youth are moving away from that sort of strict observance because it's the only way the world will ever come to a census [sic] that will allow everyone to be who they are without retribution and condemnation.

A baby boomer who reads the paragraph above would probably tell the person who left the comment to grow up because the comment is immature and egocentric. However, it points to a major disconnect; it sounds like the person who posted it does not feel like his or her voice is heard or that the things he or she values are valued by the church. The silence of personal involvement is deafening. Where are the pastors, parents, or small group leaders who might have a conversation or a relationship with this person? Perhaps the person has never been to church and is slinging judgments from afar, but it is possible that he or she represents the statistic of those teenagers who gave up on the church.

I kept hearing about the students who left for various reasons, so I decided to conduct some informal research. First, I spent some time with my own two children, asking them about the highs and lows of church for them. They both acknowledged that we had modeled and encouraged involvement in church that went beyond mere attendance. While I admit I did not do everything right as a father, my kids were not outsourced to the church. Yet their observations were astute. They did not really feel challenged to great things like they were in their athletic or theater endeavors. They felt like there was a lot of repetition and that many of the programs or events seemed so similar as to be interchangeable.

Moving on from my own children, I realized that I had students in my classes at seminary who were emerging adults, who were in a generation where the norm was to leave the church or faith of their childhood (if any) and who represented the 10 percent or "devoted" minority of the National Study of Youth and Religion. I also realized that they were an accessible representation of students who did not leave the church or faith of their youth. So I asked them why they stayed. Assuming that seminary students represent young adults with a "connected" faith post–high school, I asked them about things that they connected with their decision to go into ministry.[12]

This was not quantitative data collection but rather a qualitative process in which I listened a lot and tried to find categories. I used a grounded theory approach by which I assigned each student to write an essay about their life from middle school through college. I gave very few guidelines and allowed them to use bullet points, stream of consciousness, and partial sentences—whatever kept the flow of recollection going. I then coded their responses to try to identify the friendship patterns, school configuration, family dynamics, church involvement, and extracurricular activities. My assumption was that I could identify at least some patterns that were different from those of students who did not remain active in their faith.

Their faith stories fell into three categories. Some students had never "strayed" (though some of them went through a "disconnected" or "apathetic" season in their faith journey). Some students had returned from a walk on the wild side (some wilder than others). Some students came to faith after high school.

About 75 percent of them indicated that their parents or grandparents were influential in faith formation. All who indicated that family faith was strong described it as "authentic" or "real," though some described parents as "controlling." About half indicated that "surrogate" or other adults besides parents (extended family, church, community) were spiritually influential. Adult volunteers in youth ministry were often described as "mentors." I rarely heard that church was positive unless friends were mentioned.

Most worked between ten and twenty hours per week in a part-time job or played varsity sports. If family was not the catalyst for faith, then a friend had usually been the influence. "Youth group" was mentioned more positively than "church." All of the young adults who said that they were far from God, either because they strayed or because they were lost, were brought into or back to a vibrant faith by a friend. Even the young adults who never strayed indicated the presence of a spiritual mentor.

Most interesting in my conversations was that ninth and/or tenth grade was pivotal. More than three-fourths of the students indicated that something significant happened in one of these school grades. They wrote statements such as, "I became a Christian at camp"; "I knew I was called to ministry"; and "I knew it was real on a mission trip." From my perspective, it seems as if someone was there to guide them when they were able to process abstract thought in terms of application. If psychologist Jean Piaget is right and concrete thought gives way to the abstract cognitive ability, it is not surprising that these young adults appreciated and accepted the challenges that came from a deeper understanding of what it means to be a follower of Christ.

Finding Balance

As in most things that generate emotional response, it is sometimes difficult to appreciate the merit of positions that seem to be polar opposites. Yet a balanced perspective is both appropriate. It is important to hear the concerns voiced by the Family Integrated Church and at the same time acknowledge that age-segregated youth culture exists in every area of life. A healthy position acknowledges that some youth ministers and youth ministries have alienated families. In an interview with Rick Lawrence in *Group* magazine, Richard Ross says, "It is so obvious to those of us that have been doing this awhile that the family environment around young people is a major variable in how things go for them in adulthood."[13] If students credited parents with spiritual direction, they described parents who *authentically* lived out their faith. A healthy position digs into statistics for accuracy while at the same time being honest about the need for change. Jones writes,

> The news that youth ministry had failed to keep kids connected to the church resonated with these young leaders' existing feelings of frustration. This widespread frustration yielded some very positive results. This frustration fueled the development of healthier ministry strategies than the fun-and-games approaches the youth ministers had inherited. The results included ministry approaches that emphasized discipleship, community, and the cultivation of intergenerational relationships.[14]

Jones edited a book that summarizes the spectrum of youth ministry models regarding youth ministry and family.[15] In summary, "Family-Integrated Ministry" involves an emphasis on intergenerational discipleship but considers age-segregated ministry as humanistic and nonbiblical. "Family-Based Youth Ministry," a term made popular in a

1994 book by Mark DeVries with the same name, places emphasis on programs according to ages and interests, but with facilitation of family interaction through intentional activities and training events.[16] "Family-Equipping Ministry" involves maintaining age-organized ministry while reorganizing the congregation to call parents to become active partners in the discipleship of their children.

In all three models, the value of parents as primary disciple makers is stated. Parents do need to see themselves as the main source of discipleship for students, but they also need to recognize value in the community and collective discipleship that takes place in youth ministry.

My friend Walt Mueller from the Center for Parent Youth Understanding (CPYU) penned a concise synthesis on the reconciliation of the tension between jettisoning youth ministry as harmful outsourcing and the tendency of families to yield the work of discipleship to youth ministry.[17]

Let me offer some brief and direct thoughts on the relationship between church, youth group, and family that are restatements of things we've been saying here at CPYU since the get go:

- The Scriptures are clear: parents are primarily responsible for the spiritual nurture of their children.
- The youth group, Sunday school, youth pastor, youth workers, teachers, and congregation are to offer deliberate secondary spiritual guidance and nurture in support of parents.
- Youth ministries that establish separate youth worship services at times when the "big people" are in "big people church" are nurturing kids into a needs-based understanding of worship and the Chris-

tian faith. Not only that, but they are dividing up the body of Christ. Children, teenagers, young adults, parents, middle-aged adults, senior citizens . . . all of them need to be worshiping together to experience the full breadth and depth of the body of Christ and to exercise and benefit from the giftedness of all.

- Youth workers should be recruiting and equipping an army of adults to love, relate to, and mentor kids.
- The church and youth group cannot ignore the growing number of young people who are growing up without a parent or parents in the home, and the growing number of kids whose search for redemption in the absence of home-based spiritual nurture lead them to the church and youth group.

One Size Doesn't Fit All

In 1993, George Barna published a book titled *The Future of the American Family*. Barna lists a number of living arrangements that might be called (by some) as families. He contrasts the traditional family (people related by marriage) with the "nouveau" family (two or more people who care about each other).[18] His point is that families in Western culture are moving away from traditional families and toward the nouveau model.

The 2010 Census revealed that more and more Americans are living alone, in blended or extended families, non-married cohabitation, domestic partnerships, and so on—pretty much what Barna predicts.[19] Homes with mom and dad, 2.1 children, and a white picket fence are becoming a minority if not a rarity.

Married couples were present in 48.4 percent of households, but only 20 percent of households contain married couples who have children living with them. According to MetLife, almost 20 percent of households have children (of any age) from a prior relationship(s).[20] Almost one in ten of the families represented by the census are single parents living with their children.

On the one hand, the ideal incubator for spiritual formation is an intact family. Ben Freudenburg, in a critique of the errant strategy that discipleship happens only in the church, suggests that church leaders demonstrate a greater awareness of family discipleship by changing the thinking from a church-centered, home-supported ministry to a home-centered, church-supported ministry.[21] On the other hand, families should be able to count on the church for a little help.

One of the most repeated questions of models that view discipleship as the exclusive responsibility of families is, "What about students who have no family spiritual involvement?" I asked Dr. Smith about the place of youth ministry in such cases. He indicated that in the absence of parents who are actively pouring faith into the lives of teenagers, the only other significant predictor of a devoted student is the presence of a youth minister in his or her life: "I did investigate what factors predict that teens are highly religiously involved when their parents are not. And there were only a few things that stood out—one of them was that the teen is in a church that has not only a youth ministry program but a full-time, paid youth minister."[22]

One size doesn't fit all. Different families need different influences to help them to guide their children down a productive spiritual path. Adolescence is fluid, and declarative statements about the best youth ministry model are not always helpful. Predictability goes out the window with teenagers because

their faith choices are not always based on rational or normative factors. Consider the contrast between the journeys of my son and me: I found my way into church without spiritual nurture at home, and my son found his way out of the church (and thankfully back in) even though he had spiritual nurture at home. In these and all cases, the human dynamic is the X factor. Statistics are meaningless in the face of individual stories. Furthermore, God is not limited by our strategy, our circumstances, our models, or our expectations.

Abandonment in a Culture of Specialists

The purpose of this chapter is to think critically about youth ministry and families. Hopefully, the interaction between church and family is one that facilitates discipleship. However, the model of youth ministry is only one of several issues that come to mind. The pace of life for adolescents and adults is frenetic, and the lack of mental health resources, quality education options, and even recreational options for teenagers is well documented.[23] The feeling of isolation from adults that Chap Clark describes as "abandonment" is almost a paradox in a social-media-driven culture. Despite constant connectivity, Clark observes that "those who control and define the systems and structures charged with nurturing and training up our young (and especially those who have the power associated with them) are either ignorant of how destructive life is for today's adolescents or unwilling to take the wide array of indicators seriously."[24]

Finally, the aforementioned trend of outsourcing has placed many adolescents in the care of adults—but not always with adults who are motivated by the best interest of the teenager. Anecdotal conversations with students reveal tremendous pressure from teachers who act like "their class is the only class I have," coaches who say, "You have to choose between football and anything else," or juvenile justice workers who gauge success by the lack of another arrest.

Changing educational models have muddied the waters as well. I recently read that New Orleans has the greatest per capita percentage of charter school enrollment of any city in the nation and that the New Orleans suburb Jefferson Parish is the number two county in the United States for private school participation.[25] Only Hawaii and Delaware have a greater percentage of children in private schools than Louisiana. The movement to private and charter schools, as well as home schools, seems to indicate that parents—particularly middle- and upper-class parents—have decided that the education afforded in public schools is inadequate. In the article I read about New Orleans schools that largely emerged as charter schools following the rebuilding effort after Hurricane Katrina, one parent said, "It's the size of the classes and the community (feeling) at the school." "Also, every kid has a computer, they have all the tools they need."[26]

While it is not the purpose of this chapter to debate the flight from public schools, the question "What about other peoples' kids?"[27] is appropriate for both school and church. If middle- and upper-class students are taken out of schools and if age-segregated church programming (i.e., youth ministry) is eliminated, the influence of families who are willing and able to be part of the process is taken from students who do not have such involved families. Clark calls this the benefit of the "tribal connection."

In the not-too-distant past, even in the United States, communities were just what the name implied—networks of friends and neighbors who knew one another and carved out a life together. . . . The benefits of this tribal connection are obvious, especially in light of how far our culture has drifted from that. Not too long ago, even single parents were not alone in raising their kids, for someone was always looking out for them. Even as "rebellious" adolescents, young people knew they were valuable members of the community, were genuinely enjoyed and appreciated, and therefore were given boundaries and protected.[28]

Sadly, many students do not have intact or healthy family environments. I volunteer as a minister in the juvenile detention center in New Orleans, and one inmate remarked to me, "I don't know anyone who knows anyone who has a father living at home." Some parents have allowed their own agendas to take precedence over the identity and faith development of their teenagers. Clark states, "The mid-adolescent students who struggled the most in nearly every category of adolescent development— for example, self-concept, sexual behavior, substance abuse, and trust in friends or authority figures—almost universally came from a family system in which the home was not a safe, supportive environment."[29]

What if parents who are involved in a local church youth ministry served as an advocacy group for all teenagers in the community? What if they organized to speak on behalf of students who might not have a voice? Clark goes on to suggest that students need parent advocates who might speak for more inclusion in sports, more reasonable and accessible school environments, and "regular meetings at which all those who work with adolescents . . . come together to help one another assess their unique and collective efforts to care for each child and adolescent in the community."[30]

What Do Students Need from the Faith Community?

I said earlier that I believe that parents can use a little help from the faith community. I mean all parents: parents like me who are wondering what they did wrong, parents who are raising children on their own, parents who are making the best of a blended or extended family, and parents who could care less about spiritual things. I also believe that the privilege and responsibility of youth ministry is to partner with all families to intentionally create environments that combine the best of families with the best of the faith community in order to see students mature physically, mentally, emotionally, socially, and spiritually. I don't think it is coincidental that following the "Where's Jesus?" episode of Luke 2, the author states that Jesus "grew in wisdom and stature, and in favor with God and man" (Luke 2:52).

It is time to land the plane that is this chapter, so I will conclude with two lists and a quote. The first list is from Kenda Creasy Dean in her book *Almost Christian*, with an understanding (stated near the conclusion of the book) that the faith of teenagers is "the legacy of communities that have invested time, energy and love in them, and where the religious faith of adults (especially parents) inspires the faith of their children"[31] and that faith formation is a "labor of love."[32] Working under the assumption that churches partner with parents to minister to adolescents, she says that the community of faith should give five things to students.[33]

1. A creed to believe in—the articulated beliefs that students develop and defend. Dean's premise is that students need a sense of certainty about their faith. Statements of faith from their community of faith are powerful statements of God's involvement and concern for their lives.

2. A community to belong to—peer involvement as well as relationships with other adults who befriend them, with whom they enjoy talking, and who give them lots of encouragement

3. A call to live out—a sense that students exist for a purpose greater than themselves, that they are on earth to be the hands and feet of Jesus in helping and serving others

4. A hope to hold on to—inspire and equip toward a confidence that this world is not all there is, that there is a promised "next," and that God controls the future of this world and the next

5. A world to share with—as Dean writes, "The essential mark of maturity in Christians—as in peach trees—is generativity. Mature faith bears fruit."[34] Her emphasis is on both an evangelistic generativity and the presence of the fruit of the spirit (Gal. 5:22–23).

The youth ministry is a part of the larger congregation, not a kiosk outside the store at the mall. As such, youth ministry should integrate and facilitate the greater goals, including the ones Dean identifies.

Richard Ross describes the partnership between family and church, identifying at least three ways in which youth ministry might extend the faith lessons from home.[35]

1. *Give opportunity for leadership roles at church*. Part of the "silo" problem in youth ministry design is that churches treat students like they will one day be the church but not now. Ross advocates helping students to identify and deploy their spiritual gifts in significant roles in the faith community.

2. *Allow and facilitate challenging experiences*. Challenges like missions and internships and gap-year programs help students to move toward adulthood and to see that they can accomplish great things. Ross quotes Tim Elmore, saying, "Our message to [the young] has been more about safety and maintenance than about adventure and calling. We have been protecting them rather than preparing them and coddling them instead of calling them out—challenging them to seize opportunities and make a significant contribution."[36]

3. *Intergenerational relationships*. One of the clearest ways churches can augment family discipleship is to surround students with persons who are younger than and older than they are. Certainly siblings, parents, and grandparents are part of their home orbit, but at church they may be taught in Bible study by a senior adult or be asked to assist with Vacation Bible School for children. Part of spiritual maturity is what psychologists call "de-centering"—the realization that the world is bigger than one person. Students can observe mature faith in older persons and see the eyes of a child light up when a student shows interest in them.

Conclusion and Discussion

Here comes the quote. In the final chapter of Chap Clark's book *Hurt 2.0*, the last section on the last page is titled "Communities Must Make Sure That Each Student Has a Few Adult Advocates Who Know and Care for Him or Her." The last three sentences on that page read: "Every adult must attempt to add to the cumulative message of protection, nurture, warmth, and affection. It takes several consistently supportive and encouraging messages to counteract the effects of systemic abandonment. By far the best way to help our young is by being a chorus of support and a choir of commitment."[37]

What Clark says in *Hurt 2.0* about abandonment sets the pattern for healthy youth ministry.[38] Students need both family and surrogate family. They need Mr. Clint to be crazy about them, and they need the senior adult who sends them notes; they need the pastor and youth pastor to know both their names and their dreams. They need to see discipleship lived out in families so that they will have a vision and a pattern for passing on faith to their own children. They also need to see church as an organic and local body that worships together, works together, and does life together. They need local bodies that are not self-contained but are part of a larger family called the body of Christ.

When adolescents are launched into adulthood, they do not leave without the expectation they will attach themselves to a community of faith wherever they go so that they can be a significant part of a greater effort—being salt and light and voice in a culture that needs them.

Thinking Globally

An Asian American Case Study Approach

DAVID JIA HWA DOONG AND JINNA SIL LO JIN

The world has changed, and is changing, at a rate few could have envisioned even a few decades ago. One of these changes is the reality that what many have viewed as a Western if not exclusively North American phenomenon—the nature and impact of adolescence—is now worldwide. For today and tomorrow's youth workers this fact alone may not seem all that important, unless one were to travel to parts of the world affected by this massive social shift. But another impact of global change is the way in which our cities, schools, and churches are facing an ever-increasing globalization in our own communities, whether we have sought it or not. Immigration, international education and business opportunities, ease of travel, and even entertainment and cultural trends have created a global culture impossible to evade. This chapter, then, helps us to understand the world we now live in, especially as it relates to ministry in today's global society.

The question we are asking at this point is how does a person who is committed to a theologically grounded ministry in our rapidly changing world "think globally"? We are intentionally not asking whether one should be thinking globally but rather making the case that global thinking is a de facto requirement for contemporary ministry. Regardless of where we are or what we specifically do, our ministries will interface with people of other ethnicities, lands, and peoples. How we think about them theologically is an important aspect in ministry—especially youth ministry—as we seek before the Lord to faithfully represent the gospel as God's love for his whole world. More directly, most youth workers will engage students who come from different backgrounds and bring with them different assumptions and needs, all of which are related to the universal issues that come with adolescence.

David Doong, PhD, and Jinna Jin, PhD, from Taiwan and South Korea respectively, study practical theology, with an emphasis in youth, family, and culture. While their experience flows from an Asian immigrant context, their interaction with youth and family ministry people and ministries around the world gives them a broad perspective on the issues related to youth ministry in a global context. In this chapter, they report that systemic abandonment (as described in Hurt 2.0) is not simply a US or even Western cultural phenomenon but rather is part and parcel of every culture that has ready access to the internet and American movies and television. They also note that there is great upheaval around the world when it comes to understanding and dealing with this new generation of global young people. Following this assessment, Jin and Doong offer a helpful primer on global adolescent worldviews and values emerging from different cultures, the issue of identity in these contexts, and a description of how this plays out specifically in an Asian and Asian American adolescent community.

As you read, our hope is that you will consider the assumptions and even racial and ethnic prejudices you carry concerning people and adolescents outside your ethnic heritage. Whether you encounter an exchange student from Chile, a second-generation Asian American, a first-generation Latina who recently moved to town, or an African who has immigrated with his mother, you will have the cultural awareness of what it means to honor Christ as you connect to and honor them.

As you read this chapter, consider these questions:

1. In what ways does your experience growing up hinder your ability to "think globally"? How does your background enhance your ability to "think globally"?

2. What people and/or cultural groups outside your own do you believe you are most familiar with? What would you describe as the major differences between you and the majority of the students you work with when it comes to worldview, values, identity struggles, or other issues?

3. Which people and/or cultural groups are you least familiar with? What would you describe as your assumptions regarding their worldview, values, identity struggles, or other issues?

4. In considering the youth ministry you envision being involved in, what are some things you need to consider and/or be aware of when it comes to minority, immigrant, or simply different kids?

Esther is a second-generation Asian immigrant. Before her family came to the United States, her father was the department head of a large corporation and her mother was a middle school art teacher. When they moved to America, they couldn't find jobs equivalent to their previous ones due to language and cultural barriers. Instead, they opened a restaurant. After years of diligent work, they bought a decent house in a good school district.

Esther is now a junior in high school. Like many other Asian Americans who live at the intersection of two cultures, she is going through an identity crisis that indigenous teenagers do not face. Although her family's financial situation is stable, they continue to work late hours. Esther is often home alone. Her parents, committed to her integration into American society, arrange many after-school programs to ensure that she takes full advantage of her education and maintains high grades. Her parents are also involved in church in their new neighborhood and had encouraged, even forced, Esther to attend the youth group. Esther's parents expect their daughter to assimilate into mainstream American culture.

After going on a short-term summer missions trip to a developing country with the youth group, Esther started to see a bigger world and felt challenged to live differently. One day Esther asked her parents whether she could quit one of her after-school programs and volunteer for an organization that does social work instead; she even told them she would like to be a social worker herself one day. Her parents reacted angrily and said that social work is not a good job to have as an immigrant. Esther was upset and argued with her father. Her response made her parents even angrier, and they grounded her from the youth group. Esther sent a text message to her youth pastor about what happened. She had been touched and moved by both the youth group and the trip, and now her parents, who had forced her to get involved, were trying to get her to walk away.

Imagine you are Esther's youth pastor. What would you do?

Understanding Global Teenagers

Today's youth ministry is rarely homogeneous. Even a few decades ago, most youth workers needed to concern themselves only with the single culture of the youth and families they served. In contemporary society, however, it is vital that those called to minister to the young in God's name work to understand the cultural heritage and practices of the youth and families whom they work with; not only does this help youth workers be culturally sensitive, but it also helps them to connect the gospel with their daily lives. In beginning this process it is important to keep in mind that there are basic universal characteristics of adolescents regardless of their cultural background and that these characteristics become the backdrop against which we can look more deeply into the uniqueness of a family's particular culture.

First, the concept of adolescence is relatively new around the world. It is constantly morphing and changing, and every society struggles as they respond to this new transitory population. Up until the past few decades, only two basic life stages were recognized around the globe: childhood and adulthood. While there has been some discourse throughout the centuries (in the times of Plato and Aristotle and in the Middle Ages) concerning the nature and behavior of the young (some even use the term *adolescence*), these references generally focus on people who were either older children or young adults.[1] As Chap Clark states, it was in about 1900 when the universal idea of adolescence (as we understand it now) was first noticed.[2] At the turn of the twentieth century in the United States, scholars and researchers began noticing that a new stage—no longer child but not yet adult—had emerged in contemporary society. This stage soon became known as adolescence.[3]

People often seem to have negative attitudes about this uncertain and constantly changing stage of life. Instead of treating adolescence as "a unique phase of life that must be understood and [dealt] with on its merits,"[4] adults tend to think adolescents are a problem. Christian Smith and Melinda Lundquist Denton strongly state that adults "typically frame adolescence in ways defining teenager life per se as *itself* a social problem and adolescents as alien creatures, strange and menacing beings, perhaps even monsters driven by raging hormones, visiting us from another planet."[5]

A second aspect of adolescence that carries global implications—in addition to the prevailing uncertainty and negative attitudes regarding adolescence—is that rapid cultural changes across the world make adolescence more confusing for youth and society alike.

In the midst of this confusion, and perhaps because of it, the general consensus is that young people have been isolated from the adult world.[6] As Clark states:

> Some researchers believe that culture has changed so quickly that the developmental, societal, and relational needs of children have been neglected in recent decades and that by the time children reach adolescence they have been left on their own to attempt to navigate the path toward adulthood.... The adolescent is left to discern how to handle the multi-conflicting messages related to home, stable relationships, and internal security— all while trying to figure out how to survive lengthened adolescence. This only adds to the aloneness most feel.[7]

Although each culture may vary slightly depending on cultural factors, evidence suggests that in every society with access to the internet and American movies around the world children and adolescents have received less interpersonal nurture, fewer opportunities for being around adults, and less social capital than in any time in history.

Third, having lost the normative and ongoing proactive nurturing relationships with adults that all children in every culture once experienced[8] and therefore being left to navigate the journey toward adulthood that adolescence requires, adolescents have created their own subculture. Clark refers to this as "A world beneath, a world in which rules, expectations, a value system, and even social norms are created to maintain an environment in which the middle adolescent can achieve the single most important goal of this life: *survival*."[9]

To survive—to feel safe and included— adolescents create their own world where adults are not invited or welcomed. Although younger generations feel they have no choice but to create a world apart in which they rely on one another for social support, life guidance, and mutual self-protection for their own survival, they further encourage this cycle of separation from adult society.

Different Cultural Assumptions

Worldview and Values

While all young people find themselves having to rely primarily on themselves and their peers to navigate the complexities of today's world, this process is even more difficult for minority and immigrant youth. For those ministering to minority youth (often referred to as "people of color")—even those raised in the United States and especially immigrant minority children and youth—it is vital that youth workers recognize that the pull toward isolation and loneliness is even greater; therefore, they must work hard to develop appropriate cultural sensitivity. We acknowledge that it is unrealistic to expect a youth pastor or leader to learn everything about every culture. There are, however, three distinct areas of which any person serving a minority, immigrant, or community must make a careful study: family, relationships, and perspectives on human development.

The definition of *family* differs from culture to culture according to its worldview and values. *Family* can mean different things to different people in different cultures. For example, the dominant Anglo-American definition of family emphasizes the nuclear family; Africans focus on a network of kin and community; and Asian families include both their kin and community as well as their ancestors.[10] Puerto Ricans tend to have more flexible boundaries among the family and surrounding communities, while African Americans esteem mothers and especially grandmothers. As opposed to Puerto Ricans, Italians and Greeks have very definite family boundaries.[11]

People from different cultures interact differently. Take, for example, verbal communication: people from a Jewish heritage often value cognitive clarity when communicating verbally, while people from an Anglo background (especially the United Kingdom) tend to use verbal communication in a utilitarian way. Chinese tend to avoid direct communication and employ symbolic means of communication, and while Norwegians also tend to avoid verbal expression, they do it more out of an ethic of respect and politeness and do not employ symbols. Italians tend to use words to express the emotional intensity of an experience, while the Irish are more reserved in expressing feelings toward one another, and especially toward outsiders. (What's more, they generally cringe when an American tells them, "I'm part Irish!" because every American they have ever met, including African Americans and Latinos, claim to be "part Irish.")[12]

The assumptions and worldview behind people's interactions also differ from culture to culture. Consider the behaviors of students in a youth Sunday school class when the teacher asks a question. Students from some cultural backgrounds are more comfortable raising their hands to express their opinions while students from other cultural backgrounds are more likely to stay silent. Though it may seem natural to read disengagement into the silence of the students, this may simply be an example in which cultural heritage and training is the culprit, rather than disinterest. Certainly this is also true at a microlevel with children or anyone from the same culture. A boisterous seventh-grade boy who is a recent immigrant from Korea and a wildly fun African American girl may both be far more vocal and directly engaged than a naturally shy girl from Colombia. Temperament, unique family dynamics, and a parent's modeling are all as important as cultural heritage for those trying to care for a child or teenager. The key, then, is that the person working alongside young people of all shapes and stripes must take great care not to pigeonhole a child or adolescent without getting to know them, their family, and their unique personality in order to serve them well.

A more egalitarian assumption of social relations operates in some cultures, such as the majority (or dominant) culture in America, whereas a more hierarchical assumption operates in other cultures, like those of Korea and China. The egalitarian assumption of social relations assumes that everyone is "equal" and considers interpersonal relationship to be two autonomous individuals who are similar in status.[13] It is important to be aware that while the assumption of social equality is the prevailing social worldview in the majority culture in America, it is not universal. This also affects how children and youth act and interact, especially in controlled settings such as church and ministry programs.

Last, different cultures have different understandings of basic human development. Psychologist Monica McGoldrick and her colleagues argue that "eastern cultures tend to define the person as a social being and categorize development by growth in the human capacity for empathy and connection. Many Western cultures, in contrast, begin by positing the individual as a psychological being and define development as growth in the capacity for autonomous functioning."[14] The cultural vision of adulthood influences people's decisions and priorities through their transition from adolescence to adulthood. What does it mean to be an "adult"? For most Americans, being an adult is associated with one's ability to be independent. For most Asians, being an adult is more associated with one's ability to look after one's family; being independent is just a means to get there.

Identity Issues Related to Cultures

Adolescence is a period of identity formation and exploration. Youth in general experience an identity crisis, seeking to find out who they are and where they fit in the larger society. Youth from minority or immigrant cultures in America particularly experience another layer or dimension of identity crisis. Not only do they have to navigate the question "Who am I?" along with their dominant culture peers, but they must also answer this question with the need to determine how their ethnicity and identifiable community relates to their understanding of self.

There are many variables that can influence a person's ethnic identity, including their family history (immigration, social and economic status, etc.) and their own trajectory for the future. Narrative is very influential in shaping a person's individual and ethnic identity. Almost all American families have experienced migration, either forced or chosen. McGoldrick notes that "the hidden effects of this history, especially when it goes unacknowledged, may linger for many generations."[15] The following questions are helpful in naming a person's narrative of migration: Why did the family migrate? What were they seeking? What were they leaving behind? Understanding how the shared migration memory of a group shapes the way they live in the present as well as the future is vital. For example, whether a group of people has experienced oppression or been given the opportunity to thrive impacts how they see themselves in relationship to America and how their ethnic identity is shaped.

Most scholars agree that, for the most part, people who have lived in America longer are usually more assimilated into the majority culture. However, it is also important to distinguish a group of people's enculturation in their public and private lives. It is much easier for people to act according to the majority culture of America in public settings. However, for many subgroups who do not feel automatically included in the dominant culture, the influence of people's original culture may take much longer to change in their private lives, if it ever does. In the film *The Butler*, an example of this is brilliantly played out by Forest Whitaker in the character of Cecil Gaines. At the White House, Cecil is impeccable in his ability to live, work, and serve, and at home with his friends and family he is able to be who he is without needing to "fit in" to the dominant culture. Most minority communities are not actually interested in "assimilating" into someone else's culture. They would rather be honored for who they are and included, welcomed, and, yes, "adopted" by siblings who embrace them for who they are, as they are as Jesus's siblings.

Characteristics of Asian American Youth and Family

The American Dream

America historically considers itself a melting pot of different cultures and ethnicities. Each ethnic group has a unique migration history; some came to seek liberty and others to find refuge. Especially for those who did not migrate by their own will but did so by either force or enslavement, the term *melting pot* has always been a hard one to accept (few use the concept today, seeking rather to welcome without "melting" another's heritage). For Asians, however, migration has generally been motivated by economic drive and opportunity. In the nineteenth century, the Chinese were the first to arrive in the United States, followed by Japanese, Korean, and Filipino immigrants. The first Chinese immigrants came to work for the gold mining industry in California. Later, other Asian groups such as the Japanese, Korean, and Filipino people came to Hawaii as sugar farm worker recruits. Asian immigrant history starts with the yearning to seek better work and a better standard of living. Sucheng Chan states, "Asian immigrants came to the states primarily to earn a living,"[16] which is the primary reason most come today. Recent immigrants still seek better lives, although they no longer have to work on sugar farms.

Still, working and living in a foreign land as strangers has been a difficult journey. The first Asian immigrants were often treated like slaves, receiving unfair wages and unjust treatment.[17] In the midst of hardship and under tremendous pressure to merely survive, they have had little chance to achieve their understanding of the "American dream."[18] While enduring hardship and sacrificing themselves (usually without the ability to claim their own rights), the earnest hope and prayer for all first-generation Asian immigrants is that their children will be given better lives—the life they dreamed of that never came true. For them, the American dream represents the end of suffering as second-class citizens and an end to racial and ethnic injustice. No matter how hard early Asian immigrants worked, they

were not considered American citizens. They were treated as "forever foreigners."[19]

Like all Americans, Asian immigrant families depended on education as the chief means for upward social mobility[20] because most believed that education was the only way to save their children from the unfairness and hardship they endured. Moreover, Asian immigrants demonstrate some particularities regarding their approach to education. Min Zhou states that "what is unique about the emphasis on education among Asian Americans lies in the family's control over educational choices and the community's institutional support. Families set high expectations for their children and instill in their children that educational achievement is a family honor as well as a means to secure future livelihood."[21]

Both the immense support and the strong pressure from their families has led Asian children to perform exceptionally well in academics.[22] At the same time this tremendous pressure can be a significant burden for the children, who are trained and prodded to sacrifice everything—their interests and desires and dreams—to faithfully fulfill the family's dream for them and to honor their family.

In this light, when Esther (in the opening story) expressed her desire to quit the after-school program to become a social worker, it was seen as a threat to her family's hope and future security. This conflict within an Asian American family is not resolved by simply debating the merits of social work as a respectable job or a benefit to society. Their long history of hurt, anxiety, and the earnest wish to achieve a better life (especially for the children) has driven families to make tremendous sacrifices on behalf of their children. The elusive but nonetheless perceived reality of the American dream lies at the root of this tension for Asian immigrant families. For an outsider to step into this familial space uninvited (no matter how credentialed or well-meaning) and without an understanding of this powerful dynamic and worldview will make things only worse for both the parents and the child.

Interpersonal Relationships

Different cultures have different assumptions and concepts regarding interpersonal relationships. The concepts of "self" and "community" can mean different things to people in different cultures. As youth pastors, it is important to be aware of how different cultures attach different meanings to the same words, such as *identity*, *community*, and *self*.

When I (David) first came to America, I was flattered when I heard people call me "friend." I had great expectations toward my new "friends." However, it only took me a couple of weeks to realize that when people call me "friend" in America, it often means that we are, at best, acquaintances and that my expectations for these new "friends" were never going to be met. This personal experience in my own life showed me how people from different cultures use the same words but the meaning and worldview attached to them can be very, very different.

The most important principle of relationships in Confucianism and in Confucian-influenced cultures is *ren*—not justice, equality, or freedom. *Ren* is the moral ideal in Confuciansim, and it is a comprehensive term encompassing love, benevolence, human-heartedness, sympathy, and perfect virtue. *Ren* flows out from one's affection to his or her family based on filial piety toward the whole of humankind, which means that a person treats others differently according to their relationships. A

person's loyalty lies with his or her family. For example, a person is expected to treat his or her parents in certain ways and other older adults in other ways. Children are expected to submit to their parents as a way to share their loyalty to the family. Luo Lu writes, "A person in the Confucian tradition is seen primarily as a relational being defined in specific dyadic relationships."[23] People raised in Confucian cultures relate to others depending on the status and history of their relationships with them. A person is expected to follow different expectations and rules in different kinds of relationships. The closer one's relationship with the other person, the more duties one will have toward him or her.

This strong emphasis on filial piety is passed on through various rituals and has significant implications in terms of the way people incorporate faith in their lives. Take, for example, ancestral worship. In traditional East Asian culture, ancestors who pass away become gods who watch over the family, bringing prosperity and blessing to one's descendants. People worship ancestral gods for protection and blessing over their own families. For Esther's parents, going to church might mean similar things. On the surface, the family goes to church regularly to worship, but they might unconsciously take worship as an exchange for God's provision and blessing on the family. Esther's loyalty and obedience to her parents comes prior to her self-fulfillment. One is expected to live for one's family first. At the same time, God is perceived as the One who watches over and blesses one's family.

For most Americans in the majority culture, community is a group of individuals who gather under the banner of common causes, interests, or tasks. For most people from Asian cultures, however, community is more than a mere gathering of individuals; it is an extension of self, a place where people pledge mutual commitment to one another. The American concept of community emphasizes personal rights, individual goals, and freedom rather than harmony, while the Asian/Confucian concept emphasizes duty, societal goals, and harmony rather than freedom. In the case of Esther, most Americans from the majority culture might consider the decision hers to make, a personal "choice" that is her right. Most Asians, on the contrary, are more likely to consider career as a communal decision, impacting everyone in the family. In the eyes of her parents, Esther is not just an independent individual on her own personal journey toward adulthood; she is also a highly connected, integral extension of the family. Through the lens of Confucian culture, Esther's decision to change her major and drop biology class is something that *must* concern the whole family, and to make this all the more complicated and difficult for an American to understand, *she should have known this*! Esther's example illustrates the need to deeply probe the core values that govern and regulate relationships in Confucian-influenced cultures in order to seek to understand how a single series of events can engender so much anger, pain, and conflict.

Identity, then, is interwoven with interpersonal relationships. One of the major differences between the Confucian and Western understandings of identity is whether identity is constructed or assumed. In Confucian culture, a person's identity is built into his or her place in the existing web of relationships; therefore, people do not choose their identities but assume the roles given to them by society. Mainstream American culture encourages youth to explore and construct their own identities, while Confucian culture emphasizes a youth's given role in family and society.

Hierarchical Cultures

To communicate effectively with people from Asian cultures, even to the third generation, it is important to understand the meaning and reasoning behind social hierarchy in Confucian cultures. When I (David) first came to study at Fuller Theological Seminary in Pasadena, California, from Taiwan, I had a hard time addressing my professors by their first names. In Taiwan, one should address a professor by his or her title, "Professor." It was very uncomfortable for me to drop the formal title and address my professors by their first names. In my Taiwanese/Chinese culture, one is expected to treat people who hold higher authority with a different set of rules. For example, children are expected to submit to their parents without shaming them in public, and students are expected to respect their teachers without questioning their authority directly.

As youth pastors, understanding the meaning and reasoning behind social hierarchy enhances our ability to connect and communicate with students and their parents who were raised in and/or are from Confucian cultures. Confucian social hierarchy is embedded in a concept called *li*. Li is the ritual that guides people's behaviors. People in Confucian culture are taught to comprehend and express *ren* (love, sympathy, virtue) by observing *li*. Observing *li* is not blind submission to a ritual; rather, it is a process of learning and the cultivation of a highly held value (of *ren*) through observation and participation in rituals, followed by reflection on the meanings behind the rituals in order to more fully embrace and comprehend *ren*.

Confucianism identifies five primary relationships in society and forms corresponding *li* to ritualize how one should interact with people in these relationships. These five primary relationships are ruler and subject (government and citizen), parent and child, husband and wife, older sibling and younger sibling, and friend and friend. Confucianism teaches that peace and harmony can be achieved only if every person knows his or her proper place in society and upholds his or her responsibilities in relationships. A set of *li* ritualizes how people should interact in these five relationships. It is significant to point out that four out of the five primary relationships exist in a clear hierarchical structure; citizens are expected to submit to the ruler, children to their parents, a wife to her husband, and younger siblings to their older siblings.

Due to *li*, direct confrontation and communication usually does not work well within Confucian hierarchy. How should children express disagreement with their parents when they are expected not to express disagreement in public? How should students express disagreement with their teachers when they are expected to submit to the teacher's authority? Under these circumstances, indirect communication is not a means of being dishonest but a way in which to express disagreement while abiding *li* and maintaining appropriate politeness. Direct confrontation is not how people in Confucian culture usually handle conflicts. In the example of Esther, her parents did not come to the youth pastor to address their concern directly but rather expressed their concerns through indirect ways, such as grounding her from youth group.

Individuals in Confucian culture find their place in society through assuming roles defined by *li*. In the majority culture of America,

people tend to value others based on their occupational roles and their contribution to the society.[24] While this is also partly true in a Confucian culture, people give a higher priority to relational roles tied to one's family (such as being a father, a daughter, etc.) over one's occupational roles (such as being a teacher, a pastor, etc.).

According to Confucianism, in the mind of parents the role of a youth pastor is similar to that of a teacher. Teachers are highly regarded by both students and parents. Parents expect teachers to teach students the concept of *ren* and ways in which to observe *li*. Youth pastors are also expected to encourage their children to be good students and study hard. They should be role models not only in faith but also in academics. One study shows that Chinese eleventh graders are more likely than their American counterparts to identify teachers as significant role models.[25]

In the majority American culture the role of children differs from that in Confucianism. In Confucian culture, the proper role of the children is to submit to their parents, honor their families, and carry on the family legacy. In American society, children are expected to grow into autonomous individuals and eventually become independent from their parents and interdependent with adults. In Confucian culture academic achievement is an important aspect of being a "good child" because it links to the demonstration of good character and honoring one's family. For parents, academic achievement is more than an achievement; it is proof of one's moral character. A child's academic success means more than being brilliant and smart; it means being diligent, perseverant, and responsible. Academic achievements are tied not only to a child's grade but also to one's major. Asian parents typically regard law school, medical school, and PhDs in engineering as successful majors. In the eyes of Esther's parents, her shift from biology to social work is not just a change; it also represents a downgrade in her academic performance.

Shame-Honor Culture

Although there are many arguments on this matter, generally speaking, shame is the primary ethos for Asian culture, while guilt holds that position in the West.[26] Because of this difference, both cultures have different values and patterns of behavior. Miller Creighton defines shame as "awareness of inadequacy or failure to achieve a wished-for self-image which is accompanied by, or originally arises from, the fear of separation and abandonment,"[27] while guilt is "generated whenever the boundaries of negative behavior, as established by the superego, are touched or transgressed."[28] The anxiety of shame arises from the fear of separation or loss of the loving parent; conversely, the unconscious threat in guilt anxiety is not abandonment but punishment or retribution.[29]

This shame is deeply related to the collectivist character in Asian culture. Young Gweon You states, "Asians put high value on the harmonious integration of group members. So shame, possibly evidence [*sic*] by its emergence during the bounding stage, is more profoundly associated with the fear that one's inadequacies will result in the loss of union with or expulsion from the group."[30]

In other words, Asians may feel shame when going against the harmony or expectations of the community, which is not sinful or criminal. In Asian culture, it is of primary importance to uphold the expectations and harmony of one's group. For Asian families, the goal of rearing a child is to create an individual who is in harmony with the community.[31] If a child fails to carry any obligation that is expected of him or her as a member of the family, the child may feel extreme shame. This failure also brings shame for parents who have failed to raise their children to keep the harmony of family and society. Thus children in shame-based and collectivist cultures are under constant observation, supervision, and control.[32]

Because of this fear of separation in a collective shame culture, both children and parents feel shame when children fail to keep up the expectations and obligations of family and community. One of the representative examples in this matter relates to academic achievement. For Asian families, choosing a major or job is not an individual matter, and both a child and parents feel shame if the child fails to get into a good college. While a child may certainly feel frustrated toward him- or herself for failing to get a good SAT score or get in to a good college, the primary cause of shame for the child would be his or her failure to meet the parents' and community's expectations, which would also result in fear of abandonment by them. The parents also would feel shame for failing to raise the child well, fearing separation from mainstream society as well as the immigrant community.

Multiple layers of shame can be uncovered in the story of Esther. First of all, by expressing a desire and interest that is against the ideal expectations of her family and immigrant community, Esther caused them great shame. As a result, she probably feared separation and abandonment from them. For her parents, Esther's actions also prompted tremendous shame and fear, as her divergence from expected norms indicates their failure to raise their child well. Finally, because Esther revealed this issue to a youth pastor who is not only a complete outsider but also a representative of God and church, her parents felt terrible shame. This inflamed their feelings of shame and failure to present a wished-for self-image of parent and child that is loving and harmonious, without any family issues.

Theological Reflection

In regard to the overall theme of adoption in this book—that is, making the youth faithful disciples of Christ by adopting them as co-siblings into the family of God—we must remember that adoption is not simply a ministry strategy but a biblical truth that shapes all followers of Christ. We are all adopted into God's family as his sons and daughters, and therefore we are all brothers and sisters, one to another. Being in God's family is a radical message, especially for many cultures around the globe. It changes our relationship with God and others; it alters how we view one another and how we relate to one another. The author of Hebrews says that Jesus is not ashamed to call us brothers (and sisters) (Heb. 2:11). We are accepted and embraced into God's family.

Three questions can help us to deepen our understanding of this adoption narrative and its implications for youth from any nondominant culture:

- What are the youth adopted into?
- How does adoption change people's life trajectories?
- How does adoption change our relationships and communities?

In an East Asian cultural context, these three questions have lasting implications.

First, what are we adopting the youth into? Of course, the easy and theologically correct answer is the family of God or God's kingdom. In practice, however, we are often tempted to adopt the youth into something else. In mainstream American church, it is tempting to adopt the youth from a minority culture into the dominant American culture (which is not really adoption at all, as defined in the introductory chapter). Conversely, it is also tempting for ethnic churches to adopt youth into a reinvestment in their culture of origin. It is natural to adopt the youth into the culture that we are used to, particularly if we don't give it much thought. Adoption of those from minority or immigrant cultures does *not* mean forcing others to look like, talk like, think like, and behave like the dominant culture, the church, or society. Adoption has great power because it enables the ones being brought into the family to come as they are. To be the adoptive "family" of one Father (Eph. 4:6) is to be a family in which no single culture is dominant and everyone's background, heritage, and cultural values are honored.

Theological reflection on what we are adopting the youth into enables us to be aware of the difference between our cultures and the gospel. It is tempting to associate the culture we learn in our local church with the Christian message of the gospel. However, local church life is shaped not only by the gospel preached from the pulpit but also by the congregation's tradition and history, socioeconomic factors, surrounding cultural contexts, and so on. Instead of assuming that the culture we are used to is Christian, we should consider other cultures as God's gift to help us better understand our own culture through comparison; in this way, we can discern gospel and non-gospel influences.

The goal of youth ministry is to adopt the youth into the family of God, recognizing that the ministry is located within a certain culture and is called to witness the gospel to that culture. The church is not called to import the American majority culture to youth, nor is it called to preserve one's minority cultural heritage. The church is the eschatological community of God; as such, it is called to witness the gospel in all cultures, adopt people from all cultures into the family of God, and shape people through the gospel revealed in Jesus Christ.

Second, how does adoption change people's life trajectory? As mentioned earlier, the narrative of Asian immigration is dominated by an economic drive—the desire for better opportunities and better lives. Asian immigrants are constantly under pressure—first to survive and then to prove themselves in a foreign land. This Asian version of the American dream is driven by fear and insecurity; as they seek a better life for their children, their insecurities diminish. For Asians, the American dream is less about possibilities and opportunities and more about security. The most obvious way for many Asian immigrants to achieve social mobility and economic stability is through education. Education is not about identity exploration or career exploration; it is primarily about social mobility.

Third, how does adoption change our relationships, belonging, and value? The shame culture that is embedded in Confucianism is about acceptance and being valued in the community; people are driven by the fear of being rejected and considered worthless. On the surface, a shame culture is about honor, but the fear of rejection lies just beneath the surface. When Adam and Eve sinned against God, shame was one of the first consequences; they hid from each other because of their shame. Shame is a feeling of inadequacy about oneself. People living in shame try to live in community with one another by covering themselves up. Because of this shame culture in Confucianism, people try to act appropriately in order to be accepted by their families and the greater community. One of the most powerful idols that people worship in Confucianism is not ancestral worship but rather the idol of "pleasing others." People constantly evaluate how others are evaluating them. This constant evaluation causes people to act in more reserved and cautious ways toward one another, especially before they feel accepted and recognized.

The gospel frees people in shame cultures from the fear of rejection. God adopts people into his family who trust in him by grace, through his son, Jesus Christ. People are accepted into God's family as they are. Church is a gathering of people who are all adopted into God's family by this same grace. If a person from a shame culture truly believes the gospel, then it changes the way he or she evaluates him- or herself and how he or she interacts with others. Shame culture tells people to perform in order to be accepted and valued by their community. The gospel tells people the opposite: they are accepted and valued as they are. Therefore, they can live according to God's grace.

Adoption into the divine family first changes our relationship with God. Then we can learn how to relate with God and others according to this new relationship. It opens up a new way for people to belong and find their value in community. It is not only the youth that need to be adopted into the family of God; the adults need it as well.

Practical Implication

So far, we have addressed the particular characteristics of Asian American culture and the unchanging biblical concept of adoption. Next we want to ask: What does it mean to think globally in terms of youth ministry? How should youth workers connect with kids who are from various cultural backgrounds? In a cross-cultural setting, what are practical ways to help minority young people become more integrated into the family of God as disciples of Christ (even if only one minority teenager is involved)?

We close by offering some practical steps for practicing youth ministry while thinking both biblically and globally.

First, cultural sensitivity does not mean that we need to learn and understand everything about every culture. Rather, it means that we should acknowledge our ignorance and be willing to learn. The reason why we use Asian American culture and its particular way of thinking as an illustration is to demonstrate how different and complicated the invisible cultural forces are and how difficult it is to understand them with only a cursory look. Doing ministry while thinking globally requires that those who are involved with youth humbly seek to learn how to carefully observe and be attentive to what is going on in the families and cultures of the youth (current practice), avoiding judgment of their behaviors and/or giving them immediate answers.

Second, cultural sensitivity does not mean that we must simply accept all cultural differences without dialogue, relationship, and respectful conversation before the Lord. Rather, it means that we respect the beauty and benefits of other cultures while recognizing that all cultures manifest both good and negative

aspects; the goal is to create an environment in which the Bible guides our way. Theological reflection on adoption with cultural sensitivity, serious listening, and observation enables us to be aware of the difference between cultural forces and the gospel.

Third, doing youth ministry while thinking globally means being with people as they take the risk to believe in God's love and entering into a new adopted family together from our respective cultures. Through authentic listening, observation, and analysis, we must discern the cultural ills that need transformation and restoration in order for the church to become the biblical culture of God's family. We then need to provide a safe environment for people from different cultures so that they can risk practicing unfamiliar yet biblically driven faithful action. Recognizing cultural differences does not mean that people change their perspectives or adjust deeply held convictions and values overnight. Being culturally sensitive in God's family recognizes that all of us are on a path of learning and growth; we need each other so that we can help each other be transformed. In reality, doing youth ministry in cross-cultural settings is a messy picture of facing fears, taking risks, failing, and retrying new ways of life, which requires much patience from everyone, but especially those in leadership. In terms of practicality, training volunteers in youth ministry to have cultural sensitivity is a great place to start.

Last, doing youth ministry in a cross-cultural setting requires continuous discernment of and surrender to the Holy Spirit, who is already at work in every culture. Our work is not adopting young people into our own culture but rather into the community of God. Our work is not saving them from their inferior cultural background so that they can be part of our superior culture; it is helping them have an authentic relationship with God so that they can live as a member of God's community and participate in God's mission. Thus, we should not assume that our culture is better than the cultures of others. We need to continuously remember that the Holy Spirit is everywhere, working within every cultural context. Our job is to discern how the Holy Spirit is working with the particular people in our ministry. As we have said, it is impossible to learn about and know every culture or to understand people completely. However, it is possible for us to be faithful servants, to discern and follow the Holy Spirit, who is already at work and has a perfect plan for our people.

12

Thinking Long Term

CHERYL A. CRAWFORD

A great deal has been written in recent years regarding the number of young people who "leave the church" after graduating from high school. Regardless of which study we use, the numbers are depressing at best and staggering at worst. Compared to generations past, the idea that most children raised in the church will grow up to be involved, faithful members is showing itself to be all but obsolete, at least for Western expressions of the Christian faith. This has created quite a stir among those who study church trends and especially among those focused on children and adolescents. Research is ongoing, and books, articles, blogs, seminars, websites, and the like continue to wrestle with ways in which we can enhance the likelihood that young people will remain committed to the church when they move out and head into their adult journey. Dr. Cheryl Crawford of Azusa Pacific University is one of those researchers.

While several different methods have been used to get at the issues that affect young people's interest in their parents' version of active Christian faith, Crawford devotes herself to a method known as qualitative research. Rather than relying solely on surveys and group interviews, she deeply engages and consistently walks alongside several adolescents-turned-emerging-adults as they wrestle with the faith that they will carry into the early years of adulthood. Crawford takes us into this experience and helps us to get to know the people beneath the statistics, enabling us to hear the stories that shape their journeys.

For each twist and turn, every explanation and rationalization, Crawford introduces us to faces and voices seeking to make sense of their newfound freedom from convention and authority as they move toward independence and spiritual autonomy. Depending on your age, your particular story, and your understanding of how precarious the tightrope is between the relative safety of the teenage years and the transition into an adulthood rife with big questions and little support to navigate them, you might identify with one or more of the people Crawford introduces. You might even know someone who shares a similar story. Regardless, there are two lessons we hope you take *away from this chapter. First, every person's story is unique, worthy of our respect and attention, and constantly being reshaped and rewritten through the emerging and early adult years. There is no one way someone comes to own his or her faith, and for almost everyone the road is windy and filled with obstacles. Second, our hope is that you develop a long view of youth ministry: the way we prepare the child for the road is far more important than how we try to prepare the road for the child. This is the psychosocial as well as theological reasoning behind our advocacy for adoptive youth ministry. Young people both long for and need a substantial number of people (what we call convergence) who offer a unified message of encouragement and support (what we call congruence)[1] in order to develop the sense of self they will need to allow for the faith of their parents and adult community to be a meaningful component of their development. In both parenting and youth ministry, there are no guarantees concerning ultimate spiritual outcomes; what looked like or indeed was a powerful inner commitment to faith may or may not thrive, much less last, into the twenties and beyond. Yet there is ample evidence in this chapter that those children and teenagers who received what we are calling an adoptive style of ministry focus seemed to have a clearer path to making their own decisions.*

Our goal in this chapter is for you to remember that youth ministry is one part of a marathon, or one leg of a triathlon, as opposed to a single-focused hundred-yard dash during high school. Ministry to the young doesn't begin when they reach ninth grade or end when they graduate from high school. It is what happens along a young person's lifespan that contributes the most to that person making a decision regarding Jesus Christ and the

kingdom of God. We do know that what tends to make a difference in the long haul is ultimately the depth and quality of the relationships a person experiences while growing up. As with the other chapters, the issues presented here are neither complete nor final. Crawford is committed to making this a major part of her work for years to come, and through this book's website she will be updating her findings and conclusions, doing what she can to make herself available for conversation.

As you read this chapter, consider these questions:

1. *If you were to draw a timeline of your life, what would be the high points, and why? What would be the low points? Can you identify some of the factors that contributed to both? Who was standing with you during these times? What, in reflection, have you learned from these experiences?*

2. *Ask yourself the same questions in terms of your spiritual life. What are the high and low points, contributing factors, and people who were part of these seasons of your life? What have you learned by going through these times?*

3. *With which of the three people Crawford mentions do you most identify, either now or during your most spiritually formative years? With which do you least identify during this same time period? What can you take from their stories and apply to your growth in faith?*

4. *If you are in ministry, can you identify three adolescents who may be headed down the roads discussed by each of the three emerging adults? While they are still in your youth ministry, what could you do in response to this chapter to give*

them a better opportunity for faithful discipleship following high school?

Miguel begins his freshman year at a large public university with a bang. Tall, athletic, and socially adept, he easily finds fun and friendship by hanging out with his roommate and other freshman guys from his dorm floor. The partying begins Wednesday night and doesn't end until the wee hours of Monday morning. Drinking eight to twelve beers and smoking pot become a mainstay of Miguel's daily regimen. He has decided not to look into the Christian fellowship groups or a local church because he feels like he doesn't have the time. Besides, one of his friends told him that the fellowship group on campus was cliquey. His faith is "on hold" for now; maybe after college he'll think about God again. But still he misses what he used to feel as God's presence in his life. When he is honest with himself, even fleetingly, he feels rather empty. But Miguel just can't seem to drum up the motivation to find his way back to faith right now.

Julia attends a well-known private school in the northeast. She has a Christian roommate with whom she has bonded. She's a bit surprised by the pervasive nature of alcohol at her school but decides, along with her roommate, to go ahead and drink occasionally so they can hang out with their new dorm friends. Julia and her roommate go to parties simply to be social and not miss a significant part of college life. She is committed to limiting herself to one drink per party and reports never indulging further. Julia has gotten involved in a campus fellowship group and local church; she describes her faith as challenged but growing.

Robert knew he was headed for a life in engineering since his junior year of high school. A regular at youth group, he also felt like he was committed to the basic tenets of the Christian faith. Accepted to a large, prestigious university, he pursued both his faith and academics with rigor. Although very shy, Robert was befriended by boys and girls on his dorm floor. He did *everything* with this small group of friends—meals, basketball games, and even parties. But he refused to drink or do drugs—even on a campus that canceled classes and provided a quad for students to smoke pot on 4/20.[2] During his first two years he did well academically and soon became a leader with the on-campus Christian fellowship group. But something changed toward the end of his junior year. He not only began drinking but also stopped actively pursuing his faith. He decided that it was something from his past, that it was irrational, and that it no longer made sense or was relevant for him.

Three young people active in youth ministry. Three stories. Three different faith trajectories after high school.

What determines whether someone will continue to pursue a relationship with God during college and perhaps the rest of his or her life? All three of these college students hail from at least marginal Christian homes and solid youth group involvement throughout high school. So what's the difference? While Miguel seems to have put his relationship with Jesus on hold, Robert has decided to walk away, and Julia has continued to develop hers. Was Julia prepared to pursue her spiritual relationship with Jesus more than the other two? Was something more decisively and clearly resolved for Julia before entering college than it was for Miguel and Robert?

Youth workers typically want to talk about implications: What should we do to ensure that our students will choose Julia's path rather than Miguel's or Robert's? But it's not that simple. Obviously there are no guarantees, and every person will go through his or her own journey of faith. A growing body of evidence indicates that youth ministry makes at least some difference in whether a young person will continue to own his or her faith into adulthood. In this chapter we look at the general impact parents, church, other adults, and peer practices can have on adolescents as they grow into their faith and into their adoptive family of God.

It is important to say from the outset that salvation and sanctification (growth in our relationship to Jesus) are God's work—not ours. It is God who draws us to himself, plants a desire to know him in our hearts, and adopts us into his family. But as fellow believers, we are called to be God's hands and feet on this earth, meaning that there are ways we can crack open doors (and sometimes very small windows) of opportunity for students to desire a growing relationship with their Maker and Savior. In an adoptive ministry, the family of God on earth—the local expression of the "body of Christ"—represents Jesus to all disconnected outsiders, which includes kids in youth ministry as representatives of the God who is called Father. A family-like environment in which the adults proactively seek to include and welcome young people to participate as members of God's family gives long-term ministry a much better foothold for lifelong faith to develop.

Parents

At the outset we must begin with a basic discussion about parenting in general. As a researcher who has interviewed parents, observed hundreds of parent teams, and researched parenting, some general themes

emerge in relation to lifelong faith. Among these themes are age differences, marital issues, continuity versus discontinuity, and specific practices that are helpful for creating an environment where lifelong faith can take root and flourish.

Parental Age Differences

I visited new parents and their newborn in a hospital recently. When I visited the nursery, most of the babies looked about the same size, weight, and so on, but I was unprepared for how varied the ages of their parents would be. My friends were thirty, while other parents cuddling their newborns looked to be nineteen, in their mid-thirties, and over forty. The same is true of the parents whose kids attend your youth group. Just add thirteen years—not only to the newborns but also to their parents! Although middle school kids are all twelve to fourteen years old, the parents of these kids could range anywhere between thirty and the mid-fifties! We may be somewhat aware of the developmental stages of children and adolescence, but have we considered how the ages of the parents of particular young people might affect them? Most youth workers think of parents as homogeneous—one size fits all. When we talk about "parents," we rarely consider how different parents may be.

If, for example, you have a student in the middle school youth ministry whose parents are in their early thirties, it is safe to assume that they had this child at an early age, possibly a *very* early age. You might also consider that the couple (if there is a couple) may not actually be the birth parents, or perhaps only one of them is a birth parent. It is possible that, due to their ages at the time of the child's birth, they had a rough go of it along the way. They were barely out of high school and nowhere near adulthood, and yet they took on the responsibilities of partnership (sometimes marriage) and parenting. When they were barely able to take care of themselves, they became responsible for someone else. The odds are fair that the parent(s) had to depend on extended family to support them, perhaps financially and practically. It is also possible that they had to play catch-up with adulthood for most of their journey; some might even rely on others to provide the bare necessities of life.

To continue this scenario, what happens in this family when the parents find out that their child's favorite leader gives their child a flyer during Sunday school and says, "I can't wait to take you to camp! Tell your mom you're going!" Excited and ready to sign up, the child hands over the flyer, and the first thing Mom does is look at the price (buried at the lower right-hand corner of the handout): $400! The ministry opportunities we often take for granted are way beyond this family's reach. Not only is this enough to keep the student from attending camp, but it may be enough to drive the family from church out of frustration, anger, or even guilt.

As a youth group leader you may not see this parent much and may even conclude she is negligent because of her absence or lack of involvement. While we have no idea what struggles this parent faces daily, we are often quick to judge on the basis of her "uninvolvement." Having borne a heavy weight of responsibility since her adolescence, this parent is weary. How do we best support her?

For many in middle- to upper-middle-class and/or suburban Caucasian settings, typical youth group parents are likely in their early to mid-forties. Most likely they are still married and on average started a family around the age

of thirty. Their family plans coincided with their careers and (subconsciously) with their maturity level. They began a family as adults. They had time to get their heads and hearts together, so their parenting might be more consistent. They were generally prepared for starting a family—mentally, psychologically, and financially. Buying the necessary stroller, car seat, bassinet, and diapers was all part of the plan.

For adults, the forties are an interesting developmental stage. Careers are moving and shaking. In describing the psychosocial development of humans, Erik Erikson labels this stage "generativity vs. stagnation."[3] He is calling attention to the focus of the forties: production. For those who have successfully made it through the six prior stages of psychosocial development, focus now turns to "making a mark" on the world. The two most common pursuits during this stage are raising children and work production. While most parents are heavily invested in their children, they are also in the throes of their career. Concerns about promotion, a job change, or layoffs hover continually as they balance the onset of puberty within their families.

These parents are constantly torn between family and career choices. Walking into several homes, I have been welcomed by the multicolored "family calendar" that parents use to debate who will take on which family responsibility for the upcoming week. Although most parents in this age group want to be consistently there for their kids, they constantly feel the pull of work obligations. Few at this stage of their lives are willing to risk their jobs, even for deeply held family commitments. Most US workers have difficulty turning off the phone, coming home early, or saying no to trips; as a result, they are available to their work 24-7.

For many who are employed in youth ministry (depending on the demographics of your community), these forty-year-old parents might be typical. Communication with them is difficult because they are often busy and distracted. They commit to events they end up being unable to attend because of last-minute work demands, communication gaffes, family needs, double-booking, or plain exhaustion. They may forget to sign or even return a permission slip because it was lost in the shuffle of life. In attempting to involve them in ministry, leaders may get frustrated by what seems like the parents' unwillingness to commit. In reality, they are simply torn—caught in the continual squeeze of daily life demands.

Finally, what about the parents who had your youth group kid when they were forty-one years old? These parents either married late, are on a second (or more) marriage and wanted children, or were surprised by an unplanned pregnancy. Perhaps the child you work with is by far the youngest in the family or has only stepsiblings. While the parents in this case may be more attentive to the needs of their child than to the needs of their careers, they can have their own unique challenges, such as managing a multigenerational household or navigating stepfamilies and ex-spouses. When this late-birth infant knocks on the door of your high school ministry, the parents will have already qualified for AARP membership (being in their mid- to late fifties). They must concurrently plan college and retirement. Not only are health issues beginning to concern them but also their parents are now elderly and struggling with the multiple and complex issues of aging and death. On the one hand, they are experienced parents who have "made their mark" with family and work, but on the other hand, they struggle to keep up with a contemporary

teenager and the culture that surrounds him or her. While they may be engaged as their older children journey through adolescence, they are typically unaware of current trends in media or youth culture.

Different ages and stages: it is important to recognize that although kids in your youth group are similar in age, the ages of their parents may range from thirty to sixty. Uniting this group of parents will present challenges, yet the diversity of your parents can greatly enrich your youth group. Recognizing their various challenges and strengths is vital in terms of your assumptions, expectations, communication, and engagement. Take a minute to think about your youth group. Do you know (roughly) the ages of your parents? Consider what assumptions you make about them. Do you have the same expectations for all parents? What is your mode of communication? Finally, how can you best engage parents of all ages with your youth ministry?

Relationships: Continuity and Discontinuity

Most parents report an astonishing increase in tension with their kids beginning in early adolescence (think middle school).[4] Some of this tension is the result of puberty, given all the hormonal and body changes. Some researchers believe it has to do with an adolescent's increased cognitive ability. He or she no longer accepts the "because I say so" reasoning from parents, questioning their authority and wisdom.

Researchers who look at adolescent relationships hail from two different perspectives. Those who argue for continuity maintain that a good, connected relationship early on leads to a good, connected relationship during adolescence. Based on attachment theory, psychologists propose that a good infant-bonding relationship leads to a healthy child-parent relationship, which is followed by a positive, communicative adolescent-parent relationship.[5] Those who maintain a discontinuity perspective argue that as humans mature, we develop more sophisticated cognitive and social skills, leading to distinct ways of interacting during each developmental stage.[6] Therefore, a good relationship between a daughter and her mother may not necessarily lead to an honest, open, and positive relationship during puberty.

It seems that the key to this distinction is found in holding the two perspectives in tension. Yes, a positive, healthy initial relationship most assuredly paves the way for healthy future relationships. However, if parents do not adapt the way they relate to their children as they mature, the relationship will deteriorate.

Jude is raised by two loving parents who almost overly coddle him as an infant. He is a happy baby who senses the security and love his parents offer. They are tuned in to his feeding and diaper needs and take every opportunity to express their unconditional love to him. As Jude becomes a toddler, diapers and bottles are no longer necessary. So how do they show their unconditional love? Spending time playing and reading with him, encouraging his creativity, and being present when he has a need. Although Jude will still need to know their presence and experience their unconditional love during adolescence, it takes on a different appearance. His parents' love need not be as conspicuous. It might mean being available when least expected and tuned in to the ups and downs of relationships or being willing to talk but not pushing an agenda.

Building a solid relational foundation during the early years but adjusting the way we communicate presence and unconditional love during the years when kids are working so hard to become increasingly independent is vital. As adolescents grow up, they may act as if, and even occasionally believe, they want to be totally independent from adults, but the reality is that they still very much need our support, presence, and undying love. They need and long for the blessing of both *continuity* and *discontinuity*.

Parental Practices

Back to our three friends whom I introduced at the beginning of this chapter: Miguel, Julia, and Robert. At the outset it is essential to make this disclaimer: raising kids is not template-worthy. There is no secret formula, no list that begins, "If you do x, y, and z, your child will continue to follow God throughout his or her life." No insider's classified list of do's and don'ts. Such lists and formulas ignore the uniqueness of each child—their DNA, temperament, skills, abilities, and backgrounds. What's more, they ignore the uniqueness of each parent and their marital relationship.

While interviewing students and their parents for a research project on lifelong faith in young people, I grew more aware of the incredible complexity involved in parenting adolescents. Each situation is extraordinarily unique. There will never be a masterful how-to book that provides all the answers for lifelong faith. What follows, however, are some common experiences of those who sustained faith a few to several years out of college. Based on research and interviews with both adolescents and their parents, these practices may add a few tools to the resource kit you carry as a youth worker.

If you met Miguel, for example, you would like him from the minute he walked in the room. He is a sensitive, reflective, expressive twenty-something who loves adventure. He showed up to one of our interviews fully geared up for skiing in frigid temperatures the rest of the day. He has traveled all over the world with friends and family. Recently settling into a stable job, he lives in an urban area populated with young professionals. On summer weekends, he enjoys motoring out as far as his gas will take him to catch some deep-ocean fish. He also loves basketball and beer—I'm not certain in what order.

Miguel's parents were very open and candid with me about where their son is at spiritually. They knew he had wandered and did not know why. Miguel was raised in a small town where his family was very involved in a local church. His father was on the elder board, and his mother volunteered in various ministries throughout his school years. According to Miguel's parents, Friday night was a popular party night for both parents and high school students in their hometown. Although they were frequently invited out to adult parties, Miguel's parents stayed home and weekly hosted large groups of kids at their house. The kids played games, watched movies, and just hung out under Miguel's parents' sober supervision. They intentionally chose to become the place kids wanted to be—the *safe* place. And so they hosted, week after week.

Every night before Miguel went to bed, his father prayed over and with him. And every Sunday he woke up Miguel and drove him to church. During the later years of high school Miguel opted to go to church rather than youth group. Especially during his senior year, he felt his youth group had become cliquey and judgmental.

Miguel was a different kid at school. He did not want other kids to know he was a Christian because he did not want to be held accountable to a certain lifestyle standard (drinking, sex, pot, etc.). In reality, when Miguel began his college freshman year he had already checked his faith at the door. His parents simply did not know.

Julia has a different story. When her family (parents and three sisters) moved to a new town when she was in seventh grade, they visited multiple churches and agreed not to choose one until they all agreed. Once they settled into a church, each member of the family became involved. Mom joined the women's ministry team, and Dad found a men's Bible study group; the girls all jumped into their appropriate age-group ministry. Dad was asked to become an elder about two years later.

Two parenting practices make Julia's experience unique. Every night her family sat down for dinner and evening devotions, which consisted of a Bible reading and story and then prayer. Everyone participated without exception. Perhaps even more unique is the commitment Julia's dad made when they relocated to this new town. He became a telecommuter so that he could adjust his work commitments according to *his* priorities, not his boss's. He committed to taking each daughter out for breakfast individually one day each week. They spent time at breakfast talking about what was going on in each of their lives, sharing prayer requests, and, finally, praying together. Perhaps I am somewhat of a cynic, but I actually questioned the reality of this kind of familial commitment. Yet one day three summers ago I saw this father and one of his other daughters sitting in a car outside a restaurant at breakfast time. And yes, they were praying together. There's a lot more to Julia's story, but in terms of parental practices, the commitment and consistency of this family is noteworthy.

Robert is an interesting guy. When I first interviewed him, I noted how painfully shy he is. He is probably one of the most introverted people I have ever encountered. Yet he was drawn into a small crowd of college students who journeyed through college together. Although his friends partied throughout college, Robert would not take a drink until the end of his junior year. He was heavily involved in a campus Christian organization, spending time outside regular meetings with the adult adviser. He asked a lot of questions and enjoyed being treated as an adult in terms of their conversations.

By the beginning of his senior year, Robert decided he was an atheist, posting his resolution on Facebook. Although his parents had encouraged him in his faith, he decided against it, saying it was illogical. In one of my conversations with him, Robert told me he had believed because his mother believed, but over time, he decided his father was a more credible resource for such important life decisions. After all, he was an engineer like Robert. Although his father is not an atheist, he is what Robert refers to as a "minimally committed" or "Sunday only" believer. At least somewhat influenced by his father's lukewarm faith, Robert chose an even more extreme route—atheism.

The greatest lesson I have learned from Robert about parenting is that we need to help our kids understand their faith with all of who we are. If we don't help them connect both the mind and the heart to their faith, they develop a dualistic understanding of faith: I can be a "Sunday Christian" and yet not consider my faith to mean much outside that. However, according to this understanding of faith, a choice will need to be made—faith by heart (feeling) or faith by mind (logic). For those who sustain a faith well beyond high school, most were encouraged to connect and integrate their faith in both heart (emotions, time) and mind (conviction) in some way during high school. As a result, the different aspects of their faith were not competing and eventually negating each other in the years after high school.[7]

Parenting Conclusions

Most parents would agree that parenting adolescents is probably the hardest thing they have done in their lives. The terrain is ever-changing and the issues never-ending. Consistency from both parents is essential. Active, not-in-their-face engagement and presence is required. Sharing family devotions or other spiritual disciplines seems to help build the foundation of their growing faith, and ensuring that our kids know that we love them unconditionally is key. How else will they experience the unconditional love of God?

But the story does not end when they graduate from college. Emerging adults are far from figuring out who they are by the time they receive their degree.[8] Although these twenty-somethings think they are adults and have life figured out, parents and the other adults who love them need to continue to engage them in reflective and hopeful conversations. For the most part, they still need to process who they are as they navigate their first real jobs and living situations. Oftentimes, they do not take the time to reflect. They still require the thoughtful, compassionate conversations parents can offer.

Faith that lasts is faith that continually develops. Growing in faith requires thoughtful reflection on one's life and circumstances. Parents can be our best conversation partners, if perceived as safe and loving. Regular phone calls, texts, and emails assure our kids that they are still on our minds, even though they have moved out and moved on. As parents we still need those one-on-ones with our kids. One of the parents I interviewed fishes regularly with his son, traveling into the deep waters for one to two days at least three times a year. That kind of quality time together provides opportunity for conversations that are more than 255 characters, the maximum length for a standard text message. For some reason, *doing* something together encourages more openness than simply sitting across the table from each other. Maybe it's the perceived casualness that prompts more honest conversations, or maybe it's the subconscious awareness that we have taken significant time out of our schedules to be with our kids. That in itself signals value and love.

Parenting is not a job. It is a lifelong commitment to love, support, and encourage growth in our sons and daughters. It is a huge commitment and requires the support of both the church and other adults.

Church and Other Adults

Churches are as diverse as the families they serve. No two are alike. Interestingly, the smaller churches seem to gravitate toward intergenerational ministry more than the larger ones do, perhaps out of necessity. In this section I will talk about the necessity of changing the way we think about church and family.

The United States is probably most guilty of elevating the nuclear family above the extended family and the church. In his groundbreaking and provocative book, Rodney Clapp asserts, "The negative declaration: The family is not God's most important institution on

earth. . . . And the positive declaration: The church is God's most important institution on earth."[9] In America, we seem to almost idolize the nuclear family, thinking that it is God's primary vehicle to accomplish his work. Clapp spills a lot of ink in his book outlining a biblical view of the family, which in essence he extends to the local church—in other words, church *as* family.

What does it mean when we advocate for church as family? We extend the boundaries of our nuclear family to include our church family. Dr. Diana Garland explains, "The Christian family is one of adoption. From the account of Jesus's conception and adoption by Joseph into David's line, to Jesus's last act from the cross, God provides us with the hope and reality of adoption as a way of forming families when we follow Christ. All followers of Christ belong in a family, and it is the work of Christ's church to turn this hope into reality."[10]

Beginning in the early years of childhood, other adults from church are naturally included in our lives. Most churched parents drop their children off at Sunday school before entering the sanctuary (or the "mother ship," as some have been known to call it). The people who care for our children during church have a natural relationship with our children. Rather than pigeonholing them in our minds as simply "Micah's Sunday school teacher," what prevents us from engaging that person and inviting him or her into our family? If the teachers already have a positive relationship with our child, isn't it natural to include them in our broader family?

If we begin to embrace "church as family" when our children are young, other adult voices are granted the right to be heard with little debate. Sarah, who is forty, single, and

Micah's Sunday school teacher, has been part of his life since he was in second grade. She has been an assumed family member as long as he can remember. She's been there for family holidays, birthdays, illnesses, and graduations. When Micah hits high school and seems to distance himself from most adults, he continues to share with Sarah. She has proved herself to be "safe" and has literally been adopted as family.

When Micah goes away to college and struggles with alcohol, drugs, or sex, Sarah is most likely the person with whom he will confide. She's been there with him through a lot of tough stuff over the years and continues to be his advocate and confidant. She's not only considered "safe" but has demonstrated an unwavering love and concern for Micah since he was in second grade. There is great power in close, extended family relationships.

I asked one of the male students I had been interviewing since high school who he would go to if he was in a crisis. At the time, he had graduated college and was twenty-three years old. He told me it would be his eighty-five-year-old mayor. It turns out she befriended him and was invited into his family when he was in junior high. They met on an all-church community service project and worked side by side picking up trash. From that day forward, she was welcomed into his family, by his invitation. They ended up co-teaching a Sunday school class throughout his high school years, deepening their connection. When he went off to college and struggled with some substance abuse issues, she's the one who called to check up on him. And she was the only one with whom he shared his struggle with pot and alcohol.

Church as family demands intentional intergenerational vision and strategy. For a long time many churches have embraced the "one-eared Mickey Mouse" model of youth ministry.[11] This model perpetuates the separation of youth ministry from the other ministries of the church. Although the initial reasoning was to enable youth pastors to minister specifically to the developmental needs of adolescents, it ended up cutting them off entirely from the rest of the church congregation. When our kids left to go away to college, they returned to a church they never knew, which is yet another reason they fall off the map during the college years.

But for those college freshmen who return to home churches that function as their extended family, they run into welcoming arms—a homecoming! They naturally become part of the entire church family because they *always* have been part of the family. These emerging adults have many relationships in and among the congregation, maintaining a sense of belonging that supersedes generations.

Churches can perpetuate this sense of family by encouraging staff and congregational contact with students as they journey through and beyond college and young adult life. What college student or person in the military does not love a care package with home-baked cookies? Regular texts, emails, letters, and phone calls can and do maintain the bonds created while in middle and high school over the years and miles. When a student graduates, when a young adult takes a step toward a career or achieves a milestone in his or her young life, when a young couple gets married, the entire faith community celebrates alongside and with them as they move into adulthood and maturity.

Church as family responds affirmatively to our call to adoption. By adopting all members of the church into our family, we are able to provide the necessary support for our youth as they traverse the arduous terrain of adolescence and emerging adulthood. Once someone is adopted into a family, they become a permanent member of that family. I am suggesting that churches embrace a family culture by adopting its members into their family. It not only provides a cohesive experience for kids as they move through the various ages and stages, but it also invites other adults to speak into their lives. It provides a broader foundation of support for kids as they enter into adolescence—guided by the presence of concerned and loving adults who are already known to be supportive of them.

In 2002, Dr. Chap Clark correctly noted the dangerous trend resulting from the "one-eared Mickey Mouse" model of youth ministry. At that time, Clark challenged youth ministers with a new goal: "to assimilate authentic disciples into full participation in the life of the community of faith and the church."[12] This goal appropriately describes the nature of ministry as adoption. Welcoming kids into the church family by means of adoption and inviting them into the full life of the community, where the church operates as a family, is what it takes to provide the kind of environment in which kids have the best chance to explore and ultimately embrace their faith.

Many will argue against such a practice because kids don't want to hang out with adults. But this is not true, especially when adults initiate respectful and meaningful relationships with young people. In today's world—where young people feel far safer and more comfortable with one another than with adults—peer influence significantly impacts adolescents today. The next section addresses that concern, recognizing the impact of same-age friends without giving in to the cultural myth that kids do not want to be with adults. They do, but they also need one another.

Peers versus Friends

Although I have used *peers* in the title of this section, the term is a misnomer. Researchers today have clarified what has been misconstrued in the past. *Peer* refers to "a person of the same age, the same social position, or having the same abilities as other people in a group."[13] The argument against using such a word to describe influence among friends is that most people are not influenced by people just because they are the same age, maintain the same social position, or have the same abilities. Adolescent psychologists prefer to call this "friend influence," noting that one of the more influential forces in adolescents' lives is their friends, not their peers.[14]

Ask adolescents who has the most impact on their life and without missing a beat they will tell you it is their friends.[15] And, given the onslaught of social media outlets (Facebook, texting, Twitter, Instagram, etc.), they are in constant contact with their friends. In the past parents could monitor whom their kids were spending time with, but today, with the advent of social media, kids can be connecting with a range of friends within a span of minutes. They are impacted not only by the shared messages but also by the shared photos and taglines. Both fact and fiction travel among friends in a moment's time.

Most adolescents function in that "need to know" mode so fear being out of touch from their friends. They are afraid if they miss something, they will be left out in the cold. Every parent and youth worker has noticed this shift in urgency. Adolescents do not want to be separated from their cell phones for any length of time because they need to stay "connected" with their friends.

Since 1950, Erikson's "Eight Ages of Man" (the central chapter in his *Childhood and Society*) has mapped out the developmental psychosocial sequence for infants through senior adults.[16] Each of Erikson's stages relies on the resolution of specific "crises" that lead toward mature and healthy development. Adolescence is identified as the time period in which young people either figure out who they are, resolving the identity crisis by exploration and commitment, or leave this stage failing to define themselves.

Erikson's Eight Ages of Man*

Age	Psychosocial Conflict
Infancy (0–1 year)	Basic trust vs. mistrust
Early childhood (1–3 years)	Autonomy vs. shame
Play age (3–6 years)	Initiative vs. guilt
School age (6–12 years)	Industry vs. inferiority
Adolescence (12–19 years)	Identity vs. identity confusion
Early adulthood (20–25 years)	Intimacy vs. isolation
Adulthood (26–64 years)	Generativity vs. stagnation
Old age (65–death)	Integrity vs. despair

*Erik Erikson, *Childhood and Society* (New York: Norton, 1950).

Robert Kegan added to Erikson's developmental sequence in 1982. Kegan's research led him to believe the identity task did not occur until later in adolescence. He proposed the addition of the stage "affiliation vs. abandonment" during adolescence.[17] Kegan recognized the intense need for adolescents to feel connected, to feel like they belong. Kegan's work provides an explanation as to why adolescents are so impacted by their friends during this stage of life.

Remember Julia, the college freshman whose faith was pretty foundational to her life decisions? One of the unique aspects of Julia's life is the connections she shared with one of her high school friends. She and Emily went to the same high school, played in the same orchestra, participated in the same small Bible study group, attended the same Christian camp, and ran track together. Although they did not identify each other as a best friend, they ran in the same circle in multiple venues.

Why is this important? Kids' lives today are very fragmented. They live in multiple friend circles. The kids who attend their high school probably are not on the same travel sport teams. They most likely do not attend the same church, never mind small group. Rarely would they attend the same Christian camp. This fragmentation of life allows adolescents to fragment their identity: they can be different people in different settings.[18] Social media only complicates matters. How an adolescent presents herself on Facebook or Twitter can be dramatically different from the kid who leads worship at youth group. Her language on the soccer field might just be a little *grittier* than her language at church.

But if an adolescent has a friend who travels in the same circles, identity becomes more integrated in every aspect of his or her life. An adolescent cannot fluctuate his or her identity based on setting if the same friend is present in most settings, holding him or her implicitly accountable.

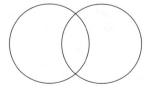

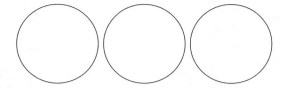

Julia had the advantage of a consistent friend in multiple circles. Miguel and Robert did not. They had friends at school and friends at church, but there was no crossover. Miguel didn't want anyone at school to even know he was a Christian because that would mean he would have to act differently. Robert was shy; he primarily kept to himself at school but connected somewhat at church. Neither had the support of a trusted friend in the many settings in which they found themselves. They lived different lives in different settings, leading to a lack of integrated faith.

Julia sought out Christian friends when she arrived at college because being a Christian was core to her well-integrated identity. Miguel decided to "shelve" his faith during college, wanting to "do the college thing."[19] He graduated three years ago and has not yet resolved his faith identity. He believes he will come back to his faith once he gets married and has kids, "because I was raised with it." Robert has disconnected from his high school and college friends but remains close with his parents and sister. He simply knows he is an engineer and an atheist and does not seem to be searching for anything more.

Conclusion

Three stories, three different faith trajectories. Parents, church, other adults, and friends all impact spiritual growth. Although I have addressed each of these in terms of their effect on adolescents, the key is integration. If the church embraced adoption as a model of youth ministry, not only parents but also other adults and friends would be considered family; they would live out what it looks like to remain faithful and serve throughout one's life. If all generations of our churches were to come alongside parents—as family members—to help raise "our" kids, we would be able to provide the consistent relationships kids need as they traverse the difficult terrain of adolescence.

Ultimately, youth ministry as adoption rests on an understanding of the church (what we call *ecclesiology*) by which members live into their calling of church as a family, extending the borders of the nuclear family to embrace those with whom we worship on Sunday morning. It involves expanding our ministries to include multigenerational opportunities so that all church members can get to know one another. The church needs to be a place where kids are *known* because they have been invited to do life with their church as family. Are we willing to expand our idolized view of the nuclear family and to include other believers—for the sake of our kids? That is our challenge and our call to adoption as a model for youth ministry.

Part 3

The **Practice** of Adoptive Youth Ministry

Adoption Extended

Creating a Welcoming Space

PAMELA ERWIN

Adoptive youth ministry rises and falls on creating welcoming spaces for teenagers and emerging adults. There are few welcoming spaces for the young. Growing up today means leaping from adult-controlled agenda to agenda, within which a child is welcomed and received when and if he or she is able to serve the needs and expectations of that agenda. Whether it is in school, in a sport, or playing an instrument, those who present as smart, "gifted," and talented are welcomed. Those who, for whatever reason, do not seem to be as adept at playing up to the performance demands placed on them recognize that if they don't "measure up" they won't be welcomed. Yet all young people today—even, and in many cases especially, those who rise to the top— know that they are one missed extra point, one exam, and one poor performance away from being welcomed. In our society, by the time adolescents reach high school, they are wondering who wants to welcome them regardless of their performance.

One of the great benefits of seeing ministry, especially youth ministry, as participation in what God has done by claiming us as his own children (thereby making us siblings) is that a (healthy) family doesn't impose an agenda. During my last Sunday in our little church after I graduated from college, the pastor defined the church as a family: "And a family is where when you show up, they always take you in!" Likewise, this chapter addresses what we are about in youth (and every) ministry: we take in anyone who would but come. That is what it means to create a welcoming space. We strategically and proactively structure and design our ministry, our programming, and our life together in order to join in what God has done.

Pamela Erwin is the right person to write this chapter. She has always epitomized the idea of a welcoming space. From her years as an urban youth minister to her time in seminary as a surrogate "mom" and big sister to the younger students—in her leadership everywhere she goes—Erwin personifies the Lord's desire to receive and welcome all who would come. An outstanding teacher, a warm counselor, an honest colleague, and a committed friend, Erwin helps us to think deeply about *what it means to create the kind of environment that fosters an adoptive ministry.*

As you read this chapter, consider these questions:

1. *Discuss the meaning of* shalom-friendship *as defined in this chapter. How can youth ministry programs foster an environment of shalom-friendship?*

2. *Why is it important to create a welcoming space for others?*

3. *Describe the relationship between programming and building relationships in the context of youth ministry. Are these entities at odds, are they in partnership, or do they simply coexist?*

4. *The author adapts Alan Roxbury's discipleship rules for the purposes of this chapter. Discuss these rules and how they might be appropriately applied to a specific youth ministry context.*

The time passed quickly. I had spent the past five days visiting ancient Roman ruins and churches, attending an Italian cooking class, and walking down the cobblestoned streets of Florence and Rome. The weather was flawless: brilliantly blue skies, warm but not too hot, and crisp, gentle breezes. Springtime in Italy. My senses were bombarded at every level: from the brilliant hues of the flowers—vivid pinks, reds, and purples of oleander and bougainvillea; the scintillating smells of roses and jasmine intermingling with the smells of fresh bread and Italian sausage; and the clipped sound of shoes on cobblestones and the rapid-fire conversations of people hurrying past.

On my last night in Rome, I walked through Campo dei Fiore and past the Pantheon to a delightful restaurant where I shared a meal with two young women who were studying and living in Rome for a semester. Over eggplant parmigiana and risotta con carciofi e funghi, I listened as they shared with me the ups and downs of a semester abroad. Both were students in small, Midwestern Christian liberal arts universities. Each had different reasons for studying in Rome. One came from an Italian-American family and wanted to make a connection with her family history. The other wanted to have a different kind of experience from what her small, close-knit community offered. They had become friends in part because of their similar Midwestern background but also because they both shared a strong Christian faith. Their first few weeks in Italy had been exciting. They experienced lots of firsts: a different climate and culture; a new language; vivacious, boisterous people; and people of conviction and faith—people very different from their own experience.

One of the most challenging discoveries was that many if not most of the other American students did not share their faith convictions. Some of the students had some level of religiosity, but many wanted nothing to do with conversations about religion, faith, or God. These two young women had welcomed each other because they found in each other a kindred spirit—a kinship—of joy and love for Jesus Christ.

As we talked about the new and unfamiliar things they were experiencing and learning, they talked about their struggles and loneliness because of the lack of a Christian community. Both of these students were naturally outgoing and quick to engage others in conversation. One of the young women, Mara, related an experience that happened in the first few days after their arrival in Rome—an experience that left her quite discouraged. They had just arrived in Rome after completing two weeks of intensive language orientation. Each of the students moved into the separate apartments that would be home over the next four months, apartments they would share with several other young women from the States. Mara was eager to develop a community that would sustain her during her study abroad. The study-abroad group had a Facebook page set up to help students connect, and she decided that she would post a message inviting others to start a regular Bible study. Mara was extremely discouraged by the responses she received. She felt ridiculed and mocked. One student, she said, responded with, "I'm an atheist. Can I come to your Bible study?" Another chimed in, "I'm Muslim. Can I come?" And on and on with a variety of other negative responses. Mara felt humiliated and isolated. We spent the next few minutes talking about ways that they could support, care, and pray for each other and opportunities to seek out Christian community beyond the boundaries of the American student network to which they were connected.

As I headed back to my hotel, I pondered many things from my conversation with these two delightful women. They shared a precious faith and sincere desire to love and serve God, and I prayed for God to provide them with a strong support network that would strengthen their faith and develop and mature them as believers during their stay in Rome. But I kept hearing the questions posed by the other students on Facebook. Sure, these students may have made their comments in jest and derision, but the questions remained: "I'm an atheist, can I come to your Bible study?" "I'm a Muslim. Can I come?" Other questions began to spill forth in my consciousness as I began to drift off to sleep, "I'm _____,

can I come?" My final thought as the street sounds lulled me to sleep was a phrase from my childhood, "Whosoever will, let him take the water of life" (Rev. 22:17 KJV). Over and over in the Gospels—particularly in the King James translation, the Bible of my childhood—you hear the phrase *whosoever will*. Lexicons note that the word for *whosoever* is a word for which we don't have a good English equivalent. When *whosoever* is coupled with the word *will*, we get the understanding that anyone who determines to do something can. *Whosoever will*. While the students who posted those comments meant to be hurtful, the answer to their question is the one that was rolling around in my head as I went to sleep: *Of course you can come. Whosoever will, may come.*

What would a Bible study—or a youth ministry—look like if we extended an invitation and truly envisioned that all were invited and that any who desired to be with us were welcome? What if our youth ministries were places of generous hospitality where each person felt valued and honored? This chapter explores what youth groups might look like if we created a welcoming space for those who don't look like us, for those who don't think like us—a space for others.

At this point you may ask, "Why would we want to do that?"

At a philosophical level most youth workers probably believe that the gospel is for *whosoever will may come*, but the day-to-day messiness of living that out in a youth ministry setting often pushes us into the reality of *only the ones who look right, act right, and play by our church rules are welcome*. What that really means is *people who look like us*. I served for many years as a youth pastor in a downtown church. The small, family-like neighborhood of houses around the church had over time been replaced with apartment buildings and small businesses (years later, the church building became the downtown police station!). As the neighborhood became more urban and longtime church members moved to the suburbs, the church membership became predominantly older, commuter congregants. I was the part-time youth director for a handful of teens who lived in well-kept manicured suburban neighborhoods but whose parents maintained ties to the church of their youth. Each week as young people came to youth group activities they passed through an urban community of kids who were rough around the edges and had no place to go but to the front door of our church. In my tenure as youth director I worked hard to engage youth leaders and teens in reaching out to the young people in the neighborhood. By the time I left to pursue a seminary degree, the youth group was about fifty-fifty suburban youth and urban, neighborhood teens. You can imagine how messy that youth group was, as well as the conversations I had with parents concerned for the "safety of their kids" and the discussions I participated in with church leaders about the mission of the church. The night a teen pulled a knife at Wednesday night supper on another teen who was sitting next to a couple of sweet eighty-year-old ladies was a night I'll never forget.

After I had been at seminary for about six weeks, I had a conversation with the pastor of my former church. He was excited to share with me that they "had finally gotten rid" of all of the neighborhood kids. Things could finally calm down. "It was just too messy with them showing up." Clearly, there are significant and real concerns that need to be addressed in opening up the doors of a youth ministry

to the neighborhood. However, the assumption that church (or youth ministry) should not be messy is a fallacy of the purpose of church and thereby youth ministry.[1] As I listened to the pastor's joy in ridding the church of the neighborhood teens, Jesus's words to the Pharisees who questioned his hanging out with "tax collectors and sinners" were blasting in my head, "Healthy people don't need a doctor, but sick people do. Go and learn what this means: I want mercy and not sacrifice" (Matt. 9:12–13 CEB). Showing mercy is fluid and organic; it forces us into face-to-face encounters with others. Being the church *is* messy, no doubt about it.

Creating Welcoming Space

As we consider creating welcoming spaces for the "others" in our church communities, three foundational principles frame the discussion. First, God has issued an invitation to *whosoever will* to be adopted into kinship relationship with God and the people of God. The Holy Spirit is at work, as Paul reminds us in 2 Corinthians 5, reconciling the world to God through Jesus Christ. God is doing the sending and invites the church to participate (John 20:21: "As the Father has sent me, I am sending you"). A second guiding theological foundation is that the reign of God extends beyond the doors of the local church. The church—the youth ministry—serves as a sign and foretaste of the present reality of the reign of God. Our youth groups are instruments of the Spirit's activity in the world and point toward the coming reality of God's reconciled people. The third theological principle that frames this discussion of creating welcoming space is that youth ministries are *launching pads*, not the destination.

It Is God's Mission, Not the Mission of the Church

Mission. We talk a lot about mission, and often we assume that we know what we mean by that word. But do we? At a minimum, mission is about going and doing, the efforts exerted in pursuit of a specified goal. The word *mission* came into the English language in the mid-sixteenth century from the Latin word *missio* meaning "to send" and denoted the sending of the Holy Spirit into the world.[2] The Triune God sends out the Holy Spirit to accomplish the reconciliation of God's creation, which is effected through the redemptive work of Jesus Christ.

This understanding of mission has been turned on its head over the past five hundred years; what began as the sending of the Holy Spirit has become the sending of the church. Mission—the ministry of reconciliation—is God's mission, not the mission of the church. The idea that it is the church's mission is a philosophical underpinning of most youth ministries; we tend to believe that the responsibility is ours—we are the ones on mission. Success or failure belongs to us. As the church, we are fulfilling the mission of God.

At first glance, this may seem a quibbling over semantics, but this underpinning shapes the choices we make about the way we do ministry. For example, we say youth ministry is not about numbers and size, but if you ask a youth worker how it's going, the quick response will typically be about numeric growth or the latest big event. If we dig below the surface, two assumptions are often at play. The first is a conviction that the success or failure of a ministry is *our doing*. A second parallel assumption is that it is also *our work*. Underlying these twin assumptions is what Brian Kirk and Jacob Thorne call the "fear factor."[3] Our ministries and our actions are driven by a fear that if we don't have high energy and if we aren't growing in numbers then we are failing. Youth workers (me included) often run at a fast pace, like hamsters running in a cage; we schedule activities, run Bible studies, and plan for retreats and mission trips. At the root of this activity is the belief that we are the ones doing the sending and that the accomplishments of the youth group are our responsibility. We measure our worth (our success) by how much we do and how many youth show up. Kirk and Thorne rightly note, "One of the most amazing results of letting go of our fears and trusting God is that we discover youth ministry isn't all about us. We discover that it isn't about how charismatic we are, or how many teenagers we attract to the ministry, or how competent we are at developing great programming."[4] It is about the Holy Spirit at work. As we turn our understanding of mission upright and acknowledge that the mission belongs to God, we are acknowledging that it is not up to us alone to fulfill this new sending but to align with it and serve it until God has accomplished the

> God's mission in this world is [God's] and [God's] alone. The glory of God, not the church, is the ultimate goal of mission. Our role as the church . . . is a humble participation in [God's] grand scheme. (Frost and Hirsch, *ReJesus*, 29)

mission. This attitude calls us to let go and shift our emphasis from what we are doing to what God is doing. If the mission is God's, the role of our youth ministries must then shift to bearing witness to the good news that God is active in the world.

Craig Van Gelder and Dwight Zscheile, ministry scholars who have spent decades considering the mission of the church, contend that youth ministries must adopt an eschatological dimension—that is, by embodying the present the reality of the Holy Spirit's work and presence in our lives we serve as a sign and a foretaste pointing toward the future reality. God's work is a work of reconciliation that draws people (young people) "from every tribe, language, people, and nation" (Rev. 5:9 CEB). Creating a welcoming place for the diversity of people in our neighborhoods is an act of pointing toward the future reality of God's reign.

In his book *Missional: Joining God in the Neighborhood*, Alan Roxburgh describes a Monday morning visit to a neighborhood coffee shop. As he sat drinking his coffee, he overheard a conversation at a nearby table (who of us hasn't done that on occasion!). As the people at the other table talked about "finding spiritual moorings in a world complicated and unmanageable," his mind began to drift to the kind of standard questions that we ministry types ask, questions that focus on getting people through the church doors: *How can the church be more relevant to these people? How do we get these people in the coffee shop to church on Sunday?*

As Roxburgh posits, we typically think that the answer to people's spiritual questioning lies

> It is God's mission that has a church rather than a church that has a mission. (Van Gelder and Zscheile, *Missional Church in Perspective*, 4)

in getting them to come to church. His conclusion is that we are asking the wrong questions. If the mission, as noted above, is God's mission, the rightly framed question is "What is God doing?" along with the follow-up question, "And how do I join in?" Roxburgh ends his ruminations by stating emphatically: "When we are truly seeking to know what it means to be God's people, we will want to know what God is up to in our neighborhoods and communities and what it means for the gospel to be lived out and proclaimed in this time and place."[5]

The implications for embracing the mission of God and inviting the youth group to participate is that we move from a WWJD (what would Jesus do?) perspective to a WTSD (what's the Spirit doing?) perspective. The former is about a moralistic, individual decision (a good thing). The latter, however, is the more valuable question for a youth group seeking to embrace God's mission in its community. *Youth ministries, like the broader physical church, are launching pads for ministry, not the destination.*

The result of understanding mission as God's doing and not our own is that the emphasis shifts in terms of what we do in our youth ministries. Youth ministries are no longer the destination but the launching pad for sending young people into the world to participate in the work of the Holy Spirit. As the launching pad, our youth ministries become places where we recharge (worship) and refuel (educate, train, and equip) students to be involved in their neighborhoods, schools, and families. This idea is really a reclaiming of the Great Commission in which Jesus gives the biblical mandate to "go and make disciples" (Matt. 28:19). Suffice it to say that the focus for youth ministry shifts from programming to preparing. I would argue that the first step in creating an inviting and welcoming space for young people is to get outside the walls of the youth ministry and into our neighborhoods and communities. We have to develop the reputation for being a place where others are welcomed. We often think we develop such a reputation by getting people to come in so they can experience how welcoming we are on the inside. People come because they have already experienced our welcoming embrace from the outside.

These three principles provide the context for a discussion about creating a welcoming space, and I will return to these ideas throughout this chapter.

Fostering Shalom: A Generous Hospitality

Kayla lives to dance. Since she was a little girl, she has taken dance lessons and performed at every opportunity and venue available. She is passionately committed to dance, practicing two to three hours most days. As a fourteen-year-old, Kayla is also involved in her youth group at a church she has been a part of since birth. When she was in fifth grade, her parents and her youth pastor began to talk about Kayla's transition to the youth group. As Kayla is a child with Down syndrome, her youth pastor and her parents wanted to ensure that the transition to youth group was a good one and that the youth group was a welcoming space for Kayla. There have been bumps along the way, as is typical for any youth group, but Kayla loves going to youth group almost as much as she does dance. Almost.[6]

Jake and Amy are fifteen-year-old twins

who live in a large metropolitan area and attend a large public high school that is culturally and ethnically diverse. Their parents are members of a church near their home and in the neighborhood in which they live, a neighborhood that in the past thirty years has also become very diverse. In the past couple of years Jake and Amy have resisted attending church with their folks. Most Sundays, they stay at home while their parents go alone. Jake and Amy would readily tell you they don't feel like they belong in the youth group at church and that they don't feel very welcome. The church is almost exclusively white. Jake and Amy are African American. Their youth pastor wants the youth group to be more diverse but doesn't quite know where to start.

Jaynace's best friend is Jasmeen. Jasmeen's family moved to the United States so that her mom could teach at the local university. She and her family are Muslim. All Jaynace knows is that she and Jasmeen have great fun together and spend most of their free time together. Jasmeen has gone to youth group with Jaynace on occasion, and she seems to have a good time when she is there, but she tells Jaynace that it all feels very strange and the other students look at her weird if she says the wrong thing or asks the wrong question.

Kayla, Jake, Amy, and Jasmeen are typical teens. In every small town, rural community, or large metropolitan area, there are hundreds, if not thousands of teens just like them. What would it look like, what *does* it look like, to create a welcoming space for them?

Shalom Paradigm: A Generous Hospitality

Creating a welcoming and safe place for young people, especially ones who don't look or act like the *typical* youth in our youth groups, compels us to seek the shalom of the neighborhood. The ancient Hebrew understanding of *shalom* is a multifaceted concept that defies a simple definition of "peace." A shalom paradigm seeks to offer generous hospitality to any young person in our community. Youth groups offer shalom as they encounter their communities as an immigrant-stranger and as a welcoming host.

> But you are a chosen race, a royal priesthood, a holy nation, a people who are God's own possession. You have become this people so that you may speak of the wonderful acts of the one who called you out of darkness into his amazing light. Once you weren't a people, but now you are God's people. Once you hadn't received mercy, but now you have received mercy.
>
> Dear friends, since you are *immigrants* and *strangers* in the world, I urge that you avoid worldly desires that wage war against your lives. Live honorably among the unbelievers. (1 Pet. 2:9–12 CEB, italics added)

Immigrant-Stranger

Stories of immigrants (i.e., foreigners) and strangers are interwoven throughout the biblical story. In the Old Testament we hear the story of Abraham and Sarah, called by God to become strangers in a foreign land, a land that God established for them. We hear the story of Moses growing up as a stranger in Pharaoh's house and later called to return to that land in which he was a stranger to serve God in leading the Israelites out of Egypt. Furthermore, the Israelites are encouraged to remember their time as strangers in a foreign land and extend hospitality to strangers in their midst: "Do not mistreat foreigners who are living in your land. Treat them as you would an Israelite, and love them as you love yourselves. Remember that you were once foreigners in the land of Egypt. I am the LORD your God" (Lev. 19:33–34 GNT).

The image of God's people as strangers is carried forward into the New Testament story. Peter calls us to remember that God's people are immigrants and strangers in this world and we are to conduct ourselves as such in our encounters with the others among us. If we are to understand our role as God's people and how to participate with what the Holy Spirit is doing in the world, we must endeavor to comprehend this notion of stranger and immigrant.

Peter, in using the two words *immigrant* and *stranger*, gives us a clear and emphatic picture. The first word, *paroikos*, describes a person (or community) that is without any rights of citizenship. Citizenship in the ancient Roman world (of which Peter was a part) held great significance. Roman citizenship granted, at minimum, legal and political protections, including protection against taxation, slavery, and physical punishment. Citizenship also granted citizens freedoms to enter into contracts and to own property.

The second word Peter uses, *parepidemos*, is a word that connotes a person living in a country that is a foreign place, a place where the customs, language, and values are not one's "first language." With these two words, Peter paints a picture of a people who don't readily speak the language or understand the customs of the place where they live. What's more, they don't experience the rights of citizenship. They do not have an expectation that they will experience the same freedoms, rights, and privileges of the citizens of the place. In the broader Roman society, Peter is suggesting that disciples should have no expectation that they will be treated with the same dignity and respect as those who have citizenship. This idea of being God's people, of being noncitizens and foreigners on the one hand, can be traced all the way back to Abraham and Sarah. But on the other hand, God is calling us toward God's reign over creation through the power of the Holy Spirit and the redemptive work of Jesus Christ, restoring spiritual citizenship to all who desire to enter in. The Scriptures affirm that God's call goes even further—to adopting us as God's own children. Thus, as we remember that we have been accepted into God's family, our calling as the expression of that gift is to participate in God's kingdom work as agents, seeking to adopt "foreigners" and "strangers" as our rightful vocation.

As an outcome of our own adoption in Christ, the concept of gracious hospitality plays into this stranger-immigrant conversation. Again, thinking about the ancient worlds of the Old and New Testaments is helpful. Hospitality—the receiving and welcoming of guests—is rooted in a sense of generosity. The typical notion of extending hospitality involves the host welcoming as a guest the lost, the immigrant, the foreigner, and the stranger. This idea of being kind and generous to friends and strangers can be seen in the biblical stories. But, as Roxburgh notes, the primary emphasis is of God's people remembering that they were once a stranger and foreigner to God—that they received hospitality from God and thereby those in God's family.

> After these things, the Lord commissioned seventy-two others and sent them on ahead in pairs to every city and place he was about to go. He said to them, "The harvest is bigger than you can imagine, but there are few workers. Therefore, plead with the Lord of the harvest to send out workers for his harvest. Go! Be warned, though, that I'm sending you out as lambs among wolves. Carry no wallet, no bag, and no sandals. Don't even greet anyone along the way. Whenever you enter a house, first say, 'May peace be on this house.' If anyone there shares God's peace, then your peace will rest on that person. If not, your blessing will return to you. Remain in this house, eating and drinking whatever they set before you, for workers deserve their pay. Don't move from house to house. Whenever you enter a city and its people welcome you, eat what they set before you. Heal the sick who are there, and say to them, 'God's kingdom has come upon you.' Whenever you enter a city and the people don't welcome you, go out into the streets and say, 'As a complaint against you, we brush off the dust of your city that has collected on our feet. But know this: God's kingdom has come to you.' I assure you that Sodom will be better off on Judgment Day than that city." (Luke 10:1–12 CEB)

In this passage, we see a vision of hospitality. Jesus tells his disciples to be ready and willing to receive the hospitality of the townspeople they visit. They are the strangers, without resources or rights of citizenship. They are to sit in the midst of the people who extend hospitality. "They are to become like the stranger who needs to be welcomed as a 'guest' and welcomed to the table of others who may be very different from us."[7] When we come to our relationships in our communities and youth groups from the vantage point of a stranger, we set aside our superiority. When we remember, like Israel, that God has adopted us—we who have done nothing to deserve such a gift—we can freely welcome others as our adopted siblings. We come with open hands to receive what young people have to bring and offer us. Yes, we are the adult leaders, and yes, we can and should offer hospitality to the young people in our youth group, but we start with the posture of stranger.

As we follow Jesus's command and go into our neighborhoods, we not only go as an immigrant-stranger, but we also go as host, joining the Spirit at work by extending the shalom and the invitation to adoption through gracious hospitality to those we encounter. As noted above, the Hebraic concept of shalom is multifaceted, reflecting the restorative work of God in God's humanity.

Shalom-Wholeness

One component of pursuing shalom in a neighborhood is to pursue wholeness and soundness. What that looks like depends on the community one lives in and the young people who inhabit these spaces. Our street has a sign at each end of the block that states "Blind Child Area." One could debate the sensitivity of the framing of that statement (and we have!), but the motivation is commendable. A young woman who is visually impaired lives on our block. The sign stands as a commitment to the neighborhood's pursuit of her wholeness and protection.

On the west end of this same city block that I call home live eight other young girls, ages one month to seventeen years. Each of these nine daughters of God represents a variety of ethnicities and cultural backgrounds: African, French, Irish-American, African American, Chinese, Swiss, and a Midwestern Scandinavian. Each brings to their world a variety of talents and abilities (e.g., dancing, soccer, piano, basketball, biology and physics, acting, etc.), along with unique personalities, individualities, and a few challenges. If I am going to be a part of creating a welcoming and safe place for these young women I will need to pay attention, first, to who they are and, second, to how the Spirit of God is at work in their lives. God is already present in their lives. My role is to participate with what God is doing. To do that, I need to know them, to learn them—to hear their stories and listen for their voices. I need to invite them to tell their stories, to share their lives. Only then can I know what we—the church/youth ministry—can do to foster wholeness. A pivotal understanding of a shalom-wholeness is that we are instruments of God's life-giving shalom.

Shalom-Welfare

After God cleaned house in Jerusalem and almost everyone had been carted off to Babylon, the prophet Jeremiah, paying attention to what God was doing, sent a letter to the elders in exile. In this familiar story, the prophet counsels them to settle into their new neighborhood: get married, have children, build houses, and plant gardens. Jeremiah paints a picture of a neighborhood that is healthy and whole (a shalom-wholeness) and further encourages them to "promote the welfare [*shalom*] of the city where I have sent you into exile. Pray to the LORD for it, because your future depends on its welfare [*shalom*]" (Jer. 29:7 CEB).

The image that God draws for these exiled Israelites through the proclamation of Jeremiah is of a vibrant people living in the very heart of a society that does not know God; at the same time, however, it is a society in which the spirit of God is very present and active, bringing the possibility of well-being *through God's people* as they join in with God in the work that God is doing. When I bake chocolate chip cookies with my neighborhood teens, I am taking a step toward participating in what God is already doing in their lives. All I have to do is show up and pay attention. The simple act of living life together opens us up to the possibilities of partnering with God's Spirit in bringing sha-lom-welfare to the young people in our world.

Shalom-Flourishing

Another side of the multifaceted aspect of shalom is the notion of flourishing and pros-pering. Inextricably intertwined with shalom-like wholeness and welfare is the image of a neighborhood that is thriving and prospering, a place where good things are happening. I am a wannabe gardener; plants seldom thrive in my yard. Every once in a while—more by coin-cidence than by my green thumb—a plant will be awash in blooms. Last year I had a squash plant that simply would not stop producing squash. Every day there would be three or four more squash to collect. Only with the first frost in October did that little plant stop producing. It was flourishing! The Spirit is at work, often in ways unseen by us, bringing the possibilities of flourishing and prospering to young people. Kayla, the young dancer mentioned previously, got involved in dance because a church friend of her parents noticed how much the tiny tod-dler loved music and thought that dance might be a way to provide healing and wholeness to her body. Through dance she has discovered a way to thrive and flourish.

Shalom-Friendship

A fourth aspect of shalom is to extend friendship. In the context of youth ministry, extending friendship is twofold. First, we must help youth in our youth groups identify ways to extend friendship to their peers. A simple gesture is sometimes all that is needed to extend shalom friendship. A couple of years ago I was observing a youth ministry student as she com-pleted her internship in a large suburban church south of the Twin Cities. The Wednesday night senior high youth group often had about two hundred youth in attendance. This night was no different. As the worship time began, stu-dents began to gather with their friends in the youth worship area. As a nonparticipant ob-server, I sat outside the circle, watching from a distance. It was easy to spot the students who were by themselves; they didn't seem to have a natural connection to the broader group. As several of these students hung back along the edges of the room, I noticed three or four stu-dents break away from their clusters of close friends and introduce themselves to the visitors. "Good," I thought, "their youth leaders have been teaching them well about being welcom-ing." As each of the students invited guests to join their groups in worship, I noticed one young woman introducing her new "friend" to her cluster of friends and clearing a spot for her in the middle of the group. Each of her friends made sure to introduce him- or herself and as-sisted the visitor in finding her way through the service. These are but simple gestures of friend-ship that promote shalom and offer a foretaste of the future reality of the reign of God.

A second aspect of shalom-friendship in-volves the role of adults. As Jason Linker de-scribes, a welcoming space for youth demands that adults be active and involved—not sim-ply as volunteers but as mentors. He describes the role of natural mentors as "non-parental adults, such as extended family members, teachers or neighbors" who "provide support and guidance as a result of a relationship de-veloped with the help of a program."[8] These kinds of relationships, according to Linker, go through the following general phases:

1. *Listening and asking probing questions.* The first phase demands lots and lots of listening. A friend of mine talks about

ironing while her son talks to her about his day. She has no need to iron, but the iron and the ironing board provide a safe space for listening. Somehow it provides safety because the focus is not on him. I have used this insight repeatedly. Sometimes I come up with a joint project, or sometimes it's a simple task. Always it diverts the direct focus from the young person I am talking with and allows him or her a measure of safety.

2. *Mutual self-disclosure.* This is not a time to unload one's dirty laundry but a time to allow the young person to know that you are real and human and that you have your own struggles. This phase comes after a significant period of time during which you simply listen.

3. *Wrestling with issues together.* This phase involves talking it out together. I often start with questions such as "What do you think is appropriate?" and "What does your gut tell you?" Then I toss in some soft questions: "Have you thought about . . . ?" "What about . . . ?" We dig deep together.

4. *Serving as a guide.* As an adult mentor, one never leaves students at the wrestling phase, if at all possible. They need to have a clear sense of guidance and direction. We don't direct. We guide—typically by asking questions and allowing the student to process them.

5. *Genuine caring—authenticity.* In this kind of adult-teen relationship, there is no room for projects. Their successes and failures are not things for us to revel in or discuss with others. This phase is the foundation for our relationship with young people: genuine and authentic

care, trusting God for the work that the Spirit is doing. Jake and Amy, the African American teens in the predominantly white church, didn't need to be someone's project; they needed someone to talk alongside them, someone with whom to wrestle through the issues of race and identity in our society and, particularly, in our churches. Cierra, my sixteen-year-old granddaughter, is biracial and struggles with some of the same issues Jake and Amy do. She is fortunate to live in a neighborhood where she has several natural mentors. In a recent incident in which she was hurt by some racist comments, an adult in our neighborhood, who is also a member of our church, invited her to a book discussion of the book *The Skin I'm In*. She felt so empowered by the discussion and the support of her adult mentor that she gave a speech in her English literature class about the experience.[9]

Shalom-Justice and Reconciliation

A final aspect of shalom is the intertwined aspect of justice and reconciliation. A neighborhood committed to shalom is a neighborhood "that embraces outcasts and foreigners." In the case of our youth ministries, outcasts and foreigners are the young people who don't look like us. Perhaps they are students with cognitive or physical disabilities. Perhaps they are students who come from different ethnic or socioeconomic backgrounds. Perhaps they are young people from a different faith background (a different Protestant denomination, Catholic, Jewish, Muslim, etc.). Perhaps they are young people with no religious background or experience. Whatever attribute defines them as "other" puts them in an outcast or foreigner category. A true shalom community offers an open door to *whosoever will*. As Jeannine Brown describes this aspect of shalom:

> Jesus focused His new community around two central commandments that bring together the law and the prophets—to love God whole-heartedly and to love one's neighbor fully. One's neighbor is broadened and specified to include those outside one's own circle. Even a person's enemies are now included in the category of neighbor. . . . The divine vision for the covenant community now centered in Jesus is the actualization of the truth that in Christ "there is no longer Jew or Greek, there is no longer slave or free, there is no longer male and female" [Gal. 3:28 NRSV].[10]

A little over three years ago, I met a young woman in the local coffee shop that I frequent. I noticed immediately that she had the most vivacious laugh and embodied a love of life and people. I, like everyone else, was drawn to her. As she made my Americano, I would talk with her. Over time, we began to ask each other more personal questions. She learned about my teaching at a Christian university. I learned that she and her family had moved here from Tunis and that she was Muslim. I also learned that she finished up around the time I would typically drop by, and she began to stop by my table. I didn't come to our friendship as a blank slate (nor did she), but I didn't need to flaunt my Christianity. My faith is a natural part of who I am. It was evident to her, and she would sometimes ask me questions. Our deep friendship also allowed me to ask her questions about her faith. And here we are three years later. We are still talking. She has a great interest in the God I love. I am trusting that the God who is working in my life is at

work in hers too. Beyond that, I have a friend whom I deeply love and respect.

If you have gotten this far in the chapter, you will have already determined that what I am arguing for is ministry that is less about programming and more about building deeply rooted relationships in one's community—about being a welcoming stranger to the young people in your neighborhood networks. A primary emphasis of this chapter has been that we need to know and learn the young people in our community *first*; as we come to know them, we can begin to see what the Spirit is doing and where the Spirit is moving, and *then* we can begin to think about we do. In that vein, I return to my earlier suggestion that the youth group is not the destination but the launching pad. As a launching pad, the youth group offers opportunities for young people to recharge and refuel (worship) and a place to prepare (educate, train, and equip).

In my thirty-plus years of youth ministry, I have developed a well-earned reputation for organization and attention to developing structured programs. However, as I have become convinced that the mission is God's—not mine—I am convinced that my energies should be less devoted to programming and more devoted to fostering an environment in which students can engage with adults, who must always keep an eye toward moving them out the door so that they can encounter the gracious hospitality of strangers (the other) as they live as strangers in their world. In these last few paragraphs, I'll unpack a few ideas about ways to contemplate a kind of youth ministry that fosters a welcoming space and pays particular attention to students outside our typical frameworks.

Throughout his book *Missional: Joining God in the Neighborhood*, Alan J. Roxburgh offers a list of "rules" for aspiring missional church leaders.[11] I have adapted them to this discussion for being a community that seeks shalom and gracious hospitality in our youth ministries.

The Rules

Be Local

"Buy local" is a common admonition these days, encouraging us to support local businesses and farms. In a similar vein, gracious hospitality that seeks to participate in the Spirit's shalom-making invites us to be local. Identify what local looks like for your ministry and community, and be local. Being local involves imagining how you can develop close-knit relationships that move beyond church boundaries and intersect the places where you live and work. Being local might take the form of small group ministries, a neighborhood school, a homeschool network, or a city block. The main idea is that being local takes one outside the confines of the youth ministry.

Leave Your Baggage at Home

In Jesus's words to his disciples, he admonishes them to "carry no wallet, no bag, and no sandals" (Luke 10:4 CEB). Leaving those things behind ensures that we will be strangers, not guests. Jesus's disciples show up with nothing and are thereby dependent on those in the community to extend gracious hospitality. Notice that Jesus doesn't send them out to the ones in their community who don't have wallets, bags, or sandals. He sends them as *the ones in need of hospitality*—not the ones offering it. When we approach our participation with the Spirit from that vantage point, we leave behind our agendas, assumptions, and self-confidence at the boundaries of relationship.

Don't Move from House to House

In other words, stay put. Each admonition from Jesus draws his disciples further and further from a world programmed and controlled by their own self-determination. Hang in there and let the relationships develop on their terms, not your own. Take time to really get to know one another. It is easy to look for a new neighborhood, a new church, or a new youth ministry when times are challenging, and they always get a little more challenging once you get to know one another.

Eat What Is Set before You

"The rule of eating what is set before us is about our readiness to enter into the world of the other on his or her terms rather than on our own."[12] As a teacher, every year I get a new group of students. I don't get to choose. They are my table. When you move into a new home, you may choose the home, but your neighbors are your neighbors. You haven't chosen them. They are your table. Maybe in your effort to be present in your neighborhood you hang out in your local coffee shop. You have chosen to do that. But you haven't chosen the people who show up each day. They are your table. As Roxburgh notes, the rule of eating what is set before you involves a commitment to "be present with someone else in ways that meet them in their context and environment."[13]

Listen People into Speech

I spend a fair amount of time each week driving teens from one place to another. When I was younger, I used to try to be the energetic, vivacious mom and youth pastor. It was draining for me and often awkward and embarrassing for the teens in the car. These days I'm more inclined to be quiet. I'm respectful and polite. I talk, but more often I listen, especially if there is, as is often the case, a car full. I don't listen to be nosy but to learn. It's amazing what you can learn about what's important in their lives when they see you simply as the chauffeur.

Conclusion

In the Gospels we discover many instances in which Jesus encounters others in the context of their world, their relationships, and their lives. One such example is the woman at the well. In this story, we see Jesus encounter her as an immigrant-stranger. "Will you give me a drink?" (John 4:7). She responds as a welcoming host. But then he returns the favor and offers her shalom—life-giving water and gracious hospitality. Like Jesus, youth ministries that want to create welcoming spaces for young people will need to join the Spirit-led movement of extending the reign of God in the world beyond the walls of the church.

14

Spiritual Formation

It's a Matter of Time

TONY JONES

When it comes to spiritual formation—sometimes called "discipleship"—the most common understanding is that it is something we do with those we lead. Typically, this is where most youth ministry people spend the bulk of their "content" time and energy. We "teach," we do "small groups" to study the Bible or discuss an important topic, or we engage in a few other practices or activities where young people "learn" what they need to "know" about the Christian faith. In everyday parlance, spiritual formation is what happens when content is delivered and those being "discipled" take in what they learn and are somehow changed.

While this is a vital topic—certainly the understanding and passing on of the content of the gospel does encourage faith to be formed in us—this chapter takes us in a slightly different direction. We are not saying that Bible study, corporate prayer, and other spiritual disciplines are not the means by which the Holy Spirit grows us in our faith and resultant holiness. Rather, Dr. Tony Jones reminds us that it is in the practice of our faith—what he refers

to as experience, in community—that God does his best and lasting work in us.

Jones is a teacher, thinker, pastor, and theologian. He is steeped in youth ministry and a mentor to those seeking to understand spiritual formation. In a style all his own, Jones opens his chapter by quoting Aristotle and listing several Greek words for knowledge and wisdom; he understands that as we are formed spiritually we grow in our knowledge of our God as well as in wisdom concerning how to live out that knowledge. While Jones generally writes in a warm, conversational style (there are fewer endnotes than in most chapters), as a seasoned theologian, thinker, and leader he does tend to get a little technical at times: "[we] are called to be an earthly instantiation of the very eschatological kingdom that Jesus inaugurated." Yet his counsel is clear and approachable, and provides a helpful understanding of the process of spiritual formation.

In setting the stage for his perspective, Jones's citation of Aristotle teaching "teenagers," while chronologically correct, could lead the reader to assume that a seventeen-year-old *hundreds of years before Christ was the developmental equivalent of a high school junior today. The current debate centers on how different today's adolescent experience is from the post-child, pre-adult era of centuries past. Most who study adolescence, including me, see this as a relatively new phenomenon in which the process of adolescence takes much longer. What is clear in this chapter, however, is that Jones isn't as much comparing today's adolescent development with ancient Greece as he is acknowledging that mid-teens have the capacity for high-level thinking and accomplishments but lack the life experience to function as adult peers in society (as brain development studies show). His point is that spiritual formation is a process that requires time and experience to be maturely realized. Regardless of the amount of Bible studies, mission trips, or service projects an adolescent attends, a teenager needs a laboratory to practice what he or she knows, in the context of the continuity of others who have gone before him or her, to grow into adult spiritual maturity.*

This chapter culminates in Jones's reminding us that our faith is a "lived human endeavor" and that practice and experience lead us toward maturity. This is why adoptive youth ministry is so vital to how we conceptualize even the most traditional aspect of youth ministry—what we typically call discipleship. Although Jones doesn't say it directly, adoptive ministry is participating in what God has declared is true, and as older brothers and sisters embrace, encourage, train, and equip the young to participate in the body and the kingdom, they must remember that adolescents still need the support and guidance offered to them by youth leaders, mentors, and other adults committed to them and their developmental journey. The community of siblings is

what they need to grow as followers of Christ and as men and women. Moreover, it gives them the experience they need to become fully functioning peers.

As you read this chapter, consider these questions:

1. *Remember what it was like when you were learning to drive. What do you know now, even instinctively, that you didn't when you were starting out? How, specifically, can you relate this to how adolescents can be embraced and included in the congregation?*

2. *Jones talks about the marginalized and reminds us that adoptive ministry is not reserved for the young but is for anyone who feels "outside." In your context, who are some of the people and/or groups that may (or do) feel like "outsiders"? How can youth ministry become a part of drawing these people further into the center of the family?*

3. *One of Jones's more salient points is that because adolescents lack "experience" in the adult world of things—like the process of worship structures, business meetings, and church organization—the presence of kids in these settings can in itself cause problems in the community. Consider one such setting where this could happen in your church. What could be done to adequately prepare teenagers and emerging adults to be able to function as participants while still being nurtured, trained, and equipped as adolescents?*

Aristotle would have made a good youth pastor.

He was a youth worker, of sorts. The great philosopher lived 350 years before Jesus was born, and mentored and tutored Alexander the Great while the future conqueror was just a teenager. Then Aristotle moved to Athens and founded the Lyceum, a school where he taught philosophy, natural history, and science to teenagers and young adults.

Perhaps all that work with teens provided Aristotle with the keen insight that he developed concerning youth and their development. Aristotle's *Nichomachean Ethics*, likely written during his time at the Lyceum, is among his most famous and influential works. Therein he spells out the concept of *phronēsis*, a certain type of wisdom.

A lot of the terms Aristotle and Plato use for knowledge have English derivatives—*theōria, sophia, epistēmē, technē, praxis*—but not *phronēsis*. That's because it's one of the ancient world's less-remembered concepts. Traditionally, it's been translated "prudence," but that's not quite right. These days, authors tend to render it "practical wisdom," but that's not quite right either. It's easiest to understand *phronēsis* by contrasting it to other forms of knowledge and wisdom in Aristotle's view.[1]

First comes *epistēmē*, from which we get the word *epistemology* (the study of knowledge). *Epistēmē* is scientific knowledge: universal, testable, and independent of context.

Next comes *technē*, from which we derive the words *technical, technique*, and *technology*. Essentially pragmatic in nature, this knowledge is entirely context-dependent and developed by practice, not intellect. Aristotle uses this term to talk about craft workers and tradesmen.

Finally, *phronēsis*: Always directed toward action, *phronēsis* is the kind of knowledge that requires both intellect and experience. It's

dependent on context too and varies across situations. *Phronēsis* is laden with values—unlike the other two types of knowledge. It is the wisdom that we use to make ethical and moral decisions.

As you might guess, I'm arguing that *phronēsis* is the type of knowledge that best describes the Christian faith. It's a combination of intellectual study and real-world experience. It demands of us ad hoc decision making based on a value system that we have internalized. It's based on the interplay with generalities and particulars. Aristotle is very clear on this point: *phronēsis* cannot be attained simply by memorizing a universal set of rules. *Phronēsis* demands experience; a human must put this knowledge to the test in a real-world situation, learn from that situation, then repeat the process. That's how *phronēsis* is developed.

Why You Can't Find a Wise Teenager

You know what scares me? In some states, kids who live on farms can start driving when they're twelve. As I write this, my three kids are fourteen, thirteen, and ten, and the thought of any one of them driving makes me go hide under the bed. If I send the fourteen-year-old to the basement to get his socks out of the dryer, he'll come back thirty minutes later having done thirteen things—and getting his socks won't be one of them.

We know why adolescents are terrible drivers: they get distracted by every little thing that crosses their mind or line of vision. And we know why, as they age, they become better drivers: the prefrontal cortex of the brain—the part that regulates behavior and enables judgment—is the last part of the human brain to develop, not reaching maturation until about age twenty-five. In other words, there is a physiological explanation as to why a thirteen-year-old has less impulse control than a thirty-three-year-old.

Aristotle didn't have the benefit of pediatric neurological studies, but he did have his own experience of teaching teenagers. With that under his belt, he was able to write:

> An indication of what has been said is that while young people become geometers and mathematicians and wise in such things, they do not seem to become practically-wise [*phronetic*]. The explanation is that practical wisdom [*phronēsis*] is concerned also with particulars, knowledge of which comes from experience. But there is no young person who is experienced, since it is quantity of time that produces experience.[2]

The reason that you don't have to count "one-one thousand, two-one thousand, three-one thousand" between you and the car that you're tailing on the freeway is that you have enough experience driving that you have a feel for it. If you're tailgating the car in front of you, you have a sense that you're too close, and you back off. No matter how much they pounded that into your head in driver's-ed class, you had to learn it on the road, from experience.

The Christian faith is no different. You can get kids memorizing all the Bible verses you want in Sunday school and Vacation Bible School, but until they have got to put their Christianity into practice, those verses aren't worth the piece of candy that the kids get for reciting them.

Christianity is fundamentally a *lived human endeavor*. No amount of study is a substitute for that. Youth group, camp, retreats, lock-ins,

you name it—each serves a purpose and each is valuable in its own way, but none of those activities or events has anything like the effect of living the Christian life on a day-to-day basis, over time.

There's a reason that, when an adolescent learns to drive, there's a progression: first there's class, then a behind-the-wheel lesson, then time with a learner's permit. Even after the license is attained, it's provisional. In my state, for the first six months any driver under twenty can't drive between midnight and five o'clock in the morning and can't have more than one passenger. That's because the state of Minnesota knows what Aristotle knew: it is quantity of time that produces experience.

The church needs to learn this lesson.

Experience Takes Time

My ten-year-old is a hockey goalie, and in Minnesota, that's a big deal. It means lots of ice time and expensive pads and emails every week from goalie coaches who want me to buy lessons.

Our city's rink happens to also be the practice rink of the Minnesota Wild, a National Hockey League (NHL) team. A couple of times last season, the Wild practiced right after my son's team, so we stuck around to watch. Because he's a goalie, and goalies are a bit thick in the head, he wanted to stand right behind the goal during the Wild practice. When NHL players take the ice, they have a tradition of shooting the practice pucks as hard as they can at the goal posts, making various clanging tones. I'll never forget the look on my son's face the first time we saw those shots from that vantage point, through the plexiglass just behind the empty net. His eyes were like saucers. Then the goalie skated into the net.

At ninety miles per hour, an NHL slap shot travels from the blue line to the goal in .456 seconds. If the shooter is inside the blue line and the goalie is at the top of the crease, halve that. It's about a quarter of a second of reaction time. Yet when the Wild goalie took the net, he saved four out of every five shots, gloving them nonchalantly, kicking them out with his leg pads, swatting them away with his stick.

In the car on the way home, I asked my son what he was thinking. He was stunned at the speed of the shots in the NHL practice. "I'll never be able to save shots like that!" he said. Yet the Wild goalie is only thirteen years older than my son. What happens in those intervening years?

Of course, it would be terribly irresponsible for me to send my kid out on the ice with the Wild. He'd be injured or worse within seconds. There's no way that he has the reflexes and technique to make a save on an NHL slap shot.

However, as he advances through the ranks of hockey, his reflexes and technique will develop. He'll get coaching, and he'll learn from experience in practices and games. If he decides to stick with goaltending, he'll move from Mites to Squirts to Pee-Wees to Bantams. If he's good enough, in five or six years he'll play high school hockey and face sixty-mile-per-hour slap shots. If he's really good, he'll see seventy- and eighty-mile-per-hour shots in college. And if, by some dint of fate and exceptional talent, he were to make the NHL, well then he'd obviously be capable of gloving a ninety-mile-per-hour slap shot.

But he would see thousands and thousands of shots between now and his purely hypothetical NHL career.

In the church, we have an unfortunate habit of treating Christianity like it's one-size-fits-all, and that size is adult. Sure, we have Youth Sunday, and we have got children's worship. But when you go into the sanctuary and look at the big show on Sunday morning, it's designed with adults in mind. The prayers, the music, the sermon—each is developmentally appropriate for adults, not for adolescents.

The same goes for how the church is run. The council or elder board or vestry meetings are very adult-ish. So are committee meetings and votes that are run on parliamentary procedure. (I move, I second, all in favor, Aye!) Each of these processes privileges the adults in the congregation, and each marginalizes the teenagers. Asking a teen to sit on a board or a committee is a bit like asking my son to practice with the Wild—it's not developmentally appropriate.

If we are serious about adopting adolescents into the center of congregational life rather than leaving them on the margins or, worse yet, outsourcing our adolescent ministry to parachurch groups, then we have to seriously consider how our churches are formed and organized. We can't simply make accommodations for teenagers, like we do for other marginalized groups. Instead, we have to make the developmental needs of teenagers constitutive of congregational life itself.

Implications for Adoption

At the heart of the adoption model of youth ministry is the metaphor of family. Like you, I know many families for whom adoption is part of their story. And although each family's adoption story is unique, they share the common experience of adoption fundamentally changing their families.

One couple I know has adopted two children—one from an Asian country and one from a Latin American country. They have made it a point to incorporate aspects of those countries' cultures into their family, including food, holidays, history, and travel. The parents in the family did not simply assume that their kids would become enculturated to the parents' northern European ancestry, even though their kids joined the family as infants. Instead, they allowed the children's native cultures to change their family. That family is now the mixture of the ancestries of the parents and the children in a very tangible way.

Another couple I know had two biological children of their own when they adopted two adolescent brothers out of foster care. Because of their ages, these boys already had ten years each of their own history, which included abandonment by their parents, the foster care system, and their Mexican ancestry. The adopting family—both parents and children—knew they were in for a challenge, but their struggles were more difficult than they expected. Their family is different as a result.

Perhaps you built a papier-mâché volcano as a child. After you added the baking soda you poured in the vinegar to produce an impressive—but safe—fountain of lava. The chemical reaction that takes place when sodium bicarbonate (baking soda) mixes with dilute acetic acid (vinegar) produces carbon dioxide gas. When those two elements mix, an altogether new element is formed.

That's what happens in an adoptive family. It's not that adoptive children are absorbed into a biological family and the family doesn't change. It's that when the adoptive children and the biological family mix, a new family is formed.

However, when adolescents are "adopted" into the life of a congregation, the congregation rarely changes. Maybe a youth room is built along the edges of the building; I have even been in churches where the youth room is a converted closet, sending a very clear message to the teens.

The Sunday morning worship is not changed to accommodate the adolescents' different learning styles. Instead, the teenagers are expected to dress, sit, and act like adults, even though nearly everything in the teenage constitution cries out against this.

Neither does the organizational structure of the congregation change. Instead, meetings are held at night (when adults can come), coffee is served, long and often boring reports are presented, and Robert's Rules of Order are observed—all of which militate against the active participation of teenagers.

Teenagers are a chemical catalyst in any group of people. They ask questions that adults have been socialized not to ask, and they wear clothes and speak in cadences that adults find distracting or even disrespectful; they are not developmentally able to sit still and listen to monologues for extended periods of time. But instead of inviting the chemical reaction that occurs when adolescents are vigorously mixed into the central life of a congregation, most church bodies do everything they can to avoid the potentially volatile chemical reaction. They push teenagers to their own space, assign them their own minister, and hope they don't disrupt their congregational stasis.

Theological Foundations of Adopting a Marginalized Population

Likely the most common way to interpret the miracles of Jesus is as a sign of his messianic power. Indeed, that's the way that many of his contemporaries interpreted them. Often, when Jesus performed a miracle, accompanied by a brief saying or teaching, the crowd dispersed and, the Gospel writers tell us, the people were amazed at the power of Jesus. His miracles around Galilee and even in Jerusalem led him to be feted as the Messiah on Palm Sunday, welcomed into Jerusalem as a heroic victor.

But there's another way to look at Jesus's miracles, particularly the healing miracles. Jesus was born into a culture that, like many in the ancient world, took a very dim view of any human who had a physical ailment. In first-century Judaism, that view had been codified into laws, regulations, and rituals. Anyone with a physical infirmity was considered "unclean" and therefore shunned. They could not, for instance, worship in the temple, the very center of Hebrew religious life. Further, if a "clean" person even touched an "unclean" person, the former would have to go through a ritual ablution before being allowed to again worship in the temple.

Who was considered unclean? A paralytic, a leper, a demoniac, a blind person, and even a menstruating woman. Yet each of these persons Jesus touched and healed, effectively bringing them back into cleanliness and back into the center of Hebrew religious life.

Among the most telling of stories in the life of the earliest church is recorded by Luke in Acts 3:1–10. Sometime after Jesus's crucifixion and resurrection, Peter, John, and some of the other disciples are in Jerusalem, walking together to the temple to pray at the appointed hour. There, a man who has been lame from birth and regularly sits by the gate to the temple is asking for alms. Notice that this paralytic man is sitting right at the boundary of the sacred space, but he is barred from crossing the threshold.

When the crippled man reaches out to them, Peter does not hand him loose change. Instead he looks the man in the eye and says, "I don't have any silver or gold, but what I have I give you: In the name of Jesus Christ, stand up and walk." Then, Luke tells us, the man's ankles and legs grow strong before their eyes; he stands up, and he grabs his mat.

You may remember what comes next from the chorus of the old Vacation Bible School song: "He went walking and leaping and praising God, walking and leaping and praising God. . . ." But what that song leaves out is *where* the man does his dance. After being healed, he immediately runs into the temple. He crosses the threshold, into the very space from which he had previously been forbidden. He moves from the margins of Jewish religious life right into the center. When he gets inside, we're told the people say, "Isn't that the man who sits outside asking for alms?" Yep, that's the same guy.

Now, we don't know what happens next. But it would be nice to think that he spent some time telling all those "clean" people in the temple what it's like to be "unclean," to be at the margins, and to be shunned. There's no question that he remembers that feeling. It is part of his story, even though his legs now work.

Materially, time and time again Jesus healed those who'd been officially pushed to the margins of Judaic life. Spiritually, Jesus's miracles were a foretaste of the eschatological kingdom that he promised is coming in God's ultimate reign. In this way, the miracles can be seen as signposts pointing to the time when *no one* will be on the margins, when all people will be at the center of God's life and rhythm.

As long as we have free will as humans, some people will be at the center of power, and others will be at the margins. That's inevitable. It's the price we pay for the freedom we enjoy.

But Jesus showed in his healing miracles that a time is coming when that will no longer be the case.

Here's the rub: the church is supposed to be a foretaste of that kingdom. We who make up the "body of Christ" are called to be an earthly instantiation of the very eschatological kingdom that Jesus inaugurated. In other words, the onus is on the church to ensure that marginalized people are ushered into the very center of our communities of faith. And guess what? That's going to change our churches.

From the Margins to the Center

I know of a church, a very old church—over one hundred years old—that didn't have any seating for disabled persons. Week after week as the pastor preached from the pulpit, he watched a wheelchair-bound parishioner jockeying for a place in the sanctuary. If he rolled in the aisle, the ushers asked him to move because of fire code. Same thing if he stopped in the doorway. His chair couldn't fit behind the last pew unless he positioned it sideways.

The pastor became so frustrated that he came into the sanctuary on a Saturday, with a chainsaw. He cut off half of a pew in the middle of the sanctuary, making a space for his congregant. That pastor has moved on to another church, but the sawed-off pew remains. They didn't even sand off the rough edges. The congregation wants to leave it in its rough state as a reminder of how difficult it can be for someone on the margins to make it to the center of a church community.

Any number of similar anecdotes can be proffered for any number of marginalized peoples in the life of the church. For many years, churches were officially segregated—now they're just informally segregated. And the list of stigmatized people in the church is longer than your arm: unwed mothers, divorcees, LGBT (lesbian, gay, bisexual, and transgender) persons, the mentally ill, the obese, the homeless.

And teenagers.

Think of where the teenagers sit in your Sunday morning worship service (that is, if they attend). Probably, it's not at the center. More likely it's in the back row.

And think of the sermon illustrations used by the pastor. Probably, they're not about when she was in middle school. More likely, they're oriented toward adults.

What about the litanies of prayer? Do they include prayers about school, peer pressure, the temptations of alcohol and drugs and sex? Probably not.

Even the version of the Bible that's used in worship is most likely a translation favored by the adults.

If we're going to get serious about adopting adolescents into the family of faith, then we really do need to get serious about it. We need to usher them into the center of our worship life, into the organizational structures of congregation. They need to have a say on the budget, on the staffing, on the mission.

Central to the adoption thesis is that adolescents aren't an "unreached people group" in need of specialized evangelism. They are as much members of the family of faith as any other group. And as a group that has been traditionally marginalized, they deserve an extra effort from those of us who traditionally hold the power in these communities.

So let's return to Aristotle. Remember, he said that young people learn *phronetically*— that is, by a combination of intellect and experience. Think about my son learning to play goalie, or a person learning to drive, or a kid who's really into chess or cello. In all of these cases, a person takes lessons and practices. Intellect and experience combine to create wisdom, a brand-new compound of the initial two elements.

Prayer is a central practice of our faith; it has been since the time of ancient Israel. It's no surprise that we emphasize prayer in our churches—both adult-oriented worship and youth ministry. But how are we teaching young people to pray? Are we doing it in a developmentally appropriate way, or are we firing the equivalent of ninety-mile-per-hour slap shots at them?

One very concrete way that we can heed Aristotle is by introducing our adolescents to prayer in ways that are appropriate. After experiencing success at a primary level, they can gradually step up to a secondary level. For instance, every middle school teacher knows that the attention span for a thirteen-year-old is limited. Can you imagine a teacher at a public middle school asking the kids to go from playing a high-energy game to listening to a twenty-minute monologue to closing their eyes and sitting in silence for five minutes? No way. They'd know that it's unfair to ask an adolescent for such a quick mental and kinesthetic turnaround. Yet that's how many middle school ministries are run.

Spiritual formation happens, guided by the Holy Spirit, when we attend to the needs of the adolescents in our care and when we provide ways for them to develop that they can handle.

At the risk of repeating myself, let me say that there is no substitute for experience. Aristotle said it, and we know it in our bones. If our congregations are really serious about adopting adolescents and ushering them into the center of congregational life, then we have to continually remind ourselves that they are gaining experience every day. Teenagers are bound to mess up, to make mistakes that we think are totally preventable and avoidable. That's endemic to adolescence. What these adolescents need is a community into which they can be adopted—a community that understands that they are gaining experience; a community that surrounds them with supportive adults who help them process those experiences; a community that provides experiences of spiritual formation and development that are appropriate to their ages. Ultimately, adolescents need to be adopted into communities that are flexible enough to change when teenagers are moved from the margins of communal life to the center.

Can I Ask That?

Imagining a Church Big Enough for Teenagers' Hard Questions

KARA POWELL AND BRAD GRIFFIN

Kara Powell and Brad Griffin help lead the Fuller Youth Institute (FYI): an interdisciplinary research-based center at Fuller Theological Seminary with a mission of equipping young people with the lifelong faith they need. The FYI team has spent the last decade commissioning, organizing, and translating research into resources that elevate leaders, families, and churches. Most recently, the Sticky Faith research projects, articles, e-journal, books, website (www.stickyfaith.org, which can also be accessed through this book's website, youth ministry.fuller.edu), and consulting have made a significant impact on how churches and faith-based youth organizations consider the impact of their ministries on faith longevity.

In this chapter, Powell and Griffin specifically address an issue that research demonstrates is vital for young people exploring faith. When teenagers and children are given stock, inadequate, or even dismissive answers to complex or difficult questions, they learn that faith is best lived by ignoring the uncomfortable. While many adults may be more comfortable with living with ambiguity in terms

of their understanding of faith and the rest of life, few young people are. Youth workers are more aware than most how important it is that young people be allowed to ask any and every question, but young people must also be taught how to navigate the journey into mysterious and faith-threatening shadows. However, this process makes parents, and even pastors, nervous (and can have an impact on youth worker jobs!). This chapter, then, is vitally important as we partner with the congregation in convincing young people that the church is their family.

Powell and Griffin help us to understand the role of doubt in both identity and faith development. In addition, they give us insight into communally dealing with doubt—not just adolescent doubt, but real faith crises in which all believers confront their struggles without the traditionally easy answers that religious culture is so proficient at disseminating. As we lead young people into sibling relationships with adults in the adoptive community— doubts and all—it is not so much that we are able to answer their doubts but that we come alongside them as family members. This is the power of familial community.

As you read this chapter, consider these questions:

1. *Describe a time when you have had questions of doubt in your own faith journey. Did you voice these? What was the response?*

2. *Name some practical ways that a youth ministry program could foster a safe space for doubt.*

3. *How could the concept of lament be integrated into a youth ministry philosophy?*

"Pastor, if I raise my finger, will God know which one I'm going to raise even before I raise it?"

Thirteen-year-old Steve attended church every week with his parents, and he had stayed after church to get an answer to his pressing question from his pastor. The pastor replied, "Yes, God knows everything."

Steve, who was haunted by the plight of African children suffering from dire famine, then pulled out a *Life* magazine cover depicting two hungry children. He asked the logical follow-up, "Well, does God know about this and what's going to happen to those kids?" The pastor gave a similar response: "Steve, I know you don't understand, but yes, God knows about that."[1]

Would you be inspired by that answer?

Steve wasn't. He walked out that day and never returned to a Christian church again. When he tried to talk with his pastor about some of his faith dilemmas, the pastor's answer, though well-intentioned, repelled Steve from the faith.

Maybe you have heard of Steve. His last name was Jobs. The young Steve Jobs, founder and CEO of Apple Inc., was a churchgoing junior high student who had doubts about faith.

Now imagine if Steve had been greeted by a different answer from his pastor. One that was less of a conversational dead end and more of an on-ramp to a deeper discussion about faith. Imagine if the pastor had replied to thirteen-year-old Steve, "That's a great question, Steve. How about if you and I and your dad meet for breakfast this week and talk about it?" Or imagine if Steve's parents had been attentive enough to initiate a discussion with Steve. Imagine if some adult hit the conversational ball over the net to Steve instead of letting it slowly roll off the court.

Imagine if Steve's questions were taken seriously by an adoptive community and he poured his entrepreneurial brilliance not just into furthering high-tech interfaces but also into furthering the gospel. Imagine what our world might be like if Steve had funneled his leadership resources into both Silicon Valley and the kingdom.

Unfortunately, no adult had those conversations with Steve.

Many of us can relate to Steve; perhaps you have a story of your own. A time when you were faced with an injustice or a tragedy and felt completely helpless to do anything about it. A time when you wondered why God didn't just fix it. Why God couldn't figure out how to make the suffering stop.

Why, God?

Those two words have punctuated faith crises for more than a few believers through the ages. Unfortunately, the questions of too many adolescents are met in the church with silence, trite fix-it Bible quotations, or a well-meaning

"Just have faith" from those around them. In short, their questions and doubts are pushed underground and either blocked out or left to grow like cancer cells that eventually consume faith.

Whether students in your ministry are disturbed by today's wars and famines or wondering about God's goodness in the midst of fifth-period algebra, their questions and doubts are begging to be unearthed. The question before us is, "Will we *let them* be known?"

Doubts Happen

Some teenagers come from traditions or training that suggests that doubt is troubling or even sinful. But our research found that doubt can actually help form our faith in stronger and perhaps more lasting ways.[2] Below are a few illustrations of the role of questioning in the spiritual growth of adolescents.

Thanks in large part to a sizable research grant from the Lilly Endowment, the Fuller Youth Institute launched the College Transition Project. Our six years of quantitative and qualitative research with students was fueled by two goals: to better understand the dynamics of youth group graduates' transition to college and to pinpoint the steps youth workers, churches, parents, and students themselves can take to help students stay on the path of long-term faith.[3]

At the center of the research stood two longitudinal studies that focused on 384 youth group seniors during their first three years in college. In many ways, these students represent "typical" youth group seniors transitioning to college (they come from different regions across the United States; they attend a mix of public, private, and Christian colleges and vocational schools; 59 percent are female

and 41 percent are male). Yet in comparison to the typical student headed to college, the students in our sample tend to have higher high school grade point averages and are more likely to come from intact families. Students were recruited from churches with full-time professional youth pastors, which means they are likely to come from larger-than-average youth groups (average youth group size is fifty to seventy-five students). These factors bring a certain bias to our findings, which we diligently tried to counter by examining other research studies and by conducting face-to-face interviews with students with more diverse academic, family, and church backgrounds.

Seventy percent of the students in our longitudinal study of youth group graduates reported that they had doubts in high school about what they believed about God and the Christian faith, and just as many felt like they wanted to talk with their youth leaders about their doubts. Yet *less than half* of those students actually talked with leaders. Likewise, less than half talked with their youth group peers about their doubts. In other words, a lot of young people are wrestling with tough questions *alone* and in *silence*.

When college students were asked to reflect back on the doubts they remembered having during high school, their responses were wide-ranging, from "Will God still love me if I have sex?" to "Why do I feel like I am never able to hear God?" Overall, responses tended to cluster around four central questions (listed in no particular order):

1. Does God exist?
2. Does God love me?
3. Am I living the life God wants?
4. Is Christianity true/the only way to God?

As we have shared these questions with leaders and parents across the country, one of the resounding responses has been that these are questions adults have too. Perhaps when adults are silent about their own faith questions, teenagers don't know that they can ask their questions aloud.

Developmentally, adolescents are calling everything into question: Who am I? Do I matter? Where (and with whom) do I belong? These questions come right alongside questions about faith: Who is God? Does God matter? Does God care about me? How do I fit into God's family? As adolescence surges on, these important questions cycle in and out of consciousness and are more pressing at times than others. You may know young people who live in constant torment about the meaning of life while their peers seem hardly able to skim the surface of the identity-development waters.

Meanwhile, conversations pop up that surprise young people in more confronting ways. Consider the following examples of four common adolescent attitudes, drawn from a composite of actual teenagers.

Eli: Faith is a personal thing. I will always respect what you believe. All I'm asking for in return is that you respect what I believe. To say that my religious beliefs are false is intolerant. I think Jesus is a wonderful example, but there are other ways to find great truth too.

Carla: I'm not concerned about getting into arguments with people, but I do believe Jesus is the true way to know God. People will know Jesus by the way I love others, and I have to share Jesus whenever I can so everyone can know the truth.

Scott: Everyone is so afraid of offending other people that we lose a sense of what makes us different and unique. Christianity *is* different, and we need to make sure people know what those differences are. People might call me intolerant, but aren't they just being intolerant of me too?

Sarah: Christians I know who claim to know all the truth make me so mad. How can they be so arrogant? What about people who were born in cultures where they grew up learning a different faith? How can we be so convinced that they aren't also right?

Chances are good that your students are wondering about these and a host of other questions. But they may not feel they have permission to ask.[4]

Safety and Support Matter

Safety to express doubt seems to be connected with stronger faith. We found that high school seniors who feel most free to express doubt and discuss their personal problems with adults also showed greater faith maturity in college. Further, among those who had doubts and did talk with leaders or peers about them, about half found these conversations helped them. This helpfulness was also linked to stronger faith across the transition. It might be that simply creating safe spaces for young people to explore hard questions can deepen faith. In other words, it's not necessarily doubt that is toxic to young people's faith; it may be silence.

We also found a relationship between young people feeling safe to share doubts and struggles and their feeling of being supported by God. Our study explored correlations between a scale measuring the concept of "God support"—the extent to which someone feels that God cares about their life, feels close to God, and feels valued by God[5]—and a number of other factors. Safe environments for expressing doubts were positively correlated with God support in those analyses. Talking with adults about doubts was also linked to feeling supported by God, and feeling more supported by God was linked to stronger faith maturity as measured in other scales. It seems as though there is a connection between students' perception of God, their perceived safety to express doubt, and their actual faith maturity.

Doubts Are Not Necessarily the End of Faith

Lest we be misunderstood, simply *having* doubts does not transfer into more mature faith. For many students, struggling with faith is connected to weakened faith, at least in the short term. One of the scales incorporated in our third-year survey of the longitudinal study was the "Spiritual Struggles Scale."[6] Students were asked to indicate the extent to which each item on a list of religious struggles (e.g., "Felt distant from God," "Questioned my religious/spiritual beliefs") had described them in college. An inverse relationship was found between students' experiences of struggling with belief and their tendency toward lasting faith. This left us to wonder whether these students received the support they needed in the midst of their struggles.

On the other side of struggle, students were asked about various events and the extent to which they strengthened or weakened faith.[7] Interestingly, experiences of loneliness, anxiety, and feeling overwhelmed seem to push students toward God. These feelings were reported as forces that strengthened faith, and when analyzed alongside measures of faith maturity and practice, exhibited strong correlations.

The same was true of dialogue with other students. The stretching experiences most connected to faith longevity were interactions with other students, particularly with people of other faiths and with students of other cultures or ethnicities. Leaders and parents often fear that the increased diversity of lifestyle and belief that many students encounter in college will weaken their faith; in our research, the opposite seems to be true.

Other research has found similar correlations between young people's faith and experiences. Research has shown that faith can grow as it encounters the following sorts of significant struggles as well as engagement with new people:[8]

1. Exposure to diverse ways of thinking, whether through other students, classes, or some other source
2. Multicultural exposure through mission trips, living in another culture, befriending someone from another culture, or even reading about people from other cultures
3. Relationship, health, or emotional challenges like significant illness, conflict with parents, or other negative experiences

In her classic study on crisis and faith, Margaret Hall discovered that those who showed the most spiritual depth after experiencing crises were those who had consciously reoriented their faith in order to overcome the crisis. In other words, they were attentive to the ways their faith must change so they could climb out of the pit of despair.[9]

One student in our study described a similar experience.

Entering my sophomore year of college, I became very, I guess, disappointed with life. I had all these ideas about college and it wasn't necessarily going how I wanted. I was feeling very far away from God and very dry spiritually, struggling to find a church and a church family where I could fit in at school. And as I went through that long struggle, basically spiritual darkness . . . when I came out of it I found God kind of waiting for me on the other side, and realized that he'd been with me through that struggle, through that time of question and doubt and searching.

Richard Niebuhr once described this kind of journey as a progression from *shipwreck* to *gladness* and eventually *amazement* at the transformation God brings.[10] Tools like lament can be helpful companions on this journey, as we will discuss in the last section of this chapter.

The Role of Adoptive Community in Adolescent Doubt: Learning from Other Perspectives

Doubt as a Force That Shapes Identity

In the midst of the adolescent process of identity formation, psychologist James Marcia has suggested that crises—such as doubts—play a crucial role.[11] Marcia believes that the healthiest state of identity development is the status of "identity achievement," meaning that individuals (both young and old) have made clear identity choices and commitments (related to faith, sexuality, ethnicity, and other areas of identity). These commitments emerge only on the other side of identity crisis experiences, which lead young people into deeper exploration.

The majority of adolescents do not reach that "achieved" state; they tend to land in two of the other states. They are either in a "diffused" state, meaning they are unable or unwilling to explore or commit to any identity, or they are in a "foreclosed" state, meaning that they have embraced certain identity commitments but those commitments are really the commitments of adults who are important to them or their culture rather than the result of their own exploration. According to Marcia, while there is no definitive path from a "foreclosed" or "diffused" identity to an "achieved" identity, it is often struggles—such as wrestling with doubt—that help adolescents and emerging adults pin down a clearer sense of who they are and what they believe. These crises lead to a necessary state of "moratorium" during which commitments are temporarily placed on hold while other alternatives are explored. As unnerving as this sounds to adults attempting to shepherd the spiritual formation of young people, this period of moratorium is actually a good sign that students are in the midst of a critical process.

Doubt and the Gift of Adoptive Community

While Marcia doesn't exhaustively describe the role of community in the identity formation process, others highlight the potential of the adoptive faith community to be the soil in which seeds of doubt can bear fruit in young people's lives—whether that fruit is related to identity formation or other types of formation, such as spiritual vibrancy or emotional health. Chris Heuertz, former international director of Word Made Flesh, chronicles lessons learned through twenty years of living in community with others who are involved in advocacy and service among the poor.[12] He writes that in spite of the brokenness we find in any community, we also find unexpected gifts. The gifts are themselves born out of the very struggles and failures we usually hope to avoid when we enter a community.

One of those gifts is the way that community helps us to hold our faith through doubt. Heuertz relays advice given to him by a priest in the midst of a season of doubt: "The opposite of faith isn't doubt but certainty."[13] In other words, faith is sometimes erroneously reduced to intellectual assent to a reasonable set of beliefs, but that formula does not actually require true faith. Faith requires humility and courage to hold something mysterious, something beyond our understanding.

Heuertz goes so far as to suggest, "Doubt is necessary for faith. Being out of touch with our doubts is an indication that we're probably not in touch with the gift of faith."[14] Perhaps it is true that without a period of questioning and exploring our belief, we continue to carry a faith that has been given to us by someone else rather than a faith we have wrestled with and internalized. When intellectual faith comes up against real-life tragedy or exposure to injustice, the walls often come crashing down. This is the experience of many of our students after high school.

But there is an unexpected gift that doubting in community offers: others hold faith for us when we struggle to believe. Heuertz writes, "One of the surprising gifts of faith, then, is that it's often not for yourself but for someone else. . . . Community is an incubator in which faith and doubt can coexist."[15]

The life of Mother Teresa offers a vivid example. When her personal writings and confessions were published after her death, they revealed more than fifty years of darkness and doubt. Perhaps what is most amazing is how she remained committed to God and to her community throughout that spiritual blackout. She never ran away, and she never stopped serving diligently among the poor. Mother Teresa had doubts, but she *never stopped having faith*.

In her research on supporting emerging adult spirituality, Sharon Parks once asked a pastor, "Why do you think that so many young adults are present in your church?" His thoughtful response is one we might want to emulate: "I think it is because we are willing to welcome a lot of questions."[16] Parks highlights the importance of "mentoring communities" for emerging adult identity and faith. She explains:

> A mentoring community offers hospitality to the potential of the emerging self, and it offers access to worthy dreams of self and world. . . . It offers a network of belonging in which young adults feel recognized as who they really are, and as who they are becoming. It offers both challenge and support and thus offers good company for both the emerging strength and the distinctive vulnerability of the young adult.[17]

"Good company." That is a good descriptor of what is missing from many of our students' lives. Our church might offer great ministry programs, but what young people most need are good—and faithful—companions. Based on his own phenomenological research with young people, Andrew Zirschky similarly urges, "If we are going to respond adequately to the doubting experiences of youth, we need to ensure that young people . . . have patient, understanding companions who can guide and care for them through the twists and turns of the journey of doubt."[18]

Acknowledging the Incredulity of Scripture

National Public Radio (NPR) recently ran a series titled "Losing Our Religion,"[19] which explores why so many young people seem to be running from faith and the religious institutions surrounding it.

In one interview, NPR's David Green speaks with six young people who are wrestling with the role of religion in their lives. Many of their concerns are not that surprising, including their discomfort with the idea of "hell" as well as with the church's response to homosexuality and why a good God would allow suffering.

One short interview brings a different twist to why young people walk away from faith. A thirty-three-year-old who was raised Muslim describes how, even as a child, stories (such as the story of Abraham being willing to sacrifice Isaac) seemed unbelievable. As this former Muslim points out, if a father today said he needed to sacrifice his son because God said to do it, he would be "locked up."

We who have come to accept the Bible as the inspired Word of God may at times lose sight of how downright strange it can seem. Donkeys talk. Seas part. Someone who has been crucified comes back to life three days later. As we expose young people to the Bible, let us not lose sight of how extraordinary certain passages are. Let us use those passages as opportunities to invite students to ask tough questions as they enter into the mystery of God.

Making Space for Doubt

Thankfully, we do not need to leave young people who are doubting alone in our ministries or our homes. Below are some ideas for creating space in our relationships and programs with adolescents so that their questions can be both heard and unpacked within the adoptive community.

Creating Safe Zones

The perception that "good Christians don't doubt" can easily (and sometimes unintentionally) be fostered in youth ministry. This understanding can be intensified by the letdowns that may follow retreat and camp highs and hype, haunting students who wake up the next week and do not "feel God" as viscerally as before. Somehow, many youth ministries today have failed to embrace the teaching of Jude 22 to "be merciful to those who doubt."

Our responsibility to the kids in our care includes creating safe places for questions that emerge along the faith journey. In the family, small group settings, mentoring relationships, and in the context of the broader youth ministry, how are doubts and struggles being voiced? How are they being received?

Sociologist Tim Clydesdale relays the following findings from his research on college students, specifically those who had walked away from faith.

In many cases, these teens reported having important questions regarding faith during early adolescence (12–14 years old) that were ignored by their parents or pastors rather than taken seriously and engaged thoughtfully. It is in early adolescence that faith trajectories (along with other life trajectories) are set. . . . Sadly, most youth ministries are long on fun and fluff and short on listening and thoughtful engagement. The former produces a million paper boats; the latter produces a handful of seaworthy ships. Launching a million paper boats is an amazing spectacle on a clear summer day, but only a ship can weather storms and cross oceans.

Paper boats versus seaworthy ships. Which are we building?[20]

One ministry works to create space for struggles and doubts to be safely heard. The leaders close each session of their fifth- and sixth-grade group with fifty-six seconds of silence, during which kids can write down any question on a note card. The hope is to make asking questions a normal part of faith development starting in early adolescence, even if all of those questions are not answered right away.

Another church is working hard to foster honesty in the midst of its confirmation program. At the conclusion of the six-month process, most students write a statement of faith. Last year one student felt safe enough to write a "Statement of Doubt" instead. This allowed her to share openly with the community that her own journey of faith was not yet at the place of trusting Christ. Several months later, she came to the point where she had wrestled through her doubts and decided to be baptized as an expression of her newfound trust. Alongside her were several adults who had supported her, prayed for her, and walked with her through her valley of doubt to the other side of faith.

Learning to Lament

While Scripture does not always give us answers to all our questions, the Bible does include a section in which doubts and struggles are freely expressed: the book of Psalms. While Psalms is commonly thought of as a book of praises, the writers of the Hebrew songs and prayers that became their worship book were not afraid to ask God to show up in the midst of ugly situations. Out of the 150 psalms, over one-third are considered laments.[21]

A lament can be defined simply as a cry to God. It is both an act of grief and a plea for help. Lament is usually something we do in the dark places, often during the darkest points of our life journeys. For example, Psalm 88 ends with the phrase "darkness is my closest friend" (v. 18). Walter Brueggemann calls the laments the psalms of "disorientation." He urges that our worship in community with others should not just focus on the cheerful aspects of life and faith but must also consider the disturbingly incoherent and painful realities as well. Brueggemann suggests that lament is necessary in faith formation, arguing that

> where capacity to initiate lament is absent, one is left only with praise and doxology. God then is omnipotent, always to be praised. The believer is nothing, and can praise or accept guilt uncritically where life with God does not function properly. The outcome is a "False Self," bad faith that is based in fear and guilt and lived out as resentful or self-deceptive works of righteousness. The absence of lament makes a religion of coercive obedience the only possibility.[22]

One of the most frequently asked questions in Scripture is "How long, O Lord?" (see Ps. 13 for several examples). It is an important question because it calls God to act in order to end our pain or the pain of others. Laments like this do not answer all of our questions, but lamenting can be a helpful part of strengthening our faith by reminding us that answers are not everything. As the psalmists proclaim over and over, the unfailing love of God is not wiped out by anything: not our crises, not our doubts, not even our sins. By weaving lament into our corporate worship and prayer life, we open up the possibility that kids might feel freer to share their own hard questions and maybe even write or sing their own psalms of lament.

The book of Job offers an extended lament that closes with a surprising response from God. When we interviewed one of Fuller Seminary's Old Testament experts, John Goldingay, we asked him whether there is anything we cannot say to God. He cited Job in his response.

> A great thing about the story of Job is that Job beats on God's chest for ages and ages, and eventually God answers back. Job perhaps slightly wishes he hadn't said some of those things, but that doesn't take away from the fact that it's a real relationship. Real things go on between Job and God. When we do speak to God like that, we risk hearing back from God, but that's great because there's a relationship! Nobody has to mince words. So I don't think there's anything that you can't say to God. But when you speak to God, you may find there are no limits to what God may say back![23]

In response to traumatic experiences in particular, it is critically important for a community of faith to offer space for this kind of response to God. As youth workers, we may fear taking students to those places of anger and disappointment with God. However, failing to create an environment for authentic lament can result in spiritually and psychologically short-circuiting the necessary healing process. Authentic trust in God may take a long time, and kids need faithful adults to walk that difficult road with them. Youth leaders have the opportunity to offer the hope of Christ and his reorienting power to lives that have been plunged into trauma and disorientation.

Preparing Seniors for Doubt and Dialogue

During our Sticky Faith research, one youth pastor from Tennessee shared with us, "Every year in the fall I get phone calls—usually in the middle of the night—from freshman college students after they get a campus ministry visit where they're asked if they ever doubt. If they say yes, they're told they don't have enough faith. They call me back confused, asking, 'Is it okay to doubt or not?'"

Some students will leave our ministries and face new questions and doubts in college that they have not wondered about before. Giving them a healthy heads-up about this before they leave home can help doubt become a building block for new, deeper faith.

Alongside new doubts in college often comes new dialogue. Students need to understand the basics of Christian faith in order to discuss their faith with others, and training in core beliefs (sometimes called apologetics) can be helpful. However, learning to argue about faith may not be the most helpful approach. Reflecting on her teenage years, author Alisa Harris writes about her own experience of being trained to give these kinds of responses: "I was taught that faith was so simple and easily grasped that I could argue someone into it, which ended up shaking my faith when I found that belief wasn't simple, and argumentation and evidence could only take me so far."[24] Leaders preparing seniors for talking about faith after high school would do well to avoid oversimplifying belief into neat tenets that resolve every question with an overly simplistic answer.[25]

In a letter to a younger version of himself, author Brian McLaren offers words I suspect many of our high school seniors and former youth group students might benefit from hearing.

I want to whisper a few possibilities to you—whisper them, not shout them; pose them as possibilities, not as yet more requirements for you to try to believe. First, God is real. God is faithful. God is good.

But not exactly in the ways you have been taught, and not exactly in the ways you wish.

. . . There aren't any shortcuts from where you are to where you will someday be. But maybe this second possibility will help you: there is a difference between trusting God and trusting your current ideas about God.[26]

Setting Up Scaffolding

In the midst of all this doubt and struggle, leaders play a significant support role. Developmental theorist Lev Vygotsky coined two interrelated concepts that help us to think more deeply about the kinds of support young people need: *zone of proximal development* and *scaffolding*.[27]

The *zone of proximal development* refers to a range of tasks and concepts that are just beyond a student's current field of mastery, for which he or she needs some assistance from another person to learn. In the case of a student struggling with new ideas about God based on what he or she has read in the Bible or heard from a friend, part of what is happening is the expansion of the student's ability to assimilate the new information into his or her current understanding. But rather than depending entirely on that student's personal competence, intelligence, or grit, Vygotsky asserts that relationships are the key to building skills in this zone. It is through relationships with adults that adolescents gain the support they need to safely explore and tackle tasks just beyond their mental, physical, or emotional reach.

Similarly, *scaffolding* serves as the safe structure around the emerging adolescent that supports growth and fosters co-learning with adults and other kids. Just as scaffolding on a building allows workers access to each part of the structure as it rises, adults become the steadying force that is carefully added (when kids are most in need of that support) and removed (when they need to be set free to try on their own). Just as scaffolding is made of many interlocking pieces in order to balance the weight and surround the building, no one adult can provide all the scaffolding in a young person's life. To truly thrive, every adolescent needs an interlocking network of caring adults. In the midst of experiences of doubt that challenge and stretch them, adolescents need safe people and places to support the overwhelming amount of internal processing taking place.

Can I Ask That? Responding to Hard Questions as They Arise

Like the pastor at the start of the chapter with thirteen-year-old Steve, have you ever been in a conversation with a teenager where you weren't sure what to say next? The question that catches you off guard in the hallway just as you are stepping into youth group. The one that comes by text around eleven o'clock at night, just as you are shutting down your phone to collapse in bed. Or the question right at the end of Bible study when you really do not have the time or energy to entertain it.

With the theme of companionship in mind from earlier in our discussion, here are the four words we recommend every parent, leader, and mentor keep handy in their back pocket for moments like these as we practice adoptive youth ministry: "I don't know, but . . ."

There are a handful of great ways to complete that sentence. *I don't know, but . . .*

that's an important question.

let's find out together.

I wonder that too.

I bet you're not the first person to ask that.

who do you think we could ask about that?

I wonder what stirred up that question just now?

that question isn't too big for God.

thanks for sharing it with me.

You might, of course, have an answer to the question. Even if you do, it might be wise to step back and probe a bit before unleashing your "right" answer. It might turn out that being heard is more important than the answer itself, at least at that moment.

When students around us fall into seasons of uncertainty, let us help them fall in the light of Christ and Christ's people, ready to catch and hold them through doubt and back into faith, as children of God and members of the family.

A Call to Adoptive Ministry

Middle School Distinctives

HEATHER FLIES

Middle school ministry is crucial in youth ministry, especially in a ministry that is seeking to partner in God's adoptive work with those he loves. The middle school age group is a unique population. On the one hand, they have clearly entered into what scholars view as contemporary adolescence, roughly coinciding with the onset of female puberty. (While there are many theories, we are not certain of the specific causes of earlier menses. We do know that the average age of puberty, which is the age that correlates with the beginning of early adolescence, continues to get younger in girls.[1] On average, it begins around eleven, until the shift into mid-adolescence around the age of fourteen.) This is the time when adolescents have the body of an adult and the brain of a child.[2] On the other hand, this is also the time when middle school students are significantly vulnerable, as they are not yet abstractly aware and reflective about their environment but are relationally intuitive. It is during this time that adult leaders must be able to offer young teens the ethos or feel of the adoptive work of Christ and ministry of the body, perhaps even more so than the content of the gospel. Content is obviously important, but according to brain researchers like Daniel J. Siegel and the Mindfulness Institute, content takes root best when it is accompanied by an experience that matches it.[3] Therefore, middle school adoptive youth ministry needs to be marked by kindness, warmth, and nurture while offering encouragement to lift their young voices; they need to learn what it means to become a participant in the kingdom of God.

Because of the uniqueness of this ministry and the vital nature of the leadership these early adolescents require, we have asked Heather Flies to write this chapter. Flies is one of the most well-respected and sought-out leaders of middle school ministry in the country. Her credibility begins with her longevity, inspiring training ability, and faithful commitment to the vitality required of middle school ministry. But what sets Flies apart is both her depth of insight into this unique population and her understanding of their fragile and tender spirits (often hidden beneath a sheen of chaos and noise). She is also among the most gracious, uplifting, and warm people I have ever encountered. She is one of a kind.

We wanted to invite Flies as an author because we believe that every youth worker needs to hear from her. She uses few (if any) footnotes, but her work is grounded in solid research and scholarship. She regularly consults with academics, and she works hard at the deepest issues related to her ministry. As you read, know that we are not lifting Flies up simply because she is a gifted and deeply loved youth worker—although that should be reason enough—but because in our view she is among the very best at getting at the heart of adoptive middle school ministry.

As you read this chapter, consider these questions:

1. *Discuss the distinctive characteristics of middle school students that Flies describes. How could these unique qualities positively contribute to the life of a church?*
2. *A section of this chapter is devoted to being a good listener. What are some practical ways that youth leaders can become better listeners?*
3. *Name three ways in which middle school students could be integrated into the larger community of a church as adopted siblings of the congregation.*

If an average adult were to walk into a room filled with middle schoolers, he might just turn around and walk right back out. The sight of lanky and awkward boys and girls with way too much makeup on their faces and way too much metal in their mouths is overwhelming. The noise is deafening. The chaos is disturbing. It makes you want to run, and that's understandable. For many adults, the sight

(and the smell!) brings back painful memories from their dramatic middle school years. For others, the thought of trying to interact with a thirteen-year-old leaves them speechless and sweaty.

I'm glad I'm not average. The Lord, in his goodness, has given me a love for middle schoolers that is supernatural and eternal. When I walk into a room full of young adolescents, I am energized. As I approach that mascaraed girl, my mind is flooded with questions I want to engage her in because I believe she is capable of so much more than most adults give her credit for. When that lanky boy awkwardly bounds up to me, I see beyond the awkwardness to the heart that just wants to be noticed and loved. The smell? Well, one never gets used to that. I have simply learned to breathe through my mouth.

I hope and pray that you aren't normal either. As a middle school pastor in Minnesota, I pray for more adults like you and me every day. More than ever, middle school students need godly, grounded, passionate, and interested adults to not only walk into that room but also to walk alongside them as they move through their teenage years and into adulthood.

Students don't typically realize the need for this kind of investment while they are in middle school, but the benefits are obvious to those outside the early adolescent world. When *Sticky Faith* by Kara Powell and Chap Clark came on the scene, it validated what adults, especially youth ministers and parents, had been sensing for years: developing faith-filled young adults requires surrounding those students with adults who are faith-filled and interested in them. *Sticky Faith* didn't just confirm what we were seeing in the lives of our students; it inspired us to be more intentional in fostering those kind of influential relationships between students and adults.

Parents and Middle School Ministry

Middle school ministries are in danger of becoming the enemy of the parent of a middle schooler. For one of the first times in the child's life, she developmentally and naturally begins to want space from her parents. She begins to place more emphasis on the opinion of her friends than the input from her parents. She starts to push back on Mom's ideas and begins to question Dad's way of doing life. At the same time, she enters the middle school ministry at the church. In the car ride home from youth group, the daughter talks about how cool the youth leaders are and how the youth pastor said something that was simply life changing! Meanwhile, mom sits behind the steering wheel thinking, *I used to be the cool one . . . and I've been saying exactly what the youth pastor said for twelve years!*

To address that danger, our ministry does everything in our power to be allies, not enemies, of parents. One practical way we do this is by giving parents windows into their children's lives. Take summer camp, for instance. Each year, we whisk busloads of middle school students away from their parents to an exotic place in the north woods. We have incredible experiences, can't-stop-laughing kind of fun, powerful group worship, and relational bonding. When we get home, rather than put those happy, rank, and tired students into their families' cars only to answer their parents' excited questions with grunts and one-word answers, we have a summer camp celebration.

The summer camp celebration is a one-hour event meant to be the climax of a student's camp adventure and a large window for a parent to see into their child's life in the last five days. All week at camp we talk about the celebration. The entire bus ride home is a ramp-up to the celebration. Parents are waving enthusiastically from the sidewalk as the buses pull up, and the students—bodies halfway out of the bus windows—are doing the same. We sweep all that energy inside the church building and the party begins!

As a student sits next to his parent, he is encouraged (from the stage) to color commentate on each image that comes across the screen in our highlight video. The room erupts with conversation as kids describe the camper hunt, skeet shooting, funny mail, and the reason leaders are being pied in the face and students doused with ice-cold buckets of water. The look on the faces of the parents is anything but hostile!

During that intentional hour, we also highlight chapel teaching from the week, do worship with the parents (three of the campers' favorite songs, led by the camp worship leader), perform skits, and reveal the winners of the week's cabin clean-up competition. At the end of the night, parents in tow, students proudly introduce their counselors. During an earlier counselor meeting, I encourage the counselors to have a "camper party" when they first meet the parent. "Tell them all the qualities you discovered and came to admire in their camper. The parent will appreciate it, and the kid will love it!" As families walk to their vehicles after the celebration, smelly luggage in hand, parents know in that moment (if they didn't know before) that we are allies with them. We are partners in helping to develop young men and women who fear and love the Lord. Another way we partner with parents during the middle school years is by offering to be part of "the five" for their child. Research found that students whose faith stuck into adulthood had webs of relationships surrounding them. These young adults had five or more adults in their lives, aside from their parents, who modeled faith and intentionally invested in the faith of those students.[4] Whether or not volunteer or even paid staff members play that kind of role in the lives of young adolescents, our commitment is to create the kind of atmosphere where every kid feels what it is like to be adopted by people who treat them like the family they are.

Planning for Adoptive Middle School Ministry

Making that happen, practically, takes deliberate and careful reflection, communication, and intentionality. First, we need to gather a team of volunteers who are as diverse as the students we minister to. While some pastors believe that an effective youth worker fits a certain profile, experience has convinced me that there is not a single profile. In over twenty years of youth ministry I have been around a few hundred effective youth workers, and each one is unique. As Paul in 1 Corinthians 12 describes the body of Christ as having many members with different gifts, each placed by God, so it is with volunteers in the family of God. What youth workers have in common is a love for the Lord and a sincere love of young people. In almost every other way, they are different.

Here is a sample of youth workers we have served alongside. Micah is in his mid-twenties. He is strong and athletic. He plays the guitar and is creative. The boys adore him, and he's able to model a softer, more creative aspect of athleticism. Yo became a single mother shortly after committing her life to the Lord. At thirty-eight she is strong, passionate, and dedicated. She can arm wrestle the boys (and win!) and encourages the girls to pursue their passions. Greg is in his late fifties. He is single and committed to holiness in all he does. He knows nothing of pop culture (nor does he want to) but is able to connect with students because of his genuine care for them and his consistent presence in the ministry. Victoria is in her late forties. She is married with two boys, and yet one of her favorite things to do is hang around early teens. She is a wild kid-magnet. She draws them in with flare and then goes deep in conversation and relationship.

There is great beauty in a diverse team! When our team walks into the youth room on a Wednesday night, they see a sea of students as diverse as they are. Naturally energetic leaders scream and run toward the out-of-control middle schoolers. Quiet leaders quietly lean up against the wall beside the shy students. Athletic leaders grab a ball or Frisbee and send it down to the crowd of agile students at the other end of the room. Intelligent leaders approach the students reading in the corner and ask, "What books did you read this last week?" The only thing better is watching the athletic leader teaching the reader how to throw a football or the quiet leader being taught a new dance move by my (literally) off-the-wall students. As you can see, "the five" will soon be identified!

Outside the Walls

Second, for volunteers to be significant adoption guides and mentors (or become part of "the five" for a young person), they need to catch a vision to engage with middle school students outside normal programming. On a really good week, we see a middle schooler for three and a half hours. We see him for two hours on Sunday morning if he comes to our Sunday school hour *and* sits in the big service with us and for an hour and a half during our midweek program. That means that 98 percent of his life is spent outside the walls of the church building. If we, as youth workers, are not engaging them outside the walls of the church, we are missing 98 percent of kids' lives!

How can we help early adolescents, who are fragile and needy to begin with, to believe that the church is truly their family and that the adults they pass by are actually their siblings, if we're missing 98 percent of a student's life? We can't. We need to infiltrate their lives outside the church! If this vision is cast and volunteers are willing to give it a shot, they'll see the benefits almost instantly with middle schoolers.

Making the Effort to Care beyond the Program

Lydia was a student in our middle school ministry. Lydia's mom desperately wanted her to connect with the students and leaders in our group, but Lydia wasn't up for it. One Sunday morning, I saw her mom in the commons, and she said, "Heather! I want you to meet Lydia!" She then called out to Lydia across the room. When Lydia turned toward us, I waved, and she turned and ran away. Not the response either her mom or I was hoping for. Lydia didn't know it, but her actions that day automatically put her on my hit list. No matter what it took, I was going to "get" Lydia.

I did all I knew to do when I saw Lydia. I smiled, tried to engage her in conversation, complimented her on her hair, introduced her to other girls. Nothing worked. I continued to be greeted with arms crossed over the chest and a look of indifference. One day in our doctrinal class, I overheard her tell another student that she was part of the color guard at school. I must be honest with you, I'm more of a football and softball girl myself, but I said, "What? Lydia, you're on the color guard squad?! I love color guard! Can I come watch you . . . do color guard?" (Does one "do" color guard?) I didn't even know what terminology to use, but that didn't seem to matter to Lydia. She was surprised, but she agreed that she would get me her schedule.

That night I sat down at my computer thirty minutes after the class had ended. In my in box was an email from Lydia with her upcoming color guard events. The only one I could make, of course, was twenty miles away and on a Friday night. My boyfriend (now husband) Chad and I made a date night of it and traveled twenty miles one way to see Lydia perform for three and a half minutes. I was down on the gym floor taking pictures and hollering for all I was worth at what I hoped were the right times.

When the performances were finished, Lydia came bounding up the bleachers and threw her arms around me. She was jumping up and down with giddiness. By a simple act of entering her world, I had earned Lydia's trust. I had communicated that I "got" her. And how? By showing up outside the walls of the church. By showing her that I was interested in *her*, not just her church attendance. We took a picture that night—Lydia, Chad, and me—and it's one I'll keep as long as I am on this earth. Lydia's arms around both of us and her beaming smile are proof of what it means to a middle schooler when you take time to invest.

Baby Steps

To make engagement with students easier, those of us who engage outside the walls of the church often invite newer volunteers along with us. Rather than going on their own and possibly feeling as awkward as the middle schooler they're ministering to, they attend with us as we walk them through all that we do.

When Nicki came to Emily's band concert with me, we stopped at the convenience store to purchase snacks for Emily. Take note: bringing candy and caffeine is a must when working with teenagers—it makes any event a success. Since Emily was playing her flute in the concert that night, I passed by the Snickers and got her lip balm instead. And a Mountain Dew. Both her lips and her body need hydration!

As we walked in, I explained to Nicki how connecting with the parent at an event is just as important as connecting with the student. Parents need to know we are allies. Plus it means the world to parents to have another adult care for and invest in their child. We sat down next to Emily's mom and told her all the qualities we admired in her daughter. When Emily walked out in her black concert outfit, we screamed her name over and over, much to the dismay of the clueless adults around us. But not Emily's mother; it was obvious that she was overcome with gratitude that we were there, simply because we cared about Emily.

Many volunteers would love to spend more time engaging with young people, but often they cannot afford to pay for concerts, games, movies, and meals. Our church makes it a priority for volunteers to engage with students by allotting budget money for events and one-on-ones. Our youth workers already give of their time, energy, insight, and love; we don't want them to have to give financially as well.

If leaders connect with a student outside our programs and turn in a receipt, they are reimbursed. For leaders who are college students, this is especially encouraging and freeing.

Knowing Is Understanding

Third, for our volunteers to convince our kids that they are part of the family, they need to understand how middle schoolers think, what they are dealing with, and how best to come alongside them. As we lead volunteers and new interns, we don't need to make the process overly detailed or complicated, but some level of training is needed to be an effective, influential adult in the life of an early adolescent. In our case, we offer large group formal training four times in a school year, but our veteran leaders also model what it means to be a competent, engaged leader in all of the settings where we engage kids— at regular programs and events as well as in the more informal settings of the van, on the bus, and before-and-after time in the youth room. The topics for the staff training sessions are composed of four essential areas: early adolescent culture and development, listening and relational skills, the content of the gospel (especially as it is translated for an early adolescent brain), and how the overall program and structure of the ministry enables and fosters the kind of environment and relationships where students literally feel as if they have been adopted by a family. Because little of this comes naturally to very many people, every leader, regardless of his or her role, goes through this basic training.

The following scenario happens as a matter of course in middle school ministry for both men and women leaders, and therefore we must be prepared to respond to what kids need as well as what they say. Audrey, an eighth grader, and I were having one-on-one time, eating Reese's Peanut Butter Cups and Pringles and drinking Mountain Dew, when she said, "Heather, do you know why I like talking to you?" I thought it was probably because I fed her junk food but didn't want to assume, so I asked, "Why?" She said, "Because you don't freak out on me." As she shared more, it was clear that from her early-teen perspective, her mom "freaked out" either verbally or emotionally whenever Audrey shared personal information with her. While I didn't place too much stock in this feedback (middle schoolers are known for their exaggeration, for a variety of reasons), I knew that I needed to empathize with her without overtly taking sides. Developmentally, early adolescents need to believe that someone cares about them more than they need an adult to necessarily buy their whole story. Stories are often shaped to get the most attention possible. What Audrey needed from me that day was to have her feelings affirmed and to know that I was willing to stand with her. The content of her complaint about her mom could have been imagined or quite serious. As Audrey's confidant, I would eventually have to make that determination to know how to proceed, but at that moment she needed my focused compassion.

Oftentimes, middle schoolers will test the waters with a caring adult. A seventh-grade boy will tell you something that happened to another kid at school—let's say that kid got caught with vodka in his water bottle (true story). All the while the seventh-grade boy is gauging your response, and he doesn't even know that he is doing this! Early adolescents, both boys and girls, want to know one thing when dealing with an adult: Do you like me? If you were to overact to a given story, for example, or fail to engage and respond in a way that shows genuine interest, they would simply avoid you instead of coming to you to tell *their own* story. In the adolescent's mind and heart, his or her story is much more dramatic, difficult, and painful than anyone else's story. In my years of ministry, I have heard amazing, heartbreaking, and shocking statements and stories from students. I suspect that many, if not most, were exaggerations, if not outright fabrications. When a boy or girl wants me to know what happened to someone else, my outward response is to be as consistently kind and attentive as possible and to project a calm "Really? Wow. Tell me more about that." Internally, I am praying for supernatural guidance from the Holy Spirit.

Another skill in working with middle school students is listening. Seems simple, I know, but most adults in the world of middle schoolers don't listen well. I see it often: a student is chatting with leaders and friends after youth group when his mom comes up, in a hurry. "Let's go!" She marches off down the hall with the student trailing behind her saying, "But, mom, it was such an awesome night! Bryan did this thing with a blender and a McDonald's Happy Meal . . ." His mom's already turned the corner, so he stops talking and just follows her out the door. Unfortunately, sometimes it is this same mom who laments to me, "My son just doesn't talk to me anymore!"

In his book *Hurt 2.0: Inside the World of Today's Teenagers*, based on a nationwide ethnographic engagement with teenagers, Chap Clark shares a high school junior's response to Clark's desire for adults to know what life is like for teenagers. "Tell them our story. Tell them the truth—that nobody cares, that nobody listens, that teachers and coaches and cops and parents don't even know who we are.

Tell them *that* and see if anybody listens. Ha! Not a chance."[5]

Are You Listening?

Middle schoolers need and deserve undivided attention. They deserve someone who is willing to block out everything and everyone else to hear their hearts and ideas. I call it "putting on my blinders." Picture the blinders placed on racehorses to keep their eyes focused on what's ahead. Figuratively, I put on my blinders each time I'm talking with a middle school kid. I want that student to know and believe that he or she is my only focus in that moment. This is a tough task in a room filled with young adolescents bursting with overt needs and raw social skills! I have learned, however, how to ignore even the most persistent (euphemism for annoying) students and parents in order to stay focused on the individual I'm engaging. I believe that our ability to focus sends a strong and needed message: I care about you.

Many adults are poor listeners because they are uncomfortable with silence. So much is going on inside a young teen—new brain connections, raging hormones, newly experienced emotions—that sometimes it just takes a while for the words to make their way out of the mouth. Let's look at the emotions of a middle schooler for a moment. Sure, when he was in the third grade, he felt sad. His bike got run over by a neighbor, and he cried. Tough stuff. But the intensity of the sadness he feels now hardly compares. "Sad" doesn't do justice to what he's feeling. He'll need some time to label this new emotion. He might even need help from you to label the emotion. In the moment, though, he needs some time to externally process and be given the gift of communal silence.

A lot of adults have a hard time offering that time and silence. Instead of waiting as the student processes, we jump into stories about ourselves. Our intent is not malicious, but we automatically take the care and attention away from the student and turn it back to ourselves. Some of us might immediately ask the student another question when he hasn't even figured out his answer to the first one. A youth worker who wants to influence for the good learns to become comfortable with silence while ministering to a middle schooler.

Validation is another important gift you can offer a young teen. Something happens to you as you age; you forget. You forget how annoying it was when your mother forgot to wash the pair of jeans you wanted to wear to school *and* the football game on Friday. You forget how tragic it was when none of your friends were in your new quarter classes. You forget how devastating it was when the guy you liked decided to like your best friend. You forget the embarrassment of the swimming unit in seventh-grade PE.

Whenever I am with adults, I encourage them to look back. I ask them to share their answers to questions like: Who was your biggest crush in middle school? What are three words that your parents would have used to describe you when you were a teenager? Where did your deepest wound come from when you were a teenager? Parents, grandparents, youth leaders, teachers, and coaches need to remember the intensity and all-consuming nature of being a middle schooler if they desire to relate effectively with them!

When middle schoolers work up the courage to share with an adult, one of their primary hopes is to have their feelings validated. So often they feel shut down, often unintentionally, by adults who have forgotten how it feels to be a vulnerable post-child attempting to make sense of the life they have been handed. The early adolescent brain and psyche may not be able to understand what it is they feel when nobody seems to listen or to care, but they feel the rejection nonetheless. Our role as adoptive brothers and sisters of these budding peers must be to do all we can to honor them as we listen not only to their words but also to their hearts, validating their feelings with our focused responsiveness. The next time you interact with an early adolescent who shares something with you, regardless of how important (or unimportant) it sounds to you, remember he or she needs your encouragement and presence. It is vital that we respond by saying something like, "Wow, that must be frustrating! I'd be upset, too, if I were you." As you respond and empathize, carefully watch the reaction of the person before you. It may be imperceptible to the uncommitted eye, but if you look closely enough you will be able to see her shoulders relax and her eyes open a bit in surprise as she nods her head. You get it. You get her.

I have learned over the years how important it is to focus and to listen. When I keep a poker face (even in the midst of an outrageous story), work hard to listen, and validate feelings, I can feel the trust of that student begin to grow. Though it takes years for trust to be fully realized, especially in today's climate of abandonment, that is what a family does. As Chap Clark notes in *Hurt*, "The process of helping an adolescent develop a consistent faith takes time, patience, and perseverance. Faith is a long, complex journey, and adolescents need someone who will walk alongside them as long as it takes."[6] That's no small task! A long-term journey like that takes prayer, thoughtfulness, and intentionality. Obviously, a middle school

youth worker can't make that commitment to a huge number of kids. For example, a man may not be able to promise with integrity that he will be there for all of the boys in his small group, but he could choose two or three of those young men to follow into adulthood.

Ryan, a dedicated volunteer in the middle school ministry, has been practicing the elements of adoptive youth ministry instinctively for the past seventeen years. As the classes move through our three-year program, he chooses a few from each grade to follow as they grow. Although he never left the middle school ministry staff, he is at high school volleyball and football games. Ryan's a staple at graduation open houses, Eagle Scout ceremonies, and prom pictures. He initiates lunches with college students as they come home for Christmas break and is invited to their weddings. Ryan understands the long-term commitment, but he devotes himself to it anyway because he sees the long-term value in walking alongside students as they navigate life and faith. He is the prototype of an adoptive older brother who sees youth ministry as a vehicle for convincing kids that they matter and that they belong.

Adoption in Action: "The Senior Adult Pasta Dinner"

During the third year of the middle school ministry, our students engage in an eight-month systematic theology course on Sunday afternoons. The class—which covers the doctrines of revelation, Holy Spirit, Christ, angels and demons, and more—is intended to provide space for students to wrestle with the faith of their parents, teachers, and youth ministers in order to make it their own. The experience is entitled "AUG," which stands for Approved unto God. The name comes from 2 Timothy 2:15, "Do your best to present yourself to God as one approved, a worker who does not need to be ashamed and who correctly handles the word of truth." I realized years ago, as the primary teacher of the AUG program, that my students have an incredibly limited view of "the church." To most, it means youth group. To a few, it means "big church." To many, it's a building. Part of the issue lies in their development. Developmentally, middle schoolers inhabit a place of self-focus. The world, from their perspective, revolves around them. They consistently ask questions like "What's in it for me?" "What about me?" or "How will this affect me?" Seeing the church in the same way that the students and leaders around them in the youth room see the church is normal.

As leaders in the church, however, we must also take responsibility for their limited view of the church. Churches all over America have expended much energy in keeping students, especially middle school students, as far away from the rest of the church, and therefore the community, as possible. Growing up in my church, our youth rooms were in the back corner of the basement, as far from the sanctuary and adult Sunday school classrooms as possible. Being next to the boiler room offered warmth all throughout the calendar year, and the mold caused issues only for the students with allergies. At least we were out of the way. The only more effective strategy would have been to put us in a completely separate building.

When it comes to adoptive youth ministry, our students' view of the church isn't big enough. In response, we began the Senior Adult Pasta Dinner during the two-week section of the class that covers the doctrine of the church. In the first week's session, students learn about how the church was started, the ordinances of baptism and communion, and Christ's challenge to go and make more disciples. In the second week, students enter their classroom to find it filled with round tables covered with fancy white tablecloths. At each table sits four adults, all over the age of fifty-five.

The two-hour event brings together two groups of people that often feel unappreciated and marginalized, even in the Christian community. They have a great deal more in common than they know! At the beginning of the event, the anxiety in the room is palpable, in both the young and the old. The senior adults wonder what in the world they have in common with the teenagers and whether they'll get more than a few grunts in response to their questions. Students fear making and holding a conversation with someone who used to hold a phone that was connected to the wall.

I take the stage and microphone to do all I can to lessen the awkwardness and hesitancy in the room. "While we wait for dinner to be served, let's get to know each other! Students, walk your new adult friend through an average day in your life. Seniors, explain to your student the process you went through in order to obtain your driver's license."

From my perch, I see the students speak timidly at first. Of course they do. Many of their interactions with adults involve lectures, reprimands, or conversation about their new dentures or chronic back pain. Although I can't read their minds, I am certain my students are surprised as the seniors turn up their hearing aids, lean in, and listen intently.

When the students are done sharing about their day, I watch as the adults recount the experience of getting a license. The students, even the shy ones, are engaged; many offer active listening as the adults talk about driving on the farm when they were twelve and getting their licenses for a quarter down at Woolworth's. The students give their attention to the adults not only because of their common interest in driving but also because of the attention given to them just moments earlier.

Following dinner, we work to give the adults an idea of the kind of fun we have in the junior high ministry on a weekly basis. A trivia game is played, and the mix of questions includes everything from politics in 1952 to current pop culture. "If your table knows the answer, an adult needs to be the first to ring the roaming bell. For the adult to ring the bell, he or she must be in a piggy back position on a student." I can't explain the energy, laughter, and teamwork that is produced in those fifteen minutes! It's powerful and palpable.

Once these two groups of people have endeared themselves to one another, we progress into more personal territory. Students are matched with an adult and sent around the church building for a one-on-one faith interview. A three-page document is given to the AUG students that contains questions for the seniors about their families, friends, and faith.

For sixty minutes, students engage and take notes as the adults give testimony to what the Lord has done in, around, and through their lives. Some adults bring photos of themselves when they were teenagers or in the military. All senior adults share stories of the past, smiling, sighing, and sometimes shedding a tear. The students' notes will give structure to the paper they will write for the doctrine of the church section of the class. As another step toward endearment, students are required to send a copy of their profile paper to the adult they wrote about.

By the end of the evening, both the students and adults leave fulfilled, grateful, and often smiling. I feel like the church has genuinely worshiped together and been seen for what it is truly intended to be—children and adults, co-siblings in Christ, brothers and sisters called not only to love one another (John 15) and know one another (intergenerational ministry) but also to actually enjoy the gift of sharing life together. Every year we receive notes and emails from the seniors. Here is a sample:

Ron: Sean seems like a great kid with sensitivity to God and desire to know God's Word. Although he is new to Wooddale, he seems like he has received some good parenting and some good instruction (at least this year in the Jr. High ministry and in AUG!). I perceive him to be a very smart person and his homeschooling by his mother will probably send him far. He was by far the best dressed student at the event.

Helen: It was our pleasure to attend and meet those wonderful kids—we had a wonderful time and enjoyed the dinner, and so on. I think the senior/9th grade group is so beneficial to all—who knew it would be such a success? I was interviewed by Charlotte, a beautiful young girl—we had "adoption" in common and I enjoyed her immensely. I look forward to her report and commend you for your work with these kids. Talk about a crucial age—and they seem so enthused. Do you ever get feedback as to how their lives are affected by this amazing study? We continue to pray for you as well as the other staff for their great work.

Lois: I loved getting to know Summer. She is a remarkable, well-balanced young lady and we discovered we related well to each other. Her family is very busy getting a business started and she's taking on a lot caring for her brother and managing her life very well.

Lois is a regular at this event. The first year she came, she was matched with Libby. To say the two hit it off is an understatement! Within a month, Lois had been invited to Libby's for a family meal. Lois took her connection with Libby seriously—writing her notes, praying for her daily, and keeping up with her life's happenings. Libby is finishing her sophomore year in college and is still in touch with Lois.

The senior adults are not the only ones surprised by the beauty of connecting with the other generation. Within the context of their papers, students express the impact the stories of the adults had on them. Holly, a fifteen-year-old, summarized a portion of her interview in this way:

A lotus flower is a flower that grows straight out of mucky waters into a beautiful creation of God's. Sandra Jeanne Miller-Waters reminds me very much of a lotus because she was born into a broken family, but grew to be one of God's finest creations. Born on January 4, 1940, to a mother who loved her dearly and a father with a severe alcohol addiction, you would never expect Sandie to have her life turn around in the way it did. At only age 5, her mom was thrown out of her house by her dad due to his alcoholism. This created fear from the start of her own father, because she saw how he treated his wife and knew it was wrong. Sandie's childhood was filled with her parent's constant turmoil which led to her living without her dad for the duration of her adolescence.

For financial reasons, Sandie and the rest of her non-Christian family moved over five times from her birth till the time she moved out. They lived all over South Minneapolis, then to Mound, and then to Spring Park where Sandie lived until she was married. Sandie's extended family members were a big part of her life as well. Her grandma took care of her often, but she didn't get along well with her mom. Also, her aunt and uncle, who are in their 90's today, were a huge part of Sandie's life as she grew up. They're Christian, and were always consistently there for Sandie even when her parents were fighting and things were rough at home.

The last question students ask in their interview is "What advice do you have for me as I move through my teenage years?" Coming from the mouths of those who have experienced so much more life than the students, the answers are incredible and are received with seriousness by my students.

In the weeks leading up to the Senior Adult Pasta Dinner, I enthusiastically bound into the Sunday senior adult gatherings to invite them to be a part of this night of formation. I highlight Judges 2:10: "After that whole generation had been gathered to their ancestors, another generation grew up who knew neither the LORD nor what he had done for Israel." This happened in the nation of Israel just after Joshua died. A whole generation grew up without knowing God because the adults had failed to proclaim to the younger generation what God had done. I tell our seniors, "I refuse to let this happen under my watch! Will you help me tell this young generation who God is and what he has done in your life?"

Conclusion

The biggest hindrance to adoptive youth ministry, especially as it relates to middle school ministry, is that adults expect kids to equally initiate with them. It is important to understand that early adolescents, indeed almost all adolescents, will *at best* need a reason to interact with adults. It's a rare twenty-year-old, much less a twelve-year-old, who has the confidence to walk up to an unknown adult and hold a conversation. The average student will need an excuse. Even though I work with kids on a daily basis, they need a reason to talk with me. When I have the opportunity to speak at middle school conferences, from the stage I invite the students to find me during the breaks. "Girls, I want to paint your nails! Guys, I won't paint your nails, but I'll arm wrestle you and beat you in the name of Jesus!" Amazingly, mobs of students crowd around a table during the breaks to interact with me. As we sit painting nails or locked in a death grip, we converse. We laugh. We connect. Within our churches, we need to create excuses for students to interact with the older people in the congregation. Once the connections are made, the interactions will happen naturally, but at first, we need to offer a little help.

This highlights an axiom of adoptive ministry that has the potential to further the relationship between adolescents and adults in a way too seldom seen in the church: *it is the responsibility of the mature to initiate conversations, relationships, and ministry partnership with the young.* Besides creating events to foster student/adult interactions, we need to encourage students to serve throughout the church, which allows middle schoolers to sustain more contact and develop relationships with adults. If an eighth grader volunteers in the kindergarten class, an adult will be in the classroom as well. It is not enough for adults to know about kids or to even *know* kids. But adoptive ministry is not essentially about serving together either, though that is an oft-repeated sentiment. For a community to authentically participate in helping young people to be convinced that they are not only "members" of that community but also little brothers and sisters, they must actively engage them relationally, seek out their opinions and perspectives, and invite them into meaningful partnership in the mission of the community.

Are you in?

> An axiom of adoptive youth ministry: it is the responsibility of the mature to initiate conversations, relationships, and ministry partnership with the young.

No Church in the Wild

Urban and Multiethnic Contexts as the New Frontier of Youth Ministry

DANIEL WHITE HODGE

Dr. Daniel White Hodge is a much beloved, gifted leader who comes to us with an uncomfortable message, at least for some. In today's world we are continually assaulted with injustice, inequities, and multiple reminders that the rhetoric of equality and Christian community is often inadequate, if not empty. The issue of race and class continues to be a real force, threatening both the nation and the institution of the church. Hodge reminds us of our own history—a history that most who have grown up in suburban as well as middle- and upper-class settings have been immune to. Those days are gone.

As we seek to be God's family and to participate in God's adoption of all his children, we must recognize that we have hindered the family from living as a family. We all carry assumptions, biases, prejudices, and even methodology that perpetuate oppression and segregation. Hodge's chapter reveals to us that we must find a better way to empower the powerless, share leadership, and listen more keenly to the voices of those outside our comfortable

circles, even when those messages are uncomfortable or even offensive.

We chose Hodge because he has earned the right to lead us in this vital and rarely exposed conversation. May you take him seriously and commit before the Lord to be a faithful witness to God's call to all of his children.

As you read this chapter, consider these questions:

1. *As you read the first section, identify how Hodge's words hit you. Depending on your own history, background, and ethnicity, you might be wrestling with many emotions. Explore your reaction.*

2. *For many who have lived in the suburban context that Hodge describes, it is very difficult to see outside that history. The reality, however, is that the time has come for those who have enjoyed economic and racial privilege to listen to those who live on the margins. If you are a white North American, what are some ways you can invite others of color*

or socioeconomic separation to help you understand another perspective? If you are a person of color, how can you help your privileged brothers and sisters to hear and enter into your story?

3. As Hodge relates, the pastor who felt like service projects and missions should go only one way—from the suburbs to the city—simply could not see the benefit of being served. If we are in a suburban setting, how can we help young people to realize that they have much to learn from people who are different, possibly poor, or even homeless? What are some ways you can move beyond good intentions and actually change how you think about and do youth ministry in the world we are part of today?

4. Name some practical ways that youth leaders can implement appropriate ministry opportunities for urban, multiethnic settings.

By the time he got to me he was flustered, exasperated, and defeated. As soon as he walked over to me, he exploded. "These kids are lost! Lost, I tell you!" He began pacing, trying to make sense of the experience he had just come from, talking as much to himself as to me. "These are the end times, Dan! That's all that I can figure out!" As he sat down and began to regain his composure, I gently asked, "What exactly are you referring to here?" He responded, "These kids at camp! They are so lost!" I was still somewhat puzzled because I knew that this outreach pastor had just come from a youth ministry "outreach" camp.

"It was a disaster! It started out badly, and it got worse from there. They didn't even give the gospel a chance."

I have known my friend for a long time, and I knew that he had had plenty of experience as a youth speaker, but something about this camp had really gotten to him. My pastor friend, who is white and from a suburban church ministry context, felt out of place, not "welcome," and—more significant—that "these kids," as he continually called them, were "lost." As we continued to talk, he shared with me his frustration: the way that he had been taught to do ministry—especially camping ministry—was now outdated. As he relayed his next grievance, the light bulb came on.

"They didn't give *me* a chance! It was like they were in gangs!"

It turns out that not only were these particular kids not from white suburban churches but also most were ethnic minorities living in urban contexts. He is white, and most of the campers were not. He confessed that his message was not relevant for them, and rather than looking at his own youth ministry teaching philosophy and methodology, he blamed the students. It never occurred to this friend that in order to connect with young people who had come from different contexts than he did, it would go a long way to attempt to build a bridge of trust and understanding. He would later reveal to me that because most of the campers were Latino and black, he assumed membership in gangs and also associated them with being "lost" and "unsaved" without first seeking to know them. As we talked, I realized that not only was this weekend difficult for both him and the kids he had spoken to but also what he and those at the camp experienced was a signpost to a new trend that few can see or are even willing to look at.

A good friend of mine has been doing urban youth ministry for thirty years. Every summer an affluent, mostly white youth group comes out to do "mission work" in his community in the inner city of Seattle. Over the years my friend had seen close up what many have been noting for years, especially in suburban, white church youth groups. Students coming to serve had changed over the years. Fewer students were coming, and those who did come demonstrated a deeper sense of theological apathy and personal entitlement. Most lacked the spiritual zeal that used to mark these experiences. Eventually my friend in Seattle discussed this with the director of that church: "What if we do something different this year? Our group has grown significantly and our students' faith is growing. What if we came out to you guys this summer and worked with your group?" My friend told me that the pastor was so put off by this suggestion that he said, "What do you all have to offer us? That's not how it works."

A change and shift has occurred over the past few decades—and even more acutely over the past few years—that has shifted how we think of urban, suburban, rural, and youth ministry. This "shift" involves much more than just pedagogy. The change is comprehensive: it is methodological, missional, philosophical, theological, sociological, and ministry-driven. The two narratives I have relayed reveal a worldview that the "urban" is "out there" and still in need of "help." It reveals ideologies and perspectives that are rooted in long-standing mantras of racism and social ignorance by many in white, suburban church contexts. The urban and multiethnic reality is now, and what used to be the "inner city" has become the reality for all of us, to at least some extent. The growing gentrification in most cities, fragmenting of central business districts into "uptowns," and an increase in "progressive planning" have created a dislocation for many

who once called the inner city home.[1] Suburban churches are now finding a more "colorful" demographic in their contexts, and most have little to no intercultural and/or interethnic training or awareness, complicating the issues even further.[2]

Jay Z and Kanye West title their opening song on the album *Watch the Throne* "No Church in the Wild." In the lyrics, they reveal an almost humanist ethos, which is rooted in an even more ambiguous theology regarding "church." "What's a god to a nonbeliever? / Who don't believe in anything?" What might that mean for youth ministry? Further, how does that affect youth ministry in both suburban and urban contexts? What does it mean for the youth pastor when the methods of old aren't working anymore? Do we blame the young for our inability to understand and, more important, adapt? What happens when the model of youth ministry and our youth ministry formulae have run their course? Jay Z and Kanye aptly answer: there is no church in the wild because those contexts are difficult and ambiguous, thus creating a gap in the way we understand youth ministry and the engagement of nontraditional youth ministry settings.

This chapter asserts that urban and multiethnic contexts are becoming the new future for youth ministry, making them not only imperative to understand but also to engage. A church in the wild is needed—that "wild" being the unknown, the foreign, the complex, and the ambiguous. Urban and multiethnic settings are growing and changing. The image of the suburban, white, relatively homogeneous youth ministry will have to adjust to and adopt new ways of thinking, ministering, and engaging this new generation of young people. I will give a brief overview of the changing urban context and then suggest some concepts of engagement regarding urban and multiethnic youth ministry. Let's begin by exploring how some of these changes occurred in the first place.

The Urban Emergence

This chapter is not intended to offer an exhaustive treatment of the rise of the post-industrial society and urban gentrification. Great scholars and urban ethnographers such as Daniel Bell,[3] Mike Davis,[4] Andrew Wiese,[5] Melvin Webber,[6] Josh Sides,[7] and Harvey Cox[8] treat these issues well and give insight into the urban emergence. For our purposes it is enough to briefly highlight the key areas of significance over the past thirty years with the help of these and other scholars and to expound on certain moments that have created the urban-suburban blend we see now.

The later years of the 1960s marked the beginning of what most scholars and cultural theorists call the postmodern[9]/post-soul era.[10] The 1970s brought in a significant rise in urban populations, and the number of poor almost doubled from that of the prior two decades for blacks and Latinos.[11] Cities were growing, but not in a functional way. To understand this better, it's necessary to take a brief look into what was happening in the prior two decades.

In the late 1950s and early 1960s the first wave of what would be called *deindustrialization* began to occur. Businesses began to find it more profitable to outsource their work, pay less in benefits, use cheaper labor, and ultimately generate larger profits for the shareholders. This adversely affected black and brown communities. A fragmentation of the middle class began to take place, and the number of people in poverty began to rise. The

American economy was beginning to change, shifting from an industrial economy to one more focused on technology and highly skilled labor, which paid a lot more but required more specialized training and education. Because of sweeping and sometimes subtle discrimination in colleges, many blacks and Latinos found it difficult to compete with peers who had specialized degrees. The aerospace industry, for example, did not typically hire blacks. Moreover, if an applicant did not have the necessary training or pedigree, there was no point in applying. Todd Boyd notes, "We're not talking about people who had careers. We're talking about people who had jobs. If you have a job you are dependent on *that job*. So when that factory closes, you are in essence assed out."[12] By the late 1960s, most of those thriving factories had disappeared. In the wake of this loss, nothing was put into place for the thousands of workers now out of a job.

By 1968, with deindustrialization in full swing, many corporations left the United States to go to Mexico, India, and China.[13] The once hopeful, growing, and generally enthusiastic black and Latino middle class was being systematically dismantled and began to crumble. The black generation born during the mid- to late 1960s was in worse financial and social shape than the preceding generations. These new generations were growing up without black leaders and visionaries such as Martin Luther King Jr., Bobby Seal, and Malcolm X. What's more, there were very few programs that could handle and deal with the significant rise in black families who were jobless. To add insult to injury, many blacks—some who volunteered in search of work—were recruited into the army and went on to fight and die in the Vietnam War. During the height of the US involvement in Vietnam

(1965–69), blacks, who formed only 11 percent of the population at that time, made up nearly 13 percent of the soldiers in Vietnam, with the majority serving in the infantry. Although some statistics are not precise, the percentage of black combat fatalities was roughly a staggering 15 percent.[14]

On Thursday, March 10, 1975, eleven years after the height of the civil rights movement, an entire section of the *Los Angeles Times*, "A Ghetto Is Slow to Die," was dedicated to this very real phenomena in the black community. John Kendall researched families and the economic structures from 1963 to 1975, stating, "The fearful live behind protective bars and double locks. High schools are graduating functional illiterates." He also asserts that "little has changed in the basic conditions of the black ghetto in 10 years since the Watts riots erupted." The article brings to light a sobering reality—one that did not offer a very promising future for anyone living in ghetto-like conditions, which principally meant blacks. Kendall continues by saying, "Some black people have got businesses; some professionals have gotten into significant jobs. But if you talk about the masses or that guy who was in trouble in '65, it is more difficult now." The social manifesto that so many black churches fought to create and instill was surmised in one word: survival.

In essence, once deindustrialization began and developed, large swatches of the black and Latino community lay in financial ruin.[15] What little capital and access to education that blacks and Latinos had by the early 1960s began to wither away and create a distinct ghetto that was ripe with anger, people searching for answers, and an increasing disenfranchisement from the rest of American society. Combine that with police brutality (a fundamental element in the anger behind the Watts riots in 1963[16]), racism within almost every system in America, and social structures that tended to see blacks and Latino youth as rebels, communists, and those "outside" American society, and you have a volatile mixture for social upheaval and shifting. Additionally, the young people who witnessed this societal shift would become the grandmothers and grandfathers of the first hip-hop generation.[17] The 1970s ended with large, overcrowded ghettos and a lack of hope for many youth.

The 1980s did not present a better "America" for ethnic minorities living in urban conditions either. Unemployment, further disenfranchisement, and the rise of the suburban complex took place during this decade. "White flight," as it came to be known, was the sign of affluence for those who could afford it, and the first wave of black and brown families began to emerge in the suburban context. This "moving up" within the social class system was reflected in television shows like *The Cosby Show*, *The Fresh Prince of Bel Air*, and even *Different Strokes*.[18] Shows like these showcased educated black families living an idealized "American Dream" and also highlighted the increase in multiethnic families moving into suburban areas, giving white America its first transmediated glimpse into black America.[19]

But by the 1990s *urban renewal* was a term synonymous with gentrification, and the inner city would once again change and shift. While not all "urban renewal" was detrimental to those who were poor and/or disenfranchised, the bulk of it displaced multitudes of families, many of whom were black and Latino. For example, the addition of the Staples Center in Los Angeles displaced over one thousand families living in that community, either through coerced placement or property tax increases, which left families, many of whom had owned homes in that area for three generations, without a home in a difficult rental market. The displaced families had little to no recourse as they did not have strong political networks or connections with civil lawyers. Moreover, many of these families were already living at or near the poverty line, so the cheaper place to move and live was the *suburban context*. Thus began the first wave of the suburban-urban blend. By the late 1990s many black, Latino, and lower-middle-class whites/Euro Americans saw themselves living in the suburban landscape, trying to survive. As inner cities were becoming transformed and "renewed," the suburbs were beginning to change demographically, and few churches were prepared to receive these families, much less welcome and embrace them as their own.[20]

The 2000s ushered in a new type of youth: the millennial. As Bakari Kitwana reminds us in his book, *Why White Kids Love Hip Hop*, the urban and black element of popular culture was a fascination for many white youth because it became a voice for them in their developmental years.[21] The 2000s also saw the largest growth in ethnic minorities leaving cities because factors such as rent, cost of living, and education were more manageable in the suburbs.[22] Further, suburban, white youth became enthralled by black popular culture—especially hip-hop—and suburban, white/Euro American youth welcomed the hip-hop cultural style from their newfound neighbors.[23]

In the 2000s, according to Elizabeth Kneebone and Alan Berube, suburban poverty began to outgrow urban and inner city poverty.[24] Furthermore, the color of poverty—which had primarily been a black and Latino urban issue—was and is now shifting. Many white, suburban, once upper-middle-class families are experiencing severe forms of poverty. The Census Bureau and The Department of Labor of Statistics reports that one in four children in America lives in poverty conditions,[25] and many of those children do not live in what was once considered to be "the hood" or "bad parts" of town. They live in suburban cities like Lakewood City, Ohio, a suburb of Cleveland. In 2000, only 7 percent of its population lived below the poverty line; between 2008 and 2010 that number rose to 16 percent.[26] Orange County, California, which is stereotypically mediatized as white, rich, and "well-off," is one example of this trend. More than one-third of residents are ethnic Latino.[27] Between 2000 and 2011 suburbs surrounding Seattle, Washington, saw a 79 percent increase in poverty; around Austin, Texas, a 143 percent increase; and around New York, a 27 percent increase.[28] Couple that with how, in 2011, racial and ethnic minorities made up more than half of the US births in a twelve-month period, which ended in July of that year. While whites are still the dominant racial group in the United States, ethnic minorities are rapidly closing the gap at nearly 40 percent of the population.[29] Our country, and therefore our ministry context, is clearly changing.[30] But does our training, philosophy, theology, and social engagement reflect these changes? More important, are we as youth workers, pastors, educators, and practitioners able to respond to these demographic changes, especially in terms of how we think about and do youth ministry? Could we learn from our brothers and sisters in ethnic and urban communities "another way" of doing youth ministry?

In the next section of this chapter, I will assert the importance of multiethnic youth ministry as well as the main issues that underlie moving forward with valuing, engaging, and training a multiethnic generation of leaders and youth.

Adopting the Urban Multiethnic Youth Ministry in the Wild

The pastor friend of mine at the beginning of this chapter continued to struggle through his own issues regarding race, class, and the shifts needed in youth ministry. He and I met for a number of months and continue, to this day, to have some tough yet honest conversations about this subject. But I am proposing much more than a conversation—more than just a sidebar to your ministry. What I am proposing involves actual change. It is about embracing and adopting a multiethnic theology for youth ministry, diving into issues of race, class, and even gender to increase our love and care for those whom God loves and has called. Not everyone is prepared to think, much less to act, differently. The other pastor I mentioned earlier, who refused the offer of urban youth coming to serve his youth ministry, has not spoken to my friend in Seattle for almost five years, and his ministry continues to decline and struggle. The issues of multiculturalism and diversity are never easy to engage; we all have layers of hidden agendas, assumptions, and expectations that can derail our attempts to learn and grow. Further, the issues of race and ethnic identity are a phenomenon that the United States, at large, has yet to fully delve into as a social issue. But the gospel never called us to take the easy road. Jesus's ministry was not one of ease and simplicity, and the apostles encountered many obstacles in spreading Christianity. Yet we often equate Christianity with safety, security, and comfort, compressed with the concept of "being blessed." As the context of youth ministry

continues to change, let us take a closer look at what this movement might involve in terms of an urban multiethnic ministry, especially as we seek to participate with God in adopting all those whom he calls as members of his family.

Three Suggestions for Change

What follows are three suggestions that I have found to be powerful agents of change in the advancement of urban, multiethnic youth ministry. As I wish to avoid the five-step process that is sometimes employed to "repair" the worldview problem rather than deal with it in its entirety, these suggestions stand as guideposts that have worked in a variety of contexts.[31]

First, *good intentions never work*. Good intentions are just what they are: good intentions. While the *intent* may be noble, righteous, and principled, it is the *effect* that makes all the difference. Youth workers may feel they are doing a "good" work for the ethnic minority community of young people they are working among, but without knowing the real need of the community, they are perpetuating a form of destructive neocolonialism in that setting.[32] If the leadership of a church, for example, is not willing to encourage or even allow leaders from an ethnic minority population to hold positions of power and influence, positive rhetoric and good intentions become meaningless. The intentions may themselves be biblical, yet without both a willingness to surrender their own ethnic power and better understand race and ethnic identity for themselves, they will only replicate their initial biases. This, then, perpetuates a white colonial model of ministry and an actual captivity of the gospel in terms of "right" and "acceptable" forms of doing ministry and theology. This is a barrier to the very idea of an urban and multiethnic youth ministry call. When one assumes that his or her racial, economic, or class-driven brand of the Christian faith is "the right way," the power of the gospel is lessened and at times completely lost. To authentically serve Christ in today's world, we in leadership must foster both an attitude and a theology by which we can honestly wrestle with how issues of race and class in the United States impact our life and ministry in the church. In that sense, it is strongly recommended that white youth leaders immerse themselves in opportunities to learn, grow, and, in many cases, repent. Excursions like Sankofa,[33] which pairs up leaders from a variety of ethnic backgrounds as they tour museums and historical locations in the South, can provide the impetus for honest inquiry and faithful change. Experiences that bring God's people together help to tear down walls, making it possible for us to move and work toward a biblical appreciation for much-needed racial reconciliation. We need to take an honest look at the issues of racism and classism as an urban multiethnic generation of young adults makes their way into the leadership of our churches and ministries.[34]

Second, we must *move beyond the great-white-hope mentality*. This mentality paralyzes ethnic minorities because it places white/Euro Americans above and over "them" in terms of power, authority, and status. Privileged and racially unconscious white/Euro Americans tend to come to multiethnic relational and institutional settings from a stance of power and domination, usually without even realizing it.[35] It stands to reason that this attitude and internal elitism carries itself into ministry settings, especially ones in which there is a "hero" role involved. While this tendency is not limited to white and Euro American

leaders (the sin associated with the abuse of power knows no race or gender), it can be aggravated when the "hope" becomes that of a white, male, seminary-educated, heterosexual leader to "save" "those people" from whatever is defined as their need or sin.

Moreover, when key positions in ministry are not reflective of the community that is being served, then neocolonialism once again becomes the default and the "great white hope" is squarely placed on white leadership. Examples of this abound, even when people mean well. A renowned urban ministry in Southern California, for instance, has been in the Hollywood area for almost two decades. Because they do good work and ministry, they have gained national attention. And yet, in a predominantly black, Latino, and Asian community, their senior leadership remains primarily white/Euro American. This is but another example of the "great white hope" in action, even if the leadership cannot see it. "We," meaning the white/Euro-American leadership, will "save you"; therefore the grip on power remains controlled by individuals who do not reflect the community.[36] What is needed is a communal approach to engagement, an approach that says, "We are with you and we are on the journey with Christ together. In this way relationship and community can be built eye to eye and soul to soul rather than from a position of power."

Third, *we serve a multiethnic Jesus, so let us start representing that in the curriculum, teaching, and theologies of our youth ministries*. For decades, urban, multiethnic youth have been subjected to the image and theological meme of a white, blond, blue-eyed Jesus who is ultimately foreign to them. James Cone tells us that there needs to be an image of a Jesus that is both relational and racially appealing to people; one that ethnic minorities in America can adjoin to; one that is socially aware of the struggles of blacks, Latinos, and all nondominant groups; and one that will have compassion on them because of their hardships.[37] Rap artist and ghetto mystic Tupac Shakur took the ideology of the black Jesus a step further, talking about a Christ figure for the ghetto.[38] A heaven for the thug. A Jesus for the poor, disinherited, and dislocated. A Jesus who did not live a "safe" life.[39] An image of Jesus that moves against the Western norm of a Jesus who is white and therefore unrelatable. A Christ who is radical, at times angered, forceful, uses strong language, and yet is consistent and loving while maintaining his God status in a context of the urban environment.

For many, especially those living in the dominant Christian culture, this is a difficult image of Jesus to comprehend. This is not the traditional form of Jesus found in Christian bookstores and on church walls. For many Christians—including many other evangelical Christians—this image is simply too irreverent and sacrilegious. Yet this is a vital contextual and theological discourse for those who seek to bear witness to the God who has made himself known and is therefore relatable to any people group—particularly those who are seeking a church in the wild. The image of a radical, activist, multiethnic Jesus who connects with the downtrodden, the sick, and the person in pain is the Jesus who, as the opening chapter of Matthew reveals, was and is a multiethnic Messiah—for two reasons. First, his lineage is an example of the diversity within the human genome, and second, God created us in his image, and that image encompasses every expression of humanity. Clearly, then, our ministries should reflect at least an appreciation of

and unity in that diversity.[40] Thus, we need an engagement with the Jesus of Scripture and his multiethnic heritage; we need to move away from the domesticated and theologically incomplete image by which he is all too commonly known. A new theological pathway is waiting to be discovered and carved out for those who are willing to take the challenge of adopting an urban multiethnic youth ministry in the wild.

Conclusion

There is much work before us, and the rise of urban, multiethnic students will continue in the future. It is imperative that we move out of our comfort zones and into the realness of what youth ministry is becoming. As Soong-Chan Rah reminds us,

> We face a challenging reality. We live under the reality of the oppression of the Western, white captivity of the church. We may claim that our version of evangelicalism is culture-free, that we are merely trying to be culturally relevant, or that we are trying to maintain the church's tradition, and thereby ultimately reject the claim of cultural captivity. But, the reality of the situation is that Western, white culture dominates American culture and, in turn, dominates American evangelicalism.[41]

Rah challenges us to move past this sobering reality. Recognizing and addressing these realities will help us to engage with the family of God and work alongside urban and multiethnic youth ministries to incorporate, at least at some level, these new ways of thinking about and doing youth ministry in any context.

This chapter represents only a basic primer of the complexity and depth of the issues we face in today's society. My purpose has not been to fully address in depth the various issues we must work through as we seek to live together as brothers and sisters in God's family. Even though I have only scratched the surface of such issues as intercultural communication, diversity competencies, gender issues, and our historical understanding and methods of youth ministry, my intent has been to start you on the road to awareness and action as you lead and love young people in the body of Christ. Each of these areas needs our dedicated attention, but we need to recognize immediately that the infusion of multiethnic youth and emerging adults is upon us in every setting, church, and ministry. We can no longer ignore this demographic shift or the church's historical biases and injustices. The future of youth ministry, and indeed the church as we know it, rests on our ability and willingness to cast new vision, empower men and women of diverse backgrounds and communities to use their gifts, and see ourselves as siblings of one Father and one family. To be a church in the wild challenges us to deal with the issues and struggles that divide us and disempower the diverse gifts and hearts of the body. As my friend discovered at camp that weekend, we can no longer blame the kids or the culture. The day has come to rather grab one another by the hand and work together to heal the church.

Adoptive Youth Ministry

A Latin American Perspective

HOWARD ANDRUEJOL

Any comprehensive book concerning the foundations of youth ministry must take seriously how the world is changing. One of the most significant changes in recent years is the reality that we do not do ministry in a single-culture vacuum. We live in a global world, and in the United States we are part of a global society. According to the Census Bureau, in 2013 there were 54 million Hispanics living in the United States; this population is now the nation's largest ethnic or racial minority group.[1] To serve in ministry within the context of contemporary culture—especially ministry to young people—it is vital that we learn how leaders in non-Caucasian groups view and practice youth ministry. Not only do we need to walk alongside one another in ministry, but we also need a clearer grasp on what God is doing around the world and across our nation.

When we began the search for someone who could bring his or her history and perspective to Adoptive Youth Ministry, the single name that kept surfacing was Howard Andruejol. As Youth Specialties has spread throughout the Hispanic (Spanish-speaking) world, offering

conferences, books, media, and magazines, Andruejol has been a central figure in shaping youth ministry training both in Latin America and around the world (Hispanics reside in nearly every nation). He knows youth ministry—not only Hispanic expressions of youth ministry but also the theological reason for and necessity of youth ministry in every context.

We are excited for you to read Andruejol's chapter and watch his video at youthministry .fuller.edu so that you can learn what youth ministry looks like in Latin America. In so doing you will not only have a deeper grasp on what brothers and sisters are doing in the name of Christ for kids, but you will also be able to more clearly see how participating in God's adoptive ministry can strengthen your own call and practice of ministry. As Andruejol puts it in this chapter, "Adopting a younger one is the biblical ministry in the church; it's the real youth ministry. To help kids feel safe with us, in a protected zone as the sheep when they are taken care of by their shepherd. This is the kind of leadership that we need today."

As you read this chapter, consider these questions:

1. *How would you describe youth ministry as you know it to be different from how Andruejol describes youth ministry from a Latin American perspective? In what ways are they similar?*

2. *What are three specific insights or statements from this chapter that can help you practice adoptive youth ministry more effectively?*

3. *Where have you seen power in leadership affect ministry? Describe what it looked like. Have you ever seen empowering leadership in ministry? Describe what that looked like.*

4. *How can adoptive youth ministry be practiced in a setting that is controlling? What can a youth worker do to encourage an adolescent or emerging adult to be connected to a community in which they may not necessarily be embraced and welcomed?*

Latin America is a young region. According to the Statistics Division of the Economic Commission for Latin America and the Caribbean (ECLAC), more than 40 percent of our population is under twenty-five.[2] According to UNICEF, more than 100 million are between ten and eighteen, and about 15 million of them live in extreme poverty.[3] Corporación Latinobarómetro reports that eight out of ten of those between sixteen and twenty-five consider themselves a religious person—either Catholic or evangelical.[4]

The way we do youth ministry today in our countries will affect the future of the church here and around the world.

Our Heritage in Latin America

I confess that defining our context in one word seems a little bit bold; nevertheless, I feel it is something both simple and necessary to do. The best description is oppression. In any circle of our societies, it is tangible. We have grown up under oppression, and that's the only thing we have seen.

It is not necessary to go back to the times of the conquest in order for our cultural environment to stand out. Just a simple glance at the governments of the past century will show how those who have reached power have been looking to take advantage of their size to dominate, control, manipulate, and oppress the people who have elected them by their sovereign will. Of course, certain cases of absolute tyranny in some of our countries stand out.

This system of oppression is notorious in the family environment as well. There are far too many stories of adults (also called "greater" in the sense of superiority) who abuse children and adolescents, including verbal, physical, and emotional abuse, or all of the above. This is because one person is always on top, and the rest are under—one who dominates and others who are dominated. A victim and a victimizer.

Are we safe at the church? No way. It takes only a shallow observation of the pastoral office to know that we suffer within this ecosystem of oppression as well. In this case, the abuse extends is tentacles to the spiritual domain. Titles and positions in organizations are a symbol of great power. It is true that power corrupts, and absolute power corrupts absolutely.[5] In the church's realm, there is one on top and the rest lay below. There is one who commands and many who obey (or at least are expected to do so). According to those in leadership, power is to control those who are called their followers. This is the perfect bait for the unsuspecting victim to fall into the claws of abuse.

We have become so used to oppression as a way of life that we do not need social scientists to describe it. In some cases oppression may be subtle, but for those who live in Latin American, it is simply a fact. In terms of a ministry perspective, people are used to living under submission to a superior power. Decision making belongs to those who are in higher levels of authority. It is very obvious that this responsibility belongs to certain people within organizations, so when it comes to making decisions concerning one's personal life or family, it is easy to yield that right. People unquestioningly follow those who are in control. Accordingly, the expression of creative ideas or alternative points of view is for the most part unacceptable. Whether it is in society, family, or church, even mild dissent is considered a sign of rebellion. In the church one does not question the pastor; you obey him (and it is almost always a him). You don't query his word, or you are seen as causing division. One is in command, and the rest obey.

As I write these lines, I imagine the expression of some Latin youth leaders that I know. I am sure that they would look at me with worried eyes. "Isn't this the way things are supposed to work?" As I say, oppression is so much a part of our ecosystem that it is hard to show a fish the water where he swims. How I am opening this chapter might cause many to call me rebellious or audacious for opposing what pastors, leaders, bishops, and modern apostles teach—and how they teach and how they lead is with power and authority. To question this, even in the church, goes against everything we have been taught about living under leadership. They rule; we follow.

In the Latin America context, you don't question that authority. If someone dares to try escaping from this prison, there are only two ways out: confront and dispute in protest or ascend to a position of power. You become one of them, or you are against them. We are either the victim or the victimizer. In the Latin psyche, there is no middle ground.

A Different Church?

Once again, we don't need to go very far to asseverate that at church the pastor is king. And in youth ministry, the leader is king—simply a smaller version of his or her immediate supervisor. As leaders would describe this arrangement, the vast majority of Christians are incapable of making right choices, either morally or in ministry, unless they seek the opinion and receive the approval of their leadership. They are incapable of feeding their own spiritual lives because they are trained to believe that they are incapable; the pastor or youth leader must tell them the proper way to pray, to read the Bible, or practice any spiritual discipline. We haven't been taught to grow and learn—only to obey those above us.

Therefore, Christians are immobilized when it comes to showing leadership. They will not develop their spiritual gifts or fulfill their unique calling unless they have the approval of their spiritual superior. And if they refuse to do so, there isn't much to do about it. People clearly know that they shouldn't embark on any ministry opportunity, especially outside the walls of the church, unless they have the *cobertura* (coverage) from their pastor. Even if you think about going to a conference or an event outside your church, the pastor needs to approve it. You can only do something that pleases God if you have the blessing and protection from your superior. Period.

One way to describe this situation is to say that Christians in Latin America suffer from codependency. They wait for their leaders to tell them what to do, and in some cases, this includes all aspects of life: personal, family, financial, professional, and spiritual matters—the list goes on. This is why our churches flutter around any character with charisma, with an attractive personality to hypnotize us with his so-called leadership. Spiritual oppression is subtle, and yet it is a powerful force in our church communities. There is one leader and perhaps a few lesser leaders; all others serve as complacent followers.

Implications for Youth Ministry in a Latin American Context

In light of the state of our church culture, youth ministry inevitably is and has long been considered a springboard to "real" ministry. Even though youth ministry may be a platform to exert power—the well-known youth ministry leaders exert great influence—the "real" ministry of leading a church stands above any status someone could enjoy in youth ministry. Being a senior pastor, often called the "pastor general" (not for the wide responsibility of leading the church but in the sense of a military leader), is who and what God blesses. Herein lies respect, and with that respect there is power.

After spending more than ten years in full-time youth ministry in our local church, I had the privilege of watching a group of our kids grow as leaders. One of our young adults was ready to take over the team of youth leaders and lead the ministry. In the midst of that transition, our church needed a senior pastor. After refusing to accept several times, I finally agreed to help in that position. (I love our church, but I love youth ministry in a very special way!) The news of my new responsibility quickly spread, and when I saw a friend in the halls of a seminary in our city, he immediately greeted me with a happy "Congratulations!" I said, "What for?" Without hesitation, he replied, "You've made it! Now you are a real minister!" I felt so sad and angry.

To so many in our faith communities, working with teens is just a technical stopover on the way to greatness. As some would say, "Practice with kids. If you mess them up, no problem; we can always find some more." In youth ministry, a successful program is what matters most. And by that I mean that one that exhibits a sense of activism, commitment, and other evidence of how powerful and capable one is in leadership. If the youth leader is skilled enough to mobilize the masses, if he (again, in our context this type of leadership is generally limited to men) gets them to follow him and builds a following, then his ability to demonstrate his talent to be a real leader will get noticed. Up the ladder he goes.

This is why in our context the focus centers on the creation of a model that focuses on the mechanics of ministry. Procedures are described concerning how to run the church, how to be spiritual, and how all followers are expected to comply with those instructions. Each of our kids becomes simply a number, a perishable statistic, a face with no name in the crowd. Their stories don't matter, and their crises don't matter; their destiny is not important. We just want them to obey, follow along gladly, and live within the system.

In Latin American Christianity, we lack an understanding of a healthy biblical concept of community and servant leadership. While we may read the books, listen to the speeches, and follow the well-known Christian leaders—even using the words that they use—unfortunately these words do not convey the meaning intended.

Sadly, leadership in our context involves as least one if not all of the following conditions:

- individuals in power
- authority and privileges
- program engineers
- codependency promoters

And regrettably, community is usually defined as one of the following:

- a group of people in the same room
- all those who attend an event
- participants or collaborators of a program
- just another face in the crowd

A Tragic Consequence

Our young are not provided with a healthy environment for their development. A safe atmosphere in which they can grow through the travails and heartache of adolescence is nonexistent. There is no individual response to crisis and no provision of ministry opportunities because individuals don't exist in the community. Young people are simply attendants of a weekly meeting. As a matter of fact, many leaders would prefer not to know their stories because it would imply involvement, or lack of involvement, in their lives. Young people are consumers of programs,

and the few who are taken into account are at best coproducers of those programs, not people to be individually affirmed, listened to, or honored. They have never experienced a spiritual church, much less a healthy community in which they are treated as siblings of those in leadership. The idea that children and adolescents must be included, welcomed, and nurtured by the adult community as members of the same family—the concept that the leaders are not "surrogate parents" but actually co-siblings—is foreign. This biblical concept of adoptive ministry is so countercultural that it is completely unknown.

Some leaders do eventually wake up to their lack of care and interest when they perceive that kids are leaving the church. However, this response is rarely due to an authentic desire to nurture the young as Christ has taught (see Mark 10:13–16) but rather because it is important that a powerful leader does not to lose them. If success is measured in programs and attendance, less equals failure. Those youth who leave do so because they don't find their needs met. These could range from deep intrinsic issues such as struggling with a sense of identity or purpose in life to issues as superficial as being discontent with an irrelevant and boring program. Many sincere and faithful young people today believe that it is better to leave in search of new spiritual horizons. They might seek out a new church that offers better events with more resources that impress the crowd. There are many churches to choose from; in our countries there are churches on every corner. The options are many. Yet even if they walk in new fields, the same problem persists: the lack of spiritual support that true community can provide is rare across many if not nearly all of the church communities in Latin America.

Eager to keep their adolescents from straying, leaders have begun to think of strategies for retention. They typically fall into the default response of raising their programming standards to create new and better events that compete with those deemed attractive at other churches. Of course, the cycle of performance and oppression over staff, volunteers, and even parents continues as more financial and human resources are required. But the church still depends on a few people who administer the youth program. In most cases, those faithful volunteers are ultimately responsible for leading the youth group and youth programs. They tend to feel exploited as they are left alone to solve the urgency of bigger and better programs that will attract even the most disinterested teenager. The lack of resources, encouragement, time, and people in youth ministry is self-evident, and willing volunteers are scarce at best. Young volunteers lead and execute the ministry; the absence of adults in youth ministry is undisputable. And since youth ministry is program based, it becomes just another department managed by someone, external to the life of the church. Adults are excluded. Youth ministry is seen as a necessary evil. "We've got kids—somebody has to do something with them," the adults might say. "And it's not going to be us! We don't know what to do with them."

The church and adults have abandoned the nurturing of youth. They are strangers, and yet they demand tangible results. That is why youth ministry in Latin America is reduced to a weekly activity prepared with great effort for an anonymous audience. Success is measured by attendance, enthusiasm, and budgets. The less trouble, the better. Even pastoral care in youth ministry, something that North American youth ministry has worked hard to incorporate, is totally absent in Latin America. Many youth leaders would argue that the name says it all: if it is supposed to be *pastoral* care, then that is something reserved for pastors, which they are not. At least, they don't see themselves that way.

Even discipleship itself, the core calling of ministry, has been reduced to a thirteen-week curriculum—in particular, a program specially designed as preparation for baptism and the indoctrination of new believers.

Is There Hope?

Though some leaders are sincere, they can still be sincerely wrong. It is true that most youth ministry leaders, and especially volunteers, have not been exposed to any other way of doing things. Is it fair, then, to demand from them a more effective ministry, a more communal and adoptive-focused ministry? Of course it is. None of us exercises ministry perfectly, and none of us has the ideal point of view. When we allow our cultural history, experiences, and assumptions to dictate how we go about our ministry to the young, we are responsible for the outcome. We cannot do youth ministry or any ministry on our own, with our own resources and perspective. We must return to the voice of the one who calls us in the first place. It is our God, primarily through the gift of the Scriptures, who can lead us into what can authentically be called Christian ministry. This is the key to adoptive youth ministry, in which we do everything we can to design and practice a ministry that lines up with what God is doing in bringing young people to faith. They have been, in Christ, adopted as his sons and daughters. It is, then, the church's job to join in that work. That is adoptive youth ministry.

Emerging generations need a new style and practice of leadership that can nurture and equip them to be fully embraced by the body of Christ. Although many youth leaders haven't been exposed to any other model of Christianity, if we return to the biblical text we can become a transition generation. As we follow how God teaches us to function as leaders and equippers, we will lead our young with a model of relationship rather than oppression. This is the power of Paul's use of the term *adoption*, for when we see ourselves as family, and especially as co-siblings with all other believers, both the young and the old, regardless of status, are empowered to live into their calling as members of God's family.

Working within such distorted history and practice, how can we mobilize the church to embrace adoptive youth ministry? What can we do to teach a church lacerated and abused by oppression and power to become a community that adopts new generations and encourages them to come into our midst as family, just as they are? For such a long time we have tried to make kids become us, to convert them into our adult molds, with the intention of controlling them. We think that if they become like us, then we will be able to understand them and have them under our command.

What should a new leadership and a new youth ministry look like in a Latin American context? How can we come closer to our kids in order to impress on them a fingerprint rather than the scars of power and abuse? I firmly refuse to offer a model because it would be my model, and then I would become the authority and impose it on others. Instead, I appeal that we urgently come back to the biblical text and let the Scriptures shape our new lens.

I understand this means going against the flow, and I know it won't be very attractive to some. In a world where more is better, it doesn't sound good to talk of growing until you become a mini-church, for example. Nevertheless, my hope is that some leaders will be wise enough to understand that the church is not ours. Neither our lens nor our wisdom should reign. This is why we need to come up with new metaphors that can communicate the biblical sense of Christian leadership and community.

Until today, the concepts that have been used fall too short and divert completely. To see God's work as a business scheme, a military structure, or a mere hierarchy is to follow the guidelines of this world, which is controlled by the prince of darkness. Christ said that he would build his church. Why are we so anxious for the statistics of church growth? Is this really what Jesus had in mind?

Allow me to clarify a couple of things. First, I totally agree with the creation and implementation of organizational structures that allow us to communicate and cooperate better. If we get better organized, we will better fulfill our mission. The biblical text didn't give us instructions on how to accomplish the Great Commission; we are told what to do but not how to do it. This invites us to exercise our creative freedom. It reminds us that somebody has to think and create a good way to come together and get organized, an effective way according to our context, needs, and opportunities. What I completely disagree with is imposing the organizational structure on the community dimension of the church. When did we forget that we don't have authority over people's lives? Only Christ has complete authority in the heavens and the earth. When did we forget that he is the Good Shepherd who lays down his life for his sheep and that it's his voice that each one of us should listen to and obey? The supremacy is Christ's and not ours, especially not those in leadership.

Second, this is not a new problem. As I'll address later, Jesus emphatically declared that our model for leadership should not follow the guidelines of this earth. It is proper to explore again the relational dimension of the church and the pastor's role as a way of life rather than a position in an organization.

A Look at Scriptures with New Lenses

Forgotten Responsibilities

To the elders among you, I appeal as a fellow elder and a witness of Christ's sufferings who also will share in the glory to be revealed: Be shepherds of God's flock that is under your care, watching over them—not because you must, but because you are willing, as God wants you to be; not pursuing dishonest gain, but eager to serve; not lording it over those entrusted to you, but being examples to the flock. And when the Chief Shepherd appears, you will receive the crown of glory that will never fade away. (1 Pet. 5:1–4)

Someone must have read these verses incorrectly and interpreted them to mean that our calling is to "be shepherds of God's programs that are under our care." The pastoral responsibility is to dedicate the necessary attention to the lives of the people who constitute the flock of Christ. It is a privilege entrusted from heaven, not a mere designation that puts us in charge of a program.

This flock belongs to the Lord Jesus Christ (Acts 20:28). Thus we should be reminded that Christ is the one whom the sheep should listen to; he is the one to whom they should submit and whom they should consult for any decision in their lives—not the pastor/CEO of the church/organization.

The work of each youth leader is the same work as the pastor with the sheep of the flock. It involves five main responsibilities:

1. Feed the sheep. Train kids to read, understand, apply, and proclaim the biblical text. If we suffer today from spiritual malnourishment, it's because in our ministries we have too many meetings called "Bible study" where we don't study the Bible (1 Tim. 3:16–17).

2. Guide the sheep. Help them know the will of God and obey it. This requires biblical discernment and surrender to the will of God (Matt. 28:20).

3. Protect the sheep. The main danger is the intrusion of ideas apart from biblical truth in the minds of kids; their worldview cannot proceed from the values of this world (2 Tim. 4:1–4).

4. Heal the sheep. Those who are hurt by the crises in life, the slavery of sin, and the shamefulness of bad choices need pastors who love them unconditionally. Only a ministry that becomes a safe zone will be able to lead them to restoration (Gal. 6:1–2).

5. Gather the sheep. This has nothing to do with weekly meetings but rather with the strengthening of a community and the construction of relationships that are healthy, spiritual, and mutually edifying (Heb. 10:22–25).

It is impossible that an event, meeting, or program can fulfill these responsibilities. These responsibilities demand time, tenderness, and personal attention, and they certainly cannot be achieved from a platform of oppression. They cannot be done from above. They require men and women who are spiritual and faithful to the call—leaders who can relate at the same level with teenagers as they nurture them. It is so sad that many leaders read the word *pastor* and immediately associate it with the boss or CEO of their local church. This is not in keeping with the thinking of the biblical authors. They used the term to refer to those who gently cared for the well-being of the believers. It's a gift from above, not an organizational designation.

The apostle Peter gives us a concise look at the wrong way to develop pastoral care (1 Pet. 5:2–3). The following ways of doing ministry will only hurt our kids:

1. Ministry as an imposed, forced obligation
2. Ministry that seeks any kind of personal gain or benefit
3. Ministry that assumes we own their lives and master them

A clear distinction can be made between ministry that hurts kids and ministry that leaves a legacy, an indelible fingerprint on their lives. The right way to do ministry as a pastor includes:

1. Ministry by our own will, in response to God's call
2. Ministry with enthusiasm and internal motivation
3. Ministry that kids follow not because we force them to but because we are an example

Major erudition is not required to understand this great pastoral commission. Of course, the lack of Bible reading means that these fundamental passages for our ministry philosophy end up being ignored or never even noticed. While understanding this kind of pastoral ministry may be simple, exercising it is complicated. It requires engagement; it demands time and energy, sacrifice and commitment. It's much easier to make programs than to care for people. Nevertheless, how glorious the moment will be when those who have responded faithfully to their work and have genuinely cared for Jesus's sheep will receive from his very own hand the imperishable reward (1 Pet. 5:4). Dear leader, be faithful to your call.

Abused Exhortations

Obey your leaders and submit to them, for they keep watch over your souls as those who will give an account. Let them do this with joy and not with grief, for this would be unprofitable for you. (Heb. 13:17 NASB)

But we request of you, brethren, that you appreciate those who diligently labor among you, and have charge over you in the Lord and give you instruction, and that you esteem them very highly in love because of their work. Live in peace with one another. (1 Thess. 5:12–13 NASB)

Someone once said that to the boy with a hammer, everything looks like a nail. Likewise, the way that we see the Scriptures depends on the lens with which we read the Scriptures. Generally speaking, we tend to bring our own worldview to the text rather than allowing the text to shape our minds. Far too many leaders have seen texts like Hebrews 13:17 and 1 Thessalonians 5:12–13 as the biblical basis for demanding unconditional obedience, respect, and (why not?) a few presents from time to time. Given the paradigm of oppression, these passages fit very well in this framework and justify the victim and the victimizer by the codependency that unites them. But I firmly believe that the biblical authors were not communicating this message to the believers back then, and thus it's not what the Spirit wants to communicate to the believers today.

We should remember that both passages are addressed to believers who were still growing in their faith. Regarding the readers of Hebrews, we know that they should have been teachers already but they needed to be reminded of the basics of faith (see Heb. 5:11–12). Concerning the believers in Thessalonica, their discipleship lasted only about one month, during the time that Paul stayed in that city. As a result, there were many topics left to discuss and truths to be clarified.

But a sober reading of the passages gives us sufficient light by which to see a proper interpretation. If we read with no prejudice, we will note that neither text pleads for leaders to have a position of superiority or authority over the lives of the believers. It's just the opposite.

The text in Hebrews highlights that there are leaders who look after the souls of their flocks to such an extent that they know they'll be accountable for their actions. Without a doubt, this evokes the great pastoral commandment that Peter talks about in his first letter. There are those who recognize the divine gift in themselves to gently and patiently nurture the flock. They know that it's a responsibility carried out under the gaze of the Chief Shepherd Jesus Christ, and with all their heart they focus on feeding, guiding, protecting, healing, and gathering the sheep. Their work is an invaluable gift to those for whom they care. In other words, what a privilege

to count on men and women who sincerely make the effort to take care of us! To people like them, why shouldn't we pay attention? To those who point us toward the voice of Jesus, the Good Shepherd, why shouldn't we listen?

It seems to me that the author of Hebrews was telling those believers, "Look! What great spiritual leaders you have! Listen to them; follow them. Support them." In spite of organizational titles, there are people who exercise a pastoral ministry with our teens. We don't call them pastors, but that's the role they play. It is to these mentors, counselors, and teachers that our kids should listen. They should seek out these leaders when they need to make choices because these are not people who want to rule over them; these leaders want to guide our kids to their Lord.

Of course, there are CEOs in our organizations and churches, people with the title of "pastor" who don't do this. They demand to have the last word on every matter and are offended if their opinion is not taken under consideration. They attack with texts like Hebrews 13:17: obey your pastors. There's no reason why we should be following these people. In the case of 1 Thessalonians 5, we find an exhortation to be considerate with those who exercise a very particular ministry in our lives. It has nothing to do with the position they have at church but with the relationship they have with us. Note that the passage says that these people labor, have charge over us, and give instruction.

Those who see through lenses of programs and oppression interpret "labor" as the responsibility of a full-time, paid person, with an office schedule and public roles in the local church; "have charge over" as the ones who organize events, meetings, or programs and possess a title and a position in projects, committees, or departments in the local church; and "give instruction" as the rebuke that they should generously share with all those who don't submit to their authority. But once again, this interpretation doesn't seem to be what the author had in mind when he wrote these exhortations.

The work that was expected from those in leadership in the early church was pastoral—to look after the flock, as we have mentioned in 1 Peter 5:2 and Acts 20:28. This is a special role; working in an office can be done by anyone. To have charge over and to give instruction are pastoral tasks that recall the interest for the care and well-being of the person, not a position over him or her. The passage highlights the relationship of cordiality, unity, and fraternity that should exist between a believer and those who care for him or her pastorally. It is not a position or a personality; it is relational ministry.

The Path to Greatness

Jesus called them together and said, "You know that those who are regarded as rulers of the Gentiles lord it over them, and their high officials exercise authority over them. Not so with you. Instead, whoever wants to become great among you must be your servant, and whoever wants to be first must be slave of all. For even the Son of Man did not come to be served, but to serve, and to give his life as a ransom for many." (Mark 10:42–45)

Success in our world is often measured in the wrong ways; too many boast of the number of people who serve them. Because Jesus affirmed that leadership is service, the behavioral framework we seek cannot be built on business or military models. Peter reminds us that we are not lords over those we serve but an example to follow. Jesus is the example,

the perfect reason to convince us to follow his steps. Why should we lead by example and service? Because Jesus showed us that way. If we are going to become leaders who don't abuse their power and are not tyrants, it's because the very Lord of Lords, the sovereign one, humbled himself and gave his life on the cross.

When we forget that leadership is about giving and not receiving, we walk on the wrong path. We stop talking in terms of loving, caring, and serving kids. When we as pastors stop caring for the sheep and expect the sheep to care for us, we walk away from being a true disciple. We follow our own dreams, our own glory.

The service we can provide to those we care for has nothing to do with activities inside a program. That is a matter of collaboration. It's good, but it's not service or ministry per se. To serve is to give your life to rescue people from their deep need, just as Jesus gave his life for our rescue. It implies engagement in what's happening in the life of others. Service is not limited to a meeting; it's a sacrificial relationship. Service is leadership; it is being disciples of Jesus (John 15:12–13).

Needless to say, this greatness doesn't fit with the publicity models and marketing campaigns that resound with such fanfare. As a friend used to say, many leaders dream of seeing their names on a billboard or the poster of a big event when they should be seeking to see their names in their kids' contact lists as someone whom their young people trust and would call with any need.

An Intergenerational Ministry Inside and Outside

Up to this point I have emphasized the shortcomings we face in the Latin American context regarding youth ministry and the whole church. We need to come close to Scripture with no prejudice so that we can discover, as if for the first time, the divine instructions that allow us to see our calling with new lenses. We are pastors who care for the new generations, who guide them gently and patiently. We are not superiors; we are servants.

This unequivocally means that youth ministry is not for just a few.

Traditionally, we have delegated the responsibility to a small group of volunteers (or victims, as some would say). Not only do we segregate, but we also measure success by the impact of the events they organize. Totally wrong. While youth ministry is certainly the call of that small group, it is also the call of every believer. I know that many adults don't like to participate in specific activities for youth. Many of us don't like to stay up late, eat junk food at camps, run and get dirty, or go showerless for several days. But that doesn't disqualify us from working with kids; it just means we don't work certain events, and that's fine.

If leadership means influence, then we need to offer as much positive influence as we can, surrounding the new generations with mentors. This is both strategic and relational; what's more, it is God's expectation for the entire church. In Titus 2 we find Paul's instructions to his faithful teammate regarding some problems in the communities of believers in Crete. Verse 1 begins with a reminder to Titus of the need to communicate sound doctrine, with no contamination. In the following verses, the sound doctrine is described, and it doesn't resemble what we'd read in a book of systematic theology. Sound teaching should always result in sound application. As some would say, orthodoxy and orthopraxis go hand in hand.

In the first verses of Titus 2 we read about the character and behavior of the believers. As Eugene Peterson paraphrases: "Your job is to speak out on the things that make for solid doctrine. . . . We don't want anyone looking down on God's Message because of their behavior" (Titus 2:1, 5 Message). In Titus 2:2 Paul speaks of the older men. As we read the entire passage, note that it does not refer to those who play a role in leadership in the community of believers; it refers to every older man. Verse 3, similarly, talks about older women. I once asked our church at what age a woman was considered old, though I didn't encourage that conversation because I didn't want to hurt anybody's feelings. In the case of these women (as well as the men mentioned in v. 2), qualities of character and behavior are mentioned. These women are called to be righteous with a purpose: to teach the younger women (v. 4). Again, I asked our church at what age a woman is still considered young, which was a much easier conversation to manage! But beyond that, it's fascinating to realize the connection that exists between the women in verse 3 and those in verse 4. The word that Paul uses to refer to the older women can be translated as "women of advanced age." Although it doesn't say how old these women are, we know that these they are further along the path of life, in front of the younger ones.

My daughter is ten years old as I write this, and for her, almost all the women in our church are of advanced age, ahead of her in the trail of life. Many of them have already made choices regarding their spiritual lives, families, marriages, professions, and ministries. They have gone through stages of crisis, victory, tears, happiness, loneliness, abundance, and scarcity. They have felt close to God and far from God; they have had questions and doubts. These are women of faith who have experienced assurance, convictions, and fears. They have known God in that walk of life and possess experiences that have enriched them. On top of that, they are righteous women, examples to follow in character and behavior. No, they don't form part of the team that organizes youth activities; no, they don't go to camps or come for lock-ins. But they are called youth pastors. They are called to invest their lives in other girls like my daughter so that they can be surrounded by mentors who teach them how to become women of God.

We see the same regarding boys. Verse 6 reminds us of what boys need to learn: self-control. The example for them is Titus (v. 7) and other men who show that same character and behavior (v. 2). This is an intergenerational ministry in which everyone is called. This is the whole church exercising a powerful influence in the lives of the new generations. All of us, advanced in age, leaving a legacy and an indelible print. A position is not required, just a relationship. It's not about one on top of all but one next to others.

Therefore, when we talk about getting only parents involved in youth ministry, we are falling very short. In reality we should talk about all of us sharing the youth ministry as a church: parents and anyone advanced in age, young adults, single mothers, the elderly, couples with no kids. Not in programs, but in meaningful relationships. We should encourage everyone in the church to take the initiative and build spiritual friendships with children, adolescents, and youth—to become mentors and models. Adopting a younger one is the biblical ministry in the church; it's the real youth ministry. It means helping kids feel safe with us, in a protected zone, just like the sheep when they are taken care of by their shepherd. This is the kind of leadership that we need today.

Given the oppression that exists in leadership, by which people are seen only as laborers for programs, we don't hear this kind of message from the pulpit. At the church the program is king, not relationships. Ministry means participating in a program, not in somebody's life. This unfortunate reality leads me to denounce a very serious problem that limits the way in which many people could fulfill their call to youth ministry in a formidable way. This same tyranny in leadership preaches that ministry happens only inside the walls of the church; they say that ministry means being involved in the operational machinery of the local programs, and they condemn any effort that is done outside the control and the territory of the local church.

Many schoolteachers don't know how important their ministry is, as a consequence of this oppression. Many leaders who are propelling parachurch projects wouldn't dare to say they are genuine youth pastors. The church has called them rebellious and excommunicated them from the ministry's benediction. They are anything *but* ministers. They are labeled employees, academic professors, administrators, or sport coaches, all of whom are disconnected from the kingdom of God. But this is not true. The influence they exercise in the life of kids is genuine and much deeper than what many so-called youth pastors achieve in a ninety-minute weekly meeting. These "excluded ones" are doing the true work of God—with God's blessing and with God's lenses—even though they have been told otherwise.

It is very sad to see that many church leaders demand that these faithful ones abandon their spheres of influence just because they are outside the church. Instead, many leaders require that these people give their time and energy to the service of the organization in which they have a membership rather than to their calling. These heroes are divested of their powers and told to give their lives to setting up chairs and passing out handouts at the door. Youth ministry doesn't happen just in a meeting. It's about adults interacting with kids at the church and outside the church. It's a community of leaders who are mentors, who care for kids until they see those kids reach maturity. It's people who walk alongside young people and one another, during good times and bad times. Youth ministry is the positive influence that draws us closer to Jesus, that interferes with sin, that heals us in crisis, and that rejoices in obedience. Youth ministry is men and women who love the new generations. It's a network of people who represent a safe zone in which younger ones are protected, helping them feel secure, encouraged, cheered, instructed, and corrected.

The young in our region of the world don't need more events; they need more of these pastors. We should equip others and encourage those who already serve in that role.

Some Critical Recommendations

We Should Not Impose New Models

Although it is still necessary to create models and it is vital to continue to develop strategic intents, we should not think that we have the solution and the only answer. Imposing the same style of ministry for all would result in stagnation. Every innovation should arise from the effort to create a healthy community in which intergenerational youth ministry flourishes. And there are many ways to do this.

The Tyranny of Authority Should Be Stopped

We await a leadership driven by genuine and unconditional love. We seek pastoral care and service as a critical element for effective discipleship. Though in the past we have produced supporters—fans of some leader with great charisma—rather than disciples of Christ who learn his Word, follow his example, and share his mission, we need to break that mold now.

Let's Build a New Intergenerational Ministry

This relational approach should be modeled and intentionally developed. Very few leaders today have experienced the gift of a mentor or leader in a biblical sense. But it's a disadvantage, not a disability. That said, we need to learn carefully and quickly in order to become a transition generation. We have the opportunity to pass on new lenses—which show us God's perspective—to the next leaders of the church.

Final Thoughts

Latin America today is a force in the preaching of the gospel. While there's much to correct, its presence and influence are undisputed. Thus, Latin America cannot be ignored if we want to develop a real global perspective of the church. Furthermore, in countries like the United States, the contact is more direct. Due to immigration, many youth leaders have been working with kids from a Latin American background for quite some time. Some of those teens are from a third culture. The information in this chapter might also help us to understand their behavior or the kinds of ministry their families are used to. In addition, the opportunity for cross-cultural mission from and to Latin America is great.

Many leaders from Latin America are leaving their countries for the United States, Europe, or even the "10/40 Window," a region between ten and forty degrees north latitude that missiologists since the 1980s have targeted as being strategically significant.[6] These sent ones will surely bring with them (without noticing) the lenses they inherited from their culture. Knowing their context will help us to understand them and encourage them with patience. I also have in mind the good number of youth groups and adults who travel to our cities for short-term projects. I value tremendously the love that brings them and the heart that moves them. I am truly convinced that we can generate great projects when we work together—and I don't just mean material resources. It's obvious that people with more financial resources can support initiatives that relieve urgent needs in our communities. I am referring to working one next to the other rather than the model of one on top of the other. Unfortunately, this was the scheme used by some missionaries who came with

good intentions, invested, and left a legacy. Too often their mentality was to instruct—or should we say impose—a way to see and live Christianity. They became the figures of authority and we, domesticated by oppression, took everything they said and taught us as the only right way to do ministry.

If people come to our region with the wrong lenses and don't allow the locals to talk about their true needs and opportunities, they will retain the ideas they already have—the ones they brought with them. In many cases, those ideas will be the ones they want to keep. It would be very different if short-term missionary experiences focused on learning from the local people. What if the local people helped their visitors understand their context, exegete their culture, and create their own models of ministry? The richness of the experience would be of great value for all.

May the Lord help us in his grace to be faithful, good servants who leave a legacy to the following generations. May we assume, in his power and through his Word, the responsibility of adjusting the course of the church so that we all may become the salt of the earth and the light of the world.

Part 4

The Skills for Adoptive Youth Ministry

Adoptive Leadership

BILL MacPHEE

Some leaders are kind controllers. Others are relational encouragers who let people "do" their ministry. Still others seem more concerned with pleasing their supervisors, or in the case of youth ministry, their multiple supervisors (parents, pastoral staff, other youth workers, and even kids). Yet in order to lead a theological ministry in which our goal is further reaching than the immediate results we so often seek, we need healthy, trained, and committed leaders who know that they are called to encourage and empower their peers to serve well, as well proactive leaders who are willing to be honest, to teach and train, and to guide those exploring their ministry gifts. At least on the surface, we need people who are both collaborative and in charge. How can one be both a guiding and an empowering leader? That is what Bill MacPhee shares in this chapter.

MacPhee knows what he's talking about. For more than two decades he led large and powerful adoptive youth ministry programs (before anyone called them that!). He always had a stable full of "senior" volunteers and

another large group of new and inexperienced volunteers and staff. During the last five years of MacPhee's high school ministry, there were several hundred students attending Sunday ministry, midweek youth group and small groups, and over 125 adults involved in direct ministry. MacPhee knew each one—every student, (almost) every family, and every leader. This chapter tells what he learned from his ministry experience, from others along the way, from what he experienced with leaders who supervised him, and from ministry and congregational friends. MacPhee is as competent and accomplished a leader as I have ever been around, in large part because he leads with humility; he listens and encourages others to live into their own calling. Perhaps that's why for the past five years he has been giving his life to lead the spiritual formation of students, faculty, and staff at a large Christian school. MacPhee lives as—and knows what it means to be—an adoptive leader, one who sees every person as a gift from God and who is able to do whatever it takes to ensure that *he or she is given every opportunity to find a place in God's kingdom family.*

As you read this chapter, consider these questions:

1. *Describe a situation in which you have experienced poor leadership as a result of a leader's inappropriate use of power.*
2. *How can a praxis-committed leader exercise hierarchical-necessary leadership? Is it ever appropriate?*
3. *Define* primus inter pares *and explain how it applies to leadership.*
4. *Using the situational leadership model, describe which style of leadership you currently describe yourself as using.*
5. *Design a sample volunteer application packet.*

Introduction

The church that takes seriously the New Testament call to embody vital community recognizes that this calling is much deeper than mere programming or even strategy. It is a way of thinking, an attitude that drives everything else a church says or does in the name of Christ. Leadership that has done its work to reflect the calling to be unified in Christ knows that this attitude begins with the leadership. In terms of youth ministry, community doesn't simply happen; few young people will naturally feel drawn to initiating relationships with an adult community that sits back and waits for them. Adults must be the initiators of relationships with the young. More than this, it takes the church community as a whole to recognize that they are the ones called to welcome and include children and young people even as they nurture their journey into full

adulthood and Christian maturity. In a church that heeds Jesus's "one command" in John 13:34 to "love one another," both staff and lay leadership recognize that they must lead as an extension of this command. Thankfully, churches are discovering that the role of building lasting and authentic relationships with teenagers can't be relegated to a lone youth pastor but is the call of every adult within the church family.[1]

In *Bowling Alone: The Collapse and Revival of American Community*, Robert D. Putnam details ways in which we are increasingly disconnected from our family, friends, and neighbors.[2] Our networks of connections are diminishing. Putnam's title is drawn from the reality that more people are bowling but fewer are joining leagues. What he refers to as "social capital" the New Testament calls "fellowship."[3] William Damon offers this profound warning, "Isolation is the one condition that can turn a family adversity into a developmental tragedy for a child," and calls for the support of a community-wide, "virtual extended family."[4] Dennis Guernsey, author of *A New Design for Family Ministry*, describes this community appropriately as an embracing church—a "family of families."[5] Within the church, as networks of families connect with one another and do life together in partnership with local youth ministry leadership teams and other caring adults, adolescents are caught up into a community of welcome, embrace, and spiritual nurture.

To create a youth ministry environment in which the young are valued requires a new yet timeless leadership mind-set and approach. Those serving as the point person for local church ministry to adolescents must lead the way by inspiring, informing, inviting, and modeling for the rest of the church.

Models of Leadership in (Youth) Ministry

How do you define leadership? The *US Army Field Manual* defines it as "influencing people."[6] For anyone who is in Christ, the question becomes more pointed, regardless of the actual setting: what is unique about *Christian* leadership? For our purposes, then, how is leadership practiced or how is power structured in typical youth ministry and church environments? In *Leadership by the Book*, Ken Blanchard, Bill Hybels, and Phil Hodges argue that leaders need to ensure that the development of people as a primary goal is at least on the same priority level as bottom-line agendas for money, numbers, profit, prestige, or any other current ministry motivations and measurements.[7] As leaders who see their vocation as an expression of their calling as agents of the kingdom of God, regardless of the role in which we are placed, we must constantly ask ourselves, do we *develop* or *deplete* people? In adoptive youth ministry, where we participate in God's declaration of our familial status as siblings, the way in which we see leadership—either as using or controlling people for our own ends or as serving and setting free God's people to welcome and invite young people into the church family—determines whether we are adoptive or simply trying to do a "good job."

How are the pressures and demands of life and leadership manifested in most churches and youth ministries? A youth worker, especially someone who is young, eager, and (usually) just beginning to gain life and call experience, may get hired by a local church because he or she seems to love kids. Inevitably, pressure mounts to produce a certain number of kids and programs to justify the job, or maybe even a sense of personal identity. Where there is ministry "success," programs multiply, volunteers need to be recruited, and the machine is more difficult to keep going. Things are busier and more chaotic, but for what purpose? In our more honest, stressful moments, we discover that we easily resort to using and directing people in order to help run "my ministry," with "my kids," using "my volunteers." We may think we are serving and setting people up for their ministry of adoption, but in fact we have succumbed to the call to "be good" in our "work" of youth ministry.

This all-too-common scenario could be called the "pre-Jethro" Moses style of leadership. Moses was on point "from morning till evening," with people standing "around *him*." Jethro wisely inquires, "Why do you alone sit as judge?" Moses assumed his only option was to lead solo as the lone conduit of God's information and decision. Jethro gives timeless advice: "What you are doing is not good. . . . You and these people . . . will only wear yourselves out. The work is too heavy for you; you cannot handle it alone." Jethro prescribed a new plan that placed Moses as part of a team, enabling him "to stand the strain" and, in turn, assuring that "all these people [went] home satisfied."[8] Jethro urged Moses to learn *a new way* to lead.

In the midst of overwhelming responsibility and need, this is the tension every leader faces in ministry: we, like Moses, may also want to be, even feel the need to be, the master helmsman functioning at the pinnacle of leadership focus, identification, influence, and power over the needs and expectations in our ministry. But Jethro's intervention provides an important correction to Moses's controlling nature: he provides an alternative to the more common, autocratic, and hierarchical leadership style of his son-in-law.[9] Trina Soske and Jay Conger, writers on the Harvard Business Review Blog Network, note, "Despite the continued popularity of the 'great man' theory of leadership and our romantic attachment to the idea of an individual that's going to 'ride in and save the day,' leadership is a team sport."[10]

A key issue every leader must wrestle with is *the appropriate use of power.* How one chooses to wield power ultimately reflects one's sense of identity as a leader in dialogue with the expectations of how power can be used within a particular cultural context.

Robert K. Greenleaf is credited with coining and helping to define our modern understanding of servant leadership, both in business and in the church. His perspective focuses on the two essential realities of leadership: *orientation* and *motivation.*

> The servant-leader *is* servant first. . . . It begins with the natural feeling that one wants to serve, to serve *first.* Then conscious choice brings one to aspire to lead. That person is sharply different from one who is *leader* first, perhaps because of the need to assuage an unusual power drive. . . . The difference manifests itself in the care taken by the servant-first to make sure that other people's highest priority needs are being served. The best test, and difficult to administer, is this: Do those served grow as persons? Do they, *while being served,* become healthier, wiser, freer, more autonomous, more likely themselves to become servants?[11]

Greenleaf grounds his understanding of servant leadership in a Latin phrase used in Roman times to designate the key leader: *primus inter pares*—"first among equals." Green-

leaf maintains, "There is still a 'first,' a leader, but that leader is not the chief. The difference may appear subtle, but it is important that the *primus* constantly test and prove that leadership among a group of able peers."[12] This model refers not so much to the organizational structure but instead highlights the key relationships; this fosters an openness of communication that leads to greater collaboration among leaders, no matter the organizational structure. A *primus inter pares* leadership mind-set can be fostered effectively even within a hierarchical structure.[13]

A *primus inter pares* leadership mind-set is found within the apostle Paul's letters to the family of families, especially in Romans 12:3–8; 1 Corinthians 12; and Ephesians 4:1–16, where he focuses on how the household of God can function not only with unity and diversity but also with hospitality, especially as it embraces the youngest members. His words, like Jethro's, invite a new way to look at family relationships and leadership in the church—even if the organizational structure is hierarchical. The role of the youth minister serving those he or she leads as *primus* is to nurture the gifts and power of others in order for the whole church to function in such a way that every person is included and needed in the body of Christ. In this new paradigm,

> [Leaders] would still function in significant roles and positions, but they would operate from among rather than over others, seek participation more than make a presentation, establish connections before expressing content, and ask questions as much as give answers. They would also recognize that change emerges as people are encouraged to make unique contributions and as conversations take place within various parts and levels of an organization.[14]

Living and Leading as the Beloved Child

When a leader's identity has been securely formed and saturated in the life-giving grace of God's love, power is wielded with more equity and responsibility for the good of all, especially the young. Few Christian leaders have articulated a *primus inter pares* approach to authentic identity formation as it flows into spiritual leadership better than Henri J. M. Nouwen, who put power on display in books such as *In the Name of Jesus*, *The Return of the Prodigal Son*, and *Life of the Beloved*.

A plethora of opportunities and experiences in life, especially in ministry, engender discouragement to the point of making us want to quit or tempting us to bear down and use the power of our office without regard for the best of those we lead. In these times and moments it is easy to feel as if our sense of self and our ability to fulfill the expectations of our vocation are called into question. In these moments we must pause and, with settled assurance in our relationship to God, lean into the fundamental question, "Who am I?" The answers that we and others give to this question largely determine what kind of leadership environment and ethos is created.

In his brief yet penetrating book *In the Name of Jesus*,[15] Henri Nouwen articulates three common yet inadequate answers we and others give to this nagging yet indispensable question of identity:

- "I am what I . . . *do*."
- "I am what others . . . *say about me*."
- "I am what I . . . *control* or *influence*."

The dilemma Nouwen explores involves how we try but can't control the ultimate answer to these questions because of our own human frailty, the whimsy of others' opinions, or the fate of circumstances. In trying to form an identity with answers to these three questions we are tempted to define ourselves *by opinions and circumstances outside ourselves.* We constantly shore up our inner angst by trying to make ourselves look and feel better than we know we truly are, often at the expense of those we seek to lead. This defensive response eventually creates chaos within a leadership team and ministry environment. Is it an overstatement to suggest that the vast majority of organizational conflict and confusion is likely traced back to leaders using their power to heal a void with their own sense of identity?

What sets Christian leadership apart, according to Nouwen, is our ability and willingness to settle into our own true identity by listening to the voice of our first love, the love of our heavenly Father. The apostle Paul, having heard that voice on the road to Damascus, said it this way: "I urge you to live a life worthy of the *calling* you have received" (Eph. 4:1, italics added).

In *Life of the Beloved*, a follow-up to *In the Name of Jesus*, Nouwen helps us to grasp that, in order to discover and embrace our true identity, we need to hear the Holy Spirit speak from *within* instead of listening to the external, dark voices yelling lies of self-rejection. "Do something relevant, or spectacular, or powerful."[16] This takes great courage, determination, and a community of grace. What's more, this gets at the fundamental issue of leadership: if we lead others seeking to be satisfied in our ability or reputation to feed our need for acceptance and love, we will use others. It may be subtle for some and overt for others, but when one's motive is twisted by self-need and brokenness, using others is difficult to overcome. If, however, we believe the gospel and are able to discover who we are apart from what we do or what others say, we find we have the ability to lift others above ourselves. So which voice(s) are you listening to?

Nouwen asks, "What voice did Jesus listen to?" and "When did he hear it?" Certainly Jesus matured in his ability to listen to and recognize the voice of his Father, but at a pivotal point a declaration from heaven rang out, "You are my Son, the Beloved; with you I am well pleased" (Luke 3:22 NRSV). Jesus's power to resist the devil's temptations came from his settled sense of identity, which was deeply rooted in his relationship to his Father; everything about his life and ministry flowed from that relationship!

Nouwen urges us to also consider the timing of the Father's public declaration of Jesus. God was "well pleased" *prior* to Jesus's public ministry—before he performed miracles, taught the crowds, called the disciples, or did anything especially newsworthy. In terms of ministry start-up, Jesus hadn't done anything yet to deserve this statement. The Father's love and declaration did not depend on Jesus's *doing* or *controlling* anything; these things didn't come about as a result of the *opinion* of others. "This is my Son, whom I love." According to Nouwen, that voice is what helped Jesus discover and live into his true identity as the beloved Son.

The implications of Nouwen's observation are profound, especially as we contemplate our leadership and its impact on the vulnerable lives of adolescents. We must hear and listen to this same voice. Nouwen declares that we too are, in Christ, granted the status of "beloved child."[17] This same voice sustained Jesus throughout his ministry, convincing him of what he knew to be true ("*Abba*, Father, . . .

everything is possible for you"; Mark 14:36). As we listen to this same voice and hear this same affirmation, we are granted the assurance that who we are is settled long before we are right, or good, or gifted.

According to the Scriptures, in Christ the Father has declared, "You are my beloved child!" This message is for you and the world around you to hear. Furthermore, the second sentence adds texture to the first—"with you I am *well pleased*." You belong to the Father as his beloved, and *he is pleased with you*—regardless of your title, position, or performance. There are voices from the outside measuring us by what we *do* or *control*. But there is a more important voice that comes from heaven. We can choose to listen to the external noise or the internal voice of the Spirit. This is a lifelong struggle for any leader, informing our understanding of identity, call, and mission. Parker Palmer, noting that our standing before God is what empowers our vocation, says,

> Today I understand vocation quite differently—not as a goal to be achieved but as a gift to be received. Discovering vocation does not mean scrambling toward some prize just beyond my reach but accepting the treasure of true self I already possess. Vocation does not come from a voice "out there" calling me to become something I am not. It comes from a voice "in here" calling me to be the person I was born to be, to fulfill the original selfhood given me at birth by God.[18]

Our spiritual life and leadership will be determined as we let this calling grow inside us, letting our leadership flow out of an inner reservoir of grateful yet secure humility. This is our anchor—the voice from above that says, "You are my beloved child." Prayer, according to Nouwen, is to stop talking and *listen* to that voice, do the hard work to *believe* that voice, and then progressively *discover* what it means to become the beloved of God.[19]

In practice, what do we do to begin living into the life of the beloved (to live *in the name of Jesus*)? How do we cultivate a climate conducive to a beloved community? In addition, how does our knowledge of our belovedness impact our leadership? Nouwen gives the following pastoral counsel to young leaders:

1. Remind yourself daily that though the world speaks lies, the Spirit speaks truth (good things) about who you are.
2. Find and spend time with people and in places that will affirm the same Spirit-given message.
3. Celebrate and say "thank you" to God and to all those who "remind you of your chosenness."[20]

This is the beginning of leadership, but it will continue to be a lifelong and career-long journey. "If you don't love Jesus, you will soon discover that being a pastor or a church leader is not really a very good job. You will be overworked, underpaid, overstressed, and underappreciated. But if you do love Jesus, you will discover as so many others have that it can be the most wonderful and exciting job in the world."[21]

Leading Volunteers

When we lead out of the authentic sense of vocation as God's beloved children set free, we are forced to ask, "Which is the preferred leadership model—*primus inter pares* or top-down hierarchical controllers?" Is one style exclusively better than the other? In *Building*

Strong People, Bobbie Reed and John Westfall frame the thesis of their book with a penetrating question: "Are you building a strong *ministry*, or are you building strong *people* who minister?"[22] The answer not only reveals our motivation but also the focus of our efforts, which manifests our preference.

Jesus said, "The greatest among you will be your servant" (Matt. 23:11). With these words Jesus summed up his critique of his foes. The Pharisees considered themselves great leaders, having taken the mantle from Moses to guide Israel. But Jesus unmasked their hypocrisy as he addressed his disciples: "Do not do what they do, for they do not practice what they preach. They tie up heavy, cumbersome loads and put them on other people's shoulders, but they themselves are not willing to lift a finger to move them" (Matt. 23:3–4). Jesus exposed their leadership as mostly for show, used to control and to impress others for their personal gain. Jesus wanted his followers to take note as they prepared to become the leaders of the church. Should not we, as disciple leaders, heed this warning ourselves?

Our attitude creates a leadership ethos that eventually leaks out. Ron Martoia calls it the "leadership leak."[23] Are we more concerned with assuring our status or facilitating a platform for leadership in the service of those we lead? Does our positional power benefit us or alleviate the burden of others? Are we building a ministry to be recognized, one that is spectacular and powerful, at the expense of helping others, or do we see our roles as empowering those we lead? While it may seem obvious that "first among equals" is the preferred posture of Christian leadership, virtually every model of leadership in the church, especially those that have been extracted from the business world (another world?), is at best learning how to be a benevolent and kind hierarchy. It is true that the disciples in the church had a leader—first Peter, then James—but they were *primus* leaders who functioned as equals. On the one hand we can easily recognize that our theological responsibility in the body of Christ is to love, nurture, and lift up one another as co-disciples and co-siblings. On the other hand, when leadership involves a paycheck or a title, by default we know it falls to us to "make it happen."

How do we navigate this dichotomy? To use Paul's metaphor of the body in 1 Corinthians 12, how can we encourage the "hand" who holds all the cards when we, as the "eye," are the ones who can see the cards (notice, there is one Head, and that is Christ; the rest of us are merely body parts working together)? To put it another way, is there a place and theological justification for hierarchical leadership in ministry? Does the *primus inter pares* leadership model make room for command and control? Consider Jesus cleansing the temple, or Peter doling out discipline to Ananias and Sapphira, or the apostles leading the early church in Acts 6. What about Paul, especially when he was in conflict with Peter, Barnabas, and John Mark? These and other challenges convince us that love is not the opposite of power and strength. Rather, it is our use of power and our belief in the giftedness and calling of all we lead as equals that is the foundation for Christian leadership.

Churches and people need and want strong leadership that exerts loving power for the greater good of each individual and the whole. In this kind of relational environment more and diverse leaders are raised up, with deeper loyalty, to meet a greater variety of ministry needs and goals. At times leaders must make decisions, often without the full agreement of the community they serve. Though some call this hierarchical leadership, it is actually delegated authority on behalf of the whole. Essentially, this is what it means to be a leader: to know how to discover and maintain the appropriate balance of *primus* leadership as a general style and commitment and yet risk being seen as hierarchical when it is necessary and appropriate.

Situational Leadership

Paul Hersey and Kenneth Blanchard introduced the situational leadership model in *Management of Organizational Behavior*.[24] In the words of Walter C. Wright, Hersey and Blanchard "developed a leadership model that sees leadership as a relational continuum with four distinct styles of leadership behavior tied directly to the specific follower."[25] Core to situational leadership is the determination of the leader to adapt his or her leadership style in any given situation to fit the *competence* and *commitment* level of the follower within his or her real-time context. Situational leadership presents four quadrants or leadership styles that are consistently *primus* and yet appropriately hierarchical.

- The vertical axis: *relationship* behavior (support in developing people)
- The horizontal axis: *task* behavior (guidance or direction in getting tasks done)

As you consider applying situational leadership to your ministry context, think about specific people you know who might fit in each of the four quadrants.

S1—Directing. This person is probably an inexperienced and relatively new vol-

Supporting	*relationship* behavior (support in develop- ing people)	Coaching
task behavior (guidance or direction in getting tasks done)		
Delegating		Directing

unteer who is enthusiastic and ready to go. In this quadrant, your leadership style is mostly hierarchical, though still grounded in love—"do this now, in this way." We give this person specific and simple tasks, with few details. The conversation might be mostly one-way, though we will wisely take time to clarify instructions. While permeated with love and confidence, this leadership style may feel mostly hierarchical.

S2—*Coaching*. This person has a few initial experiences in actual ministry but may be a bit disillusioned. His or her experience of ministry and adolescents may have been initially overwhelming and discouraging. This person's initial excitement is wearing off because actual ministry is more difficult than he or she imagined. Many leaders lose volunteers at this stage because they fail to give the right kind of supportive attention that breathes courage back into a shell-shocked newbie. This person still need lots of direction and also support, encouragement, and a sounding board to check reality. "You can do this!"

S3—*Supporting*. This volunteer is now more capable; having pushed through inevitable obstacles and difficult kids or parents, he or she has some significant and fruitful ministry experience behind him or her. But fruitful leaders in this quadrant are typically still unsure whether they can do this task alone, without being held by the hand. They still need and want your support, but that support gravitates toward encouragement of their leadership strengths, trusting they have what it takes to lead. You are mostly encouraging them to figure out next steps—you trust them, and you tell them so.

S4—*Delegating*. This leader is now able and willing to make ministry happen and to train and raise up other leaders. You are able to give this leader less time in both direction and support. As a trusted team partner, you have not only gained loyalty and love but have also multiplied leadership.

Situational leadership reminds us that we need to know our partners in ministry and apply the appropriate kind of support and direction depending on their commitment and competence. Whenever a new skill or responsibility is required, any given leader can quickly move back to the S1 quadrant, needing clear and straightforward direction until he or she builds new competence and confidence, which will lead to greater commitment. This requires a *primus* leader to pay close attention to the team, offer timely and appropriate support, hand over real responsibility, and empower others to live into the call God speaks to them.

But situational leadership is not the goal. The goal is increasing the maturity, confidence, and competence of specific volunteers and entire teams. The more confident and competent the volunteer, the more important it becomes to function as a fully equal *primus* leader. The more insecure and immature the person being led, the more he or she will want and need you to be hierarchical and seemingly directive in style, at least for a season, while maintaining the attitude of mutual respect and equality. Our goal must always be to lead volunteers and teams into maturity and interdependence by intentionally moving them along the continuum toward confidence and competence. Our goal is individual, team, and community transformation and empowerment. *Primus* leadership needs to be adaptable and flexible, which is why the model of situational leadership is so important.

Cultivating Healthy Leadership Environments

The word *recruiting*, when applied to church ministry, is a bit distasteful—it can sound manipulative and self-serving. Rather than recruiting, we are essentially *inviting* people to consider participating on an adoptive leadership team, becoming a part of the family that embraces young people.[26] A common perceived plight and/or question voiced by many leaders is, "I don't have enough helpers for *my* program. How do *I* get more leaders?" Most likely you have felt the panic and desperation that comes from knowing you need others to join you in loving, leading, and adopting kids.

Health breeds health, so in Christian leadership people come first. Considering what I have discussed, does your theology and practice of leadership lead you to treat people as objects to fulfill your agenda or as individuals discovering and living out the emerging call that God is growing in their lives? Jesus calls all of us, as we align our lives to his purposes, to participate in his kingdom work. We have the great honor of connecting with all sorts of laborers in God's great rescue operation. Every person is a potential candidate for the ministry to which God has called each one. Everyone is called to serve others, regardless of whether they know it or not, and all of us are on a continuum of personal development and gift discovery, increasing our confidence and competence as we enter into ministry.

Consider some of the reasons we avoid inviting volunteers onto a youth ministry team.[27] We may lack faith—we possess a shaky belief that God and people will come through. Recruiting takes a lot of work—it is messy and complicated. Our pride gets in the way—no one can lead the ministry as well as we can. We struggle with nearsightedness—we perpetually get caught up in the *urgent* rather than *important*.[28] We have an inability to relate to adults; as a result of our work, we have become isolated from an adult community. We are stubbornly unwilling to empower others through mentoring and delegation; we define our identity by what *we* do rather than what *others* do. In addition to all of this, insecurity may continue to fester deep inside.

A Secure Leader versus an Insecure Leader*

A Secure Leader	An Insecure Leader
Encourages others' attempts	Sabotages others' efforts
Points out others' strong points	Brings attention to others' faults
Overlooks flaws	Uses others' flaws as ammunition

A Secure Leader	An Insecure Leader
Readily admits own mistakes	Is defensive and justifies mistakes
Gives away credit to others	Demands or manipulates credit
Rejoices when others succeed	Is jealous of others' successes
Is excited when others do it better	Is easily intimidated
Is willing to risk to improve	Plays it safe to retain position
Is content to remain anonymous	Requires others to notice
Is quick to build teams	Wants to do things himself or herself

*Wayne Cordeiro, *Doing Church as a Team* (Ventura, CA: Regal, 2001), 112.

We must build people first and then allow ministry programs to flow out of our relational response to need and gifting. For example, we often start a summer program planning process with the question, "What do you want to *do*?" We fill the calendar and then must go out and find (and even beg) adults to staff and lead the programs we planned—whether or not they sense a call or the gift to lead within the purpose of this effort. When we understand our primary or ultimate task to be running programs, we will be tempted to use people through coercion, even if they are not the right people for the role. Frustration, discouragement, lack of trust, and burnout often result.

An alternative is to ask God, "Who are the people, both adults and students, you have given us, and how can we develop these people in order to fulfill the calling you have for them,

> I don't ever care what a person's spiritual gifts are. I want to know two things: Do they authentically love Jesus Christ, and do they like people? —L. David Cowie, former senior pastor, University Presbyterian Church, Seattle[32]

and for us, in the ministry you have given us this summer?" "Us" language reveals a more conducive attitude toward both people and programs, within the family of families.[29]

Characteristics of Exceptional Volunteers

What kind of adults do we seek to influence the lives of students through our relational and programmatic networks in ministry? Be on the lookout for leaders who are willing to make one of their highest priorities the acceleration of healthy development in adolescents.[30]

When it comes to thinking about the prototypical volunteer we might seek for leadership in a ministry to adolescents, what kinds of stereotypes exist in our churches? What image gets flashed across our minds? Doug Fields lists ten stereotypes: young, funny, athletic, good in front of crowds, strong teacher, lots of Bible knowledge, outgoing personality, charisma, understands youth culture, and owns a van.[31] To create an embracing culture in which young people are drawn into life-altering and inclusive relationships within the wider spiritual family, we must force ourselves and convince others to break out of stereotypes and consider the relational dynamics and actions that *matter to kids*.

When you are building a team and consider a potential volunteer, ask, "Are they relationally driven?" This doesn't mean your team can't benefit greatly from task-oriented folks, but it is imperative that every member can get along with people and is able to work through conflicts. If you have been in ministry for even a short time, you have probably encountered people who have a passion for working with kids but don't like or can't relate to anyone else, especially other adults. This will sabotage a ministry; it creates toxicity and prompts kids to run.

If volunteers are moving toward allowing Jesus to form their lives spiritually, are grounded in their love of God, and like people, you will be able to address inevitable challenges and resolve relational difficulties. Notice that the emphasis is on liking *people*, not just *kids*. This matters. *Everyone* in the church body is a potential contributor for service in support of adolescents. We must open our eyes and expand our vision about the possibilities and calling of a wide variety of people who can surround students with care, both up close and at a distance.

Cultivating Strategies for Finding Volunteers

What would you do if you had ten potential and capable volunteers right now? Do you have a plan for how you would care for and deploy them into ministry? The plan needs to include their ministry description, assignment, parameters for leading, and ways they will be trained and led. A clear and simple pathway to real ministry is attractive to potential volunteers. Your well-thought-through plan will take you to the next level in developing a thriving volunteer team.

The *plan* helps transition from *maintaining* to *building* a ministry.[33]

Here is a profound relational ministry axiom: take good care of the few volunteers you have and let that investment spill over into the rest of the church and organization. How you treat the few will determine how many and what kind of other leaders are drawn to

join the team. Are you looking past your current team, wistfully moaning about the lack of volunteers?

As you take care of the people God has given you, you will discover a significant cultivating strategy: *your best recruiters are your current team members*. Outstanding volunteers are drawn to the ethos created by a high-functioning leadership environment. Vital volunteers who love their ministry experience will naturally tell others about the team.

> For leadership, achieving a vision requires motivating and inspiring people to stay on board and move together toward a common goal. To do this well, a leader must recognize basic human needs such as the need to make a meaningful contribution and to belong. Individuals in an organization bring with them their values and deeply held beliefs, their aspirations and desires to achieve. Leaders who can acknowledge and tap into these sources of creativity and passion will find the fuel needed to transform the idealism of their vision into a lived reality.[34]

As we learn to love one another on the team, we determine to *be* the people of God before *doing* the work of God. A word of caution: don't let the desire for rich adult community overshadow ministry to students. We must hold the two in balance. Stoking the vision of each individual team member, including the impact each can make as a member of a dynamic team, leads to healthy interdependence—"we are better together." Max De Pree wisely taught his leadership team that "effectiveness comes about through enabling others to reach their potential—both their personal potential and their corporate or institutional potential."[35] Inviting potential volunteers into a loving team of like-minded leaders who are making something happen that is bigger than them is compelling.

As we design a programmatic response that leads to adoption, we discover that every youth ministry program is an opportunity not only to accomplish ministry goals but also, and primarily, to facilitate transforming relationships between healthy adults and students who are connected to their families. A healthy team is facilitated when volunteers know experientially that they are indispensable to the fulfillment of the ministry vision and dream.

Volunteers often worry about their effectiveness—their fit, skill, and relational capacity with kids. People are not afraid to give of themselves and invest deeply in ministry, as long as they are not left alone to figure out what to do next. Volunteers need support, encouragement, and resourcing. As *primus* leaders we must curate materials, opportunities, and people who will invest in the ongoing development of the team.

Highly developed volunteers can't afford to waste their time investing in busywork or babysitting; they need to know that, along with the kids, they are moving toward deeper formation in Christ. If you ask most people about their experience of being on a typical church committee, more than we may want to admit will likely reflect that their relationship with Christ suffered while serving. Remember, we *develop* rather than *use* people. *Be* the people of God before you *do* the work of God.

This is the primary responsibility of the *primus* in a Christian ministry. We do this in response to the needs of the individual people God is calling our way. Our path is intentional because we care not only for what the volunteer produces or gives to us but also for him or her as a unique and valuable person. As a result, healthy people attract other healthy people.

Leader Selection

When selecting potential leaders for ministry, we will refuse the temptation to fling wide the door, giving cavalier access to students. We will be *selective*—since it is easier to hire than fire. We will be *protective*—of kids, other leaders, our own reputation, and our church. We will be *direct*—by asking pointed questions as we pursue concerns. We will be *discerning*—by taking the time to evaluate motivation. We will be *clear*—by providing tangible steps for a potential volunteer to take in order to be on the team.

In *Purpose Driven Youth Ministry*, Dough Fields provides ten clear steps a potential volunteer will take to get formally placed on a ministry team.[36] You may want to adapt this list for your ministry context. The potential volunteer will move through the following steps:

1. Express interest
2. Be contacted by someone on the youth staff
3. Receive the student ministries application packet
4. Observe programs (*before* formal involvement)
5. Complete the application (get this *before* you set up an interview!)
6. Participate in a face-to-face interview
7. Prayerfully consider the commitment
8. Return the signed commitment sheet
9. Begin ministry
10. Benefit from a thirty-day checkup and/ or evaluation meeting

Though there is flexibility in the precise order of these steps, this flow ensures prospective team members are guided through the process in a way that helps them, and you, make an informed decision.

Provide a Volunteer Application Packet

A volunteer packet that includes everything volunteers need to understand the nature of serving in the ministry should be readily accessible to interested people. This packet will also provide the information you need to make a good decision about their involvement.

The volunteer packet potentially includes: a welcome letter; an overview of what students need in a caring adult; the purpose statement and values of the church and ministry; general job descriptions; the involvement steps; the application; and a request for references and background check. Healthy teams have clearly established roles, responsibilities, and expectations.

An effective volunteer application includes general information—like name, contact information, marital status, education, and church affiliation. Be sure to ask about the leader's spiritual pilgrimage, ministry background, and experience but also include an opportunity for personal responses. Give space and ask a few open-ended questions about the volunteer's motivation, preferred roles, character issues, and criminal history. Finally, be sure to ask for references and seek permission to conduct a background check.

Meet for an Interview, Face-to-Face

Be proactive and set up a face-to-face interview for the purpose of discerning the appropriate fit and placement for each potential volunteer. Once again, it is important to receive the completed application prior to any interview. This will ensure that you have adequate and helpful information as you dialogue about possible roles. Meet in a comfortable setting so that you can be relaxed yet intentional in getting together. Review the application *before* the interview and develop a list of questions that can guide the discussion. Get in the practice of holding back a promise about involvement in the ministry until after you meet for an interview. Invite the volunteer to talk more about his or her application, life journey, ministry experience, and passions. It is in this interview that you can begin to get clarity together on whether that person fits best in a support or direct ministry role.

Contact Their References

Find a way—whether through phone, in person, or electronically—to receive honest feedback about the character of the potential volunteer. This assumes you have already requested the names of several people who could serve as a reference. Ask the reference, "What are some strengths this person brings to youth ministry, and do you have any reservations you can share with me?"

Invite Them to Observe the Ministry

Make sure that during the selection process, and preferably early on, you give the potential volunteer a mandated monthlong opportunity to observe several of your ministry programs that include students. This is not the time to engage in direct ministry roles or demonstrate ministry skills but rather to observe "who we are and what we do." It is important he or she gets a feel for the nature of what the ministry is about and to see students and other volunteers in action.

Assign a Mentor or Coach for the Volunteer's First Year

It is vital that no volunteer be sent into ministry without proper orientation and support. A mentor or a coach is someone who has been around student ministry, especially within your church context, for a while. Some of the best coaches are longtime leaders who are ready for the transition to being a "leader of leaders." This is the kind of veteran who can walk alongside and offer support, encouragement, and training on the go while keeping a watchful and caring eye on the new recruit. This is especially important during the first three months. Most volunteers who quit in frustration do so early on. The coach can provide all the initial orientation and training to help the new leader not only get off on the right, confident footing but also get the sense that he or she is truly a full-fledged member of the team. This is a good place for careful situational leadership, which was discussed earlier.

Conclusion

In youth ministry, leaders represent the community of faith. As a *primus* leader, your role is to call the church to adoption. Leaders become adoption mentors as they model welcoming care, inviting children and adolescents to fully participate in the life of the community. Adoptive youth ministry *exists only to invite young people into the community*. This is why youth ministry is so valuable and important. The ministry itself is a bridge between the abandoned world of adolescence and the family of God. Recruiting, choosing, training, nurturing, and leading volunteers and staff is a vital part of helping young people to know that they matter—and that people care about them.

The Communication of Adoption

Hearing and Making Known

DUFFY ROBBINS

Without fanfare, Dr. Duffy Robbins has consistently served as one of the more influential youth ministry leaders in modern history. His unassuming, lighthearted manner, his self-deprecating humor, and his willingness to readily lift up and defer to others is what draws so many to him. As one of the pioneering youth ministry professors in the country, Duffy has led the way to a depth of theological thinking about youth ministry that is in the service of Jesus Christ and the kingdom of God. As a communicator, Robbins is as good as it gets.

One of the most important practices of adoptive youth ministry is the care with which we communicate, both as hearers of the Word and listeners to the Word. In this chapter, Robbins shares how communication is at the heart of the gospel story. In the beginning God spoke, and all things sprang to life. As the fall took root, God continued to speak. God's voice reverberates across creation in the incarnation, and in the end all things will be restored as "every creature" speaks and sings praise to God. Between the reality of redemp-

tion and the culmination of restoration, Robbins reminds us, "We are no longer lost, but we are not yet fully home." As facilitators of adoptive youth ministry, we are encouraged by Robbins to be faithful and deliberate in our communication.

As you read this chapter, consider these questions:

1. *What does Robbins mean by respecting "the power of words"?*
2. *Think of someone who is a great listener. What characteristics does he or she demonstrate that make you feel heard? Think of someone who is a poor listener. What are the things he or she does that cause this person to come to mind?*
3. *Communication has been defined as "the art of being understood." In this chapter, understanding is the first step in making sure that our message is received as we intended. What are some ways that this chapter can help you be an effective communicator in youth ministry?*

"Everything that I learned from my Father I have made known." (John 15:15)

We begin with a family in a full-on dash to get ready for work and school: family members hustling in and out of bathrooms and bedrooms, music playing behind one door, a TV blaring somewhere down the hall, and the smell of overcooked toast wafting up from downstairs.

A brief interaction ensues:

Daughter #1 (yelling to nobody and everybody at the same time): "Has anybody seen my sweater?"

Daughter #2: "You mean the one you never let me borrow?"

Dad: "You mean the one that cost me eighty dollars?!"

Mom: "Do you mean the one I have to hand wash in cold water?"

Grandma: "Do you mean, honey, the one with the low neckline that seems a little snug on you?"

Little brother: "Oh, you mean the one that makes you look fat!"[1]

Ah yes, what a wonder—the family that communicates!

Adoption and Communication

Adoption is a family word. And, as the dialogue above reminds us, communication—or the lack of it—is a key component of family life. To focus on the theme of adoption (or on family and relationships, or on ministry and adolescence) without talking about communication is like talking about music without talking about melody or talking about painting without talking about color. *Communication*, a term that has its roots in fourteenth-century words for community, fellowship, and a life lived in common, is what makes our relationships come alive.

Theology of Communication

The great fact of human history is that God has chosen to make himself known (Col. 1:26–27). In the words of apologist Francis Schaeffer, "He is there and he is not silent."[2] This truth is the main story line of a drama that plays out over four grand chapters of human history.[3]

Chapter 1—Creation: "God Said . . . and There Was . . . " (Gen. 1:3)

Four stunning truths light up the stage in this opening act of human experience. (1) God speaks. He is not some carved deity who exudes a menacing air, majestic and mute. In a volley of creative masterstrokes, God speaks all creation into being (Gen. 1:1–25). (2) When God speaks he brings into existence human beings, and he speaks *with them* (Gen. 1:26–30). (3) God creates humans, both male and female, because he realizes the inherent goodness of community—that is, sharing life together (Gen. 1:28). (4) In this narrative we're given a glimpse of the relational (i.e., communal) nature of God: "Let *us* make mankind in our image" (Gen. 1:26, italics added).[4]

Chapter 2—Fall: "Did God Really Say . . . ?" (Gen 3:1)

Almost immediately the story takes a dark turn as the serpent begins to sow seeds of doubt and confusion about what God has spoken: "Did God really say . . . ?" This confusion about the words of God ushers in a tragic fall, and what follows is a cosmic fail that extends its darkness into our lives today: hurtful words, deception, slander, anger, suspicion, confusion, misunderstanding, gossip, country music, YouTube cat videos, and long commencement speeches (just kidding about the last three . . . sort of).

We discover right away that sin and the fall are no laughing matter. Its poisonous blossoms begin to flower almost immediately with lies and false accusations between Adam and Eve. Only a few chapters later, we see the devastation of sin on human communication. God begins to see humans, to whom he gave the gift of speech, fashioning that gift into a tool of rebellion.

> Now the whole world had one language and a common speech. As people moved eastward, they found a plain in Shinar and settled there.
>
> They said to each other, "Come, let's make bricks and bake them thoroughly. . . ." Then they said, "Come, let us build ourselves a city, with a tower that reaches to the heavens, so that we may make a name for ourselves; otherwise we will be scattered over the face of the whole earth."
>
> But the LORD came down to see the city and the tower the people were building. The LORD said, "If as one people speaking the same language they have begun to do this, then nothing they plan to do will be impossible for them. Come, let us go down and confuse their language so they will not understand each other."
>
> So the LORD scattered them from there over all the earth, and they stopped building the city. That is why it was called Babel—because there the LORD confused the language of the whole world. From there the LORD scattered them over the face of the whole earth. (Gen. 11:1–9)

As this second act of the divine drama unfolds through the text of Scripture we begin to see two broad story lines: (1) God's communication—God's speaking—goes unheard and ignored by the humans he has made: "For this people's heart has become calloused; they hardly hear with their ears" (Matt. 13:15; see Isa. 6:8–13; Ezek. 12:2); and (2) even when we hear God's words, we fail to obey them:

> The wrath of God is being revealed from heaven against all godlessness and wickedness of people, *who suppress the truth by their wickedness . . .*
>
> Furthermore, just as they did not think it worthwhile to retain the knowledge of God, so God gave them over to a depraved mind, so that they do what ought not to be done. They have become filled with every kind of wickedness, evil, greed and depravity. They are full of envy, murder, strife, deceit and malice. They are gossips, slanderers, God-haters, insolent, arrogant and boastful; they invent ways of doing evil; they disobey their parents; they have no understanding, no fidelity, no love, no mercy. (Rom. 1:18, 28–31, italics added)

Thus we begin to see the fall in its full fury. No wonder James warns us about the power of the tongue (James 3:5–12). It divides people, divorces families, and devours relationships. Broken communication makes orphans of all of us (Jer. 3:21).

Chapter 3—Redemption: "The Word Became Flesh." (John 1:14)

The third chapter of this grand story opens with an astonishing proclamation: "The Word became flesh and made his dwelling among us. We have seen his glory, the glory of the one and only Son, who came from the Father, full of grace and truth."

It's clear from the way John constructs the first chapter of his Gospel that he means for us to hear in this stunning news an echo of those opening words from Genesis (see John 1:1–5; Gen. 1:1–5). God spoke "in the beginning," but now he speaks in a different way. The Word is incarnate or in-fleshed. In the Phillips paraphrase of John 1:1 we read, "At the beginning, God expressed himself."[5]

As explained by the apostle Paul, humanity needs no longer to be confused and deceived by "fine-sounding arguments" (Col. 2:4), taken captive by "hollow and deceptive philosophy, which depends on human tradition" (Col. 2:8), for in Christ, "God was pleased to have all his fullness" (Col. 1:19).[6] In Jesus, we have the full expression, the most complete communication of the Word. Once again we have an Adam (a man) who walks and speaks with God. But this time, there is no breach in the relationship; there is no fall. And with Christ's coming, we see the first promise of communication redeemed, because in Christ we have what we lost in the fall: the Word, "*full* of grace and truth" (John 1:14, italics added).

If the fall blew out and distorted all of our communication systems, Jesus's coming offers us the opportunity for reconnection (2 Cor. 5:18–20). It is he who brings us within the range of reception (Eph. 2:13). It is he who restores the circuits (Rom. 12:2). It is he who deals with the interference so that we can clearly engage with God and our neighbor (Eph. 2:17–22). To get a glimpse of the fall undone, turn to Acts 2 and read about the day of Pentecost. "Now there were staying in Jerusalem God-fearing Jews from every nation under heaven. When they heard this sound, a crowd came together in bewilderment, because *each one heard their own language being spoken*" (Acts 2:5–6, italics added). It is Babel remixed and reversed. This time people speak and people understand; rather than build a tower to make a great name for themselves, they build a church to proclaim the great name of Jesus (Acts 2:37–47).

It was a sign that the family would one day experience a true reunion.

Chapter 4—Restoration: "And I Heard Every Creature . . . Saying . . ." (Rev. 5:13)

We see that day, in all of its mystery and majesty when John describes a multitude in heaven, which is composed of

> every creature in heaven and on earth and under the earth and on the sea, and all that is in them, saying:
>
> > "To him who sits on the throne and to the Lamb
> > be praise and honor and glory and power,
> > for ever and ever!" (Rev. 5:13)

This is now a picture of communication fully redeemed and restored. It's a vision dominated by the dramatic entrance of one who is "called Faithful and True." He is clothed in a robe dipped in blood, "and his name is the Word of God" (Rev. 19:13).

In a world orphaned by sin and isolated by communication gone bad, here is an invitation to a new creation, a new earth, where we are restored as children of the eternal Father.

God has spoken indeed!

Living in the In-Between

But we're not there yet. Long-lost members of the family are still being found. Wayward children are returning home. The orphaned and forgotten are discovering that they have a Father they never knew. The table is being set, but the family is not yet fully reunited. We are no longer lost, but we are not yet fully home. We live in a land between. Redemption is reality, but restoration is yet to be.

So, still we continue to struggle with the barriers, filters, and flaws of broken communication. Like adopted children in a new family, we are learning how to communicate, how to express feelings, how to speak truthfully, how to confront graciously. We're trying to regain what we lost in the fall; we're trying to learn how to share life together.

And (perhaps you've noticed) it's not easy.

The Challenge of Communication

Think of a flannelgraph with several wooly figures bunched together wearing brightly colored bathrobes, flat and fuzzy, stuck against the dark blue flannel of the board, which is propped up in front of a Sunday school class. There's Jesus, of course, some "Bible-looking" adults (both men and women), some children posed in positions of permanent attentiveness, and, for the sake of realism, some flat and fuzzy sheep nestled at the feet of Jesus. From the right-hand side of the board, Jesus is teaching in a scene meant to recall a moment in John 7:1–43. He's in an earnest conversation about who he is and why he's come, but he's met mostly by confusion and ridicule. Stop for a moment and read through the slightly abbreviated passage below, then come back to the flannelgraph.

At that point some of the people of Jerusalem began to ask, "Isn't this the man they are trying to kill? Here he is, speaking publicly,

and they are not saying a word to him. Have the authorities really concluded that he is the Messiah? But we know where this man is from; when the Messiah comes, no one will know where he is from."

Then Jesus, still teaching in the temple courts, cried out, "Yes, you know me, and you know where I am from. I am not here on my own authority, but he who sent me is true. You do not know him, but I know him because I am from him and he sent me."

At this they tried to seize him, but no one laid a hand on him, because his hour had not yet come. Still, many in the crowd believed in him. They said, "When the Messiah comes, will he perform more signs than this man?"

The Pharisees heard the crowd whispering such things about him. Then the chief priests and the Pharisees sent temple guards to arrest him.

Jesus said, "I am with you for only a short time, and then I am going to the one who sent me. You will look for me, but you will not find me; and where I am, you cannot come."

The Jews said to one another, "Where does this man intend to go that we cannot find him? Will he go where our people live scattered among the Greeks, and teach the Greeks? What did he mean when he said, 'You will look for me, but you will not find me,' and 'Where I am, you cannot come'?" . . .

On hearing his words, some of the people said, "Surely this man is the Prophet."

Others said, "He is the Messiah."

Still others asked, "How can the Messiah come from Galilee? Does not Scripture say that the Messiah will come from David's descendants and from Bethlehem, the town where David lived?" Thus the people were divided because of Jesus. (John 7:25–36, 40–43)

Now, imagine some "talk bubbles" hovering over each of the flannelgraph figures facing Jesus from the left side of the board.

Figure #1 (big, bearded guy, bright red robe): "Isn't that the one they were trying to kill?"

Figure #2 (younger woman smiling from the back of the crowd, with a red scarf on her head): "He's a good man!"

Figure #3 (older guy, halfway from the front of the crowd, wearing a suspicious-looking yellow-and-green-striped robe): "He's demon-possessed."

Figure #4 (long, gray beard, royal blue robe): "Look, if this guy were truly the Messiah, don't you think he'd be doing more miracles?"

Figure #5 (older woman, black hair, brown robe, and large gold ring): "What does he mean that he's going somewhere and we won't find him?"

Figure #6 (young woman, purple robe, with cool sandals): "Surely this man is a prophet!"

Figure #7 (young man, standing with her, wearing gold and red robe): "Why do we have to wear these hot flannelgraph clothes?"

Figure #8 (young girl, bright green robe): "I feel really two-dimensional."

Figure #9 (kid wearing a blue suit coat, nice slacks, and dress shoes): "Hey, mister, can you help me get back to the proper flannelgraph?"

Now, think about this: If Jesus, the master teacher, the Word himself, the full expression, struggled this much with being understood, how much more will we need to wrestle with the difficulties of speaking with "grace and truth" (John 1:14)? Add to that the unique challenges that those of us in youth ministry face when we embrace the privilege of communicating all of this good (and bad) news to an adolescent audience that feels acutely orphaned and abandoned and that, in way too many instances, has never fully experienced what it means to be in a family. Makes you want to pray about a career change.

Communicating Adoption

We'll take the remainder of this chapter to think about how these challenges play out in the arena of youth ministry and how we can in a broken world—by God's grace and through his Spirit—be more effective in communicating the Word. Let's consider three basic principles for communicating adoption.

Principle 1: The Communication of Adoption Respects the Power of Words

The photo on the website (www.juvenile.org) was poignant and effective. Looking up and to the right, as if asking a question he didn't dare to speak, the young boy's tear-marked face showed fear and betrayal. In the form of a sinister grip around the boy's neck, the artist had intimated the outline of a hand. But the choking hand was formed by an artistic portrayal of hurtful words and phrases: "You're such a moron," "fatso," "fool," "pig," "worthless," "Is that all you can do?" At the bottom corner of the picture, in a simple white font, were the words, "Verbal abuse is still abuse."[7]

It's a powerful reminder of the importance of words. In the communication of adoption, one of the first fundamental truths is that *words have power*. God brought all of creation into being by the power of his words. "God said . . . and there was . . ." (Gen. 1:3).

Reading through passages like Ephesians 4–5, in which Paul is talking about community and family, it's striking how much he talks about the importance of the words we use. In just one section of Ephesians (4:17–32),[8] Paul warns his readers to

1. put away lying (4:29): speaking that which isn't true;
2. put away evil talk (4:29, cf. 5:4):[9] speaking that which doesn't build up; and
3. put away bitterness and . . . all malice (4:31–32): speaking that which isn't kind.

This passage from Ephesians underlines Jesus's warning in Matt. 12:36–37, "I tell you that everyone will have to give account on the day of judgment for every empty word they have spoken. For by your words you will be acquitted, and by your words you will be condemned" (see also Matt. 15:10–18).

Implications: "By Your Words You Will Be Acquitted . . . By Your Words You Will Be Condemned."

Although there is some disagreement among Bible scholars about what Jesus meant by these sobering words, what is clear to any experienced youth worker is that on the playing field of everyday youth ministry, words can mean the difference between good communication and poor communication.

What does it mean to respect the power of words in everyday youth ministry practice?[10]

1. *Be clear and concrete in communication.* This is true whether you're talking to a youth group, a parent, a member of the church staff, or a volunteer colleague. Steer clear of vague messages that call your students to "Be a blessing out there!" Be as concrete as possible. Words are the brushes we paint with; use your brush wisely.

Avoid drive-by criticism or ambush conversations where clarity is almost impossible. If you have affirmation to offer, offer it; if you have criticism, offer it. Try to be as concrete as possible so that the other party can translate your meaning accurately. Rather than saying to your senior pastor, "When you shut down discussion in staff meetings like that, it makes me want to go Katniss on you," it would be more concrete and truthful to say, "When you didn't allow me to ask what I thought was a serious question in today's staff meeting, it made me feel like you don't value my input, and it makes me want to push back against your leadership."

2. *Don't be too electronic.* The *way* we communicate will have an impact on *what* we communicate. That's why your roommate's boyfriend proposed to her in a romantic restaurant on one knee with candles burning and a ring beautifully wrapped in a gift box, which was balanced carefully on a brand-new iPad that was playing her favorite song from the *Frozen* soundtrack. He understood the delivery method was a part of the delivered message. Just because you can save time by texting a message to a staff colleague doesn't mean that you should. Face-to-face interaction (think *word become flesh*) is the best way to communicate most ideas.

3. *Don't hide behind humor.* How many times have we heard someone make a comment, with more than a bit of sarcasm, followed up with the disclaimer, "Just kidding"? Even as the speaker disavowed the words, we knew or suspected those words spoken in jest represented some genuine sense of what the speaker was feeling and thinking. This is a cowardly approach to honest dialogue that indiscriminately wounds the hearer. What is that person supposed to do with this remark? Laugh?

Cry? Take it seriously? Apologize? Proverbs 27:6 insightfully reminds us, "Wounds from a friend can be trusted, but an enemy multiplies kisses." Don't allow humor to be a distraction from honest conversation. And by all means (as Paul put it in Eph. 4:29–32):

4. *Don't lie.*

5. *Don't use foul language* (even if you think it will help you connect with your students).

6. *Avoid slander, gossip, and speaking unkind words.* Sticks and stones will break bones, but words will often leave the deeper scars.

Principle 2: The Communication of Adoption Respects the Power of Context

Consider the following riddle. Don't look immediately to the answer. Take a minute to think about it first. If you have already heard this riddle, turn to your study partner and look smug, but don't say anything.

> Romeo and Juliet lie dead on the floor. Water and broken glass surround them. The cat peeks out from behind the curtain. How did they die?

One of the reasons riddles are tricky is that every time we hear a story, we hear that story in the context of stories we have already heard. Like many riddles, this riddle is essentially a short story. When we hear this particular story about Romeo and Juliet lying dead on the floor, we immediately think of Shakespeare's story of two star-crossed lovers who die tragically in a suicide pact. Were we not distracted by our memories of *that* story, we might simply surmise (get ready: here's the answer to the riddle) that Romeo and Juliet are goldfish and that a cat has knocked over their bowl so that he can make a meal of them.

So what? Just this: every time we share God's story, we are sharing it with people whose lives and perceptions have been shaped by their own stories. Words are not just spoken—they are heard—and meaning is created on both ends of that equation. That's why one of the most basic principles of communication is this: *It's not what we say but what is heard that makes all the difference.*

The communication of adoption requires us to pay careful attention to context and perspective. There are no words that stand alone; there are no words that already come packed in their purest sense with an absolute universal meaning. Our words mean what they mean to our hearers. That means we better pay careful attention to the hearers.

Implications: Listening before We Speak

1. *Faithful communication requires holistic exegesis.*[11] Because everything we see and hear is impacted by everything we have seen and heard, faithful communication will entail three kinds of exegesis:

- the exegesis of Scripture—taking pains to make certain that we understand the original message of the biblical text that God intended us to hear (2 Tim. 2:15);
- the exegesis of (youth) culture[12]—making the effort to listen carefully before we speak to make sure that we communicate with relevance and sensitivity— "How does this text speak to the needs of *my students* in *their world*, and how will they hear the message of this text?"; and
- the exegesis of self and community—taking time to reflect thoughtfully about how my own culture and background

might lead me to misrepresent, distort, taint, or otherwise miscommunicate what God wants these students to hear from this text—"How might my story distort how I hear or communicate God's story?"[13]

2. *Faithful communication requires attention to context.* Take a minute to think about how you would respond to the following scenarios. They represent real-life situations faced by actual youth workers.

- A youth worker is speaking to teenagers in a weekly Bible study. He uses profanity to vividly make the point that sin is a really bad thing. Word gets back to the parents, and some of them complain about the coarse language. The youth worker says he was only trying to relate to the students in their own language. Was he right to do so?

- A youth worker wants to use a scene from a music video to illustrate a truth in her Bible study. Some of the adults in the church are concerned that this might represent a tacit endorsement of the artist herself. Are their concerns valid? Should she do it anyway?

- A youth worker is doing a session on the scriptural teaching regarding premarital sex. A student says that this is all well and good, but what if she chooses to be sexually active anyway—"not sleeping around with anything that moves, but maybe later on with my fiancé?" She wants to know whether the youth worker is going to say anything about contraception. Is it appropriate for the youth worker to teach about various means of birth control?

In one form or another, each of these case studies represents that place where the pure message of God's Word meets the impure realities of today's world. It is the place where the Way meets the street corner, where the Word becomes flesh. Massaging biblical truth into a body of real live people with complex problems can cause as much soreness as relief. But it can be done.

Contextualization is giving attention to the soil into which we hope to sow the seed (Matt. 13:4–23). It's taking the time to listen to the questions before we start spouting God's answers. It's recognizing that God is at work in a culture or in a student before we get there, and it's taking seriously what we might be able to give to and receive from that culture. Think of Paul in Athens, walking around and carefully observing the local objects of worship (Acts 17:23). Think of Jesus with the Emmaus pilgrims, listening attentively to their questions before jumping in to identify himself (Luke 24:13–27).

Dietrich Bonhoeffer crystallizes the mandate in this way:

> The first service that one owes to others . . . consists in listening to them. . . . Many people are looking for an ear that will listen. They do not find it among Christians, because these Christians are talking when they should be listening. . . . Christians have forgotten that the ministry of listening has been committed to them by him who is Himself the great listener and whose work they would share. We should listen with the ears of God that we may speak the Word of God.[14]

This is the work of contextualization. It is listening well in order to speak clearly.[15]

3. *Faithful contextualization will require a combination of grace and truth.* I was sched-

uled to speak at a large youth event out West, and about two weeks prior to the event I received a phone call from a woman on the design team who wanted to review with me some basic details regarding conference schedules and travel plans. All in all, it was pretty routine.

That was when she added, without a hint of irony, this additional word of direction: "Please, when you give your talks to the kids, we've decided as a design team to ask that you not mention the name of Jesus. We don't mind if you talk about God; in fact, we hope you will. But we hope you'll understand that talking about Jesus will offend some of our young people, and we don't want to do anything that will make them feel uncomfortable."

Please understand, I am completely sympathetic with the motives that must have led these good folks to "design" the Designer out of their youth event. After all, they wanted to make the conference a safe place for young people to ask questions, to feel accepted, and to feel comfortable. That's important. But just because we want all patients—no matter how sick—to be welcomed into the hospital, that doesn't mean that we have to be hospitable to every sickness and germ, and it certainly doesn't mean that we have to be modest about the Cure.

William Temple, archbishop of Canterbury, commented several years ago that the Church of England was "dying of good taste."[16] Perhaps it's in poor taste to say so, but sometimes the same thing happens in the name of contextualization within the youth ministry landscape.

To be sure, there's a very important and a very fine line between being bold to speak the truth and speaking the truth in such a way that we sound rude and cranky. This is likely what Paul had in mind when he asked his friends in Colossae to pray that he would proclaim the Word with clarity, adding, "as I should" (Col. 4:4). But he also counseled them to "be wise" in the way they act toward outsiders—to "make the most of every opportunity" (Col. 4:5).

For Paul, good teaching means a *combination* of grace and truth, sweetness and salt (Col. 4:6), and for good reason. On the one hand, truth without grace has a bold and salty taste, but it can be so strong that not many "outsiders" will come back for more. In the words of that great theologian Mary Poppins, "A spoonful of sugar helps the medicine go down."

On the other hand, grace without truth is sweet and appealing—everybody loves it—but it isn't a clear proclamation. Jesus warned us in very grave terms that salt, if it loses its flavor, is virtually useless (Matt. 5:13). Paul doesn't want to sound rude and cranky, but that doesn't mean he wants to sound bland and sweet. What he wants to sound is clear.

From the very beginning of Jesus's story we see two elements combined in a way that fully expresses the Word of God: grace and truth (John 1:14). Not surprisingly, we see those two ideas tied together throughout Scripture because grace and truth are absolutely essential for family communication. At the core of Paul's teaching about church life (Eph. 4:11–24) and family life (Eph. 5:1–6:9) is the mandate to speak "the truth in love" (Eph. 4:15). That's important to note because there are two equal and opposite mistakes to make in contextualization: (1) be so "loving" and audience-sensitive that we cease to be truthful; and (2) be so "truthful" and faithful to the message that we ignore the feelings and questions of those who will hear it. One approach is very loving but not fully truthful; the other approach is fully truthful but not very loving. True contextualization will be marked by both grace and truth.

Principle 3: The Communication of Adoption Takes Initiative

"God so loved the world that *he gave . . .*" (John 3:16). Missiologist Charles Kraft[17] reminds us that the first communicator/bridge builder was God himself. From the beginning of time, it was God who sought us out, God who revealed himself to us, God who spoke to us (see Gen. 3:9; Ps. 19:1–4; Heb. 1:1–2). And it was God who came to this planet as a human being (John 1:1–14; Phil. 2:6–7) to heal the tragic and cosmic misalignment between God and us.

When we communicate the good news of adoption to adolescents, we're addressing the gap not only between them and their God but also between them and their parents, them and their friends, them and people of other ethnicities, and them and kids in the various other clusters of their school or youth group—middle school and high school, boys and girls, surfers, goths, jocks, and homeschoolers—gaps between those who know Jesus and those who don't. How in the world can we do it?

We do it the way God did it.

Implications: Youth Ministry as Bridge Building

Here are four basic lessons[18] about communication that we can learn from the One who in the beginning was the Word (John 1:1).

1. *To communicate as God communicates means that we'll do whatever is necessary to make sure that our students understand.*

What do all of the following have in common?

- a burning bush (Exod. 3:2)
- a talking donkey (Num. 22:28)
- an illustration using a mustard seed (Matt. 13:31)
- a potter working his wheel (Jer. 18:2–3)
- a fig tree that met an early death (Matt. 21:19)
- a distant star (Matt. 2:2)
- a story about a man and his pet lamb (2 Sam. 12:1)
- strange graffiti on the banquet-room wall (Dan. 5:5)
- a swarm of frogs and locusts (Exod. 8:2; 10:4)
- countless dreams and visions (see Gen. 37:5; 1 Sam. 3; Isa. 1:1; Rev. 9:17)
- stunning miracles (Matthew, Mark, Luke, John)
- a prophet commanded to marry a whore named Gomer (Hosea 1:1)
- the Word become flesh (John 1:14)

All of these events remind us of the amazing lengths to which God will go to make himself known. God understood that if a bridge were going to be built between God and humankind, it would have to start from God's side. Surely this is what Paul is saying when he writes, "But now in Christ Jesus you who once were far away have been brought near by the blood of Christ. . . . He came and preached peace to you who were far away and peace to those who were near" (Eph. 2:13, 17). Adoption almost always begins with the adoptive parents, not with the orphaned child. *God came to us.* God made the first move. But he also understood that he could not reach us if he didn't fully understand us—that is, what life is like on our side of the bridge (Heb. 4:15).

All of God's communication is geared to the contours and contexts of life on our end of the bridge. He starts high and stoops low (see Phil. 2:6–7) because God is *receptor-oriented*. He is determined to do whatever he needs to do to communicate to specific people in specific places and specific times. It isn't always easy or convenient, but he wants to make himself known.

I remember back when I first started giving talks as a rookie youth pastor, I gave to my youth group the kind of talks that I liked to hear: thorough exposition, clear outlines, lots of notes, meaty teaching. If I had been sitting under my own teaching, I probably would have really liked it!

But after a few months it became painfully clear that my students and I did not see eye to eye about what made good teaching. By the time I had whittled the group down to a few diehard kids whose parents must have been bribing them to come, it dawned on me that if I really wanted to communicate with teenagers, I would have to adjust my methods a bit. I still wanted to offer meat and sound, biblical teaching, but I wanted to offer it in ways that my students could receive it.[19] That's what it means to be receptor-oriented.

In terms of the bridge between our students and us, there are elements of life on our end of the bridge that are quite different from life on their end. If we want to take seriously the lessons God teaches us about communication, we'll need to take the initiative and make the effort to bridge the gap. The apostle Paul puts it this way: "I have become all things to all people so that by all possible means I might save some" (1 Cor. 9:22; see also vv. 19–23).

2. *To communicate as God communicates is to remember that the most important place to speak is not in the front of the room.*

Thankfully, Scripture does not announce, "God so loved the world that he became a Facebook friend," or "God so loved the world that he invited us to join LinkedIn," or "God so loved the world that he texted us." God understood that if ever we were to comprehend his love for us, it would have to be done in a way that was up close and personal. It could not just be the Word become word. It would have to be the Word become flesh, God incarnate. Jesus says, "*Come* to me," in Matthew 11:28, not "*listen* to me" (italics added).

One of the pivotal elements of Christian communication is that it's got to be more than informational; it must also be highly relational. We don't just read teenagers the operator's manual—we join them in the car. We come alongside them on the journey. Our students are much more likely to remember what we said walking *beside* them than they are to remember what we said standing *in front* of them. In fact, if we walk beside them, they're more likely to be interested in what we say when we *are* speaking in front of them.

Does this kind of intentionality somehow filter the relationship? Does it mean our relationships are conditional? No more so than when Jesus sat in Zacchaeus's dining room and explained, "the Son of Man came *to seek and to save the lost*" (Luke 19:10, italics added). That sounds pretty intentional. Intention doesn't nullify incarnation, but incarnation can help to verify intention.

Is it any wonder that in the three years of Jesus's public ministry he spent only a fraction of his time preaching to large crowds and the bulk of his time in the company of individuals and small groups of disciples? One of my mentors drove this principle home to me with these words: "If you want to make a big impression, speak to a crowd; but if you want to make a big impact, speak to a person."

3. *To communicate as God communicates is to take seriously both method and message, form and content.*

It is not uncommon to hear someone say, "God doesn't care about our methods; what he cares about is our message. It's *what* we say, not *how* we say it that really defines faithful communication." But when we read through the hundreds of verses in Exodus in which God gives attention to minute details of tabernacle design or note the care with which Jesus and his disciples observed the Passover on what he knew would be their last night together, it becomes quite clear that the neat and clean boundaries we draw between form and content, method and message, *how* and *what*, are not so neat and clean.

In Marshall McLuhan's groundbreaking text, *Understanding Media: The Extensions of Man*,[20] he makes his famous observation: "The medium is the message." In simplest terms, it is the notion that a message does not stand alone; the medium through which we communicate a message is, itself, a part of the message. The medium isn't neutral. The medium actually shapes the message.

- If we worship in a room that is mostly dark, except for the lights on the stage, what does that say about the focal point of our worship? And what does speaking in that dark room—where reading from one's own Bible is difficult, if not impossible—teach our students about corporate study of God's Word?
- If it's essential for me to be funny when I speak, how does that limit the range of topics I can talk about, and in what kinds of situations would that approach limit my effectiveness?
- If I limit my communication only to creative and engaging stories, it might win me a wide audience. But what implicit message am I communicating to my students when I am timid about taking them into the text of Scripture?
- Suppose I encourage my students to be discerning about what they watch and what they listen to, but then I find a strong illustration from a video that comes from a raunchy movie. Do I use it, and what is the message of that medium?

Someone who chooses to communicate by means of smoke signals is, by default, limiting the kinds of topics that can be talked about and the depth with which he or she can dialogue. The medium impacts the message. Maybe this is why God married form and content, word and flesh. He understands that, to some extent, *how we speak determines what we say.*

In practical terms, what I mean is this: the ways by which we communicate to students—the way we use media and language; the way we approach Scripture; the way we talk about our family, the church, or authority figures in the church; the way we use humor and whether we send a text or a handwritten note—become a part of the message we communicate to our students.

A Final Word on Communication

It could be that you're thinking, "Wow, I thought I could just share my heart and that would be enough to communicate the gospel."

The bad news first: that's not exactly how it works, any more than you can call someone on your cell phone, share your heart with them, and expect that to impact them even though (1) they haven't answered the phone; or (2) they're not listening to you speak on the phone; or (3) they have a bad sound connection on their end of the phone; or (4) they don't speak the language you're speaking into your end of the phone. It would be great if communicating adoption were that simple, but it's not.[21]

The good news is that God isn't waiting for the perfect talk, the slam-dunk lesson, or the ideal youth ministry conditions to do a mighty work. Men and women of God have been announcing this good news of adoption for centuries, and many of them were untrained, ill-equipped, and under-resourced. But God used them to extend his amazing story of grace and restoration.

That's why the most important element of communication always comes back to prayer. Adoption doesn't start with a child or even a really passionate adoption agency. It starts with loving parents who want to bring someone into a family to which they could not and would not otherwise belong. If we want to communicate adoption, let's begin by approaching the adopting Father. Perhaps it seems unusual to conclude a chapter in an academic textbook with a summons to prayer, but adoption into the family of God begins with God's initiative. For that reason, the most important act of communication is not our communication with teenagers but our communication with God.

> When I came to you, I did not come with eloquence or human wisdom as I proclaimed to you the testimony about God. For I resolved to know nothing while I was with you except Jesus Christ and him crucified. I came to you in weakness with great fear and trembling. My message and my preaching were not with wise and persuasive words, but with a demonstration of the Spirit's power, so that your faith might not rest on human wisdom, but on God's power. (1 Cor. 2:1–5)

Teaching for Adoptive Ministry

JAY SEDWICK

I have known Dr. Jay Sedwick for more than a decade. He has served in a variety of contexts in both the church and community and is a full professor in educational ministries and leadership at Dallas Theological Seminary. Sedwick is a highly acclaimed consultant for the church and parachurch, and his students know him to be more than a professor; he is a friend and a leader. What adds credibility to Sedwick as a professor and author is his consistent commitment to youth ministry in the local church throughout his career. When many of us shift into teaching, writing, and speaking, we are forced to be less involved in direct ministry, but Sedwick has maintained his commitment to listen to and walk with ninth graders even while preparing to teach doctoral students.

One of our core commitments in this volume is to gather together a team of scholars and leaders to speak into what it means to create a church culture in which adolescents are welcomed as adopted siblings in diverse settings. Sedwick does not bring ethnic or gender diversity but rather theological and

even geographic diversity. As a professor at Dallas Seminary, Sedwick views the Scriptures in ways that are different, perhaps vastly different, from some of the other authors in this book. For example, he interprets Deuteronomy 6 to mean that parents are the "primary disciplers" of their children, while I interpret it as a command to Israel as a community. Some included authors share his perspective, and some do not. This is exactly what we want to happen in this book. Our hope is that people and traditions who are typically seen as being somewhat isolated from one another will come together with a common commitment to God's call to live as God's family on earth. The theological issues that we may hold in tension are serious and worthy of dialogue, and yet the body of Christ seeks to be the people whom God has called us to be. Therefore, our unity is of utmost importance.

Sedwick brings a history and expertise in the teaching ministry of the church—a voice that in much of youth ministry literature is neglected. Yes, there is plenty of curriculum, books, and resources that we can use as we seek to help equip adolescents in their faith. But what we lack is a guide to thinking critically and theologically about faith education. This chapter offers an excellent correction in that regard.

As you read this chapter, consider these questions:

1. *In recent years teaching has become a "back-burner" consideration in many churches, especially in youth ministry. As you read, how do you answer Sedwick's question "Why do we teach?"*

2. *Who does Sedwick say is responsible for teaching young people? What is his rationale?*

3. *In your background and experience, who were your teachers? Consider those who made the greatest impact on your faith journey. What about them do you remember?*

4. *What is the relationship between teaching that happens in the home, teaching that happens formally in the church, and teaching that happens informally in relationships?*

Mark is sixteen years old and, by most measures, has everything together. He is kind, compassionate, considerate, polite, friendly, and makes his spiritual development a priority. He has never been in trouble with the law, never used or abused any illegal substances, never been involved in an inappropriate relationship, and never demonstrated any rebellious tendencies or attitudes. He is a dream teenager so far. Most people don't believe adolescents like Mark exist today. He is like bigfoot. Some believe he exists, but no one has any solid proof he's really out there. Mark is real. I know Mark personally. How did Mark become the ideal

teenager at sixteen years old? I'm convinced that adoptive relationships have played a huge part in his development.

Mark has two loving parents who are still married and lead his family to love and honor the Lord. He has grandparents who fear the Lord and spend intentional time encouraging him along the way. He has two close uncles he sees on a regular basis who are also walking with the Lord and leading their own families by example. They have both spoken into his life on many occasions. He has a football coach who leads the school team with integrity and spends time building Mark up in the Lord. He has a campus pastor at his Christian school who leads small group Bible studies and regularly mentors Mark, who is the chaplain of his sophomore class. He has a youth pastor he highly respects and who regularly challenges him to seek the Lord in all he does. These are the people who have "adopted" Mark and hold him accountable to the calling in his life to serve the Lord. Mark is blessed. I wish every teenager had this kind of support structure. Things would be very different.

Mark has been taught by all of these significant adults in different contexts, and they have all influenced him in remarkable ways. An adoptive teaching approach encompasses all of the adults in his life who continue to play a role in discipling him. So, what are the characteristics of adoptive teaching?

Adoptive Teaching

Why Do We Teach?

The disciples had just seen Jesus! He was *alive*! They touched him, spoke with him, and even ate a meal with him. How could this be? Every experience they had with him between his resurrection and ascension would be replayed in their minds again and again. All doubt and fear now gone, they followed whatever he said or told them to do without reservation. Acts 1:3 says that Jesus spent forty days interacting with his disciples and friends to further prepare them for what he had called them to do. The last words Jesus spoke to his disciples before ascending into heaven are critically important: "You will receive power when the Holy Spirit has come upon you; and you shall be My witnesses both in Jerusalem, and in all Judea and Samaria, and even to the remotest part of the earth" (Acts 1:8 NASB). He was sending them to lead and to serve what would become the church, his body and bride, for the rest of their lives. These were his marching orders, given to motivate and guide them as they spread the gospel throughout the known world. This was what they had spent over three years preparing to do; this was the goal. But how were they to accomplish this incredible task?

Jesus briefly outlined a simple strategy during his post-resurrection interaction with the disciples. Matthew's Gospel records this strategy, which we commonly refer to as the Great Commission: "All authority has been given to Me in heaven and on earth. Go therefore and make disciples of all the nations, baptizing them in the name of the Father and the Son and the Holy Spirit, teaching them to observe all that I commanded you" (Matt. 28:18–20 NASB). When discussing this passage with my students, I often ask them to identify the command in this statement. Many will say it is to "go" or "baptize" or "teach." However, these verb forms are participles that support the imperative verb, which is translated "make disciples." The simple strategy Jesus commands is to "make disciples." The way disciples are

made involves three steps—going, baptizing, and teaching. He assumed that his disciples would be going (Acts 1:8); after all, they were apostles, which means "sent" ones (John 17:18; 20:21). The action of obedience in taking the gospel to every part of the world is the first step. They took it seriously. Over two billion people alive today—and the countless others who have believed through the centuries—owe their knowledge and understanding of Jesus Christ to this handful of faithful followers.

The second step in the process of making disciples is baptizing through evangelism. I am relating the process of evangelism (presenting the gospel to an individual whom the Holy Spirit moves to belief) with baptism for those who have heard the gospel and believe that Jesus is Lord, that he died on the cross to pay the penalty for our sins, and that he was raised from the dead, resulting in salvation (Rom. 10:9). The word *baptize* means "to identify." The new disciple identifies with Jesus as Savior in baptism after believing in him through faith. Throughout the New Testament, the rite of baptism was performed on those who had first believed. Jesus, in telling the disciples to baptize in the name of the Triune God (Matt. 28:19), infers that the gospel has already been presented and believed through evangelism.

The third step in making disciples is to teach all that Jesus commanded. The things that he taught his disciples were to be taught to subsequent disciples throughout the generations until his return to earth. Amazingly, Jesus prayed for you and me (John 17:20–21) and every future Christian who would come to believe in him because of the teaching handed down across the ages by the disciples through Scripture. The teaching ministry of the church is crucial for communicating the truth of God's Word to every generation. The ongoing health of the church and the propagation of the gospel depend on how well that job is done. It has been said that "the church is one generation from extinction." If at any point in the sequence the next generation is not taught the essential elements of the faith by the current generation, then the church will struggle to remain effective in its calling.

It is my contention that every aspect of the ministry of the church in all of its various forms should be viewed as part of making disciples. As Paul wrote in Colossians 1:28, "He is the one we proclaim, admonishing and teaching everyone with all wisdom, so that we may present everyone fully mature in Christ." The disciple-making process is, therefore, a lifelong commitment to becoming like Christ. I want to focus more intently now on the vital role of teaching in the development of the young disciple of Jesus Christ.

Whose Responsibility Is It?

Scripture directly addresses the question of whose job it is to make sure children are taught the things of God: parents and the nation of Israel are primarily responsible. The Lord commanded the nation of Israel to make sure the children learned his commandments in order to obey and be blessed. Although written to the newly formed nation, the principles are applicable to us today. "These commandments that I give you today are to be on your hearts. Impress them on your children. Talk about them when you sit at home and when you walk along the road, when you lie down and when you get up. Tie them as symbols on your hands and bind them on your foreheads. Write them on the doorframes of your houses and on your gates" (Deut. 6:6–9).

The Lord gave the Hebrews a simple pattern to follow. As the psalmist writes:

> He decreed statutes for Jacob
> and established the law in Israel,
> which he commanded our ancestors
> to teach their children,
> so the next generation would know
> them,
> even the children yet to be born,
> and they in turn would tell their
> children.
> Then they would put their trust in God
> and would not forget his deeds
> but would keep his commands.
> (Ps. 78:5–7)

Paul, having been trained in the Old Testament as a Pharisee, knew the commandments well. He reiterated the primary responsibility of the parents to teach their children the things of God. Ephesians 6:4 states, "Fathers,[1] do not exasperate your children; instead, bring them up in the training and instruction of the Lord," which places the burden of "training" on the shoulders of the parents, and likely the fathers in particular. Extended families are to play a role too. Paul reminded Timothy of the influential teaching of his mother and grandmother,

> For I am mindful of the sincere faith within you, which first dwelt in your grandmother Lois and your mother Eunice, and I am sure that it is in you as well. . . . You, however, continue in the things you have learned and become convinced of, knowing from whom you have learned them, and that from childhood you have known the sacred writings which are able to give you the wisdom that leads to salvation through faith which is in Christ Jesus. (2 Tim. 1:5; 3:14–15 NASB)

Although the evidence is slim, it appears that Timothy's mother and family played a key role if not *the* key role in his development as a disciple of Jesus Christ.

When the Family Breaks Down

The ideal situation, and what I believe God intended, was for the family to be the "cradle of theology." The influence that parents have over their children is more powerful than any other factor. Timothy was taught from birth in the home. The Israelites were commanded to do so as well. The problem with this approach today is the deteriorating health of the family. Can we realistically expect parents to do the job of teaching their children the things of God? The answer to that question is not straightforward. Parents who are still married and who take the responsibility to teach their children seriously can and should be expected to do so. However, their tribe continues to decrease in numbers. One parent often understands the responsibility and the other doesn't, or doesn't care. So many youth have experienced the pain and brokenness of their parents' divorce. At best, they now split their time between two households. At worst, they have limited or no exposure to one of their parents for the rest of their adolescence. Although we cannot be certain of this, Timothy's father was likely not a believer and perhaps had little to do with Timothy's spiritual development (Acts 16:1). What we do know is that his mother and grandmother clearly provided significant spiritual modeling and nurture, which Timothy relied on throughout his life (2 Tim. 1:5). He was fortunate. Some youth don't have either parent as a spiritual guide, nor do they have extended family to help fill the void.

Surrogate Family and Friends

In his groundbreaking research, presented in the books *Hurt* and *Hurt 2.0*,[2] Chap Clark argues that the health and well-being of a teenager is directly proportional to the number of adult influencers in the teen's life. In other words, the more adults who speak into the life of a teen the better off that teen is, particularly in terms of a number of factors deemed important for success in life. Clark found that those teenagers who have a relationship with an average of five significant adults navigate their way through adolescence with relative success. The problem, as Clark puts it, is that the adult population of our society has "abandoned" (his word) its youth. Whether intentional or not, many adults simply let teens fend for themselves during what many would say is the most difficult developmental stage of life. Just when adolescents need the influence of mature adults to help them navigate life's many questions and challenges, they end up turning to the youth culture and their peers for answers. Unfortunately, the youth culture does not have their best interests in mind, and their friends are just as needy and confused as they are.

Research and Scripture affirm that the two most significant influencers in a teen's life, for better or worse, are parents. When that doesn't happen, and sometimes even when parents are actively in the picture, there are thankfully any number of places where other adults have influence on teenagers outside the home. A youth pastor could fill the role. A small group leader, a Sunday school teacher, a football coach, a dance instructor, an aunt or uncle, a neighbor, an employer, or a family friend might fill the role. These relationships are highly beneficial for healthy adolescent development. An adoptive teaching approach takes advantage of these meaningful adult relationships. The apostle Paul encourages this approach when he exhorts the older men and women to have influence over the younger (Titus 2:2–8). Peter also instructs the younger men to be subject to the shepherding of their elders (1 Pet. 5:5). Jesus, who brought a new level of connection, intimacy, and mutual responsibility, affirms that people in the church make up his "family" as God's adopted children (Matt. 12:48; 25:40).

With all of the influence parents have, God gives us siblings in his earthly body to mutually care for and nurture one another, and this clearly includes the children. The church community is one of the best contexts where this can happen. Paul explains that every believer is spiritually gifted and an important part of the body (1 Cor. 12). Each part is valued and essential for the body's overall health—that is, we are stronger together than when apart. The writer of Hebrews reminds believers to meet together regularly for the purpose of encouragement and accountability (Heb. 10:24–25). Adolescents benefit greatly by being around the influence of other, more mature, believers—their older brothers and sisters—in the church. An adoptive teaching approach takes advantage of these significant adult relationships.

What Should Be Taught?

All curriculum publishers use the guiding concepts of *scope* and *sequence* to help them determine the content of what to teach and the order in which to teach it. Their materials are organized in such a way that the essential Bible stories, doctrinal concepts, and theological views are presented in a systematic way. Some publishers strive to make their curriculum as comprehensive as possible, especially given that an age-graded and formally organized teaching format may last only six years for grades seven through twelve. The obvious downside of this strategy is that few if any children or adolescents will attend programs consistently enough to benefit from a cumulative curriculum. This strategy might be appropriate for a math class where attendance is mandatory, but it is untenable in the local church. Youth come and go throughout their adolescence, checking in and out through the years. Some are faithfully involved and do regularly attend, but most, for many reasons, are not as consistent. The other issue with sequential curricula that builds lessons on input from previous lessons concerns new or visiting students. How can a high school junior who has recently responded in faith but who has missed the last several years of teaching participate? We should be able to foster the discipleship process with every teenager no matter what his or her level of spiritual understanding and maturity is.

Should we give up and haphazardly teach whatever we feel is "relevant" at the moment? While that may sound exciting and immediately effective, I don't believe it is the most beneficial in the long run. What I have found is that systematically teaching through books of the Bible provides the opportunity to address "relevant" topics as they are discussed in context—that is, as Scripture deals with those issues. If your leadership team made a list of all the "hot topics" they feel should be addressed in their teaching, many if not most of those "hot topics" will be covered when Scripture is properly interpreted and contemporarily applied, helping teenagers to discover the truth of God's Word. The Bible is relevant for today and for tomorrow (2 Tim. 3:16–17).

Many quality curriculum series systematically cover the Bible; a few of them do so in a six-year cycle. Most publishers will send a free copy of their products for your review. David C. Cook offers a free downloadable curriculum evaluation guide that can be used to compare different curriculum.[3] Select what best fits your purposes. Some churches choose to write their own curriculum—a task that takes more time than most people realize in order to produce appropriate material, but can be worth the effort in certain contexts. The advantage of writing your own curriculum is the immediate relevancy to the culture and context of your church and community. A publisher one thousand miles away does not know you, your teenagers, or your context and therefore must produce curriculum that is generic so that it can be used by various churches from different traditions.

Another approach is to anchor the scope and sequence of what to teach with what I call the Discipled Student Profile, or DSP.[4] Ask yourself, "What are the essential qualities or characteristics a disciple of Jesus Christ should demonstrate or exemplify in life?" There are various lists like this available in print, with as many as thirty qualities enumerated,[5] but no one outside your ministry knows your teenagers better than you do. Start by creating your own list of eight qualities that you believe every youth in your church should "own" by graduation, which will constitute your DSP. Your curriculum selection or writing can be guided by these qualities, supporting and teaching them on a recurring basis throughout the years. Basically, you are drawing a target that will help you to focus your aim in everything you teach.

Essential Bible stories, doctrinal concepts, and theological views can form still another organizing approach to scope and sequence.

Teens are capable of studying the Bible for themselves and should regularly have the opportunity to dig into Scripture to discover truth. The word *doctrine* scares some people, but our Christian faith is constructed on doctrinal concepts such as the Trinity, the sinfulness of humanity, and the deity of Christ and his resurrection, to name but a few. Don't shy away from tackling the important doctrines of the faith. In addition, theology is not a four-letter word, yet many people avoid it like it is. Youth are capable of understanding different theological views and should study them before they encounter other youth and young adults, especially in college, who will challenge their beliefs. There is nothing worse than having your faith challenged by someone who has developed answers to questions that haven't even entered your mind. Many of our youth are unprepared and unarmed in the defense of their faith because we are no longer teaching them the essentials. A book like *Truth Matters*,[6] which deals with many of the contemporary challenges to Christianity and is written for youth and young adults, could be used to build confidence in their faith.

Moreover, there has been a renewed interest in the catechetical process for youth. Catechesis, which is simply "oral religious instruction," has been a mainstay of the church for centuries, especially since the Reformation. Historically speaking, catechesis was used to instruct the young convert in the essential Bible stories, doctrinal concepts, and theological views in preparation for confirmation or baptism. The Roman Catholic and Eastern Orthodox Churches have a very defined content for their catechisms. The mainline Protestant church denominations have specific content in their catechisms as well, perhaps the best known being the Westminster Shorter Catechism.

Tim Keller has more recently produced the New City Catechism, which is an update of the Heidelberg Catechism. These instructional materials can be used effectively by an adoptive teacher who deeply cares for those with whom he or she has influence.

Where Should We Teach?

Most of us associate teaching and learning (in a formal sense) with a location—a school, an office, a church. Is content discipleship limited to a church building and during a particular time period (Sunday morning or Wednesday night)? My answer is no, for *where* we teach is limitless. Following Jesus's example, the where is less important than the who, the why, and the what. The New Testament presents a picture of the local *gathering* as the place where worship, instruction, fellowship, evangelism, and service either happen or are fostered, but it does not specify the place (other than "breaking bread" in homes; Acts 2:42–47). In Paul's letters—written to the churches he planted over the years of his missionary journeys—he instructs the churches on doctrinal and theological issues, often correcting their misunderstanding of Scripture or their behavior toward one another. His letters were meant to be read in the gathering place for the benefit of the entire local body. *Where* they gathered was rarely mentioned.

Most churches have a formalized educational program for the purpose of teaching the things of God to their members. For youth, the most common program is an age-graded Sunday school. If your church has a Sunday school program, capitalize on it. An adoptive teaching strategy involves every Sunday school teacher and leader for the purpose of influence in teenagers' lives. These well-trained adult leaders can have a tremendous amount of impact if they will take the time to do so. Youth desire relationships with adults who actually listen to what they have to say, spend time demonstrating the love of Jesus, and genuinely care about their needs and concerns. However, the relationships need to go beyond the forty-five minutes together on a Sunday morning. Often we do not ask enough of our leaders. The spiritual formation of our youth demands more of our time than we are typically willing to give. Therein lies a huge part of the problem.

Other formal settings in which teaching commonly happens are small groups or weekly large group celebrations. Small groups are often held in the homes of church members on a weeknight. This setting is more intimate and less threatening than the church, lending itself to a more relaxed atmosphere and the possibility of more transparency and authentic discussion. Adoptive discipleship relationships can grow strong through a small-group structure. The large-group celebration meetings are still a staple in many churches and, if used properly, can provide the catalyst for promoting the interaction necessary for relationships between adult leaders and youth.

Churches should also take advantage of casual, informal opportunities to teach the things of God and influence teenagers. Summer camps, weekend retreats, and simply being away from the regularity of daily life have been proved to provide the kind of environment in which God clearly works, especially for teenagers (but also for the rest of us). Being out in creation and experiencing the wonder and awe of God's handiwork (Ps. 19) has the potential to get our attention in ways that buildings do not. There is something about getting away from the busyness of daily life to focus on God's mercy and goodness for a few days or a week that moves teens to respond in powerful and often life-changing ways. Mission trips, both domestic and foreign, often break the hearts of youth for those who do not know Christ as Savior and for the needs of others in difficult life situations. Adult leaders with an adoptive teaching commitment should consistently seek opportunities to discuss the experiences the teens are having, giving them the chance to debrief and process as they construct their own biblical worldview.

The church is not the only place where discipleship instruction can happen. Since parents have a significant calling to help their children by teaching them how to worship and serve the Lord, they should take strategic advantage of the time available at home with their teens and their teens' friends. Whether formally or—better yet—informally, they can use this time to focus on the Lord, discussing what it means to know and follow him together as a family. This may also mean opening our homes so that several young people or several families can share lives in the Lord with one another. Using the informal and comfortable settings of our homes in this way, as we learn not only about the Bible but also about how the Bible changes lives and how God is calling us to live as his children, is more in line with the early church than rows of chairs in a building.

The commandment in Deuteronomy 6 involves instructing children at all times of the day in various places and circumstances. We are a mobile society, and parents struggle to have any quality time together with their children. The concept of quality time is intriguing. I have found that scheduling quality time is impossible because it can't be forced. It happens when people connect at a level that is infused by the Holy Spirit. What I have discovered is that quality time cannot happen unless a quantity of time together is scheduled. Quality time happens in the midst of quantity time. Those special moments we seek to have with our teenagers will happen only if we are willing to sacrifice our time in order to make time for them. Have a conversation with your son while driving to soccer practice about the opportunity to represent Christ with his teammates. Discuss the meaning of the play your daughter is in and the worldview it communicates. Process relevant and important news stories together in light of God's Word. Make interaction like this a habit and a way of life, not a special occasion. Encourage the parents of youth in your church to change the way they view the time spent with their children. It must be more intentional.

Adoptive teaching can also involve those in the broader community. Many teens have the opportunity to attend a Christian school. There can be great opportunities to connect with godly teachers who desire to model and extend God's love through the subject matter of the classroom. A number of public school teachers are faithful believers and can be a source of encouragement in a young person's faith, although the opportunities may be harder to realize given the restrictions of that context. Campus fellowship opportunities and Bible studies can provide the setting for significant interaction with God's Word, combined with the discipleship influence of the adult teacher/sponsor of the group. Young Life, K-Life, Student Venture, and other similar group meetings (all ministries that seek to reach and teach youth in high school) employ mostly young adults to build relationships with those who attend. These leaders can fill the role of one of the five adults who speak into the lives of the youth.

As King Solomon says, "As iron sharpens iron, so one person sharpens another" (Prov. 27:17). To sharpen and refine a tool, another tool as strong or stronger is used to reshape it. The modeling and teaching of faithful living in Christ takes place in other relationships in the community as well. Any ongoing group function, like a sports team or musical group, can foster the life-on-life opportunities for influence between a Christian coach or band director and a teen. These are often cited as some of the most significant relationships that foster change and development toward following Christ.

When Do We Teach?

An adoptive teaching approach will change the way we think about when teaching takes place. If we don't confine teaching to a particular location, parents and other adults can have influence on teens whenever they are together and even when they are apart. In Deuteronomy 6, Moses instructs the people of Israel as a group but uses singular pronouns to emphasize the individual responsibility that each family has to teach *all* the "statutes," "judgments," and "commandments" of the Lord. It is clear from the passage that this should be done at all times throughout the day, whenever there is an opportunity. Adoptive teaching means that parents spend lots of time with their children demonstrating a godly life, teaching godly principles, and consistently encouraging them to live "in Christ" (1 Pet. 5:14).

Teaching shouldn't just happen during Sunday school, small group, or summer camp either. Adult leaders need to be much more intentional about the time that they spend with youth. The proliferation of smartphones for most youth means that connecting with them

is easier than at any time in recent history. Social media tools like Facebook, Twitter, and Instagram provide the means to influence youth throughout the week in ways that were never dreamed of in the past. Of course, the technology can be overused and even abused, so appropriate safeguards must be in place to protect both adults and teens. Used effectively, social media can provide a level of accountability, interaction, and influence not seen before in the modern era.

The order in which you decide to teach certain content is the second part of scope and sequence. Rather than a haphazard "What do I want to teach this week?" approach, giving proper thought to sequencing can be useful in organizing your teaching calendar. We should not only be cognizant of the time of day or week when teaching takes place, but we should also think through the times of the year when certain Bible stories, doctrines, and theological views are best presented. The liturgical calendar used by many mainline denominations can serve as a guide for effectively teaching specific and critical aspects of the faith on an annual basis and when they coincide with religious holidays like Christmas and Easter. The Jewish calendar is full of festivals and feasts—holidays and celebrations that constantly reminded the Jewish people of who God is and what he has done for them. Christians should take a page from their practices and better instill a sense of awe and reverence toward our sovereign God by being reminded regularly of all he has done for us.

How Should We Teach?

The idea of teaching usually conjures up the image of a formal setting in which a teacher stands in front of a classroom of students and delivers a boring and lengthy lecture. Thankfully, most teaching situations aren't as bad as that. There is a scene in the movie *Dead Poet's Society* I ask my students to watch each semester that illustrates the difference between what I would call an adoptive teacher, who values mutual relationship and creativity in teaching, and the stereotypical authoritarian teacher, who values total control and rote memory. On the first day of school the film presents several teachers monotonously drilling students and threatening them with severe consequences if they don't do exactly as instructed. Mr. Keating, played by Robin Williams, walks into his classroom whistling the "1812 Overture" and then walks out into the hallway, inviting the students to follow him. Once gathered around the trophy cases displaying pictures of Welton students from the past, the teacher uses the unorthodox location, a question-and-answer format coupled with the visuals of the pictures, and some conversational monologue to motivate the students to "seize the day." The three "orthodox" teachers are depicted as engaging only the cognitive learning domain, that which is concerned with knowledge and understanding. Mr. Keating's teaching methods are more experiential, engaging the affective domain—that which is concerned with attitudes, values, and feelings—in addition to the cognitive domain.

Adoptive teaching is more concerned with life transformation than with information transfer. To be sure, life transformation is predicated on information transfer, but we cannot stop with simply providing information. What the teenager does with the information is vitally important. Caution must be taken to make sure that the application of the Bible does not supplant the content; the two are inextricably connected and necessary to

each other. Some published curriculum is so application heavy that very little of what the Bible actually says is taught. Be wise in evaluating and selecting your curriculum to make sure it is properly balanced between content and application.

Parents, as already mentioned, need to intentionally spend *quantity* time with their teens in order to be available for teachable moments—those *quality* times that can't be planned—to happen. The key is being ready to take advantage of the opportunity when it arises (Col. 4:5). These informal teaching moments can happen at any time during the day as we live life together. Parents should also plan to use some formal contexts, like family devotions and family prayer time. Several Christian publishers produce useful materials that can help parents by providing them with guidance on what and how to teach. Lake Pointe Church in Rockwall, Texas, has developed HomePointe, a promising family-centric strategy complete with well-developed materials (many available for free) to help parents "become intentional about building a God-honoring home one step at a time."[7]

Adult leaders in the church also have responsibility to teach and will typically do so in a more formal setting. In their book *Grounded in the Gospel*, J. I. Packer and Gary Parrett argue that recent educational methods have failed to produce committed believers who know how to stand firm in their faith and defend their beliefs.[8] They propose a return to a catechetical process in order to rectify this situation. A formal catechesis involves the teacher asking questions, which are followed by a specific answer. The Westminster Shorter Catechism's well-known question, "What is the chief end of man?" is asked by the teacher, to which the student replies, "To glorify God and enjoy him forever." This back-and-forth Socratic teaching method can still be very effective today. "At its core, catechesis is a way of helping people understand and internalize the core doctrinal teachings the church has held for hundreds of years, with the hope of transforming their hearts with the power of the gospel. It also serves as a way for people to renew their minds (Rom. 12:1–2) and be ready for every question that is asked about their faith (1 Pet. 3:15)."[9] Will youth learn using this method? That's a difficult question to answer directly because the teaching/learning process is complicated.

Researchers have developed dozens of niche learning theories, each with a particular emphasis. Not one of them is exclusively correct in terms of how learning best takes place, but each contributes something to our understanding. One field of study that can be helpful if applied in our adoptive teaching contexts is the recognition and use of learning styles to plan instruction. It is helpful to realize that teenagers bring different dominant learning styles, or preferred ways of learning, to the context. It can also be helpful for youth to be aware of their own dominant learning style. Teens perceive and process information best when their preferred style is used. However, they can still learn when the other styles are used and should be helped to grow in their ability to do so.

One of the more common classifications of learning styles is presented by Bernice McCarthy in her 4-Mat System,[10] in which she identifies four learning styles: innovative, analytical, common sense, and dynamic. Innovative learners are primarily interested in personal meaning. They need to have reasons for learning—ideally reasons that connect new information with personal experience and establish that information's usefulness in daily life. Some of the many learning methods effective with this type of learner are cooperative learning, brainstorming, and integration of content areas. Analytic learners are primarily interested in acquiring facts in order to deepen their understanding of concepts and processes. They are capable of learning effectively from lectures and enjoy independent research, analysis of data, and hearing what "the experts" have to say. Commonsense learners are primarily interested in how things work; they want to "get in and try it." Concrete, experiential learning activities work best for them—using manipulatives, hands-on tasks, kinesthetic experience, and so on. Dynamic learners are primarily interested in self-directed discovery. They rely heavily on their own intuition and seek to teach both themselves and others. Any type of independent study is effective for these learners. They also enjoy simulations, role-play, and games.

According to this theory, my dominant learning style is analytic (the theory claims that everyone has tendencies in all four but typically has one dominant style). I prefer to learn with more information-based methods like lecture. I dislike interactive and creative methods like drama or artwork. Consequently, when I teach, I'm always tempted to teach the way I prefer to learn and have to remind myself that two-thirds to three-fourths of the youth in my group prefer to learn differently than I do. I have to get out of my comfort zone and use a variety of learning methods to make sure that the youth I teach have an opportunity to really enjoy learning. Dan Lambert has provided a great resource in his book *Teaching That Makes a Difference* called the "World's Longest List of Teaching Methods."[11] He lists 217 ways to teach a concept, from acrostics to writing newspaper headlines. What is the best method to use? There is no clear answer to that question, but it should definitely be a method you haven't used in the last several weeks. Providing variety in learning methods will greatly help you to stay creative as a teacher and will also help to keep the youth interested. Howard Hendricks, a greatly revered and longtime Dallas Seminary professor, used to regularly quote his friend Jim Rayburn, the founder of Young Life: "It is a sin to bore a kid with the gospel."

Adult leaders may also need help organizing the teaching period. Total Period Teaching (TPT) is an old concept I learned in seminary years ago. TPT means that every moment, from the time the first teenager walks in the door until the last teenager leaves, is intentionally used for the purpose of teaching and learning. It doesn't matter what the published start and end times are. There can be no unplanned dead time. The music that is playing, the lighting that's used, the chair arrangements, those greeting youth as they arrive, food that is provided, games that early arrivers play—everything is done with purpose. Many curriculum publishers will provide suggestions in their lesson materials to help with this.

Curriculum publisher materials also have a suggested flow for each lesson that involves three sections: an introduction, a study of the Bible, and an application. I have found Larry Richard's system of Hook, Book, Look, Took (HBLT)[12] to be very helpful and easy to remember and teach others. The Hook section is the introduction, which is used to grab the teenagers' attention. How will you motivate them to want to learn and listen to what you have to say? The best hooks involve every single student in the group. The Book section is when the students, guided by the teacher, actually study the Bible passage(s) that form the focus of the lesson. Every lesson should include reading, observing, and interpreting a portion of God's Word. The Look section involves the teacher and students identifying together the timeless principle(s) derived from the text of Scripture just studied. What is the general application that applies to all people at all times in all places? The Took section is the conclusion; each teenager chooses a personal application to act on that moment, that day, that week, and so on. This personal application does not need to be, nor should it be, the same for every teenager. The Holy Spirit can and will work in the hearts of each of his children to practically apply the truth of his Word in a meaningful way.

Adoptive Teacher Training

> Not many of you should become teachers, my fellow believers, because you know that we who teach will be judged more strictly. (James 3:1)

My church usually does it. Your church probably does it too. It's August, and the new education year is about to start. That means it's time for the obligatory teacher-training seminar to kick off the new year. Yea! Except the people who really need the training never come. The church heavily advertises, hires an outside expert speaker, feeds everyone, and even provides childcare—sometimes to great expense. The enthusiastic teachers, the ones who are already trying to be the best that they can be, are there taking notes, filling in blanks, and paying close attention. The expert speaker may actually say something they have never heard before and give them something they can use in their teaching right away. For all the time and effort, there is little return on investment. How much better at teaching are those who attend?

A better way to train teachers is Adoptive Teacher Training. Every church has a master teacher, the one who most people recognize as really good at teaching. Often it is the Christian educator hired by the church to supervise the discipleship programs of the church. That person "adopts" another teacher for six months of team teaching. These two meet together weekly to plan the lesson, brainstorming creative ideas and learning methods. They divide up the lesson section responsibilities and truly team-teach. Some weeks the master teacher teaches while the adopted teacher observes and critiques. Other weeks the adopted teacher teaches while the master teacher observes and critiques. After twenty-six weeks of teaching together the adopted teacher will be well trained in the philosophy of teaching that the master teacher espouses. You now have two great teachers. These two master teachers then adopt two new teachers and train them in the same way for six months. At the end of one year there will be four master teachers. They will then adopt four new teachers and train them for the next six months. At the end of eighteen months there will be eight master teachers. They will then adopt eight new teachers and train them for the next six months. At the end of two years there will be sixteen master teachers. The pattern is obvious. I would trade sixteen master teachers who have been very well trained for two annual teacher-training meetings in a heartbeat. For most youth ministries, sixteen master teachers will meet the teaching position needs. Adoptive Teacher Training takes a commitment of time to each other and to the Lord, but the return on investment is amazing.

The Role of the Holy Spirit

I'd like to offer one last thought, and it may be the most important one. If you are involved in teaching the Bible in any context, then the Holy Spirit is working in and through you. The apostle John writes, "I will ask the Father, and He will give you another Helper, that He may be with you forever. . . . But the Helper, the Holy Spirit, whom the Father will send in My name, He will teach you all things and bring to your remembrance all that I said to you. . . . And He, when He comes, will convict the world concerning sin and righteousness and judgment" (John 14:16, 26; 16:8 NASB).

When you are engaged in making disciples by going, baptizing, and teaching, the Holy Spirit empowers you in a supernatural way, distinguishing what you are doing from any other endeavor. If you feel called and gifted to teach, then step out in faith, knowing that the Holy Spirit will help you every step of the way.

Rethinking Church Strategies and Structures

STEVEN ARGUE

The best way to understand Steve Argue is to read his Twitter page (@steveargue):

> PhD. i teach. Pastor. study topics on adolescence, emerging adulthood, and spirituality. speak. write. eat vegetarian. love running.

Except for the vegetarian and running references, Argue is one of a kind. He is a thinker, a well-trained trainer, a great youth worker, and an even better teacher of youth ministry at Fuller Theological Seminary. He completed his PhD at Michigan State University, and he was until recently a core leader (they call it "Life Development Director") at one of the more influential churches in the country (Mars Hill in Grand Rapids, Michigan). He is also one of the kindest, most intentionally compassionate people I have ever met. When you look at his picture (you can see it on this book's website at youthministry.fuller.edu) you can see that he is unique.

Argue is exceptional not only because he is an experienced church person, a deep thinker, and a significant leader who needs to be heard,

but he also gets how much we need to change how we do youth ministry. In this chapter on strategy and structure Argue suggests that change should begin with who we are as youth ministry leaders. His advice is practical and real. As we close out this book, Argue's call to inspire our congregations to intentionally engage adoptive ministry as learners is vital for anyone who wants to bring change to an institution that may be somewhat stuck. By focusing on those in front of us, whether that person is a middle school early adolescent or an exhausted volunteer, Argue gives helpful insight into pastoral care with a deeper calling—adoptive ministry.

Although Argue does not spend a great deal of time using the language of adoptive ministry, throughout this chapter he makes it clear that intergenerational connectedness matters only when there is a commitment to authentic family-like relationship. While Argue focuses on practicalities, it is important to read this chapter within the framework of the rest of Adoptive Youth Ministry. Argue's insights and advice are vital practices for any *youth worker, and especially for someone attempting to move a congregation from the inside of the organization. Keep in mind, however, that the ultimate goal of adoptive youth ministry is for every young person to come to know and believe that he or she is an important part of God's family on earth.*

As you read this chapter, consider these questions:

1. *What is your reaction to the job description that opens this chapter? Do you think it is typical? If you could change anything, what would it be?*

2. *What does Argue mean when he writes about being a "learner-centered teacher"? When have you seen this practiced by someone? What did it look like?*

3. *What does Argue say about youth ministry leaders taking care of volunteers? What especially resonates with you?*

4. *In considering adoptive youth ministry, what does it mean or look like to be a person committed in a time and season of transition?*

"We want to hire a youth pastor . . .

who's smart and funny
and relevant and traditional
and young, but not immature
and mature, but not too old
and a leader who can follow
and creative and organized and musical
but not too artsy
and radical in an acceptable way
and married or married to Jesus
and masculine yet sensitive
and feminine but not too feminine
and can hang with our students and our parents
while hanging with her/his own family
in a perfectly balanced way
and spiritual in a practical sort of way
and practical in a spiritual sort way
and up on current events and historical events
and can predict the future of all things youth-related
and get our kids "on fire" for Jesus
in a safe environment
that avoids controversial issues like sexuality, poverty, or war
and can fill in on Sundays when the senior pastor is gone
and keeps office hours (this person should be in the office)
and goes out to meet students in their individual environments (this person should not be in the office)
and knows something about children's ministry
and college ministry and small groups and programming
and can give his or her all but not burn out
and is willing to commit for the long haul
though we may not commit to him or her.

Furthermore, since youth ministry is changing, this person needs not only to understand family ministry and intergenerational ministry but also must solve the problem of young people leaving the church.

Do you know of someone?"

I have encountered forms of this montage with church leaders often—too often. It's an impossible list forced into an impossible "youth pastor" job description with the intention of solving what seems to be an impossible challenge for youth ministry. The demands placed on the "ideal" youth pastor grow more and more overwhelming as we continue to learn about adolescent development, spiritual formation, sociological forces, neuroscience, theological turns, multiculturalism, pluralism, sexuality, and so on (the topics keep growing). We're only beginning to discover how deep the youth ministry project hole goes.

As we realize that youth ministry challenges are broader and deeper, the expectations concerning what the youth pastor needs to be, know, and do keep expanding. As ridiculous as the above "job description" seems, it's not measurably different from the expectations that are placed on youth pastors by desperate senior pastors, visionary boards, students, and overwhelmed parents. Mix these demands with present and future youth workers who desire to serve God through ministry, care about students, and establish themselves in the ministry world, and you have a cocktail for disaster that sets up everyone for failure.

If we care about our (typically) younger pastors who serve in the majority of youth pastor roles, churches cannot stuff one more line item into their job descriptions. It is time (it's been time) for youth ministries in church contexts to reframe what "youth ministry" means and what role the "youth pastor" plays. Thinking about the place of youth ministry and the role of the youth pastor within a church context challenges churches to step back and consider—both theologically and missionally—what they are trying to accomplish.

Before we proceed, allow me to offer a few assumptions that frame my approach to addressing this challenge. First, while some will agree that youth ministry needs to be rethought, they will argue that youth ministry has failed and even damaged young people's spiritual lives. There are movements within the church to eradicate youth ministry and to get churches to repent of this practice, which they see as ineffective, damaging, and unbiblical. I share their concern for advocating for young people but reject their conclusions; I believe that arguments to eliminate youth ministry are biblically unfounded and practically disingenuous. Yes, there is poor youth ministry out there (just like there is poor ministry for any demographic), but that does not take into account the great ministry that is being done or capture the faithful work of so many youth pastors (paid and volunteer) who love and walk with adolescents as society's marginalized.

Second, youth ministry doesn't need knee-jerk responses to the growing research we have on adolescents and their spirituality. Churches, youth ministries, and youth pastors don't need the zeitgeists perpetually bombarding them with the latest and greatest topics and methods, which only oppress local ministries and drive them to ministry attention deficit disorder, insecurity, and impotence. When I first entered ministry as a youth pastor, my senior pastor told me that most pastors overestimate what they can do in a year and underestimate what they can do in five years. The topics raised in this chapter and book appeal to the five-year vision that values process and incremental change. Chasing the youth ministry flavor of the moment is not necessary or helpful to you or your ministry.

Third, youth ministry has come of age, and we must think critically on this whole experiment. Ministry fueled on good intentions is not enough. You probably picked up this book (or your professor assigned it) because part of being a youth pastor and ministering involves being critically self-reflective about your theology, assumptions, and practices. Rooted in the youth ministry experiment are the essential components of question asking, ministry innovation, and doing whatever it takes to thoughtfully and carefully connect the gospel and adolescence. Any good youth pastor is haunted by the question "What is good news to our students?" and is dissatisfied with prepackaged, generic answers. Therefore, we must be vigilant in our youth ministry practice; doing something "because we did it before" is woefully shortsighted (at best) and dangerous (at worst). Further, any reimagining of youth ministry practices means a reimagining of youth ministry roles. The two are inseparable, and I often see youth pastors who want to change their students, their parents, their church, and their world but are unable to change themselves. Be thoughtful. Be careful.

Fourth, context matters. My own ministry interactions and friendships have exposed me to ministry in urban, suburban, rural, national, and international venues, and I am convinced that context affects ministry practice. What works in one context won't work the same way in another. Youth ministry is not generalizable. At best, we can learn from one another. In addition, each of us is tasked with understanding information pertaining to youth ministry and translating it into our contexts. For the sake of your students—no matter how great the resource—every Bible study tool needs to be rewritten and every book needs translation; while every success story can be celebrated, it cannot be replicated. Valuing context requires the hard work of taking ideas and reworking

them for your contexts. It also means rejecting two responses that I hear often from youth pastors. I have seen some youth pastors hide behind their context, rejecting any challenge to their theology or praxis by saying, "Well, it's different here." Of course your context is different, but that does not mean youth pastors can be irresponsible and dismiss research, theology, or the challenges of our day. On the other end of the continuum I have seen youth workers trying to replicate everything they hear and read, with little success. There is no singular "biblical" approach, perfect formula, or timeless ministry idea (no matter what the promotional piece says). There's only you. Youth ministry requires you to understand and test ideas against your contexts so that you can best serve your church.

Fifth, I recognize that my own personal background has brought insights and limitations to my perspectives. I am a white male who has grown up and ministered primarily in suburban contexts. While I have worked as a volunteer youth pastor, experienced parachurch ministry, and taught and trained youth pastors in seminar, college, and seminary settings, most of my proper youth ministry experience has been in larger, multistaff churches. My ministry journey has given me insights and given me blind spots; this chapter will likely highlight both.

Sixth, as someone who has been invested in the church, please understand that any critique I offer on youth ministry is not from afar. The questions I raise, the struggles I feel, and the hopes I cling to emerge from a desire to critique and improve youth ministry, of which I am part. Any critique one offers requires that person not only to point out the problem but also to work toward solutions. Thus I extend a hand of friendship to my readers, asking that they join together with me in loving God, loving others, and being courageous enough to contribute to innovative youth ministry.

The changing and challenging demands piled on the youth pastor have raised important questions about what youth ministry should be doing and what role the youth pastor inhabits within this context. It starts, however, with reimagining the youth ministry within church contexts.

Reimagining the Youth Ministry List (by Looking behind It)

The youth pastor superlist described above both humorously and grievingly captures the challenge facing youth ministry. As youth ministry has successfully attended to adolescents, it has also unearthed the complex challenges associated with young people. Unfortunately, as we have identified new challenges associated with serving adolescents, the "solution" has been to add corresponding correctives to the youth ministry list and the youth worker job description. This is problematic for a number of reasons. First, and most obviously, youth workers don't have space for one more thing. Typically, they don't have the time, experience, resources, or authority to address the multi-faceted challenges facing adolescents. When youth workers are expected to do everything, they run the risk of doing nothing. We must reimagine their role.

Second, the complexities associated with advocating for adolescents require churches to recognize that the challenges associated with teenagers are not a youth ministry problem but a church and societal problem. Any hope of addressing adult abandonment, poverty, education, mental health, family dynamics, or loss of social capital requires a systemic

perspective that calls for the investment of all adults—of which youth workers and the church are one resource, directly and indirectly serving young people and the worlds in which they live and move.[1]

While the challenges we are discovering open a Pandora's box of challenge and possibility, I will remain focused on youth ministry within the local church while recognizing that many youth ministry initiatives beyond the local church share the church's passion and conviction and are doing some very good work. Still, the local church is theologically unique in its mission to proclaim the gospel through the reenacting of God's story within a tangible community—word, sacrament, mission, and love gain context within a local faith community.[2]

Youth ministry in local church communities must reimagine its approach by first ceasing the additive practices that cram more things into youth worker job descriptions. This does not mean that churches do not need to change and that youth ministry must ultimately be seen through the lens of adoptive ministry, but youth workers must begin to bring this corrective in whatever ways they can. In the meantime, churches must commit to refrain from adding to the list without first reimagining what forms the list. This requires systemic and creative thinking that is not simply outsourced to the youth pastor job description but also is embraced by the whole faith community. The practice of reimagining youth ministry begins by reworking the youth worker role. Those of you seeking a new job as a youth pastor can use this as a guide for your next call. Those of you who have current youth director/pastor positions may find reimagining your role more challenging for your church. Remember that a revamped list doesn't mean simply editing the youth pastor's list so that he or she can keep doing similar, but fewer, things. It means challenging youth pastors to reimagine their role, competencies, training, and trajectory.

For the sake of simplicity, I will use the term *youth pastor* to refer to the main person who thinks and implements youth ministry initiatives. I will assume this title to be broad, covering everyone from volunteers to part-time and full-time staff. I recognize that even this continuum assumes certain challenges and resources. However, I hold to the idea that pastors are volunteers, and part-time and full-time staff dedicated to working with adolescents; they respond to God's call in their lives to serve adolescents, their families, and their communities. Pastors care for those entrusted to them, create spaces for people to follow Jesus and, at times, lead them where they may not want to go. Through it all they ensure that every leader aligns his or her ministry and rhetoric toward adoptive ministry. I remind my seminary students that the difference between a "youth director" and a "youth pastor" is that directors respond to what people want while pastors shepherd people where they need to go. This is the heart of being a "youth pastor," no matter what the title.

To reimagine the youth ministry approach and the youth pastor role requires theological and philosophical shifts that reframe the way both are situated within the missional practices of the local church. The youth ministry "list" and the youth pastor role must change when youth pastors prioritize learner-centered pedagogy, commit themselves to pastoring adults as much as adolescents, and focus on transitional moments as the space in which transformative faith happens. For each of these categories, I will explore in practical terms what it means

for the youth pastor and, systemically, for the whole church.

Reimagining the Youth Pastor as a Learner-Centered Teacher

Most youth pastors know that they need to teach somewhere, somehow. What I have discovered, however, is that most youth pastors, no matter what form they use (large group, small group, one-on-one, writing, etc.) tend to think that a "good" lesson, sermon, talk, or Bible study is one that they *deliver* well. The reality is that how well we deliver a lesson doesn't equate to learning. Asking "How did the teaching go?" is the wrong question. A better question is "How did the learning go?" This is learner-centered pedagogy (teaching). In learner-centered pedagogy, attention is placed on the learner—who they are, what they think, and what story they bring to the teaching/learning space.

Learner-centered pedagogy assumes that adolescents (the learners) are not blank slates, empty vessels that need to be filled, or passive individuals to whom teachers download information. They are active learners who seek to connect what they have already known, perceived, or experienced with the new information or experiences they encounter.[3] I have heard too many youth pastors lament or complain that their students "don't know the Bible" or "don't care about the Bible." A learner-centered teacher takes the perspective that if learners aren't learning it's the youth pastor's responsibility. Assuming that you have given them the right Bible verse or the best talk on sexuality fails to take into account where the learner is or what the learner needs. It also reduces the Bible to a list of magical statements that change people. Good teaching learns to value and cultivate good learning, which encourages active learning that invites the learner into the idea, the story, or the question. This approach is a much more challenging task for the youth pastor and for the entire church.

What This Means

A learner-centered posture is more than theory. It frames the way teaching and learning are done in a church context. When I explain this to pastors, I say that they must be committed to excellent content embedded in nurturing contexts. Both content and context require careful attention that encourages teaching and learning in relational spaces that allow for questions and meaning making. By *content* and *context* I mean the following: *Content* gives attention to the curricular scope and sequence that have been developed to ensure theologically sound and developmentally appropriate teaching and learning. This includes weekly programming, small group resources, and retreat materials that encourage students to further their understanding, questions, meaning making, and formation. Content calls students to connect their stories to God's story. It is the responsibility of the youth pastor to faithfully tell this good story, which is rooted in the faithful teaching of Christianity's narrative theology.

Context gives attention to the relational environments needed to create safe and open dialogue with peers and volunteers. Relational connection can be cultivated through volunteer training, formal small groups, and mentoring. Volunteers must be trained to interact with students in ways that communicate they are present and available, inviting them to articulate and ask questions of faith as they make sense of themselves in relation to God and others. Good youth ministry contexts create space for

students to connect their understanding and experiences with God's story.

In Philippians 3:10, Paul declares that he wants to "know Christ." This concept of truly "knowing something" is established through the intersection of what one learns (content) and what one experiences (context). Formation happens at this intersection.

What This Means
for the Youth Pastor

In practical terms, a learner-centered pedagogy that emphasizes content and context will impact the way youth pastors do ministry in some of the following ways:

1. When youth pastors are committed to learner-centered teaching and learning, they will evaluate their teaching in terms of how well their students are learning, invite students' questions, and nurture spiritual formation that encourages students to make the teaching their own.[4]

2. When youth pastors are committed to delivering good content, they spend time preparing theologically sound, developmentally appropriate, and culturally relevant teachings. This requires vigilant study, the pursuit of robust theology, and sensitivity to developmental and sociological considerations. More broadly, youth pastors have a plan—a scope and sequence that maps out what students need to explore regarding their faith.[5]

3. When youth pastors are committed to creating good contexts, they create spaces for students to wrestle with the intersection of God's story and their story. Youth pastors train themselves and their volunteers to create spaces for explora-

tion, questions, struggle, and honesty. Context encourages students to imagine and talk about their faith in a way that is articulate and their own.[6]

What This Means for the Youth Pastor's Church

Beyond good youth ministry, the perspectives described above are essential for the whole church. When it comes to teaching and learning, many churches have conflicting values that often divide "big church" from youth group and contradict learner-centered teaching with teacher-centered teaching. Youth pastors must advocate for the values stated above not because they're just "good for the kids" but because they are good for everyone. I am not suggesting that youth pastors square off against senior pastors (youth pastors are sure to lose!) but that they consider the following:

- If you are applying for a youth pastor position, ask the senior pastor about her or his teaching style. What does the pastor value? How does the pastor know when he or she has given a "good" message?
- If you are a youth pastor, help the main teachers understand who is in their audience. Most teachers (youth pastors included) tend to narrow their perspective, raising questions or using examples that apply to a fairly limited demographic. A youth pastor can be an informant to the church's teachers: tell them stories about their audience; affirm the types of approaches or examples that resonate with the younger population in the church; and gently remind them that negative examples of middle schoolers aren't helpful. This helps senior pastors to grow in their peripheral vision when it comes to the people in the pews.

- Youth pastors can encourage the value of content and context beyond youth ministry. If content is taught with learner-centered pedagogy, then context, in the broadest sense, comes by encouraging people who come together at church to talk about the weekly topic with each other over the next week. Youth pastors can help by offering questions for families to ask one another. Over the past two summers, our congregation participated in a teaching series that, at the end of each week, encouraged everyone to share their answers to these questions: (1) What in this story was new to you? (2) How does this story make you want to live differently? The questions and answers were important. Even more important were the people creating contexts in which these conversations could happen.

The goal, then, is to create learner-centered environments in which learning is valued, people are encouraged to be active (vs. passive) learners, and the entire church becomes a learning community in which questions are valued and faith conversations are expected. The challenges that arise from this approach include the absence of simplistic answers, the disruption of black-and-white thinking, and the dominance of a single perspective. The hope is that faith for the whole community becomes relevant and the church becomes a space where the real questions of life and faith can be explored. Table 1 below describes how we have tried to think about creating learner-centered environments, emphasizing the intersection of content and context.

Table 1

Content and Context for Learner-Centered Learning

	Middle School	High School	Emerging Adult
Content	• Learning the story of God • Questions of content *We must teach them the story and how the pieces connect together. We must avoid moralism.*	• Practicing the story of God • Questions of congruency *We must help high school students see that what they know must be integrated with what they believe and do. This is a learning process. Experience and knowledge inform each other.*	• Extrapolating the story of God • Questions of meaning *Emerging adults bring new questions to the narrative; there must be room to question, doubt, and make sense of their complex world. Pat answers will not do.*
Context	• Space to explore and experience *Be sensitive to the development of middle school students and that they need space to learn, understand—and learn and understand!*	• Space for honesty of fears and doubts *Questions are abundant, and space needs to be made for them to ask the hard questions as they begin to make their faith their own. Failure to do this damages the formational process.*	• Space for dialogue and creativity *Emerging adults need more than conformity. Growing up does not mean bowing to the status quo; it means actively interacting with it. Everyone must change.*
Learning Killers	An uninteresting environment *Faith/formation matters in daily life.*	An unsafe environment *Questioning faith is essential, expected, and encouraged.*	An undynamic environment *Faith looks different from that of parents. It needs community.*
	An unshared environment *We are in this together. Learning and transformation is desired and expected by all, not just those we think we're ministering to.*		

Reimagining the Youth Pastor as Promoting Sacramental Volunteerism

Youth pastors must begin to see their role as pastoring not only adolescents but also those who volunteer in their ministry. On the surface, this doesn't appear to be a radical idea, but I would like to propose a definite shift in the youth pastor and volunteer relationship. Too often, we witness youth pastors recruiting volunteers to do only that—volunteer. Often the word *volunteer* communicates the expectation of "giving a few hours," "helping out," "chaperoning," or "making a difference in someone's life." These types of expectations affect the way we invite adults to serve in our youth ministries. We often invite volunteers into our youth ministries expecting more of them than we should and promising them more than we can deliver. No wonder volunteers drop out and burn out. No wonder youth pastors sometimes maintain a love-hate attitude toward volunteerism.

Volunteering isn't essentially about giving a few hours, showing up to supervise, or even changing a teenager's life. We want volunteers to love God and love the youth. What's more, our spiritual journeys don't end when we reach adulthood. Most volunteers have their own questions, doubts, fears, hopes, and aspirations. When we ask people to join us in working with our youth ministry communities, we are not getting youth ministry experts; these are people who have lived life a little bit longer than our adolescents and who are willing to engage in the adolescent community. We are all in this spiritual journey together.

When youth pastors take this perspective seriously, they must realize that they need to reframe their relationship with their volunteers. Volunteers are not experts. Neither are they the supporting cast of the youth pastor superstar. They are simply people willing to follow Jesus in community with adolescents. In your youth ministry community, you will likely discover that volunteers are working through their own formational and personal challenges. Youth pastors, then, must pastor their volunteers as much as they pastor their adolescents. While there are pragmatic reasons for doing so—such as increased retention, longevity of volunteer involvement, and benefits to volunteer-adolescent relationships—I suggest that volunteerism is, in its purest sense, sacramental.

What This Means

A sacramental perspective toward volunteerism shifts a youth pastor's mind-set from getting volunteers to "help their ministry" or "change a kid's life" to highlighting the theological possibility that when volunteers choose to participate in the lives of teenagers, they encounter the living Jesus. Where two or three are gathered, and wherever we serve the least of these, Jesus is present. And where Jesus is present, everyone is transformed. Volunteering isn't just an option or something people do in their spare time. Rather, volunteering is

a necessity—primarily for the spiritual lives of *the volunteers*. People need to volunteer as though their spiritual lives depend on it. In serving and encountering others we see the resurrected Jesus and are transformed.

Volunteers in youth ministry, therefore, are not needed to stand at a distance, monitoring spiritual behaviors. They are invited to join in the journey of following Jesus themselves—a journey that involves us in the tension, pain, hope, controversy, insecurities, and hopes of life. There is nothing safe about it, not for adolescents or volunteers.

What This Means for the Youth Pastor

When it comes to youth pastors inviting volunteers into youth ministry, we must reimagine what volunteerism looks like. A vision of healthy volunteerism includes both expectation and support. In terms of expectations, I suggest that a sacramental view of volunteerism will inform the way we reimagine our work in the following three areas: the way we recruit, the way we train, and the way we evaluate.

We Recruit Differently

As I mentioned above, let us repent of making promises we can't keep. You cannot guarantee that volunteers will change a student's life. It is more truthful (and likely) to promise that students will mess up volunteers' lives. (Try saying that at your next recruiting push!) But the deeper issue is this: we don't recruit volunteers because students need volunteers; we recruit volunteers because adults need to volunteer for the sake of their own spiritual formation.

We need to convey to our volunteers that when we give of ourselves—whether to youth, emerging adults, young couples, or senior citizens—we are putting ourselves into the relational space of another. In the case of youth ministry, we are inviting potential volunteers into the life of a shared community so that we can begin to understand the lives and worlds of adolescents as they begin to understand the lives and worlds of the adults who spend time with them. Who is changing whose life? Exactly. I have seen many volunteers quit because, as they told me, "I didn't sign up for this." I realized they were right. I promised them impact, not pain. I promised them they'd see lives change, just not their own. And I realized that I failed them by the way I recruited them. No more. State your expectations up front. Accurately frame who a volunteer is and what a volunteer is stepping into. You owe it to them.

We Train Differently

Volunteer expectation and support can be articulated in volunteer training. Volunteers need two things: a clear vision of their role and a community who nurtures their formation. Space does not permit me to go into great detail here, but I want to suggest that both of these volunteer needs can be addressed through the following initiatives.

First, create a volunteer handbook that frames the role volunteers have in the youth ministry. This is more than creating a job description. The job description is only one, small element. The way you actually create the handbook models the priorities you have for your volunteers. Keep these things in mind:

- Make sure your volunteers understand what "faithfulness" looks like in the youth ministry. Do not assume volunteers know what you mean, as they will attach their own meaning to generic expectations.

- Make sure you explain to your volunteers what they need to do and what they don't need to do. Some volunteers attempt to do too little, while others attempt to do too much. Especially when it comes to crisis situations, make sure volunteers know who to contact and how. Professionally and legally, the youth pastor must address the more serious issues that may arise in their youth ministries. Volunteers must know how to identify and resource what they see and hear. Consider drawing up a decision tree[7] for volunteers and training them to use it for potential situations.

- Be clear on how volunteers are to address more controversial issues. We want them to be themselves, but there are appropriate ways to talk about politics, sexuality, gender roles, and theology. Volunteers should not use their position as a platform to promote their own agendas.

Second, create a volunteer training arc in which the primary goal is to nurture the spiritual formation of your volunteers. If volunteerism is about volunteers following Jesus, youth pastors must take this seriously. Spiritual formation coupled with serving provides the perfect intersection of content and context in the lives of our volunteers. Our church has come up with a yearly training arc that invests in our volunteers. Below is the rhythm we have implemented.

Summer

- We work with youth ministry staff to explore and assess topics, research, and resources that we deem important for

the development of our youth ministry. (Note: the key is to critically reflect
on your youth ministry's strengths and
weaknesses, needs and aspirations.)

- Once a topic is chosen, our youth ministry staff studies relevant research and
literature that pertains to our chosen
topic, and we map out the salient elements we want to train and implement
through our volunteers.

Early Fall

- We implement our annual and required
all-volunteer weekend retreat. This weekend is designed to gather the volunteer
team before the ministry year kicks off.
We prioritize this weekend, delaying fall
kickoffs in order to invest in our volunteers. At this retreat we offer introduction seminars for our new volunteers—
establishing our theology, philosophy of
ministry, and expectations—and elective
seminars for our veterans.

- For the whole team, the retreat centers on
the training topic we have prepared during
the summer. We take the weekend to teach
on the topic and provide practical tools
for volunteers to use as they prepare to
meet with students throughout the year.

- Past topics we have emphasized include:
"What do volunteer relationships look
like in light of the incarnation?"; "How
do we cultivate a present-future faith that
grows with the student?"; "How do we
understand and talk about the gospel
with one another and our students?";
and "How do we practice faith individually and as a community?"

- Note that our topics encourage volunteers
to articulate and grow in their own faith
as they invite students into this process.

Late Fall

- By this point, volunteers have had time
to meet with their students and have
tried out some of the training we have
offered. Hopefully, they are connecting
the theoretical teaching to real-life volunteer experiences.

- We regroup to remind the volunteers of
the teaching, get feedback from them
on what's working, what's not, where
they feel empowered, and where they feel
stuck. This space provides a way to revisit the expectations we have established
and to support and encourage everyone
to stay the course and to seek extra help
where needed.

Winter

- By winter, our youth ministry volunteer team has heard us talking about
our topic for six months. Terminology,
approach, and concepts should be relatively familiar.

- At this point we bring in an expert on
the subject we are addressing for the year.
Likely, we have referred to this expert and
have made articles and videos available
to our volunteers so that they know who
the expert is and, generally, what this
person will teach.

- The rationale behind bringing in the
expert at this point in the year is that
our volunteers are familiar with the concepts and have attempted to implement
them in their volunteering spaces, giving
a deeper quality to their understanding
and questions. Also, hearing from the
expert provides a different angle to and
a fresh perspective on the way we have
been teaching the subject. In addition,
volunteers feel deeply invested in.

TABLE 2

Training Arc for the Formation of Volunteers

Timing	Summer	Early Fall	Late Fall	Winter	Spring
Topic	Discern and Decide *Work with youth ministry staff and core leaders to discern the training-arc topic for the ministry year.*	Train *Introduce the topic to your volunteers. Establish this theme as your focus for the year and provide ways for volunteers to express the theme in their volunteer ministry.*	Retrain *Volunteers have had time to think about the training theme and work with it within their volunteering experiences. Remind and retrain based on volunteer feedback (what's sticking, what's unclear, what new questions have surfaced?).*	Go Deeper *Invite an expert on the topic to formally train your volunteers. Volunteers will now be familiar with the topic and will likely have deeper questions. This promotes new perspectives and encourages deeper understanding.*	Celebrate *As the ministry year ends, take time to reflect on your theme. What have volunteers learned about God, themselves, and ministry? Celebrate the ways they have grown and been challenged.*

Spring

- As the ministry year begins to wrap up, we use our spring training to address any additional questions and to reflect on what our volunteers have discovered over the year. While we certainly care about our students, we are more interested in how our volunteers have made sense of their own spiritual growth through their learning and ministry experiences.

- We use this time to celebrate the things we have discovered and the ways we have grown individually and together.

- We also use this time to begin to reflect on the new questions or challenges our volunteers raise, which will inform our training arc for the following year. The process begins again in summer with our youth ministry staff searching for resources for the upcoming ministry year.

We Shepherd/Assess Differently

Let's face it: simply having volunteers makes a youth pastor grateful. The thought of assessing their performance seems counterintuitive, especially since we aren't going to give them raises! If we situate assessment within the context of formation, however, we begin to realize that assessment is part of the formational process we owe to our volunteers. Without a clear assessment process, assessment often gets reduced to whether we like the volunteer. But there's a better way. If you have established solid recruiting promises, clear expectations, and consistent support through training (formal and informal), you can have a fruitful conversation with your volunteers at the end of the year—and you need to have that conversation. There are many approaches to this process, so I'll offer just one as an example. I encourage you to develop your own.

Assessments may have the following categories:

Expectations

- Did you consistently show up to events and volunteer trainings?

- Were you available to your students, and did you pursue them per our guidelines?

Competencies

- Describe the quality of the relationships you have with your students.
- What were some highlights and challenges?

Personal Formation

- In what ways did you grow this year?
- In what ways have you become more mature (in your thinking/living)?
- What personal gaps were exposed, and how can we help you?

Future

- Where do you want to grow this next year?
- How can we help you?
- Here's one thing I see . . .

Reimagining the youth pastor in terms of pastoring volunteers is essential because it acknowledges the role the youth pastor plays in the spiritual formation of her or his volunteers, reframes volunteerism as sacramental and formational for volunteers, and reverses the flow of formation—rather than adults doing things for students, students are invited into a shared formational process.

What This Means for the Youth Pastor's Church

I have made the assumption regarding the pastoring of one's youth ministry volunteers that the annual calendar fits into the broader church calendar. While I think this is a reasonable assumption, it is important for youth pastors to compare their plan with the broader calendar of the church to prevent conflicting priorities. For example, we realized that our volunteer weekend was typically the same weekend as the fall kickoff for the whole church. Asking our volunteers, who are invested members in our church, to be absent from that gathering was a disservice to them and to our broader church. We now end our retreat by going to church together. In addition, many of our volunteers are younger and also serve in our kids' ministry. To be gone for youth training affected their volunteer needs, and we had to carefully ensure that everyone was cared for.

More broadly, this approach to pastoring our volunteers has a dramatic effect on raising the volunteer expectations and support of all those who volunteer in the church. Expectations, theology, investment, and support can help other ministries but also have the potential to create tension between ministries. Also recognize that if you are shepherding your volunteers well you are preparing them not only for your ministry but for any future ministry as well.

Reimaging the Youth Pastor as Bridge Builder within (Necessary) Transitions

It is old news that churches continue to segment ministries and thereby solidify the silos those segments create. Cries for churches to break the barriers and even deconstruct the segments are heartfelt but, in my estimation, misguided. Churches must hold generalizability and specificity in tension. It is true that segments can turn into silos; for some churches, these silos, in turn, become minikingdoms that fight other ministry kingdoms for resources and attention. It gets ugly, but I don't blame pastors for being passionate about their ministries and ferocious in advocating for their constituencies. As I see it, the silos have developed through a combination of unhealthy practices and a passion for a particular ministry.

What This Means

Dismantling silos by creating generic ministries like "family ministry" may offer a better structure, but it fails to address the unique formational needs of kids, students, and emerging adults. At the same time, siloed ministries that don't communicate and work together to create a broader developmental and formational arc are also shortsighted. The youth pastor role cannot be eliminated, but again, it is essential that her or his role be reimagined. Gone are the days when youth pastors can be "hip with the kids" and simply be concerned with their own ministries. I won't hire a youth pastor who can't speak to children's ministry issues, explain to me what emerging adulthood is, or talk to me about the pastoral needs parents have. Through the youth pastor role we can address both the need for youth ministry to include a broader, generalized view of ministry and the need for youth ministers to be experts in their field, ensuring attention is paid to the transitions in a young person's life.

What This Means for the Youth Pastor

Therefore, the role of the youth pastor must include being a bridge builder. In learning theory, bridge building is a crucial element for those transitioning from one way of knowing to a new, more mature way of understanding. The transition is also a time of great anxiety as a young person leaves one way of relating to faith and community and moves toward new, more complex expressions. From a church perspective, we must recognize that young people are constantly navigating new ways of relating to their faith community as they transition from childhood to emerging adulthood. They are changing, and we must change with them.

The role of the youth pastor, then, is to build bridges between old and new forms of knowing and relating. Too often, ministries "graduate" young people from one siloed ministry to the next, assuming that they will assimilate. Research and experience show that as students get older, attrition increases and often culminates in youth "leaving the church." Youth pastors can address siloing, attrition, and transition better by being the bridge builders. Bridge building acknowledges that young people are being challenged to move from one form of knowing toward another. Bridge builders are advocates who start where young people *are* and provide intentional ways to walk *with* young people until they are willing to let go and journey to other side of the bridge. Too often in youth ministry we yell from the other side of the bridge, "Come here! It's *awesome*! We're cool!" Young people need more than that.

While young people who have graduated from high school are often accused of "leaving the church," interpreting this through the perspective of "transitions" and "bridge building" can help us to see the situation differently. Consider, first, that those graduating from high school are faced with one of the biggest shifts in their spiritual lives—they are forced to relate differently to their faith community. They no longer have youth group or age-graded programming and are asked to relate to their church as adults, but they are typically given very few cues to help them through this transition (unless they get married!). Second, churches have not provided clear bridges that emerging adults can use to relate to their faith community. Worse, many churches blame emerging adults for their failure, accusing them of "leaving the church." Imagine how an emerging adult feels—they no longer have a clear way to relate to the church and have received no help in making these transitions, and then they're blamed for it.

What This Means for the Youth Pastor's Church

As bridge builders, youth pastors can address this challenge and advocate for young people by focusing on two important transitional perspectives that affect the whole church: developmental transitions and epistemological transitions.

Developmental Transitions

The most obvious transitions are those that happen between the developmental breaks young people experience between grade school, middle school, high school, and post–high school (college, military, work, gap year, etc.) ministries. Space does not permit us to debate whether these transitional gaps in church should follow the educational system. It is enough to say that culturally there are established transitions in your community that most families experience and to which the local church must pay attention. Again, for young people, each transition represents a shift in the way they relate to their faith community. The way they are treated, the expectations we place on them, and the support we give them change. We must help them and their parents make these transitions. Remember that the questions, fears, and anxieties that surface have less to do with whether young people like the program and more to do with young people and parents learning to relate to your church in

a new way. The student who is suspicious of a new program may just miss their old teachers and friendships. The parent who wants you to take care of their kid the way their church programs did for them (or at least how *they* think they did) in grade school must learn that, as parents, they must play a more active role in their child's spiritual development. As you pastor, you can promise to walk with them, help them to interpret this new relationship, give them resources to participate well, and challenge them in their own spiritual development. Great ideas have surfaced in light of developmental transitions.

Here are a few ideas that we have tried to capture.

- Parent meetings rarely work because few parents want to look as if they need help. A rare exception is during times of transition. Parents are looking for resources when their child's relationship with the church is changing and when their child is encountering new life experiences associated with middle school, high school, and post–high school. This is where we can meet them.

- Silos are broken down when ministries on either side of the "bridge" work together to ensure a supportive transition. If you want to begin to break down siloed ministries, have leaders work on the transitional periods together. Bridge building can happen only when all invested leaders work together to ensure transitions from one ministry to the next.

- In our church's context, we recognized that the post–high school transition is very important. As a result, we developed a whole new job description and reframed our senior high pastor as the high school and post–high school pastor. This was more than a title change. With it came resources and the responsibility to ensure that our graduating seniors are cared for, walked with, and supported as they transition from one way of relating to our faith community to whatever is next for them (work, military, gap year, local college, out-of-state college, etc.).

Epistemological Transitions

I'd like to take this idea of transitions and the youth pastor as bridge builder a bit further. If we talk only of structural and developmental elements, we miss the deeper, underlying essence of Christian formation. Transition ultimately challenges us to reimagine our understanding of faith. For many, faith has been taught, communicated, and believed to be something that most people "get" when they are young. The resulting mentality, then, is to provide programming that preserves and protects them from "losing" their faith. Transitions become more about church retention and attrition, which contributes to the misguided understanding that many churches have concerning young people "leaving" church (assuming that they have lost their faith).

Epistemologically—how we know what we know—youth pastors need to recognize that faith is actually one giant transition. It is dynamically changing, and the role of youth ministry is not to preserve young people's faith as much as it is to help them mature it. Maturity is about transformation, change, and transition from less mature forms of faith to more mature and reliable ways of living our faith.

When understood in this way, faith has verb-like qualities. It may be more accurate to call it "faithing." Faith is a verb more than a nounlike possession on which young people act.[8] Faith

is the way humans make sense of their world. People make meaning in order to connect and hold together the barrage of information they are continually learning and experiencing.

In light of epistemological transitions, faithing is a difficult task. First, new information is constantly bombarding people, increasing the amount of information they must juggle. Second, people need to find epistemological equilibrium. In other words, if pieces of information they acquire don't fit, the human psyche is compelled to find a way to make them fit. People can't live in disequilibrium; life has to make sense. Failure to see faith as a verb and relegating it to a noun we fear they'll "lose" misses the role we must play in building bridges that encourage their formation within their complex worlds, rather than the simplistic preservation of a world that no longer exists.[9]

When the amount of information or the depth of an experience overwhelms the existing ways in which people process data, people can't assimilate it all. They must accommodate it. Accommodation requires a destroying of one's current way of faithing in order to reconstruct a new, bigger, and more complex way to handle the new information/experience.[10] Accommodation occurs as one works through crises and disorienting experiences by constructing a more reliable way to faith.[11] When we hear students who have traumatic experiences say, "I'm not sure I believe in God anymore," understanding their struggle as faithing in more mature ways rather than losing their faith affects the way we support them.

When we think of faith as perpetual transition, we begin to see faith as a process that is owned by the whole church. We must work together to ensure that our young people are given support and opportunities to grow their faith, creating ministries that prepare them for a life of faith that is dynamically changing and growing. The youth pastor's role can no longer be to protect the faith and create "safe places" for young people (as though faith were safe!). Instead, he or she must provide space for young people and the whole community to journey together as their faith changes, grows, and matures.

For our church, this has informed many of our ministry approaches. Below are a few examples.

What Does It Mean to Bring Young People into "Big Church"?

I lament the common term *big church* because it communicates that many young people see the main church gathering as being for "them and not us." I have been told that large church services are not for young people because the topics discussed are too complex for young minds. This assumes, however, that church and faith are merely intellectual exercises and that the main service is a lecture hall. Adoptive ministry advocates and mentors need to be reminded that the "main service" of word, sacrament, symbol, and ritual is not a lecture hall as much as it is a family gathering where people from diverse backgrounds join together to reenact the story of God *together* as a *family*. Young people may not understand everything, but they see adults praying, singing, taking communion, and responding to God's story. We learn more about the family of God when the family gathers. The more that we (and the leaders we serve) focus on adoption as the goal of youth ministry, the better we can help young people understand that this gathering is not just for others but is also actually where they belong.

In our church's context, we recognized that we needed to prepare young people to engage in our gathered community time, but we also needed to prepare our adults to welcome and receive those young people. To prepare relationally separated adolescents for participation in the community gathering, we take them through recordings of our services, starting and stopping the video to point out what is happening and what we are doing while kids (and parents!) ask questions. As we are preparing the kids to join the family room we are reminding the adults that young people are not guests but participants, *even siblings*, in the community. We try to emphasize—to everyone—that we are all formed through the faith of one another as the family of God.

Summer Is for Everyone

We have discovered that when we scale back segmented programming in the summer, we have an opportunity to deliberately address the whole community through creative teaching and by placing an emphasis on the conversations people have with one another when they leave church. It has been observed that the best conversations happen not only when older people ask questions of younger people but also when both groups mutually ask and answer questions. This is another way in which faith grows.[12]

"Post-High School" Starts Junior Year

One of the ways we can prepare our students for faith after high school is to begin preparing them during their junior year. The teaching arc that we have established for our juniors and seniors shifts toward helping them think about the faith questions they are already starting to ask regarding their identity, belonging, and life's purpose. Giving them permission and space to express doubt, ask questions, make sense of their faith prepares them for a dynamic faith that must change and mature.[13]

Resist College-Age Ministry

One of the commitments we have made is to resist creating a college-age ministry program that looks like our youth ministry programs. This is tough for two reasons. First, having a ministry where college kids show up always feels really good and makes churches feel like they're doing something. Second, many college-aged students (especially the more spiritually immature) want a college-age ministry.

In light of our emphasis on faith as dynamically maturing, we recognize that we want all of our programming to promote a "formation-forward" approach. This means that our programming must do more than meet the needs of our age groups; it must move them forward in their faith maturity. If it is true that emerging adults are challenged to relate to their faith community differently, then we do them a disservice by providing them "adolescent" forms of programming. "Youth group" for college students is formation "backward" not "forward." Youth pastors and those working with emerging adults must reimagine the

relationship between emerging adults and the church. What is "good news" for them? What kind of community do they need? How does their involvement and service grow us as a community? Can we take their questions, critiques, and doubts seriously? This approach ultimately challenges every church's theology, values, assumptions, and purpose.

Reimagine

The youth pastor list can't get any longer. Youth ministries in the church need youth pastors to reimagine the way in which they advocate for young people as well as their own role in that process. This brief exploration suggests that we can start by reimagining youth pastors who are committed to promoting learner-centered pedagogy, forming adults through the sacrament of volunteerism, and being bridge builders in the dynamic transitions of faith. Hopefully, these necessary perspectives can contribute to rethinking both youth ministry's purpose in the local church and the youth pastor's role, affecting churches' priorities, strategies, and structures. I hope these ideas inspire more ideas as we continue to live into this great youth ministry experiment together.

A Call to Adoption

Integration of Youth Ministry to the Church

APRIL L. DIAZ

Imagine moving from suburban Chicago, a successful staff member of one of the most influential churches in the country, to a warehouse in Irvine, California. Imagine a highly energetic, widely gifted middle school leader who has never let gender or ethnicity hold her back, even while serving in a predominantly Asian American church. This is April Diaz.

Diaz's experience and background are unparalleled; she was trained and entrusted by leaders at Willow Creek and Newsong in Irvine, California. Diaz is a mother of three children (two are adopted Ethiopians) and has been a pastor for seventeen years. She is also a writer, a speaker, and a leader committed to the health and equipping of youth workers. She is a sought-after speaker and coach, primarily because she continues to stay close to youth ministry in the local church. We have invited Diaz to offer her take on what it means and looks like for a youth worker to integrate adolescents into the faith family. She is an adoptive mom and has worked for years at a church that has been working hard at adoptive ministry.

As you read this chapter, consider these questions:

1. *In what ways might the church you go to (or grew up in) treat adolescents as "siblings" in the future? In what ways do they treat adolescents like siblings in the community now?*

2. *What makes someone an "expert" on adolescents? What are his or her qualifications? Who are the experts in your church?*

3. *The 5:1 ratio states that every young person needs five adult advocates who know them and are committed for the long haul. How many adults knew you well, and who was there for you in middle and high school? How many do you have now?*

in·te·grate

verb

to bring together or incorporate (parts) into a whole

to give or cause to give equal opportunity and consideration to (a racial, religious, or ethnic group or a member of such a group)

to unite or combine

synonyms: merge, unify, fuse, mingle[1]

When I was a young girl, I never imagined that I'd be an adoptive mom. I didn't dream much of being a mom at all. I dreamed of changing the world, or at least becoming the first female president of the United States of America.

It's funny how dreams change.

Years into marriage, my husband and I began dreaming of starting a family of our own. After a trip to Kenya, our "Plan A" became solidified: first have biological children and then adopt from Africa. Simple enough. We tried having a biological child the old-fashioned way, which led to an infertility diagnosis, which led to countless fertility treatment cycles. The entire three-year process led us to a broken heart and an empty crib.

As a result, God's Plan A was revealed: adopt now. With battered hearts still glistening with hope, we began the adoption process.

Nearly five years after our original dream formed, we became parents to two of the most beautiful Ethiopian children the world has ever known. Judah came home forever when he was two-and-a-half years old; Addise was just shy of one year old. Though the four Diaz family members (at that time) shared no biological DNA, we were family. We were becoming integrated as close as flesh and blood can be.

It's funny how dreams expand. Merely nine months after Judah and Addise became our own, we miraculously became pregnant with our son. (Note: though you may have heard of this phenomenon before, research confirms that less than 10 percent of infertile couples conceive after adoption. Fertility post-adoption is a rare occurrence—a miracle.) Terrified throughout most of my pregnancy of what adding a third child to our family would do to our barely adjusted multiracial and trauma-filled family, we increasingly allowed our fear to be transformed into trust in God's Plan A for our family.

In just fifteen months Brian and I went from zero to three little ones in our home. Almost instantaneously we were parents to a three-and-a-half-year-old son, a barely two-year-old daughter, and a newborn son. Chaos became a way of life.

Vocationally, when I compare my dreams to God's Plan A, things haven't been all that different.

When I became a youth worker at the youthful age of eighteen, I never thought about the goal of youth ministry being "integration into the whole body of Christ." I didn't dream all that much about teenagers' faith beyond high school. I dreamed about how they would receive the gift of salvation, impact their high school campus for Christ, discover their spiritual gifts, experience the power of community, and grow in their faith in Jesus Christ. I had lots of dreams for my students, but I honestly didn't consider what would happen the day after they turned their tassels on graduation day.

It's funny how dreams change.

Fast-forward nearly a decade. In my pastoral work with teenagers I started noticing a trend (I can be a slow learner). There weren't nearly as many youth group graduates loving Jesus as there were when they were in the safety of their family and our youth ministry. A brutally painful trend emerged: there was an alarming percentage of youth ministry graduates who were no longer engaged in a local church or passionately following Jesus. These students (who were now emerging adults) whom I loved for years had left their faith somewhere after high school. They were too old for youth groups but hadn't found their place within a church family; too many of them were no longer following Jesus like they had when they were in our youth ministry.

Sadly, our church's statistics were not very different from the national statistics. It's common knowledge these days that at least 50 percent of adolescents walk away from faith after high school. Six out of seven high school graduates say they're not prepared for life after high school. For most college-bound students, if they don't find a local church to be a part of within two weeks of entering college, it's likely they'll flail in faith for the rest of their college tenure (Fuller Youth Institutes' Sticky Faith research captures these realities). The research was mirroring our church's experience.

Something had to change.

First, the implicit, expressed goal needed to be revised. It was no longer enough for droves of students to be a part of our church's program. Success could no longer be defined as *x* number of students participating in our youth ministry. The goal needed to be defined as students following Jesus for a lifetime.

So our church entered into a several-month-long honest, thorough, and discerning assessment and evaluation of our ministry, and the Holy Spirit graciously revealed a "new way" for our local community to raise, equip, and empower the adolescents in our midst. The Lord challenged us with Isaiah 43:18–19:

> Forget the former things;
>   do not dwell on the past.
> See, I am doing a new thing!
>   Now it springs up; do you not perceive it?
> I am making a way in the wilderness
>   and streams in the wasteland.

He reminded us that all was not lost. The God of all time—and now!—is doing a new thing among us that requires a new carrier, a new wineskin to hold the valuable gift. "And no one puts new wine into old wineskins. For the old skins would burst from the pressure, spilling the wine and ruining the skins. New wine is stored in new wineskins so that both are preserved" (Matt. 9:17 NLT; see also Mark 2:22 and Luke 5:37–38).

God's Plan A was illuminated for our community: the integration of teenagers into the whole body of Christ. With a grief-filled heart and bruised ego still full of hope, our local church began to dismantle the system that systematically abandoned our teenagers by isolating them from the whole body of Christ and began exploring a practical theology of adoption and integration.

If we were going to see more teenagers loving Jesus beyond graduation day, we needed to stop following old models and cease some of the practices that led teenagers to abandon and walk away from their faith. God was doing a new thing in our midst, and we needed to explore a new way of raising up the younger generation.

The New Way: Integration

After our evaluation and discernment process concluded, we determined a clear way for us to move forward. We would get about the business of integrating our students into the life of our whole church. No longer would our teenagers (or children or college students, for that matter) be isolated in their age-specific ministry programs. We would broaden the influence and exposure of our students, including them into the entire church community. "Far too often and for too long, the students' immediate families and their spiritual family have been downplayed in our efforts to create safe youth ministry havens for teenagers. We believe it takes a village to raise a child, and that village needs to be much larger than a siloed youth ministry."[2]

In order to become a more integrated community, or a family of siblings, the people of God must align with a few core principles.

Adolescents are a part of the family of the church now. If adolescents are a part of the church today—which means siblings with other members—they need opportunities and environments to participate, explore, and experience relationships within the entire church. They need exposure to spaces outside the walls of the youth room. They need to interact with those who have earned their gray hairs, make decisions alongside middle-aged folks, and, of course, join in the changing of babies' diapers. They need a vision and experience of what life and faith look like outside the confines of their high school boundaries.

Perhaps one of the reasons adolescents don't find themselves a part of the church once they graduate is that they don't really see themselves as a part of the church today. If they participate only in their designated service, in their assigned room, with predetermined leaders, why should it surprise us when they can't find their way into service, worship, and community beyond their youth group years?

What if we expanded their vision—and ours!—and included them in the life of Christ, community, and cause no matter their age?

God is at work in our whole church. Scripture is clear that out of the mouths of babes come praise and wisdom and strength (Ps. 8; Matt. 21:16). When older followers of Jesus Christ have the humility and take the time to listen to a sixth-grade boy's thoughts about creation or a tenth-grade girl's questions about the Sermon on the Mount, God's transformational activity materializes. When we open the space for a gifted middle school student to run the soundboard for our Sunday services, we affirm the gifting of the Holy Spirit in her life. When a worship pastor takes the time to invest in a younger musician, teaching him the techniques and heart of worship, the church is better. When an older person reveals their insecurity about a particular text to a high school student who engages with her, the body is built up.

The question needs to turn from "How do we tolerate 'them'?" to "Where is God at work in our church, and how do we join him?" John 5:19 illuminates how Jesus engaged the kingdom: Jesus did only what he saw the Father doing. If our churches and communities are going to become more integrated by adopting teenagers into our lives, we have to recognize where God is at work in their lives and join God's activity there. Knowing that God is at work with our youngest members of the body and that we have something to learn from them fosters humility. This mind-set results in far more than the recruitment of small group leaders for the youth ministry. It's a paradigm shift that opens the church's eyes to the transformation at work all around us.

Youth pastors and workers are not the sole experts of adolescents. The professionalization of youth ministry hasn't been an entirely bad thing. We place a certain value on teenagers when we develop college degrees and church staffing positions for the purpose of caring for and developing teenagers. Undoubtedly, the rapid growth of youth ministry in the last generation is correlated to the professionalization of youth ministry.

However, one of the unintended consequences of this movement is that youth pastors and youth workers have become the academic authority on adolescents. Parents released their "I'm the expert on my child" card, and professional youth pastors willingly took it from them. The rest of the church abandoned their responsibility to spiritually form the younger generation.

The emphasis changed from "caring relationship" to "trained expert." Perhaps we forgot that even without training or degrees "love covers a multitude of sins" (1 Pet. 4:8) and that there's no substitute for parents—whether familial or spiritual.

I'm not suggesting a "throw the baby out with the bathwater" approach. Yes, we need adolescent experts among us who help us to understand youth culture and adolescent development, especially in a rapidly changing environment. But the rest of the church needs to increase their engagement with teenagers so that teenagers know their place in the larger body of Christ.

With these core beliefs in hand and heart, integration becomes more than possible. It becomes probable and essential. There is no argument that middle school and high school students have developmentally appropriate needs that are different from each other, not to mention different from a ten-year-old, a thirty-year-old, and a sixty-year-old. Those developmental needs must be considered, honored, and met in order for healthy development to continue into adulthood.

However, instead of looking for youth ministries to become the be-all and end-all for students, what if we focused on the developmentally specific actions that only a youth ministry can provide and looked to the whole church to meet other needs of the students? What if our faith community's approach was to provide developmentally specific experiences within an intergenerational context? If our mindset shifted only a few degrees, the long-term trajectory shift would be enormous. Adolescents would be seamlessly integrated into the whole body of Christ without being ignored, displaced, or isolated because of their specific developmental needs.

The Centrally Related Elements and Issues

As churches move toward becoming more integrated, consider the following ways, discussed in *Redefining the Role of the Youth Worker*, to focus on the developmental and holistic needs of adolescents without cutting off their connection to the whole community:[3]

- *Think initiatives, not programs.* Be careful not to create another program. Instead, examine what may be required for the next season of their lives. Consider short-term initiatives that will perpetuate connection and belonging to their peer group and beyond.

- *Find meaningful places for adolescent involvement in the church.* This may look like making your church's missions trips intergenerational or inviting a sixteen-year-old to serve in the new believers' ministry. It may involve inviting a gifted middle-school-aged drummer to join the church's worship team or calling out a group of freshmen to serve in the children's ministry. Whatever the place of involvement, make it meaningful to both the adolescent and the rest of the church.

- *Create specialized experiences for community and learning, keeping in mind formation-forward, theologically sound, and developmentally specific experiences for teenagers.* Reflect for a minute about your closest friendships and how significant they've been for your holistic development. If you've benefited from a healthy, spiritual community, you know how important those relationships are for your growth. Adolescents need the same relational spaces for community to be nurtured and nourished. Teenagers' desperate felt need is for peers who "get" their current reality, yet their deepest real need is for someone to know and love them. It is at the intersection of their real and felt needs that age-specific and intentional integration can happen.

Think for a moment about your understanding of the entirety of Scripture. There was likely a process to your learning about creation, the fall, the Israelites and judges, and hopes for the coming Messiah. You may have learned about the birth, life, death, and resurrection of Jesus before the Old Testament stories, but there was probably a progression to your biblical understanding. The same is true for teenagers. What my preschool-age daughter knows about the Bible and the story of the good news is radically different from what it will be in ten years, which is in keeping with her cognitive and spiritual development. Likewise, her comprehension of moral and social issues will broaden and become more complex over the years.

The church as an integrated body must pay attention to those needs along the way. This is why God commanded the Israelites in Deuteronomy 6:7 to "talk about them [the commandments] when you are at home and when you are on the road, when you are going to bed and when you are getting up." Learning and teaching cannot be quarantined to Sunday school and religious education, yet both must be intentional. They function as building blocks for the soul.

- *Invert the 5:1 ratio, with five adults investing in every teenager instead of one adult ministering to five teenagers.* This key idea for nurturing long-term faith has long been trumpeted by Dr. Chap Clark and found throughout Fuller Youth Institute's Sticky Faith research. This upside-down ratio is not about finding five youth group leaders for every teenager but five adults who love every teenager and are committed to his or her lifelong faith. These five adults can be relatives, educators, family friends, or church people.

- *Host regular retreats.* Participating in one weekend retreat is like a whole year in a weekly small group. The foci of teenager-specific retreats can be communal and experiential in nature, allowing them to hyperfocus on an area to catalyze spiritual formation.

- *Host multiple mission experiences in a variety of contexts.* One of the primary ways we grow is when we are outside our comfort zones and daily rituals. In addition to the fact that a teenager's brain is begging for new experiences to grow the brain's capacity, these learning adventures can be exceptionally foundational. Uncomfortable experiences can become catalysts for transformation. A few examples of mission experiences might include a weekend in a local setting outside normal life patterns, one global experience, and one neighborhood experience exclusively for mid-adolescents.

- *Customize the development of juniors and seniors in high school to more intentionally prepare them for life after high school.* If the research is correct, six out of seven graduating high school students don't feel prepared for life after high school. Focusing on training them for life beyond their school, family, and church will reap significant fruit. Consider how you can engage current college students, professionals in occupations your students are interested in, and others in your faith community as a way to better equip students during this important transition.

- *Weave Jesus into everyday life.* Find ways to train and equip students to connect with Jesus's presence in every circumstance. (See Skye Jethani's book *With: Reimagining the Way You Relate to God* for an excellent theology of how we have messed up our understanding and relationship with Jesus.[4]) By helping our students see that all of their life is with God, their faith becomes integrated beyond their church involvement.

- *Share stories of a future hope where all of the above is already happening within the church.* Since God is always at work in our midst, one of our primary responsibilities is to note where God is at work and tell those stories to others. These stories build faith and love by reminding us that God is indeed working in our lives and our church, increasing our hope in God's presence with us today and in the future. Stories fan the flames of vision for the kind of community we want to become. As we tell these stories

of a future hope, we invite people into the story of God in our midst.

Some time ago I was at our church's Sunday morning worship gathering, headed off to pick up my then-five-year-old son, Judah, from his classroom. As I walked through the door of his classroom, I quickly paused and instinctually took a step backward as I saw what was happening. Tears filled my eyes as I watched the scene unfold. Judah was sitting at a short, little table with his fellow adopted Ethiopian friend, Hallelujah (yes, that's his birth name), a couple of other five-year-olds, and three high school students—Devin, Stephanie, and Abby. Together they were playing a made-up game around the table, laughing and joking with one another. A few other teachers were in the room: a Caucasian adoptive dad, who was leading alongside his Chinese middle school daughter, as well as Stephanie's mom and elementary-age sister. The room was full of life, energy, and connection. The presence of love was palpable.

In that holy moment, the Lord affirmed a few truths to me. First, adoption is not easy. Whether you physically adopt a child or spiritually adopt another person into your faith journey, it will be messy. You won't all look the same or carry the same bloodlines, but you might as well. You are family. You are family because that's what the redemptive work of the Holy Spirit does for believers.

Second, it's important to realize that discipleship matters. The investment you make in another person is always worth it. Before I was Judah's mom, Devin, Stephanie, and Abby were students in my middle school spiritual leadership group. For two years I spent my time, energy, and prayers investing into their spiritual lives and leadership gifts because I believed in them—both in that moment and into the future.

As I stood in that doorway with tears spilling down my cheeks, I sensed the Father showing me that the pursuit of integration is worth it. Just as that adoptive dad and Stephanie's mom had invested in their own kids, they were now doing the same with a room full of lively five-year-olds. Just as I had invested my life into Devin, Stephanie, and Abby, they were now investing in my son. Multiple generations were beautifully relating with one another. Faith was being integrated, woven into each person as they loved, served, and played together. I'm confident the kingdom came that Sunday morning, a little more on earth as it is heaven.

That scene in Judah's classroom reminded me again of God's word to the Israelites in Deuteronomy 6 when the Lord commands his chosen people to instruct their children at every opportunity, in any circumstance, with whatever truth is required. Yet we often misinterpret this passage as God's word to parents. The Lord wasn't exclusively instructing parents to do this for their children. He was calling forth the entire community—"all y'all"—to raise up the younger generation. It would require the entire village, all of the Israelites, to ensure that the next generation would know the great "I AM."

That same directive was at work that Sunday in Judah's classroom. "All y'all" was in action in that moment. But the village instructs my children at times and in ways I don't even know. Only a few weeks ago I was with a dozen middle school students who serve in our children's ministry. I had stepped in that day for our children's pastor, who facilitates a monthly leadership meeting with these students. I hadn't met several of the sixth, seventh, and eighth graders, and yet when I asked them

whether they knew my kids—Judah, Addise, and Asher—they were quick to tell stories and squeal about them. I couldn't conceal a silly grin as they exclaimed about what they had said or done in class with my kids. Joy exploded in my heart as I saw integration at work in our community.

Other Perspectives on Integration

Like Me, Not like Me

An often-voiced challenge to integration is that adolescents need a unique place to call their own. I couldn't agree more. Needing to be with others "like me" is a basic human instinct. Affinity is a powerful force. I love to be with others who look like me, talk like me, are in similar seasons of life as me, and engage in similar passions and interests. This need is particularly strong in adolescence. One of the three primary tasks of adolescence is affinity. Teenagers are constantly asking the question (if not consciously, then subconsciously), "To whom and where do I belong?" Therefore, fostering places of connection and belonging is crucial for adolescent development.

Yet I also know from personal experience and studying the Scriptures that this doesn't eliminate my need to be with others not like me. Many of the greatest transformations and times of growth in my lifetime have come from being with those not like me in age, race, socioeconomic status, season of life, religious beliefs, and family of origin. I also know that coming alongside teenagers to help them find affinity and a place of belonging with those who are not like them can be a powerful force. While the American church has done an incredible job of setting up small group ministries, age-specific ministry, and even entire churches around those who are "just like me," Scripture gives us another picture.

The question we need to ask when we consider integrating teenagers into the life of our churches is, "Who is my neighbor?" The story Jesus told of the Good Samaritan illustrates this truth. (My lead pastor, Dave Gibbons, at Newsong Church in Orange County, California, does an incredible job of communicating this story in his book, *The Monkey and the Fish*.[5])

> One day an expert in religious law stood up to test Jesus by asking him this question: "Teacher, what should I do to inherit eternal life?"
>
> Jesus replied, "What does the law of Moses say? How do you read it?"
>
> The man answered, " 'You must love the LORD your God with all your heart, all your soul, all your strength, and all your mind.' And, 'Love your neighbor as yourself.' "
>
> "Right!" Jesus told him. "Do this and you will live!"
>
> The man wanted to justify his actions, so he asked Jesus, "And who is my neighbor?"
>
> Jesus replied with a story: "A Jewish man was traveling from Jerusalem down to Jericho, and he was attacked by bandits. They stripped him of his clothes, beat him up, and left him half dead beside the road.
>
> "By chance a priest came along. But when he saw the man lying there, he crossed to the other side of the road and passed him by. A Temple assistant walked over and looked at him lying there, but he also passed by on the other side.
>
> "Then a despised Samaritan came along, and when he saw the man, he felt compassion for him. Going over to him, the Samaritan soothed his wounds with olive oil and wine and bandaged them. Then he put the man on his own donkey and took him to an inn, where he took care of him. The next day he handed the innkeeper two silver coins, telling him, 'Take care of this man. If his bill runs higher than this, I'll pay you the next time I'm here.'
>
> "Now which of these three would you say was a neighbor to the man who was attacked by bandits?" Jesus asked.
>
> The man replied, "The one who showed him mercy."
>
> Then Jesus said, "Yes, now go and do the same." (Luke 10:25–37 NLT)

The Western church has inaccurately identified our neighbor as someone who is "just like me." We have built churches and designed ministries, including youth ministry, around descriptors and strategies that aim at a specific demographic. But this is not what we see in Jesus's story.

The Jewish people were at the pinnacle of first-century Roman society. They were the revered ones, the religious and socioeconomic elite. Samaritans were the opposite. In this culture, Samaritans were half-breeds and misfits—half Jew and half gentile, which didn't make them half as good as the Jews. It placed them at the bottom of the social hierarchy; it was more like they were half human. Samaritans were pushed to the margins of society because they weren't really like anyone else. And yet this is the illustration Jesus chooses to bring to life the question, "Who is my neighbor?"

It is the Samaritan—a marginalized, isolated, and misunderstood member of society—who steps into relationship with the societal elite. Jesus makes a shocking and painstakingly clear point concerning how we are to interact with one another. Not only are we to walk toward someone who is not like us, but we are also to sacrifice our resources and pride for their personal benefit.

I can only imagine how our world would be different if the church were to walk toward and sacrifice our resources on behalf of teenagers, those who are not like us. The time has come for the church to once again respond to Jesus's question, "Who is my neighbor?"

"It Takes a Whole Village to Raise a Child"

This popular African proverb advocates a powerful theological truth: my kids are your kids. My kids need you. I need you to help me grow my kids to be all God's created them to be. My husband and I cannot do this alone. We were parents only for about five minutes before we realized we'd need an army of people to support us in the calling of parenting our children.

Visit a smaller American church or a community somewhere halfway across the world, and you'll see integration at work. In many of these faith communities, they have recognized the truth of this proverb. Due to the perceived lack of resources in smaller American churches, our brothers and sisters have been "divinely forced" to use the whole community as they train up the younger generation. Church budgets haven't allowed them to hire a youth pastor with the latest training or an expert, veteran youth worker. So they have "resorted" to the community to care for and love their teenagers. I have heard leaders from smaller churches or urban ministries lament that they can't hire a youth pastor or additional paid staff to serve teenagers. But I want to commend our co-laborers for how they have intentionally—or even haphazardly—integrated teenagers into their faith communities. The ways in which they are investing in teenagers encapsulate what our larger churches or

megachurches want more of—more care from the whole church, more parental involvement, and a long-term view of faith development. The silos that many churches must tear down in order to bridge the generational gap (by building relationships that cross the divide) simply aren't a problem in those smaller contexts. Smaller ministries are resource-laden in this respect and are leading the way.

I was invited to speak on this vision of integrating teenagers into the life of the whole church at a conference a few years ago and after I'd finished speaking, a key influential leader in Latin America came up and immediately hugged me. I wondered what exactly the hug was for! And then he whispered in my ear, "This is what the church in Latin America has been doing for years. You're right on. Thank you!" He quickly walked away, giving me a "thumbs up" and performing a little victory dance. I chuckled and thought, "We have so much to learn from the global church."

To the smaller American churches and global church, *thank you* for your faithful service and leadership—especially when you were told you were doing something wrong, that you needed larger crowds, fancier technology, flashier gizmos, or more "fun events" on your calendar. Please forgive our large-church arrogance, and please continue to speak up so that we can learn from your heritage.[6]

Don't Throw the Baby Out with the Bathwater

I'm not sure I believe in balance. My friend Mark Oestreicher often says, "Balance is something you swing through on your way to the other extreme." Integration is not swinging to the other extreme and eliminating youth ministry. Integration is not firing your youth pastor and mindlessly absorbing teenagers into the whole church. This is not about an "all-or-nothing" approach to working with teenagers.

It's quite the opposite. Where traditional youth ministry (over the past couple decades) has hired out the care and spiritual development of teenagers to the youth department of the church, integration is about bringing people together for greater care and spiritual development. Integration is about increasing the engagement of the whole church because we deeply love the younger generation and desire relationship with them now and in the future. Integration is affirming that we are better together than we are apart.

I believe youth ministry is critical for the future, but it must be far more integrated and far less segregated if we are to see generations of students rise up to radically love God and his kingdom.

Building Blocks and Customized Development

So, if the church is to integrate students but not "throw the baby out with the bathwater," what's the best response? My suggestion is a both/and approach, which capsizes a one-size-fits-all model of youth ministry. We need to *both* integrate students into the life of the broader church whenever and wherever possible *and* provide the building blocks they need for their long-term spiritual formation. This requires customized spiritual formation that pays particular attention to adolescent brain development.

Most of the time, a baby needs to learn how to crawl before she learns how to walk, and she needs to walk before she runs. A baby needs to babble before words are uttered and sentences are formed. But not all babies learn to crawl, walk, and run at the same age, just as toddlers don't all speak in sentences by their second birthday.

The same is true for spiritual formation. For example, people need to receive the gift of salvation before they can be baptized or receive spiritual gifts from God. Teenagers need to doubt and question their faith before it becomes their own. Therefore, as we look to the developmental changes in adolescents, we need to put the proper building blocks into place so that the next block can be laid solidly on that foundation. This demands that we be thoughtful and flexible concerning teenagers' development. Families, churches, and young ministries need to be mindful that as we integrate students they are each in different places, requiring unique next steps for their holistic development.

Conclusion

It's time for the church to go back to God's Plan A for raising up the coming generations to fully know, passionately love, and radically follow Jesus for a lifetime. This is not a new idea. It's an ancient way of life that desperately needs to be reclaimed "for such a time as this" (Esther 4:14).

In my immediate family and now in our church family we echo the belief of the Israelites' way of life, repeating God's commands "again and again to [our] children." We "talk about them when [we] sit at home and when [we] walk along the road, when [we] lie down and when [we] get up" (Deut. 6:7). We desperately rely on our village to help us in this mighty calling because we are painfully aware of our inadequacies and limitations. Most of all, we pray. We pray our kids will experience a Romans 8 kind of love that will tether them to their Creator.

Isn't this the prayer of us all? The more we can individually customize the spiritual formation of every young disciple while communally integrating and attaching them to the spiritual family of God, the more depth and breadth and length of faith we will see in the teenagers we love. As each disciple, young and old, considers not only the interests of themselves, but also the interest of others (Phil. 2:4), we will see the kingdom of God come on earth as it is in heaven because our teenagers will be introduced and integrated into a way of life that is greater than anything the world has to offer.

Just as we have been adopted into the family of God, so we have the privilege and calling of spiritually adopting adolescents to be fully engaged participants in our faith communities. May the miracle of spiritual adoption and this fullness of life become increasingly true in your immediate family, church community, spiritual family, and beyond. Yes and Amen.

Notes

Introduction: Adoption

1. Hezekiah Walker, "I Need You to Survive," www
.azlyrics.com/lyrics/hezekiahwalker/ineedyoutosurvive
.html.

2. The origins of the term predate the New Testament.
It is defined as "a political assembly of citizens of ancient
Greek states" (www.merriam-webster.com/dictionary
/ecclesia). The first use of this term in Christian usage, at
least according to the Gospels, is in Matt. 18:17.

> I will build my church.—It is significant that this is
> the first occurrence of the word Church (*Ecclesia*)
> in the New Testament, the only passage but one
> (Matthew 18:17) in which it is found in the whole
> cycle of our Lord's recorded teaching. Its use was
> every way significant. Partly, doubtless, it came
> with the associations which it had in the Greek of
> the Old Testament, as used for the "assembly" or
> "congregation" of the Lord (Deuteronomy 18:16;
> Deuteronomy 23:1; Psalm 26:12); but partly also,
> as soon at least as the word came in its Greek form
> before Greek readers, it would bring with it the
> associations of Greek politics. The *Ecclesia* was
> the assembly of free citizens, to which belonged
> judicial and legislative power, and from which
> aliens and slaves were alike excluded. The mere
> use of the term was accordingly a momentous
> step in the education of the disciples. They had
> been looking for a kingdom with the King, as its
> visible Head, sitting on an earthly throne. They
> were told that it was to be realised in a society, an
> assembly, like those which in earthly polities we
> call popular or democratic. He, the King, claimed
> that society as His own. (*Ellicott's Commentary
> for English Readers*, biblehub.com/commentaries
> /matthew/16-18.htm)

See also Veli-Matti Kärkkäinen, "Ecclesiology," in *Global
Dictionary of Theology* (Downers Grove, IL: InterVarsity,
2008), 251–61.

3. Merriam-Webster online, www.merriam-webster
.com/dictionary/adoption.

4. One of the most recent comprehensive theological
resources is Moody Bible professor Trevor J. Burke's
*Adopted into God's Family: Exploring a Pauline Meta-
phor* (Downers Grove, IL: InterVarsity, 2006). In this
book, however, and in reviews and blogs, the focus is
on exploring the metaphor—history, ancient sources,
etc.—especially as it relates to our standing before God
as his adopted children. The back cover summarizes this
aspect: "The relationship between God and his people
is understood in various ways by the biblical writers,
and it is arguably the apostle Paul who uses the richest
vocabulary." See also Keith Graber Miller, "Adoption," in
Joel Green et al., eds., *Dictionary of Scripture and Ethics*
(Grand Rapids: Baker Academic, 2011), 41–43, and the
article "Adoption" in Leland Ryken et al., *Dictionary
of Biblical Imagery* (Downers Grove, IL: InterVarsity,
1998), 14–15: "The adopted child has developed a new
family narrative, Israel's story, and is expected to live and
act in accordance with that story and its exemplars like
Abraham. This responsibility involves God's child in a
life of faith and a struggle with sin." Notice there is no
mention of the power of the community or the primary
necessity to "love one another" (John 15:17) as the base

from which to live out this faith. In my research on a "theology of adoption," I have found almost no mention of what this means for our life together, how the Spirit works in and through community, or what Jesus and Paul meant when calling disciples to "maintain the unity of the Spirit." I find this an amazing and frightening omission in theological literature.

5. For years I had been growing in my understanding of how the church needed to help young people become more integrally related to the larger congregation. Both from my own history and biblical theology I learned that the end goal of youth ministry cannot be limited to an individualistic faith disconnected from the people of God. However, the term *assimilate*, which I had been using for several years in reference to adolescents, is actually a negative term because it means the one assimilating must adapt to the norms of the dominant. This is neither my experience nor good theology.

6. The Greek term is *huiothesia*, which he uses in Rom. 8:15, 23; 9:4; Gal. 4:5; and Eph. 1:5. "It is a spiritual adoption which replaces the natural familial relationship with God that had been forfeited through the fall." A. C. Myers, "Adoption," *The Eerdmans Bible Dictionary* (Grand Rapids: Eerdmans, 1987), 29.

7. Chap Clark, ed., *Youth Ministry in the 21st Century: Five Views* (Grand Rapids: Baker Books, 2015).

8. Trinity professor Mark Senter coined this term in the early 1990s to describe the ministry of Jim Rayburn, the founder of Young Life. He referred to Rayburn as "the father of modern youth ministry," distinguishing what we now think of as youth ministry from the early years of the Sunday school movement in England and Christian Endeavor in the nineteenth century.

9. Duffy Robbins's *This Way to Youth Ministry* (Grand Rapids: Zondervan, 2004) is an exception to this. His excellent, comprehensive textbook covers much of what Dr. Robbins covered in his Introduction to Youth Ministry class at Eastern University for years.

10. The 5:1 ratio of adults for every child originated with an article I wrote in 2004 in the online magazine of the Billy Graham Evangelistic Association. Here's the bottom line: Every kid needs five adult fans. Any young person who shows any interest in Christ needs a minimum of five people of various ages who will say, "I'm going to love that kid until they are fully walking as an adult member of this congregation." www.billygraham.org/articlepage.asp?ArticleID=461.

11. Andrew Root, *Revisiting Relational Evangelism: From a Strategy of Influence to a Theology of Incarnation* (Downers Grove, IL: InterVarsity, 2007), 82.

12. David Kinnaman, *You Lost Me: Why Young Christians Are Leaving the Church . . . and Rethinking Faith* (Grand Rapids: Baker Books, 2001), states, "Authentic community banishes loneliness, and alienation" (50, 225).

13. For a more detailed description of the erosion of adult nurture and support, see Theresa O'Keefe, "Growing Up Alone: The New Normal of Isolation in Adolescence," *JYM: The Journal of Youth Ministry* 13, no. 1 (2014): 63–85, and the two responses by Chap Clark and Michael Langford.

14. To read a prominent scholar discussing social capital, see Robert Putnam, *Bowling Alone: The Collapse and Revival of American Community* (New York: Touchstone, 2001).

Chapter 1 The Strategy of Adoptive Youth Ministry

1. Marc Yoder, "10 Surprising Reasons Our Kids Leave Church," *Church Leaders*, February 2013, www.churchleaders.com/children/childrens-ministry-articles/166129-marc-solas-10-surprising-reasons-our-kids-leave-church.html. I discovered this article by reading Philip Yancey's *Vanishing Grace* (Grand Rapids: Zondervan, 2014), 17.

2. I credit Dr. Scott Cormode, dean at Fuller Theological Seminary, with this example.

3. Ronald A. Heifetz and Marty Linsky, *Leadership on the Line: Staying Alive through the Dangers of Leading* (Boston: Harvard Business School Press, 2002), 11.

4. While many claim that the three most prominent "gifts" passages—Rom. 12, 1 Cor. 12, and Eph. 4—do not emphasize *prescriptive* and therefore limited understanding of gifts of the Spirit, careful exegesis of these texts reveals that Paul's point in each was to stress the *descriptive*, and therefore not exhaustive, list of gifts, which are given primarily for unity in diversity.

5. There is significant evidence that Aristotle advocated civil community to function for mutual commitment to citizen peers. As Alfredo Ferrarin notes, "For Aristotle the city-state was based on the bond of friendship." He goes on to assert, "Rather than being equally subject to the sovereign's law, citizens actively taking part in the rule of the polis (i.e., community) actually constitute the city-state." Aristotle envisioned the members of the citizenry to see one another as equals with different roles while still recognizing a leader. The New Testament affirms this same view of leadership; leaders are peer servants of those they lead based on gifts. *Hegel and Aristotle* (Cambridge: Cambridge University Press, 2004), 354–55.

6. Pope Francis, address to the Roman Curia, December 22, 2014, www.theguardian.com/world/2014/dec/22/pope-francis-scathing-critique-vatican-officials-curia-speech.

7. Stuart Cummings-Bond, "The One-Eared Mickey Mouse," *YouthWorker Journal* 6 (Fall 1989): 76–78.

8. Mark DeVries, *Family Based Youth Ministry* (Downers Grove, IL: InterVarsity, 1994).

9. Mike Yaconelli, "The Failure of Youth Ministry," www.sundaysoftware.com/yaconelli.htm.

10. A particular group offers a "research project" (dubious at best) that concludes, "Youth groups driving Christian teens to abandon faith." See www.charisma news.com/us/41465-youth-groups-driving-christian-teens -to-abandon-faith.

11. For an overview of many of these perspectives, see Chap Clark, ed., *Youth Ministry in the 21st Century: Five Views* (Grand Rapids: Baker Books, 2015).

12. For more information on the work of the Fuller Youth Institute (FYI), see www.fulleryouthinstitute.org, www.stickyfaith.org, and youthministry.fuller.edu.

13. As an example of this, Kara Powell, executive director of Fuller Youth Institute, and I, on the executive committee for FYI, both teach annually at the Young Life New Staff Training conference to all new Young Life staff.

14. Chap Clark, "The Myth of the Perfect Model," in *Starting Right: Thinking Theologically about Youth Ministry*, ed. Kenda Creasy Dean, Chap Clark, and Dave Rahn (Grand Rapids: Zondervan, 2001), 118–23.

Chapter 2 Understanding the Changing Adolescent

1. John Santrock, *Adolescence*, 12th ed. (Boston: McGraw-Hill, 2008), 26–34.

2. Ibid., 26.

3. Susan Harter, *The Construction of the Self* (New York: Guilford, 2012), 10.

4. Ibid., 72–157. Harter demonstrates this reality in her own treatment of adolescence and emerging adulthood.

5. John Santrock, *Adolescence*, 4th ed. (Dubuque, IA: William C. Broan, 1999), 28–29.

6. G. Backman, "Accelerated Development in Girls: Premature Menarche, Delayed Menopause, Extended Lifespan," *Acta Anat* 4 (1948): 421.

7. Susan Euling et al., "Role of Environmental Factors in the Timing of Puberty," *Pediatrics* 121 (2008): 167.

8. L. Aksglaede et al., "Recent Decline in Age at Breast Development: The Copenhagen Puberty Study," *Pediatrics* 123 (2009): 932.

9. M. E. Herman-Giddens et al., "Secondary Sexual Characteristics and Menses in Young Girls Seen in Office Practice: A Study from the Pediatric Research in Office Settings Network," *Pediatrics* 99, no. 4 (1997): 505–12. See also T. P. Mendola Wu and G. M. Buck, "Ethnic Differences in the Presence of Secondary Sex Characteristics and Menarche among US Girls: The Third National

Health and Nutrition Examination Survey," *Pediatrics* 110, no. 4 (2002): 752–57.

10. S. Cesario and L. Hughes, "Precocious Puberty: A Comprehensive Review of Literature," *Journal of Obstetric, Gynecologic, and Neonatal Nursing* 36, no. 3 (2007): 264.

11. Sherril Sellman, "Precocious Puberty: Teens before Their Time," *Total Health* 26, no. 6 (2003): 41.

12. Ibid.

13. Medha Talpede and Salil Talpede, "Early Puberty in African-American Girls: Nutrition Past and Present," *Adolescence* 36, no. 144 (2001): 789–94; Medha Talpede, "African American Child-Women: Nutrition Theory Revisited," *Adolescence* 41, no. 161 (2006): 91–102.

14. Aksglaede et al., "Recent Decline," 935.

15. Jay Belsky, Laurence Steinberg, and Patricia Draper, "Childhood Experience, Interpersonal Development, and Reproductive Strategy: An Evolutionary Theory of Socialization," *Child Development* 62 (1991): 647–70; Michelle Wierson and Patricia Long, "Toward a New Understanding of Early Menarche: The Role of Environmental Stress in Pubertal Timing," *Adolescence* 28, no. 112 (1993): 913–24; K. Smith and P. K. Smith, "Family Relations in Early Childhood and Reproductive Development," *Journal of Reproductive and Infant Psychology* 17, no. 2 (1999): 133–48; Bruce Ellis and Judy Garber, "Psychosocial Antecedents of Variation in Girls' Pubertal Timing: Maternal Depression, Stepfather Presence, and Marital and Family Stress," *Child Development* 71, no. 2 (2000): 485–501; Robert Quinlan, "Father Absence, Parental Care, and Female Reproductive Development," *Evolution and Human Behavior* 24 (2003): 376–90; Line Trimblay and Jean-Yves Frigon, "Precocious Puberty in Adolescent Girls: A Biomarker of Later Psychosocial Adjustment Problems," *Child Psychiatry and Human Development* 36, no. 1 (2005): 73–94; Bruce Ellis and Marilyn Essex, "Family Environments, Adrenarche, and Sexual Maturation: A Longitudinal Test of a Life History Model," *Child Development* 78, no. 6 (2007): 1799–1817; Julianna Deardorff et al., "Father Absence, Body Mass Index, and Pubertal Timing in Girls: Differential Effects by Family Income and Ethnicity," *Journal of Adolescent Health* 48, no. 5 (2011): 441–47; Bruce Ellis et al., "Quality of Early Family Relationships and the Timing and Tempo of Puberty: Effects Depend on Biological Sensitivity to Context," *Development and Psychopathology* 23 (2011): 85–99.

16. Deardorff et al., "Father Absence," 441.

17. J. J. Arnett, *Emerging Adulthood* (Oxford: Oxford University Press, 2004).

18. Ibid., 15.

19. Harter, *Construction of the Self*, 76.

20. Ibid.

21. Ibid., 97.

22. Ibid., 83.

23. Ibid.

24. Ibid., 85.

25. K. W. Fischer, "A Theory of Cognitive Development: The Control and Construction of Hierarchies of Skills," *Psychological Review* 87 (1980): 477–531.

26. Harter, *Construction of the Self*, 122.

27. M. J. Karcher and K. W. Fischer, "A Developmental Sequence of Skills in Adolescents' Intergroup Understanding," *Applied Developmental Psychology* 25 (2004): 259–82.

28. Andrew Root, "Stop Calling Them Students: Discovering a New Word for Personhood," *Immerse Journal* 3, no. 4 (2012): 23.

29. John Zizioulas, *Being as Communion* (Crestwood, NY: St. Vladimir's Seminary Press, 1997), 18.

30. Bogdan Lubardic, "Orthodox Theology of Personhood: A Critical Overview (Part 1)," *The Expository Times* 122, no. 11 (2011): 525.

31. Ibid.

32. Immanuel Kant, *Groundwork of the Metaphysics of Morals*, ed. Mary Gregor (Cambridge: Cambridge University Press, 1998), 42.

33. Louis Pojman, *Ethics: Discovering Right and Wrong* (Belmont, CA: Wadsworth, 2002), 150.

34. Lina Papadaki, "What Is Objectification?," *Journal of Moral Philosophy* 7 (2010): 17.

35. Steven Bonner and Brandon Fredenburg, "The Madness of Millennials and Academic Program Design: Two Worlds Collide," paper presented at the annual conference of the Southern Association of Colleges and Schools Commission on Colleges, Orlando, Florida, December 3–6, 2011.

36. Steven Bonner and Dean Culpepper, "Extended Midadolescence and Entering College Students: Quantitative Evidence of Diminished Logical and Moral Cognitive Development," paper presented at the annual meeting for the Association of Youth Ministry Educators, Chicago, Illinois, October 19–21, 2013.

37. Chap Clark, *Hurt 2.0* (Grand Rapids: Baker Academic, 2011).

38. Harter, *Construction of the Self*, 122.

39. R. E. Dahl, "Adolescent Brain Development: A Period of Vulnerabilities and Opportunities," in *Adolescent Brain Development: Vulnerabilities and Opportunities*, ed. R. E. Dahl and L. P. Spear (New York: New York Academy of the Sciences, 2004), 1–22.

Chapter 3 Welcoming Wounded and Broken Adolescents into the Family of God

1. Chap Clark, *Hurt 2.0: Inside the World of Today's Teenagers* (Grand Rapids: Baker Academic, 2011), 23.

2. The term *silos* has gained in popularity to describe anything that is operationally isolated from others. In academic circles, silos are disciplines, such as psychology and sociology, in that often scholars in these realms generally do not integrate perspectives, methods, or other aspects of their frameworks. How the term is used here, and elsewhere in *Adoptive Youth Ministry*, refers to how people have been separated, or "siloed," from others due to age. This is especially true in most church communities.

Chapter 4 Technology and Adoptive Youth Ministry

1. The full video can be viewed at www.youtube.com /watch?v=kl1ujzRidmU.

2. John Horrigan, *New Internet Users: What They Do Online, What They Don't, and Implications for the 'Net's Future* (Pew Internet and American Life Project, 2000), 13.

3. K. Moore, ed., "Tech Usage over Time," pewinternet.org/Trend-Data-(Teens)/Usage-Over-Time.aspx.

4. Elishiva Gross, "Adolescent Internet Use: What We Expect, What Teens Report," *Journal of Applied Developmental Psychology* 25, no. 6 (2004): 635, 641–42.

5. Ibid., 646.

6. Paul Adams, "The Future Is Already Here," *Brand-Connect*, LinkedIn.com, 2012.

7. Lisa Lee, "Young People and the Internet: From Theory to Practice," *Young* 13, no. 4 (2005): 360.

8. For a description of the ages, stages, and unique characteristics of adolescence, see Chap Clark, *Hurt 2.0: Inside the World of Today's Teenagers*, 2nd ed. (Grand Rapids: Baker Academic, 2011); Chap Clark and Dee Clark, *Disconnected: Parenting Teens in a Myspace World* (Grand Rapids: Baker Books, 2007).

9. Danah Michele Boyd, *Taken Out of Context: American Teen Sociality in Networked Publics* (Berkeley: University of California Press, 2008), 10.

10. Sonia Livingstone, "Taking Risky Opportunities in Youthful Content Creation: Teenagers' Use of Social Networking Sites for Intimacy, Privacy, and Self-Expression," *New Media and Society* 10 (2008): 400.

11. Gross, "Adolescent Internet Use," 646.

12. Nancy J. Cobb, *Adolescence: Continuity, Change, Diversity*, 2nd ed. (Mountain View, CA: Mayfield, 1995), 195.

13. Amanda Lenhart, "Teens, Kindness and Cruelty on Social Network Sites: How American Teens Navigate the New World of Digital Citizenship," pewinternet.org/Reports/2011/Teens-and-social-media.aspx.

14. Ibid., 28.

15. Kim Thomas, "Teen Online and Wireless Safety Survey: Cyberbullying, Sexting, and Parental Controls,"

14–15, 28, www.cox.com/wcm/en/aboutus/datasheet/take charge/2009-teen-survey.pdf?campcode=takecharge-re search-link_2009-teen-survey_0511.

16. See Clark, *Hurt 2.0*, and Clark and Clark, *Disconnected*.

17. Melissa Pujazon-Zazik and M. Jane Park, "To Tweet, or Not to Tweet: Gender Differences and Potential Positive and Negative Health Outcomes of Adolescents' Social Internet Use," *American Journal of Men's Health* 4, no. 1 (2010): 83.

18. Clark, *Hurt 2.0*, 18–19.

19. Clark and Clark, *Disconnected*, 136–39.

20. Paul Adams, "The Real Live Social Network," 53–60, www.slideshare.net/padday/the-real-life-social -network-v2.

21. Clark, *Hurt 2.0*, chap. 3.

22. Danah Boyd, *It's Complicated: The Social Lives of Networked Teens* (New Haven: Yale University Press, 2014), 352.

23. Patti M. Valkenburg and Jochen Peter, "Social Consequences of the Internet for Adolescents: A Decade of Research," *Current Directions in Psychological Science* 18, no. 1 (2009): 4.

24. Clark, *Hurt 2.0*, 60–72.

25. Paul Hodkinson and Sian Lincoln, "Online Journals as Virtual Bedrooms? Young People, Identity and Personal Space," *Young* 16, no. 1 (2008): 29.

26. Patsy Eubanks Owens, "No Teens Allowed: The Exclusion of Adolescents from Public Spaces," *Landscape Journal* 21, no. 1 (2002): 156–63.

27. Daniel Levi, Camille Passon, and Vicente del Rio, "Implications of Adolescents' Perceptions and Values for Planning and Design," *Journal of Planning Education and Research* 28 (2008), jpe.sagepub.com/content/28/1/73.

28. Hodkinson and Lincoln, "Online Journals," 40.

29. Lenhart, "Teens, Kindness, and Cruelty," 12.

30. Boyd, *Taken Out of Context*, 22.

31. Boyd, *It's Complicated*, 275.

32. Artemio Ramirez Jr. and Kathy Bronek, "'IM Me': Instant Messaging as Relational Maintenance and Everyday Communication," *Journal of Social and Personal Relationships* 26, no. 1 (2009): 309.

33. Levi Baker and Debra Oswald, "Shyness and Online Social Networking Services," *Journal of Social and Personal Relationships* 27, no. 7 (2010): 885.

34. Danielle Couch and Pranee Liamputtong, "Online Dating and Mating: The Use of the Internet to Meet Sexual Partners," *Qualitative Health Research* 18, no. 2 (2008): 272.

35. Catalina Toma and Jeffrey Hancock, "Looks and Lies: The Role of Physical Attractiveness in Online Dating," *Communication Research* 37, no. 3 (2010): 345.

36. Couch and Liamputtong, "Online Dating and Mating," 269–77.

37. K. Subrahmanyam and P. Greenfield, "Connecting Developmental Constructions to the Internet: Identity Presentation and Sexual Exploration in Online Teen Chat Rooms," *Developmental Psychology* 42 (2008): 395–406. This study reports that 40 percent of emerging adults are apt to post sexually explicit material versus 13 percent of mid-adolescents.

38. Laura M. Padilla-Walker et al., "Generation XXX: Pornography Acceptance and Use among Emerging Adults," *Journal of Adolescent Research* 23, no. 1 (2008): 16–24.

39. Erik Erikson, *Childhood and Society* (New York: Norton, 1950), 261–66.

40. Cuihua Shen and Dimitri Williams, "Unpacking Time Online: Connecting Internet and Massively Multiplayer Online Game Use with Psychosocial Well-Being," *Communication Research* 38, no. 1 (2011): 140–41.

41. Sherry Turkle, *Alone Together: Why We Expect More from Technology and Less from Each Other* (New York: Basic Books, 2011), 273.

42. Ibid., 294.

43. Ibid., 245–46.

44. Boyd, *It's Complicated*, 324.

45. Ibid., 274–83.

46. Paul Adams, *Grouped: How Small Groups of Friends Are the Key to Influence on the Social Web* (Berkeley, CA: New Riders, 2012), 185.

47. Eyal Ophir, Clifford Nass, and Anthony D. Wagner, "Cognitive Control in Media Multitaskers," *Proceedings of the National Academy of Sciences of the United States of America* 106, no. 37 (2009): 15583–15587.

48. Roy Pea and Clifford Nass, "Media Use, Face-to-Face Communication, Media Multitasking, and Social Well-Being among 8-to-12-Year-Old Girls," *Developmental Psychology* 48, no. 2 (2012): 327–36.

49. To view the commercial and follow marketing stats, see: http://www.ispot.tv/ad/7RZB/amazon-fire -phone-hipster-kids.

50. Clark, *Hurt 2.0*.

51. Lenhart, "Teens, Kindness, and Cruelty," 7.

52. A. Hope, "Risk Taking, Boundary Performance and Intentional School Internet Misuse," *Discourse* 28, no. 1 (2007): 87–99.

Chapter 5 Screen Time

1. Check out more about the excellent programs at the Los Angeles Film Studies Center at www.bestsemes ter.com.

2. Kara E. Powell and Chap Clark, *Sticky Faith: Everyday Ideas to Build Lasting Faith in Your Kids* (Grand Rapids: Zondervan, 2011).

3. Kenda Creasy Dean, *Almost Christian: What the Faith of Our Teens Is Telling the American Church* (New York: Oxford University Press, 2010).

4. My first book was cowritten with Barry Taylor, *A Matrix of Meanings: Finding God in Pop Culture* (Grand Rapids: Baker Academic, 2003).

5. My doctoral dissertation from Fuller Theological Seminary became *Into the Dark: Seeing the Sacred in the Top Films of the 21st Century* (Grand Rapids: Baker Academic, 2008).

6. Victora J. Rideout, Ulla G. Foehr, and Donald F. Roberts, "Generation M2: Media in the Lives of 8- to 18-Year Olds," Kaiser Family Foundation, January 2010, kaiserfamilyfoundation.files.wordpress.com/2013/01/8010.pdf

7. Eugene H. Peterson, *Working the Angles: The Shape of Pastoral Integrity* (Grand Rapids: Eerdmans, 1989), 127–28.

8. For a helpful primer, see David P. Setran and Chris A. Kiesling, *Spiritual Formation in Emerging Adulthood: A Practical Theology for College and Young Adult Ministry* (Grand Rapids: Baker Academic, 2013).

9. Alex Strachan, "Meet *Glee*'s Real Mr. Schues," *Vancouver Sun*, September 20, 2010, www.vancouversun.com/entertainment/Meet+Glee+real+Schues/3533547/story.html.

10. *Glee*. Season 2, episode 3, first broadcast October 5, 2010, by Fox. Directed by Alfonso Gomez-Rejon and written by Brad Falchuk.

11. Christian Smith and Melina Lundquist Denton, *Soul Searching: The Religious and Spiritual Lives of American Teenagers* (New York: Oxford University Press, 2005).

12. Denise Martin, "Are You There, God? *Glee*'s Twist on Faith," *TV Guide*, October 4, 2010, www.tvguide.com/News/Glee-Grilled-Cheesus-1023969.aspx.

13. Ibid.

14. Ibid.

15. Ibid.

16. Ibid.

17. Ibid.

18. Ibid.

19. Ibid.

20. H. Richard Niebuhr, *Christ and Culture* (San Francisco: Harper & Row, 1951).

21. Robert K. Johnston, *Reel Spirituality: Theology and Film in Dialogue*, 2nd ed. (Grand Rapids: Baker Academic, 2006).

22. Brett McCracken, *Gray Matters: Navigating the Space between Legalism and Liberty* (Grand Rapids: Baker Books, 2013).

23. Tambay A. Obenson, "What Are You Watching? Top 10 Primetime Shows among Black Viewers," *IndieWire*, November 4, 2013, blogs.indiewire.com/shadowandact/whatre-you-watching-top-10-primetime-shows-among-black-viewers.

24. Lynette Rice, "Ratings Alert: What You're Watching if You're 11, 50, or 34 Years Old (the Results May Surprise You!)," *Entertainment Weekly*, March 15, 2011, insidetv.ew.com/2011/03/15/ratings-by-age/.

25. See Douglas Rushkoff's investigative report, "Generation Like," *Frontline*, PBS, February 18, 2014, www.pbs.org/wgbh/pages/fronline/generation-like/.

Chapter 6 Reflective Youth Ministry

1. Even youth who are in rural communities have access to a much broader perspective via technology.

2. Peter Berger, *The Sacred Canopy* (New York: Anchor, 1967), 3–28.

3. For more information about the Youth Theological Initiative (YTI) see yti.emory.edu. I have written about the research interviews I conducted at YTI in other works, but here I reflect on the life and model of critically reflective communal youth ministry, which YTI also embodies. Also, it is important to acknowledge that I do not lift up either of these communities as 100 percent perfect. In particular, I am aware of and take seriously the criticism of each, but it would be disingenuous for me to undervalue the many ways that my understanding of ministry with youth and the power of young people to transform the world as public theologians was shaped in this context.

4. For a longer description of the types of transformation many youth experience at YTI see Elizabeth W. Corrie, "Christian Liturgy Spilling Out into the World: Youth as Public Theologians," *Liturgy* 29, no. 1 (2014): 13–22.

5. Over the years, YTI observed this phenomenon repeatedly and implemented measures, such as assigning staff and connecting youth with a spiritual leader in their home community who committed to continuing the reflection process with the youth.

6. James Fowler, *Faith Development and Pastoral Care* (Philadelphia: Fortress, 1987). According to Fowler, praxis is both the way a community "does its business" and the ways the community strives to align itself with the purpose and vision of God. Fowler writes, "Praxis is both customary and transformative . . . it involves the ways in which things get done in community . . . the ways in which a community does it business . . . praxis also involves strategic initiatives and intentional action aimed at the transformation of the community toward a more effective realization of its purpose and a more faithful alignment with its master story and vision" (16).

7. See my discussion of practical theology as both a method of thinking/researching youth ministry and a model of ministry with youth in Mary Elizabeth Moore

and Almeda Wright, *Children, Youth, and Spirituality in a Troubling World* (St. Louis: Chalice, 2008). Both James Fowler and the editors of *Starting Right: Thinking Theologically about Youth Ministry* (Grand Rapids: Zondervan, 2013) note this connection as well. I point not simply to the disciplinary home of youth ministry or the significance of theology for youth ministry, but I also want to emphasize the practice of reflection (critical reflection) as essential to all ministries with youth. This is reflection that must be done by youth, not simply for youth or by concerned youth leaders who are seeking to improve their ministry.

8. Howard W. Stone and James O. Duke, *How to Think Theologically* (Minneapolis: Fortress, 2013), 2.

9. Material in the previous section represents a slightly revised version of material that was published in *Reflections*, Yale Divinity School, spring 2014.

10. Fowler, *Faith Development*, 27–32, 53.

11. Parker J. Palmer, *Let Your Life Speak: Listening for the Voice of Vocation* (San Francisco: Jossey-Bass, 2000).

12. Paulo Freire, *Pedagogy of the Oppressed* (New York: Continuum, 1970), 43–44.

13. Ibid., 81.

14. Ibid., 83.

15. Allen Moore, ed., *Religious Education as Social Transformation* (Birmingham, AL: Religious Education Press, 1989), 1–10.

16. Freire, *Pedagogy of the Oppressed*, 87. Freire repeatedly cautions against attempting to have only action or only reflection. He argues that without action, there is a tendency toward *verbalism*, and without reflection, it is *activism*. This definition parallels but differs slightly from Fowler's definition of praxis.

17. Freire defines coming to critical consciousness, or *conscientização*, as "learning to perceive social, political, and economic contradictions, and to take action against the oppressive elements of reality" (*Pedagogy of the Oppressed*, 35 [see translator's note]).

18. Katherine Turpin, *Branded: Adolescents Converting from Consumer Faith* (Cleveland: Pilgrim Press, 2006), 59.

19. Both Freire and Turpin offer concrete strategies and methodologies for empowering people to engage in the process of critical reflection. Other religious educators, such as David White, also offer a model of discerning and perceiving more clearly how one should act in response to the deep passions that emerge or the places where youth experience injustice. White's method parallels with Freire's praxis model but also includes listening, understanding, dreaming, and acting. See David White, *Practicing Discernment with Youth* (Cleveland: Pilgrim Press, 2005).

20. Evelyn Parker, "Sanctified Rage," in *Children, Youth and Spirituality in a Troubling World*, ed. Mary Elizabeth Moore and Almeda Wright (St. Louis: Chalice, 2008), 196–209. Parker outlines several examples of tapping into the rage of black youth and reconnecting it with the traditions. I am more hesitant to offer strategies or examples of how this rage can be used to benefit churches. I do not believe that it cannot happen, but I am uncertain that any way I perceive or name as "appropriate" for expressing "holy indignation" would not already demonstrate a domestication and attempt to normalize the breach youth are naming/calling for.

21. Ibid., 197.

22. Fowler, *Faith Development*, 116. In the conclusion, Fowler leaves us with questions to "begin an inventory" of whether we as communities of faith "constitute environments of developmental expectation." Do we signal that ongoing growth and change in faith and vocation are expected and will be supported? Do we provide images and understandings that will sponsor persons in moving into the questions and issues that seem to lie on the frontiers of their commitments in faith and vocation? I offer a similar inventory here.

Chapter 7 Thinking (Practical) Theology

1. William Treadwell was the professor for my leadership class. He had spent most of his career working as a conflict resolution consultant for churches. What unfolds throughout this chapter is my recollection of the first conversation I ever had with professor Treadwell. It may not be 100 percent word for word, but I assure you the content is not exaggerated. In all, the conversation lasted less than fifteen minutes, but I still find myself learning from it and the many other incredible discussions that would follow. I am so thankful for Professor Treadwell's wisdom and guidance in my life. I would go on to serve as Professor Treadwell's teaching assistant until he passed away before my final year of seminary. He is an outstanding example to me of someone who embodied the ministry of adoption.

2. Douglas John Hall, *Thinking the Faith: Christian Theology in a North American Context* (Minneapolis: Augsburg, 1989).

3. Chap Clark, "Youth Ministry as Practical Theology," *Journal of Youth Ministry* 7, no. 1 (2008): 18.

4. These observations are not critiques of a specific congregation but rather a blunt generalization of what we often feel like our jobs as youth ministers boil down to. This list is not meant as an indictment toward any particular person or congregation; rather, it is meant as a written caricature to help us reflect on what should and should not be the focus of student ministry.

5. S. R. Covey, *The 7 Habits of Highly Effective People: Powerful Lessons in Personal Change* (New York: Free Press, 2004), 99.

6. Andrew Root, "Practical Theology: What Is It and How Does It Work?," *Journal of Youth Ministry* 7, no. 2 (2009): 56.

7. Richard Robert Osmer, *Practical Theology: An Introduction* (Grand Rapids: Eerdmans, 2008), 240.

8. Hyun-Sook Kim, "The Hermeneutical-Praxis Paradigm and Practical Theology," *Religious Education* 102, no. 4 (2007): 429.

9. James W. Fowler, "Practical Theology and the Shaping of Christian Lives," *Practical Theology* (1983): 149.

10. Ray Sherman Anderson, *The Shape of Practical Theology: Empowering Ministry with Theological Praxis* (Downers Grove, IL: InterVarsity, 2001), 59.

11. Osmer, *Practical Theology*, xiv.

12. M. L. Branson, *The Missional Church in Context: Helping Congregations Develop Contextual Ministry*, ed. Craig Van Gelder (Grand Rapids: Eerdmans, 2006), 110.

13. Root, "Practical Theology," 66.

14. Osmer, *Practical Theology*, 4.

15. Clark, "Youth Ministry," 21.

16. Thomas H. Groome, *Sharing Faith: A Comprehensive Approach to Religious Education and Pastoral Ministry: The Way of Shared Praxis* (San Francisco: HarperSanFrancisco, 1991), 152.

17. Kim, "Hermeneutical-Praxis Paradigm," 421.

18. For a good background on the evolution of praxis see Kim's essay, "Hermeneutical-Praxis Paradigm," esp. 421–22.

19. Paul H. Ballard and John Pritchard, *Practical Theology in Action: Christian Thinking in the Service of Church and Society* (London: SPCK, 1996), 80.

20. Clark, "Youth Ministry," 22.

21. Scott Cormode, "Constructing Faithful Action," *Journal of Religious Leadership* 3, no. 1–2 (2004): 237.

22. This phrase was inspired by Amy E. Jacober, who uses the phrase "secular discipline" in describing the import of correlation in practical theology. Citing the work of James Poling and Donald Miller, Jacober (*The Adolescent Journey: An Interdisciplinary Approach to Practical Youth Ministry* [Downers Grove, IL: InterVarsity, 2011], 42) states:

> Three types (of correlation) are also on a continuum: *critical scientific* uses a secular discipline as the framework and norms, while tradition (theology) plays a secondary role; *critical correlation* seeks a collaborative dialogue between the Christian tradition (or theology) and the secular discipline; in the *critical confessional* type, Christian tradition is considered normative while cautiously considering the secular sciences and

minimizing the influence of norms outside of the Christian tradition.

I agree that the term *secular disciplines* is a more holistic descriptor, so I have borrowed it for our purposes.

23. Root, "Practical Theology," 67.

24. Ballard and Pritchard, *Practical Theology in Action*, 49.

25. Clark, "Youth Ministry," 17.

26. David F. White, "A More Excellent Way: A Response to Chap Clark's Youth Ministry as Practical Theology," *Journal of Youth Ministry* 7, no. 1 (2008): 52.

27. Root, "Practical Theology," 66.

28. Osmer, *Practical Theology*, 59 (italics in the original).

29. Osmer uses the specific terms of episodes, situations, contexts, and systems to explain contextual analysis. While this chapter does not use Osmer's specific terminology, each of these concepts can be applied within the content of this work.

30. The practice of using the tools of social science to understand our current context has been around since biblical times. On more than one occasion Paul quotes the work of ancient philosophers to lay a foundation for introducing the gospel. In Titus 1:12, Paul quotes the Cretan philosopher Epimenides, "One of Crete's own prophets has said it: 'Cretans are always liars, evil brutes, lazy gluttons.'" And in Acts 17:28, Paul quotes both Epimenides and the Cilician Stoic philosopher Aratus, "'For in him we live and move and have our being.' As some of your own poets have said, 'We are his offspring.'" Although they are not named, I believe we can see in Acts 17 the main elements of practical theology supported in this chapter.

31. Clark, "Youth Ministry," 27 (italics in the original).

32. Ibid.

33. Ibid., 28.

34. Hall, *Thinking the Faith*, 91 (italics in the original).

35. Ibid.

36. Root, "Practical Theology," 70.

37. Clark, "Youth Ministry," 32.

38. Kenda Creasy Dean, Chap Clark, and Dave Rahn, *Starting Right: Thinking Theologically about Youth Ministry* (Grand Rapids: Zondervan, 2001), 225.

39. White, "More Excellent Way," 52.

40. Anderson, *Shape of Practical Theology*, 109.

41. The imagery I use here comes from a model of practical theology that Chap Clark and I created to help students better understand and incorporate practical theology into their ministry. I use this imagery not as the standard of theological reflection but as an illustration of how I choose to organize and understand the work necessary for good theological reflection to occur.

42. Osmer, *Practical Theology*, 4.

43. Gerben Heitink, *Practical Theology: History, Theory, Action Domains: Manual for Practical Theology* (Grand Rapids: Eerdmans, 1999), 9.

44. Anderson, *Shape of Practical Theology*, 21; Osmer, *Practical Theology*, 4.

45. James W. Osmer, Richard Robert Schweitzer, and Friedrich Fowler, *Developing a Public Faith: New Directions in Practical Theology: Essays in Honor of James W. Fowler* (St. Louis: Chalice, 2003), 239 (emphasis added).

46. Gilbert G. Bilezikian, *Community 101: Reclaiming the Church as Community of Oneness* (Grand Rapids: Zondervan, 1997).

Chapter 8 Youth Ministry, Adoption, and Culture

1. Jerram Barrs, *The Heart of Evangelism* (Wheaton, IL: Crossway, 2001), 216.

2. *Time*, May 31, 1963, "Barth in Retirement," http://content.time.com/time/subscriber/article/0,33009,896838,00.html.

3. John Stott, *The Contemporary Christian* (Downers Grove, IL: InterVarsity, 1992), 110–11.

4. To learn more about how to "read" and contextualize the gospel in ways that speak to the emerging generations, I encourage you to read my book, *Engaging the Soul of Youth Culture: Bridging Teen Worlds and Christian Truth* (Downers Grove, IL: InterVarsity, 2006). I have also written about the unique cultural challenges and pressures of youth culture in *Youth Culture 101* (Grand Rapids: Zondervan, 2007) and *The Space Between: A Parent's Guide to Teenage Development* (Grand Rapids: Zondervan, 2009). You can also visit the regularly updated online home of The Center for Parent/Youth Understanding at cpyu.org.

5. Gary Parrett, "Becoming a Culturally Sensitive Minister," in Elizabeth Conde-Frazier, S. Steve Kang, and Gary A. Parrett, *A Many Colored Kingdom: Multicultural Dynamics for Spiritual Formation* (Grand Rapids: Baker Academic, 2004), 145–46.

6. A. Scott Moreau, Gary R. Corwin, and Gary B. McGee, *Introducing World Missions: A Biblical, Historical, and Practical Survey* (Grand Rapids: Baker Books, 2004), 12.

7. Steve Scott, *Like a House on Fire: Renewal of the Arts in a Postmodern Culture* (Chicago: Cornerstone, 1997), 6.

8. Stott, *Contemporary Christian*, 27.

9. Sherwood G. Lingenfelter and Marvin K. Mayers, *Ministering Cross-Culturally: An Incarnational Model for Personal Relationships*, 2nd ed. (Grand Rapids: Baker Books, 2003), 22.

10. Dean Borgman, *When Kumbaya Is Not Enough: A Practical Theology for Youth Ministry* (Peabody, MA: Hendrickson, 1997), xiii.

11. John Stott, *The Lausanne Covenant: An Exposition and Commentary* (Minneapolis: World Wide Publications, 1975), 26.

12. W. Stanford Reid, "Christianity as Counter-Culture," in *Readings in Christian Sociology*, ed. Russell Heddendorf (privately printed, 1974).

13. Harold Netland, *Encountering Religious Pluralism: The Challenge to Christian Faith and Mission* (Downers Grove, IL: InterVarsity, 2001), 328.

14. William D. Romanowski, *Eyes Wide Open: Looking for God in Popular Culture,* rev. and exp. ed. (Grand Rapids: Brazos, 2007), 44.

15. Ibid., 49.

16. Albert M. Wolters, *Creation Regained: Biblical Basics for a Reformational Worldview* (Grand Rapids: Eerdmans, 1985), 36 (italics in the original).

17. Ibid., 38.

18. To learn more about what it means to make culture, see Andy Crouch, *Culture Making: Recovering Our Creative Calling* (Downers Grove, IL: InterVarsity, 2013).

19. David J. Hesselgrave, *Communicating Christ Cross-Culturally: An Introduction to Missionary Communication*, 2nd ed. (Grand Rapids: Zondervan, 1991), 100.

20. To understand the concept and function of "clusters," see chap. 4 in Chap Clark, *Hurt 2.0: Inside the World of Today's Teenagers* (Grand Rapids: Baker Academic, 2011).

21. Hesselgrave, *Communicating Christ Cross-Culturally*, 100.

22. Ibid.

23. Patty Lane, *A Beginner's Guide to Crossing Cultures: Making Friends in a Multi-Cultural World* (Downers Grove, IL: InterVarsity, 2002), 18.

24. The best and most helpful working definition of *worldview* that I have found comes from James Sire. He says, "A worldview is a commitment, a fundamental orientation of the heart, that can be expressed as a story or in a set of presuppositions (assumptions which may be true, partially true or entirely false) which we hold (consciously or subconsciously, consistently or inconsistently) about the basic constitution of reality, and that provides the foundation on which we live and move and have our being" (*The Universe Next Door: A Basic Worldview Catalog*, 4th ed. [Downers Grove, IL: InterVarsity, 2004], 20).

25. The basic worldview questions that I use when exegeting subjective culture are:

"Where am I?" "What is real?" and "What is the nature of the world?"

"Who am I?" and "What is my reason and purpose for being on this earth?"

"What's right and what's wrong?" and "It's obvious that in our world we encounter good and bad. But how do we explain the bad things that happen in the world? And how can we differentiate between that which is bad and that which is good?"

"What happens when I die?" and "Is that it? Or is there something else awaiting me when my heart stops beating on this earth?"

"Is there a cure for the evil and brokenness in the world?" and "Will things get any better? And if so, how?"

For a more in-depth explanation and discussion of the worldview questions, see Sire, *Universe Next Door*, 20; and J. Richard Middleton and Brian J. Walsh, *Truth Is Stranger than It Used to Be: Biblical Faith in a Postmodern World* (Downers Grove, IL: InterVarsity, 1995), 11.

26. Lane, *Beginner's Guide to Crossing Cultures*, 18.

27. Ibid., 27.

28. Francis A. Schaeffer, *The God Who Is There*, in *The Complete Works of Francis Schaeffer: A Christian Worldview*, vol. 1, *A Christian View of Philosophy and Culture*, 2nd ed. (Wheaton: Crossway, 1985), 9.

29. Francis A. Schaeffer, *The Complete Works of Francis A. Schaeffer: A Christian Worldview*, vol. 1, *A Christian View of Philosophy and Culture* (Wheaton, IL: Crossway, 1982), 269.

30. For more explanation of these basic principles, I recommend reading Steven Garber, *The Fabric of Faithfulness: Weaving Together Belief and Behavior*, exp. ed. (Downers Grove, IL: InterVarsity, 2007).

31. Russell Heddendorf, *In the World: An Introduction to Christian Sociology*, TMs (photocopy), 1973, chaps. 2–3.

32. George Gerbner, quoted in Romanowski, *Eyes Wide Open*, 55.

33. J. I. Packer and Gary A. Parrett, *Grounded in the Gospel: Building Believers the Old-Fashioned Way* (Grand Rapids: Baker Books, 2010), 22.

34. Ibid., 27.

35. Ibid., 29.

36. Darrell L. Guder, *Missional Church: A Vision for the Sending of the Church in North America* (Grand Rapids: Eerdmans, 1998), 151.

37. Denis Haack, "Christian Discernment 202: Pop Culture: Why Bother?," available from www.ransomfellowship.org/D_202.html.

38. Ibid.

39. C. S. Lewis, *Christian Reflections*, ed. Walter Hooper (Grand Rapids: Eerdmans, 1967), 33.

40. Wolters, *Creation Regained*, 49.

41. Ibid.

42. Ibid.

43. John R. W. Stott, *Christian Mission in the Modern World* (Downers Grove, IL: InterVarsity, 1975), 122.

44. Henri J. Nouwen, *In the Name of Jesus: Reflections on Christian Leadership* (New York: Crossroad, 1989), 10.

45. Ibid.

46. Ibid., 31.

47. Ibid., 65.

48. Marva J. Dawn, *Is It a Lost Cause? Having the Heart of God for the Church's Children* (Grand Rapids: Eerdmans, 1997), 244.

49. Millard J. Erickson, *Postmodernizing the Faith: Evangelical Responses to the Challenge of Postmodernism* (Grand Rapids: Baker Books, 1998), 67.

50. For an explanation of how Paul engaged the Athenian culture in Acts 17 along with a practical framework for engaging in "Mars Hill Ministry" (cultural exegesis) today, consult chap. 9 of my book, *Engaging the Soul of Youth Culture: Bridging Teen Worldviews and Christian Truth* (Downers Grove, IL: InterVarsity, 2006).

51. Borgman, *When Kumbaya Is Not Enough*, 34.

52. Ibid., 34.

53. Gene Edward Veith Jr., *Postmodern Times: A Christian Guide to Contemporary Thought and Culture* (Wheaton: Crossway, 1994), xii.

54. Dawn, *Is It a Lost Cause?*, 17.

55. Duane Elmer, *Cross-Cultural Conflict: Building Relationships for Effective Ministry* (Downers Grove, IL: InterVarsity, 1993), 14.

56. As quoted in Erickson, *Postmodernizing the Faith*, 155.

57. Francis A. Schaeffer, *Complete Works of Francis A. Schaeffer*, 285.

Chapter 9 Thinking Ecclesiologically

1. Christian Smith with Patricia Snell, *Souls in Transition: The Religious and Spiritual Lives of Emerging Adults* (New York: Oxford University Press, 2009), 256.

2. Ibid., 227.

3. Lisa Pearce and Melinda Lundquist Denton, *A Faith of Their Own: Stability and Change in the Religiosity of America's Adolescents* (New York: Oxford University Press, 2011), 70–71 (italics added).

4. Dave Coryell, "Three Ways Churches See Teenagers," *Group* 36, no. 6 (2010): 55.

5. Charles R. Swindoll, *Improving Your Serve* (Nashville: Thomas Nelson, 1981), 34.

6. Marcia J. Bunge, "Biblical and Theological Perspectives on Children, Parents, and 'Best Practices' for Faith Formation: Resources for Child, Youth, and Family Ministry Today," *Dialog* 47, no. 4 (2008): 353–54.

7. Ibid., 357.

8. Todd Erickson (executive director of student ministries, Second Presbyterian Church, Memphis, Tennessee), in an interview with the author, January 12, 2012.

9. Mark Dever, *What Is a Healthy Church?* (Wheaton: Crossway, 2007), 94–95.

10. Joshua Harris, *Why Church Matters: Discovering Your Place in the Family of God* (Colorado Springs: Multnomah Books, 2011), 37–38 (italics in the original).

11. Charles W. Colson and Ellen Santilli Vaughn, *Being the Body* (Nashville: Thomas Nelson, 2004), 306–7.

12. Dever, *What Is a Healthy Church?*, 95.

Chapter 10 Thinking Critically about Families and Youth Ministry

1. Richard Ross, *Accelerate: Parenting Teenagers toward Adulthood* (Bloomington, IN: CrossBooks, 2013), 119.

2. Jon Walker, "Family Life Council Says It's Time to Bring Family Back to Life," *SBCnet*, June 12, 2002, www.sbcannualmeeting.net/sbc02/newsroom/newspage.asp?ID=261.

3. www.lifeway.com/Article/LifeWay-Research-finds-reasons-18-to-22-year-olds-drop-out-of-church.

4. Youth Transition Network Staff, "Youth Transition Network Launched," *Assemblies of God*, 2007, ag.org/top/Events/General_Council_2007/News/index_articledetail.cfm?targetBay=071e05e0-f702-4a75-bc1d-18df19349beb&ModID=2&Process=DisplayArticle&RSS_RSSContentID=16121&RSS_OriginatingChannelID=1158&RSS_OriginatingRSSFeedID=4539&RSS_Source=.

5. www.barna.org/barna-update/article/16-teensnext-gen/147-most-twentysomethings-put-christianity-on-the-shelf-following-spiritually-active-teen-years#.VbLhWqRViko.

6. Timothy Paul Jones, "Debunking the Dropout Myth," *Children's Ministry Magazine*, July 11, 2012, childrensministry.com/articles/debunking-the-dropout-myth.

7. The National Study of Youth and Religion is a research project directed by Christian Smith and Lisa Pearce. It began in 2001 and is currently funded through the Lilly Foundation and the John Templeton Foundation through December 2015. See www.youthandreligion.org/research.

8. Christian Smith with Melinda Lundquist Denton, *Soul Searching: The Religious and Spiritual Lives of American Teenagers* (New York: Oxford University Press, 2005); Christian Smith with Patricia Snell, *Souls in Transition: The Religious and Spiritual Lives of Emerging Adults* (New York: Oxford University Press, 2009); Christian Smith with Kari Christoffersen, Hilary Davidson, and Patricia Smell Herzog, *Lost in Transition: The Dark Side of Emerging Adulthood* (New York: Oxford University Press, 2011).

9. Merton P. Strommen and Richard A. Hardel, *Passing on the Faith: A Radical New Model for Youth and Family Ministry* (Winona, MN: Saint Mary's Press, 2007), 7.

10. See Scott Brown, *A Weed in the Church: How to Recover the Original Generational Design for Discipleship in the Church* (Wake Forest, NC: The National Center for Family Integrated Churches), 2010.

11. Jon Nielson, "3 Common Traits of Youth Who Don't Leave the Church," *Church Leaders*, n.d., outof theoverflow.com/2013/07/03/jon-nielson-3-common-traits-of-youth-who-dont-leave-the-church/.

12. Data was collected in youth ministry classes at the New Orleans Baptist Theological Seminary from August 2011 to April 2012. One hundred students completed essays that were usable.

13. Rick Lawrence, interview with Richard Ross in "Giving Parents What They Deserve," *Group Magazine*, July–August 2004.

14. Jones, "Debunking the Dropout Myth."

15. Timothy Paul Jones, ed., *Perspectives on Family Ministry: Three Views* (Nashville: B&H, 2009).

16. Mark DeVries, *Family-Based Youth Ministry* (Downers Grove, IL: InterVarsity, 1994).

17. From Walt Mueller, "Youth Groups Driving Christian Teens to Abandon Faith?," *Learning My Lines*, November 18, 2013, learningmylines.blogspot.com; http://www.cpyu.org/2013/11/18/youth-groups-driving-christian-teens-to-abandon-faith-some-issues/.

18. George Barna, *The Future of the American Family* (Chicago: Moody, 1993), 26.

19. US Census Bureau cited in Debra Caruso and Sandra Timmermann, "Disappearing Nuclear Family and the Shift to Non-Traditional Households Has Serious Financial Implications for Growing Numbers of Americans," January 25, 2013, www.huffingtonpost.com/debra-caruso/retirement-plan-the-disappearing-nuclear-family_b_2534622.html.

20. Ben Freudenburg and Rick Lawrence, *The Family Friendly Church* (Loveland, CO: Group, 1998), 10.

21. Strommen and Hardel, *Passing on the Faith*, 18.

22. I exchanged emails with Dr. Smith in 2008, and he affirmed a statement I heard him make at an earlier plenary session at the Association of Youth Ministry Professors.

23. See, e.g., "Increasing Access and Coordination of Quality Mental Health Services for Children and Adolescents," American Psychological Association, www.apa.org/about/gr/issues/cyf/child-services.aspx.

24. Chap Clark, *Hurt 2.0: Inside the World of Today's Teenagers* (Grand Rapids: Baker Academic, 2011), viii.

25. Danielle Dreilinger, "N.O. Tops List of Charter Enrollment," *The Times Picayune*, December 13, 2013, and Bob Ross, "Louisiana Is 3rd in Nation in Private School Enrollment," *The Times Picayune*, May 6, 2012.

26. B. Ross, "Louisiana Is 3rd."

27. Chris Lubienski, "Whither the Common Good? A Critique of Home Schooling," *Peabody Journal of Education* 75, no. 1–2 (2000).

28. Clark, *Hurt 2.0*, 192.

29. Ibid., 93.

30. Ibid., 193.

31. Kenda Creasy Dean, *Almost Christian* (New York: Oxford University Press, 2010), 194.

32. Ibid., 122.

33. Ibid., 70–81.

34. Ibid., 22.

35. R. Ross, *Accelerate*, 113–19.

36. R. Ross cites Tim Elmore, *Generation iY* (Atlanta: Poet Gardner, 2010), 58.

37. Clark, *Hurt 2.0*, 202.

38. Ibid.

Chapter 11 Thinking Globally

1. John W. Santrock, *Adolescence*, 9th ed. (Boston: McGraw-Hill, 2005), 16. There is new evidence that this long-held theory regarding adolescence as an "invention of modernity" may not be completely accurate. Scholar Crystal Kirgiss (Purdue University), in an unpublished but well-researched PhD dissertation, contends that adolescence as a unique and transitional experience was present throughout the Middle Ages and for centuries afterward, especially in the West. While this data is too new and, by the author's admission, understudied at this point, it is important to note.

2. Chap Clark, *Hurt: Inside the World of Today's Teenagers* (Grand Rapids: Baker Academic, 2004), 7.

3. Santrock, *Adolescence,* 7.

4. Clark, *Hurt*, 27.

5. Christian Smith and Melinda Lundquist Denton, *Soul Searching: the Religious and Spiritual Lives of American Teenagers* (Oxford: Oxford University Press, 2005), 264 (italics in the original).

6. Theresa O'Keefe, "Growing Up Alone: The New Normal of Isolation in Adolescence," *JYM: The Journal of Youth Ministry* 13, no. 1 (2014): 63–85.

7. Clark, *Hurt*, 26, 34.

8. Ibid., 50.

9. Ibid., 54 (italics added).

10. Monica McGoldrick, Joseph Giordano, and Nydia Garcia-Preto, "Ethnicity and Family Therapy," in *Ethnicity and Family Therapy*, ed. Monica McGoldrick, Joseph Giordano, and Nydia Garcia-Preto (New York: Guilford, 2005), 24.

11. Ibid., 31.

12. Ibid., 29–30.

13. Juan F. Martinez, "Defining Social Relations," in *Churches, Cultures and Leadership: A Practical Theology of Congregations and Ethnicities*, ed. Mark Lau Branson and Juan F. Martinez (Downers Grove, IL: IVP Academic, 2011), 136.

14. McGoldrick, Giordano, and Garcia-Preto, "Ethnicity and Family Therapy," 3.

15. Ibid., 19.

16. Sucheng Chan, *Asian Americans: An Interpretive History* (Boston: Twayne, 1991), 25.

17. Ibid., 100.

18. Tazuko Shibusawa, "Living Up to the American Dream: The Price of Being the Model Immigrants," *Psychotherapy Networker*, n.d., www.psychotherapynetworker.org/magazine/recentissues/130-living-up-to-the-american-dream.

19. Min Zhou, "Intragroup Diversity: Asian American Population Dynamics and Challenges of the Twenty-First Century," in *Asian America: Forming New Communities, Expanding Boundaries,* ed. Huping Ling (New Brunswick, NJ: Rutgers University Press, 2009), 38.

20. Ibid., 34.

21. Ibid.

22. Asian American students frequently appear as high school valedictorians and on competitive academic decathlon teams, and they win prestigious awards and honors at the national, state, and local levels. They are also gaining admission to Ivy League and prestigious colleges in disproportionate numbers. In the past few years, Asian American students represented more than 20 percent of the undergraduate student population at all nine University of California (UC) campuses and close to 60 percent at UC Irvine and 40 percent at UCLA, UC Berkeley, and UC Riverside. They are also visible, at 15 to 30 percent of the total undergraduate student population, at Harvard, Yale, Stanford, MIT, Caltech, and other renowned colleges. As of 2000, Asian Americans have attained the highest level of education of all racial groups in the United States: 44 percent of Asian American adults (aged 25 and over) have attained bachelor's degrees or higher, and the ratio for those with advanced degrees (for example, master's, PhD, MD, or JD) is one in seven. Ibid.

23. Luo Lu, "Culture, Self, Subjective Well-Being: Cultural Psychological and Social Change Perspectives," *Psychologia: An International Journal of Psychology in the Orient* 51, no. 4 (2009), 291.

24. Martinez, "Defining Social Relations," 151.

25. Chuansheng Chen et al., "Beyond Parents and Peers: The Role of Important Non-Parental Adults (Vips) in Adolescent Development in China and the United States," *Psychology in the Schools* 40, no. 1 (2003): 42.

26. This does not mean that shame-based culture does not have a guilt mechanism. See Miller R. Creighton,

"Revisiting Shame and Guilt Cultures," *Ethos* 18, no. 3 (1990): 279–307.

27. Ibid., 285.

28. Ibid.

29. Ibid., 286.

30. Young Gweon You, "Shame and Guilt Mechanism in East Asian Culture," *The Journal of Pastoral Care* 51, no. 1 (1997): 59.

31. Ibid., 60.

32. Ibid.

Chapter 12 Thinking Long Term

1. I have discovered the value of these concepts primarily through the work of Stanford University's William Damon and his speaking and writing. A particularly salient book describing the value of both convergence of the community and congruency of the message is William Damon and Richard M. Lerner, eds., *Handbook of Child Psychology*, 5th ed. (Oxford: Wiley, 2000).

2. 4/20 is a well-recognized date among college students. During the course of my interviews for *Sticky Faith*, I learned that although it is Hitler's birthday, it has become better known in recent years as National Weed (or Pot Smoking) Day. Sadly, it is also the day of the Columbine High School Massacre (1999), which was related to Hitler's birthday.

3. Erik H. Erikson, *Childhood and Society* (New York: Norton, 1950).

4. Isabella Granic et al., "Longitudinal Analysis of Flexibility and Reorganization in Early Adolescence: A Dynamic Systems Study of Family Interactions," *Developmental Psychology* 39, no. 3 (2003): 606–17.

5. John Bowlby originally proposed continuity of attachment based on an intrapsychic understanding of the self in *Attachment and Loss* (New York: Basic, 1982). Researchers have also discovered environmental support for the same theory; see Michael E. Lamb et al., eds., *Infant-Mother Attachment: The Origins and Developmental Significance of Individual Differences in Strange Situation Behavior* (Hillsdale, NJ: Lawrence Erlbaum, 1985). A more recent review of the literature can be found in Everett Waters et al., "Attachment Security in Infancy and Early Adulthood: A Twenty-Year Longitudinal Study," in *Child Development* 71, no. 3 (2000): 684–89.

6. Discontinuous theories abound among the stage theorists, who postulate that each stage is qualitatively unique from the others. Consider Jean Piaget. An adolescent who operates at the concrete stage of cognitive development processes information in a qualitatively different manner from one who has entered formal operations. Yet the manner in which a teenager *approaches* formal operations depends largely on his or her successful accomplishment of concrete operations.

7. This is one of the most significant findings of the Fuller Youth Institute research, as detailed in the Sticky Faith books and website (stickyfaith.org).

8. Developmental psychologist J. J. Arnett was the first to recognize, research, and eventually "discover" this new developmental period in nontraditional Western cultures. It describes the 18–25/27 age bracket and is marked by identity exploration, mobility, self-focus, feeling between stages, and an ability to see endless possibilities for oneself. See "Learning to Stand Alone: The Contemporary American Transition to Adulthood in Cultural and Historical Context," *Human Development* 41 (1998): 306.

9. Rodney Clapp, *Families at the Crossroads: Beyond Traditional Modern Options* (Downers Grove, IL: InterVarsity, 1993), 67–68.

10. Diana R. Garland, *Family Ministry: A Comprehensive Guide*, 2nd ed. (Downers Grove, IL: InterVarsity, 2012), 110–11.

11. The "one-eared Mickey Mouse" model was first coined by Stuart Cummings in Stuart Cummings-Bond, "The One-Eared Mickey Mouse," *YouthWorker Journal* 6 (Fall 1989): 76–78.

12. Chap Clark, "Strategic Assimilation: Rethinking the Goal of Youth Ministry," *YouthWorker Journal* (July/August 2002), http://www.youthworker.com/youth-ministry-resources-ideas/youth-ministry/11624001/.

13. Cambridge Dictionary online, dictionary.cambridge.org/us/dictionary/american-english/peer_2.

14. J. J. Arnett, *Adolescence and Emerging Adulthood: A Cultural Approach* (San Francisco: Pearson, 2013), 211.

15. Researchers have verified that both quantity and quality of time adolescents spend with friends increases during this stage of life. B. B. Brown and J. P. Bakken, "Parenting and Peer Relationships: Reinvigorating Research on Family-Peer Linkages in Adolescence," *Journal of Research on Adolescence* 21 (2011): 153–65.

16. Erikson first outlined the Eight Ages (now commonly called "stages") of Man in his groundbreaking book, *Childhood and Society* (New York: Norton, 1950).

17. Robert Kegan states in *The Evolving Self*, "I believe Erikson misses a stage between 'industry' and 'identity.' His identity stage, with its orientation to the self alone, 'who am I?,' time, achievement, ideology, self-certainty, and so on—captures something of late adolescence or early adulthood, but it does not really address the period of connection, inclusion, and highly invested mutuality which comes between the more independence-oriented periods of latency and [late adolescent] identity formation" (*The Evolving Self: Problem and Process in Human Development* [Cambridge, MA: Harvard University Press, 1982], 87).

18. Susan Harter describes the development of multiple selves in *The Construction of the Self: A Developmental Perspective* (New York: Guilford, 1999).

19. Miguel defined "the college thing" for me as "you know, party, drink, smoke, and have sex." Recognizing the inconsistency of these priorities with his faith, he intentionally sidelined his faith so he did not have to modify his behavior.

Chapter 13 Adoption Extended

1. A presupposition for me as I consider a welcoming youth ministry is that youth ministry is part of the work and calling of a local church, which seeks to be the visible reality of the *ekklēsia*—God's people. In that regard, the theological principles for the local church also apply to our youth ministries. The practice may be and probably will look very different, but the theological principles are the same.

2. "Mission," Oxforddictionaries.com, from http://www.oxforddictionaries.com/us/definition/american_english/mission.

3. Brian Kirk and Jacob Thorne, *Missional Youth Ministry: Moving from Gathering Teenagers to Scattering Disciples* (Grand Rapids: Zondervan, 2011), 19–20.

4. Ibid., 22.

5. Alan J. Roxburgh, *Missional: Joining God in the Neighborhood* (Grand Rapids: Baker Books, 2011), 26.

6. It is estimated that somewhere between 5 million and 8 million young people in the United States have physical or cognitive disabilities. As Amy Jacober notes in her qualitative study of families with children who have disabilities, churches often are not welcoming spaces for these young people. Amy Elizabeth Jacober, "Youth Ministry, Religious Education, and Adolescents with Disabilities: Insights from Parents and Guardians," *Journal of Religion, Disability & Health*, 14, no. 2 (2007): 167–81. http://dx.doi.org/10.1080/15228961003622310.

7. Roxburgh, *Missional*, 141.

8. Jason Linker, "Life-Long Guides: The Role and Relationships of Natural Mentors in the Lives of Christian Adolescents," *Journal of Youth Ministry* 1 (Fall 2012): 38.

9. Out of respect for my family, I have Cierra's permission to share this story.

10. Jeannine Brown, "Shalom: A Biblical/Theological Vision for God's People." Paper written in collaboration with Bethel Anti-Racism and Reconciliation Commission and published on the internal Bethel University website 2003, St. Paul, MN. https://jeanninekbrown.files.wordpress.com/2015/07/shalom-paper.pdf.

11. Roxburgh, *Missional*, 160–78.

12. Ibid., 172.

13. Ibid.

Chapter 14 Spiritual Formation

1. For the following categorization, see Bent Flyvbjerg, *Making Social Science Matter: Why Social Inquiry Fails and How It Can Succeed Again* (Cambridge: Cambridge University Press, 2001), 55–57.

2. Aristotle, *Nichomachean Ethics*, trans. C. D. C. Reeve (Indianapolis: Hackett Publishing, 2014), 120.

Chapter 15 Can I Ask That?

1. Walter Isaacson, *Steve Jobs* (New York: Simon & Schuster, 2011), 14–15.

2. Portions of this chapter are adapted from prior Sticky Faith publications, primarily Kara Powell, Brad M. Griffin, and Cheryl Crawford, *Sticky Faith: Youth Worker Edition* (Grand Rapids: Zondervan, 2011), and "I Doubt It: Making Space for Hard Questions," *FYI*, March 10, 2014, fulleryouthinstitute.org/articles/i-doubt-it. Also see stickyfaith.org/about-sticky-faith for more details about the research behind *Sticky Faith*, which spans eight years and includes over 500 students and parents from across the United States.

3. The College Transition Project was composed of four separate research initiatives: an initial quantitative pilot study involving 69 youth group graduates; two three-year longitudinal (primarily quantitative) studies of high school seniors during their first three years in college, involving 162 and 227 students, respectively; and additional qualitative interviews with 45 former youth group graduates who are currently in college, conducted by Dr. Cheryl Crawford. For more on our research methodology, visit www.stickyfaith.org.

4. This dialogue and others were developed out of conversations with teenagers and published in Jim Candy, Brad Griffin, and Kara Powell, *Can I Ask That? 8 Hard Questions about God and Faith* (Pasadena, CA: Fuller Youth Institute, 2014).

5. W. E Fiala, J. P. Bjorck, and R. Gorsuch, "The Religious Support Scale: Construction, Validation, and Cross-validation," *American Journal of Community Psychology* 30 (2002): 761–86.

6. Adapted with permission from A. W. Astin, H. S. Astin, and J. A. Lindholm, *Cultivating the Spirit: How College Can Enhance Students' Inner Lives* (San Francisco: Jossey-Bass, 2015). See also A. W. Astin, H. S. Astin, and J. A. Lindholm, "Assessing Students' Spiritual and Religious Qualities," *Journal of College Student Development*, forthcoming.

7. The scale used was adapted from the HERI 2007 College Students' Beliefs and Values Follow-Up Survey, University of California–Los Angeles.

8. For example, see Gay Holcomb and Arthur Nonneman, "Faithful Change: Exploring and Assessing Faith

Development in Christian Liberal Arts Undergraduates," in *Assessing Character Outcomes in College* (San Francisco: Jossey-Bass, 2004), 93–103.

9. Margaret Hall, "Crisis as Opportunity for Spiritual Growth," *Journal of Religion and Health* 25, no. 1 (1986): 8–17.

10. Richard R. Niebuhr, *Experiential Religion* (New York: HarperCollins, 1972), 91–104. See also Sharon Daloz Parks's expansion on this idea related to young adults in *Big Questions, Worthy Dreams: Mentoring Young Adults in Their Search for Meaning, Purpose, and Faith* (San Francisco: Jossey-Bass, 2000), 27–31.

11. See James E. Marcia, "Development and Validation of Ego Identity Status," *Journal of Personality and Social Psychology* 3 (1966): 551–58. See also James E. Marcia, "Identity in Adolescence," in *Handbook of Adolescent Psychology*, ed. Joseph Adelson (New York: John Wiley & Sons, 1980). We first began writing about the connections between Marcia's typology and youth ministry in Brad Griffin, "Through the Zone: Creating Rites of Passage in Your Church," *FYI*, June 12, 2006, fulleryouthinstitute.org/articles/through-the-zone.

12. Christopher L. Heuertz, *Unexpected Gifts: Discovering the Way of Community* (New York: Howard, 2013).

13. Ibid., 24.

14. Ibid., 27.

15. Ibid., 23, 30.

16. Parks, *Big Questions, Worthy Dreams*, 198.

17. Ibid., 93, 95.

18. Andrew Zirschky, "How Youth Doubt Is Different than We Expected," *Center for Youth Ministry Training*, February 19, 2014, www.cymt.org/how-youth-doubt-is-different-than-we-expected.

19. National Public Radio, "Losing Our Religion: One-Fifth of Americans Don't Identify with Any Religion. Who Are They? What Do They Believe?," January 2013, www.npr.org/series/169065270/losing-our-religion.

20. Tim Clydesdale in an interview with Derek Melleby, "Life after High School: The First Year," College Transition Initiative, 2012, www.collegetransitioninitiative.com/files/2012/10/cti_clydesdale.pdf.

21. For example, see Pss. 6, 10, 13, 61, 79, 80, 88, 94.

22. Walter Brueggemann, *The Psalms and the Life of Faith* (Minneapolis: Augsburg Fortress, 1995), 103–4.

23. See Jesse Oakes and Annie Neufeld, "A Book We Read That Also Reads Us: A Conversation about the Psalms with Dr. John Goldingay," *FYI*, March 24, 2014, fulleryouthinstitute.org/articles/a-book-we-read-that-also-reads-us.

24. Alisa Harris, *Raised Right: How I Untangled My Faith from Politics* (Colorado Springs: WaterBrook, 2011).

25. Interestingly, Christian education doesn't inoculate students from doubt either. In an opposite twist, one study of nearly 3,500 college students found that students at private Christian colleges were actually more likely to struggle spiritually than students at public universities or nonreligious private schools. Alyssa N. Bryant and Helen S. Astin, "The Correlates of Spiritual Struggle during the College Years," *The Journal of Higher Education* 79, no. 1 (January 2008): 1–27.

26. Brian McLaren, in Dan Schmidt, *Letters to Me: Conversations with a Younger Self* (self-published, 2012), 117–19.

27. Vygotsky's work is well described and illustrated by Jack O. Balswick, Pamela E. King, and Kevin S. Reimer in *The Reciprocating Self: Human Development in Theological Perspective* (Downers Grove, IL: InterVarsity, 2005), 90–97.

Chapter 16 A Call to Adoptive Ministry

1. While examples abound, one recent study is an example of how researchers are attempting to understand and deal with this phenomenon: Sylvie Mrug et al., "Early Puberty, Negative Peer Influence, and Problem Behaviors in Adolescent Girls," *Pediatrics* 133, no. 1 (2014): 7–14.

2. See Daniel J. Siegel, *Brainstorm: The Power and Purpose of the Teenage Brain* (New York: Tarcher, 2014). Siegel also mentions what a significant shift takes place in the brain around fourteen years of age, when we move from "early" to "mid-adolescence" (230).

3. Ibid.

4. Flipping the typical five students to one youth worker ratio on its head is not new, as both Jim Burns and Wayne Rice discussed in the late 1980s the importance of many adults in the life of a young person. But the particular research leading to the five-to-one ratio, or five nonparental adults who know a student deeply and make a lifetime commitment, came about as an article Chap Clark wrote for the Billy Graham Association's *Decision Magazine*, August 17, 2004, billygraham.org/decision-magazine/september-2004/in-spite-of-how-they-act.

5. Chap Clark, *Hurt 2.0: Inside the World of Today's Teenagers* (Grand Rapids: Baker Academic, 2011), xv.

6. Chap Clark, *Hurt: Inside the World of Today's Teenagers* (Grand Rapids: Baker Academic, 2004), 189.

Chapter 17 No Church in the Wild

1. See Edward W. Soja, *Postmetropolis: Critical Studies of Cities and Regions* (New York: Blackwell, 2000).

2. Dr. Soong-Chan Rah argues this in his book *The Next Evangelicalism: Releasing the Church from Western Cultural Captivity* (Downers Grove, IL: InterVarsity, 2009).

3. Daniel Bell, *The Coming of Post-Industrial Society: A Venture in Social Forecasting* (New York: Basic, 1973).

4. Mike Davis, "Fortress L.A.," in *The City Reader*, ed. Richard T. Le Gates and Frederic Stout (New York: Routledge, 1996).

5. Andrew Wiese, *Places of Their Own: African American Suburbanization in the Twentieth Century* (Chicago: University of Chicago Press, 2004).

6. Melvin Webber, "The Post-City Age," in Le Gates and Stout, eds., *The City Reader*.

7. Josh Sides, *L.A. City Limits: African American Los Angeles from the Great Depression to the Present* (Berkeley: University of California Press, 2003).

8. Harvey Cox, *The Secular City: A Celebration of Its Liberties and an Invitation to Its Discipline* (New York: Macmillan, 1965); idem, *Religion in the Secular City: Toward a Postmodern Theology* (New York: Simon & Schuster, 1984).

9. Many scholars have argued that the actual "beginning" of the postmodern era began to develop during the period following 1959 and into the decade of the 1960s—what year specifically is debated—however, a strong collection do agree that the birth of the era of public distrust, nihilism, and wariness of institutions began with events such as the Vietnam War, civil rights movement, several major assassinations, and the rise of women and ethnic minority rights, which revealed some of the deceptions from these institutions. See Zygmunt Bauman, "Postmodern Religion?," in *Religion, Modernity, and Postmodernity*, ed. Paul Heelas (Oxford: Blackwell, 1998); Daniel Bell, *Cultural Contradictions of Capitalism* (London: Heinemann, 1976); Todd Boyd, *The H.N.I.C.: The Death of Civil Rights and the Reign of Hip Hop* (New York: New York University Press, 2002); Ronald L. Johnstone, *Religion in Society: A Sociology of Religion* (Upper Saddle River, NJ: Pearson, 2009); Cornel West, "The New Cultural Politics of Difference," in *Out There: Marginalization and Contemporary Culture*, ed. Russell Ferguson (Cambridge, MA: MIT Press, 1990); idem, *Prophetic Thought in Postmodern Times: Beyond Eurocentrism and Multiculturalism*, vol. 1 (Monroe, ME: Common Courage, 1993).

10. The post-soul era has many similarities with postmodern traits, mores, characteristics, theory, pedagogy, and philosophy. Likewise, post-soul adheres to similar chronological dates of emergence. In actuality, post-soul is a rejection of modern (or soul) values, traditions, metanarratives, theological accounts, and societal structures stemming from hierarchal systems attempting to control various societal areas. Further, the post-soul vernacular better suits the black and brown societal structure in ways that the term *postmodernity* does not because many postmodern scholars are white and male, thereby ignoring important events such as the civil rights movement, hyper-masculinity in black contexts, gospel-tinged optimism in soul music, the decline of soul culture, and the significance of hip-hop culture. See Nelson George, *Post-Soul Nation: The Explosive, Contradictory, Triumphant, and Tragic 1980s as Experienced by African Americans (Previously Known as Blacks and before That Negroes)* (New York: Viking, 2004); Mark Anthony Neal, *Soul Babies: Black Popular Culture and the Post-Soul Aesthetic* (New York: Routledge, 2002).

11. Sides, *L.A. City Limits*; Wiese, *Places of Their Own*.

12. Interview taken from the DVD *Crips and Bloods: Made in America* (Docurama, 2008).

13. Sides, *L.A. City Limits*; Wiese, *Places of Their Own*.

14. Taken from John Whiteclay Chambers, *The Oxford Companion to American Military History* (Oxford: Oxford University Press, 1999).

15. Wiese, *Places of Their Own*.

16. Sides, *L.A. City Limits*.

17. This generation also fueled the white, suburban generation of youth listening to and consuming rap music. It cannot be overlooked as a major part of the lives of many suburban, white youth.

18. One of the first television shows to capture this monumental movement was *The Jeffersons*. This was a show about a black family moving up into "high society," which included a maid and a penthouse apartment in New York City, luxuries typically associated with white, affluent families. The theme song narrates this move, "We're a moving on up, / To the East Side. / To a deluxe apartment in the sky. . . . / We finally got a piece of the pie." This show also represented the coming wave of black and brown families who were able to afford moving out of the inner city to suburban-like contexts.

19. Bakari Kitwana discusses this in *Why White Kids Love Hip Hop: Wankstas, Wiggers, Wannabes, and the New Reality of Race in America* (New York: Basic Civitas, 2005), 17–50.

20. See also Brian Joe Lobley Berry, *Urbanization and Counterurbanization* (Beverly Hills, CA: Sage, 1976); Allen John Soja and Edward W. Scott, *The City: Los Angeles and Urban Theory at the End of the Twentieth Century* (Berkeley: University of California Press, 1996). They discuss postmodern challenges to urban renewal and the rise of the white lower class in the United States. Also note that Los Angeles can be seen as a case study of what a post-soul metropolis will look like as it has become the school of thought for urban and city design. This was once only held by cities such as Chicago and New York because of their donut-shape city design (central business district ring moving outward to a suburban and exurban

ring design); Los Angeles does not have this element and is a fragmented, decentralized central business district city. Soja, *Postmetropolis*.

21. Kitwana, *Why White Kids Love Hip Hop*. This is illustrated well in the 2003 film *Malibu's Most Wanted*, in which actor Jamie Kennedy plays the role of a privileged white male who has grown up with hip-hop as his ethnic identity. Hip-hop has shaped and formed his life as a result of his parents being withdrawn from him. This is a crucial element in hip-hop's attractiveness to many suburban, white youth because it is about personal consciousness and connecting with those who are suffering. Daniel White Hodge, *Heaven Has a Ghetto: The Missiological Gospel and Theology of Tupac Amaru Shakur* (Saarbrucken, Ger.: VDM, 2009); idem, *The Soul of Hip Hop: Rims, Timbs and a Cultural Theology* (Downers Grove, IL: InterVarsity, 2010); Bakari Kitwana, *The Hip Hop Generation: Young Blacks and the Crisis in African-American Culture* (New York: Basic Civitas, 2003).

22. See Leigh Gallagher, *The End of the Suburbs: Where the American Dream Is Moving* (New York: Portfolio, 2013); Patrick Sharkey, *Stuck in Place: Urban Neighborhoods and the End of Progress toward Racial Equality* (Chicago: University of Chicago Press, 2013).

23. Hodge, *Soul of Hip Hop*, 55–62.

24. Elizabeth Kneebone and Alan Berube, *Confronting Suburban Poverty in America* (Washington, DC: Brookings Institution, 2013), 13–36.

25. The poverty line is defined as a family of four living at or below $23,050 a year, according to the US Census Bureau.

26. From the US Census, "American Fact Finder," http://www.census.gov/quickfacts/table/RHI725213/53,39416 64,00. Also see Berube and Kneebone, *Confronting Suburban Poverty in America*, 12–15; and The Working Poor Families Project managed by Brandon Roberts, "Working Poor Families," www.workingpoorfamilies.org.

27. US Census, "American Fact Finder," http://www.census.gov/quickfacts/table/RHI725213/06059,3941664,00.

28. US Census data "American Fact Finder," http://www.census.gov/quickfacts; see also Kneebone, *Confronting Suburban Poverty in America*.

29. US Census Bureau data sets on racial categories. "American Fact Finder," http://www.census.gov/quickfacts/table/RHI725213/53,3941664,00. Also see Daily Mail Reporter, "Number of Babies Born to Ethnic Minorities Surpasses Whites in U.S. for First Time," *Daily Mail*, May 17, 2012, www.dailymail.co.uk/news/article-2145687/Non-white-births-outnumber-white-Ethnic-minorities-surpasses-whites-US-time.html.

30. I would also argue that youth ministry training resources and materials have consistently not reflected this ethnic minority and demographic shift. I make this argument here because, with the growth of the multiethnic and multicultural youth groups in many churches, the training materials have continued to focus on white, suburban, and affluent styles of ministry while issues such as gangs, poverty, and generational mobility are rarely discussed. More important, the issue of race is almost completely absent.

31. These suggestions flow out of a six-year research project in which I studied urban/suburban youth ministry organizations and their relationships with the community and the students they served. I then followed fifteen multiethnic youth into their early adulthood to see how these organizations affected their theology, worldview, and perceptions on race/ethnicity. These suggestions are to aid in pushing past and dealing with good intentions, tokenism, racial ignorance, and paternalism so that the widening gulf between white/Euro Americans and ethnic minorities can be reduced.

32. Several scholars have addressed the issue of neocolonialism in the Christian ministry setting. See Roy L. Brooks, *Racial Justice in the Age of Obama* (Princeton, NJ: Princeton University Press, 2009); J. Kameron Carter, *Race: A Theological Account* (New York: Oxford University Press, 2008); James H. Cone, *The Cross and the Lynching Tree* (Maryknoll, NY: Orbis, 2011); James E. Evans, *We Have Been Believers: An African American Systematic Theology* (Minneapolis: Fortress, 1992); Soong-Chan Rah, *The Next Evangelicalism: Releasing the Church from Western Cultural Captivity* (Downers Grove, IL: InterVarsity, 2009).

This issue is exacerbated even more when the white/Euro American youth worker approaches the ministry table believing he or she "knows" more and can "teach" "these people" something—similar to the leaders of the organization in the opening story of this article, which is an attitude sometimes found in white/Euro American missionaries (76–80).

33. This Ghanaian term translates into either "reaching back to get it" or "looking back, moving forward." It is an experience that North Park University in Chicago uses to train, educate, and encourage leaders of all ethnic backgrounds as they ponder and discover the issues of race for their own context.

34. Moreover, one must understand that the issues of gentrification, systemic racism, and "urban renewal" did not happen in a vacuum. In other words, systemic sin is not a coincidence. As Christians and especially youth ministers, we must take a hard look at and engage the legacy of racism and systemic sin in our country. For example, when I speak at camp and talk on "sin," rather than asking students what sins they have committed, I ask, "What sins, systemically, have been committed against

you?" This shifts the conversation and begins the necessary dialogue in this matter.

35. Also see Matthew Desmond and Mustafa Emirbayer's historical account of the social construct of whiteness in their seminal book *Racial Domination, Racial Progress: The Sociology of Race in America* (New York: McGraw Hill, 2010), 60–63.

36. Why is this a problem? Because the people in that context have much to give, and their perspective is needed to push the conversation past suburban stylized ministry. When introducing his classes on intercultural engagement for missionaries, Professor Dan Shaw of Fuller Theological Seminary's School of Intercultural Studies states that if you are doing great missionary work, allowing the people group to dictate the gospel for themselves, but arrive at church and feel a bit culturally uncomfortable, then—and only then—is contextualization of the gospel taking place. If the church looks the same as it did in your context, then contextualization is not happening. In other words, what do ministry leaders fear by allowing the Holy Spirit to move and contextualize worship, praise, and theology for the people and by the people?

37. James H. Cone, *God of the Oppressed* (New York: Seabury, 1975), 127–34.

38. I use rap and hip-hop here because of their relevance to youth ministry and the rising tide of white/Euro American suburban youth who admire rapper and hip-hop artist Tupac Amaru Shakur. In my own work I found that a large group of white/Euro American youth identified with Tupac's lyrical messages about God, pain, life, death, and Jesus. As a youth worker, this cannot be ignored. See Hodge, *Heaven Has a Ghetto*.

39. Ibid., 250–55.

40. For a broader view of this concept see Tyron Inbody, *The Many Faces of Christology* (Nashville: Abingdon, 2002); and Volker Küster, *The Many Faces of Jesus Christ: Intercultural Christology* (Maryknoll, NY: Orbis, 2001), which discuss the varieties of Jesus and Christology.

41. Rah, *Next Evangelicalism*, 200.

Chapter 18 Adoptive Youth Ministry

1. US Census Bureau, "Hispanic Americans by the Numbers," *infoplease*, n.d., www.infoplease.com/spot/hhmcensus1.html.

2. CEPALSTAT, Databases and Statistical Publications, n.d., statistics.eclac.org.

3. UNICEF América Latina y el Caribe, n.d., www.unicef.org/lac.

4. Corporación Latinobarómetro, n.d., http://www.latinobarometro.org/lat.jsp.

5. "Lord Emerich Edward Dalberg Acton," *Acton Institute for the Study of Religion and Liberty*, n.d.,

www.acton.org/pub/religion-liberty/volume-3-number-1/lord-emerich-edward-dalberg-acton.

6. The term "10/40 Window" is said to have been coined by Luis Bush at the 1989 Lausanne II Conference in Manila. See Luis Bush, "The 10/40 Window, Getting to the Core of the Core," AD2000 & Beyond Movement, http://web.archive.org/web/20051118223835/http://www.ad2000.org/1040broc.htm.

Chapter 19 Adoptive Leadership

1. See Kara Powell and Chap Clark, *Sticky Faith: Everyday Ideas to Build Lasting Faith in Your Kids* (Grand Rapids: Zondervan, 2011). See also Chap Clark, "In Spite of How They Act . . . ," *Billy Graham Evangelistic Association*, August 17, 2004, www.billygraham.org/articlepage.asp?ArticleID=461; Mark Cannister, *Teenagers Matter: Making Student Ministry a Priority in the Church* (Grand Rapids: Baker Academic, 2013).

2. Robert D. Putnam, *Bowling Alone: The Collapse and Revival of American Community* (New York: Simon & Schuster, 2000).

3. Carlos Raimundo describes this as "relational capital." Cited in Robert Banks and Bernice M. Ledbetter, *Reviewing Leadership: A Christian Evaluation of Current Approaches* (Grand Rapids: Baker Academic, 2004), 96. Peter C. Scales and his colleagues warn about "the presence or absence of various ecological supports, and adolescents' reduction of risks and attainment of positive developmental outcomes." Peter C. Scales et al., "Contribution of Developmental Assets to the Prediction of Thriving among Adolescents," *Applied Developmental Science* 4, no. 1 (2000): 27–46.

4. William Damon, *The Youth Charter* (New York: The Free Press, 1997), 87–88.

5. Dennis Guernsey, *A New Design for Family Ministry* (Elgin, IL: David C. Cook, 1982). See also "Congregations as Family," in Merton P. Strommen and Richard A. Hardel, *Passing on the Faith* (Winona, MN: St. Mary's Press, 2000), 155–85.

6. *US Army Field Manual* (Lawrence, KS: Neeland Media, 2007), 1–4.

7. Ken Blanchard, Bill Hybels, and Phil Hodges, *Leadership by the Book* (New York: HarperCollins, 2001).

8. Exodus 18:13–23 (italics added). Robert K. Greenleaf argues that Jethro did not go far enough because he allowed Moses to maintain his leadership identity as the lone leader on top of a pyramid with lesser worker bees below. Nonetheless, Jethro's new paradigm moved Israel toward a team model rather than an autocratic leader. The nation would have to wait for Jesus to show them a better, more perfect way. Robert K. Greenleaf, *Servant Leadership: A Journey into the Nature of Legitimate*

Power and Greatness, 25th anniversary ed. (New York: Paulist Press, 2002), 96–98.

9. Larry C. Spears, "Character and Servant Leadership: Ten Characteristics of Effective Caring Leaders," *The Journal of Virtues and Leadership* 1, no. 1 (2010): 25–30.

10. Trina Soske and Jay A. Conger, "It's Time to Focus Executive Development on Real Business Isues," *Harvard Business Review*, June 4, 2010, blogs.hbr.org/2010/06/time-to-shift-the-paradigm-of.

11. Greenleaf, *Servant Leadership*, 27 (italics in the original).

12. Ibid., 74.

13. Ed Brenegar, "Leading Questions: A Circle of Impact," November 24, 2008, edbrenegar.typepad.com/leading_questions/2008/11/primus-inter-pares-a-strategic-ethic-of-leadership-success.html.

14. Robert Banks and Bernice M. Ledbetter, *Reviewing Leadership: A Christian Evaluation of Current Approaches* (Grand Rapids: Baker Academic, 2004), 109.

15. Henri Nouwen, *In the Name of Jesus* (New York: Crossroad, 1992).

16. Henri Nouwen, *Life of the Beloved* (New York: Crossroad, 1992), 26–29.

17. Ibid., 26.

18. Parker J. Palmer, *Let Your Life Speak: Listening for the Voice of Vocation* (San Francisco: John Wiley and Sons, 2000), 10.

19. Nouwen, *Life of the Beloved*, 62.

20. Ibid., 49–52.

21. Mark Allan Powell, addressing graduating seniors at Trinity Lutheran Seminary, Columbus, Ohio.

22. Bobbie Reed and John Westfall, *Building Strong People: How to Lead Effectively* (Eugene, OR: Wipf & Stock, 1997), 12 (italics added).

23. Ron Martoia, *Morph: The Texture of Leadership for Tomorrow's Church* (Loveland, CO: Group Publishing, 2003).

24. Paul Hersey, Kenneth H. Blanchard, and Dewey E. Johnson, *Management of Organizational Behavior: Leading Human Resources*, 9th ed. (Upper Saddle River, NJ: 2007). See also Dr. Paul Hersey, *The Situational Leader* (New York: Warner, 1984); Ken Blanchard and Spencer Johnson, *Leadership and the One-Minute Manager* (New York: Berkley, 1983).

25. Walter C. Wright, *Relational Leadership: A Biblical Model for Influence and Service* (Waynesboro, GA: Paternoster, 2000), 36.

26. Doug Fields, *Purpose Driven Youth Ministries* (Grand Rapids: Zondervan, 1998), 274.

27. Adapted from Les Christie, *Unsung Heroes: How to Recruit and Train Volunteer Youth Workers* (Grand Rapids: Zondervan, 1987), 30.

28. See Stephen R. Covey, *The Seven Habits of Highly Effective People: Powerful Lessons in Personal Change* (New York: Free Press, 2004), 151.

29. Kenda Creasy Dean, Chap Clark, and Dave Rahn, *Starting Right: Thinking Theologically about Youth Ministry* (Grand Rapids: Zondervan, 2001), 109–24.

30. This perspective is influenced by "the field of positive psychology, with its emphasis on empirical research about what leads to positive individual and community functioning." L. A. Schreiner, "The 'Thriving Quotient': A New Vision for Student Success," *About Campus* 15 (2010): 2–10. The emphasis of Schreiner, and others with this perspective, leans toward helping students not just survive their time in adolescence but *flourish* and *thrive*.

31. Fields, *Purpose Driven Youth Ministry*, 275. Speaking of stereotypes, here is a guest post by Rob Schwinge, written for Josh Griffin's blog, on youth pastor stereotypes: I Have a Dream.

32. Chap Clark, lecture in YF502 "Leadership in Youth Ministry," Fuller Theological Seminary, 2009.

33. This idea comes from Bo Boshers with Kim Anderson, *Student Ministry for the 21st Century: Transforming Your Youth Group into a Vital Student Ministry* (Grand Rapids: Zondervan, 1997), 155.

34. Banks and Ledbetter, *Reviewing Leadership*, 18.

35. Max De Pree, *Leadership Is an Art* (New York: Crown Business, 2004), 16, 31–37.

36. Fields, *Purpose Driven Youth Ministry*, 292–98 and also appendix F.

Chapter 20 The Communication of Adoption

1. This story has been attributed to the humorist Erma Bombeck.

2. Francis Schaeffer, *He Is There and He Is Not Silent* (Wheaton: Tyndale House, 1972).

3. For a fuller account of this grand story, see Albert M. Wolters, *Creation Regained: Biblical Basis for a Reformational Worldview* (Grand Rapids: Eerdmans, 2005).

4. While this passage may not point convincingly to the trinitarian nature of God, it does point to what Victor Hamilton calls a plural, *cohortative* (from the word *cohort*) element in the Godhead. For a review of six different ways this passage might be understood, see Victor Hamilton, *The Book of Genesis: Chapters 1–17* (Grand Rapids: Eerdmans, 1990).

5. J. B. Phillips, *The New Testament in Modern English* (New York: Simon & Schuster, 1958).

6. Note here that Paul is also responding to echoes from those first seminal chapters in Genesis.

7. The poster was designed by Eugene Fuller for the Juvenile Protective Association. All three photos used in the campaign can be seen at eugenefuller.com/creative/juvenile/.

8. This section mirrors the "put off/put on" instruction that we see repeated in Col. 3:5–17. Notice that in both places the instruction is connected to family communication and interaction.

9. Paul's words here point to obscene language—that which is disgraceful, shameful, or indecent. One of the nouns here, *morologia*, is composed of two words: *moron* and *speak*. That should give us a pretty good idea of Paul's thinking. For more, see Klyne Snodgrass, *Ephesians* (Grand Rapids: Zondervan, 1996), 268.

10. Duffy Robbins, *Youth Ministry Nuts and Bolts: Organizing and Managing Your Youth Ministry* (Grand Rapids: Zondervan, 2010), 138.

11. Dean Borgman, *When Kumbayah Is Not Enough* (Peabody, MA: Hendrickson, 1997), 13.

12. For some practical questions to ask in this process, see John R. W. Stott, *The Contemporary Christian* (Downers Grove, IL: InterVarsity, 1992), 247–48.

13. I also discuss this material and other issues related to cultural exegesis in Len Kageler and Duffy Robbins, *This Way to Youth Ministry: The Companion Guide* (Grand Rapids: Zondervan, 2002), 258–63.

14. Dietrich Bonhoeffer, *Life Together*, trans. John W. Boberstein (New York: Harper and Bros., 1954), 97–99.

15. I also discuss this material and other issues related to cultural exegesis in *This Way to Youth Ministry*, 258–63.

16. Cited in an address by George Carey to the Clergy of the Chelmsford Diocese, 2000, www.anglicannews.org/news/2000/02/the-way-ahead-preparing-the-church-of-england-for-the-challenges-of-the-new-millennium.aspx.

17. Charles Kraft, *Communication Theory for Christian Witness* (Maryknoll, NY: Orbis, 2002), 2–3.

18. Ibid., 15. These lessons are adaptations of principles set forth by Kraft. See also the discussion in Doug Fields and Duffy Robbins, *Speaking to Teenagers* (Grand Rapids: Zondervan, 2007), 32–39.

19. Note this same kind of receptor sensitivity in the New Testament (John 16:12; 1 Cor. 3:2; Heb. 5:12–14).

20. Marrshall McLuhan, *Understanding Media: The Extensions of Man* (Cambridge, MA: MIT Press, 1994), 7.

21. Fields and Robbins, *Speaking to Teenagers*, 236–37.

Chapter 21 Teaching for Adoptive Ministry

1. Note in the NIV: "Or *parents*."

2. Chap Clark, *Hurt: Inside the World of Today's Teenagers* (Grand Rapids: Baker Academic, 2004); idem, *Hurt 2.0: Inside the World of Today's Teenagers* (Grand Rapids: Baker Academic, 2011).

3. To download the free David C. Cook curriculum evaluation guide, go to http://www.davidccook.com/curriculum/index.cfm?N=2,2,3,1.

4. This is a slight name modification of the Description of a Discipled Person, or DDP, that Sonlife Ministries used to promote.

5. Randy Frazee, *The Connecting Church* 2.0 (Grand Rapids: Zondervan, 2013); Andy Stanley and Stuart Hall, *Seven Checkpoints*, rev. ed. (New York: Howard Books/Simon & Schuster, 2011).

6. Andreas Köstenberger, Darrell Bock, and Josh Chatraw, *Truth Matters* (Nashville: B&H, 2014).

7. Lake Pointe Church parent resources: https://www.lakepointe.org/homepointe/intentional-parents/.

8. J. I. Packer and Gary Parrett, *Grounded in the Gospel: Building Believers the Old-Fashioned Way* (Grand Rapids: Baker Books, 2010).

9. Ben Espinoza, "Toward a Revival of Catechesis in Youth Ministry," *Youthworker eJournal*, March 4, 2014, www.youthworker.com/youth-ministry-resources-ideas/youth-ministry/11706730/.

10. Bernice McCarthy, *Teaching around the 4mat Cycle: Designing Instruction for Diverse Learners with Diverse Learning Styles* (Newbury Park, CA: Corwin, 2005).

11. Dan Lambert, *Teaching That Makes a Difference* (Grand Rapids: Zondervan, 2004), 147–62.

12. Larry Richards and Gary Bredfelt, *Creative Bible Teaching* (Chicago: Moody, 1998).

Chapter 22 Rethinking Church Strategies and Structures

1. Chap Clark, *Hurt 2.0: Inside the World of Today's Teenagers* (Grand Rapids: Baker Academic, 2011); P. E. King, "Religion and Identity: The Role of Ideological, Social, and Spiritual Contexts," *Applied Developmental Science* 7, no. 3 (2003): 197–204; Peter Scales and Nancy Leffert, *Developmental Assets: A Synthesis of the Scientific Research on Adolescent Development* (Minneapolis: Search Institute, 2004); R. Wuthnow, *Loose Connections: Joining Together in America's Fragmented Communities* (Cambridge, MA: Harvard University Press, 1998).

2. F. P. Edie, *Book, Bath, Table, and Time: Christian Worship as Source and Resource for Youth Ministry* (Cleveland: Pilgrim Press, 2007); R. E. Webber, *Ancient-Future Worship: Proclaiming and Enacting God's Narrative* (Grand Rapids: Baker Books, 2008); N. T. Wright, *Paul and the Faithfulness of God* (Minneapolis: Fortress, 2013).

3. P. Freire, *Pedagogy of the Oppressed*, 20th anniv. ed. (New York: Continuum, 1993); M. Weimer, *Learner-Centered Teaching: Five Key Changes to Practice* (San Francisco: Jossey-Bass, 2002).

4. S. Arthur, *The God-Hungry Imagination: The Art of Storytelling for Postmodern Youth Ministry* (Nashville: Upper Room Books, 2007).

5. K. C. Dean, *Almost Christian: What the Faith of Our Teenagers Is Telling the American Church* (New York: Oxford University Press, 2010); K. C. Dean and R. D. Martinson, *OMG: A Youth Ministry Handbook* (Nashville: Abingdon, 2010).

6. Arthur, *God-Hungry Imagination*.

7. A decision tree [diagram] helps map out potential opportunities, challenges, and outcomes and aids leaders in planning and anticipating the ministry choices they make. It helps leaders consider the intended and unintended consequences of their choices, programs, initiatives, etc. It is a "type of tree-diagram used in determining the optimum course of action, in situations having several possible alternatives with uncertain outcomes. The resulting chart or diagram (which looks like a cluster of tree branches) displays the structure of a particular decision, and the interrelationships and interplay between different alternatives, decisions, and possible outcomes." http://www.businessdictionary.com/definition/decision-tree.html#ixzz3jCG2Uvur.

8. J. W. Fowler, *Stages of Faith: The Psychology of Human Development and the Quest for Meaning* (San Francisco: Harper & Row, 1981); S. D. Parks, *Big Questions, Worthy Dreams: Mentoring Young Adults in Their Search for Meaning, Purpose, and Faith* (San Francisco: Jossey-Bass, 2000).

9. B. Christerson, K. Edwards, and R. Flory, *Growing Up in America: The Power of Race in the Lives of Teens* (Stanford, CA: Stanford University Press, 2010); A. Jacober, *The Adolescent Journey: An Interdisciplinary Approach to Practical Youth Ministry* (Downers Grove, IL: InterVarsity, 2011).

10. Parks, *Big Questions, Worthy Dreams*; J. Piaget, *Biology and Knowledge* (Chicago: University of Chicago Press, 1971).

11. J. Mezirow, *Learning as Transformation: Critical Perspectives on a Theory in Progress* (San Francisco: Jossey-Bass, 2001).

12. K. E. Powell and B. M. Griffin, *Sticky Faith, Youth Worker Edition: Practical Ideas to Nurture Long-Term Faith in Teenagers* (Grand Rapids: Zondervan, 2011).

13. G. A. Boyd, *Benefit of the Doubt: Breaking the Idol of Certainty* (Grand Rapids: Baker Books, 2013).

Chapter 23 A Call to Adoption

1. dictionary.reference.com/browse/integrate?s=t.

2. April Diaz, *Redefining the Role of the Youth Worker: A Manifesto for Integration* (San Diego: Youth Cartel, 2013), 50.

3. Ibid., 36–38.

4. Skye Jethani, *With: Reimagining the Way You Relate to God* (Nashville: Thomas Nelson, 2011).

5. Dave Gibbons, *The Monkey and the Fish: Liquid Leadership for a Third-Culture Church* (Grand Rapids: Zondervan, 2009).

6. Ibid., 45–46.

Scripture Index

Old Testament

Genesis

1:1–5 291
1:1–25 289
1:3 289, 293
1:26 289
1:26–27 122
1:26–30 289
1:28 113, 122, 289
2:15 113, 122
2:18 113
3:1 289–90
3:9 298
11:1–9 290
37:5 298

Exodus

3:2 298
8:2 298
10:4 298
18:13–23 364n8

Leviticus

19:33–34 204

Numbers

22:28 298

Deuteronomy

6 302
6:4–9 128

6:6–9 305
6:7 345
16:16 153
18:16 347n2
23:1 347n2

Judges

2:10 244

1 Samuel

3 298

2 Samuel

12:1 298

1 Chronicles

12:32 120

Esther

4:14 345

Psalms

2:19 309
8 338
13 229
19:1–4 298
23 69
26:12 347n2
42:1–2 42
68:6 48

78:5–7 305
88:18 229
100:3 2

Proverbs

27:6 295
27:17 311

Isaiah

1:1 298
6:8–13 290
43:18–19 337
55:1 42
56:5 82
56:7 82

Jeremiah

2:13 43
3:21 290
6:13–14 49
18:2–3 298
29:7 206

Ezekiel

12:2 290

Daniel

5:5 298

Hosea

1:1 298

New Testament

Matthew

2:2 298
5:13 297
5:13–14 17
5:13–16 3
5:21–22 70
6:9 2
6:10 112
9:12–13 200
9:17 337
9:36 70
11:28 299
12:36–37 294
12:48 307
13:4–23 296
13:15 290
13:31 298
15:10–18 294
18:2–5 141
18:17 347n2
19:14 141
21:12–13 91
21:16 338
21:19 298
22 19
22:36 113
22:37–40 114
23:3–4 279
23:11 279
25:31–46 19

25:40 307
28:18–20 304
28:19 203, 304
28:20 263

Mark

2:22 337
3:1–6 91
10:13–16 260
10:14–15 91
10:15 3
10:31 91
10:42–45 266
14:36 278

Luke

2:41–52 152–53
2:44 153
2:47 91
2:49 91
2:52 163
3:22 278
5:37–38 337
10:1–12 205
10:4 210
10:25–37 92, 343
19:10 3
24:13–27 296

John

1:1 291, 298
1:1–5 291
1:1–14 298
1:12 2, 3, 11, 17, 19
1:12–13 117
1:14 47, 70, 118, 290–91,
    291, 293, 297, 298
3:7 133
3:16 112, 298
4 92
4:7 211
4:14 42
5:19 338
7:1–43 292
7:25–36 292
7:40–43 292
9:25 69
10:10–30 119
13:34 274
14:13 1
14:16 314
14:26 314
15 243

15:12–13 266
15:17 347n4
16:8 314
16:12 366n19
17:18 304
17:20–21 304
20:21 1, 200, 304

Acts

1:3 304
1:8 2, 3, 304
2 15
2:5–6 291
2:37–47 291
2:42–47 309
3:1–10 218
4:32 15
5:14 15
6 280
8 70–71, 81–82
16:1 306
17 70, 133
17:23 296
17:28 354n30
20:28 148, 263, 266

Romans

1:18 290
1:28–31 290
5:8 50
8 345
8:14 51
8:15 348n6
8:17 51
8:18–23 130
8:23 348n6
8:28 1
9:4 348n6
10:9 304
12 147, 348n4
12:1–2 313
12:2 291
12:3–8 276
12:4–5 147
12:5 17
12:10 138
13:8 138
14:3 79
15:7 138
16:16 138

1 Corinthians

2:1–5 301
3:2 366n19

8 79
9:19–23 299
9:22 299
12 147, 236, 276, 280, 307,
    348n4
12:25 138
12:27 51

2 Corinthians

5 200
5:17–21 112
5:18 43
5:18–20 291

Galatians

3:26–29 4
3:28 209
4:4–5 114
4:5 348n6
5:13 138
5:22–23 163
6:1–2 263

Ephesians

1:5 348n6
2:10 50
2:13 291, 298
2:17 298
2:17–22 291
2:19 2
3:14–15 3
4 147, 348n4
4–5 294
4:1–6 16
4:1–16 276
4:6 176
4:11–16 148
4:11–24 297
4:13 149
4:15 297
4:17–32 294
4:29 138, 294
4:29–32 295
4:31–32 294
4:32 138
5:1–6:9 297
5:4 294
5:21 138

Philippians

2:4 346
2:6–7 298, 299

3:5 110
3:10 322

Colossians

1:19 291
1:26–27 289
1:28 305
2:4 291
2:8 291
3:5–17 366n8
3:16 138
4:4 297
4:5 297, 312
4:6 297

1 Thessalonians

4:18 138
5:11 138
5:12–13 264

1 Timothy

3:16–17 263

2 Timothy

1:5 305, 306
2:15 242, 295
3:14–15 305
3:16–17 307
4:1–4 263

Titus

1:5 15
1:7–9 15
1:12 354n30
2:1 267
2:2 267, 268
2:2–8 307
2:3 267
2:4 267
2:5 267
2:6 268
2:7 268

Hebrews

1:1–2 298
2:11 176
4:15 299
5:11–12 265
5:12–14 366n19
10:22–25 263

10:23–25 139, 146
10:24–25 307
12:2 112
13:17 148, 264, 265

James

3:1 314
3:5–12 290
5:16 138

1 Peter

2:9–12 204
3:15 313
4:8 339
5:1–4 263
5:1–5 15–16
5:2 266
5:2–3 264
5:4 264

5:5 307
5:14 311

1 John

1:7 138

Jude

22 228

Revelation

5:9 202
5:13 291
9:17 298
19:13 291
22:17 199

Subject Index

abandonment, systemic, 32–33, 37–38, 40, 161–63
abuse, verbal, 293–94
achievement, identity, 226
adolescence
  culture and, 68–82, 167–79, 358n1
  development and, 27–36, 46–49, 214–15, 233, 342
  early, 56–58, 235–45
  middle, 37–38, 44–46, 58–61
  parents and, 185–86, 235–36, 331
  technology and, 56–61
adoption, theology of, 2–4, 11–12, 347–48n4, 348n6
  (introduction). *See also* family
adoption level programming, 20
adulthood, 29–30, 37–38, 61–63
adults. *See* intergenerational interaction
advertising, 64, 128
affiliation vs. abandonment, 192, 359n17
affinity, adolescence and, 342
age, 7, 25–26, 183–85
agency. *See* choice, adolescence and
American Dream, the, 170–72
analytical learners, 313
Anderson, Ray, 102
Andruejol, Howard, ix, 256
anger, reflection and, 95–96
antecedent, biblical, 109
AOL, 54
application packet, volunteer, 285–86
Approved unto God (AUG), 241–42
Argue, Steven, ix, 316–17
Aristotle, 213–14, 348n5 (chap. 1)
Asian-American culture, 170–76, 358n22

assessment, volunteer, 328–29
assimilation, adoption and, 4–5, 19
attainment, cognitive, 36–37
AUG, 241–42
authenticity, welcome and, 208
authority, leadership and, 257–69

Babel, tower of, 290
baggage, mission and, 210
baptism, 140, 304
bargaining, prayer and, 73–74, 76–77
behavior, culture and, 169
beliefs, youth and, 163
Bible, the
  communication and, 289–91, 295
  culture and, 70–71, 118, 133, 263–66
  doubt and, 228, 229–30
  education and, 307–9
  practical theology and, 109
"big church," youth and, 333–34
body, church as, 147–49
body mass index (BMI), 28–29
Bonner, Steven, ix, 22
Boyd, Danah, 63
bridge building, 298–99, 329–34
Bronfenbrenner, Urie, 99, 100
Browning, Dan, 102
Byrne, Jim, 144

calling, 93–94, 163
camper party, 235
Cannister, Mark, ix–x

canopy, sacred, 87
capital, social, 8, 40, 274
catechesis, 128–29, 308–9, 312–13
cell phones, 63
change, 13, 123, 130–32
childhood, 44, 45
choice, adolescence and, 46–47
Christ. *See* Jesus
Christian nurture, 87
Christopraxis, 111
church, the
    adolescence and, 35–36, 137–49, 241–44
    adoption and, 2–4, 11–12, 216–19, 347n4, 348n6
        (introduction)
    community and, 86–89, 236–40, 333–34
    as *ecclesia*, 1–2, 347n2
    family and, 15–17, 152–64, 189–91, 338
    oppression and, 257–66
    reflection and, 91–93
    suffering and, 48–49
cities, 249–51
citizenship, Roman, 204–5
clarity, communication and, 294
Clark, Chap, x, 104
cleanliness, ritual, 218
coaching, leadership as, 281
cobertura, 258–59
codependency, the church and, 259
cognitive attainment, 36–37
cognitive development, 43–44, 56–58, 214–15
cognitive propagation, 30–31
cohortative, God as, 365n4
college-age ministry, 334
College Transition Project, 223–32, 360n3
commitment, church as, 147–48
common-sense learners, 313
communication, 289–301
community
    Aristotle on, 348n5 (chap. 1)
    the church as, 86–89, 138–49, 152–64, 344
    communication and, 295–96
    creation and, 112–14
    in Latin America, 260, 262–63
    personhood and, 33, 172–76, 226–27
community-building level, 18
competencies, volunteer, 329
concrete, communication as, 294
concrete thinking, 56–58
Confucianism, 172–75
conglomerates, culture and, 128
congruence, 181
conscientization, 95
content, educational, 307–9, 322, 324

contextualization, 119, 295–98, 322, 324
continuity, relationships and, 185–86
contributions, youth, 140–45
convergence, 181
conversion, ongoing, 95
core needs, 42–43
corporations, culture and, 128
correlation, theology and, 354n22
Crawford, Cheryl, x, 180
creation, 112–14, 122, 130–32, 289, 291. *See also* world, the
creed, youth and, 163
culture
    the Bible and, 70–71, 118, 130–31, 133, 263–66
    communication and, 295–96
    globalization and, 167–79, 257–70, 358n1, 358n22
    ministry and, 120–34, 160–63
    popular, 68–82
curriculum, educational, 307–9
cynicism, ministry and, 100–101

data, education and, 15
dating, online, 61–62
deal-making, 73–74, 76–77
decision-tree, 326, 367n7
deindustrialization, 249–50
Deism, Moralistic Therapeutic, 74
delegation, leadership and, 275–76, 281
descriptive-empirical task, 103, 105–6
Detweiler, Craig, x, 67
development
    adolescent, 27–36, 46–49, 233, 342
    cognitive, 43–44, 56–58, 214–15
    culture and, 169–70
    proximal, 231
    psychosocial, 192, 359n6
    transitions and, 331–32
Diaz, April, x, 335
diffusion, identity, 226
digital technology. *See* technology
directing, leadership as, 280–81
direction, creation and, 130–31
directive, culture as, 127–29
disabilities, welcome and, 203, 217–19, 360n6 (chap. 13)
Discipled Student Profile (DSP), 308
disciples, making, 304–5
discipleship. *See* formation, spiritual
discipleship level, 18
discontinuity, relationships and, 186
disorientation, doubt and, 229
disruption, reflection and, 95–96
diverse relationship level, 20
diversity, 78–82, 167–79, 206, 236, 342–44
doctrine, education and, 308

Doong, David Jia Hwa, x, 165–66
double listening, 118–19, 129
doubt, 222–32, 361n25
DSP. *See* Discipled Student Profile (DSP)
duration of adolescence, 27–30
dynamic learners, 313

early adolescence, 56–58, 233, 235–45
ecclesia, 1–2, 347n2
ecclesiology. *See* church, the
Ecology of Human Development, The (Bronfenbrenner),
   99, 100
education
   adolescence and, 31, 34–35
   Asian Americans and, 171, 174–75, 358n22
   community and, 162, 303–15
   faith and, 94–95, 361n25
   institution of, 14–15
   leadership and, 321–24
egalitarianism, culture and, 169
"Eight Ages of Man" (Erikson), 192
emergence, urban, 249–51
engaging level programming, 20
entry level programming, 18
environment, leadership, 282–83
episteme, 214
epistemology, 332–33
equals, first among, 16
Erickson, Todd, 144
Erikson, Erik, 192
Erwin, Pamela J., x–xi, 197–98
eschatology, 202, 291
Ethiopian eunuch, the, 70–71, 81–82
ethnicity, ministry and, 170–76, 249–55, 257–70, 358n22,
   363n34
evangelism, 201–3, 210–11, 340–41
evil, problem of, 75–76. *See also* suffering
exegesis, 71, 295–96
exhortation, abuse of, 264–66
exodus, youth, 155–59
expectations, volunteer, 328
experience, 109, 214–16, 219–20
experts, leaders as. *See* outsourcing, parental
extracurricular activities, 33–34

faith, 91–93, 222–32, 332–33
fall, the, 130–31, 289–90
family
   adoption and, 2–4, 11–12, 216–19, 347n4, 348n6
      (introduction)
   the church as, 15–17, 152–64, 189–91, 338
   culture and, 168–69, 170–77
   education and, 305–7, 309

Family-Based Youth Ministry, 159–60
Family-Equipping Ministry, 160
Family Integrated Church, 157, 159–60
Fast and the Furious, The, 81
Father, God as, 3
fear factor, mission and, 201
fellowship, social capital and, 274
film, role of, 72–73
first among equals, 16, 276, 279–80
five, the, 7, 236, 306, 340, 348n10
Flies, Heather, xi, 233–34
flourishing, welcome and, 207
foreclosure, identity, 226
formation, spiritual, 214–20, 329, 339–41, 345
4-Mat System, 313
4/20, 359n2
Fowler, James, 102
fragmentation, technology and, 59, 62, 64–66
freedom, religious, 74–75
Freire, Paolo, 93–95
friendship, 56–61, 172, 191–93, 207–8
Fuller Youth Institute (FYI), 221
Funnel of Programming, 18–20
FYI. *See* Fuller Youth Institute (FYI)

gaming, online, 62
gay rights, 74–75
gender, friendship networks and, 57–58
general revelation, 68–70, 73–78
generations. *See* intergenerational interaction
generativity vs. stagnation, 184
gentrification, urban, 250–51
geophysical space, 60–61, 64–66
ghettos, 250
gifts, 226–27, 348n4 (chap. 1)
Glee, 70, 73–78, 81
globalization, culture and, 167–79
God, 3, 42–43, 365n4
going, discipleship and, 304
good, culture as, 122
good intentions, 252–53
grace, 47, 296–98
grandparents, role of, 49
great white hope, the, 253
Griffin, Brad, xi, 221–22
"Grilled Cheesus," 73–78
guide, adult as, 208
guilt, culture and, 175

HBLT (Hook, Book, Look, Took), 314
health, leadership and, 282–83
hermeneutics, pop culture and, 71
Heuertz, Chris, 226–27

hierarchy, culture and, 169, 173–75
hierarchy, leadership and, 257–69, 279–80
Hispanics. *See* Latin Americans
hodegesis, pop culture and, 71
Hodge, Daniel White, xi, 246
holy indignation, 96
Holy Spirit. *See* Spirit, the
Hook, Book, Look, Took (HBLT), 314
hope, youth and, 163
hospitality, ministry and, 203–9, 210
Howell, Bradley, xi, 53
humanization, calling to, 93–94
humor, communication and, 294–95

identity, personal
    adolescence and, 44–46, 93–94, 226, 342–44
    culture and, 170, 173
    leadership and, 277–79
    online, 61–62, 63
IMDB (Internet Movie Database), 80
immigrants, 170–72, 204–5, 210
inadequacy, suffering and, 48
incarnation, the, 70–71, 94, 118, 290–91, 299–300
indignation, holy, 96
information, education and, 15
information superhighway, 54–55
initiative, ministry and, 298–300, 339
innovative learners, 313
insecure, leaders as, 282–83
insiders, adoption and, 2
institution, ministry as, 13–18
integrated, culture as, 123
integration, ministry and, 337–46
integration, selves and, 32
intentions, good, 252–53
intergenerational interaction
    community and, 207–8, 242–44, 337–46
    ministry and, 12, 49–50, 152–64, 266–69
    technology and, 64–66
internet, the, 54–56
Internet Movie Database (IMDB), 80
interpretation, pop culture and, 71
interpretive task, 103, 106–7
interview, volunteer, 286
intimate relationship level, 18–19
invitation, leadership and, 282–87, 325–26
isolation, systemic. *See* abandonment, systemic

Jackson, Allen, xi–xii, 150
"Jeremy," 131–32
Jesus
    communication and, 290–91
    culture and, 91–92, 132–33, 341

leadership and, 266, 278–79
marginalization and, 217–19, 253–54
practical theology and, 111
teaching and, 303–5
two natures of, 94, 118
Jethro, 275–76, 364n8
Jin, Jinna Sil Lo, xii, 165–66
Job, book of, 230
Jobs, Steve, 222
Jones, Tony, xii, 212–13
justice, welcome and, 208–9

Kegan, Robert, 192
kingdom, the, 109–11, 112, 146
knowledge, education and, 15

lament, 229–30
Latin Americans, 257–70
launching pad, ministry as, 202
leadership
    church, 15–17, 257–69, 275–87, 321–34
    youth and, 164, 338–39
leak, leadership, 279–80
learned, culture as, 123, 133–34
learner-centered teaching, 321–24
li, 173–74
liberty, religious, 74–75
Linker, Jason, 207–8
list, youth ministry, 317–21
listening, 118–19, 129, 207–8, 210–11, 239–41
local, mission as, 210
location, education and, 309–11
loss, resistance to, 13
love, leadership and, 277–79

MacPhee, Bill, xii, 273–74
map, culture as, 127–29
Marcia, James, 226
marginalization, 55–56, 217–20
markers, developmental, 27–36
marriage, traditional, 160–61
master teacher, 315
McEntyre, Michael, xii
mediated interaction, 65–66. *See also* technology
medium, communication and, 300
membership, church, 145–49
menarche, 28–29, 233
mentoring level programming, 19
mentors, 208, 286–87
methodology, 300, 311–14
mid-adolescence, 37–38, 44–46, 58–61
middle-school youth. *See* early adolescence
minorities, cultural, 168–70

miracles, marginalization and, 217–19
mirror, culture as, 129–30
misattribution, cultural, 125
mission, 201–3, 210–11, 340–41
Moore, Allen, 94–95
"Moore's Law," 117
Moralistic Therapeutic Deism, 74
moratorium, identity, 226
Moses, 275–76, 364n8
Mother Teresa, 227
Mueller, Walt, xii, 115–16
multiethnic ministry, 249–55
multiple selves, 30–32
multitasking, 63–64
mutual self-disclosure, 208

narrative, 98–100, 295, 341–42
National Youth Study of Religion (NYSR), 155–57, 357n7
needs, core, 42–43
neocolonialism, ministry and, 252–53
neutrality, culture and, 130–32
Nielson ratings, 79–80
Nones, the, 6–7
normative task, 103, 107–10
norms, cultural, 87, 127–29
nouveau family, 160–61
Nouwen, Henri J. M., 277–79
NYSR. See National Youth Study of Religion (NYSR)

obedience, church and, 147–48
obesity, puberty and, 28–29
objectification, adolescence and, 32–36
objective culture, 124–25
observation, volunteers and, 286
oppression, Latin America and, 257–58
organic, culture as, 123
organism, ministry as, 13–18
organization, ministry and, 257–63
Osmer, Richard, 101–3
outreach, programming and, 18, 19
outsiders, adoption and, 2
outsourcing, parental, 155–57, 161–63, 338–39, 344–45.
    See also abandonment, systemic

pain. See suffering
Palmer, Parker, 93
parents
    adolescent development and, 235–36, 331
    education and, 305–7, 309, 312
    the internet and, 65–66
    role of, 49, 155–64, 183–89, 338–39, 344–45
Parker, Evelyn, 95–96
Parks, Sharon, 227

participation, community and, 140–45
pastors, 263–64, 321–33
Pearl Jam, 131–32
peer groups. See friendship
Penner, Marv, xii, 39–40
personhood, objectification and, 33
Philip, the apostle, 70–71, 81–82
phones, cell, 63
phronesis, 214
physical space. See space, geophysical
Piaget, Jean, 43–44
pop culture, 68–82
post–high school youth, 331–32, 333–34
postmodernism, 362n9
post-soul era, 362n10
potential, leadership and, 284
poverty, 249–51
Powell, Kara, xii–xiii, 221–22
power, 2, 257–69, 276
practical theology, 101–14
practice, religious, 91–93, 103
practices, parental, 186–88
pragmatic task, 103, 110–11
praxis, 95, 103–4, 352n6 (chap. 6)
prayer, 73–78, 220, 278–79
preteens, technology and, 63–64
Pretty Woman, 68–69
pride, suffering and, 48
primus inter pares, 16, 276, 279–80
process, practical theological, 102–11
profiles, online, 61–62
Programming, Funnel of, 18–20
proliferation, selves and, 31
propagation, cognitive, 30–31
prospering, welcome and, 206–7
proximal development, 231
Psalms, book of, 229–30
puberty, adolescence and, 28–29, 233
public space. See space, geophysical

qualitative research, 180

race. See ethnicity, ministry and
Raging Bull, 69
ratio, 5:1, 7, 236, 306, 340, 348n10
receivers, teenagers as, 138
receptor oriented, communication as, 299
reconciliation, 112, 208–9
recruiting, leadership and, 282–87, 325–26
redemption, communication and, 290–91
references, volunteer, 286
reflection, theological, 85–96, 103, 107–10
reflective, definition of, 90

relationship level programming, 18–20
relationships, 169, 172–73, 185–86, 280–82, 283–84. *See also* community
religious freedom, 74–75
ren, 172, 173
renewal, urban, 250–51
reservoirs, teenagers as, 138
responsibilities, leadership, 263–64
restoration, communication and, 291
retention, youth, 6
retreats, integration and, 340
revelation, general, 68–70, 73–78
ritual, Confucianism and, 173–74
Robbins, Duffy, xiii, 288
rocks, teenagers as, 138
Rome, ancient, 204–5
Roxburgh, Alan J., 209–11
rules, missional, 210–11

sacramental volunteerism, 324–29
sacred canopy, 87
safety, doubt and, 224–25, 228–29
Samaritans, 343–44
Sankofa, 253, 363n33
sarcasm, communication and, 294–95
scaffolding, 32, 37–38, 231
Scripture. *See* Bible, the
second fiddle, 140–41
secure, leaders as, 282–83
Sedwick, Jay, xiii, 302–3
selection, leadership, 285–87
self-disclosure, mutual, 208
self-reflection, calling and, 93–94
selves, multiple, 30–32
Senior Adult Pasta Dinner, 242–44
sequence, curriculum and, 307, 311
service, leadership as, 266, 276, 279
Se7en, 68
sexuality, online, 62
Shakur, Tupac, 254
shalom, 203–9
shame, culture and, 175–76, 177
shared, culture as, 122–23
shepherds, pastors as, 263–64, 321
siblings, 2–3, 49
silence, listening and, 240
silos, 350n2 (chap. 3). *See also* intergenerational interaction
sin, 130–31, 289–90, 363–64n34
situational leadership, 280–82
size, congregational, 139
social capital, 8, 40, 274
social comparison, adolescence and, 31

socialization, education and, 14–15
social media. *See* technology
social networks. *See* friendship
society, culture and, 122–23
space, geophysical, 60–61, 64–66
Spirit, the, 101, 201–2, 315
spiritual formation. *See* formation, spiritual
Spiritual Struggles Scale, 225–26
stages, developmental, 25–26, 192, 359n6
standards, practical theological, 109
Stanley, Andy, 143–44
story, 98–100, 295, 341–42
strangers, hospitality and, 204–5, 210
structure, culture and, 130
struggles, spiritual, 225–26
subcultures, 122–23, 168
subjective culture, 124–25. *See also* worldview
suburbs, the, 250–51
suffering, 42–51, 75–76
Sunday school, 309
support, 32, 37–38, 224–25, 231, 281
survival, culture and, 168
systemic abandonment. *See* abandonment, systemic
systemic isolation. *See* abandonment, systemic

table fellowship, 210
task behavior, leadership, 280–82
tasks, practical theological, 103, 105–11
tattoos, culture and, 125–26
teachers, Confucianism and, 174
teaching. *See* education
techne, 214
technology, 54–66, 191–92, 294
television, 73, 79–80
telos, 104
theodicy, 75–76. *See also* suffering
theology
    community and, 89–96, 200
    early adolescence and, 241–42
    education and, 308
    practical, 101–14
    story and, 98–100, 289–91
time, education and, 311
timing of adolescence, 27–30
Total Period Teaching (TPT), 314
tradition, 91–93, 109, 160–61
"traditional" faith, 6–7
training, youth ministry, 238–40, 314–15, 326–28
trajectory, kingdom, 109–11, 112
transformation, education and, 312
transitions, leadership and, 329–34
tree diagram, decision, 326, 367n7
trust, 48, 59–61

truth, 47, 296–98
Turkle, Sherry, 63
Turpin, Katherine, 95
"tweens." *See* preteens, technology and

unclean, ritually, 218
universal, culture as, 122
urbanization, 249–51

values, culture and, 168–70
verbal abuse, 293–94
victimization, adolescent, 46–47
Vietnam War, 249–50
volunteers, leadership and, 279–87, 324–29
vulnerability, adoption and, 3

web, worldwide. *See* internet, the
Web 2.0, 55–56, 59–60, 63
weed, youth ministry as, 157
welcoming level programming, 19–20
welfare, welcome and, 206

white flight, 250
white man's burden, the, 253
whole, culture as, 123
wholeness, welcome and, 206
window, culture as, 129–30
wisdom, 15, 214
witness, 3–4, 146, 147
Word, the. *See* Bible, the; Jesus
words, communication and, 293–95
world, the, 94–95, 112–13, 163. *See also* creation
worldview, 124–25, 168–70, 355n24
worldwide web. *See* internet, the
worship, community and, 88
Wright, Almeda M., xiii, 85–86

"Youth Ministry as Practical Theology" (Clark), 104
Youth Theological Institute (YTI), 88–89, 352n3 (chap. 6)
YouTube, 73
YTI. *See* Youth Theological Institute (YTI)

zone of proximal development, 231

FULLER THEOLOGICAL SEMINARY,

in partnership with

BAKER ACADEMIC,

has created a website dedicated to this book at

YOUTHMINISTRY.FULLER.EDU

• • •

This site will provide supplemental content for *Adoptive Youth Ministry: Integrating Emerging Generations into the Family of Faith* as well as author interviews introducing and describing their various contributions, dialogue between the authors, and a variety of other resources—video and print—that extend the conversation found in this book.

We encourage professors and leaders who would like to have their students or others dialogue with one or more of the authors to invite them to participate in a video chat through this website.

This website also hosts resources related to Chap Clark's recent book *Youth Ministry in the 21st Century: Five Views* (also from Baker Academic) as well as other books, people, and topics that move the faithful to think differently about youth ministry.

• • •

Baker Academic
a division of Baker Publishing Group
www.BakerAcademic.com

FULLER
THEOLOGICAL SEMINARY